The Hellenistic world
from Alexander
to the Roman conquest

The Hellenistic world from Alexander to the Roman conquest

A selection of ancient sources in translation

M. M. AUSTIN
Lecturer in Ancient History
University of St Andrews

CAMBRIDGE
UNIVERSITY PRESS

Published by the Press Syndicate of the University of Cambridge
The Pitt Building, Trumpington Street, Cambridge CB2 1RP
40 West 20th Street, New York, NY 10011–4211, USA
10 Stamford Road, Oakleigh, Melbourne 3166, Australia

First published 1981
Reprinted 1984, 1988, 1989, 1992, 1994, 1995, 1998

Printed in the United Kingdom at the University Press, Cambridge

Library of Congress catalogue card number: 81–6136

British Library Cataloguing in Publication Data

The Hellenistic world from Alexander to the Roman conquest
I. Greece – History – Sources
I. Austin, M. M.
938   DF222

ISBN 0 521 29666 8 paperback

Contents

Maps

Preface

'After the generation of Alexander, the political action of Greece becomes cramped and degraded – no longer interesting to the reader, or operative on the destinies of the world [. . .] As a whole, the period between 300 B.C. and the absorption of Greece by the Romans is of no interest in itself, and is only so far of value as it helps us to understand the preceding centuries.' Thus George Grote in the Preface to his great *History of Greece* (12 volumes, first published 1846–56). Few nowadays would subscribe to this view, at least publicly; indeed, the ground had already begun to disappear from under Grote's feet thanks to the German historian J. G. Droysen, the modern inventor of Hellenistic history, who published successively histories of Alexander (1833), of the Successors (the *Diadochi*, 1836), and of subsequent rulers down to 220 B.C. (the *Epigoni*, 1843). Droysen's impact was initially restricted, but a second edition of the whole work (1877) was much more influential.[1] The great upsurge of epigraphic and papyrological studies at the end of the nineteenth century then brought the Hellenistic period to the forefront of scholarly research, where it has since remained.

Yet in spite of this the Hellenistic period has tended to remain the province of specialists and has on the whole not yet found its deserved place in academic curricula. The reasons for this are not far to seek. The Hellenistic world was diverse, divided and unstable; it lacks a single point of reference and is difficult to grasp. It did not stand up to the challenge of Rome and so can be thought of as a 'failure'. Despite the large and increasing volume of documentary evidence (much greater than for the Classical period) it suffers from the lack of a good literary source to serve as a guide for most of the third century until the beginning of Polybius' account (contrast the availability of e.g. Thucydides for the fifth century, Cicero for the late Roman Republic, or Tacitus for the early Empire).

This book is an attempt to help fill this gap by presenting in one volume a selection of ancient sources in translation, intended to illustrate the main lines of development of the Hellenistic states, their institutions, society and economy. Chronologically the period covered extends from the reign of Alexander to the mid- or late second century, the precise lower limit depending on the region concerned. Geographically the coverage concentrates mainly on Macedon and the mainland of Greece, the Aegean, Asia and Egypt; the West is largely sacrificed except for a passing glance at Agathocles and Pyrrhus in chapter 2. It is hoped that the selection will convey to the non-specialist reader something of the interest of this period and of the richness and diversity of the available source material, and so encourage him to further study.

The limits of this book must, however, be clearly understood. Though meant to be self-contained, it is not a substitute for a history of the Hellenistic world; in particular, as regards political and military narrative, only the outlines could be presented. The selection is also based exclusively on written evidence, from literary, epigraphic and (in the case of Egypt) papyrological sources; it therefore largely omits, save for passing references, the important (and growing) contribution of archaeology in general, and in particular of the coinage of the Hellenistic states.[2] Furthermore, it only reproduces a small proportion of the total volume of written evidence available. Any selection is bound to be arbitrary; the reader must not imagine that all the texts that matter are collected here. Finally, translations are at best only approximations and an inadequate substitute for the originals. The attempt seemed nevertheless worth making.

As will be seen, the layout of the material is normally chronological within each chapter, except for chapter 4 where it is mainly thematic, and chapters 5 and 7 where some of the material is arranged geographically. The division of the Hellenistic world into the separate spheres of influence of the dominant monarchies in chapters 3, 5, 6 and 7 is purely for convenience and occasionally involves the arbitrary placing of a text in one chapter rather than another. It also has the disadvantage of obscuring interrelations within the Hellenistic world; Polybius would no doubt have been shocked. It is hoped that extensive cross-referencing and the chronological table will partly offset this. The annotation seeks in general to put the passages cited in context, to clarify essential details and to provide cross-references with other related passages; but a full commentary is beyond the scope of this volume. Bibliographical references are very selective and give preference to works in English. References that seemed self-evident have usually been omitted. It is assumed, for instance, that for any passage of Polybius the reader will wish to consult F. W. Walbank's *Commentary*, or that constant reference will be made for all narrative history to E. Will's *Histoire politique du monde hellénistique*. Similarly, for inscriptions and papyri the reader can refer to the editions cited for a fuller discussion of the texts concerned. The translations are all my own, except for a few Oriental sources (**138, 141, 165, 189**)[3] where I have necessarily relied on published translations.

For Polybius I have frequently drawn on E. S. Shuckburgh's translation (2 vols., 1889) and also on suggested translations of particular phrases or sentences in F. W. Walbank's *Commentary on Polybius*. I am very grateful to him for permission to do so.

In preparing this book I have had the benefit of help and advice from a number of colleagues and friends, notably A. E. Astin, D. J. Crawford, J. K. Davies, G. T. Griffith, G. E. Rickman and F. W. Walbank. I am very grateful to them all; they must not be held responsible for the many imperfections of this book. Finally, I wish to thank the Cambridge University Press, and Mrs J. Ashman for the speed and efficiency of her typing.

St Andrews, August 1980   Michel Austin

1. See A. Momigliano in *History and Theory* 9 (1970), 139–53, reproduced in *Quinto Contributo alla storia degli studi classici* (Rome, 1975), 109–26 and in *Essays in Ancient and Modern Historiography* (Oxford, 1977), 307–23. I use the word 'inventor' deliberately: the concept of a 'Hellenistic period' was unknown to ancient sources and was created by Droysen (and invested by him with misleading connotations); on this see C. Préaux, *CE* 40 (1965), 129–39 and also Préaux I (1978), 5–9.
2. See G. K. Jenkins, *Ancient Greek Coins* (London, 1972); N. Davis and C. M. Kraay, *The Hellenistic Kingdoms* (London, 1973); Will II (1967), index s.v. 'monnayages' (pp. 532f.); Préaux I (1978), 106–10 and 280–94.
3. Numbers in bold type refer here and throughout this volume to the numbered sequence of texts.

Abbreviations

AJA	*American Journal of Archaeology*
AJP	*American Journal of Philology*
AM	*Mitteilungen des Deutschen Archäologischen Instituts. Athenische Abteilung*
Ancient Macedonia I and II	*Ancient Macedonia*, ed. B. Laourdas and C. Makaronas, vol. I (Thessalonica, 1970) and vol. II (1977)
Annuario	*Annuario della Scuola Archeologica di Atene*
Badian (1958)	E. Badian, *Foreign Clientelae* (Oxford, 1958)
Badian (1966)	E. Badian, in *Ancient Society and Institutions. Studies presented to Victor Ehrenberg* (Oxford, 1966)
Bagnall (1976)	R. S. Bagnall, *The Administration of the Ptolemaic Possessions outside Egypt* (Leyden, 1976)
BCH	*Bulletin de Correspondance Hellénique*
BSA	*Annual of the British School at Athens*
Bull.	J. and L. Robert, *Bulletin Epigraphique* in *REG*; the year is that of the *REG*, the number that of the entry
CAH	*Cambridge Ancient History*
CE	*Chronique d'Egypte*
C. Ord. Ptol.	M. T. Lenger, *Corpus des Ordonnances des Ptolémées* (Brussels, 2nd ed., 1980)
CP	*Classical Philology*
CQ	*Classical Quarterly*
CRAI	*Comptes rendus de l'Académie des Inscriptions et Belles Lettres*
Crawford (1971)	D. J. Crawford, *Kerkeosiris* (Cambridge, 1971)
dr., drs.	drachma, drachmas
Entretiens Hardt	*Fondation Hardt. Entretiens sur l'antiquité classique*
Errington (1971)	R. M. Errington, *The Dawn of Empire* (London, 1971)
FGrH	F. Jacoby, *Die Fragmente der griechischen Historiker* (Berlin 1923–)
Fraser (1972)	P. M. Fraser, *Ptolemaic Alexandria*, 3 vols. (Oxford, 1972)
GRBS	*Greek, Roman and Byzantine Studies*

Griffith (1935)	G. T. Griffith, *The Mercenaries of the Hellenistic World* (Cambridge 1935)
Griffith (1966)	G. T. Griffith, ed., *Alexander the Great: the Main Problems* (Cambridge, 1966)
Hamilton (1969)	J. R. Hamilton, *Plutarch Alexander. A Commentary* (Oxford, 1969)
Hamilton (1973)	J. R. Hamilton, *Alexander the Great* (London, 1973)
Hammond and Griffith (1979)	N. G. L. Hammond and G. T. Griffith, *A History of Macedonia* II (Oxford, 1979)
Hands (1968)	A. R. Hands, *Charities and Social Aid in Greece and Rome* (London, 1968)
Hansen (1971)	E. V. Hansen, *The Attalids of Pergamum* (2nd ed., Ithaca 1971)
Holleaux, *Etudes*	M. Holleaux, *Etudes d'épigraphie et d'histoire grecques*, ed. L. Robert, 6 vols. (Paris, 1938–69)
ICret.	*Inscriptiones Creticae*, ed. M. Guarducci, 4 vols. (Rome, 1935–50)
IDélos	*Inscriptions de Délos*
IG	*Inscriptiones Graecae*
IGLS	*Inscriptions grecques et latines de la Syrie*, ed. L. Jalabert, R. Mouterde, J. P. Rey-Coquais (Paris, 1929–)
JEA	*Journal of Egyptian Archaeology*
JHS	*Journal of Hellenic Studies*
Jones (1940)	A. H. M. Jones, *The Greek City from Alexander to Justinian* (Oxford, 1940)
JRS	*Journal of Roman Studies*
Larsen (1968)	J. A. O. Larsen, *Greek Federal States* (Oxford, 1968)
Launey (1949, 1950)	M. Launey, *Recherches sur les armées hellénistiques*, 2 vols. (Paris 1949–50)
McShane (1964)	R. B. McShane, *The Foreign Policy of the Attalids of Pergamum* (Urbana, 1964)
Magie (1950)	D. Magie, *Roman Rule in Asia Minor*, 2 vols. (Princeton, 1950)
ML	R. Meiggs and D. M. Lewis, *A Selection of Greek Historical Inscriptions* (Oxford, 1969)
Moretti I and II	L. Moretti, *Iscrizione Storiche Ellenistiche*, 2 vols. (Florence, 1965 and 1976)
NC	*Numismatic Chronicle*
ob.	obol
OGIS	*Orientis Graeci Inscriptiones Selectae*, ed. W. Dittenberger, 2 vols. (Leipzig, 1903–5)
P.	Papyrus
P. Cairo Zen.	*Catalogue général des antiquités égyptiennes du Musée du Caire, Zenon Papyri*, ed. C. C. Edgar, 4 vols. (Cairo, 1925–31), vol. v ed. O. Guéraud and P. Jouguet (Cairo, 1940)

P. Col.	*Zenon Papyri: Business Papers of the Third Century B.C. dealing with Palestine and Egypt*, vol. I ed. W. L. Westermann and E. S. Hasenoehrl (New York, 1934), vol. II ed. W. L. Westermann, C. W. Keyes and H. Liebesny (New York, 1940)
P. Cornell	*Greek Papyri in the Library of Cornell University*, ed. W. L. Westermann and C. J. Kraemer jr (New York, 1926)
P.CPS	*Proceedings of the Cambridge Philological Society*
P. Ent.	O. Guéraud, *ENTEUXEIS: Requêtes et plaintes addressées au roi d'Egypte au IIIe siècle avant J. C.* (Cairo, 1931–2)
P. Hib.	*The Hibeh Papyri*, Part I ed. B. P. Grenfell and A. S. Hunt (London, 1906), Part II ed. E. G. Turner and M. T. Lenger (London, 1956)
P. Lond.	*Greek Papyri in the British Museum*, vol. VII *The Zenon Archive*, ed. T. C. Skeat (London, 1974)
P. Mich. Zen.	*Papyri in the University of Michigan Collection*, vol. I *Zenon Papyri*, ed. C. C. Edgar (Ann Arbor, 1931)
PP	*Prosopographia Ptolemaica*, ed. W. Peremans and E. van't Dack, 8 vols. to date (Louvain, 1950–75)
Préaux (1939)	C. Préaux, *L'Economie royale des Lagides* (Brussels, 1939)
Préaux (1975)	*Le monde grec. Hommages à Claire Préaux*, ed. J. Bingen, G. Cambier, G. Nachtergael (Brussels, 1975)
Préaux (1978)	C. Préaux, *Le monde hellénistique*, 2 vols. (Paris, 1978)
PSI	*Pubblicazioni della Società Italiana per la ricerca dei papiri greci e latini in Egitto*, ed. G. Vitelli, M. Norsa *et al.* (Florence, 1912–)
P. Tebt.	*The Tebtunis Papyri*, ed. B. P. Grenfell, A. S. Hunt, J. G. Smyly *et al.*, 3 vols. in 4 (London, 1902–38), vol. IV ed. J. G. Keenan and J. C. Shelton (London, 1976)
P. Yale	*Yale Papyri in the Beinecke Rare Book and Manuscript Library*, ed. J. F. Oates, A. E. Samuel and C. B. Welles (New Haven, 1967)
RC	C. B. Welles, *Royal Correspondence in the Hellenistic Period* (New Haven, 1934)
REG	*Revue des Etudes Grecques*
Rev. Num.	*Revue de Numismatique*
Rostovtzeff (1941)	M. Rostovtzeff, *The Social and Economic History of the Hellenistic World*, 3 vols. (Oxford, 1941)
RPh	*Revue de Philologie*
SB	*Sammelbuch griechischer Urkunden aus Ägypten*, ed. F. Preisigke, F. Bilabel, E. Kiessling (Strasbourg, Berlin, Heidelberg etc. 1913–)

Abbreviations

SEG	*Supplementum Epigraphicum Graecum*
Sel. Pap.	A. S. Hunt and C. C. Edgar, *Select Papyri* (Loeb edition), 2 vols. (London, 1932 and 1934)
SGDI	*Sammlung der griechischen Dialekt-Inschriften*, ed. H. Collitz and F. Bechtel (Göttingen, 1884–1915)
Sherk	R. K. Sherk, *Roman Documents from the Greek East* (Baltimore, 1969)
Staatsv. III	*Die Staatsverträge des Altertums*, ed. H. Bengtson; vol. III ed. H. H. Schmitt, *Die Staatsverträge von 338 bis 200 v. Chr.* (Munich, 1969)
*Syll.*³	*Sylloge Inscriptionum Graecarum*, ed. W. Dittenberger, 4 vols. (3rd ed., 1915–24)
Tarn and Griffith (1952)	W. W. Tarn and G. T. Griffith, *Hellenistic Civilization* (London, 3rd ed., 1952)
Tod, *GHI* II	M. N. Tod, *A Selection of Greek Historical Inscriptions* vol. II (Oxford, 1948)
UPZ	U. Wilcken, *Urkunden der Ptolemäerzeit*, 2 vols. (Berlin, Leipzig, 1922–7 and 1957)
Walbank I (1957), II (1967), III (1979)	F. W. Walbank, *A Historical Commentary on Polybius*, 3 vols. (Oxford, 1957, 1967, 1979)
W. Chrest.	L. Mitteis and U. Wilcken, *Grundzüge und Chrestomathie der Papyruskunde*, 4 vols. (Leipzig, Berlin, 1912) (References are all to Part I, vol. II by U. Wilcken)
Will I and II	E. Will, *Histoire politique du monde hellénistique*, vol. I (Nancy, 2nd ed., 1979), vol. II (1967; new edition forthcoming)
YCS	*Yale Classical Studies*

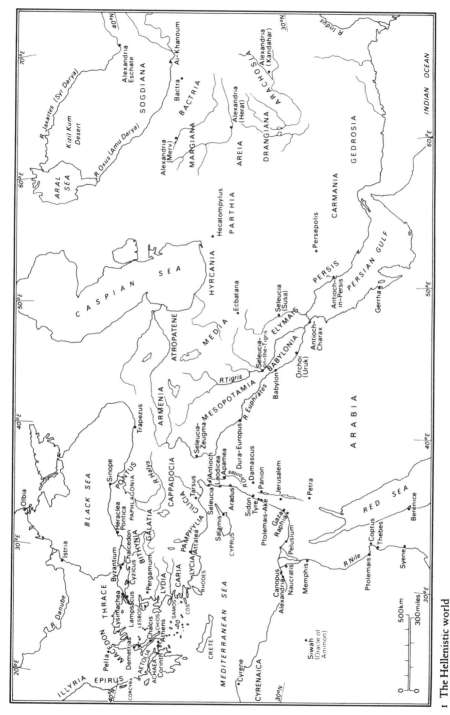

1 The Hellenistic world
adapted from E. Will, *Le monde grec et l'Orient* II (Paris, 1975). pp. 344–5

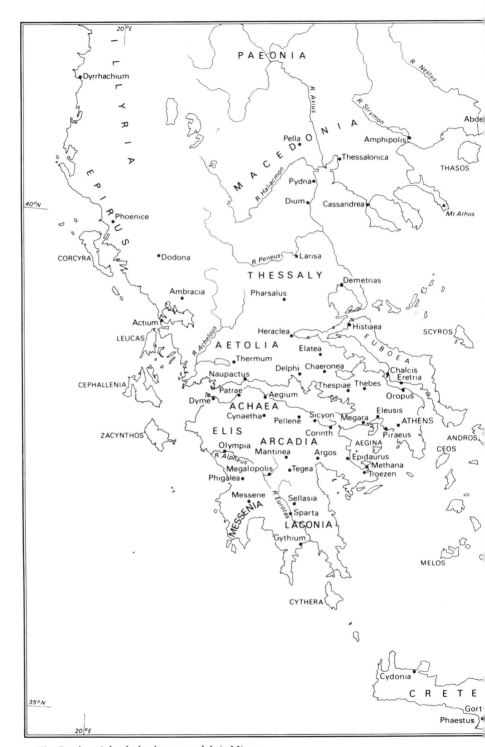

2 The Greek mainland, the Aegean and Asia Minor
adapted from W. W. Tarn, *Hellenistic Civilization* (London, 3rd ed., 1952), pp. 8–9

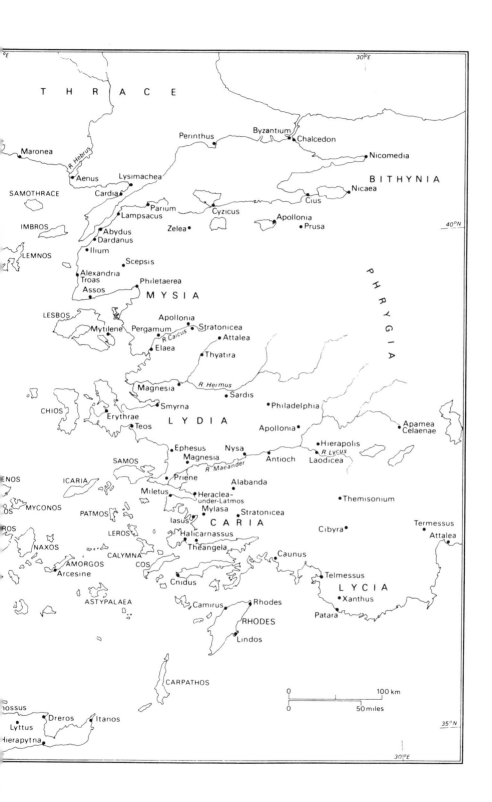

Note on the sources[1]

(§1) Two points should be made at the outset in addition to what has already been said in the Preface. First, the extant written sources for the Hellenistic age are but a fraction of what once existed. Not a single historian of the period has survived complete; many known to have existed are little but names to us, and many may well have disappeared without trace. The inscriptions and papyri that have survived are a purely random selection, not necessarily representative, of a vastly larger corpus of evidence now lost. The history of the Hellenistic age is necessarily riddled with gaps and uncertainties.

Second, our view of the Hellenistic world is largely one-sided. The world conquered by Alexander was one of many races and cultures, in which the Greeks and Macedonians, though politically, socially and culturally dominant, were nonetheless only a minority in the newly conquered territories of the east. Yet the evidence for the Hellenistic world is very largely of Greek origin and reflects Greek points of view. The Greeks were articulate. The tradition of historical writing, as well as other forms of literature, was established among them well before Alexander and continued after him. Greek cities had long been in the habit of setting up inscribed public records, and the habit spread in the Hellenistic age together with the spread of Greek civic institutions to the east. Greek was the official language of administration of the new monarchies in Asia, which were run by a Greek-speaking governing class. The coinage of the new kingdoms was purely Greek in style.

The historian is therefore confronted with a largely Greek view of a world that was only partly Greek and never became fully hellenised, and this important limitation can only be overcome to a restricted extent. The oriental evidence from Mesopotamia, abundant in previous Near Eastern history, is relatively scanty in the Hellenistic period (cf. **138, 141, 189**).[2] The two principal exceptions are the Jews and the Egyptians. The Jews had a literary tradition of their own which antedated the Hellenistic age and continued in this period; though they came under strong Greek influence, the Jews successfully asserted their separate identity (cf. **166–168, 172, 262, 276**). In Egypt the native priesthood met in synods which passed resolutions, though they were largely under the control of the Ptolemies; a few of these, inscribed in Greek, hieroglyphs and demotic, are extant (cf. **222, 227**). More generally, the evidence of published papyri from Egypt, though largely in Greek, yields much information about the Egyptian countryside that would otherwise have been almost completely lost. This is an exceptional case; elsewhere in Asia it is only rarely that the voice of the native is heard (cf. **142**; contrast in Egypt **165, 240, 245, 246, 259**).

(§2) *Alexander.* The achievements and personality of Alexander the Great stimulated more historical writing, in his time and after, than any other single figure in antiquity (cf. *FGrH* 117–53).[3] Of all this literature, only four principal accounts are now extant, all of them written well after Alexander, and so ultimately dependent on earlier writers, whether these were used directly or not. DIODORUS of Sicily (1st c. B.C.) devoted Book XVII of his *Library of History* to the reign of Alexander; the account is preserved except for an important gap between chapters 83 and 84, from 330/29 to 327.[4] QUINTUS CURTIUS (1st c. A.D.?) wrote a history of Alexander in ten books, the first two of which are lost (down to early 333). Similarities between Diodorus and Quintus Curtius indicate that they drew, in part at least, on a common source, often identified as Clitarchus (*FGrH* 137), a contemporary of Alexander. PLUTARCH of Chaeronea (2nd half of 1st c. A.D. – early 2nd c.) included Alexander in his *Parallel Lives* of Greek and Roman statesmen; he draws on a wide variety of sources, many of which are named.[5] ARRIAN of Nicomedia (2nd c. A.D.) wrote an account of Alexander's expedition in seven books, and also a separate account of India and Nearchus' journey by sea from the Indus to the Persian Gulf.[6] The account of Alexander is based primarily, as Arrian indicates (I, Preface), on two writers, Ptolemy the founder of the Ptolemaic dynasty (*FGrH* 138) and Aristobulus of Cassandrea (*FGrH* 139), both of them contemporaries of Alexander and regarded by Arrian as trustworthy sources. Arrian's account is the fullest and most detailed available for Alexander, though it tends towards apologia, as did both Ptolemy and Aristobulus; it omits or distorts important aspects and episodes of Alexander's career, as comparison with the other sources shows (cf. **9, 16**). Most of the important questions concerning Alexander, his personality, conduct and aims, remain a matter of controversy and speculation. This is due partly to the inadequacy of the ancient sources, but partly to Alexander himself and his achievements. The Alexander legend started in Alexander's lifetime and was to some extent started deliberately by Alexander himself.

(§3) *The Hellenistic world after Alexander.* For the history of the Hellenistic period as a whole, only one continuous source has survived, the *Epitome* by JUSTIN (Roman Empire) of the *Philippic Histories* of Pompeius Trogus (time of Augustus), but this work is too mediocre and unreliable to provide a solid framework (it is not represented in this selection). Otherwise the coverage of Hellenistic history in the extant sources is very uneven, some periods being known in detail, others hardly at all.

For the first two decades after Alexander (down to 302), the survival of Books XVIII–XX of DIODORUS provides an adequate framework;[7] thereafter Diodorus' text is lost, apart from brief excerpts. For this period Diodorus is thought to have relied, not necessarily directly nor exclusively, on a good contemporary account, that of Hieronymus of Cardia (*FGrH* 154), whose narrative covered the period from 323 to (perhaps) 272 (cf. **22** n. 3).

This period, and parts of later Hellenistic history, are also partially covered in some of the Lives of PLUTARCH,[8] namely those of Demosthenes, Phocion, Eumenes of Cardia, Demetrius Poliorcetes, Pyrrhus of Epirus, the Spartan kings Agis IV and Cleomenes III, and the Achaean statesmen Aratus of Sicyon and Philopoemen; there is also some material in the Lives of the Roman commanders T. Quinctius Flamininus and L. Aemilius Paullus. It will be noted that Plutarch's Greek Lives for the Hellenistic period are significantly fewer than for previous Greek history, and in particular that Hellenistic rulers are not represented except for Alexander, Demetrius Poliorcetes and Pyrrhus. This is no accident. Plutarch, in spirit a man of the *polis* though living under the Roman Empire, regarded the death of Demosthenes as marking the end of free Athens (*Demosthenes* 3; cf. the Athenian viewpoint in e.g. **26, 43, 44, 49**). He had a strong and explicit aversion for Hellenistic kings and their courts (cf. **36, 56, 57**), and his preferences went to statesmen from Greek cities of the mainland (the Spartan kings; the Achaean statesmen), whose actions seemed to him to recall something of the spirit of the classical *polis*.[9] A series of royal biographies of the Hellenistic rulers would have been invaluable for the historian, and its absence leaves a gap which can only partially be filled (cf. **163, 199, 207**; contrast the continuous sequence of biographies available for Roman emperors).

Diodorus' history and Plutarch's Lives were derivative sources written long after the event. The history of POLYBIUS of Megalopolis (*ca* 200 – after 118 B.C.) is in a different class altogether; it is to the Hellenistic world of his time (the late 3rd and 2nd c.) what Thucydides is to the fifth century.[10] Polybius was not just a witness, but to some extent also an agent in the events he narrates. An Achaean statesman who was deported to Rome as a hostage in 167, and formed there friendships with important Roman statesmen, Polybius, though not free of bias, had a deep knowledge and understanding of the Hellenistic and Mediterranean world of his time. The theme of his history was the rise of Rome to the status of a world power; it was covered in detail from 220 to 145, with (in

3

the first two books) an outline of the First Punic War (264–241) and a summary of events prior to his main starting point. Of the whole massive work in 40 books, only Books I–V survive intact (down to 216); thereafter only excerpts of varying length are preserved. The gap is filled in part (down to 167) by Books XXI–XLV of the Roman annalist LIVY (time of Augustus), who drew extensively on Polybius for the sections of his narrative that dealt with Greek affairs.[11]

Other sources may be mentioned briefly. The *Geography* of STRABO (time of Augustus), in 17 Books, contains a number of valuable descriptions of cities and regions (cf. e.g. **174, 232**), as well as frequent historical digressions (cf. e.g. **191, 193**).[12] The same is true of the *Description of Greece* (mainland only) in ten Books by PAUSANIAS (2nd c. A.D.; cf. **23, 45, 82**).[13] Mention should be also made of the Jewish sources alluded to above, notably I and II MACCABEES (cf. **168**) and Books XII–XIII of the *Jewish Antiquities* by JOSEPHUS (1st c. A.D.);[14] these provide important evidence on the Jews in the Hellenistic world and on their relations with the declining Seleucids in the second century.

(§4) *Inscriptions.*[15] Nearly half of the texts included in this selection are Greek inscriptions; this simple fact illustrates the great and ever increasing importance of inscriptions for the study of the Hellenistic world, and the texts selected do not by any means fully represent the range and variety of available epigraphic texts. (The emphasis is on inscriptions that illuminate public affairs.) Generally speaking, finds are most abundant on the mainland of Greece, in the Aegean, and in western Asia Minor, and become scarcer in the eastern parts of the Hellenistic world, though even the remotest regions are occasionally represented (cf. e.g. **192, 221**). Inscriptions were commonly displayed in public buildings and areas, and in sanctuaries, as the provisions for their engraving and publication reveal (cf. e.g. **44** (end), **115, 118** Side A, **119** (VII), **185** II, etc.). The great sanctuaries of panhellenic renown thus became veritable storehouses of inscribed texts displayed for public scrutiny. Among the profusion and variety of texts certain categories stand out: official letters of kings to cities or to officials (numerous examples, e.g. **5, 31, 40, 60**, etc.);[16] decrees of cities, or leagues, or even private associations, on a wide range of subjects, one very important category being the honorific decrees passed in praise of rulers, magistrates, or individuals for services performed (very numerous examples, e.g. **26, 32, 43, 44, 151**, etc.); treaties and alliances of various kinds (e.g. **33, 49, 89, 132**, etc.); constitutions (**42, 264**); laws and regulations, on civil or religious matters (e.g. **74, 108, 129, 216**); dedications and offerings to gods (e.g. **122, 197, 279**); lists and accounts (e.g. **104, 177, 234**), etc. Inscriptions do not merely supplement the evidence of literary sources; on many aspects of

Greek history they are the principal or indeed the sole source of information available (cf. e.g. **127, 130, 135, 218**).[17]

(§5) *Papyri*.[18] While Greek inscriptions are found in most parts of the Hellenistic world, the evidence of papyri is confined almost exclusively to Egypt (and in fact, only to certain parts of Egypt). The reason for this is simply one of climate: though papyrus was the normal writing material for everyday use in the Hellenistic world, only the desert fringes of Egypt provide conditions suitable for the virtually indefinite survival of papyrus. Thus the countryside of Egypt is represented, though not the Delta or Alexandria. Generally speaking the evidence of papyri relates mostly to Egypt itself and betrays little awareness of the wider Hellenistic world (though cf. **220, 265**, for exceptions). With these important restrictions the range and variety of extant papyri are very great. Apart from literary texts (cf. **86**), papyri are normally classified into private and public documents. Private documents include personal archives and papers (cf. **237–246**, from the archive of Zenon; **260**, from the archive of Menches), receipts (cf. **248, 260**), correspondence (cf. **241**), etc. Official documents include regulations and edicts (**231, 235, 236, 250, 275**), official correspondence (cf. **238, 249, 252**, etc.), petitions (cf. **239, 240, 255**), records of various kinds (**247, 251**), etc. Comparison of the chapter on the Ptolemies with that on the Seleucids will show how much information has been preserved on the life and administration of Ptolemaic Egypt which elsewhere has almost completely vanished. Yet the abundance of the evidence can be deceptive and misleading, and historical reconstructions are at the mercy of chance finds. For example, very few papyri survive from the reign of Ptolemy I, while they are abundant for the reign of Ptolemy II: the early days in the establishment of the Ptolemaic administration therefore largely escape us. The large archive of Zenon reveals the dynamism of the Greek governing class in early Ptolemaic times, but how typical was this of Ptolemaic Egypt as a whole, even at this period? (Cf. **240** n. 2.)

The same note of caution may be sounded for the Hellenistic world as a whole. Over the last century the study of the Hellenistic age has progressed immeasurably. Significant new finds are reported almost every year. Yet large areas of Hellenistic history are likely to remain at best a mosaic of scattered fragments rather than a connected whole.

NOTES

1. For a fuller discussion of the evidence for the Hellenistic age cf. Préaux I (1978), 77–112.
2. Cf. P. Grimal, ed., *Hellenism and the Rise of Rome* (London, 1968), 266–89.

3. For a fuller discussion of the sources for Alexander see L. Pearson, *The Lost Histories of Alexander the Great* (New York, 1960); E. Badian, *The Classical World* 65 (1971), 37–42, 46–53; P. A. Brunt, *Arrian* I (Loeb, London, 1976), Introduction §§10–23.

4. Edition by C. Bradford Welles in the Loeb *Diodorus*, vol. VIII (London, 1963).

5. J. R. Hamilton, *Plutarch Alexander. A Commentary* (Oxford, 1969).

6. Translation in the Penguin Classics by A. de Sélincourt, with Introduction and notes by J. R. Hamilton (Harmondsworth, 1971); edition by P. A. Brunt in the Loeb series, vol. I (London, 1976). Cf. also A. B. Bosworth, *CQ* n.s. 26 (1976), 117–39 and *Entretiens Hardt* 22 (1976), 1–33; P. A. Stadter, *Arrian of Nicomedia* (Chapel Hill, NC, 1980).

7. Loeb edition (vols. IX and X, London, 1947 and 1954) by R. M. Geer (there is a useful index in vol. XII (1967)).

8. Numerous translations, including those in the Loeb series.

9. For the intellectual context of Plutarch cf. E. L. Bowie in *Studies in Ancient Society*, ed. M. I. Finley (London, 1974), 166–209.

10. Translations by E. S. Shuckburgh, 2 vols. (1889); W. R. Paton in the Loeb series, 5 vols. (London, 1922–7); I. Scott-Kilvert (selections only), *Polybius: the Rise of the Roman Empire* (Penguin Classics, Harmondsworth, 1979, with an introduction by F. W. Walbank); F. W. Walbank, *Polybius* (Berkeley, 1972) and above all his *Historical Commentary on Polybius*, 3 vols. (Oxford, 1957, 1967, 1979).

11. Books XXI–XXX in *The War with Hannibal* (Penguin Classics, Harmondsworth, 1972); Books XXXI–XLV in *Rome and the Mediterranean* (Penguin Classics, Harmondsworth, 1976); J. Briscoe, *A Commentary on Livy Books* XXXI–XXXIII (Oxford, 1973).

12. Loeb edition by H. L. Jones, 8 vols. (London, 1917–33).

13. Loeb edition by W. H. S. Jones (with R. Wycherley), 5 vols. (London, 1918–35); translation and notes by P. Levi, 2 vols. (Penguin Classics, Harmondsworth, 1979).

14. Loeb edition (vol. VII) by R. Marcus, with notes (London, 1943); P. Vidal-Naquet, *Flavius Josèphe, ou du bon usage de la trahison* (Paris, 1977, Preface to *La Guerre des Juifs*, tr. P. Savinel).

15. Cf. A. G. Woodhead, *The Study of Greek Inscriptions* (Cambridge, 1959); L. Robert, *Epigraphie* in *L'Histoire et ses méthodes* (Paris, 1961), 453–97; J. and L. Robert, *Bulletin épigraphique* in *REG* since 1938 (invaluable; also reprinted separately with index volumes). For all inscriptions in Dittenberger's *OGIS* and *Syll.*³ consult W. Gawantka, *Aktualisierende Konkordanz zu OGIS und Syll.*³ (Hildesheim, 1977).

16. C. Bradford Welles, *Royal Correspondence in the Hellenistic Age* (New Haven, 1934), with translation and full commentary, for those from Asia. Many more have been discovered since (cf. **156, 158**).

17. Many inscriptions are fragmentary or difficult to read, and the texts used are often (to a greater or lesser extent) the result of scholarly reconstruction (the same is true of papyri). To give some indication to the reader of what is original text and what is restoration, I have adopted the following method:

where half or more of a word is restored, the whole word has been enclosed in square brackets, even if the restoration is virtually certain; where less than half is restored, the whole word is printed without square brackets, unless there is possible doubt about the restoration. The procedure is rough and ready; if anything it slightly exaggerates the degree of restoration. For a more precise indication of what has survived on the stone (or the papyrus) the reader must consult the original Greek text. Angular brackets < > are used to indicate words accidentally omitted by the scribe or stonecutter. For most inscriptions and papyri I have also indicated line divisions every 5 lines; again, this can only be done approximately in a translation.

18. Cf. E. G. Turner, *Greek Papyri. An Introduction* (Oxford, 1968); O. Montevecchi, *La Papirologia* (Turin, 1973); A. S. Hunt and C. C. Edgar, *Select Papyri* (Loeb edition, London), vol. i: *Private Affairs* (1932), vol. ii: *Official Documents* (1934).

1 The reign of Alexander

1 Alexander's reign in the Parian Marble (264/3)

The following text is part of a chronological list of notable events, political and cultural, from the first (mythical) kings of Athens to the year 264/3, drawn up by an unknown writer and inscribed on stone in the island of Paros, then under Ptolemaic control (hence the name 'Parian Marble' or 'Chronicle'; cf. **218**). Each event is dated in relation to the year of writing (264/3). The latter part of the inscription is lost after the year 299/8. For the continuation of the text see **21**.

B (1) [From the time when Philip] died and Alexander came to the throne, 72 years, and Pythodelus was archon at Athens (336/5).

(2) From the time when Alexander marched against the Triballians and Illyrians, and when the Thebans revolted and blockaded the (Macedonian) garrison, he turned back, captured the city and destroyed it, 71 years, and Euainetus was archon at Athens (335/4).[1]

(3) From the time of Alexander's crossing to Asia and the battle at the river Granicus, and the battle at Issus fought by Alexander against Darius, 70 years, and Ctesicles was archon at Athens (334/3).

(4) From the time when Alexander made himself master of Phoenicia, Cyprus and Egypt, 69 years, and Nicocrates was archon at Athens (333/2).

(5) From the battle which Alexander fought and won against Darius at Arbela,[2] the capture of Babylon, the dismissal of the allies,[3] and the foundation of Alexandria,[4] 68 years, and Nicetes was archon at Athens (332/1).

(6) From the time when Callippus made public his astronomical cycle,[5] and Alexander captured Darius and hanged Bessus, 66 years, and Aristophon was archon at Athens (330/29).

(7) From the time when Philemon the comic poet won the prize, 64 years, and Euthycritus was archon at Athens (328/7). And a Greek city was founded on the Tanais.[6]

Marmor Parium, *FGrH* 239 B §§1–7;
Tod, *GHI* ii, 205

1. See **2, 10**.
2. More correctly Gaugamela.
3. The Greek allies of Alexander were formally dismissed at Ecbatana, though many reenlisted (Arrian III. 19. 5f.).
4. Founded during Alexander's stay in Egypt (see **7**), and so misplaced here though not misdated.
5. Cf. E. J. Bickerman, *Chronology of the Ancient World* (London, 2nd ed., 1980), 28f.
6. Alexandria on the Jaxartes or Alexandria Eschate (Arrian IV. 1. 3f. and 4. 1), the Jaxartes (Syr Darya) being confused with the Tanais (Don).

2   The beginning of Alexander's reign and the sack of Thebes (336/5)

See further: Hamilton (1969), 27–31; *id.* (1973), 41–51.

(*a*) Philip was then murdered by Pausanias, who had been insulted at the instigation of Attalus and Cleopatra and had been unable to obtain justice. Most of the blame for this was attributed to Olympias, who allegedly encouraged and incited the young man's anger, but some suspicion was also attached to Alexander. It is said that when Pausanias came to see him after the insult he had suffered and complained about it, Alexander quoted to him the line from the *Medea*

The bride's father, the bridegroom and the bride. [1]

Be that as it may, he sought out the accomplices in the plot and punished them, and when in his absence Olympias treated Cleopatra with cruelty he showed his displeasure. [2]

(11) And so at the age of twenty Alexander took over the kingdom, which faced dangers on every side, being exposed to great jealousies and deep animosities. For the neighbouring tribes of barbarians would not submit to Macedonian rule, and longed for their ancestral dynasties. As for Greece, Philip had defeated her in the field but had not had time enough to subdue her under his yoke; he had simply introduced change and confusion into the country and had left it in a state of unrest and commotion, unaccustomed as yet to the new situation. Alexander's Macedonian advisers, alarmed at this crisis, took the view that he ought to give up Greece completely, without recourse to arms, and as for the barbarians who were inclined to revolt, he ought to apply conciliation to win them back by handling gently the first symptoms of rebellion. Alexander, however, took the opposite view, and set out to establish the safety and security of his kingdom through boldness and determination, in the conviction that if he was seen to waver in his resolve, all his

enemies would be upon him. Accordingly, he put an end to the barbarian unrest and the wars which threatened on that side by conducting a lightning campaign as far as the Danube, and in a great battle he defeated Syrmus, the king of the Triballians. On hearing that the Thebans had revolted and that the Athenians were in sympathy with them, he immediately led his army through Thermopylae, declaring that since Demosthenes referred to him contemptuously as a boy while he was among the Triballians, and as a youngster when he had reached Thessaly, he wanted to show him before the walls of Athens that he was a man. On reaching Thebes he wanted to give the Thebans a chance to change their minds, and so merely requested the surrender of Phoenix and Prothytes, promising an amnesty to those who defected to his side. But the Thebans retaliated with a demand for the surrender of Philotas and Antipater, and issued a proclamation that those who wanted to join in the task of liberating Greece should come and fight on their side. So Alexander ordered the Macedonians into battle. [. . .] The city was captured, plundered and razed to the ground.3 Alexander's calculation was essentially that the Greeks would be so struck by the magnitude of the disaster that they would be frightened into submission, but he also wished to give the appearance that he was giving in to the complaints of his allies.4 For the Phocians and Plataeans had denounced the Thebans. So, making an exception for the priests, all the guest-friends of the Macedonians, the descendants of Pindar, and those who had opposed the vote for revolt, he sold the rest into slavery, some 30,000 in all. The dead numbered over 6,000.

Plutarch, *Alexander* 10.6–11

(*b*) [. . .] The king buried the Macedonian dead, who numbered more than 500; he then called a meeting of the delegates (*synedroi*) of the Greeks5 and referred to the common council the question how to treat the city of Thebes. The debate was then opened, and some of those who were hostile to the Thebans sought to recommend that they be visited with a merciless punishment, and pointed out that they had espoused the cause of the barbarians against the Greeks. [. . .] By producing many arguments of this kind, they stirred the feelings of the delegates against the Thebans, and in the end it was voted that the city should be completely destroyed and the prisoners sold, that the Theban exiles should be liable to extradition from the whole of Greece, and that no Greek should harbour any Theban. In conformity with the decision of the council the king destroyed the city and so struck terror in the minds of those Greeks who were contemplating revolt. He sold the prisoners and raised a sum of 440 talents of silver.6

Diodorus XVII.14

1. Spoken by Creon to Medea (line 288 of Euripides' tragedy) when he says he has heard that Medea is planning revenge on himself, his daughter and Jason. The quotation would have conveyed a veiled encouragement to Pausanias to take revenge on Attalus, his niece Cleopatra, and Philip.
2. The fullest account of the insult to Pausanias and Philip's death is in Diodorus XVI.93–4, who makes no mention of Alexander's or Olympias' possible involvement. The question remains as controversial now as it was then; cf. e.g. E. Badian, *Phoenix* 17 (1963), 244–50; J. R. Hamilton (1973), 41–3; Hammond and Griffith (1979), 675–91.
3. Cf. also **10**.
4. See passage (b) below.
5. The Greek allies of the 'League of Corinth' founded by Philip in 338 (Hammond and Griffith (1979), 623–46); Alexander was appointed their commander-in-chief (*hegemon*) after Philip's death. For Alexander's subsequent relations with the Greeks cf. esp. **4, 5, 6, 16**.
6. Thebes was rebuilt by Cassander in 316 (**21** §14, **29**; cf. **23, 83** §12).

3   The start of the expedition to Asia (spring 334)

See further: Hamilton (1969), 36–8 and *id.* (1973), 53–5.

(a) As for the size of his army, those writers who give the lowest figures put it at 30,000 foot and 4,000 horse, while those who give the highest figures put it at 43,000 foot and 5,000 horse.[1] Aristobulus writes that to provision these forces he had no more than 70 talents, while Duris says that he had supplies for only thirty days, and Onesicritus relates that he even had debts amounting to 200 talents.[2] And yet, although he was setting out with such meagre and limited resources, he would not embark before enquiring into the circumstances of his Companions and distributing to one an estate, to another a village, and to another the revenue of some hamlet or harbour. Virtually all crown property had been used up and earmarked for distribution[3] when Perdiccas asked him: 'What are you leaving for yourself, Sire?' 'My hopes', replied Alexander, to which Perdiccas rejoined: 'Then we, your companions in the expedition, will share these with you.' So Perdiccas refused the estate that had been allotted to him, and a few more of his friends did the same. But to those who accepted or asked for presents Alexander gave generously, and in this way he spent in largesses most of his Macedonian estates.[4] Such was his enthusiasm and eagerness when he crossed the Hellespont. He went up to Ilium, sacrificed to Athena and poured a libation to the heroes. At the tomb of Achilles, after anointing himself with oil and taking part in a race naked with his Companions, as is the custom, he deposited crowns and remarked how fortunate Achilles was to have had a faithful friend while he was alive and a great herald of his fame after his death. While he was going sightseeing about the town someone asked him whether he wanted to see the lyre of Alexander (i.e. Paris); he replied that he was not interested in that one, but was looking for the lyre of Achilles, to which he used to sing the glorious deeds of brave heroes.[5]

Plutarch, *Alexander* 15

(b) Alexander's army

[. . .] Alexander then carried out in person a careful review of the army that was following him. Of the infantry there were counted 12,000 Macedonians, 7,000 allies, and 5,000 mercenaries; Parmenion held command over all these. They were accompanied by 7,000 Odrysians, Triballians and Illyrians, and 1,000 archers and the so-called 'Agrianians'. In all the infantry numbered 30,000. Of the cavalry there were 1,800 Macedonians, under the command of Philotas son of Parmenion, 1,800 Thessalians, commanded by Callas son of Harpalus, a total of 600 of the other Greeks, commanded by Erygius, and 900 Thracian scouts and Paeonians, with Cassander as their commander. The total number of cavalry was 4,500. Such was the size of the army that crossed into Asia with Alexander.[6]

Diodorus XVII. 17.3–4

1. See passage (b) below.
2. Cf. **15** (ch. 9).
3. An exaggeration.
4. For Alexander's generosities to his followers cf. also **9** (ch. 72), **14, 15** and in general cf. **25** n. 3.
5. For the Homeric theme in Alexander's career cf. also **7** (b).
6. This is the only detailed account of Alexander's army; for discussion cf. R. D. Milns, *Entretiens Hardt* 22 (1976), 87–136; P. A. Brunt, Loeb *Arrian* I (1976), Introduction §§56–65; D. W. Engels, *Alexander the Great and the Logistics of the Macedonian Army* (London, 1978).

4 Alexander in Asia Minor, administration and politics (334)

Alexander then[1] appointed Calas satrap of the province which Arsites had governed and ordered the inhabitants to pay the same taxes they had formerly paid to Darius.[2] All the barbarians who came down from the hills and gave themselves up he ordered to go back to their homes. He exempted the people of Zelea from blame, because he knew that it was under duress that they had been fighting on the Persian side. Parmenion he sent ahead to take control of Dascylium, which he did as the garrison evacuated the place.

Alexander himself moved on to Sardis,[3] and when he was within 70 stades (*ca* 12.25 km) of the city there came to him Mithrenes the commander of the acropolis of Sardis and the leading citizens of the town, who surrendered the city to him while Mithrenes handed over the citadel with its treasures. Alexander pitched his camp on the banks of the river Hermus, which is about 20 stades (= *ca* 3.5 km) from Sardis. Amyntas the son of Andromenes he sent ahead to Sardis to take over the citadel; Mithrenes he took with him and treated with honour, while to the people of Sardis and the other Lydians he granted the use of their ancestral laws and allowed them their freedom.[4] [. . .] He left behind as commander of the citadel of Sardis Pausanias, one of the Companions; Nicias was put in charge of the assessment and collection of tribute,[5] while Asander son of Philotas was to govern Lydia and the rest of the province of Spithridates. He gave to Asander cavalry and light-armed troops in sufficient numbers for present needs. Calas and Alexander son of Aeropus he despatched against the territory held by Memnon, with the Peloponnesians and the majority of the other allies except the Argives, who had been left behind to guard the citadel of Sardis. [. . .] Three days later, on arriving at Ephesus, he brought back the exiles who had been expelled from the city for taking his side, overthrew the oligarchy and set up a democracy; the tribute which they used to pay to the barbarians, he ordered them to contribute to the goddess Artemis. The common people at Ephesus, freed from the fear of the oligarchs, rushed to put to death those who had called in Memnon, those who had plundered the sanctuary of Artemis, those who had cast down the image of Philip which was in the sanctuary and had dug up from the agora the tomb of Heropythes, the liberator of the city. They dragged out from the sanctuary and stoned to death Syrphax, his son Pelagon, and the children of Syrphax's brothers. But Alexander prevented them from hounding down the others any further and inflicting punishment, as he knew that the common people, if allowed to do so, would kill innocent men as well as the guilty, some through hatred and others to seize their property. This action of Alexander's at Ephesus brought him as much credit as anything else he did.[6]

Arrian 1.17 (omitting 5–6, 9)

1. Immediately after the victory at the river Granicus.
2. I.e. the previous Persian system was maintained except for the substitution of a Macedonian satrap for a Persian; this was Alexander's normal practice down to 331. On the administration of Alexander's empire cf. E. Badian, *Greece & Rome* 12.2 (1965), 166–82.
3. Residence of the Persian satrap of Lydia.
4. I.e. local autonomy; in practice Macedonian rule replaced Persian rule.

5. It is not clear whether the appointment of a separate financial official represents a significant innovation in government by Alexander (G. T. Griffith, *PCPS* n.s. 10 (1964), 23–9; *contra*, Badian (1966), 54f.).

6. Support for democracies now became Alexander's declared policy with the Greek cities of Asia Minor (Arrian 1.18.2; cf. **5**), for tactical and not ideological reasons (the Persians had supported tyrants and narrow oligarchies). Whether the Greek cities of Asia Minor were admitted to the League of Corinth, as the offshore islands were (cf. **5**) is disputed; in any case, whatever their technical status, Alexander interfered in their affairs. See Badian (1966), 37–69. For the general problem of the relations between Hellenistic rulers and Greek cities cf. **29**.

5 Letter of Alexander to Chios (332?)

The disturbed internal history of Chios during the years of the Macedonian conquest of Asia Minor reflects both the vicissitudes of that conquest and the political and social instability which affected many Greek states at that time (compare the case of Ephesus in **4**). A pro-Persian oligarchy was ov·rthrown in 336 at the start of the Macedonian offensive, but Chios was then betrayed to the Persians by an oligarchic group early in 333 (Arrian 11.1.1), and not recovered by the Macedonians until the autumn of 332 (Arrian 111.2.3–7). The original letter of Alexander to Chios is usually dated to 332, after the Macedonian recovery (for an earlier dating, in 334, see A. J. Heisserer, *Historia* 22 (1973), 191–204; H. Hauben, *Ancient Society* 7 (1976), 84–6). The inscription, however, was probably set up a few years later.

See further: Badian (1966), 46–53.

[In] the prytany of Deisitheus, from King[1] [Alexander to the] people of Chios. All the exiles from Chios shall return,[2] and the constitution in
5 Chios shall be democratic.[3] Law drafters shall be appointed to record / and correct the laws,[4] to remove all obstacles to the democracy and the return of the exiles. What is corrected or recorded shall be referred back to Alexander.[5] The people of Chios shall provide twenty triremes manned at their own expense, and these shall operate at sea as long as the
10 rest of the Hellenic fleet / follows us.[6] As for those who betrayed the city to the barbarians, those who have already taken to flight shall be banned from all the cities which participate in the peace and are liable to arrest, according to the decree of the Greeks.[7] Those who have stayed behind
15 are to be brought to trial in the council of the Greeks.[8] / If any dispute arises between the exiles who have returned and the men in the city, it shall be judged in our own court. Until such time as the Chians reach a settlement, an adequate garrison from King Alexander shall remain with them; the Chians shall be responsible for maintaining it.[9]

Tod, *GHI* II, 192; *Syll.*³ 283

1. The royal title may have been added here and in l.18 (contrast l.7) when the inscription was published; it is not clear how systematic Alexander was (or became) in his use of the title. For a definite example cf. **16** and see generally A. Aymard, *Etudes d'histoire ancienne* (Paris, 1967), 92f.
2. The democratic exiles.
3. Cf. **4** n.6.
4. Cf. **40** §8.
5. Throughout the letter Alexander takes for granted his right to interfere in the affairs of Chios.
6. Alexander had disbanded his Greek fleet in 334 after the capture of Miletus (Arrian 1.20.1); if the letter is correctly dated to 332 the reference will be to the fleet operating in the Aegean under Hegelochus (Arrian III.2.3–7).
7. The Greek allies of the 'League of Corinth' (cf. **2**(*b*)).
8. Yet Alexander placed the Chian oligarchs in custody at Elephantine in 332 (Arrian III.2.5 and 7).
9. The garrison was withdrawn in 331 at the request of the Chians (Quintus Curtius IV.8.12).

6 Alexander's manifesto to Darius after Issus (332)

See further: G. T. Griffith, *PCPS* n.s. 14 (1968), 33–48.

While Alexander was still at Marathus there came to him envoys from Darius with a letter from him and a request they conveyed verbally to release Darius' mother, wife and children. The letter's contents[1] were to the effect that there had been friendship and alliance between Philip and Artaxerxes,[2] but when Artaxerxes' son Arses came to the throne, Philip was the initial aggressor against Arses, though he had suffered no harm from the Persians.[3] Since Darius' own accession Alexander had not sent any envoy to confirm the old friendship and alliance, but crossed with an army to Asia and did the Persians much harm. This was why Darius had come down to defend his country and preserve his ancestral rule. The battle had been decided as some god willed, but he, as one king to another, was asking for his captive wife, mother and children, and was prepared to make a treaty of friendship with Alexander and to be his ally. He requested Alexander to send envoys to accompany the Persian emissaries Meniscus and Arsimas and to exchange mutual assurances.

Alexander drafted a reply to this letter and sent Thersippus to accompany the envoys from Darius, with instructions to hand over the letter to Darius but not to engage in any negotiations. Alexander's letter read as follows:[5] 'Your ancestors invaded Macedon and the rest of Greece and did us harm although we had not done you any previous injury. I have been appointed commander-in-chief (*hegemon*) of the Greeks[6] and it

15

is with the aim of punishing the Persians that I have crossed into Asia, since you are the aggressors. You gave support to the people of Perinthus, who had done my father harm, and Ochus sent a force to Thrace,[7] which was under our rule. My father died at the hand of conspirators instigated by you, as you yourself boasted to everybody in your letters,[8] you killed Arses with the help of Bagoas and gained your throne through unjust means, in defiance of Persian custom and doing wrong to the Persians. You sent unfriendly letters to the Greeks about me, to push them to war against me, and sent money to the Spartans and some other Greeks, which none of the other cities would accept apart from the Spartans. Your envoys corrupted my friends and sought to destroy the peace which I established among the Greeks.[9] I therefore led an expedition against you, and you started the quarrel. But now I have defeated in battle first your generals and satraps, and now you in person and your army, and by the grace of the gods I control the country. All those who fought on your side and did not die in battle but came over to me, I hold myself responsible for them; they are not on my side under duress but are taking part in the expedition of their own free will. Approach me therefore as the lord of all Asia. If you are afraid of suffering harm at my hands by coming in person, send some of your friends to receive proper assurances. Come to me to ask and receive your mother, your wife, your children and anything else you wish. Whatever you can persuade me to give shall be yours. In future whenever you communicate with me, send to me as king of Asia; do not write to me as an equal, but state your demands to the master of all your possessions. If not I shall deal with you as a wrongdoer. If you wish to lay claim to the title of king, then stand your ground and fight for it;[10] do not take to flight, as I shall pursue you wherever you may be.'

Arrian II.14

1. According to Diodorus XVII. 39. 1–2 Alexander concealed the letter of Darius and submitted instead to his council of advisers a forged letter 'more in accordance with his own interests' (and thus secured rejection of Darius' advances). The letter paraphrased by Arrian may be this forgery; see Griffith, *op. cit.*

2. No other ancient source mentions this 'friendship and alliance', which may be fictitious (cf. Hammond and Griffith (1979), 485–7).

3. The Persians gave support to Perinthus against Philip in 240, cf. below (Hammond and Griffith (1979), 573).

4. There is no mention of the territorial and financial offers recorded by Diodorus XVII.39.1. During the siege of Tyre Darius made renewed offers to Alexander, which were also rejected (Arrian II.25.1–3).

5. The wording is Arrian's not Alexander's.

6. Cf. **2**(*b*).

7. Not otherwise attested.
8. This is pure propaganda.
9. The start of Philip's campaign in Asia Minor in 336 antedates Persian intervention in Greece.
10. For this view of kingship and the rights of conquest cf. **36**.

7 The foundation of Alexandria (332/1)

As with much in Alexander's career, the circumstances surrounding the origins of the first and most famous of his foundations in Asia easily became the subject of legend. Arrian's sober account should be compared with Plutarch's more colourful version. The foundation is usually dated to before the visit to Ammon (**8**), though some place it after. For Alexander's reputation as a founder of cities see also **18** and **19**; on Hellenistic city foundations see **40**. For a description of Ptolemaic Alexandria see **232**.

See further: Fraser 1 (1972), 3–7.

(a) Arrian

Alexander came to Canobus, sailed round Lake Mareotis, and landed on the site of the present city of Alexandria, which is called after himself. The site seemed to him to be a most favourable one for the foundation of a city and he thought that it would be prosperous. He was therefore seized with a longing (*pothos*)[1] for the task, and marked out himself the main parts of the city, the location of the agora, how many sanctuaries there should be, and of which gods, those of Greek gods and of Egyptian Isis, and the course of the city-wall. He offered sacrifice over the plan, and the omens appeared favourable. The following story is also told, and I do not disbelieve it. It is said that Alexander wanted to indicate to the builders the lines of the city-wall, but had nothing to mark the ground with. One of the builders suggested making use of the meal which the soldiers carried in vessels, and dropping it on the ground where the king indicated. In this way the circumference of the city-wall was marked out according to his wishes. The seers, and especially Aristander of Telmessus, who had made many correct prophecies to Alexander, reflected on this and declared that the city would be prosperous in every way, particularly as regards agricultural produce.

Arrian III.1.5–2.2

(b) Plutarch

If what the Alexandrians say on the authority of Heracleides is true, then it seems that Homer was no idle or useless companion to him on his expedition. They say that after his conquest of Egypt he resolved to found and leave behind him a large and populous Greek city which would bear his name. On the advice of his architects he was about to measure out and enclose a certain site, when during the night, as he was sleeping, he saw a remarkable vision. He thought he could see a man with very white hair and of venerable appearance standing beside him and speaking these lines:

> Then there is an island in the stormy sea,
> In front of Egypt; they call it Pharos.[2]

He rose at once and went to Pharos, which at that time was still an island a little above the Canobic mouth of the Nile, but which has now been joined to the mainland by a causeway. When he saw that the site was eminently suitable (it is a strip of land similar to a fairly broad isthmus, running between a large lagoon and the sea which terminates in a great harbour), he exclaimed that Homer was admirable in other respects and was also an excellent architect, and ordered the plan of the city to be drawn in conformity with the terrain. Since there was no chalk available, they used barley-meal to describe a rounded area on the dark soil, to whose inner arc straight lines succeeded, starting from what might be called the skirts of the area and narrowing the breadth uniformly, so as to produce the figure of a *chlamys*.[3] The king was delighted with the plan, when suddenly a vast multitude of birds of every kind and size flew from the river and the lagoon on to the site like clouds; nothing was left of the barley-meal and even Alexander was much troubled by the omen. But his seers advised him there was nothing to fear (in their view the city he was founding would abound in resources and would sustain men from every nation); he therefore instructed his overseers to press on with the work.

Plutarch, *Alexander* 26.3–10

1. An expression frequently used of Alexander by Arrian (cf. **8, 17**). This may go back to Alexander himself (V. Ehrenberg in Griffith (1966), 74–83; cf. P. A. Brunt, Loeb *Arrian* I (1976), 469f.), but may also be a literary phrase with no special significance.
2. *Odyssey* IV.354f.
3. A military cloak; cf. also **232** §8. On this passage cf. Fraser II (1972), 26 n. 64.

8 Alexander's visit to the oracle of Ammon (332/1)

Alexander's visit to the oracle of the Egyptian god Ammon, whom the Greeks identified with Zeus, is one of the most famous but also one of the most mysterious episodes in his career. The motives for the expedition, the question (or questions) he put to the oracle, and the answers he received, remain a matter of speculation and debate. At any rate, Alexander's close personal attachment to Ammon and his apparent belief in his descent from him (cf. **15** ch. 8) date from this visit. Arrian is reticent on what actually happened at the oracle while the other sources provide conjectures liberally.

See further: Hamilton (1969), 71–3; *id.* (1973), 75–7; P. A. Brunt, Loeb *Arrian* I (1976), Appendices 4 and 5.

At this point Alexander was seized with a longing[1] to visit Ammon in Libya;[2] his intention was to consult the god, as the oracle of Ammon was reputed to be truthful and it was said that Perseus and Heracles had consulted it, the former when Polydectes sent him against the Gorgon, the latter when he was making his journey to Libya and Egypt in search of Antaeus and Busiris. Alexander wanted to rival Perseus and Heracles, since he was descended from them both, and was also seeking to trace his birth back to Ammon, just as mythology traces that of Heracles and Perseus to Zeus. He therefore set out for Ammon in this frame of mind, with the intention of finding out more exactly about his origins, or of claiming he had found out. The journey along the coast as far as Paraetonium was through deserted, though not waterless, country, for a distance of 1,600 stades (*ca* 280 km) according to Aristobulus (*FGrH* 139 F 13). From there he turned inland, where the oracle of Ammon was to be found. The road is deserted, sandy for the most part and without water. But Alexander had the benefit of heavy rains, and he ascribed this to the divinity. Another occurrence was attributed to divine intervention: whenever a south wind blows in that country, much of the road is covered with sand and the roadmarks disappear. One is in an ocean of sand, as it were, and it is impossible to tell one's direction, as there are no mountains or trees or solid hills to serve as signs and guide the travellers on their way, just as sailors go by the stars. Hence Alexander's army was advancing aimlessly and the guides could not tell the way. Ptolemy son of Lagus relates (*FGrH* 138 F 8) that two speaking snakes preceded the army and Alexander ordered the guides to follow them and trust in the divinity; the snakes then led the way to the oracle and back again. But Aristobulus (F 4) says (and most writers agree with him) that two crows flew in front of the army and served as guides to Alexander. I can assert that there must have been some divine intervention to help Alexander, because this is what seems probable. But the truth of the matter has been obscured by the conflicting accounts of historians.

(4) The area where the sanctuary of Ammon is situated is circular in shape; it is completely deserted, covered with sand and waterless, but the site itself is small (it has a maximum breadth of 40 stades (*ca* 7 km)). It is full of garden trees, olives and palms, and is the only part of the area to catch the dew [. . .] Alexander admired the site and consulted the god,

19

and having received, as he put it, the answer which his heart desired he returned to Egypt by the same road, as Aristobulus says (F 15), though according to Ptolemy (F 9) he followed a straight road to Memphis.

Arrian III.3–4 (omitting 4.2–4)

1. See **7** n. 1.
2. Ammon's oracle lay in the oasis of Siwah in the Libyan desert, to the west of Egyptian Thebes.

9 The destruction of Persepolis and its palace (330)

The burning of the palace of Persepolis by Alexander at the end of his four-month stay in the city is briefly mentioned by Arrian (III.18.10–12) and presented by him as a deliberate act of policy to punish the Persians for their invasion of Greece in 480 (on this propaganda presentation of the war cf. **6**). More plausible is the version of Diodorus, which shows the burning to have taken place at the climax of a wild drinking-party, an act of which Alexander soon repented (cf. Plutarch, *Alexander* 38, end). The destruction of the palace was certainly in contradiction of the policy of conciliating the Persians which Alexander was about to adopt (**11, 14, 15**).

See further: Hamilton (1969), 99–101; *id.* (1973), 88f.; P. A. Brunt, Loeb *Arrian* I (1976), Appendix 10.

As for Persepolis, the capital of the Persian kingdom, Alexander described it to the Macedonians as their worst enemy among the cities of Asia, and he gave it over to the soldiers to plunder, with the exception of the royal palace. It was the wealthiest city under the sun and the private houses had been filled for a long time with riches of every kind. The Macedonians rushed into it, killing all the men and plundering the houses, which were numerous and full of furniture and precious objects of every kind. Here much silver was carried off and no little gold, and many expensive dresses, embroidered with purple or with gold, fell as prizes to the victors. But the great royal palace, famed throughout the inhabited world, had been condemned to the indignity of total destruction. The Macedonians spent the whole day in pillage but still could not satisfy their inexhaustible greed. [. . .] As for the women, they dragged them away forcibly with their jewels, treating as slaves the whole group of captives. As Persepolis had surpassed all other cities in prosperity, so she now exceeded them in misfortune.

(71) Alexander went up to the citadel and took possession of the treasures stored there. They were full of gold and silver, with the accumulation of revenue from Cyrus, the first king of the Persians, down to that time. Reckoning gold in terms of silver, 120,000 talents

were found there. Alexander wanted to take part of the money with him for the expenses of war and to deposit the rest at Susa under close guard. From Babylon, Mesopotamia and Susa, he sent for a crowd of mules, partly pack and partly draught animals, as well as 3,000 pack camels, and with these he had all the treasure conveyed to the chosen places. He was very hostile to the local people and did not trust them, and wished to destroy Persepolis utterly. [. . .]

(72) Alexander held games to celebrate his victories; he offered magnificent sacrifices to the gods and entertained his friends lavishly. One day when the Companions were feasting, and intoxication was growing as the drinking went on, a violent madness took hold of these drunken men. One of the women present (she was an Athenian called Thais[1]) declared that it would be Alexander's greatest achievement in Asia to join in their procession and set fire to the royal palace, allowing women's hands to destroy in an instant what had been the pride of the Persians. These words were spoken to young men who were completely out of their minds because of drink, and someone, as expected, shouted to lead off the procession and light torches, exhorting them to punish the crimes committed against the Greek sanctuaries. Others joined in the cry and said that only Alexander was worthy of this deed. The king was excited with the rest by these words. They all leaped out from the banquet and passed the word around to form a triumphal procession in honour of Dionysus. A quantity of torches was quickly collected, and as female musicians had been invited to the banquet, it was to the sound of singing and flutes and pipes that the king led them to the revel, with Thais the courtesan conducting the ceremony. She was the first after the king to throw her blazing torch into the palace. As the others followed their example the whole area of the royal palace was quickly engulfed in flames. What was most remarkable was that the sacrilege committed by Xerxes, king of the Persians, against the Acropolis of Athens was avenged by a single woman, a fellow-citizen of the victims, who many years later, and in sport, inflicted the same treatment on the Persians.

Diodorus XVII.70–2 (omitting 70.5; 71.3(end)-8)

1. Known to have been Ptolemy's mistress, hence probably the different and briefer version of events in Arrian (from Ptolemy), which makes no mention of Thais.

10 The triumph of the Macedonians: a contemporary view (summer 330)

The following passage comes from the speech of Aeschines in the famous trial in which he attacked his rival Demosthenes for the failure of his anti-Macedonian policies; the trial took place in Athens in summer 330. For the political context see G. L. Cawkwell, *CQ* n.s. 19 (1969), 163–80.

What strange and unexpected event has not occurred in our time?[1] The life we have lived is no ordinary human one, but we were born to be an object of wonder to posterity. The Persian king, who dug a canal through Mt Athos, who cast a yoke on the Hellespont, who demanded earth and water from the Greeks, who had the arrogance to write in his letters that he was the lord of all men from the rising to the setting sun, surely he is now fighting for his own safety rather than for domination over others?[2] And do we not see that the men who are thought worthy of this glory and of the command against the Persians, are precisely those who freed the sanctuary at Delphi?[3] And Thebes, Thebes the neighbouring city, has been erased in one day from the centre of Greece – a just punishment perhaps, for their misguided policies and for the blindness and folly that afflicted them, divinely inspired rather than human.[4] And the unfortunate Spartans, who were only involved with these events at the beginning when the temple at Delphi was captured, and who at one time claimed to be the leaders of the Greeks, are now about to be sent to Alexander as hostages to parade their misfortune.[5] Whatever he decides, they and their country shall have to endure, the verdict depending on the moderation of the victor whom they offended. And our own city, the common refuge of the Greeks, which formerly embassies from all over Greece would visit, each city seeking its safety from us, is now no longer fighting for the leadership of Greece, but to defend the land of its fathers. And all this has happened from the moment Demosthenes took over control of affairs.

Aeschines III (Against Ctesiphon), 132–4

1. Compare **20**.
2. Darius had been defeated at Gaugamela on 1 October 331; news of his murder by Bessus in July 330 had not yet reached Athens.
3. The Macedonians had put an end to the Phocian control of Delphi which had lasted from 356 to 346.
4. See **2**.
5. The Spartans had remained aloof from the 'League of Corinth'; they revolted against Macedon under King Agis III, but were defeated by Antipater at the battle of Megalopolis (exact date uncertain: at the time of Gaugamela (E. N. Borza, *CP* 66 (1971), 230–5), or later, in 330 (Cawkwell, *op. cit.*, 170–3)). Cf. P. A. Brunt, Loeb *Arrian* I (1976), Appendix 6.

11 Alexander's attempt to introduce obeisance ('proskynesis') at his court

Among Greeks and Persians, 'obeisance' (*proskynesis*) was a mark of respect performed by kissing one's fingers towards the person honoured. However, it was an honour paid by Greeks only to the image of a god, but by Persians to social superiors, and especially to the king. For Persians *proskynesis* did not imply that the person honoured was regarded as a god, though Greeks often misleadingly believed so. At the Persian court, prostration (falling on one's knees) was not necessarily a part of *proskynesis* towards the king, at least not for the Persian nobility.

Alexander's motives for attempting (unsuccessfully) to introduce the ceremony to his own court, and making it apply equally to Macedonians, Greeks and non-Greeks, are conjectural, and modern scholarship is divided on the subject. On a minimum interpretation, Alexander's aim was political and was part of his attempt to bridge the gap between the Persian and the Macedonian nobility, the old and the new rulers of the empire (see further **14, 15**). On a maximum interpretation, Alexander deliberately sought to exalt himself by receiving a quasi-divine honour (this is the view reproduced by Arrian). Whatever the truth about Alexander's intentions with *proskynesis*, it is likely that he did eventually (in 324) come to demand divine honours from the Greek states, though both fact and interpretation are disputed. On the cult of rulers after Alexander see **32**.

See further: J. P. V. D. Balsdon, *Historia* I (1950), 363–88 = Griffith (1966), 179–204; Hamilton (1969), 150–3 and (1973), 105–8, 138–41; P. A. Brunt, Loeb *Arrian* I (1976), Appendix 14.

Concerning the opposition offered to Alexander by Callisthenes over the question of obeisance, there is also the following story.[1] It had been agreed between Alexander, the sophists and the most distinguished of the Persians and the Medes at his court that the subject should be raised during a drinking-party. Anaxarchus launched the topic, saying that Alexander had much better claims to be regarded as a god than Dionysus and Heracles, not so much because of the number and magnitude of his achievements, as because Dionysus was a Theban and was not related to the Macedonians, and Heracles an Argive, only related to them through Alexander's family, since Alexander was descended from Heracles. The Macedonians would have better reason to honour their king with divine honours; there was no doubt that once Alexander departed from men they would honour him as a god. How much more justifiable it would therefore be to honour him in his lifetime rather than wait for his death, when the honour would be of no benefit to the recipient. (11) After Anaxarchus had spoken to this effect, those who were privy to the plan praised his words and wanted to begin doing obeisance to Alexander, but the majority of Macedonians were displeased and kept quiet. Then Callisthenes intervened with these words: 'Anaxarchus, I declare that there is no honour fitting to man that Alexander does not deserve. But a distinction has been drawn by men between honours fit for mortals and honours fit for gods, for example in the matter of building temples and setting up cult statues and setting apart sacred enclosures for gods, and making sacrifices and libations to them, and offering hymns to the gods but eulogies to men. Most important is the distinction observed in the matter of obeisance. You greet men with a kiss, but since a god is placed higher up and it is sacrilege to touch him, you honour him in this way with obeisance. Dances, too, are held in honour of the gods, and paeans are sung to praise them. No wonder, when one considers that different honours are appropriate to different gods, while heroes receive yet others distinct from divine honours. It is unreasonable, therefore, to obliterate all these distinctions by inflating human beings to excessive proportions through extravagant honours, while inappropriately diminishing gods, as far as is possible, by offering them the same honours as men. Alexander himself would not tolerate for a moment a private individual laying claim to royal honours on the strength of some unjust show of hands or vote. How much more justified would be the displeasure of the gods against men who assume divine honours or allow others to do it for them. Alexander has more than justified the claim that he is and is seen to be the bravest of the brave, the most kingly of kings and the greatest of all generals. More than anyone else, Anaxarchus, you ought to have put forward this point of view and opposed the rival line of argument, because of your position as philosopher and instructor of Alexander. You ought not to have launched this subject. Remember that it is not Cambyses or Xerxes you are associating with and advising, but the son of Philip, descended from Heracles and Aeacus, whose forefathers came from Argos to Macedon, and have since ruled the Macedonians by law and not by force.[2] Why, not even Heracles received divine honours from the Greeks in his lifetime, nor even after his death until Apollo at Delphi gave an oracle instructing Heracles to be honoured as a god. If one must think in foreign ways on the ground that this argument has originated in a foreign land, then do not forget Greece, Alexander. It was for her sake that you launched your whole expedition, to add Asia to Greece. Consider then whether on your return you will exact obeisance from the Greeks, the freest of men, or will you make an exception for the Greeks but inflict this indignity on the Macedonians? Or will you draw a distinction in the matter of honours generally, receiving from Macedonians and Greeks honours fit for men and acceptable to Greeks, and foreign honours only from non-Greeks? It may be said that Cyrus the son of Cambyses was the first man to receive the honour of obeisance, and that it is this which has kept the Persians and Medes submissive as you can see. But you must remember that the great Cyrus was humbled by Scythians, poor but independent men, and Darius by other Scythians, and Xerxes by Athenians and Spartans, and Artaxerxes by Clearchus, Xenophon and the Ten Thousand, and lastly our opponent Darius by Alexander – who had not yet been the object of obeisance.'

(12) These and similar words of Callisthenes greatly irritated Alexander, though the Macedonians were pleased to hear them. Alexander realised this and sent instructions to the Macedonians to forget about obeisance for the future. Silence fell after these words, but the eldest of the Persians came forward to perform obeisance one after the other. Leonnatus, one of the Companions, thought that one of the Persians had not bowed properly, and made fun of the Persian's air of submissiveness. Alexander was angry with him at the time, though later he was reconciled. The following story is also told.[3] Alexander sent round a golden cup, passing it first to those who were privy to the plan about obeisance. The first person would drink from it, stand up and offer obeisance, then receive a kiss from Alexander, and the rest likewise in turn. When it was Callisthenes' turn, he stood up, drank from the cup, and went towards Alexander to kiss him, but without offering obeisance. Alexander was then engaged in conversation with Hephaestion and was not paying attention to whether Callisthenes was going through the act of obeisance or not. But when Callisthenes approached Alexander to kiss him, Demetrius the son of Pythonax, one of the Companions, remarked that he had not made obeisance, whereupon Alexander did not allow himself to be kissed. 'Well then,' exclaimed Callisthenes, 'I shall go away one kiss the poorer.'[4]

Arrian IV.10.5–12.5

1. I.e. the story does not come from Ptolemy or Aristobulus, Arrian's two principal sources. The reliability of the account is questionable; it may be influenced by controversies of the Roman imperial period over the deification of emperors.
2. This hardly implies the existence of a Macedonian 'constitution'; cf. R. M. Errington, *Chiron* 8 (1978), 80–3.
3. From Chares of Mytilene (*FGrH* 125 F 14), court chamberlain of Alexander, as appears from Plutarch, *Alexander* 54.4–6; the story has better credentials than the previous one.
4. Callisthenes was later arrested (spring 327) for alleged complicity in the conspiracy of the Pages; the sources differ on the manner of his death (Hamilton (1973), 107f.).

12 The mutiny at the Hyphasis (326)

See further: Hamilton (1969), 170–5 and (1973), 116–18.

When Coenus had spoken[1] the bystanders shouted their approval; many even shed tears, thus making even more plain their reluctance to advance and face yet more dangers, and how anxious they were to turn back.

Alexander for the moment was annoyed at Coenus' plain talking and at the lack of courage of the other leaders, and dismissed the meeting. Then he summoned again the same men for the next day and angrily declared that he was going to pursue his advance, but would not compel any Macedonian to follow him against his will; for he would have men to follow their king of their own volition; as to those who wanted to return home, it was open for them to do so and report back that they had returned leaving their king in the midst of enemies. With these words he withdrew to his tent and would not admit to his presence any of his Companions for the whole of that day and for another two days after. He expected that the Macedonians and the allies would experience a change of mind, as often happens in a crowd of soldiers, and would then be more easily brought over to his point of view. But when there was profound silence through the camp and it was clear they were annoyed with his show of temper, though not prepared to change their minds because of it, then, according to Ptolemy the son of Lagus (*FGrH* 138 F 23), he nonetheless offered sacrifice to cross the river, but did not obtain favourable omens. At this he called together the eldest of his Companions and especially those who were closest to him, and since everything was now pointing to withdrawal, he declared to the army that he had decided to turn back. (29) At this there arose a loud shout such as you would expect from a large and joyful multitude, and many of them wept. Some drew near the royal tent and called for many blessings on Alexander, since he had allowed himself to be defeated by them and them alone. Then he divided the army into twelve parts and gave orders to build twelve altars, as high as the biggest towers and broader even than towers would be. These were meant as thank offerings to the gods for having brought him victorious so far, and as memorials of his labours.

Arrian v.28–29.1

1. Arrian has just reproduced 'speeches' by Alexander and Coenus, a Macedonian noble, arguing respectively for and against the advance further east.

13 'Maladministration' in Alexander's empire

'The difficulties of Alexander's march into the upper country, the wound he had received among the Malli, and the losses suffered by his army, which were said to be considerable, made men doubt his safety and encouraged the subject peoples to revolt. The generals and satraps were incited to commit many injustices, exactions and acts of violence; in short, restlessness and a desire for change spread everywhere' (Plutarch, *Alexander* 68.3). Loss of control by the central authority had been a recurring problem in the Persian empire and remained so in the

Hellenistic kingdoms (cf. e.g. **147, 231**); the nature and extent of the crisis in Alexander's empire in 325 have been variously estimated.

See further: E. Badian, *JHS* 81 (1961), 16–43 = Griffith (1966), 206–33; Hamilton (1969), 189f. and (1973), 128–30; R. Lane Fox, *Alexander the Great* (London, 1973), 541f.

When Alexander had reached Carmania Craterus arrived bringing with him the rest of the army and the elephants, and also Ordanes, who had revolted and started a rebellion but whom he had arrested. There also came Stasanor the satrap of Areia and the satrap of the Zarangians, and with them Pharismanes son of Phrataphernes, satrap of Parthyaea and Hyrcania. There arrived also the commanders who had been left behind with Parmenion in charge of the army in Media, Cleander, Sitalces and Heracon, bringing with them the largest part of this army. Both the natives and the army itself made many accusations against Cleander and Sitalces, charging them with plundering temples, rifling ancient tombs, and other unjust and arrogant actions towards their subjects. When this was reported, Alexander put these two to death, to inspire fear in all the other satraps, hyparchs or nomarchs who were left, that they would suffer the same fate as these if guilty of misconduct. This more than anything else kept in order the peoples who had been conquered by Alexander or who had come over to his side, though they were so many in number and so far apart – that in Alexander's kingdom the subjects were not to be wronged by their rulers.[1] As for Heracon, he was for the time being acquitted of the charge, but not long after he was convicted by men from Susa of having plundered the sanctuary at Susa, and he too was punished.

Arrian VI.27.3–5

1. An apologetic view; for a critical interpretation of Alexander's action see E. Badian, *op. cit.*

14   The marriages at Susa and Alexander's generosities (324)

See further: Hamilton (1969), 194–7 and (1973), 133f.

Then he also celebrated weddings at Susa, both his own and those of his Companions. He himself married Barsine, the eldest of Darius' daughters, and, according to Aristobulus (*FGrH* 139 F 52), another girl as well, Parysatis, the youngest of the daughters of Ochus. He had already married previously Roxane, the daughter of Oxyartes of Bactria.[1] He gave Drypetis to Hephaestion, she too a daughter of Darius and a sister of his own wife; his intention was that the children of Hephaestion should be cousins to his own children. To Craterus he gave Amastrine daughter of Oxyartes, brother of Darius, and to Perdiccas the daughter of Atropates, satrap of Media. To Ptolemy the bodyguard and to Eumenes the royal secretary he gave the daughters of Artabazus, Artacama to one and Artonis to the other. To Nearchus he gave the daughter of Barsine and Mentor, and to Seleucus the daughter of Spitamenes of Bactria. Similarly he gave to the other Companions the noblest daughters of the Persians and Medes, some 80 in all.[2] The marriages were celebrated according to Persian custom. Chairs were placed for the bridegrooms in order, and after the drinks the brides came in and sat down, each by the side of her groom. They took them by the hand and kissed them; the king began the ceremony, for all the weddings took place together. More than any action of Alexander this seemed to show a popular and comradely spirit. The bridegrooms after receiving their brides led them away, each to his own home, and to all Alexander gave a dowry. And as for all the Macedonians who had already married Asian women,[3] Alexander ordered a list of their names to be drawn up; they numbered over 10,000, and Alexander offered them all gifts for their wedding.

(5) He also thought this was a suitable opportunity to settle the debts of the army, and ordered a list of individual debts to be drawn up, with a promise to pay them. At first few put down their names; they feared Alexander was testing them to find out who thought the soldier's pay insufficient and who was living above his means. When it was reported that the majority would not put their names down, but concealed any bonds they had, he condemned the soldiers' lack of trust. A king should not say anything but the truth to his subjects, and they must not imagine their king to be saying anything but the truth to them. So he had tables set up in the camp with gold on them, and men charged with the distribution of money to anyone who could show a bond, and he ordered the debts to be settled but without now drawing up a list of names. In this way they were convinced that Alexander was saying the truth, and their pleasure at not being individually identified was even greater than their satisfaction at seeing their debts paid off. It is said that up to 20,000 talents were distributed to the army on that occasion.

He also made various presents to various men, according to the reputation each enjoyed or the courage which anyone had displayed in dangers. He also crowned with golden wreaths those conspicuous for bravery, first Peucestas who had covered him with his shield, then Leonnatus for the same service[4] and for the dangers he faced among the Indians and the victory he won among the Orians. With the forces left to him he opposed the rebelling Oreitans and their neighbours and defeated them in battle, and in other respects he seemed to have handled affairs well among the Orians. In addition Alexander crowned Nearchus for his navigation from India by the great sea; for he had now arrived at Susa. He also crowned Onesicritus the pilot of the royal ship, and Hephaestion and the other bodyguards.[5]

Arrian VII.4.4–5

1. In 327.
2. With the exception of Seleucus (cf. **46** n. 15, **174**), Alexander's Companions all repudiated their Persian wives after Alexander's death. For Alexander's attempts to reconcile Macedonians and Persians see also **11, 15**.
3. This happened independently of Alexander's wishes; after the banquet at Opis (**15**) Alexander promised to bring up the children from these marriages in Macedonian ways and send them back to Macedon (Arrian VII.12.2).
4. During an attack on an Indian village in 325 when Alexander nearly lost his life.
5. For Alexander's generosities see **3** n. 4.

15 The mutiny at Opis and the feast of reconciliation (324)

See further: Hamilton (1969), 197–9 and (1973), 134f., 142–4.

On arriving at Opis, Alexander called together the Macedonians and declared that he was discharging from the campaign and sending back to their country those who were unfit for service because of age or wounds suffered. The presents he would give would make them an object of even greater envy at home and would encourage the other Macedonians to take part in the same dangers and hardships.[1] Alexander spoke these words with the clear intention of pleasing the Macedonians, but they felt Alexander now despised them and regarded them as completely unfit for service. It was not unreasonable for them to take exception to Alexander's words, and they had had many grievances throughout the expedition. There was the recurring annoyance of Alexander's Persian dress which pointed in the same direction, and the training of the barbarian 'Successors' in the Macedonian style of warfare,[2] and the introduction of foreign cavalry into the squadrons of the Companions.[3] They could not keep quiet any longer, but all shouted to Alexander to discharge them from service and take his father on the expedition (by this insult they meant Ammon).[4] When Alexander heard this – he was now rather more quick-tempered and eastern flattery had made him become arrogant towards the Macedonians – he leaped from the platform with the leaders around him and ordered the arrest of the most conspicuous trouble-makers, indicating to the hypaspists the men for arrest, thirteen in all. He

29

ordered them to be led off for execution, and when a terrified silence had fallen on the others he ascended the platform again and spoke as follows.[5]

(9) 'Macedonians, my speech will not be aimed at stopping your urge to return home; as far as I am concerned you may go where you like. But I want you to realise on departing what I have done for you, and what you have done for me. Let me begin, as is right, with my father Philip. Philip found you wandering about without resources, many of you clothed in sheepskins and pasturing small flocks in the mountains, defending them with difficulty against the Illyrians, Triballians and neighbouring Thracians. He gave you cloaks to wear instead of sheep-skins, brought you down from the mountains to the plains, and made you a match in war for the neighbouring barbarians, owing your safety to your own bravery and no longer to reliance on your mountain strongholds. He made you city-dwellers and civilised you with good laws and customs. Those barbarians who used to harry you and plunder your property, he made you their leaders instead of their slaves and subjects. He annexed much of Thrace to Macedon, seized the most favourable coastal towns and opened up the country to commerce, and enabled you to exploit your mines undisturbed. He made you governors of the Thessalians, before whom you used to die of fright, humbled the Phocians and so opened a broad and easy path into Greece in place of a narrow and difficult one. The Athenians and Thebans, who were permanently poised to attack Macedon, he so humbled (and I was now helping him in this task) that instead of you paying tribute to the Athenians and being under the sway of the Thebans, they now in turn had to seek their safety from us. He marched into the Peloponnese and settled matters there too. He was appointed commander-in-chief of all Greece for the campaign against the Persians, but preferred to assign the credit to all the Macedonians rather than just to himself.

Such were the achievements of my father on your behalf; as you can see for yourselves, they are great, and yet small in comparison with my own. I inherited from my father a few gold and silver cups, and less than 60 talents in the treasury; Philip had debts amounting to 500 talents, and I raised a loan of a further 800.[6] I started from a country that could barely sustain you and immediately opened up the Hellespont for you, although the Persians then held the mastery of the sea. I defeated in a cavalry engagement the satraps of Darius and annexed to your rule the whole of Ionia and Aeolis, both Phrygias and Lydia, and took Miletus by storm. All the rest came over to our side spontaneously, and I made them yours for you to enjoy. All the wealth of Egypt and Cyrene, which I won without a fight, are now yours, Coele Syria, Palestine and Mesopotamia are your possession, Babylon and Bactria and Susa belong to you, you own the wealth of Lydia, the treasures of Persia, the riches of India, and the outer ocean. You are satraps, you are generals, you are captains. As for me, what do I have left from all these labours? Merely this purple cloak and a diadem.7 [. . .]'

(11) When he had finished Alexander quickly leaped down from the platform, retired to the royal tent and neglected his bodily needs. For that day and the day after he would not let any of his Companions see him. On the third day he invited inside the élite of the Persians, appointed them to the command of all the squadrons, and only allowed those who received the title of 'kinsmen' from him to kiss him. As for the Macedonians, they were at first struck dumb by his speech and waited for him near the platform. No one followed the departing king, apart from the Companions around him and the bodyguards, but the majority were unable to decide what to do or say or to make up their minds to go away. When they were told what was happening with the Persians and Medes, that the command was being given to Persians and the oriental army was being divided into companies, that Macedonian names were being given to them, and there was a Persian *agema* (squadron) and Persian foot-companions and other *asthetairoi*8 and a Persian regiment of Silver Shields,9 and a Companion cavalry together with another royal squadron, they could not endure it any longer. They ran in a body to the royal tent, cast their weapons down in front of the doors as a sign of supplication to the king, and standing before the doors shouted to the king to come out. They were prepared to hand over those responsible for the present disturbance and those who had raised the outcry. They would not move from the doors by day or night until Alexander took pity on them.

When this was reported to Alexander, he quickly came out and saw their humble disposition; he heard the majority crying and lamenting, and was moved to tears. He came forward to speak, but they remained there imploring him. One of them, whose age and command of the Companion cavalry made him preeminent (he was called Callines) spoke as follows. 'Sire, what grieves the Macedonians is that you have already made some Persians your "kinsmen", and the Persians are called "kinsmen" of Alexander and are allowed to kiss you, while not one of the Macedonians has been granted this honour.' Alexander then interrupted him and said 'I make you all my "kinsmen" and henceforward that shall be your title.' At this Callines stepped forward and kissed him, and so did everyone else who wished. And thus they picked up their arms again and returned to the camp amid shouts and songs of triumph. Alexander celebrated the occasion by sacrificing to the gods he normally sacrificed to, and offering a public banquet. He sat down and so did everyone else, the Macedonians around him, the Persians next to them, then any of the other peoples who enjoyed precedence for their reputation or some other quality. Then he and those around him drew wine from the same bowl and poured the same libations, beginning with the Greek seers and the Magi. He prayed for other blessings and for harmony and partnership in rule between Macedonians and Persians. [10] It is said that there were 9,000 guests at the banquet, who all poured the same libation and then sang the song of victory.

Arrian VII.8–9 and 11

1. Cf. **3** n.4.
2. Probably decided by Alexander in 327 (Quintus Curtius VIII.5.1); they had recently arrived at Susa, causing the Macedonians much resentment (Arrian VII.6).
3. Alexander had recently formed a new cavalry regiment recruited mainly from orientals (Arrian VII.6.3–4; E. Badian, *JHS* 85 (1965), 160f.).
4. Cf. **8**.
5. The speech is of course not literally Alexander's.
6. Cf. **3**.
7. Alexander had adopted the diadem as a symbol of royalty; cf. **36** and n. 1.
8. A title used for some of the Macedonian infantry; cf. Hammond and Griffith (1979), 709–13.
9. An élite corps of Macedonian infantry organised by Alexander (though cf. R. A. Lock, *Historia* 26 (1977), 373–8); cf. **24, 28**.
10. This does not amount to a prayer for the 'unity of mankind' (E. Badian, *Historia* 7 (1958), 425–44 = Griffith (1966), 287–306 against the view of Tarn, *ib.* 243–86). For other ancient views of Alexander's aims cf. **18, 19**.

16 Alexander's decree on the return of Greek exiles (324)

See further: E. Badian, *JHS* 81 (1961), 25–40 = Griffith (1966), 215–30; Hamilton (1973), 136–8, 140; R. Lane Fox, *Alexander the Great* (London, 1973), 542f.

Not long before his death Alexander decided to bring back all the exiles in the Greek cities, partly to increase his own glory and partly to have in each city many personal supporters to counteract the risk of revolution and revolt among the Greeks. [1] Consequently, as the celebration of the Olympic Games was imminent, he despatched Nicanor of Stagira to Greece with a letter about the exiles' recall; his instructions were to have it read out by the victorious herald[2] to the assembled crowds. Nicanor carried out the order, and the herald took and read out the following letter. 'King[3] Alexander to the exiles from the Greek cities. We were not the cause of your exile, but we shall be responsible for bringing about your return to your native cities, except for those of you who are under a curse. We have written to Antipater about this matter so that he may apply compulsion to those cities which refuse to reinstate their exiles.' This proclamation was greeted with loud approval by the crowd; for those at the festival joyfully welcomed the king's favour and repaid his generosity with shouts of praise. All the exiles had gathered together at the festival, being more than 20,000 in number. The majority of Greeks welcomed the return of the exiles as a good thing, but the Aetolians and Athenians were incensed with the matter. For the Aetolians had expelled from their country the inhabitants of Oeniadae[4] and expected the punishment that would follow their misdeeds; indeed, the king had threatened that it would not be the children of Oeniadae but himself who would punish them. Similarly the Athenians had divided up Samos into lots among their citizens and were in no way prepared to give up that island. But they were no match for the army of Alexander and kept quiet for the time being, while looking out for a suitable opportunity which chance soon gave to them.[5]

Diodorus XVIII.8.2–7

1. In 325 Alexander had ordered his generals and satraps to disband their mercenary armies, thus filling Asia with footloose soldiers (Diodorus XVII.106.2–3; 111.1). For the suggestion that the exiles decree of Alexander was in fact intended to liquidate this problem cf. Badian *op. cit.* Whatever the motive, Alexander's action violated the charter of the 'League of Corinth'.
2. Victorious in the contest of heralds which opened the games.
3. Cf. **5** n. 1.
4. A town in Acarnania. Cf. **62, 70** (end).
5. This was the prelude to the 'Lamian War' which broke out in Greece after Alexander's death (cf. **23, 26**). For the effects of Alexander's decree at Mytilene and Tegea cf. Tod, *GHI* II, 201 and 202.

17 Arrian on Alexander's ultimate aims

On reaching Pasargadae and Persepolis, Alexander was seized with a longing[1] to sail down the Euphrates and Tigris to the Persian Gulf, and to see the outlets of these rivers into the sea, as he had done with the Indus, and the ocean nearby. Some historians have even written that Alexander had in mind to sail around most of Arabia, Ethiopia, Libya (Africa), the Nomads who live beyond the Atlas range, as far as Gades, and so return to the Mediterranean.[2] By subduing Libya and Carthage he would then be truly worthy of the title of King of all Asia. The kings of the Persians and the Medes had not ruled the larger part of Asia and had therefore no right to call themselves Great Kings. After that, some say that he intended to sail into the Black Sea to the Scythians and Lake Maeotis (the Sea of Azov), others that he aimed at Sicily and South Italy;

the fame of the Romans was greatly on the increase and this was already causing him concern. As for what Alexander had in mind, I have no means of forming an accurate conjecture, nor do I care to speculate.[3] But I would venture to assert that Alexander's plans had nothing small or mean about them, and that he would not have been able to remain satisfied with his conquests so far, not even if he had added Europe to Asia and the British Isles to Europe. He would always have been seeking out some unknown land, attempting to rival himself if not anybody else.

Arrian VII.1.1-4

1. Cf. **7** n. 1.
2. On Alexander's reported western plans see also Plutarch, *Alexander* 68.1-2; Quintus Curtius x.1.17-19; and **18**.
3. Arrian does not explicitly mention the 'last plans' of Alexander referred to in **18**.

18 Alexander's 'last plans'

The authenticity of Alexander's 'last plans' has been much debated. The truth may in fact be irrecoverable, for what we have is Perdiccas' version of what these plans contained, and it was in his interest to have them rejected by the army (so E. Badian). However, the version reported in Diodorus is important in giving an indication of what the army was prepared to believe as a statement of Alexander's final intentions.

See further: E. Badian, *HSCP* 72 (1967), 183-204; Hamilton (1969), 187-9 and (1973), 154-8.

Now it happened that Craterus, who was one of the leading men, had been sent ahead to Cilicia by Alexander with the soldiers discharged from the army, some 6,000 in number.[1] At the same time he had received written instructions which the king had given him to carry out; but after the death of Alexander the successors decided not to implement what had been decided. For when Perdiccas found among the king's memoranda plans for the completion of Hephaestion's funeral monument, a very expensive project,[2] as well as the king's other numerous and ambitious plans, which involved enormous expenditure, he decided that it was most advantageous to have them cancelled. So as not to give the impression that he was personally responsible for detracting from the king's glory, he submitted the decision on the matter to the common assembly of the Macedonians.[3]

The following were the largest and most remarkable of the plans. It was intended to build 1,000 warships larger than triremes in Phoenicia, Syria, Cilicia and Cyprus for the expedition against the Carthaginians and the other inhabitants of the coastal area of Libya (Africa), Spain and the neighbouring coasts as far as Sicily;[4] to build a coastal road in Libya as far as the Straits of Gibraltar, and, as required by such a large expedition, to build harbours and shipyards at suitable places; to build six expensive temples at a cost of 1,500 talents each;[5] in addition, to settle cities and transplant populations from Asia to Europe and vice versa from Europe to Asia, to bring the largest continents through intermarriage and ties of kinship to a common harmony and feeling of friendship.[6] The temples just mentioned were to be built at Delos, Delphi and Dodona, and in Macedon there was to be a temple of Zeus at Dium, one of Artemis Tauropolus at Amphipolis, and at Cyrnus one of Athena. Likewise there was to be built at Ilium a temple of Athena which could never be excelled in size by any other. A tomb for his father Philip was to be constructed which would be as large as the greatest pyramids in Egypt, which some reckon among the seven wonders of the world.

When these plans had been read out, the Macedonians, although they approved highly of Alexander, nevertheless saw that the plans were extravagant and difficult to achieve, and they decided not to carry out any of those that have been mentioned.

Diodorus XVIII.4.1–6

1. Immediately after the reconciliation at Opis, **15** (Arrian VII.12).
2. Alexander's friend Hephaestion had died at Ecbatana in autumn 324.
3. Cf. R. M. Errington, *Chiron* 8 (1978), 115–17.
4. Cf. **17**.
5. Cf. **163** n. 4.
6. For this view of Alexander's aims compare **19**.

19   Alexander the bringer of Greek civilisation to Asia

The following passage comes from the first of two speeches by Plutarch in which the author celebrates the achievements of Alexander, portrays him as a philosopher, and attributes his success to the king's own merits (*arete*) and not to Fortune (*tyche* – on *tyche* see **20**). The speeches may only be rhetorical exercises, not to be taken literally as giving Plutarch's considered view of Alexander, nor as providing evidence for what Alexander actually set out to do. They are important nonetheless in showing how Alexander's aims and achievements lend themselves to rhetorical amplification: modern theories of Alexander the champion of the 'fusion of races' or of the 'brotherhood of mankind' have their starting point in ancient sources (cf. also **15** n. 10, **18**).

See further: Hamilton (1969), xxiii–xxxiii.

But if you consider the effects of Alexander's instruction, you will see that he educated the Hyrcanians to contract marriages, taught the

Arachosians to till the soil, and persuaded the Sogdians to support their parents, not to kill them, and the Persians to respect their mothers, not to marry them. Most admirable philosophy, which induced the Indians to worship Greek gods, and the Scythians to bury their dead and not to eat them! We admire the power of Carneades,[1] who caused Clitomachus, formerly called Hasdrubal and a Carthaginian by birth, to adopt Greek ways. We admire the character of Zeno, who persuaded Diogenes the Babylonian to turn to philosophy. Yet when Alexander was taming Asia, Homer became widely read, and the children of the Persians, of the Susianians and the Gedrosians sang the tragedies of Euripides and Sophocles. And Socrates was condemned by the sycophants in Athens for introducing new deities, while thanks to Alexander Bactria and the Caucasus worshipped the gods of the Greeks. Plato drew up in writing one ideal constitution but could not persuade anyone to adopt it because of its severity, while Alexander founded over 70 cities among barbarian tribes,[2] sprinkled Greek institutions all over Asia, and so overcame its wild and savage manner of living. Few of us read Plato's *Laws*, but the laws of Alexander[3] have been and are still used by millions of men. Those who were subdued by Alexander are more fortunate than those who escaped him, for the latter had no one to rescue them from their wretched life, while the victorious Alexander compelled the former to enjoy a better existence. [. . .] Alexander's victims would not have been civilised if they had not been defeated. Egypt would not have had its Alexandria, nor Mesopotamia its Seleucia, nor Sogdiana its Prophthasia, nor India its Bucephalia, nor the Caucasus (the Hindu-Kush) a Greek city nearby; (329) their foundation extinguished barbarism, and custom changed the worse into better. If, therefore, philosophers take the greatest pride in taming and correcting the fierce and untutored elements of men's character, and if Alexander has been shown to have changed the brutish customs of countless nations, then it would be justifiable to regard him as a very great philosopher.

Furthermore, the much-admired *Republic* of Zeno, the founder of the Stoic school, is built around one guiding principle: we should not live in separate cities and demes, each using its own rules of justice, but we should consider all men to be fellow-demesmen and citizens, with one common life and order for all, like a flock feeding together in a common pasture. This Zeno wrote, conjuring up as it were a dream or an image of a well-ordered and philosophic constitution, but it was Alexander who turned this idea into reality. For he did not follow the advice of Aristotle and treat the Greeks as a leader would but the barbarians as a master, nor did he show care for the Greeks as friends and kinsmen, while treating the others as animals or plants; this would have filled his realm with many wars and exiles and festering unrest.[4] Rather, believing that he had come as a god-sent governor and mediator of the whole world, he overcame by arms those he could not bring over by persuasion and brought men together from all over the world, mixing together, as it were, in a loving-cup their lives, customs, marriages and ways of living. He instructed all men to consider the inhabited world to be their native land, and his camp to be their acropolis and their defence, while they should regard as kinsmen all good men, and the wicked as strangers. The difference between Greeks and barbarians was not a matter of cloak or shield, or of a scimitar or Median dress. What distinguished Greekness was excellence, while wickedness was the mark of the barbarian; clothing, food, marriage and way of life they should all regard as common, being blended together by ties of blood and the bearing of children.

Plutarch, *De Alexandri Magni Fortuna aut Virtute*, I 328 C –329 D

1. A philosopher of the second century B.C., head of the Academy in Athens.
2. An exaggeration; on Alexander's foundations cf. W. W. Tarn, *Alexander the Great* II (Cambridge, 1948), 232–59 = Griffith (1966), 84–101 (in part), though see R. M. Errington, *Entretiens Hardt* 22 (1976), 163–8, cf. 218f. For city foundations and the hellenization of Asia after Alexander cf. **40, 46** ch. 57, **121.**
3. There are no 'laws of Alexander'.
4. Contrast **13, 16.**

20 The end of Persia and the rise of Macedon: a contemporary view

By contrast with Plutarch (**19**) Demetrius of Phalerum, an Athenian philosopher and statesman contemporary with Alexander (cf. **21** §§13 and 20, **23, 34, 262** and n. 1), ascribed the extraordinary events that had taken place in his lifetime to the workings of Fortune (*tyche*), a power which exercised a deep influence on religious thought in the Hellenistic age. Compare **10.**

One is often reminded of the words of Demetrius of Phalerum. In his treatise on Fortune, wishing to give the world a clear picture of her mutability, he fixed on the age of Alexander when that king destroyed the Persian empire, and writes as follows: 'If you consider not an unlimited stretch of time or numerous years, but merely these last fifty years before us, you will understand there the cruelty of Fortune. For can you imagine that fifty years ago if some god had foretold the future to the Persians or their king, or the Macedonians or their king, they would have believed that the very name of the Persians would now be lost, who at one time were masters of almost the whole inhabited world, while the Macedonians, whose very name was formerly unknown, would now be masters of it all?[1] Nevertheless Fortune, who makes no compact with our lives, causes events to happen in defiance of our expectations, and displays her power by surprises, is now, I think, demonstrating to all mankind that by establishing the Macedonians as colonists amid the prosperity of Persia, she has merely lent these advantages to them until she decides to do something else with them.'

Demetrius of Phalerum, *FGrH* 228 F 39,
quoted by Polybius XXIX.21.1–6

1. On the idea of the 'succession of empires' cf. J. W. Swain, *CP* 35 (1940), 1–21, esp. 5–8.

2 The Age of the Successors

21 The Parian Marble: events from 323 to 301

For the Parian Marble see 1. §27 referring to the year 299/8 is too mutilated for continuous translation, and the rest of the inscription is lost. For a detailed examination of the chronology down to 311, which largely vindicates the accuracy of the dates given by the Parian Marble as against those in Diodorus, the main narrative source of this period, see R. M. Errington, *JHS* 90 (1970), 75–7 and *Hermes* 105 (1977), 478–504.

B (8) From the time when Alexander died and Ptolemy took control of Egypt,[1] 60 years, and Hegesias was archon at Athens (324/3).

(9) From the Lamian War fought by the Athenians against Antipater,[2] and from the sea battle fought and won by the Macedonians against the Athenians at Amorgos, 59 years, and Cephisodotus was archon at Athens (323/2).

(10) From the time when Antipater captured Athens, and Ophellas was sent by Ptolemy to take over Cyrene,[3] 58 years, and Philocles was archon at Athens (322/1).

(11) From the time when Antigonus crossed to Asia, and Alexander was laid to rest in Memphis,[4] and Perdiccas invaded Egypt and was killed, and Craterus and Aristotle the philosopher died at the age of 50,[5] 57 years, and Archippus was archon at Athens (321/20). And Ptolemy made an expedition to Cyrene.

(12) From the death of Antipater,[6] and the withdrawal of Cassander from Macedon, and from the siege of Cyzicus by Arrhidaeus, and from the time when Ptolemy took over Syria and Phoenicia,[7] 55 years, and Apollodorus was archon at Athens (319/18). And in the same year the Syracusans chose Agathocles to be general with full powers over the strongholds in Sicily.[8]

(13) From the sea battle fought by Clitus and Nicanor near the sanctuary of the Chalcedonians, and the legislation of Demetrius at Athens,[9] 53 years, and Demogenes was archon at Athens (317/16).

(14) From the time when Cassander returned to Macedon, and Thebes was resettled, and Olympias died, and Cassandrea was founded,[10] and

Agathocles became tyrant of the Syracusans,[11] 52 years, and Democlides was archon at Athens (316/15). And Menander the comic poet won his first victory at Athens at that time.

(15) From the time when Sosiphanes the poet died at the age of 45, 49 years, and Theophrastus was archon at Athens (313/12).

(16) From the time when there was an eclipse of the sun,[12] and Ptolemy defeated Demetrius at Gaza and despatched Seleucus to Babylon,[13] 48 years, and Polemon was archon at Athens (312/11).

(17) From the time when Nicocreon died and Ptolemy took control of the island (Cyprus),[14] 47 years, and Simonides was archon at Athens (311/10).

(18) From the time when Alexander [the son of Alexander] died and also another son Heracles from the daughter of Artabazus,[15] and Agathocles crossed over to Carthage[16]. . ., 46 years, and Hieromnemon was archon at Athens (310/9).

(19) From the time when the city of Lysimachea was founded,[17] and Ophellas [marched?] to Carthage . . . and Ptolemy the son[18] was born in Cos and Cleopatra[19] died in Sardis . . ., 45 years, and Demetrius [was archon] at Athens (309/8).

(20) From the time when Demetrius the son of Antigonus besieged and captured Piraeus [and Demetrius of Phalerum was expelled from Athens,[20] 44 years, and] Caerimus [was archon] at Athens (308/7).

(21) From the time when Demetrius razed Munychia and captured Cyprus[21] and . . ., 43 [years] and Anaxicrates was archon at Athens (307/6).

(22) From the time when Sosiphanes the poet was [born (?) and . . ., 42 years, and] Coroebus [was archon at Athens] (306/5).

(23) From the siege of Rhodes[22] and from the time when Ptolemy assumed royalty[23] [41 years, and Euxenippus was archon at Athens] (305/4).

(24) [From the] earthquakes which occurred in Ionia, and from the time when Demetrius took over Chalcis by compact and . . ., 40 years, and Pherecles was archon at Athens (304/3).

(25) From the time when a comet appeared, and Lysimachus [crossed over to Asia,[24] 39 years, and Leostratus was archon at Athens] (303/2).

(26) From the time when Cassander and Demetrius made a truce . . ., 38 [years], and Nicocles was archon at Athens (302/1).

Marmor Parium, *FGrH* 239 B §§8–26

1. See **22** §5, **24** §34. Note the emphasis in the inscription on events relating to the Ptolemaic dynasty: at the time of writing Paros was under Ptolemaic control (cf. **218**).

2. See **23**, **26**.

3. See **264**.
4. See **232** §8.
5. An error: Aristotle probably died aged 63.
6. See **25**.
7. See **46** (ch. 52).
8. An earlier stage in Agathocles' rise to power in Sicily, distinct from his coup of 316 mentioned in §14 below, but not explicitly attested in the narrative of Diodorus (XIX. 1–9).
9. See **23, 34**.
10. See **29**.
11. See **27**.
12. An error: the nearest known eclipse of the sun dates from August 310.
13. See **46** (ch. 54).
14. See Bagnall (1976), 39–42 and **273**.
15. See **22** n. 1, **29, 30**.
16. See **27**.
17. See **45**.
18. The future Ptolemy II Philadelphus; cf. **268**.
19. Cleopatra, Alexander's sister, put to death by a subordinate of Alexander (Diodorus XX. 37. 3–6).
20. See **34**.
21. See **36, 46** (ch. 54).
22. See **39**.
23. See **36, 46** (ch. 54).
24. This refers to the campaign which led to the defeat and death of Antigonus at Ipsus; see **43, 45, 46** (ch. 55).

22 The arrangements at Babylon after the death of Alexander (June 323)

Alexander's sudden death at Babylon in June 323 left a political vacuum: there was no successor both qualified and able to take over his position, hence the door was open to the conflicting ambitions of the Macedonian leaders. The ultimate fragmentation of Alexander's empire was a likelihood from the moment of the king's death, or even before, and the history of the following generation was to see the emergence of several separate kingdoms and dynasties out of his once unified empire.

See further: R. M. Errington, *JHS* 90 (1970), 49–77 (detailed discussion of events from 323 to 320); *id.*, *Entretiens Hardt* 22 (1976), 137–79 (on the declining influence of Alexander and of his ideas after his death); *id.*, *Chiron* 8 (1978), 115–31 (on the political role of the armies in this period).

(a) Arrian

(1) He (sc. Arrian) also wrote an account in ten books of what happened

after Alexander. They comprise the sedition in the army and the proclamation of Arrhidaeus, a son of Philip, Alexander's father, from the Thessalian Philine, on the condition that the throne would be shared between him and Alexander, who was about to be born to Roxane from Alexander (the Great); and that is what happened when the child saw the light of day. They proclaimed Arrhidaeus king and changed his name to Philip.[1] (2) Strife broke out between the infantry and the cavalry; the most eminent of the cavalry and of the commanders were Perdiccas son of Orontes, Leonnatus son of Anteas (?)[2] and Ptolemy son of Lagus, after them Lysimachus son of Agathocles, Aristonous son of Pisaeus, Pithon son of Crateuas, Seleucus son of Antiochus and Eumenes of Cardia. These were the commanders of the cavalry, while Meleager commanded the infantry.[3] (3) They then sent numerous embassies to each other, and in the end the infantry who had proclaimed the king and the commanders of the cavalry came to an agreement, to the effect that Antipater should be general of Europe, Craterus protector (*prostates*) of the kingdom of Arrhidaeus, Perdiccas should hold the office of 'chiliarch'[4] which Hephaestion had held (this made him supervisor of the whole kingdom), while Meleager should be Perdiccas' lieutenant. (4) On the pretext of purging the army Perdiccas arrested the most conspicuous leaders of the sedition, and had them put to death in his presence, alleging orders from Arrhidaeus; this struck terror in the rest of the army. Not long after he also put Meleager to death. (5) As a result mutual suspicions were rife between Perdiccas and all the others. Nonetheless Perdiccas, pretending to act under the orders of Arrhidaeus, decided to appoint to the satrapies men who were suspected by him. Accordingly Ptolemy son of Lagus was appointed to rule Egypt and Libya and the parts of Arabia that lie close to Egypt,[5] while Cleomenes who had been placed by Alexander in charge of this satrapy was to be Ptolemy's lieutenant; Laomedon was to rule Syria next to Egypt, Philotas Cilicia and Pithon Media; Eumenes of Cardia Cappadocia and Paphlagonia and the territory along the Black Sea as far as the Greek city of Trapezus, a colony of Sinope; (6) Antigonus the Pamphylians, Lycians and Greater Phrygia; Asander the Carians; Menander the Lydians; Leonnatus Hellespontine Phrygia, which Calas had received from Alexander to govern, and which Demarchus had then ruled. Such was the distribution of provinces in Asia. (7) In Europe, Thrace, the Chersonese and all the people who neighbour on the Thracians as far as the sea at Salmydessus on the Black Sea were entrusted to the rule of Lysimachus;[6] the further parts of Thrace as far as the Illyrians, Triballians and Agrianians, Macedon itself and Epirus as far as the Ceraunian Mountains, and all the Greeks, were entrusted to Craterus and Antipater. (8) Such was the distribution of provinces;[7] but many parts remained unassigned, under the control of native rulers, as organised by Alexander.

Arrian, FGrH 156 F 1 §§1–8

(b) *Diodorus*

As for the remaining satrapies in Asia Perdiccas decided not to disturb them but to leave them under the same governors as before, and likewise to leave Taxiles and Porus in control of their own kingdoms, as Alexander himself had arranged. [To Pithon?][8] he gave the satrapy next to Taxiles and the other kings; the satrapy lying along the Caucasus,[9] which is called that of the Paropanisadae, he attributed to Oxyartes of Bactria, whose daughter Roxane Alexander had married. He gave Arachosia and Gedrosia to Sibyrtius, Areia and Drangine to Stasanor of Soli, and attributed Bactriane and Sogdiane to Philip, Parthia and Hyrcania to Phrataphernes, Persia to Peucestes, Carmania to Tlepolemus, Media to Atropates, Babylonia to Archon and Mesopotamia to Arcesilas. Seleucus he appointed to the command of the Companion cavalry, a most distinguished post, held first by Hephaestion, then by Perdiccas, and thirdly by the aforementioned Seleucus.[10] They appointed Arrhidaeus[11] to look after the funeral cortège and the construction of the chariot which was to bring the body of the deceased king to Ammon.[12]

Diodorus XVIII.3.2–5

1. There was also a son of Alexander by Barsine called Heracles (cf. **21** §18; **30** n. 3), but he had not been recognised by Alexander and his claims to the succession were very weak. On all these events see also **46** (ch. 52).
2. The name of Leonnatus' father is not certain.
3. The fullest account of these events is in Quintus.Curtius x.6–10, probably based, like the passages in Arrian and Diodorus, on the history of Hieronymus of Cardia (*FGrH* 154), the principal ancient source for the age of Alexander's Successors, now lost (see **25, 45**).
4. The commander of the Persian royal bodyguard, in effect a kind of Grand Vizir (see **25**).
5. According to one tradition (Pausanias 1.6.2) Ptolemy played a leading role in the division of satrapies which was eventually to lead to the fragmentation of Alexander's empire.
6. See **45**.
7. This omits the eastern satrapies, mentioned in the passage of Diodorus which follows.
8. An emendation.
9. The Hindu-Kush.
10. See also **46** (ch. 57).
11. Not the king.
12. Cf. **232** §8; for the sequel in Diodorus see **18**.

23 The Lamian War of 323/2: Athens under Macedonian domination

At Alexander's death the challenge to the Macedonian empire came not from the recently conquered peoples of Asia but from the Greeks. In Bactria a revolt by Greek military settlers established by Alexander was brutally suppressed (Diodorus XVII.99.5f. and XVIII.7). In Greece discontent with Macedonian rule, which had been growing during Alexander's last years, broke out in open revolt led by Athens; on the background to the war see **16**, and contrast Diodorus' other version in XVIII.111.1–3. Pausanias' short account reflects the Athenian democratic view of the struggle against Macedon; it is slanted and inaccurate in detail (see also **26**).

See further: W. S. Ferguson, *Hellenistic Athens* (London, 1911), chs. 1–2; C. Mossé, *Athens in Decline* (London, 1973), 96–108; Will I (1979), 29–33.

The disaster at Chaeronea was the beginning of misfortune for all the Greeks; in particular it brought about the enslavement[1] of those who had failed to see the threat or who had sided with the Macedonians. Philip captured most of the cities; with Athens he nominally came to an agreement, but in practice did them most harm as he deprived them of the islands and put an end to their maritime empire.[2] For some time during the reign of Philip and then of Alexander, the Athenians kept quiet. After the death of Alexander the Macedonians chose Arrhidaeus as their king, though supreme power had been entrusted to Antipater;[3] the Athenians now found it intolerable that the Greeks should forever be under Macedonian domination, and they themselves went to war as well as inciting others to action. The cities which participated in the struggle were, among the Peloponnesians Argos, Epidaurus, Sicyon, Troezen, the Elians, the Phliasians and Messene, among those beyond the Isthmus of Corinth the Locrians, Phocians, Thessalians, Carystus and the Acarnanians who belonged to the Aetolian League. As for the Boeotians who occupied the territory of Thebes, then deserted,[4] they were afraid that Athens might harm them by resettling Thebes, and so took no part in the alliance but assisted the Macedonian cause as far as they could. The allied contingents from each city were led by their own generals, while the Athenian Leosthenes was chosen to command the whole army because of the prestige enjoyed by his city and his own reputation for military ability. He had already shown himself a benefactor of all the Greeks. For when Alexander wished to resettle in Persia all the Greek mercenaries serving with Darius and the satraps, Leosthenes got in first and brought them by sea to Europe. On this occasion he performed feats beyond expectation; his death provoked despair and was to a great extent the cause of the Greek defeat.[5] A Macedonian garrison was placed in Athens, occupying Munychia and later Piraeus and the Long Walls as well.[6] After the death of Antipater, Olympias came over from Epirus and reigned for some time after killing Arrhidaeus, but soon afterwards she was besieged and captured by Cassander and handed over to the people.[7] And when Cassander became king[8] – and I shall only relate of him what concerns the Athenians – he captured the fort of Panactum in Attica and Salamis, and set up as tyrant in Athens Demetrius son of Phanostratus, a man who had a reputation for wisdom; his tyranny was brought to an end by Demetrius son of Antigonus, a young man devoted to the Greek cause.[9]

Pausanias 1.25.3–6

1. 'Enslavement' should not be taken literally.
2. Athens' maritime confederacy was formally dissolved in 338, but in fact had ceased to be of much importance since 356; despite Pausanias, Athens retained control of the islands of Samos (see **16**), Lemnos, Imbros, and Scyrus (*Staatsv.* III.402).
3. See **22**.
4. See **2**.
5. Pausanias does not mention the decisive sea battle at Amorgos (see **21** §9) which marked the end of Athens' long predominance at sea.
6. Athens' capitulation involved in addition the loss of the cleruchy at Samos, the surrender of the anti-Macedonian politicians (Demosthenes committed suicide rather than fall into the hands of Antipater), the overthrow of the democracy after nearly two centuries of existence and its replacement by a timocratic oligarchy (*Staatsv.* III.415 and see **26**).
7. See also **29**.
8. Cassander did not become 'king' till 305/4; see **36**.
9. See **20, 34**; Demetrius of Phalerum, who ruled in Athens on Cassander's behalf from 317 to 307, had strictly speaking the title of 'overseer' or 'governor' (*epimeletes* or *epistates*) and was nominally elected by the Athenians (see *Staatsv.* III.421).

24 The settlement at Triparadisus (summer 320)

In the period following the settlement at Babylon (see **22**) Perdiccas sought to secure control of the whole empire for himself; his attempt met with resistance from the other Macedonian leaders and came to an end in 320 with his invasion of Egypt and assassination. After his death Antipater arranged a new settlement at Triparadisus in north Syria; the detail of the two settlements should be compared.

See further: R. M. Errington, *JHS* 90 (1970), 67–72.

(34) Antipater in this turn carried out a distribution of provinces in Asia, partly confirming the previous arrangements and partly modifying them

when circumstances required. Ptolemy was to control Egypt, Libya and all the expanse of territory beyond it together with any further conquests he made to the west. Syria was entrusted to Laomedon of Mytilene; Philoxenus he appointed to Cilicia, which he held before. (35) Of the upper satrapies he assigned Mesopotamia and Arbelitis to Amphimachus, the king's brother.[1] To Seleucus he gave Babylonia.[2] Antigenes, who had been the first to attack Perdiccas and who commanded the Macedonian Silver Shields,[3] was granted rule over the whole of Susiane. He confirmed Persia to Peucestes, assigned Carmania to Tlepolemus, Media as far as the Caspian Gates to Pithon and Parthia to Philip. (36) He appointed Stasander governor of Areia and Drangine, Stasanor of Soli governor of Bactriane and Sogdiane, and Sibyrtius governor of Arachosia. He assigned the Paropanisadae to Oxyartes, Roxane's father. As regards India, the land bordering on the Paropanisadae he gave to Pithon son of Agenor; of the adjacent satrapies, that lying along the river Indus and Patala, the greatest of the Indian cities in the region, he attributed to King Porus, while that lying along the river Hydaspes he gave to Taxiles, another Indian ruler. It was difficult to remove them as they had received their provinces from Alexander and controlled substantial military forces. (37) In the regions stretching from the Taurus to the north he assigned Cappadocia to Nicanor; he placed Antigonus as before in charge of Greater Phrygia, Lycaonia, Pamphylia and Lycia. Caria he assigned to Asander. Lydia was given to Clitus and Hellespontine Phrygia to Arrhidaeus.[4] (38) He instructed Antigenes to bring the funds deposited at Susa and entrusted to him about 3,000 of the Macedonians who had engaged in sedition.[5] As bodyguards of the king he appointed Autodicus son of Agathocles, Amyntas son of Alexander and brother of Peucestes, Ptolemy son of Ptolemy and Alexander son of Polyperchon. His own son Cassander he made 'chiliarch' of the cavalry. Antigonus he appointed commander of the army previously under the orders of Perdiccas, with the mission of guarding and protecting the kings and also, at Antigonus' own request, of concluding the war against Eumenes.[6] Antipater himself, highly praised by everyone for all his exertions, then returned to Macedon.

Arrian, *FGrH* 156 F 9 §§34–38

1. Brother of Philip Arrhidaeus.
2. The starting point of the Seleucid empire; see **46**.
3. See **15** n. 9.
4. See **22** n. 11.
5. Troops which had mutinied over pay demands.
6. Eumenes of Cardia (see **22** §5) had sided with Perdiccas; for the sequel see **25**, **28**, **46** (ch. 53).

25 The death of Antipater and its consequences (autumn 319)

While already on his death-bed, Antipater appointed Polyperchon guardian (*epimeletes*) of the kings and general with full powers (Polyperchon was nearly the oldest member of Alexander's expedition[1] and was respected by the Macedonians.) His son Cassander he appointed 'chiliarch' and second in authority. The office and rank of 'chiliarch' was first raised to fame and repute by the Persian kings, and afterwards under Alexander it achieved great power and prestige when he became an admirer of Persian customs.[2] That is why Antipater, imitating the precedent, appointed his son Cassander 'chiliarch' in spite of his youth. (49) Cassander, however, was dissatisfied with the arrangement and incensed at the idea that his father's authority should pass to someone who was not related by blood, particularly since Antipater had a son capable of handling affairs who had already given sufficient proof of his merits and bravery. At first he went into the country with his friends,[3] where he had ample opportunity and leisure to converse with them on the subject of supreme command. Then he would take each one of them aside in private and urge him to assist in securing his dominion; by great promises he made them all willing allies in his enterprise. He also sent messengers in secret to Ptolemy, to renew his friendship with him and invite him to be his ally and send with all haste a navy from Phoenicia to the Hellespont. Similarly he sent messengers to the other leading men and the Greek cities to urge them to join his side. But he also organised a hunt for many days to dispel any suspicion that he was about to revolt. Polyperchon, on his side, assumed the guardianship of the kings and held a meeting of his council with his friends. With their approval he summoned Olympias, inviting her to assume the care (*epimeleia*) of Alexander's son who was still a child, and to take up residence in Macedon with royal authority; Olympias had previously fled to Epirus because of her disagreement with Antipater.[4] Such was the state of affairs in Macedon. (50) In Asia, as the news of Antipater's death was noised about, revolutionary stirrings began to be felt, as those in positions of authority sought to work for their own ends. Chief among these was Antigonus. He had previously defeated Eumenes in Cappadocia and taken over his army, and he had overcome Alcetas and Attalus in Pisidia and also taken over their armies.[5] In addition he had been chosen by Antipater general of Asia with full powers,[6] and appointed commander of a large army. All this filled him with self-importance and pride. He was hoping to achieve supreme power and resolved to ignore the kings and their guardians. He reckoned that his superior army would make him master of the treasures in Asia, since there was no one in a position to oppose him. He had at the time 60,000 infantry, 10,000 cavalry and 30 elephants; apart from these he hoped to procure if necessary other armies, since Asia was capable of providing an inexhaustible source of pay for the mercenaries he recruited. With all this in mind he summoned Hieronymus the historian,[7] a friend and fellow-citizen of Eumenes of Cardia who had taken refuge with him at the fort called Nora (*FGrH* 154 T 4). He attempted to win him over with lavish gifts and sent him on an embassy to Eumenes: let Eumenes forget about the battle they had fought in Cappadocia, become his friend and ally, receive far more gifts than he had ever done before and a larger satrapy, and in general be ranked the first of his friends and participate in his whole enterprise.[8] Antigonus then immediately called a council of his friends, communicated to them his ambitions for supreme power, and assigned satrapies to some of his most prominent followers and military commands to others. He filled them all with great hopes and made them enthusiastic for his own plans. For it was his intention to overrun Asia, expel the existing satraps and organise the appointments in favour of his friends.

Diodorus XVIII.48.4–50

1. On this theme cf. R. M. Errington, *Entretiens Hardt* 22 (1976), 159–62; in appointing Polyperchon instead of his son Cassander, Antipater was clearly seeking to avoid any suggestion of dynastic politics, but the legality of his action was open to challenge.
2. See **22** n. 4.
3. On the role and importance of the 'friends' of the leading men, who were to become a recognised institution in all the Hellenistic monarchies, see also **56** (A) and n.2 (general), **3, 14, 15** (Alexander), **74, 79** ch. 32 (Antigonids), **113, 139, 147, 164, 167, 175, 176, 186** (Seleucids), **199, 207, 208** (Attalids), **224** n. 2 (Ptolemies).
4. Olympias was subsequently executed by Cassander (see **23, 29**) and Roxane and her son Alexander IV placed under arrest by him, then executed (see **29, 30**).
5. A common occurrence in this period (see **33**).
6. After the settlement of Triparadisus (**24**); see R. M. Errington, *JHS* 90 (1970), 71.
7. See **22** n. 3, **45**.
8. On Eumenes see **24** n. 6.

26 Athens honours Euphron of Sicyon (318/17)

In the archonship of Archippus (318/17), in the [fourth] prytany, of the [tribe Acamantis], for which Thersippus [son of Hippotherses of Acharnae] was secretary, on the [last day] of Maimakterion[1] and the 35th of the
5 prytany; Gnosias of Halae [and the other presiding officers] / put to the vote; Hagnonides son of Nicoxenus [of Pergase moved: since Euphron]

son of Adeas of Sicyon[2] has [previously on every occasion] continued to
show himself a good man towards the people of Athens, both himself
and his ancestors; [and during] the Greek / [war] which [the people of   10
Athens began] on behalf of the Greeks,[3] Euphron, returning [from exile]
expelled [the] garrison from the [Acropolis with the support of the]
Sicyonians and [after freeing] the city made it a [friend and] ally of the
people [of Athens the first of the] cities [in] / the Peloponnese; and   15
during all the [time] that the people was [fighting the war], he collaborated with the people and [gave assistance] to the troops and all others
involved in [the war]; and when it happened that Greece suffered
[misfortune and garrisons] were sent into the cities which had [expelled
them], he / preferred death at the hand of his enemies, [fighting] for the   20
democracy, rather than to see his [own native city] or the rest of Greece
enslaved; [and] when the people of Athens honoured him with
[citizenship] and the other honours which are fitting for [benefactors], /   25
both himself and his descendants, because of his [merits and] because of
the benefactions of his ancestors, the government of the oligarchy
deprived [him] of his privileges [and] destroyed the stelae; but now since
the people has [come back] and has [recovered] its laws and the
democracy,[4] / with good fortune, be it resolved by the people, that all   30
the [privileges] granted by the [people] of Athens to Euphron in his
honour should be confirmed, both for himself and his descendants, and
that [the] secretary of the council should inscribe the [stelae] which were
destroyed and in which the privileges were [recorded], and the decree,
and dedicate / one copy on the acropolis and the other near (the altar of)   35
Zeus the Saviour,[5] just as the people decreed [previously], and should
also inscribe the present decree on both the stelae, and that the friends
and relatives of Euphron should also attend to the inscription (of the
stelae); and that [the] / council which is in office and the generals should   40
take care of the descendants of Euphron, and that they should have
precedence of access to the council [and the] people after religious
matters. And now [just as] the people has shown [care] for the child of
Euphron / and has passed a decree and sent ambassadors [to] the people   45
of Sicyon, so too it [will show care] in future should they need anything,
so that all may know [that the people] of Athens, when a good deed is
done to it, believes it must honour not only the benefactors but their
children as well / and remember the benefactions it has received. For the   50
inscription of the stelae the treasurer of the people shall give 50 drachmas
from the people's fund for the expenditure on decrees. [. . .]

Syll.[3] 317; *IG* II[2]. 448

---

1. November 318, but the restoration is uncertain (cf. *SEG* XXIII. 61).
2. Previously honoured in an Athenian decree of 323/2 (see below); the earlier

decree, destroyed by the Athenian oligarchs, was reinscribed on the same stele together with this text (*Syll.*[3] 310).

3. The Lamian War of 323/2 (see **23**).
4. Deprived of her democracy in 322 (see **23** n. 6), Athens recovered it briefly in 318, in conformity with an amnesty decree issued by Polyperchon not long after Antipater's death (see **25**) in a bid to secure support from the Greek cities (Diodorus XVIII.55f.; on this move see further **29**). The democracy was again overthrown in 317 and Athens fell under the rule of Demetrius of Phalerum (see **23**). For the tone of the inscription cf. **43, 44, 49**.
5. The present text, found in the Agora.

27 Agathocles, ruler of Sicily (316–289)

'No land was more productive of tyrants than Sicily' (Justin IV.2). After the breakdown in the second generation of the tyranny established by Dionysius of Syracuse (tyrant from 405 till his death in 367), the Corinthian Timoleon sought in the late 340s and early 330s to rid the island of its tyrants and revive the autonomy of the Greek city-states, but although he was successful in initiating a revival of the prosperity of Sicily, no long-term political stability was achieved for the island. Social tensions between rich and poor remained alive and in Syracuse led to the rise of Agathocles, whose rule was explicitly based on the support of the lower classes; his 'reign' lasted till his death in 289. It was the last time that Sicily was to play a powerful and independent role in the ancient world.

See further: H. J. W. Tillyard, *Agathocles* (Cambridge, 1908); M. I. Finley, *Ancient Sicily to the Arab Conquest* (London 2nd ed., 1979), ch. 8.

(a) Agathocles' coup in Syracuse (316)

After this[1] Agathocles summoned an assembly and accused the Six Hundred[2] and the oligarchy they had previously set up. Claiming to have rid the city of the would-be tyrants, he declared he was restoring to the people their full autonomy; his own wish was to be freed from his toils and live the life of a private citizen on equal terms with all.[3] With these words he took off his military dress and exchanged it for civilian dress, and was on the point of walking off after demonstrating that he was one of the many. In behaving so he was playing the part of a man of the people and he knew very well that the majority of the assembly, as they were implicated in his criminal deeds, would never consent to entrust the office of general to anyone else. At once these men, who had plundered the property of their unfortunate victims, shouted not to abandon them but to take over full control of affairs. Agathocles at first said nothing, but when the crowd became more insistent, he said he accepted the office of general provided he did not share it with others; he could not accept having to render accounts as one of a board of generals, as the laws required, for crimes committed by others. As the crowd agreed to let him be sole ruler, he was elected general with full powers and henceforth he ruled openly and controlled the government of the city. As for the Syracusans who had not committed themselves, some were constrained by fear to submit, while others, being no match for the crowd, were deterred from making any hostile demonstration. There were also many poor and indebted men who welcomed the change of régime; for Agathocles had promised in the assembly to carry out a cancellation of debts and to distribute land to the poor.4 This done he put an end to massacres and punishments, and undergoing a complete change showed himself considerate to the common people, conferring benefits on many, making encouraging promises to not a few, and by conversing in a friendly fashion with everyone he earned great favour. Although he wielded such great power, he did not assume a diadem, keep a bodyguard or seek to make himself difficult to approach, as is the custom with nearly all tyrants.5 He also busied himself with the revenues and the manufacture of weapons and missiles and built more warships in addition to the existing ones. He also brought under his control most of the forts and cities in the interior. Such was the situation in Sicily.

Diodorus xix.9

(b) The achievements of Agathocles and Dionysius of Sicily

As I have said, there is no similar need to write at length about such men6 as there is in the case of the Sicilians Agathocles and Dionysius and a few others who made a name for themselves in government. Of these two, the latter came from a popular and humble background, while Agathocles, as Timaeus7 says mocking him (*FGrH* 566 F 124 c), started off as a potter and left the wheel, the clay and the furnace when he came as a young man to Syracuse.8 To begin with, they both in their time became tyrants of Syracuse, a city which enjoyed then considerable fame and was very prosperous, and then they were recognised as kings9 of the whole of Sicily and even established their control over parts of Italy. Not only did Agathocles launch an expedition against Africa,10 he even maintained his position of supreme power till his death. And that is why Publius Scipio, the first conqueror of Carthage, when asked who in his opinion had been the wisest and most enterprising statesmen, is said to have replied 'the Sicilians Agathocles and Dionysius'.

Polybius xv.35.1–6

1. The massacre of many Syracusan oligarchs.
2. It is not clear whether this oligarchic body had been set up by Timoleon or had assumed power after him; cf. R. Talbert, *Timoleon and the Revival of Greek Sicily, 344–317 B.C.* (Cambridge, 1974), 140–2.
3. Compare the similar tactics of Dionysius' rise to power (Diodorus xiii.94.3).

4. Cf. **90** n. 2.
5. On the character of Agathocles' rule see also Diodorus xx.63; Polybius ix.23.2. Later Agathocles did assume the royal title in imitation of the Successors (see **36, 46** ch. 54), but this does not appear to have modified the character of his rule.
6. Polybius has just related the death of a corrupt minister of the Ptolemies.
7. Timaeus of Tauromenium, the greatest of the Sicilian historians (*FGrH* 566): a victim of Agathocles' rise to power (he was exiled from Sicily), his hatred of the Sicilian tyrants and particularly Agathocles has deeply coloured the surviving historical tradition.
8. An insistent theme in the tradition on Agathocles (Diodorus xix.1.6f.; xx.63.4f.), though it is unlikely he can have been a pauper; more probably he owned a pottery establishment staffed by slaves (M. I. Finley, *op. cit.*, 102).
9. Dionysius was never 'king' and Agathocles only took the royal title after the Successors (n. 5 above). The western corner of Sicily remained always under Carthaginian control.
10. Agathocles' daring expedition against Carthage (310–306), undertaken while Syracuse was besieged by the Carthaginians; although the expedition failed it was to influence Pyrrhus (see **47**) and later the Romans in the Punic Wars.

28 The armies of Eumenes and Antigonus at the battle of Paraetacene (autumn 316)

A detailed description of two Hellenistic armies in this period, before the battle of Paraetacene (near Isfahan in modern Iran). For other Hellenistic armies cf. **3, 149, 160, 211, 224**.

See further: on the battle itself, H. H. Scullard, *The Elephant in the Greek and Roman World* (London, 1974), 86–90; on the armies of the period, H. W. Parke, *Greek Mercenary Soldiers to the Battle of Ipsus* (Oxford, 1933), ch. 21; Griffith (1935), ch. 2; Rostovtzeff I (1941), 143–52.

The tactical arrangements of the two generals were different, as they vied with each other in military skill. Eumenes had placed on the left wing Eudemus who had brought the elephants from India, with his guard of 150 cavalry, and as an advance guard two companies of selected mounted lancers drawn up 50 deep. These troops were placed in contact with the slopes of the hill, and next to these he stationed Stasander the general with his own cavalry force 950 strong. Next he placed Amphimachus, the satrap of Mesopotamia,[1] with 600 cavalry, and next to these the 600 cavalry from Arachosia, previously commanded by Sibyrtius, but now because of his flight under the orders of Cephalon. Next came 500 men from Paropanisadae and an equal number of Thracians from the settlements in the upper country.[2] In front of all these troops he stationed 45 elephants in a crooked (?) formation, with a sufficient number of archers and slingers in the intervals between the animals. Having strengthened the left wing in this way he placed the phalanx next to it. The extremity of the phalanx was occupied by the mercenaries, more than 6,000 in number, and next to them the troops armed in Macedonian fashion though they were of all races, numbering about 5,000. (28) Next to these were placed the Macedonian Silver Shields, more than 3,000 in number, men who were undefeated and whose valour was a source of terror to the enemy.[3] Finally the men from the hypaspists, who were more than 3,000, commanded like the Silver Shields by Antigenes and Teutamus. In front of the whole phalanx he stationed 40 elephants and filled the intervals between them with detachments of light armed troops. On the right wing he placed the cavalry: close to the phalanx were the 800 from Carmania, commanded by the satrap Tlepolemus, next the 900 so-called Companions and the guard of Peucestes and Antigenes, comprising 300 men organised in one squadron. At the extremity of the wing was placed the guard of Eumenes with the same number of men, and as an advance guard two squadrons of Pages of Eumenes, each consisting of 50 men, and outside the wing to protect its flank four squadrons composed of 200 selected horsemen. In addition he placed behind his own guard 300 cavalry selected from all the hipparchies for their speed and strength. Along the whole length of his wing he placed 40 elephants as an advance guard. The entire force of Eumenes added up to 35,000 infantry, 6,100 cavalry and 114 elephants.[4]

(29) Antigonus, after observing from a vantage point the enemy's formation, arranged his own army to match it. Seeing that the enemy's right wing was reinforced by the elephants and the best of the cavalry, he placed against them his lightest cavalry, whose task it was to refuse battle at the front, open up their ranks then wheel round and harass the enemy, so as to neutralise in this way the part of the army the enemy was most relying on. On this wing he placed the 1,000 mounted archers and spearmen from Media and Parthia, who were well suited to wheeling movements, next the 2,200 'Tarentines'[5] who had come up with him from the sea, men selected for their skill in ambushes and who were well disposed to him, then the 1,000 cavalry from Phrygia and Lydia, the 1,500 cavalry of Pithon, the 300 lancers of Lysanias, and finally the so-called *asthippoi*[6] and the 800 [Thracian?][7] cavalry from the settlements in the upper country. The left wing was composed of these, and they were placed under the single command of Pithon. As for the infantry, first came the mercenaries, who numbered more than 9,000, then 3,000 Lycians and Pamphylians, more than 8,000 men of all races armed in Macedonian fashion, and finally not much less than the 8,000 Macedonians given by Antipater at the time when he was appointed guardian (*epimeletes*) of the kingdom. On the right wing, close to the phalanx, the

cavalry comprised first 500 mercenaries of all races, then 1,000 Thracians, then 500 men sent by the allies, and next to these 1,000 of the so-called Companions, commanded by Demetrius son of Antigonus, who on that occasion was going to be fighting for the first time with his father. At the extremity of the wing was placed the guard of 300 cavalry, with whom Antigonus himself was fighting the battle; as an advance guard, in front and parallel to these were three squadrons of his own Pages, equal in number, and 100 'Tarentines' fighting with them. Around the whole wing he arranged in a crooked (?) formation his 300 strongest elephants, and filled the intervals between them with selected detachments of light armed troops. The majority of the remaining animals he placed at the front of the phalanx, and some on the left with the cavalry. Having arranged his army in this way he moved down against the enemy in oblique formation; he was pushing forward his right wing, on which he relied most, while holding back the other one, as he had decided to avoid battle with one and fight with the other.[8]

Diodorus XIX.27.2–29.

1. On this and the following satraps see **22** and **24**.
2. The eastern satrapies.
3. An élite corps of Macedonian infantry, cf. **15** n. 9, **24**; they submitted with difficulty to the orders of Eumenes, a Greek, not a Macedonian, and eventually betrayed him (see Parke, *op. cit.*, 213–15).
4. The totals do not agree with the detailed figures just given.
5. The name, which appears here for the first time, refers to a certain type of cavalry and not to their origin (see Griffith, *op. cit.*, 246–50).
6. Usually emended to *amphippoi* = 'horsemen with two mounts', but cf. the *asthetairoi* in **15** (n. 8). See N. G. L. Hammond, CQ n.s. 28 (1978), 128–35.
7. An emendation, cf. the Thracians mentioned in ch. 27 above.
8. The battle was won by Eumenes, but he was worsted in another engagement not long after, betrayed by the Silver Shields, and put to death by Antigonus (winter 316/15). On his career, H. D. Westlake, *Essays on the Greek Historians and Greek History* (Manchester, 1969), 313–30.

29 Antigonus denounces Cassander and proclaims the 'freedom of the Greeks' (314)

The rise to power of Macedon under Philip and Alexander, and the predominance after them of individual rulers, raised a political problem which by its very nature was insoluble and was to persist in one form or another throughout the Hellenistic period: the problem of reconciling the Greek cities' wish for autonomy with the overriding sovereignty of the kings. For the earlier Macedonian responses to this problem see **2, 4, 15, 16** (Alexander), **23, 26** (Antipater and Cassander). Polyperchon in 319 had sought to gain support from the Greek cities by issuing an amnesty decree which aimed at restoring for the Greeks the status quo before the Lamian War (see **26** n. 4), but there was no precedent for the bold propaganda stance adopted by Antigonus in 314, in which he posed as champion of the 'freedom of the Greeks', a posture which he and his son Demetrius subsequently sought to maintain consistently (for the sequel see **30–32, 34, 40**(a) §10, **41, 42**). The sincerity of Antigonus' policy has been much discussed; it seems clear, however, that Antigonus' principal consideration was tactical – to embarrass his rivals, especially Cassander, and to win popularity with the Greek cities, an essential source of manpower, skills and revenues. On the subsequent use of the theme, cf. **49** n. 5, **199** n. 10, and by Rome cf. **68, 79, 154, 159, 200**.

See further: R. H. Simpson, *Historia* 8 (1959), 385–409.

Antigonus established friendship with Alexander son of Polyperchon, who had joined him. He also summoned a general assembly of his troops and of the resident foreigners and accused Cassander,[1] invoking the execution of Olympias[2] and the fate of Roxane and the king. Antigonus added that Cassander had forced Thessalonica[3] to marry him, that he was manifestly seeking to appropriate the throne of Macedon, and also that he had settled the Olynthians, the worst enemies of the Macedonians,[4] in the city he named after himself (Cassandrea)[5] and had restored Thebes which the Macedonians had razed to the ground.[6] As the crowd shared his indignation he moved a resolution that Cassander should be regarded as an enemy, unless he destroyed the two cities, released from captivity the king and Roxane his mother and restored them to the Macedonians,[7] and in general obeyed Antigonus, the appointed general who had received the supervision of the kingdom. All the Greeks should be free, exempt from garrisons, and autonomous. The soldiers carried the motion and Antigonus despatched messengers in every direction to announce the resolution. He calculated as follows: the Greeks' hopes for freedom would make them willing allies in the war, while the generals and satraps in the upper satrapies, who suspected Antigonus of seeking to overthrow the kings who had succeeded Alexander, would change their minds and willingly submit to his orders when they saw him clearly taking up the war on their behalf. Having done this he gave 500 talents to Alexander and despatched him to the Peloponnese with great hopes for the future. He sent for ships from the Rhodians[8] and, having equipped most of those that had been built, he set sail against Tyre. Through his command of the sea he prevented corn being imported to the city and maintained the blockade for a year and three months. The besieged were starved into submission. Ptolemy's soldiers he allowed to go away with their possessions, and after receiving the surrender of the city he placed there a garrison to defend it. (62) While this was happening Ptolemy heard of the resolution concerning the freedom of the Greeks which the Macedonians with Antigonus had passed, and drafted a proclamation in much the same words to convey to the Greeks that he cared no less for their autonomy than did Antigonus.[9] Each side saw that to gain the goodwill of the Greeks would carry no little weight, and so they vied with each other in conferring favours on them.

Diodorus XIX.61–62.2

1. See **25**.
2. Olympias returned to Macedon in 317 at Polyperchon's invitation and assassinated Philip Arrhidaeus and his wife Eurydice; Cassander, returning to Macedon, had Olympias condemned by the Macedonian army and executed (spring 315). See **23, 25**.
3. Daughter of Philip II.
4. Olynthus had been destroyed by Philip in 348.
5. Founded in 315; for other foundations in this period see **40**.
6. See **2**.
7. In fact Roxane and her son Alexander IV were put to death by Cassander after the peace of 311 (see **30**).
8. At the time in the orbit of Antigonus; cf. H. Hauben, *Historia* 26 (1977), 321–8.
9. Ptolemy had less success with the Greeks than did Antigonus and Demetrius (Simpson, *op. cit.*, 390f.); for the 280s and after see **44**.

30 The peace of 311 and the end of the Argead dynasty

After several years of indecisive warfare Antigonus' ambitions (see **25**) were no closer to realisation. The peace of 311 therefore represented a setback for him, though he managed to turn it into a propaganda victory (see **31**). Comparison between the peace of 311 and the earlier settlements of 323 and 320 (see **22, 24**) shows the progression in the power of the leading Macedonians. The elimination of the remaining members of the Argead dynasty was made virtually inevitable by an agreement in which the principal contenders for power dealt with each other as *de facto* sovereign rulers.

See further: R. H. Simpson, *JHS* 74 (1954), 25–31.

In the archonship of Simonides at Athens (311/10) [. . .] Cassander, Ptolemy and Lysimachus put an end to the war against Antigonus and concluded a treaty. It was specified in it that Cassander should be general of Europe until Alexander, Roxane's son, should come of age, that Lysimachus should be master of Thrace and Ptolemy master of Egypt and the neighbouring cities in Libya and Arabia, that Antigonus should command the whole of Asia,[1] while the Greeks should be autonomous.[2] Nevertheless they failed to abide by this agreement, and each of them put forward fair pretexts and sought to increase his power. Cassander saw that Roxane's son Alexander was growing up and that there were some who were spreading the word in Macedon that one ought to release the boy from custody and hand over to him his father's kingdom. Afraid for his own safety, he instructed Glaucias, who was in charge of the boy's custody, to assassinate Roxane and the king and conceal their bodies, and not to report the deed to any of the others. Glaucias carried out the orders, and this freed Cassander, Lysimachus, Ptolemy and even Antigonus from anticipated fears about the king. For now that there was no one to take over the empire,[3] those who ruled peoples or cities could each entertain hopes of kingship and controlled henceforward the territory under their power like kingdoms that had been conquered in war.[4]

Diodorus XIX.105.1–4.

1. The absence of any mention of Seleucus (see **46**) here and in **31** has been variously interpreted: the likeliest explanation is that he was deliberately excluded from the peace by Antigonus who wanted to have a free hand against him. See Simpson, *op. cit.*
2. Antigonus was probably behind this clause (see **29** and **31**); Diodorus' account does not make clear that the Greek cities participated directly in the ratification of the peace (see **31**).
3. The only surviving descendant of Alexander was an illegitimate son Heracles by the Persian Barsine (see **21** §18, **22** n. 1); in 309 Polyperchon thought of putting him forward as a rival to Cassander for the throne of Macedon but was then persuaded by Cassander to put him to death (Diodorus XX.20.1–2 and 28).
4. Literally 'won by the spear'; for this notion cf. **6, 36, 148, 154**.

31 Letter of Antigonus to Scepsis in the Troad (311)

On the conclusion of the peace of 311 (see **30**) Antigonus promptly sent a manifesto to many Greek cities in his sphere of control, and possibly outside it as well. Of this manifesto only the copy made of the letter addressed to the city of Scepsis in the Troad has survived in part on an inscription. In it Antigonus refers to the events leading up to the conclusion of the peace, but while he is at pains to emphasise his concern for the 'freedom of the Greeks' (see **29**), he is deliberately vague as to the precise circumstances and calculations behind the signing of the peace and as to the terms of an agreement which the Greek cities were to swear to respect though they had taken no part in its formulation (contrast **30**). As a result modern reconstructions of the diplomatic activity leading up to the peace differ substantially and several allusions in the letter remain obscure; see e.g. Welles, *ad loc.* and R. H. Simpson, *op. cit.* on **30**.

(The beginning of the inscription is lost)

. . . we displayed [zeal for the] freedom [of the Greeks] and made [for this purpose] many considerable concessions including [the gift of?]

5   money, and to this end we sent out jointly / Aeschylus [and Demar-
    chus?]. As long as there was agreement on [this] point, we took part in
    the meeting at the [Hellespont], and if [certain] men had not raised
    difficulties, the matter would have been settled then. [But now] when
10 Cassander and [Ptolemy] were discussing / a truce and Prepelaus and
    Aristodemus came to see us [on] this matter, although we saw that some
    of Cassander's demands were excessive, we thought we ought to
15 overlook them since there was agreement about the Greeks, / so that the
    essential points should be implemented as soon as possible; we should
    have thought it a great achievement to arrange something for the Greeks
    as we had wished, but because this would have been a rather lengthy pro-
20 cess and delay / can often bring about many unforeseen consequences,
    and because we were anxious to see the affairs of the Greeks settled in
    our lifetime,[1] we thought it imperative that questions of detail should
    not prevent the implementation of the essential points. How great is the
25 zeal we have displayed over this will, I think, be clear / to you and to all
    others from the actual dispositions taken. When we had reached agree-
    ment with Cassander and Lysimachus, for which purpose they had sent
30 Prepelaus with full powers, Ptolemy sent ambassadors to us / requesting
    a truce with himself and his inclusion in the same agreement. We saw
    that it was no small matter to give up part of the goal for which we had
35 taken great trouble and spent much money, / and that when we had
    reached a settlement with Cassander and Lysimachus and the rest of the
    task was easier; nevertheless, because we understood that a settlement
    with him too (Ptolemy) would speed up a solution to the question of
40 Polyperchon,[2] / since he would have no allies, and because of our
    relationship with him, and also because we saw that you and the other
45 allies were burdened by military service and by expenses, / we thought it
    was right to give way and to conclude a truce with him too. We
    despatched Aristodemus, Aeschylus and Hegesias to conclude the
50 agreement; they have returned after receiving pledges, and the envoys /
    from Ptolemy, Aristobulus and his colleagues, have arrived to receive
    pledges from us. Know therefore that the truce has been concluded and
    that peace has been made. We have written a clause into the agree-
55 ment that all the Greeks should join together in protecting / their mutual
    freedom and autonomy, in the belief that in our lifetime they would in all
    human expectation be preserved, but that in future with all the Greeks
60 and the men in / power[3] bound by oath, the freedom of the Greeks
    would be much more securely guaranteed. To join in the oath to protect
    what we agreed with each other did not seem to us inglorious or without
65 advantage to the Greeks.[4] / It therefore seems to me right that you
    should swear the oath which we have sent to you. We shall endeavour in
    future to achieve whatever is in your interest[5] and that of the other

Greeks. Concerning these matters I resolved to write to you / and to   70
send Acius to discuss them with you; he brings you copies of the
agreement we have made and of the oath. Farewell.

RC 1; *OGIS* 5; *Staatsv*. III.428

1. Antigonus was now 71.
2. By this time Polyperchon (see **25, 30** n. 3) was confined to the Peloponnese
   and had little influence; he was not one of the signatories of the peace of 311.
3. Literally 'those in charge of affairs', i.e. the chief signatories of the peace (**30**);
   the vagueness of the phrase reflects the vagueness of their constitutional
   position.
4. Antigonus is virtually admitting that the Greeks are being made to agree to a
   settlement they had no share in drawing up.
5. Some time after the people of Scepsis were made to move to Antigonus' new
   settlement of Antigonea in the Troad (Strabo 593 and 607).

32 Scepsis decrees religious honours to Antigonus on receipt of his letter (311)

The following inscription, found together with **31** and closely related to it,
provides the earliest instance known so far in the age of the Successors of divine
honours offered by a Greek city to a living ruler. Precedents are however known
for both Philip (cf. **4**) and Alexander, and in fact the earliest attested case concerns
the Spartan Lysander at the end of the Peloponnesian War (Plutarch, *Lysander* 18,
from Duris *FGrH* 76 F 71, cf. F 26). These cults represented a spontaneous
expression of gratitude by the cities concerned for benefits received from the
rulers, as the following text makes clear. For further examples in this period see
34, 35, 39, 41; for the later period cf. **139** n. 7 (Seleucids), **209** n. 7 (Attalids), **218**
(Ptolemies). There is no hint of any request for religious honours by the rulers
themselves (as there may have been in the case of Alexander; cf. **11**). The cults of
rulers set up by Greek cities are quite distinct from the dynastic cults set up by the
rulers themselves (Seleucids and Ptolemies) in the second generation or after (see
158, 217).

(The beginning of the inscription is lost)

[. . . since Antigonus has sent] Acius who [in every respect shows
himself to be] well disposed [to our city] and continues to [maintain his
zeal] and [requests] that the city declares to him its demands; and since he
has also sent / news of the agreement concluded by him with Cassander,   5
Ptolemy and Lysimachus, copies of the oath, and news of what has been
done concerning the peace and the autonomy of the Greeks; be it
resolved / by the people: since Antigonus has been responsible for great   10
benefits to the city and the other Greeks, to praise Antigonus and to

rejoice with him in what has been accomplished; let the city also
15 rejoice / with the other Greeks that they shall live in peace henceforward
enjoying freedom and autonomy;[1] and so that Antigonus may receive
honours worthy of his achievements and the people should be seen to be
20 returning thanks / for the benefits it has received, let it mark off a sacred
enclosure (*temenos*) for him, build an altar and set up a cult statue as
beautiful as possible, and let the sacrifice, the competition, the wearing of
25 the wreath and the rest of the festival be celebrated every [year] / in his
honour as they were before.[2] Let it [crown] him with a gold crown
[weighing] 100 gold [staters], and crown Demetrius and Philippus[3] with
30 crowns weighing each 50 drachmas; / and let it proclaim the crowns [at
the] contest during the festival; let the city offer a sacrifice for the good
tidings sent by Antigonus; let all the citizens wear wreaths,[4] and let the
35 treasurer provide the money / for this expense. Let friendly gifts be sent
to Antigonus, and let there be inscribed on a stele the text of the
agreement, the letter from Antigonus and the oath which he sent, as
40 he / instructed, and place it in the sanctuary of Athena; let the secretary
[supervise] the task, [and] let the treasurer provide the money for the
45 expenditure; let all the citizens [swear] the [oath which was sent], / as
[instructed by Antigonus]; and let those who have been chosen . . .
(the rest of the inscription is lost)
OGIS 6

1. See **29**.
2. This shows that Scepsis was already celebrating an annual festival in Antigonus' honour; the occasion for the establishment of this festival is unknown
   and it is not clear whether the festival already implied divine honours for
   Antigonus. At any rate the new honours voted to him (sacred enclosure, altar,
   cult statue) are divine in character (cf. **II** ch. 11).
3. Antigonus' two sons; on Demetrius see **34**, etc. Philippus, the younger son,
   died in 306/5.
4. Cf. **220** col. III.

33 Treaty between Eupolemus and Theangela and its defenders on its capitulation (ca 310?)

The political history of the age is dominated by the great figures prominent
elsewhere in this chapter. No less characteristic of the age, however, were the
careers of minor military dynasts, whose existence is often only casually attested
in the surviving evidence. Such is the Macedonian Eupolemus, known as a
general of Asander, satrap of Caria, in 314 from a passing allusion in Diodorus
(XIX.68.5–7), but who in fact ruled as dynast over part of Caria around this time.
This is shown by bronze coins issued by him in his name and by three

inscriptions from Caria, one an honorific decree of Iasus (*CIG* 2675), another from Labraunda (J. Crampa, *Labraunda* III.2 (Stockholm, 1972), no. 42), the third the text of a treaty between himself on the one hand and on the other the city of Theangela (near Halicarnassus) and its defenders, to which is appended the oath sworn by Eupolemus. The context is the capitulation of the city to Eupolemus after a siege. For other examples of the 'dynasts' who proliferated in Asia Minor, cf. **182** n. 6.

. . . [1] and there shall also be an amnesty for the people of Erinaea[2] . . . to Philippus, Demagathus and Aristodemus[3] [and the] soldiers [under their command] shall be paid the four [months' salary] that is due [to them] as well as a donative of two months' salary to Aristodemus and all the soldiers [under his command?] / who decide to remain in the service of   10
Eupolemus; for all the [soldiers] who came over to the city from the army of Eupolemus in peace or in war there shall be an amnesty; for all the slaves who came over in peace the conditions shall be as laid down in the treaties with Eupolemus and with Peucestas;[4] for those who came over in war there shall be an amnesty; to the artillerymen shall also be paid / four   15
months' salary; all the soldiers who wish to depart shall be allowed to do so taking their chattels with them and shall be exempt from custom dues on their goods on passing through the territory of Eupolemus;[5] and when Eupolemus has sworn to the people of Theangela and the troops (in the city) that he will abide by the agreement, and when he has paid the salary to the soldiers, / let him take control of the city and the (two)   20
citadels; any soldiers from Theangela who take up service with Eupolemus shall be allowed to settle at Pentachora.[6] Oath sworn by Eupolemus:[7] I swear by Zeus, the Earth, the Sun, Ares, Athena Areia and the Tauropolus and all the other gods and goddesses; I will abide by the agreement made with the city of Theangela / and the soldiers in   25
Theangela, and I will place a seal on the treaty I have made with the people of Theangela and hand it over to them sealed up, and I will not prevent the city from inscribing the treaty and the oath I have sworn on a stele and placing it in any sanctuary in Theangela they wish.[8] If I abide by my oath may I and my family prosper, / if I break the oath may the   30
opposite happen.[9]

L. Robert, *Collection Froehner* I *Inscriptions Grecques* (1936), 69–86 no. 52;

Staatsv. III.429

1. The first five lines of the inscription are seriously mutilated; the extant text begins at the end of the provisions applying to Theangela.
2. Probably a small town near Theangela and in alliance with it, otherwise unknown.
3. Also known from an honorific decree of Iasus (*CIG* 2676).
4. Earlier agreements, now lost.

5. Cf. **194**.
6. Provisions are made for the settlement of the soldiers as colonists; the location of Pentachora (literally 'the five villages') is unknown. On the conditions of service of mercenaries cf. **196**.
7. For other oaths cf. **49, 54, 61, 90, 91, 118, 133, 182, 196**.
8. Hence the existence of the present text.
9. There is no reciprocal oath by Theangela: Eupolemus controlled the city and could enforce the terms of the treaty.

34 Demetrius and the liberation of Athens (307)

See further: W. S. Ferguson, *Hellenistic Athens* (London, 1911), ch. 3; C. Mossé, *Athens in Decline* (London, 1973), 108–14; K. Scott, *AJP* 49 (1928), 137–66 and 217–39 (takes a very unfavourable view of the honours paid to Antigonus and Demetrius).

As the glory of this achievement was noised abroad,[1] Antigonus and Demetrius were filled with a remarkable eagerness to free Greece,[2] which was all under the sway of Cassander and Ptolemy. None of the kings fought a fairer or more just war than that one. The abundant resources they had gathered together by humbling the barbarians they now spent in search of glory and honour on the Greeks. As soon as they had decided to sail against Athens, one of their friends remarked to Antigonus that, should they capture that city, they must keep it for themselves, as it was the stepping-stone to Greece. But Antigonus would have none of it, and declared that goodwill was a fair and unshakable stepping-stone and that Athens, the watch-tower of the inhabited world, as it were, would quickly flash to all mankind the message of their glorious achievements. Demetrius set sail for Athens with 500 talents and a fleet of 250 ships; the city was governed on behalf of Cassander by Demetrius of Phalerum,[3] and a garrison had been installed in Munychia. By a combination of good luck and foresight he appeared before Piraeus on the 26th of Thargelion;[4] no one had spotted him beforehand and when his fleet was sighted off-shore, they all believed the ships were Ptolemy's and made ready to receive them. The generals were late in realising their mistake and coming to the rescue, and there was confusion as one would expect with a forced attempt to fight off an unexpected landing of enemies. Demetrius found the entrances to the harbour open and sailed in; he was now inside and in full view and signified from his ship that he was asking for quiet and silence. When this had been established, he proclaimed through the voice of a herald near him that his father had sent him with prayers for his success to free the Athenians, expel the garrison and restore to them their laws and ancestral constitution. (9) On hearing this proclamation the majority at once cast down their shields at their feet and applauded, and shouted to Demetrius to disembark, calling him their benefactor and saviour. Demetrius of Phalerum and his followers thought they had in any case to welcome the man who had force on his side, even if there was no certainty that he would keep his promises, but nonetheless they sent off a deputation to convey their requests. Demetrius met them graciously and sent them back with Aristodemus of Miletus, one of his father's friends. Because of the change of government Demetrius of Phalerum was more frightened of his fellow-citizens than of the enemy. Demetrius did not ignore him, but out of regard for the man's reputation and merits, he had him and his friends escorted safely to Thebes as requested. He himself declared he would not cast a glance at the city, despite his wish to do so, before he had freed it entirely and rid it of its garrison. He threw a palisade and ditch around Munychia, and sailed off against Megara, which was garrisoned by Cassander. [. . .] (10) Returning to Munychia he encamped, expelled the garrison and razed the fort. The Athenians now welcomed him and called for him, and so he came to the city, called the people together and restored to them their ancestral constitution. He added a promise that his father would send them 15,000 medimni of corn and enough timber to build 100 triremes.[5] And so the Athenians recovered their democracy after fifteen years; in the intervening period since the Lamian War and the battle of Crannon the constitution had ostensibly been oligarchical, but was in actual fact the rule of one man because of the power exercised by Demetrius of Phalerum. Demetrius had shown his magnificence and greatness in his benefactions, but the Athenians proceeded to make him offensive and obnoxious through the extravagant honours they voted to him. They were the first to give the title of kings to Demetrius and Antigonus,[6] although they had otherwise avoided the name up till now, and it was the only royal prerogative still left to the descendants of Philip and Alexander which others could not touch or share in. They were the only men to call them Saviour Gods.[7] They abolished the ancestral eponymous archonship and elected every year a priest of the Saviours, and put his name on the prescripts of decrees and contracts.[8] They also voted to weave their likenesses into the robe of Athena together with the gods,[9] consecrated the spot where Demetrius had first stepped down from his chariot, placed an altar there and called it the altar of Demetrius Cataebates (the descending god).[10] They added two more tribes (to the ten existing ones), Demetrias and Antigonis, and raised the numbers of the Council from 500 to 600, since each one of the new tribes was providing 50 councillors.[11]

Plutarch, *Demetrius* 8–10

1. Demetrius' relief of the city of Halicarnassus from a blockade by Ptolemy.
2. See **29**; Plutarch, a patriotic Greek, is inclined to take Antigonus and Demetrius' aims too literally.
3. See **20**.
4. *Ca* 10 June 307.
5. Athens' loss of her naval supremacy (see **23**) turned the question of the corn supply into a critical issue (cf. **44** n. 8).
6. Similarly the oracle of Apollo near Miletus addressed Seleucus as king in advance of the assumption of the royal title by the Successors (Diodorus XIX.90.4, and see **36, 46** ch. 54).
7. Antigonus and Demetrius are only called 'Saviours' in Attic inscriptions, not 'Saviour Gods'. For divine honours to rulers see **32**.
8. An error by Plutarch: there is no confirmation from inscriptions that the new 'priest of the Saviours' ever replaced the traditional eponymous archonship as Plutarch states.
9. Every four years at the Great Panathenaea a robe was offered to Athena (see **43, 44**).
10. This honour was probably offered to Demetrius on a later occasion, in 304.
11. See also **198**; R. L. Pounder, *Hesperia* 47 (1978), 52f. On Demetrius and Athens see further **35, 43, 44**. For other royal receptions cf. **198, 220**.

35 The 'ithyphallic hymn' in honour of Demetrius (291)

Although belonging to a later context (Demetrius' return from Corcyra to Athens in 291) the 'ithyphallic hymn' in his honour may be placed side by side with the honours mentioned in **34** as giving remarkably explicit evidence on the psychology of ruler worship. It should be noted that it is only in Athens that there is any evidence of opposition to the worship of rulers at this time, and that this opposition was not based on religious grounds (contrast the arguments in **11**) but was the result of political rivalries (the Athenian Demochares was an opponent of Demetrius and of his supporters in Athens, and Duris of Samos was hostile to the Antigonids). For a quite different Athenian view of their traditional civic religion contrast **43, 44**.

See further: V. Ehrenberg, *Aspects of the Ancient World* (Oxford, 1946), 179–98.

What then is surprising about the fact that the Athenians, the flatterers of flatterers, sang paeans and processional odes in honour of Demetrius himself? For instance Demochares writes in Book 21 of his *History* (*FGrH* 75 F 2): 'When Demetrius returned from Leucas and Corcyra to Athens, the Athenians welcomed him not just with incense, crowns and libations of wine; he was even met by processional choruses and ithyphallic[1] hymns accompanied by song and dance. As they took their places in the crowds they sang and danced, chanting that he was the only true god, that the other gods were asleep or away or did not exist, that he was descended from Poseidon and Aphrodite, that he was surpassingly beautiful and courteous in his kindness to everyone. They would address supplications to him, he says, and would offer him prayers.' So much from Demochares on the flattery of the Athenians. Duris of Samos in Book 22 of his *Histories* (*FGrH* 76 F 13) quotes the actual ithyphallic hymn:

'How the greatest and dearest of the gods have come to the city! For the hour has brought together Demeter and Demetrius; she comes to celebrate the solemn mysteries of her Daughter (Persephone),[2] while he is here full of joy, as befits the god, fair and laughing. His appearance is majestic, his friends all around him and he in their midst, as though they were the stars and he the sun. Hail son of the most powerful god Poseidon and of Aphrodite![3] For the other gods are either far away, or they do not have ears, or they do not exist, or do not take any notice of us, but you we can see present here; you are not made of wood or stone, you are real. And so we pray to you: first bring us peace, dearest; for you have the power. And then, the Sphinx that rules not only over Thebes but over the whole of Greece, that Aetolian sphinx sitting on a rock like the ancient one, who seizes and carries away all our people, and I have no defence against her (for it is an Aetolian habit to seize the property of neighbours and now even what is far afield).[4] Most of all punish her yourself; if not find an Oedipus who will either hurl down that sphinx from the rocks or reduce her to ashes.'

Athenaeus, *Deipnosophistae* VI.253 b–f

1. So called because the metre is that used in the popular songs of the phallus-bearers in the Dionysiac processions.
2. The Eleusinian Mysteries.
3. 'Poseidon' conveys a reference to Demetrius' maritime ambitions, 'Aphrodite' to his amorous exploits. Coins of Demetrius show the god Poseidon on the reverse.
4. A reference to Aetolian privateering which was a feature of the third century; cf. Rostovtzeff I (1941), 196, 198f. and 1361 n.14, and see further **52, 88**.

36   The Successors assume the royal title (306–304)

The assumption of the royal title by Alexander's Successors marked an important stage in the fragmentation of his empire: with the disappearance of the legitimate descendants of the royal house of Macedon (see **21** §§18 and 19, **29, 30**) the Successors were now free to usurp a title that had once been the privilege of the

Argead dynasty. The initiative taken by Antigonus and Demetrius probably implied a claim to succeed to the whole heritage of Alexander, and on a dynastic basis (though cf. R. M. Errington, *JHS* 95 (1975), 250f.); the Antigonid dynasty subsequently maintained its claim to be related to the Argeads (C. F. Edson, *HSCP* 45 (1934), 213–46), and Demetrius significantly refused to give the title of 'king' to his rivals (Plutarch, *Demetrius* 25.3–5). The response of Ptolemy and the others implied by contrast a refusal to recognise any authority other than their own over the territory they controlled.

Yet the significance of the event, and the change in the behaviour of the Successors which is alleged to have resulted, may not be as great as Plutarch imagines. The Successors had long been behaving as individual rulers, concluding treaties (see **30**), founding cities in their own name (see **40**), receiving divine honours from Greek cities (see **31**), and had even on occasion been unofficially addressed as kings by Greeks (see **34** and n. 6). Seleucus I reckoned his 'era' as from 312/311 (cf. **138** n. 2). The royal proclamations of 306–304 merely consecrated the existing state of affairs.

The precise timing of the proclamations is important. Antigonus and Demetrius took on the royal title after Demetrius' victory over Ptolemy in Cyprus in 306, and despite Plutarch, Ptolemy seems to have delayed his assumption of the title till he had performed a comparable military feat by defeating Antigonus' and Demetrius' invasion of Egypt in 305 (detailed discussion in A. E. Samuel, *Ptolemaic Chronology* (Munich, 1962), 4–11). For this conception of monarchy based on individual merit and military achievements see **30** n. 4, **37**, **47**(a), **150**, **199**. The precise circumstances of the assumption of the title by the other Successors (and also Agathocles in Sicily, see **27**) are not known.

The multitude then for the first time proclaimed Antigonus and Demetrius kings. Antigonus' friends tied at once a diadem[1] round his head, while Demetrius was sent a diadem by his father and addressed as king in a letter he wrote. When the news was reported, Ptolemy's followers in Egypt also proclaimed Ptolemy king, to dispel any impression that his defeat had humbled his pride. And so emulation spread the practice like a contagion among the Successors: Lysimachus began to wear the diadem, and so too Seleucus in his dealings with the Greeks (with the barbarians he had already been behaving as a king).[2] Cassander, however, although the others wrote to him and addressed him as king, continued to write letters in the same style as before, with his name only but no title.[3] Now this practice did not involve merely the addition of a title and a change of fashion; it stimulated the men's pride and raised their ambitions, and made them arrogant and obnoxious in their style of living and in their dealings with others. It is the same as with tragic actors who change their step, their voice, their posture at table and their way of addressing others when they put on their costumes. They became harsher in their judicial verdicts and no longer concealed their power, which had often in the past made them more lenient and gentle with their subjects. Such was the power of a single word spoken by a flatterer, and so great was the revolution it brought about in the world.[4]

Plutarch, Demetrius 18

1. A plain head band, symbol of royalty, regularly shown on the coins of Hellenistic kings (contrast Agathocles, see **27**). Cf. **15** ch. 9, **146, 147, 226, 228**.
2. But not formally recognised as king by them till 305/4; cf. **138**.
3. This statement cannot be tested from the available evidence; cf. R. M. Errington, *JHS* 94 (1974), 25.
4. See also **46** ch. 54.

37 The ideology of Hellenistic monarchy

A brief entry under the heading of 'monarchy' from the Byzantine compilation known as 'the Suda', which emphasises correctly individual merit and military ability as the basis of the new Hellenistic monarchies (see **36**). The ultimate source of the passage is unknown.

See further: Rostovtzeff III (1941), 1346 n. 24.

Monarchy. It is neither descent[1] nor legitimacy[2] which gives monarchies to men, but the ability to command an army and to handle affairs competently. Such was the case with Philip and the Successors of Alexander. For Alexander's natural son was in no way helped by his kinship with him, because of his weakness of spirit, while those who had no connexion with Alexander became kings of almost the whole inhabited world.

Suda s.v. Basileia (2)

1. Literally 'nature'.
2. Literally 'justice'.

38 The doctrines of Euhemerus of Messene on the gods and royalty

Striking evidence for the climate of ideas of the age of the Successors comes from the following quotation from the *Sacred Record* of Euhemerus of Messene, a friend of King Cassander (the original work has not survived; see *FGrH* 63). Cast in the form of a travel novel (fictitious, though taken literally by Diodorus), Euhemerus' work put forward the view that the gods are in reality rulers of the past who were deified for their achievements on earth. The parallel with the contemporary Hellenistic kings is inescapable (see **32, 36**).

See further: Fraser I (1972), 289–95 and notes.

Concerning the gods, then, men of ancient times have handed down to later generations two different conceptions. Some, they say, are eternal and indestructible, such as the sun, the moon and the other stars in the heavens, and also the winds and all other bodies which have the same nature as these. For each of these is everlasting in genesis and duration. Other gods, they say, were earthly beings who achieved immortal honour and fame through their benefactions to mankind, such as Heracles, Dionysus, Aristaeus, and others like them. Historians and mythographers have handed down many varied stories about the earthly gods; of the historians, Euhemerus the author of the *Sacred Record* has written a separate account of them [. . .] Euhemerus, then, was a friend of King Cassander, and so had to carry out a number of royal missions and undertake long journeys abroad. He says he travelled south to the ocean; starting from Arabia Felix he sailed for many days through the ocean, and came to islands in the sea. One of these was called Panchaea; there he saw the Panchaeans who inhabit the island, men of great piety who honour the gods with the most lavish sacrifices and remarkable dedications of silver and gold. The island is sacred to the gods, and there are many other objects in it remarkable for their antiquity and the excellence of their craftsmanship; of these we have written severally in previous books.[1] There is in the island, on a very lofty hill, a temple of Zeus Triphylius, founded by himself at the time when he was still among men and was king over the whole world. In this temple there is a golden stele on which are inscribed in Panchaean characters the main achievements of Uranus, Cronus and Zeus. Euhemerus then says that Uranus was the first king, an honourable man, beneficent and versed in the movement of the stars and who was the first to honour the heavenly gods with sacrifices; that is why he was called Uranus.[2] By his wife Hestia he had two sons Titan and Cronus, and two daughters Rhea and Demeter. After Uranus Cronus was king; he married Rhea and had as children Zeus, Hera and Poseidon. Zeus succeeded Cronus in the monarchy and married Hera, Demeter and Themis; his children by the first wife were the Curetes, Persephone by the second and Athena by the third. He then went to Babylon and was entertained by Belus, and afterwards came to the island of Panchaea which lies in the ocean and founded an altar of Uranus, his own ancestor. From there he traversed Syria and came to Casius, who ruled there at the time and gave his name to Mt Casius. He then went to Cilicia and defeated in war Cilix the governor, visited many other peoples and was honoured by all of them and proclaimed a god.

Diodorus VI.1.2–10

1. V.41–46.

2. *Ouranos* in Greek = heaven.

39 Demetrius and the siege of Rhodes (305/4)

Although eventually unsuccessful, Demetrius' siege of Rhodes in 305/4 made a powerful impression on contemporaries as a grandiose demonstration of the military inventiveness which earned Demetrius the nickname of 'Poliorcetes' (the Besieger). It also provided a flagrant contradiction of the policy of championing the 'freedom of the Greeks' which father and son had long claimed to be pursuing (see **29**). Diodorus' description of Rhodian policy applies to the Hellenistic period as a whole (down to 167) rather than to the years before 305/4. On Rhodes see also **80, 92–95**.

   See further: on Rhodes under Alexander and the Successors, H. Hauben, *Historia* 26 (1977), 307–39; on the siege, E. W. Marsden, *Greek and Roman Artillery. Historical Development* (London, 1969), 105–8; on Rhodes and Egypt, P. M. Fraser I (1972), 162–9.

(*a*) After this year Euxenippus became archon at Athens (305/4), and Lucius Postumius and Tiberius Minucius consuls at Rome. During their year of office war broke out between the Rhodians and Antigonus for more or less the following reasons. The city of Rhodes had a powerful navy and enjoyed the finest government in Greece, and so was an object of competition between the dynasts and kings, as each sought to win it over to his friendship.[1] Seeing ahead where its advantage lay, it concluded friendship with each of the protagonists separately and took no part in the wars the dynasts fought against each other. And so it happened that it was honoured by each of them with royal presents, and prospered greatly by remaining at peace for a long time. It had reached such a peak of power that it took up on its own, on behalf of the Greeks, the war against the pirates and cleared the sea of that scourge.[2] Alexander, the most powerful man in human memory, honoured it above all cities, deposited there his will concerning the whole kingdom,[3] and in general admired it and enhanced its preeminence. The Rhodians, then, by establishing friendship with all the dynasts, kept themselves immune from any justifiable complaint, but their sympathies inclined most towards Ptolemy. For it so happened that they derived the majority of their revenues from the merchants sailing to Egypt and that in general their city was sustained by that kingdom.

Diodorus xx.81

(*b*) The Rhodians, then, brought the war to a close after a siege of one year. They honoured with appropriate presents those who had shown bravery in the face of danger and conferred freedom and citizenship on the slaves who had displayed courage. They also set up statues of King Cassander and King Lysimachus, who although they held second place in the general estimation had yet made a great contribution to the salvation of the city.⁴ But as for Ptolemy, they wished to repay his favour with an even greater one, and sent sacred ambassadors to Libya (Africa) to ask the oracle of Ammon⁵ whether he advised the Rhodians to honour Ptolemy as a god. When the oracle had given its assent they consecrated a square enclosure in the city, which they called the Ptolemaeum, and constructed on each of its sides a stoa one stade long. They also rebuilt the theatre, the parts of the wall that had collapsed and the other buildings that had been destroyed, all far more beautifully than before.

Diodorus XX. 100. 1–4

1. Rhodes also enjoyed a strategic position on the sea route to the Levant.
2. See further **86, 92**.
3. This is pure fiction; Alexander left no will. See Hauben, *op. cit.*, 311–16.
4. Note the absence of Seleucus, at the time campaigning in eastern Asia (see **46**).
5. See **8**; on the worship of rulers see **32** (general), **218** (Ptolemies).

40 Two letters of Antigonus to Teos concerning the projected synoecism with Lebedus (ca 303)

The foundation or resettlement of Greek cities by Hellenistic rulers was a characteristic feature of the age and represented a continuation on a larger scale by Alexander's Successors of the precedents he had set (see **7, 18, 19**). So did the practice of giving such foundations dynastic names. One procedure commonly followed was that of 'synoecism', whereby two or more communities were made to merge into a new and larger state (cf. also **128, 133, 134, 182** II). The following two letters addressed by Antigonus to the people of Teos give by far the most vivid evidence available of what such a synoecism involved in practical, legal, and human terms for the communities concerned, and also show the complex questions of detail the ruler had to attend to. Lebedus, the smaller city, was to be abandoned altogether, but it was not clear whether the site of Teos was to be moved further west or remain as at present. The letters do not make clear whence came the initiative for the projected synoecism, and outwardly Antigonus pretends to be merely providing advice in answer to delegations sent by the two cities. On the other hand it seems clear that the plan was that of Antigonus himself, imposed on the reluctant communities, and in fact the synoecism was never carried out, owing to the defeat and death of Antigonus at Ipsus in 301. However, the people of Lebedus were later moved by Lysimachus to Ephesus (see **45**). For other foundations or resettlements in this period and later see **21** §14, **29** (Cassandrea), **21** §19, **45** (Lysimachea), **31** n. 5 (Antigonea in the Troad), **41** (Sicyon – Demetrias), **46** chs. 57–8, **153, 174, 179, 187, 190, 192** (Seleucids), **233** (Ptolemies).

See further: Rostovtzeff I (1941), 155–8; A. H. M. Jones (1940), ch. 1; *id., The Cities of the Eastern Roman Provinces* (Oxford, 2nd ed., 1971), *via* index.

(The beginning of the first letter is lost)

A (1) . . . [whoever is] sent to the Panionion[1] we thought it right [that he should perform all the] common rites for the same period of time, that he should pitch tent, take part in the festival together with [your envoys] and be called a Tean.

(2) We thought it right that every one of the [Lebedians should be given] / a building site in your city equal in size to the one he has left in Lebedus. Until they are built [all] the Lebedians [should be given] accommodation without payment, if the present city is to remain, one [third of the] existing houses, but if one must destroy it, half of the existing houses [are to be left], one third of these given [to the Lebedians] and you will have [the] other two thirds; and if part of the city is destroyed and [the] remaining [houses are sufficient] / to accommodate both you and the Lebedians, the [Lebedians] shall be given one third [of these]; but if the remaining houses are not sufficient to accommodate both you [and the Lebedians], enough [houses] should be left of those due for destruction, [and when] enough houses [have been completed] in the newly built city, the [remaining] houses [which] lie outside the perimeter of the city should be destroyed. [All the Lebedians] shall build / houses on their plots within three years; if not, the [plots] shall become public property. [We thought it] right that the roofs of the houses should be given to the Lebedians [to speed up the construction] of the houses, one quarter every [year over] a period of four [years].

(3) [We thought it] right that a place should be assigned to the Lebedians for the burial [of their dead].

(4) [Whatever sums are] owed by the city of Lebedus [with interest] should be met [every year] from the common [revenues]. / [These] debts [should be taken over] by your city on the same conditions as the [Lebedians].

(5) Concerning all those who are *proxenoi*[2] of the city of Lebedus or benefactors (*euergetai*) or have received from the Lebedians [citizenship] or some other grant or honour, [they shall enjoy the same privileges in your] city, and shall be inscribed within one year in the same place where your *proxenoi* [and benefactors are] inscribed.

(6) As to any lawsuits and contracts [which exist between members of] your two communities and others, / they shall be settled by agreement or by trial [according to the] laws [of each state] and our edict within two years of the [issuing of that edict (?)]. As to those suits (you) have against the Lebedians or the Lebedians have [against you, you should both make] an agreement and set it down in writing (?), and should there be any [objection against the] agreement, it shall be decided on by the umpire city within six months; the umpire [city is to be]

5

10

15

20

25

30 Mytilene [as] / agreed by both of you. [We think it right] that the
drafters of the agreement should write up the other provisions [according
to] their own judgement. But since we hear there is [such a mass of]
contracts and accusations that if one were [to settle them according to]
the [law, even without] any interruption, no one would be able to wait
for the outcome – for up till [now it does not appear that any progress
has been made] with these matters nor that the agreements have been
executed, as contracts in your city [have not been decided upon for a long
35 time] / – and if interests go on adding up [year after year, no one] will be
able to pay.³ We think it right that if [the debtors pay] of their own
accord, the drafters of the agreement should lay down that they will not
[repay] more than twice the value [of the original debt]; but if the debtors
need to be taken to court, they will repay three times its value.

(7) Whenever the agreement [is ratified], the lawsuits shall be filed and
40 decided within a year. Those who do not file a suit [or prosecute] /
within the prescribed period, while the courts are in session, shall not be
allowed to file suits or [prosecute] subsequently. [If any] of your citizens
or of the Lebedians is abroad during the specified period, [it shall be
allowed] to serve a summons [on him] at the town hall and at his house,
by declaring to the [magistrate . . .] in the presence of two qualified
witnesses.

(8) In future you shall pay [and receive penalties according to what-
45 ever] laws seem equitable to both your cities. [You should each appoint] /
three codifiers of the laws aged 40 or more and [above corruption]; let
the men chosen swear to draw up laws [they think are] the best and will
benefit the city. When they have sworn [let them draw up laws they
think] fair to both sides and let them present them within [six months;
and let] any one else who wishes draft a law and introduce it; of the laws
50 [that are introduced, all those] / which are agreed on and ratified by the
people should be put into practice, [but all those which meet with
objections] should be referred to us, so that we may either decide on
them ourselves [or appoint a city] to give a decision; the [laws] that have
been agreed on (by you) should be sent to me, and it should be made
clear which laws were introduced by the codifiers of the laws and which
laws [were drawn up by others, so that] if it is clear that some of the
codifiers have not provided the best laws but [some which are unsuitable]
55 we shall censure and punish [them];⁴ / all this should be carried out
within one year. [Until such time as the complete code of] laws was
drawn up, your envoys thought it right [that you should use] your own
[laws, while the envoys] of the Lebedians requested to send for laws
from another city [and to use them; and since we] think it more just to
send for [laws] from another city, [and instructed both] sides to declare
60 the city whose laws they wished to use, and both sides [agreed] / to use

72

the laws of Cos,⁵ we decided accordingly, and [invited] the [people of Cos] to give you a text of their laws to copy. We think it [right] that three men should be [appointed] immediately as soon as [this] answer is read out, and be [sent to Cos within] three [days] to take a copy of the laws, and that these envoys should [bring back the] laws bearing the seal of the people of Cos within [thirty] days; and that [when] the laws [have been brought back] / you and the Lebedians should appoint the magis-   65
trates [within] ten [days].

(9) As to those who have performed the *choregia* or the trierarchy or another [liturgy⁶ in either] city, we think it right that they should no longer [be liable to the same liturgy]. The envoys of the Lebedians also [requested] that they should in addition be exempted for some time [from the liturgies while] the synoecism is being carried out; we think it right that if you all [remain in the old] city, / the Lebedians should be   70
exempted from liturgies for three years; [and that if some of you] move to the peninsula, they too should be exempted [for the same period, but that all of you whose] houses are not demolished (?) should assume the liturgies.

(10) The envoys of the [Lebedians] also said [it was necessary] to set aside from the revenues a sum of [fourteen] hundred gold staters [for] the supply of [corn, so that] anyone who wished could take this money against security [and import corn to / the] city and sell it whenever he   75
wished for a period of one year, and after [the end of the year] should pay back to the city the money, the capital sum and the interest at [the rate fixed for the loan. And when they particularly requested] that we should now make this provision, so that there would be [a sufficient supply of corn in the city] – for you could not grow enough – your envoys also thought it right [that this should be done, and requested] that a larger sum be fixed when the synoecism [was in progress and there were more of you] / gathered together in the same place. Now previously we were   80
[unwilling] that [any] city should be given the right to import corn and that stocks of corn should be built up, [as we did not wish the] cities to spend unnecessarily large sums of money for this purpose; [we were still reluctant] to do this now, as the tributary [territory]⁷ is near by [so that if there] is [need] for corn, we believe it is easy to fetch [as much] as one wishes from [it]. / Our concern on this matter [was prompted by the   85
wish to assist] the [cities], since you [know] like every one else that [we gain] no private profit from the matter, and the instructions we give [seek to] free the cities from their debts. For in the belief [that in so far as it lies within our power] we have made [you] free and autonomous in other respects,⁸ [we thought] we ought to give some care to [this matter], / so as to relieve you as quickly as possible. [But since] the   90
proposals on the corn supply [seem useful], so that nothing [should be

omitted which is just and] advantageous [to the] people, we think it right that the [corn supply] should be organised as the envoys of the Lebedians said, and [think that the sum] made available against security should be fixed at a maximum of [fourteen hundred] gold staters.

95   (11) (We think it right) that the import and export of all [corn] / be declared [in the stoa in the agora] so that if some (dealers) do not find it profitable to bring (the corn) to the [agora and thence to] export it again, it shall be permitted to them to export it after paying the tax on [goods declared in the agora]. As to all the villages and farm-houses which lie outside [your city], we think it right that each man be instructed to
100 register [the quantity of crops] / he wishes to export from the country-side, and after making his declaration [to the *agoranomos*⁹ and] paying [the] taxes, to export them.

    (12) Your envoys [and those from the Lebedians] requested that three men should be appointed on each side to draw up [any proposals that may still have been omitted] which would help the synoecism. [It seems to use useful] that the men should be appointed within thirty days [of the]
105 reading out [of this answer], / and that the men chosen should draw up any proposal that may have been omitted [by us]. Of the proposals made, those [agreed on] by both sides [shall be valid], while disputed ones should be referred to us within the next two [months, so that] we may hear [both sides] and give our decision according to what we believe [to be advantageous to] both.

    B King Antigonus to the council and people of Teos, greetings. When
110 we [previously considered] / the quickest ways of completing the synoecism, we could not see where you would find the money [you need] in order to [give] the Lebedians the price of their [houses without delay], because of the [long time] it takes for you to get the income from your revenues; [we received] your envoys and those from the Lebedians and asked [them whether they could show] us any source of revenue, and they said they had none apart from the (usual) taxes; [we examined their
115 views] / and find that among you only the wealthiest always have to make advance contributions;¹⁰ [we therefore think it right] that 'the wealthiest' should be reckoned as numbering 600, [and that these . . .] should make advance contributions in proportion to their property, so as to raise quickly one quarter of the price (of the houses) [for the Lebedians], and that repayment be made to these men in priority from the revenues [of the city] after the lapse of one [year], all income being earmarked for that purpose.¹¹ The men who are to conduct the assessors
120 [of the houses, and the men] / who are to take a copy of the laws of Cos should be appointed as soon as the abrogation (?) [takes place (?)]¹² and should be] despatched within five days of their appointment, and the

men [sent] to copy the laws should bring them back from Cos within the number of days specified in our [answer; the men] sent [to fetch] the assessors should bring them back as quickly as possible. [We think it right . . .] that a count of the houses in your city which are to be given to the Lebedians for [residence] should be carried out [within] fifteen [days] / of the reading of this answer, and that the men who are to carry   125 out the count [of the houses and hand them] to their occupants should be elected by each [tribe] at the next meeting of the assembly.

RC 3–4; *Syll.*³ 344 (cf. *SEG* xv.717)

1. The meeting place for the religious celebrations of the league of Ionian cities in Asia Minor; cf. **129** §1. On the Ionian League cf. **143, 203**.
2. An honorific title bestowed by a city on a member of another city, and which made him into an official local representative of the interests of the city which honoured him.
3. It was not infrequent for the activity of the courts in Greek cities to come to a virtual standstill; this could provoke royal intervention (see further **135**).
4. A clear indication of how the 'advice' of Antigonus was meant to be taken. Cf. Alexander and Chios, **5**.
5. Cf. **48, 133**; S. M. Sherwin-White, *Ancient Cos* (Göttingen, 1978), ch. 5.
6. 'Liturgies' were a form of honorific taxation whereby the wealthier members of Greek cities were required to undertake certain civic duties which involved financial outlay, such as the training of a chorus for a dramatic festival (*choregia*) or the maintenance of a trireme (trierarchy). Cf. **99, 129**.
7. I.e. crown land; Antigonus thus had a vested interest in the corn trade and his claim to be disinterested was open to doubt. He also had additional leverage with Greek cities frequently in difficulties over their corn supply (see generally **112**) and cf. the case of Samothrace, **269** and n. 6.
8. See **29**; Antigonus evidently did not regard his dealings with Teos and Lebedus as contradicting that claim.
9. Cf. **107** n. 3.
10. Cf. **129** §4.
11. Cf. **97** n. 9.
12. Possibly a mistake by the stonecutter for 'this answer [is read]'.

41 Demetrius and the refounding of Sicyon (302)

The city of Sicyon was garrisoned by the soldiers of King Ptolemy, and their most illustrious general was Philip. Demetrius made a surprise attack by night and forced his way inside the fortifications. The garrison troops then took refuge in the acropolis, while Demetrius after making himself master of the city occupied the area between the private dwellings and the citadel. He was on the point of bringing forward siege engines[1] when the panic-stricken troops surrendered the acropolis by

agreement and sailed back to Egypt. Demetrius moved the Sicyonians to
the acropolis and razed the part of the city which adjoined the harbour, as
it was strategically a very weak spot.[2] He joined with the body of citizens
in the construction work and restored them their freedom,[3] for which
benefaction they granted him godlike honours.[4] They called the city
Demetrias, voted to celebrate every year sacrifices, festivals and also
competitions in his honour and to grant him the other honours of a
founder. The passage of time and changing circumstances have obliter-
ated these honours, but the Sicyonians, having moved to a much better
site, have continued to inhabit it up to our time.[5] For the area contained
by the acropolis is level and spacious and surrounded on all sides by cliffs
that are difficult to approach, which makes it impossible to bring
forward siege engines at any point. It also has an abundance of springs
which has enabled the Sicyonians to lay out numerous gardens. In this
way the correctness of the king's foresight has been demonstrated both as
regards the enjoyment of peaceful conditions and as regards protection in
time of war.

Diodorus XX.102.2–4

1. On Demetrius the 'Besieger' see **39**.
2. On such resettlements see **40**.
3. See **29**.
4. See **32**.
5. Contrast the failure of **40**. The name Demetrias, however, was not preserved.

42 The Hellenic League of 302

'And when a common council of the Greeks met at the Isthmus of Corinth and a
large crowd was gathered together, Demetrius was proclaimed Leader (*hegemon*)
of the Greeks as Philip and Alexander before' (Plutarch, *Demetrius* 25.2). This is
the only explicit reference in the surviving literary evidence to an important
event, the foundation by Antigonus and Demetrius of a league of mainland
Greek states headed by themselves, on which inscriptions have shed important
though fragmentary light. The charter of the League is partially preserved on
many fragments of a large inscription from Epidaurus, the best preserved part of
which is translated here, and the activities of one of the presidents of the League,
Adimantus of Lampsacus, are illustrated by several texts (L. Robert, *Hellenica* 2
(1946), 15–33).

The foundation of the League may have been planned by Antigonus and
Demetrius as early as 307 (cf. Diodorus XX.46.5), but it was only after
Demetrius' successes against Cassander on the Greek mainland in 304 and 303
that conditions became favourable for the attempt. The League was a revival of
that founded by Philip of Macedon in 337 (*Staatsv.* III. 403, and see **2, 5, 6, 16**),

and was intended to be permanent (lines 140–2 of the Epidaurus inscription). Its aims and chances of development have been variously estimated; while some scholars have seen in it a genuine attempt at founding a 'United States of Greece', others have interpreted it as a convenient constitutional instrument devised by the two kings to gain the moral and material support of the Greeks (see **29**) in their struggle against Cassander in Macedon. The charter of the League makes clear that so long as that struggle was in progress, the kings would control League policy; how the League might have worked in peace time never came to the test. The disaster at Ipsus in 301 and the death of Antigonus (see **43**) consigned the League to irrelevance, forgotten and never revived by Demetrius and the Greeks alike. For the very different Hellenic League of Antigonus Doson, see **58**. For the League of Islanders cf. **218**.

See further: R. H. Simpson, *Historia* 8 (1959), 396–8.

. . . and it shall not be permissible [to exercise reprisals against]   61
ambassadors [coming from the Greeks? to] the councillors, [nor] against
ambassadors [sent by the] councillors, nor against men sent out on a
[military expedition] in the common interest [nor against men starting
off] on their respective errands, nor against men [travelling] back to
[their own cities?], nor to kidnap anyone nor to seize anyone as a
security / [for any] reason. If [anyone does this, let the] magistrates in   65
each city prevent this and let the [councillors pass judgement?]. The
councillors shall meet in peace time [during the sacred competitions?],
and in war time whenever it seems expedient to the councillors (?)[1] and
[the general] left in charge by the kings for the common defence. The
council shall be in session for as many days as the presidents / of the   70
council announce. Until the common war is brought [to a close],[2]
meetings of the council shall take place wherever the presidents and the
king[3] or the general appointed by the kings announce; but when peace is
established, wherever the crowned competitions[4] are celebrated. The
decisions of the councillors shall have [the force of law]; they shall
transact business when over half of them are present, but not if less than
half attend the meeting. / Concerning decisions reached in the council,   75
the cities shall not be allowed to call to account the councillors they have
sent. There shall be five presidents chosen by lot from among the
councillors, when the war [has been brought to an end]. No more than
one president shall be chosen by lot from any single people or city. The
presidents shall [summon] the councillors [and the] secretaries of the
treasury (?)[5] [and the] / assistants, and lay before (the council) the   80
matters for deliberation and [hand over the] resolutions to the secretaries,
keeping for themselves [legible?] copies, and they shall introduce [all?]
the lawsuits (?) and take care [that business is transacted in every way as
required?], and shall have authority to punish anyone who causes a
disturbance. [Anyone who] wishes [to put forward] anything of advan-

85 tage to the kings and [the Greeks], or to denounce men acting against the interests / of the allies [or] refusing to comply with resolutions passed, or to communicate any other business to the [councillors], shall register with the presidents, and they shall lay the matter before the councillors. The presidents chosen by lot shall [render] accounts for their actions. [Anyone who] wishes to lay a written charge against [them] shall do so before the next presidents chosen by lot. [When they have received] it

90 they shall introduce it / before the [councillors] at the first session which takes place [after their[6] period in office]. Until the common war has been brought to a close [the] representatives of the kings shall [always] exercise the presidency.[7] If any city does not send the councillors to the meetings according to the [agreement], it shall pay a fine of two [drachmas] a day for [each] of [these] until the councillors are dismissed

95 unless [a councillor] declares on oath that he has been ill. / And if a city does not send whatever [military contingent] it is instructed to provide, it shall [pay a fine] every day of half a mina [for every] cavalryman, 20 drachmas for [every] hoplite, 10 drachmas for every [light armed] soldier and [ten?] for every sailor, until [the expiry of] the period of military service for all the other [Greeks. . .]

Staatsv. III. 446, lines 61–99

1. Probably a stonecutter's error for 'presidents'.
2. The war against Cassander.
3. Possibly a mistake for 'kings', though this may be a deliberate reference to Demetrius with whom the mainland Greeks had all their dealings.
4. Cf. **119** n. 14.
5. Text and meaning uncertain.
6. I.e. the previous presidents.
7. The League therefore never had its own presidents.

43 Decree of Athens in honour of the poet Philippides (283/2)

See further: T. L. Shear, *Hesperia* Supplement 17 (1978), index p. 203 under *IG* II[2]. 657.

In the archonship of Euthius (283/2), in the [third] prytany, of the [tribe Acamantis], for which Nausimenes son of Nausicydes of Cholargus was secretary, on the 18th of Boedromion and the 19th day of the prytany, at

5 a principal meeting of the assembly; / Hieromnemon son of Teisimachus from Coele and the other presiding officers put to the vote; resolved by the council and the people; Niceratus son of Phileas of Cephale moved: since Philippides[1] has on every occasion continued to show his goodwill towards the people, and / having gone abroad to King Lysimachus and

10

having previously discussed the matter with the king, he brought back to
the people a gift of 10,000 Attic measures of wheat for distribution to all
the Athenians[2] in the archonship of Euctemon (299/8), and also discussed
the question of the mast and yard-arm,[3] which were / to be presented to   15
the goddess (Athena) at the Great Panathenaea together with the robe,[4]
and these were brought in the archonship of Euctemon; and when King
Lysimachus won [the] battle at Ipsus against Antigonus [and]
Demetrius,[5] he secured burial / at his own expense for the citizens who had   20
perished in the [emergency], and [as to all those who] were taken prisoner he interceded with the [king and] secured their release; for those
who wished to serve in the army he obtained the right to enrol [in] separate formations with their own commanders, while to those who chose to
leave he provided clothes and supplies from / his own resources and sent   25
them each to their chosen destination, more than 300 men altogether; and
he also appealed for the release of all the Athenian citizens who had been
placed in custody by Demetrius and Antigonus and were captured in
Asia, and has constantly shown himself helpful / to any Athenian who   30
meets him and calls on his assistance; and after the people recovered its
freedom[6] he has constantly spoken and acted in the interests of the city's
safety, and urged the king to help with money and corn, so that the
people may continue / to be free and recover the Piraeus and the forts as   35
soon as possible;[7] the king has frequently vouchsafed for all this to the
Athenian embassies visiting him; and when he was appointed
agonothete[8] in the archonship of Isaeus (284/3), he complied with the
will / of the people voluntarily from his own funds, offered the ancestral   40
sacrifices to the gods on behalf of the people, gave to all the Athenians
. . . for all the [contests and] was the first to provide an additional contest
for Demeter and Core (Persephone) as a memorial of the people's /   45
[liberty, and supervised] the other contests and [sacrifices on behalf of
the city] and for all this he spent much money from his own private
resources and rendered his accounts according to the laws, and he has
never [said or] / done anything contrary to (the interests of) the   50
democracy. Therefore, so that it may be manifest to all that the people
knows how to return adequate thanks to benefactors for the services they
have performed, with good fortune, be it resolved by the council, that
the officers chosen by lot to preside over the people, when the days
prescribed by law / for the request have passed, should introduce these   55
matters at the first assembly according to the law and communicate to
the people the decision of the council, viz. that the council resolves to
praise Philippides son of Philocles of Cephale for his merits and the
goodwill he constantly shows towards / the people of Athens, and to   60
crown him with a gold crown according to the law, and proclaim the
crown at the tragic contest of the Great Dionysia; and to set up a bronze

statue of him in the theatre, and to grant to him and for all time to the
65   eldest of his descendants / free meals in the prytaneum and a seat of
honour (*proedria*) in all the contests organised by the city; the making of
the crown and the proclamation shall be entrusted to the officials in
charge of finance. The secretary of the prytany shall be responsible for
70   the engraving of this decree on a stone / stele and the placing of it near
the temple of Dionysus; the officials in charge of finance shall provide 20
drachmas for the inscription of the stele from the people's fund for
decrees.

*Syll.*³ 374; *IG* II².657

1. An Athenian poet of the New Comedy, friend of King Lysimachus and a
   wealthy benefactor of his native city: one example among many of the
   increasing dependence of Greek cities on such benefactors for economic and
   other assistance, as well as for mediation in their dealings with Hellenistic
   kings. Compare the similar case of Callias of Sphettus at the same period (**44**),
   that of Boulagoras of Samos (**113**), and see generally **97**.
2. See **44** and n. 8.
3. Part of the ship used in the procession of the Great Panathenaea.
4. Cf. **34, 44**; T. L. Shear, *op. cit.*, 39–44.
5. The battle of Ipsus in Phrygia (301) was won in fact by a coalition of
   Lysimachus, Seleucus and Cassander (cf. **46** ch. 55, also **148**). The defeat and
   death of Antigonus marked the end of the Antigonids' hopes of uniting
   Alexander's empire under their control, though Demetrius was to remain
   active for another decade and a half (cf. **44, 45, 46** ch. 55). The Athenians, who
   had been first to hail Antigonus and Demetrius as kings (**34**), now pointedly
   refuse them the royal title (cf. also **44**).
6. A reference to the liberation of Athens from Demetrius and the restoration of
   the democracy in 287 or 286; cf. **44**.
7. These were still in the hands of Demetrius' troops and may in fact have
   remained in Macedonian hands till the Chremonidean War (**49, 50**) and even
   later; cf. M. J. Osborne, *ZPE* 35 (1979), 191–4 and C. Habicht, *Untersuchungen zur politischen Geschichte Athens im 3. Jahrhundert v. Chr.* (Munich,
   1979), 95–112, against T. L. Shear, *op. cit.*, 27–9, 79–83.
8. Responsible for the organisation of the city's competitions.

44 Decree of Athens in honour of Callias of Sphettus (270/69)

See further, for full discussion of this important new text: the *editio princeps* by T.
L. Shear, *Hesperia* Supplement 17 (1978); C. Habicht, *op. cit.*, (**43** n. 7), esp.
45–67; M. J. Osborne, *ZPE* 35 (1979), 181–94.

5   The people (crowns) Callias, son of Thymochares, of Sphettus.¹ / In the
archonship of Sosistratus (270/69), in the sixth prytany, of the tribe

Pandionis, for which Athenodorus son of Gorgippus of Acharnae was secretary, on the 18th of the month Posideon, and the 21st of the prytany, at a principal meeting of the assembly; the motion was put to the vote by Epichares son of Phidostratus of Erchia and the other presiding officers. / 10

Resolved by the council and the people; Euchares son of Euarchus of Conthyle moved: since, at the time of the uprising of the people against those who were occupying the city,[2] when the people expelled the soldiers from the city, but the fort on the / Mouseion was still occupied,[3] 15 and war raged in the countryside because of the (soldiers) from Piraeus,[4] and Demetrius[5] was coming with his army from the Peloponnese against the city, Callias, on hearing of the danger threatening the city, selected a thousand of the soldiers[6] / who were posted with him at Andros, gave 20 them their wages and food rations, and immediately came to the rescue of the people in the city, acting in accordance with the goodwill of King Ptolemy (I) towards the people,[7] and leading out into the countryside the soldiers who were following him, he protected / the gathering of the 25 corn, making every effort to ensure that as much corn as possible should be brought into the city.[8]

And (since), when Demetrius arrived, encamped around the city and besieged it, Callias in defence of the people attacked with his soldiers / 30 and was wounded, but refused to avoid any risk at any time for the sake of the people's safety; and when King Ptolemy sent Sostratus[9] to act in the city's interests, and Sostratus summoned ambassadors / to meet him 35 at Piraeus for the conclusion of the peace on behalf of the city with Demetrius, Callias complied with the instructions of the generals and the council, acted as envoy for the people and defended all the city's interests; he remained in the city with his / soldiers until the conclusion of the 40 peace,[10] and (then) sailed to King Ptolemy, assisting in every way the embassies sent by the people and collaborating for the interests of the city.

And (since), when King Ptolemy the younger (= Ptolemy II Philadelphus) took over the monarchy (283/2), / Callias was staying in the 45 city, and when the generals called on him and described the condition in which the city was, and urged him to make haste to King Ptolemy on behalf of the city to secure the prompt despatch of help to the city in corn / and money, Callias sailed himself on his own account to Cyprus, 50 met the king there and earnestly upheld the city's interests, and brought back for the people 50 talents of silver and a gift of 20,000 medimni of corn, which were measured out from Delos[11] to the envoys sent by the / 55 people.

And (since), when the king celebrated for the first time the *Ptolemaieia*, the sacrifice and the contests in honour of his father,[12] and the people [voted] to send a sacred embassy (*theoria*) and requested [Callias to agree] to be its leader and to lead [the sacred embassy] on behalf of the people,[13] Callias eagerly complied with the request, waived the [50?] minas [which had been voted] / to him by the people to lead the sacred embassy and gave them to the [people], and led himself [the sacred embassy] from his own means in a way that was honourable and [worthy] of the people, [and] looked after [the] sacrifice on behalf of the city and [all] the other appropriate observances together with his fellow ambassadors. [And] (since) the people was about to celebrate the *Panathenaea* for (Athena) Archegetis, then [for the first time / since] the recovery of the city,[14] [Callias] interceded with the king [on the question of] the ropes which needed to be made for the robe,[15] [and] when the king presented them to the city, he endeavoured [that] they be as fine [as] possible in honour of the goddess and that the sacred envoys elected with [him] / should forthwith bring [the ropes back here].

[And] (since), now that he has been posted to Halicarnassus by [King] Ptolemy, Callias continues to exert himself [on behalf of the] embassies and sacred missions sent by the people [to King] Ptolemy, and [in private] to show [all possible] attention [to every] / fellow citizen who calls on him, and to the [soldiers who are posted there] with him, attaching the greatest importance [to the interests] and generally to the dignity of the city; . . . for the fatherland Callias never endured . . . / when the democracy had been overthrown, but during the oligarchy[16] he gave up his [own] property[17] so as not to act [in any way] against the laws or against the democracy of all the Athenians.[18]

Therefore, so that all who wish to show zeal towards the city may know that the people always / remembers those who have benefited it and repays thanks to every one of them: with good fortune, be it resolved by the council that the officials who are chosen by lot to preside at the meeting of the assembly prescribed by the law, should deliberate about these matters and communicate to the people the view of the council, viz. that the council resolves to praise / Callias son of Thymochares of Sphettus for his excellence and the goodwill which he constantly shows towards the people of Athens, and to crown him with a gold crown in accordance with the law, and to proclaim the crown at the new tragic contest of the Great Dionysia. The officials in charge of finance shall be responsible for the making of the crown and the / proclamation. The people shall also set up a bronze statue of him in the agora, and he shall have a seat of honour (*proedria*) at all the contests celebrated by the city, and the architect who is appointed in charge of sacred buildings shall assign to him the seat of honour. The people shall elect at once / three men from among all the Athenians who shall be responsible for making and dedicating the statue. The *thesmothetai* shall

60

65

70

75

80

85

90

95

100

introduce the scrutiny of his award to the *Heliaea* when the days prescribed by law have elapsed. So that there might be a record for all time / of the zealous deeds performed by Callias for the people, the secretary of the prytany shall inscribe this decree [on] a stone stele and place it beside the statue, and the officials in charge of finance shall pay the expense resulting for the inscription and the stele.

105

T. L. Shear, *Hesperia* Supplement 17 (1978), at pp. 2–4

1. An Athenian from a wealthy family, prominent in public life; as this recently (1971) discovered inscription shows, much of his career was spent as an officer in Ptolemaic service. Compare Philippides and Lysimachus in **43**.
2. The troops of Demetrius who had seized control of Athens in 295/4 and set up an oligarchy (contrast his earlier relations with Athens, **34**). On his expulsion from Macedon (**45**) the Athenians revolted against him in 287 (Habicht, Osborne) or 286 (Shear).
3. A fort on the Mouseion hill, to the south-west of the Acropolis; cf. **117**.
4. Cf. **43** n. 7.
5. Cf. **43** n. 5.
6. Mercenary soldiers in Ptolemaic service.
7. The earliest indication of the establishment of Ptolemaic influence in the Aegean; cf. **49, 50, 218**. Ptolemaic support for the liberation of Athens was previously unattested.
8. Cf. **34, 43, 50**, and generally **112**.
9. Probably Sostratus of Cnidus, cf. **232**.
10. The peace may have involved the other kings as well (Pyrrhus, Lysimachus, Seleucus); cf. T. L. Shear, *op. cit.*, 76f. *Contra*, Habicht, *op. cit.*, 62–7.
11. Cf. **114** n. 2.
12. Cf. **218**.
13. Cf. Boulagoras in **113**.
14. Perhaps in 278.
15. Ropes to secure the mast of Athena's ship, cf. **43**.
16. The oligarchy set up by Demetrius in 294/3.
17. It was probably confiscated by the oligarchic government.
18. For the democratic sentiments cf. **26, 34, 49**.

45   The career of Lysimachus

Lysimachus was of Macedonian origin and one of Alexander's bodyguards; one day in a fit of anger Alexander shut him up in a room with a lion and then found he had overpowered the beast.[1] Henceforward he always held him in esteem and honoured him as much as the noblest Macedonians. After Alexander's death Lysimachus became king[2] of the Thracians, who are neighbours of the Macedonians and who had been ruled by Alexander and earlier by Philip; these represent only a small part of the Thracian people. [. . .] Then Lysimachus made war against the neighbouring peoples, first the Odrysae, then against Dromichaetes and the Getae. As he was engaging with men not lacking in experience of war and who outnumbered him heavily, he himself only escaped after facing extreme danger, while his son Agathocles, who was serving with him for the first time, was captured by the Getae. Later Lysimachus suffered other reverses in battle, and as he was seriously concerned about his son's capture, he made peace with Dromichaetes, surrendering to the Getic chieftain the part of his empire that lay beyond the Danube and giving him his daughter in marriage, largely under compulsion. There are some who say that it was not Agathocles but Lysimachus himself who was captured and saved when Agathocles made the pact with the Getic chieftain on his behalf. When he came back he married to Agathocles Lysandra, daughter of Ptolemy son of Lagus and Eurydice.[3] He also sailed across to Asia and joined in destroying the empire of Antigonus.[4] He also founded the present city of Ephesus close to the sea, bringing as settlers to it men from Lebedus[5] and Colophon and destroying their cities, which caused the iambic poet Phoenix to write a dirge over the capture of Colophon. [. . .] Lysimachus also went to war against Pyrrhus son of Aeacides; he waited for his departure from Epirus (Pyrrhus in his career wandered far and wide)[6] and then ravaged the country until he reached the royal tombs. The sequel of the story I find incredible, but Hieronymus of Cardia[7] relates (*FGrH* 154 F 9) that Lysimachus destroyed the tombs of the dead and cast out their bones. But this Hieronymus has the reputation of being a writer hostile to the kings apart from Antigonus, to whom he was unduly favourable. [. . .] Possibly Hieronymus had grudges against Lysimachus, particularly his destruction[8] of the city of Cardia and the foundation in its place of Lysimachea on the isthmus of the Thracian Chersonese.

(10) As long as (Philip) Arrhidaeus was king in Macedon, and after him Cassander and his sons, Lysimachus remained on friendly terms with the Macedonians; but when the throne fell to Demetrius son of Antigonus, then Lysimachus expecting war from Demetrius decided to take the initiative.[9] He knew that Demetrius like his father wished to extend his power, and he also saw that, though Demetrius had come to Macedon at the invitation of Alexander son of Cassander, when he arrived he assassinated Alexander, and seized the throne of Macedon in his place. For these reasons he engaged Demetrius in battle near Amphipolis and came within inches of being driven out of Thrace, but Pyrrhus came to his help and he secured Thrace and afterwards established his rule over the Nestian Macedonians; Pyrrhus himself secured the greater part of Macedonia, having come with an army from Epirus

and being for the present on good terms with Lysimachus. When Demetrius crossed over to Asia and made war on Seleucus, the alliance of Pyrrhus and Lysimachus held good as long as Demetrius' fortunes endured; but when Demetrius fell in the power of Seleucus,[10] Lysimachus and Pyrrhus broke their friendship and went to war. Lysimachus fought against Antigonus the son of Demetrius[11] and Pyrrhus himself, gained a decisive victory and took over Macedon, forcing Pyrrhus to withdraw to Epirus.[12] Now love is a frequent cause of disaster for men. Although he was advanced in years and considered fortunate in his children, and although Agathocles his son had children of his own by Lysandra, Lysimachus nonetheless married Lysandra's sister Arsinoe.[13] This Arsinoe, fearing that on the death of Lysimachus her children would fall in the power of Agathocles, conspired, it is said, against Agathocles for those reasons. Historians have already related how Arsinoe fell in love with Agathocles, and they say that on being rejected by him she plotted his death. They say too that Lysimachus later got to know of his wife's criminal audacity, but could no longer do anything as he was by now completely abandoned by his friends. And so since Lysimachus let pass Arsinoe's murder of Agathocles, Lysandra took refuge with Seleucus together with her children and brothers [. . .][14] Alexander, a son of Lysimachus by an Odrysian woman, escaped with them to Seleucus. They all went up to Babylon and implored Seleucus to go to war against Lysimachus; at the same time Philetaerus, who had the charge of Lysimachus' treasure, incensed at the death of Agathocles and apprehensive as to his likely treatment by Arsinoe, seized Pergamum on the Caicus,[15] and sent a messenger to place himself and the treasure in the hands of Seleucus. On hearing this Lysimachus quickly crossed to Asia and, taking the initiative in the war, engaged Seleucus in battle but suffered a total defeat and was killed.[16] Alexander, his son by the Odrysian woman, after much entreaty of Lysandra recovered his body and later took it to the Chersonese and buried it. His tomb is still visible there between the village of Cardia and Pactye.

Pausanias 1.9.5–10

1. On the theme of the physical strength of rulers cf. also **46** ch. 57.
2. See **22**, **24**, but Lysimachus was not 'king' till 305/4; for his subsequent career see **30**, **31**, **36**, **39**(b), **43**.
3. In 294; Lysandra had previously (297) been married to Alexander, son of Cassander and briefly king of Macedon.
4. See **43** and n. 5; this led to an extension of his kingdom in Asia Minor.
5. See **40**.
6. On Pyrrhus see also **47**. The war referred to here is otherwise unknown, if this is not simply a confusion on Pausanias' part.

7. See **25**.
8. Cardia was not literally 'destroyed' but rather absorbed in the foundation of Lysimachea (309/8 – see **21** §19). On Lysimachea cf. **153, 154**.
9. In 288 or 287; Demetrius had been king in Macedon since 294. For a revised chronology of the end of his reign cf. T. L. Shear, *Hesperia* Supplement 17 (1978), 72f., 86 n. 235.
10. In 286 or 285.
11. Antigonus Gonatas, the future king of Macedon.
12. In 285/4.
13. Lysimachus married Arsinoe *ca* 300, before his son's marriage with Lysandra.
14. The end of the sentence is corrupt.
15. The beginnings of the later Attalid kingdom; see **193**.
16. At Corupedium in Lydia in 281; see also **46** ch. 62. Lysimachus' kingdom died with him.

46 Seleucus and the foundation of the Seleucid empire

(52) [. . .] After the Persians Alexander was king of the Syrians, as well as of all the people whom he saw. When he died leaving one very young son and another as yet unborn, the Macedonians, being deeply attached to the family of Philip, chose as their king Arrhidaeus, Alexander's half-brother, although he was believed to be dim-witted, and changed his name from Arrhidaeus to Philip. While the children of Alexander were growing up (they even placed the pregnant mother under guard), his friends divided the peoples of the empire into satrapies, which Perdiccas shared out among them in the name of King Philip.[1] Not long after, when the kings were put to death, the satraps became kings. The first satrap of the Syrians was Laomedon of Mytilene, appointed by Perdiccas and then Antipater, who after Perdiccas was guardian of the kings. Ptolemy, the satrap of Egypt, sailed against Laomedon and sought to bribe him to hand over Syria, which protected Egypt's flank and was a good base to attack Cyprus. He failed and so arrested him, but Laomedon bribed his guards and escaped to Alcetas in Caria. For some time Ptolemy ruled Syria; he sailed back to Egypt after leaving garrisons in the cities. (53) Antigonus was satrap of Phrygia, Lycia and Pamphylia, and was appointed overseer of the whole of Asia by Antipater when he returned to Europe. He besieged Eumenes, satrap of Cappadocia, whom the Macedonians had voted an enemy, but Eumenes escaped and seized control of Media. Eventually Antigonus captured Eumenes and put him to death,[2] and on his return was received in great pomp by Seleucus the satrap in Babylon.[3] One day Seleucus insulted an officer without consulting Antigonus, who was present, and Antigonus out of spite

asked for accounts of his money and his possessions; Seleucus, being no match for Antigonus, withdrew to Ptolemy in Egypt. Immediately after his flight, Antigonus deposed Blitor the governor of Mesopotamia for letting Seleucus escape, and took over personal control of Babylonia, Mesopotamia and all the peoples from the Medians to the Hellespont (Antipater was dead by now). With so much territory in his power he became at once an object of jealousy to the other satraps. And so an alliance was formed between Seleucus, the chief instigator of the coalition, Ptolemy, Lysimachus satrap of Thrace, and Cassander son of Antipater, who ruled the Macedonians in his father's name. They sent a joint embassy to Antigonus to demand that he share out between them and other Macedonians, who had been expelled from their satrapies, the territory he had acquired and his money. Antigonus treated them with scorn, and so they went to war jointly against him, while he made counter-preparations, expelling the remaining garrisons of Ptolemy in Syria and laying his hands on the parts of Phoenicia and Coele Syria, as it is called, that were still under Ptolemy. (54) Crossing the Cilician Gates he left his son Demetrius, then about 22 years old, at Gaza with his army to meet the attacks of Ptolemy from Egypt. Ptolemy won a brilliant victory over him at Gaza and the young man took refuge with his father.[4] Ptolemy immediately sent Seleucus .to Babylon to recover his rule, giving him for the purpose 1,000 infantry and 300 cavalry. With such a small force Seleucus recovered Babylon, where the inhabitants received him enthusiastically, and within a short time he greatly extended his empire.[5] Antigonus defeated an attack by Ptolemy, winning a brilliant victory over him at sea off Cyprus; his son Demetrius was in command. This splendid achievement caused the army to proclaim both Antigonus and Demetrius kings; the other kings were dead by this time, Arrhidaeus the son of Philip, Olympias and the sons of Alexander. Ptolemy's own army also proclaimed him king, so that his defeat should not place him in a position of inferiority vis-à-vis the victors. And so for these men different circumstances led to similar results; the rest immediately followed their example and from satraps they all became kings.[6]

(55) And so it was that Seleucus became king of Babylonia, and also of Media, after he had killed in battle with his own hand Nicanor who had been left by Antigonus as satrap of Media. He waged many wars against Macedonians and barbarians; the two most important were against Macedonians, the latter war against Lysimachus king of Thrace, the former at Ipsus in Phrygia against Antigonus, who was commanding his army and fighting in person although over 80 years old.[7] After Antigonus had fallen in battle, the kings who had joined with Seleucus in destroying him shared out his territory. Seleucus obtained then Syria

from the Euphrates to the sea and inland Phrygia. Always lying in wait for the neighbouring peoples, with the power to coerce and the persuasion of diplomacy, he became ruler of Mesopotamia, Armenia, Seleucid Cappadocia (as it is called), the Persians, Parthians, Bactrians, Areians and Tapurians, Sogdiana, Arachosia, Hyrcania, and all other neighbouring peoples whom Alexander had conquered in war as far as the Indus. The boundaries of his rule in Asia extended further than those of any ruler apart from Alexander; the whole land from Phrygia eastwards to the river Indus was subject to Seleucus. He crossed the Indus and made war on Sandracottus (Chandragupta), king of the Indians about that river, and eventually arranged friendship and a marriage alliance with him.[8] Some of these achievements belong to the period before the end of Antigonus, others to after his death. [. . .]

(57) [. . .] Immediately after the death of Alexander he became commander of the Companion cavalry,[9] which Hephaestion and after him Perdiccas had commanded during Alexander's lifetime, then after this satrap of Babylonia[10] and eventually after satrap, king. His great successes in war earned him the surname of Nicator (the Victorious); this explanation seems to me more likely than that it was due to the killing of Nicanor. He was tall and powerfully built; one day when a wild bull was brought for sacrifice to Alexander and broke loose from his bonds, he resisted him alone and brought him under control with his bare hands.[11] That is why his statues represent him with horns added. He founded cities through the whole length of his empire;[12] there were sixteen called Antioch after his father, five Laodicea after his mother, nine named Seleucia after himself, four called after his wives, three Apamea and one Stratonicea. Of these the most famous up to the present are the two Seleucias, by the sea and on the river Tigris, Laodicea in Phoenicia, Antioch under Mt Lebanon and Apamea in Syria. The others he called after places in Greece or Macedon, or after his own achievements, or in honour of Alexander the king. That is why there are in Syria and among the barbarians inland many Greek and many Macedonian place-names, Berrhoea, Edessa, Perinthus, Maronea, Callipolis, Achaea, Pella, Europus, Amphipolis, Arethusa, Astacus, Tegea, Chalcis, Larissa, Heraea, Apollonia, also in Parthia Soteira, Calliope, Charis, Hecatompylus, Achaea, among the Indians Alexandropolis, and among the Scythians Alexandreschate. Also, called after the victories of Seleucus himself there is Nicephorium in Mesopotamia and Nicopolis in Armenia very near to Cappadocia. (58) They say that when he was undertaking the foundation of the two Seleucias, that of Seleucia by the sea was preceded by a portent of thunder, and that is why he consecrated thunder as their divinity, and the inhabitants continue to worship thunder and sing hymns in its honour up to the present day. They also say that for the foundation of

Seleucia on the Tigris the Magi were ordered to select the day and the hour when the digging of the foundations was to begin, but they falsified the hour, as they did not wish to have such a stronghold threatening them. Seleucus was waiting for the given hour in his tent, while the army ready for work kept quiet until Seleucus would give the sign. Suddenly at the more favourable hour they thought someone was ordering them on to work and sprang up; not even the efforts of the heralds could hold them back. The work was completed, but Seleucus in despair questioned the Magi a second time about the city; they asked for a promise of impunity and then spoke: 'Sire, what has been fated, for better or for worse, no man or city can change (for there is a fate of cities as well as of men). It pleased the gods that this city should last a long time, because it came into being at this hour. We feared it would be a stronghold against us and sought to divert the decrees of fate, but they proved stronger than the cunning of the Magi and the ignorance of a king. [. . .] Fortune has smiled on the beginnings of this city of yours; it shall be great and longlasting. Fear of losing our own prosperity led us into error; we ask you to confirm your pardon to us.'[13] [. . .] (62) Seleucus had 72 satraps under him,[14] so vast was the territory he ruled. Most of it he handed over to his son,[15] and ruled himself only the land from the sea to the Euphrates. His last war he fought against Lysimachus for the control of Hellespontine Phrygia; he defeated Lysimachus who fell in the battle,[16] and crossed himself the Hellespont. As he was marching up to Lysimachea he was murdered by Ptolemy nicknamed Ceraunus (the Thunderbolt) who was accompanying him. This Ceraunus was the son of Ptolemy Soter and Eurydice the daughter of Antipater; he had fled from Egypt through fear, as Ptolemy had in mind to hand over his realm to his youngest son. Seleucus welcomed him as the unfortunate son of his friend, and supported and took everywhere his own future assassin. (63) And so Seleucus met his fate at the age of 73, having been king for 42 years.[17] [. . .]

Appian, *Syrian Wars* 52–55, 57–58, 62–63

1. See on all this **22, 24**.
2. See **24** n. 6.
3. Appointed to this post in 320 (see **24** §35).
4. In 312; this led to the peace of 311 (**30, 31**). On the Ptolemies and Syria cf. **275**.
5. The Seleucid 'era' was reckoned as starting in October 312 (in the Macedonian calendar) or April 311 (in the Babylonian calendar). Cf. **138**.
6. See **36**.
7. See **43** and n. 5.
8. The peace treaty (*Staatsv.* III.441) took place *ca* 305–303 at the end of a long series of campaigns in which Seleucus secured control of the eastern

satrapies. Seleucus also received a force of Indian elephants under this treaty; these played a decisive role at the battle of Ipsus. Cf. also **150**.

9. See **22**(b).
10. See **24** §35. For his subsequent career see also **30**, **31**, **36**, **39**(b), **45**.
11. Cf. **45** n. 1.
12. On ch. 57 see R. M. Errington, *Entretiens Hardt* 22 (1976), 163f., 167f., cf. 218f.; G. M. Cohen, *The Seleucid Colonies* (Wiesbaden, 1978), esp. 16f., 89. Cf. **40** and see further **153**, **174**, **179**, **190–192**.
13. On Seleucia on the Tigris and Babylon see further **138**, **141**, **188**, **189**.
14. An error: the total of known or likely satrapies in Seleucus' empire does not exceed *ca* 20.
15. Antiochus, his son by the Persian Apama (cf. **14** n. 2), shared the royal title with Seleucus and was in charge of the eastern satrapies from 294/3.
16. See **45**, **193**.
17. Seleucus was assassinated between 25 August and 24 September 281 (see **138**); his royalty is reckoned (incorrectly) from his appointment as satrap of Babylonia in 320.

47 Pyrrhus, king of Epirus

The restless career of Pyrrhus, king of Epirus, epitomises the age of Alexander's Successors. A great military king, Pyrrhus sought to expand his power in Macedon and Greece in the 290s and 280s (see **45**), and again from 274 till his death in 272/1. His greatest title to fame, however, was his western expedition, launched in 280 in response to an appeal from Tarentum for help against the expanding power of Rome: this led to the first direct encounter of the Romans with a Hellenistic king at the battles of Heraclea (280) and Ausculum (279). From 278–276 Pyrrhus operated in Sicily in answer to a Sicilian request for help against Carthage, then again in Italy in 276–275 against the Romans, who this time gained the upper hand at Beneventum in 275 and so forced Pyrrhus to return to Epirus (though he did not initially abandon all his western ambitions). The moralising story related by Plutarch on the eve of Pyrrhus' departure for Italy has been much discussed; the vast and carefully planned conquest aims it credits Pyrrhus with are felt by many historians to be at variance with the impulsive and improvisatory character of the rest of his career. At any rate Pyrrhus' failure had an important consequence: henceforward and until the eastward expansion of Rome (see ch. 3) the political history of the western and the eastern Greek world was to run on largely separate lines.

See further: Will I (1979), 120–31.

(a) Pyrrhus, the military king

This battle[1] did not so much move the Macedonians to anger and hatred for what they had suffered at his hands as it made them respect and admire his personal courage; it became a talking point among those who had witnessed his exploits and had clashed with him in battle. His appearance, speed and movements reminded them of Alexander, and they believed they could see in him a reflection and imitation of Alexander's dash and fire in battle.[2] The other kings resembled Alexander only by their purple garments, their bodyguards, the way they inclined their head and the arrogant manner of their speech, but Pyrrhus alone did so by his arms and his exploits. His skill and mastery in tactical and strategic matters are readily illustrated by the writings he has left behind on these subjects (*FGrH* 229). It is said that Antigonus, when asked who was the best general, replied 'Pyrrhus, if he lives to grow old'; his remark only applied to contemporaries. Hannibal used to declare that of all generals Pyrrhus came first in experience and skill, Scipio second, and he himself third, as has been related in the *Life of Scipio*. In fact it seems that Pyrrhus devoted all his practice and study to the art of war, which he thought the most royal of sciences, while other refinements seemed to him to be of no significance. It is said that he was once asked at a banquet whether Python was a better flautist than Caphisias, and he replied 'Polyperchon[3] is a better general', the point being that only the art of war was worth investigating and studying by a king.[4]

Plutarch, *Pyrrhus* 8.1–7

(b) Pyrrhus' (alleged) western ambitions

There was a Thessalian called Cineas, who had the reputation of being a wise man; he had been a pupil of the orator Demosthenes and alone of contemporary speakers he could conjure up among his audience a picture of the power and mastery of Demosthenes' speeches. He was a contemporary of Pyrrhus and on his missions to Greek cities he would prove the rightness of the saying of Euripides (*Phoenissae*, 516f.) that

'Speech can remove any obstacle offered by the enemies' sword.'

Pyrrhus in fact used to say that more cities had been won over by the eloquence of Cineas than he had captured himself by force of arms. He constantly treated the man with the greatest honour and had recourse to his services. When Cineas at that time saw Pyrrhus eager to sail to Italy, finding him at leisure he started the following conversation.[5] 'Pyrrhus, the Romans are said to be good soldiers and to rule many warlike peoples; should a god grant us success over them, how shall we use our victory?' Pyrrhus replied: 'Cineas, the answer to your question is obvious; once the Romans are defeated, no barbarian or Greek city there can resist us; we shall immediately secure control of the whole of Italy, and how large, strong and powerful she is I imagine you know better than anyone else.' Cineas paused a little then said: 'Sire, once we have taken Italy, what shall we do?' Pyrrhus, not seeing as yet what Cineas was leading to, replied: 'Sicily nearby stretches out her hands to us, a wealthy and populous island, very easy to capture; there is nothing there, Cineas, but revolution, anarchy in the cities and excitable demagogues, now that Agathocles is dead.'[6] 'That seems plausible,' replied Cineas, 'but is the capture of Sicily the end of our expedition?' Pyrrhus answered: 'May a god grant us victory and success; that will be a preliminary to great achievements. Libya (Africa) and Carthage would be within easy reach, and who could keep us away from them, when Agathocles who secretly escaped from Syracuse[7] and crossed over with a few ships very nearly captured them? Can anyone dispute that once we have conquered these none of our enemies who are at present insulting us will be able to resist?' 'Certainly not,' replied Cineas; 'clearly with such power behind us it will be open to us to recover Macedon and to rule Greece. When we have established our domination everywhere, what shall we do?' Pyrrhus laughed and said: 'We shall have ample leisure; life, my friend, will be a daily drinking-party and we shall entertain each other with conversation.' At this point Cineas interrupted Pyrrhus and said: 'Well then, what is there to prevent us having a drinking-party now and enjoying leisure among ourselves if we so wish? The possibility is already there and costs no effort, so why achieve the same result through blood, toil and dangers, after inflicting on others and suffering ourselves great harm?' These words of Cineas upset Pyrrhus but did not cause him to change his mind; he realised what happiness he was sacrificing, but was unable to give up the hope of achieving his ambition.

Plutarch, Pyrrhus 14

1. In 289, against a general of Demetrius.
2. Pyrrhus was cousin of Alexander.
3. See **25, 31**.
4. For this conception of monarchy see **36, 37**.
5. The confrontation of philosopher and king is a recurring theme of Hellenistic literature; the philosopher inevitably has the better of the argument (cf. Préaux I (1978), 226–8).
6. On Agathocles see **27**; Agathocles died in 289 and the powerful monarchy he had established disappeared with him. Pyrrhus had previously married Agathocles' daughter Lanassa and so could assert some dynastic claims to the island.
7. See **27**(b).

3 Macedon and the Greek main-land to the Roman conquest

48 Thanksgiving of Cos for the repulse of the Celtic invaders and the saving of Delphi (April–July 278)

The expansion of Celtic power in central Europe had a long history before the Greek mainland was directly affected by it (cf. the sack of Rome in 390). The disappearance of the kingdom of Lysimachus in Thrace (see **45**) and the weakening of the Macedonian monarchy helped to make possible the Celtic invasion of 280–279; it had a profound impact on the political history of the age and on the consciousness of the Greeks. Macedon fell into a period of anarchy till Antigonus Gonatas was able to defeat the invaders and begin the restoration of the kingdom (276). The Aetolians, who played an important part in the defence of Delphi, exploited their role to justify their seizure of Apollo's sanctuary and extend their power in central Greece (see further **52, 58, 72**); in 246/5 (?) they refounded for their own purposes the festival of the *Soteria*, originally founded by the Delphic Amphictyony to commemorate the saving of Delphi (cf. **122, 123**). Part of the invading Celtic tribes eventually settled in Asia Minor; for their impact there see **140, 194**, cf. also **94, 96, 97**. The decree of Cos is a valuable contemporary source on the invasion, whereas later accounts embellish the story and elaborate the parallel between Xerxes' attack on Delphi in 480 and the Celtic invasion.

See further: W. W. Tarn, *Antigonus Gonatas* (Oxford, 1913), 139–66; H. W. Parke and D. E. W. Wormell, *The Delphic Oracle* I (Oxford, 1956), 254–9; A. Momigliano, *Alien Wisdom* (Cambridge, 1975), 60–4.

Diocles son of Philinus moved: since, after the barbarian expedition against the Greeks and the sanctuary at Delphi, it is reported that the aggressors / of the sanctuary have been punished by the god (Apollo) 5 and by the men who came to defend it during the barbarian incursion, that the sanctuary has been saved and adorned with the / spoils from the 10 enemy and that of the remaining aggressors the majority have perished in combat against the Greeks; so that it may be manifest that the people / 15 shares in the joy of the Greeks over the victory and is repaying thank-offerings to the god for manifesting himself during the perils which confronted the sanctuary and for the safety of the Greeks; / with 20 good fortune, be it resolved by the people that the leader of the sacred

embassy (*theoria*) and the sacred ambassadors who have been elected
should on arriving at Delphi sacrifice to Pythian Apollo an ox with
25   gilded horns on behalf / of the safety of the Greeks and address prayers
for the prosperity of the people of Cos and the harmony (*homonoia*)[1] of
their democratic government,[2] and for eternal blessings to the Greeks
30   who came to defend the sanctuary; / that a sacrifice should also be
offered by the presiding officers to Pythian Apollo, Zeus the Saviour and
Nike (Victory). They shall sacrifice to each deity an adult victim; the day
35   on which they offer the sacrifice / shall be a sacred day, and all the
citizens and resident aliens (*paroikoi*) and other foreigners staying in Cos
shall wear wreaths (on that day). The sacred herald shall proclaim that
40   'the people is observing the day as sacred / because of the safety and
victory of the Greeks; and that all may be for the best for those who wore
wreaths'. The sacrifice shall be offered in the month of Panamus; the
45   treasurer shall give 400 drachmas for the sacrifice at Delphi / and 160 for
the sacrifice at Cos; the presiding officers shall see that the money is sent
to the sacred ambassadors and the sacrifices are offered at Cos; the sellers
50   (*poletai*)[3] shall auction / the inscription on a stone stele of the decree and
its dedication in the sanctuary of Asclepius.[4]

> *Syll.*[3] 398; G. Nachtergael, *Les Galates*
> *en Grèce et les Sôtéria de Delphes*
> (Brussels, 1977), 401–3

1. On the importance of this notion in the Hellenistic age see **51**.
2. See **40A** §8, **133**.
3. Officials who dealt with state sales and the issuing of state contracts.
4. On the Celtic raid on Delphi see also **76**.

49 Decree of Chremonides on the alliance between Athens and Sparta (between 268 and 265)

The origins and causes of the 'Chremonidean War', which aligned a coalition of
Greek states and Ptolemy II against Antigonus Gonatas of Macedon (cf. also **50,
117**), are obscure and controversial, particularly as regards the aims of the two
kings. The conflict is better known on the Greek side; for Athens it marked in
effect the end of her attempts at independence (cf. *Staatsv.* III.477; F. Jacoby,
Atthis (Oxford 1949), 107–11); Sparta's ambitions revived later under Agis IV
and Cleomenes III (see **55, 56, 57**) and the Greek resistance against Macedon was
to be taken up by the Achaean League (see **53**).
    See further: C. Mossé, *Athens in Decline* (London, 1973), 125–9; J. Briscoe in
Imperialism in the Ancient World, ed. P. D. A. Garnsey and C. R. Whittaker
(Cambridge, 1978), 145–57; Will I (1979), 219–33.

Gods. In the archonship of Pithidemus,[1] in the second prytany, of the
tribe Erechtheis; on the 9th of Metageitnion and the 9th day of the
prytany; / at a principal meeting of the assembly; Sostratus son of   5
Callistratus of Erchia and the other presiding officers put to the vote;
resolved by the people; Chremonides[2] son of Eteocles of Aethalidae
moved: since previously the Athenians, the Lacedaemonians, and their
respective allies after establishing a common friendship and alliance /   10
with each other have fought together many glorious battles against
those who sought to enslave the cities,[3] which won them fame and
brought freedom to the other Greeks; and now, when similar circumstances have afflicted the whole of Greece because of [those] who seek
to subvert / the laws and ancestral constitutions of each city, and King   15
Ptolemy following the policy of his ancestor and of his sister[4] conspi-
cuously shows his zeal for the common freedom of the Greeks;[5] and the
people of Athens having made an alliance with him and / the other   20
Greeks has passed a decree to invite (all) to follow the same policy; and
likewise the Lacedaemonians, who are friends and allies of King
Ptolemy, have voted to make an alliance with the people of Athens,
together with the Eleans, Achaeans, Tegeates, Mantineans,
Orchomenians, / [Phigaleans,] Caphyeans, all the Cretans who are in   25
[alliance] with the Lacedaemonians and Areus[6] and the other allies,[7] [and]
have sent ambassadors chosen from among the members of the council
to the [people] (of Athens), and their representatives having arrived
declare the zeal displayed by the Lacedaemonians and Areus and the
other allies / towards the people (of Athens), and have come with the   30
ratification of the alliance; so that, now that a common harmony
(*homonoia*)[8] has been established between the Greeks against those who are
presently flouting justice and breaking the treaties with the cities, they
may prove eager combatants with King Ptolemy and with each other and
in future may preserve harmony / and save the cities; with good   35
fortune; be it resolved by the people that the friendship and alliance
brought by the ambassadors between the Athenians and the Lacedaemonians, the kings of the Lacedaemonians, the Eleans, Achaeans, Tegeates,
Mantineans, Orchomenians, Phigaleans, Caphyeans and all the
[Cretans] / who are in alliance with the Lacedaemonians and [Areus] and   40
the other allies, should be valid for all [time]; that the secretary of the
prytany should have [it] inscribed on a bronze stele [and placed on] the
acropolis near the temple of Athena [Polias and that the] magistrates
should [swear] / to the ambassadors who have arrived [from them the   45
oath] on the alliance according to [ancestral custom (?); and that one
should send the ambassadors elected] by the people [to take the] oaths
[from the other Greeks; and that the people should elect immediately
two] councillors [chosen from] all [the Athenians] / to deliberate with   50

Areus [and the] councillors sent [by the allies on matters of common] interest; and that the [officials in charge of finance] should pay to those who are appointed a travel allowance for the period of their absence [as] decided [by vote] by the people; and that one should praise [the ephors of

55 the Lacedaemonians] / and Areus and the allies [and crown them] with a crown of gold according to the law, [and praise the ambassadors] who have come from them, Theom[. . . from Sparta], Argius son of Clinias from Elis [and crown them both] with a crown of gold according to [the

60 law for the zeal] / and goodwill they show towards [the other allies and] the people of Athens; and that it should be possible for [each of them] to obtain [any other] favour from the council [and the people if they are thought] worthy of it; and that one should invite them [to a meal at the

65 prytaneum] tomorrow; and that [the secretary] / of the prytany should see to the inscription [of this decree and of the treaty] on a [stone stele and] to placing it on the acropolis, and that the [officials in charge of finance] should pay [whatever expense is incurred] for [the inscription and dedication of] the stele. The following councillors [were elected]:

70 Callipus of Eleusis . . . /

Treaty and alliance [between the Lacedaemonians and] their [allies] and [the Athenians and their allies] for all [time. Both parties are to preserve their territorial integrity], remaining [free] and [autonomous and preserving their] ancestral [constitution]. If anyone [attacks the territory of

75 the Athenians] / or [subverts their] laws [or attacks the allies] of the Athenians, [the Lacedaemonians and] their [allies will come to their help with all possible strength; if] anyone attacks [the territory of the Lacedaemonians or subverts their] laws [or attacks the allies of the]

80 Lacedaemonians, / [the Athenians and their allies will come to their help with all possible strength . . . the Lacedaemonians] and their allies (to?) the Athenians [and their allies. The following] oath[9] will be sworn for the

85 Athenians to the Lacedaemonians / [and the representatives of each] city by the *strategoi*, [the council of 600,[10] the] archons, phylarchs, [taxiarchs and hipparchs: I swear] by Zeus, the Earth, the Sun, Ares, Athena Areia, [Poseidon and Demeter]; I will be true to the alliance which [has been concluded; may those who respect the oath] enjoy many blessings, may

90 the [opposite] happen to those who break it. / A similar oath will be sworn [for the Lacedaemonians] to the Athenians by the [kings, the ephors and] the *gerontes* (elders). A similar oath [will be sworn in (?) the other] cities by the magistrates. If it [seems best to the Lacedaemonians and] the allies and the Athenians [to add] or to remove [any clause] from

95 the alliance, / [whatever is mutually agreed on will not breach] the oath. [The cities] will inscribe the [alliance on stelae] and place them in a sanctuary wherever they [wish].

Syll.[3] 434–5; *IG* II[2]. 687; *Staatsv.* III.476

1. Date uncertain; e.g. 268/7, H. Heinen, *Historia Einzelschriften* 20 (1972), 213; 265/4, B. D. Meritt, *Historia* 26 (1977), 174.
2. An Athenian statesman, pupil (like Antigonus Gonatas) of the Stoic philosopher Zeno; he gave his name to the war against Macedon. For his brother Glaucon see **51**.
3. Here and below the vague references to the enemies of Greek freedom are aimed at Macedon; for the sentiments see **23, 26**; for Antigonus Gonatas' policy towards the Greeks (in the Peloponnese) see **53**.
4. Ptolemy II Philadelphus and his sister/wife Arsinoe II (died in 270); for previous Ptolemaic support of Athens cf. **44**. The theory that the Chremonidean War was planned by Arsinoe for dynastic reasons (W. W. Tarn, *Antigonus Gonatas* (Oxford, 1913), 290–310; *CAH* VII (1928), 705–8) rests on tenuous grounds. Ptolemaic support of the Athenian war effort is illustrated archaeologically by the discovery of a Ptolemaic fort at Koroni in eastern Attica which dates from the war (E. Vanderpool, J. R. McCredie and A. Steinberg, *Hesperia* 31 (1962), 26–61 and 33 (1964), 69–75); see also **50** (end), and cf. **266** n. 1, **267** n. 1.
5. On this theme and its propaganda exploitation in the age of the Successors see **29**; this is its latest attested appearance until it was taken up by the Romans (see **68**).
6. King of Sparta 309/8–265/4, sought to revive Spartan power in the Peloponnese and imitated the style of other Hellenistic courts (B. Shimron, *Late Sparta* (Buffalo, 1972), 5–7; contrast **56**(a)). Note the absence of any mention in this inscription of the other Spartan king. Areus was killed while trying unsuccessfully to break through the Macedonian defences at Corinth in order to join Athens.
7. It will be seen that apart from Sparta and Athens, the 'Greek alliance' only comprised a number of small Peloponnesian and Cretan states (the Achaeans were not as yet very powerful; see **53**); note the absence of the whole of central Greece, including the Aetolians.
8. On this theme see **51**.
9. For other oath formulae see **33** n. 7.
10. See **34** (end).

50 Decree of the Attic deme of Rhamnus in honour of the general Epichares for services during the Chremonidean War

Gods. Nicostratus son of Epiteles of Rhamnus moved: since Epichares, when elected hipparch in the archonship of Lysithides (272/1), looked after the cavalry force well and in accordance with the laws, and was crowned by the council, the people, and the cavalry; and again / in the archonship of Pithidemus[1] when the people elected him general and [placed] him in charge of the coastal region, he carried out [his defensive role] well and with zeal, and saved the fort for the people during the war,[2] and gathered in [the crops] and fruits within a range of 30 stadia (*ca*

5

97

5½ km) . . . set up covered [silos? in the] land, [kept guard] himself with
10   the soldiers at the [look-outs] / to enable the farmers [to gather in their]
crops safely;[3] and he also protected the vines as far as he [was master] of
the land; and he constructed at his private expense a portico to provide
shelter for all in any emergency, and to make it possible for help to come
[quickly]; and he also built two watch towers and provided guard dogs in
15   addition to the existing ones, supplying their food himself, / to ensure
fuller protection; and he also set up his headquarters in the sanctuary [of
Nemesis] in such a way that it should be honoured and that the
[demesmen] should remain in a state of piety;[4] and he also imported 500
medimni of wheat and 500 of barley, advancing the price himself, and
distributed them to the citizens and the soldiers at the usual price; and he
20   also made a deal about the prisoners who had been captured,[5] / that they
should be freed through the mediation of a herald on payment of a
ransom of 120 drachmas (each), that none of the citizens should be
deported and that the slaves should not be killed; he also punished those
who had introduced the pirates into the land, men from the city,[6]
arresting and interrogating them [in a way that was fitting] for what they
did; and he also provided to the troops who had come from Patroclus[7] to
25   help camp installations so that they should have sufficient . . . / causing
none of the citizens to have troops billeted on them,[8] nor of the . . .

(the rest of the inscription is too mutilated for continuous translation)

H. Heinen, *Historia Einzelschriften* 20 (1972),
152–4 (B. Ch. Petrakos, *Archaiologikon Deltion*
22 (1967), 38–52; *Bull.* 1968, 247); cf. *SEG*
XXIV.154

1. See **49** n. 1.
2. The 'Chremonidean War' (see **49**).
3. Cf. **44** and n. 8.
4. I.e. the setting up of the headquarters did not desecrate the sanctuary of
   Nemesis.
5. Captured by pirates, cf. ll. 21–23.
6. I.e. from Athens, not Rhamnus; the pirates themselves escaped punishment.
7. The admiral of the Ptolemaic fleet which fought on the Greek side in the war
   (see **49** n. 4).
8. Cf. **249**.

51 Decree of the League (koinon) of Greeks at Plataea in honour of Glaucon son of Eteocles, of Athens (between 261 and 246)

Before the discovery of the following inscription (in 1971), the earliest evidence
for the joint cult of Zeus Eleutherius (the Liberator) and the Homonoia

(Concord) of the Greeks dated from Roman imperial times; the cult is now shown to have dated from at least the time of the Chremonidean War, and perhaps earlier. The institution of the panhellenic festival of the *Eleutheria* in honour of Zeus Eleutherius (as opposed to the annual Plataean cult established in 479 immediately after the Persian defeat) dates perhaps from after the restoration of Plataea by Alexander (335; cf. **83** ch. 11), but it is not clear whether the cult of the Concord of the Greeks was created in the same period, or was added later by Glaucon brother of Chremonides (cf. J. Pouilloux in Préaux (1975), 376–82), at the time of the Chremonidean War, when Athens and Sparta appealed in their propaganda to their alliances during the Persian Wars and after (see **49**).

See further on *homonoia* in the Hellenistic age and before: Tarn and Griffith (1952), 90f.; W. C. West, *GRBS* 18 (1977), 307–19.

In the priesthood of Nicoclidas son of Chaereas, when Archelaus son of Athenaeus was agonothete,[1] resolution of the Greeks; Eubulus son of Panarmostus, of Boeotia, moved: / since Glaucon son of Eteocles of   5
Athens, when staying formerly in his native city constantly showed his goodwill publicly to all the Greeks and privately to those who came to / Athens, and afterwards when he took up service with King Ptolemy   10
(II Philadelphus) he pursued the same line of conduct, wishing to make manifest his disposition by his goodwill towards the Greeks; / and he has   15
enriched the sanctuary with dedications and with revenues which must be safeguarded for Zeus Eleutherius [and] the Concord of the Greeks; and he has contributed to making more lavish the sacrifice in honour of Zeus / Eleutherius and Concord and the contest which the Greeks   20
celebrate on the tomb of the heroes who fought against the barbarians for the liberty of the Greeks;[2] / therefore, [so that] all may know that the   25
federal assembly of the Greeks repays thanks worthy of their benefactions to those who honour the sanctuary of Zeus / Eleutherius, during   30
their lifetime and after their death, be it resolved by the Greeks to praise Glaucon and to invite him and his descendants for all time to a seat of honour when the gymnastic contests / are being celebrated at Plataea, just   35
as (is the practice with) all other benefactors; let the agonothete have this decree inscribed on a stone stele and dedicated near the altar of Zeus Eleutherius / and Concord, and let the treasurer of the sacred funds   40
provide the expense for this.[3]

R. Etienne and M. Piérart, BCH 99 (1975),
51–75, at pp. 51–3

1. Cf. **43** n. 8.
2. A reference to the Persian Wars.
3. For other examples of the appeal to 'concord' see **48, 49, 53**, cf. **90, 91, 133, 135**.

52 Decree of Chios in honour of the Aetolians (247/6?)

The Aetolian League in northwest Greece existed already in the classical period, but its rise to importance was a feature of the Hellenistic age. The Aetolians participated in the Lamian War against Macedon (see **16, 23**), but unlike Athens escaped punishment after the Greek defeat. In the confused years of the early third century they extended their power in central Greece (see **35** n. 4) and secured control over Delphi; their role in the defence of Delphi against the Celtic invaders provided them with a propaganda justification for their preponderance in the Amphictyonic Council which administered Apollo's sanctuary (see **48**). The following decree from Chios illustrates one way in which they extended their influence in the Aegean: Chios was given immunity (*asylia*, cf. **151** n. 5) from Aetolian privateering (on which see **35** n. 4, **53** ch. 43, **58, 62, 88**) and a seat in the Amphictyonic Council, and exchanged citizenships with Aetolia (*isopoliteia*: a citizen of Chios in Aetolia would have the same rights as an Aetolian and vice-versa; cf. **132**). In return the Aetolians acquired a friendly base in the Aegean.

See further: on the institutions and growth of the Aetolian League, Larsen (1968), 195–215 (p. 207 on this inscription), on its role in the third and second centuries *id.*, 303–447; on Aetolia and Delphi, H. W. Parke and D. E. W. Wormell, *The Delphic Oracle* I (Oxford, 1956), 253–61.

Resolved by the [council and people]; the [monthly president (*epimenios*)] of the polemarchs . . . son of Philistus and the monthly president [of the *exetastai*] Aiantides [son of . . . moved]: since the [Aetolian] League, because of the ancestral kinship and [friendship] which exist between
5   [our] people and the Aetolians, voted previously to grant us citizenship /
[and] forbade all to plunder the property of [the Chians] from whatever starting-base [on] pain of being liable to prosecution before the [councillors][1] on a charge of harming the common interests of the Aetolians; for this the people graciously [accepted] their goodwill and voted that the [Aetolians] should be citizens and share in all the rights the
10 Chians share in, and decided that they should have priority [of access] /
to the council and the assembly, [and] be invited to seats of honour (*proedria*) at all the contests organised [by the city]; and now the sacred envoys and the ambassadors have returned and [reported] to the people the goodwill felt [towards our] city by the Aetolian League, who display
15 their anxiety to grant [all] / the requests of the ambassadors, and especially have granted to our people one vote as *hieromnemon*[2] in the Amphictyonic Council, in conformity with the feelings of kinship and friendliness [they have] had before towards our city; therefore, so that the people may be seen by [all the] Greeks to be honouring those who chose to be its benefactors, [with good fortune], be it resolved by the
20 council and the people, to praise the [Aetolian League] / for the goodwill

100

and zeal it shows on every occasion [towards our people and] to crown it with the largest gold crown according to the law, worth 100 [gold Alexander] coins; and so that all the Greeks may know what [has been decreed by the council] and the people, the sacred herald shall make the following proclamation at the Dionysia [in the theatre when the] children's choruses are about to compete: / [the people of Chios] crowns   25
the Aetolian League with the largest gold crown [according to the law], worth 100 [gold] Alexander coins, for its merits and the goodwill and [zeal (it shows) towards] it; the agonothete[3] shall be responsible for the proclamation; when the decree has been voted a *hieromnemon* [shall be elected; let the *hieromnemon*] who is elected offer with the other *hieromnemones* the [sacrifices] customary among the [Chians, / and let him act as   30
judge] in accordance with the law and the resolutions of the Amphictyonic Council; [in future one shall send] every year a *hieromnemon* to the [Amphictyonic Council] at [Delphi . . .]; let one not appoint the same person twice; one shall give [to the] *hieromnemon* [an allowance for the customary] sacrifices offered on behalf of the city: when the Pythia [are celebrated] 2,000 [Alexander drachmas], and in [the . . .] fifteen [hundred Alexander] drachmas; / and let the [next] sacred envoys appointed   35
to go to the *Laphrieia*[4] [receive from] the treasurers the [money that has been] voted and see to the making of [the crown] as [quickly as possible] and convey [with] the *hieromnemon* the decree and the crown [to the *Laphrieia*] and the *Thermika*;[5] and [let them] request the Aetolians to make sure the crown [is proclaimed in accordance with the] proclamation written in this decree at the *Laphrieia* / and at [the *Thermika*]; and let   40
the sacred envoys [sent] to Delphi make sure that the proclamation written in this [decree is proclaimed] at the Pythia; [and so that] the resolutions of the Aetolian [League] and [of the people] of Chios concerning the vote (in the Amphictyonic Council) should be preserved for all time, let [the first *hieromnemon*] who is appointed have it inscribed on two stone stelae, [one of these to be] dedicated / [at Delphi,[6] the other   45
in] the sanctuary of Apollo Thermius; let the [expense] for the [stelae and the] inscription be provided by the treasurers; and let the present [decree be promulgated for the] safety of the people. The travel allowance for the [*hieromnemon*] was fixed [at . . . drachmas]. Gannon son of Clytomedes was elected *hieromnemon*.[7]

Moretti II.78 (*Syll.*[3] 443); cf. *Bull.* 1977, 231

1. The council of the Aetolian League.
2. The title of the delegates from Greek states participating in the Amphictyonic Council.
3. Cf. **43** n. 8.
4. An Aetolian festival in honour of Artemis.

5. The autumn meeting of the Aetolian League, held at Thermum, the religious centre of the League.
6. The present decree, found at Delphi.
7. First attested as *hieromnemon* at Delphi in a list of 246 or 242.

53 The rise of the Achaean League

The rise to importance of the Achaean League, as of the Aetolian (see **52**), was a feature of the third century, particularly its second half. Both leagues shared some common institutional features and differed from the 'symmachies' of the classical age in that they were not dominated by a single powerful city (such as Athens or Sparta) and possessed a capacity to grow organically, though within limits, through the extension of their citizenship (more so in the case of the Achaean League than the Aetolian). Both also originated in areas of Greece that did not have a distinguished *polis* background; significantly Athens refused to be included in the Achaean League (Plutarch, *Aratus* 33–34) and Sparta eventually had to be coerced to join (see **71**).

Polybius was himself an Achaean statesman; his account is biased in favour of the Achaeans and their league, and is hostile to the enemies of the Achaeans, notably the Aetolians (see also **58, 69**).

See further: on the institutions of the Achaean League, Larsen (1968), 215–40 and Walbank III (1979), 406–14; on its history, F. W. Walbank, *Aratus of Sicyon* (Cambridge, 1933); Larsen (1968), 303–498; R. M. Errington, *Philopoemen* (Oxford, 1969).

As regards the Achaean people and the (royal) house of Macedon it will be appropriate to go back in time briefly, for the latter has become completely extinct, while the Achaeans, as I have said before, have experienced in our time a remarkable growth in power and a move towards unity. Previously many attempts had been made to unify the interests of the Peloponnesians, but none had succeeded, because everyone was anxious to secure his own power rather than the freedom of all. But in our time this undertaking has progressed and been completed to such an extent that not only do they have a common policy based on alliance and friendship, but they even use the same laws, weights, measures and currency, and have the same magistrates, councillors and judges. In general there is no difference between the entire Peloponnese and a single city except that its inhabitants are not included within the same wall; in other respects, within the League and in each individual city they all have similar institutions. (38) And first it will be useful to ascertain in what way the Achaean name has established itself for all the Peloponnesians. The original bearers of this ancestral name do not enjoy the advantage of a large territory, numerous cities, great wealth, or the bravery of their men. The Arcadian people, and likewise the Laconian, surpass them greatly in size of population and extent of territory; as far as the prize for bravery is concerned they are second to none of the Greeks. Why then is it that they and the remaining Peloponnesian peoples have consented to adopt both the constitution and the name of the Achaeans? [. . .] In my opinion, the reason is this: nowhere will you find a constitution and an ideal of equality, freedom of speech, and in a word of genuine democracy,[1] more perfect than among the Achaeans. The ideal found many willing converts among the Peloponnesians; many were won over by persuasion and argument; some who were forced to join when an opportunity suddenly arose were eventually made to acquiesce in their position.[2] For none of the original members is allowed to enjoy any special privilege, and equal rights are given to all newcomers; in this way the aim has been quickly achieved with the powerful help of the dual ideals of equality and humanity (*philanthropia*). This then must be looked on as the original cause and reason for the present prosperity of the unified Peloponnese. This ideal and the form of constitution I have described existed already in the past among the Achaeans. [. . .]

(39.11) Such had been their political role at that time, but there was no achievement or notable deed which would have led to an increase in their power: they could not produce a leader worthy of the occasion, and anyone who made such a claim was overshadowed and hampered by the power of Sparta, or, and especially, by that of Macedon. (40) But when at length they found capable leaders, they quickly displayed their power by bringing about that most wonderful achievement, the concord (*homonoia*)[3] of the Peloponnese. Aratus of Sicyon must be regarded as the initiator and guide of the whole policy, Philopoemen of Megalopolis as the man who championed the plan and brought it to completion, while Lycortas[4] and the men of his party ensured its lasting durability. What each of them achieved, by what means and in what circumstances, I will try to show, making mention of them from time to time in such a way as not to conflict with the scheme of this work. The actions of Aratus I will only refer to summarily now and hereafter, as he himself has written very truthful and clear *Memoirs*[5] about his achievements (*FGrH* 231 T 3); what the others did I will relate in more detail and at greater length. I think the most convenient course, and the one my readers will find easiest to follow, will be for me to start at the time when the Achaean League was broken up into cities by the kings of Macedon and the cities then began once more to approach each other; from then on the League grew in power continuously until it reached its present completion, of which I have just given a partial account.

(41) In the 124th Olympiad (284–280) Patrae and Dyme began to unite, and this was the time when Ptolemy son of Lagus, Lysimachus

and also Seleucus and Ptolemy Ceraunus died (they all died during this Olympiad).[6] In the period before this the situation of the Achaeans was more or less as follows. They were ruled by kings from the time of Tisamenus, son of Orestes, who seized control of Achaea when he was expelled from Sparta at the time of the Return of the Heraclids. They remained under the same royal dynasty until Ogyges, when they rose against his sons because of the illegal and despotic character of their rule, and changed the constitution to a democracy. Subsequently in the period down to the reigns of Philip and Alexander their fortunes varied according to circumstances, but they sought, as I have mentioned, to preserve democracy in the institutions of the League. The League consisted of twelve cities, which are still extant, except for Olenus and Helice which was submerged in the sea before the battle of Leuctra (371). They are: Patrae, Dyme, Pharae, Tritaea, Leontium, Aegium, Aegira, Pellene, Bura, Cerynea. In the period after Alexander, before the 124th Olympiad (284–280), they fell into such a state of disunity and disarray, particularly because of the kings of Macedon, that all the cities became divided from each other and acted against their common interest. As a result some had garrisons imposed on them by Demetrius and Cassander and later by Antigonus Gonatas, while others fell under the rule of tyrants; for no one set up so many tyrannies in Greece as did Antigonus Gonatas. In the 124th Olympiad, as I mentioned above, they had a change of heart and began to work towards unity (this was at the time of Pyrrhus' crossing to Italy).[7] The first cities to come together were Dyme, Patrae, Tritaea and Pharae; that is why there does not even exist a stele recording the federation (*sympoliteia*) of these cities. About five years later (275/4) the people of Aegium expelled their garrison and joined the federation, and after them the people of Bura, after putting their tyrant to death; at the same time the people of Cerynea rejoined the League. For Iseas, the then tyrant of Cerynea, when he saw the expulsion of the garrison from Aegium, and the execution of the tyrant at Bura by Margus and the Achaeans, and when he saw that he was virtually on the point of being attacked on all sides, he abdicated his rule, received pledges of safety from the Achaeans and joined the city to the Achaean League. [. . .]

(43) For the first 25 years the cities I have mentioned constituted the League, electing in rotation a federal secretary and two generals. Thereafter they decided to appoint one general only to whom they entrusted supreme command; the first to hold this office was Margus of Cerynea (255/4). Four years after his tenure of office, Aratus of Sicyon, then only twenty years old, freed his native city from its tyrant by his bravery and daring, and joined it to the Achaean League, whose political principles he had admired from the start (251/50). Eight years later, elected general for

the second time, he made a surprise attack on the Acrocorinth, then held by Antigonus; he captured it and so freed the inhabitants of the Peloponnese from a great fear, liberated Corinth and joined it to the Achaean League (243/2). In his same year of office he secured control of Megara by guile and joined it to the Achaeans. This was the year before the Carthaginian defeat which caused them to evacuate Sicily completely and submit for the first time to paying tribute to the Romans.[8]

Having made such great progress in his aim in a short time, Aratus continued henceforth as leader of the Achaean League and directed all his thoughts and actions to a single goal: the expulsion of the Macedonians from the Peloponnese, the overthrow of the tyrannies, and the preservation for all of their common ancestral freedom. And so, as long as Antigonus Gonatas was alive, he constantly opposed his interference and the Aetolians' lust for plunder,[9] handling every situation like a statesman, though they both carried their contempt for justice and impudence so far as to conclude a treaty to break up the Achaean League.[10]

(44) After the death of Antigonus, the Achaeans concluded an alliance with the Aetolians and fought nobly with them in the war against Demetrius;[11] their feelings of estrangement and hostility were provisionally lifted and gave way to a growing sentiment of solidarity and friendship.[12] When Demetrius died after a reign of only ten years (this was at the time of the first Roman crossing to Illyria) conditions became very favourable for the policy the Achaeans had pursued from the beginning. For the tyrants of the Peloponnese were downcast at the death of Demetrius, who had been as it were their leader and paymaster, and at the pressures exercised by Aratus who wanted them to abdicate their tyrannies, holding out great rewards and honours to those who complied, but threatening those who remained obdurate with even greater perils at the hands of the Achaeans. There was therefore a general movement among them to lay down their tyrannies voluntarily, restore freedom to their cities and join the Achaean League. Thus, while Demetrius was still alive, Lydiades of Megalopolis had the foresight to take the initiative and make the statesmanlike and sensible decision to lay down his tyranny and join the Achaean federation (235). Aristomachus tyrant of Argos (229/8), Xenon tyrant of Hermione and Cleon tyrant of Phlius then layed down their tyrannies and joined the Achaean democracy.[13]

Polybius II.37.7–44 (omitting 38.5; 38.11–39.10; 42)

1. Though Polybius is positive about the 'democratic' character of the Achaean League, this is not to be taken literally. By the time of Polybius the word 'democracy' had lost its full meaning (cf. **95** §3 and **92**), and the Achaean

League, where effective power rested with the wealthy, was in no way comparable to classical Athens.

2. Optimistic: for Sparta's relations with the Achaean League see **57, 63, 71**.
3. For *homonoia* in the Hellenistic age see **51**.
4. Polybius' father.
5. Now lost (*FGrH* 231), but used and referred to by Polybius and Plutarch (see **57**) and so indirectly a major, though apologetic, source for the history of the Achaean League.
6. See **45, 46**.
7. See **47**.
8. The First Punic War (264–241).
9. On Aetolian privateering see **52**.
10. *Staatsv.* III.490.
11. King in Macedon 239–229.
12. For a critical view of the Achaean role in this obscure episode see J. A. O. Larsen, *CP* 70 (1975), 159–72.
13. For another example of this process see **54**.

54 Decree of the Achaean League on the admission of (Arcadian) Orchomenus to the Achaean League (ca 234)

See further: Walbank I (1957), 242f.

(The first three lines are too fragmentary for continuous translation)

... [let him be fined] 30 talents which will be consecrated to Zeus [Amarius, and let anyone who wishes prosecute] him on a capital
5 charge / before the [Achaean] League. [Let] the Orchomenians and Achaeans [swear the same oath], at [Aegium the councillors (*synedroi*)[1] of the Achaeans, the general], hipparch and navarch, at [Orchomenus the magistrates of the Orchomenians], as follows:[2] I swear by Zeus Amarius, Athena Amaria, Aphrodite [and all the gods, to] abide [in] every respect with (the terms of) the stele, the agreement and the decree [passed by
10 the / League] of the Achaeans; and if anyone does not abide by them, I will obstruct him as far as possible; [and if I abide by my oath] may I prosper, but if I break it may the opposite happen. Any (Orchomenian) who acquires a plot of land or a house at [Orchomenus] from the time when they became Achaeans may not alienate it for a period of twenty years. If there is any charge against Nearchus or his sons[3] relating to the time before the Orchomenians became Achaeans, they shall all be null and void, and let [no / suit be brought] either by anyone against
15 Nearchus or his sons or by Nearchus or any of his [sons] concerning the charges from the time before the Orchomenians [became] Achaeans;

[anyone who] brings a suit will be fined 1,000 drachmas and the suit will be null and void. Concerning the gold [statue of Nike] from the sanctuary of Zeus Hoplosmius which the [Methydrians who moved] to Orchomenus offered as security, subsequently sharing out the money (raised), and which some of them [brought back / to Methydrium], if   20 they do not repay the monetary value to the Megalopolitans, as [conceded by the city] of Orchomenus, let the culprits be liable to prosecution.[4]

Syll.[3] 490; IG v.2. 344; Staatsv. III.499

1. Restoration uncertain; perhaps also *damiorgoi* = magistrates.
2. For other oath formulas see **33** n. 7.
3. Most probably the 'tyrant' ruling at Orchomenus, as in other Peloponnesian cities, before it joined the Achaean League (see **53**).
4. An obscure clause: men from Methydrium, a city absorbed by Megalopolis but which claimed its independence, had removed a golden statue from one of their temples; Megalopolis, now a member of the Achaean League (see **53** ch. 44), was asking for compensation. The precise circumstances are conjectural.

55 Agis IV of Sparta (ca 263–241)

The third century 'Spartan revolution' is the best known example of the social tensions that affected many Greek states in the Hellenistic age (see generally A. Fuks, *Ancient Society* 5 (1974), 51–81; cf. **75**). The ultimate aims of the reformer kings in Sparta were, however, probably political rather than social: the revival of Spartan power in the Peloponnese through the reconstruction of its citizen army. The 'revolution' is well known thanks to Plutarch's Lives of Agis IV and Cleomenes III, which are largely based on the history of Phylarchus (*FGrH* 81), a writer severely criticised by Polybius (II.56–63) for his sensationalism and inaccuracy, but who was nevertheless perhaps the most important of the historians of the third century. Polybius' critique is motivated in part by political bias – an Achaean, and an admirer of Aratus of Sicyon (see **53**), Polybius could not accept Phylarchus' favourable presentation of the Spartan reformer kings, particularly Cleomenes III, whose action eventually threatened to destroy the Achaean League (see **57**).

See further: B. Shimron, *Late Sparta* (Buffalo, 1972), 4–27; E. N. Tigerstedt, *The Legend of Sparta in Classical Antiquity* II (Stockholm, 1974), 49–85.

(a) The concentration of wealth in Sparta after 404

The beginning of the decline and of the disease in Sparta coincided with the destruction of the Athenian hegemony when they filled themselves with gold and silver. And yet, so long as the number of households remained the same as once fixed by Lycurgus, and the lots of land were passed on from father to son, the preservation of this order and equality somehow managed to compensate for the other errors committed by the city.[1] But when a powerful man called Epitadeus,[2] who was headstrong and violent in temper, became ephor, as a result of a quarrel with his son he introduced a law allowing one to bestow on whoever one wished one's patrimony and lot of land, either by gift during one's lifetime or by bequest in one's will. In introducing this law he was indulging his own private resentment, but the other citizens welcomed and ratified it through greed and so destroyed the best of institutions. For from this date onwards powerful men accumulated inheritances without limit, pushing aside the claims of the true heirs, and in a short time[3] wealth was concentrated into a few hands and the city as a whole became impoverished. The process brought in its wake servility, indifference to what is honourable, as well as envy and resentment against those who owned property. There were only 700 Spartiates left, no more, and of those perhaps 100 owned land as well as an (ancestral) lot. The remaining mass of people lingered on in the city without resources or political rights, fighting foreign wars without energy or spirit, and always on the lookout for an opportunity for change and revolution. (6) That is why Agis, rightly believing it a fine undertaking to reestablish equality in the city and fill up the citizen body, began to sound out people's feelings.

Plutarch, *Agis* 5–6.1

(b) *The revolutionary proposals of Agis and the opposition to them (243)*

Now at that time the greater part of the wealth of Sparta was in the hands of the women,[4] and this made the task of Agis laborious and difficult. For the women offered resistance when they saw that not only were they being deprived of the luxurious standard of living which their lack of taste made them believe constituted real happiness, but that they would also forfeit the honour and power they derived from their wealth. They turned to Leonidas and urged him as the elder of the two kings to attack Agis and obstruct his plans. Leonidas was prepared to help the rich, but was afraid of the people who were anxious for the change; he therefore made no open resistance but secretly sought to damage and destroy the undertaking. He would engage the magistrates in conversation and slander Agis, saying he was offering to the poor the property of the wealthy as the wages of his tyranny, and by redistributing lands and cancelling debts he was purchasing for himself a large bodyguard, and not citizens for Sparta. (8) However, Agis secured the appointment of Lysander as ephor, and straightway introduced through him a law before the elders, the chief provisions of which were the abolition of debts and the redistribution of land. The region between the ravines of Pellene and Taygetus, Malea and Sellasia was to be divided into 4,500 lots, and the rest of the country into 15,000; the latter was to be shared out to those of the *perioikoi* who were capable of bearing arms, while the central region would go to the Spartiates themselves, whose numbers were to be filled up from all those *perioikoi* and foreigners who had received a liberal education, were sound in body and in their prime.[5] The Spartiates would be organised in fifteen public messes[6] of 400 or 200 men, and their style of living would be that pursued by their ancestors.[7]

Plutarch, *Agis* 7.5–8

1. Whether this original equality of land ever existed is open to doubt (see Walbank I (1957), 728–31), but the belief exercised a powerful influence on the Spartan reformer kings.
2. Otherwise unknown, though cf. Aristotle, *Politics* 1270 a 15–29 for the law and its effects.
3. Plutarch is compressing here a longer evolution and may in any case be exaggerating the impact of Epitadeus' law.
4. See already Aristotle, *Politics* 1270 a 23–31.
5. Agis' reforms did not extend to the Laconian helots.
6. A revival of the public messes of the Spartan men; Agis' proposals must also have included the revival of the traditional Spartan education (*agoge*), though Plutarch does not make this explicit (Shimron, *op. cit.*, 20).
7. Agis' proposals failed on the opposition of the Spartan 'conservatives' and he was tried and executed in 241.

56 Cleomenes III of Sparta (ca 260–219)

See further: B. Shimron, *Late Sparta* (Buffalo, 1972), 27–52; E. N. Tigerstedt (see **55**).

(a) Cleomenes' life style

Cleomenes himself was an example to all; his own manner of life was plain, frugal and free from insolence or any affectation of superiority, and it was like a model of self-restraint for all. This gave him some influence over Greek affairs. For when people visited the other kings, they were not so much impressed at their wealth and prodigality as disgusted with their arrogant pretensions and the offensive and haughty way they answered those who met them.[1] But when they came to see Cleomenes, a king in deed as well as in title, there were no purple garments or expensive clothes to be seen around him, no array of couches and litters. He did not surround himself with a crowd of messengers, porters and secretaries to make his approach a difficult and slow task to petitioners. They found him wearing everyday clothes and answering in person the greetings of his visitors, spending time in

conversation with them in a cheerful and friendly way; they were
charmed and won over by his popular manner, and called him the only
true descendant of Heracles. His daily meals were reduced to three
couches and were very strict and Spartan in style; if he was entertaining
ambassadors or guests, two more couches were added and the servants
would make the table look a little more brilliant, not by serving rich food
and cakes, but by making the dishes more abundant and the wine more
generous. He once rebuked one of his friends when he heard that he had
entertained guests with black soup and barley bread as was customary at
the public messes. He said that on such occasions when entertaining
guests one should not behave in a too strictly Spartan way. Once the
table was removed, a tripod was brought in with a bronze crater full of
wine, two silver vases holding a pint each and very few silver cups;
anyone who wished might drink from these, but no one was offered a
cup which he did not want. There was no music and none was asked for;
Cleomenes himself would entertain the company with his conversation,
sometimes asking questions of others and sometimes telling stories;
when he was serious his words were not lacking in charm, and when he
was joking he did so with grace and without rudeness. For the hunt for
men conducted by the other kings, who tempted and corrupted them
with money and gifts, seemed to him crude and immoral.[2] But to win
over and attract those who met him by conversation and words that
evoked pleasure and confidence seemed to him a most honourable course
of action and one well worthy of a king. The only difference he could see
between a friend and a hireling was that the former was won over by
what you were like and what you said, the latter by your money.

Plutarch, Cleomenes 13

(b) Cleomenes justifies his action by an appeal to the past (227)

The next day[3] Cleomenes proscribed 80 citizens, who had to leave the
city, and removed the ephors' chairs with the exception of one on which
he intended to sit and give audience. He summoned an assembly and
defended his actions. Lycurgus, he said, had associated the Elders with
the kings, and for a long time the city was administered in this fashion,
without the need for another magistracy. Later, as the war against the
Messenians dragged on, the kings were kept busy by the campaigning
and so chose some of their friends to administer justice, leaving them
behind as their representatives for the citizens with the title of ephors. At
first they continued for a long time to be auxiliaries of the king, then little
by little they usurped authority and so turned themselves into an
independent magistracy without anyone noticing. [. . .] So long as they
acted with moderation, he said, it was better to put up with them, but
when they usurped power and destroyed the ancestral form of govern-

ment, and went as far as to exile some kings and execute others without trial, and to threaten those who longed to see again in Sparta the fairest and most divine constitution, it could no longer be tolerated.4 Had it been possible to remove without bloodshed those foreign plagues of Sparta, namely luxury, extravagance, debts and usury, and those still more ancient evils, poverty and wealth, he would have thought himself the happiest king of all to cure his native city painlessly like a doctor. But now, to excuse a necessary recourse to violence, there was the example of Lycurgus, who was neither a king nor a magistrate, but a private citizen, and who sought to act like a king and went to the agora in arms, which caused King Charillus to take refuge in terror at an altar. Charillus was a good and patriotic citizen and so quickly joined in Lycurgus' enterprise and approved the change of constitution, but Lycurgus demonstrated by his action that it is difficult to change a constitution without violence and terror.5 He himself had made use of such means with the greatest moderation, he said, to remove those who were opposed to the safety of Sparta. To all the others he was now offering the whole land as common property and freeing the debtors from their debts;6 he would carry out an examination and inspection of the foreigners, so that the best of them may become Spartiates and save the city with their arms. 'And so', he said, 'we shall no longer see Laconia being the prey of the Aetolians7 and Illyrians for want of defenders.' (11) Then Cleomenes was the first to give his property to the common stock, followed by Megistonous his father in law and each of his friends, then all the remaining citizens, and the land was divided up. He assigned a lot to each of the men he had exiled and promised to bring them back when the situation had calmed down. He filled up the citizen body with the élite of the *perioikoi*8 and raised a force of 4,000 hoplites, whom he taught to use the *sarissa*9 with both hands instead of the spear and to carry the shield by a band and not by a handle. He then turned to the education of the young and the so-called *agoge*, in the organisation of which he received considerable assistance from Sphaerus10 who was present in Sparta. The gymnasia and public messes soon recovered their decency and good order; a few submitted under compulsion to the simplicity of the old Spartan way of life, but the majority did so willingly. Nevertheless, to make the name of monarchy more acceptable, he appointed his brother Euclidas to be king with himself; this was the only time that the Spartans had two kings from a single royal house.11

Plutarch, *Cleomenes* 10–11

1. Cf. e.g. **79** ch. 32, **223**. For Plutarch's attitude to Hellenistic kings, which echoes that of Phylarchus, see also **34** (end), **36, 47**. For other royal portraits cf. **199** n. 2.

2. On the search for followers by Hellenistic kings see **25** (n. 3); Rostovtzeff I (1941), 137 and III, 1339–41.
3. Immediately after Cleomenes' coup in Sparta in which he killed four of the five ephors who opposed his plans.
4. This version of the history of the ephorate is obviously tendentious.
5. See Plutarch, *Lycurgus* 5.5–9; the story is obviously unverifiable.
6. Cf. **90** n. 2.
7. On Aetolian piracy see **52**.
8. Cleomenes, like Agis before him (see **55**), did not envisage the freeing of the Helots and only resorted partially to this tactic in 223 as a last expedient (Plutarch, *Cleomenes* 23.1).
9. The weapon of the Macedonian phalanx; see **67**.
10. A Stoic philosopher who had taught Cleomenes (Plutarch, *Cleomenes* 2.2).
11. In effect Cleomenes' position in Sparta was virtually that of a tyrant.

57 Aratus of Sicyon turns to Antigonus Doson to save the Achaean League from Cleomenes (227–224)

See further: Walbank I (1957), 245–53; *Staatsv.* III.506; E. S. Gruen, *Historia* 21 (1972), 609–25.

This ruined the affairs of Greece, which was still able to recover somehow from its present situation and escape from the insolence and rapacity of the Macedonians. Whether it was through distrust and fear of Cleomenes,[1] or because he envied his unexpected success and believed it would be a terrible thing, after holding the front rank for 33 years, to see an upstart interloper destroy his glory and power at once and take over the control of the position he had built up and preserved for so long, Aratus sought at first to apply compulsion and prevent the Achaeans (from yielding the leadership to Cleomenes). But they did not listen to him, amazed as they were at the audacity of Cleomenes and believing even that the pretension of the Spartans to bring the Peloponnese back to the ancestral order was justified. And so Aratus turned to a course of action unworthy of any Greek and most disgraceful for him, and in complete contradiction of his previous actions and policies: he invited Antigonus (Doson) into Greece and filled the Peloponnese with Macedonians, whom he himself as a young man had expelled from the Peloponnese after liberating the Acrocorinth;[2] he had been himself suspect to all the kings and their enemy, and had heaped abuse on this same Antigonus in the *Memoirs* he has left (*FGrH* 231 F 4b).[3] He says he suffered much hardship and faced many risks on behalf of the Athenians, to free their city from its garrison and from the Macedonians; and yet he brought them in arms to his own country, his own hearth and into the women's quarters,[4] and could not accept that a descendant of Heracles and king of Sparta, who was restoring his ancestral constitution, as it were, from a disordered harmony to the plain Dorian rules and way of life of Lycurgus, should deserve the title of leader of the Sicyonians and Tritaeans.[5] His aversion to the barley bread and plain Spartan coat, and especially (this was his most serious grievance against Cleomenes) to his destruction of wealth and alleviation of poverty,[6] led Aratus to subject himself and Achaea to the diadem and the purple, and to obey the orders of Macedonians and satraps[7] so as not to appear to be executing those of Cleomenes. Aratus sacrificed at festivals named after Antigonus (*Antigoneia*), sang paeans and crowned himself in honour of a man who was wasting away with consumption. This we write not out of a desire to disgrace Aratus (he showed himself on many occasions a true Greek and a great man), but out of pity for the weakness of human nature, which even in characters like this, so worthy and so well disposed to excellence, cannot achieve a perfection that is above reproach.[8]

Plutarch, *Cleomenes* 16

1. See **56**; Cleomenes' reforms and leadership had provided Sparta with a powerful army.
2. See **53** ch. 43.
3. See **53** n. 5.
4. Philip V seduced the wife of Aratus' son (Plutarch, *Aratus* 49.2).
5. A small Achaean town; see **53** ch. 41.
6. Aratus' fear of the 'contagion of revolution' in the Peloponnese following Cleomenes' reforms in Sparta is not made clear in Polybius' account (II. 46–55).
7. Rhetorical: there were no 'satraps' in the Macedonian kingdom.
8. Contrast Polybius' apologetic account of Aratus' action (II. 46–55).

58   The Hellenic League votes for war against the Aetolians (220)

Antigonus' intervention in Greece at the invitation of the Achaean League (see **57**) promptly led to the formation (late in 224) under Macedonian leadership of a general Hellenic League (*Staatsv.* III.507) which represented a new and original approach to the old problem of the relations between Macedon and the states of the mainland (contrast esp. **2, 23, 29, 42, 49, 53**). Though the Macedonian king had the presidency and executive power in the League, the member states were granted an important measure of autonomy in that decisions by the federal council were not apparently binding on them. Another novelty of the League was that it comprised federal states (i.e. Achaeans, Boeotians, etc.) and not separate cities, an indication of the success of federal institutions at this time. It is chiefly known from its participation in the so-called 'Social War' (= war of the allies) of 220–217, which aligned the young King Philip V of Macedon and the League against the Aetolians, who were not members of it, and so may have felt threatened by its creation. Cf. **59**, also **85**.

See further: J. V. A. Fine, *AJP* 61 (1940), 129–65; F. W. Walbank, *Philip V of Macedon* (Cambridge, 1940), 24–67; Larsen (1968), 326–58 and *CP* 70 (1975), 159–72.

And when Philip (V) found the representatives from the allied states gathered together at Corinth, he consulted with them and discussed the measures that ought to be taken to deal with the Aetolians. The Boeotians accused them of plundering[1] in peace time the sanctuary of Athena Itonia, the Phocians of having attacked Ambrysus and Daulium and sought to capture both cities, the Epirotes of having ravaged their territory. The Acarnanians on their side explained how they had contrived a plot to capture Thyrium and had even dared to attack the city at night. The Achaeans in addition related how they had seized Clarium in the territory of Megalopolis, ravaged the territory of Patrae and Pharae while passing through it, sacked Cynaetha, plundered the temple of Artemis at Lusi, besieged Clitor, attacked Pylus by sea and Megalopolis by land; Megalopolis was just in the process of restoration, but they (the Aetolians) were seeking with the help of the Illyrians to destroy it completely. When the representatives of the allies heard all this, they decided unanimously to make war on the Aetolians. Prefacing their resolution with the grievances just mentioned, they drew up a decree in which they declared they would give assistance to the allies in recovering any territory or cities seized from them by the Aetolians in the period dating from the death of Demetrius, the father of Philip. Similarly as regards those who had been forced by circumstances to join the Aetolian League against their will, they promised to restore them all to their ancestral form of government; they would have possession of their own territory and cities, be without garrison or tribute and free, and would use their ancestral institutions and laws.[2] Finally they also decreed to help the Amphictyons to recover their laws and their authority over the (Delphic) sanctuary which the Aetolians had usurped, determined as they were to keep in their own hands everything that was connected with the sanctuary.[3]

(26) This decree was ratified in the first year of the 140th Olympiad (220) and so began the so-called 'Social War', which was justified by the wrongs committed and was an appropriate response to them. The federal representatives immediately sent envoys to the allies to secure ratification of the decree by the people in each state, and so to get all to wage offensive war against the Aetolians.

Polybius IV.25–26.2

1. On Aetolian privateering see **52**; Polybius' ascription of the responsibility for the war to the Aetolians is tendentious.
2. For this definition of freedom compare **29**.
3. See **48**.

59 The Peace of Naupactus (217)

See further: F. W. Walbank, *Philip V of Macedon* (Cambridge, 1940), 65–7; Walbank III (1979), 774.

To begin with, the king (Philip V) sent out all the representatives of the allies with instructions to put to the Aetolians as conditions for the peace that each side should keep what they had at present.[1] The Aetolians readily agreed to this, and there then began a continuous interchange of messages to settle points of detail; most of these I shall omit as containing nothing of interest, but I shall record the advice given by Agelaus of Naupactus at the first conference between the king and the allies who were present.

(104) Above all the Greeks should never go to war against each other, he said, but give the gods hearty thanks if speaking all with one voice and joining hands together, as when crossing a river, they managed to repel the attacks of the barbarians and save themselves and their cities. And if this was altogether impossible, they ought for the present to agree and be on their guard when they considered the size of the armies and the magnitude of the war which was being fought in the west.[2] Even now it was clear to anybody with even a slight interest in politics, that whether the Carthaginians defeated the Romans in the war or the Romans the Carthaginians, there was no likelihood that the victors would be satisfied with the empire of Italy and Sicily, but they would go further and extend their operations and their forces beyond the proper limit. And so they, and particularly Philip, must keep a watchful eye on the present critical situation. Philip would be their safeguard, if he gave up the policy of wearing out the Greeks and making them an easy prey to the enemy and instead treated them as he would his own body, and in general took care of all parts of Greece as though part and parcel of his own domains. By following this policy he would secure the goodwill of the Greeks and they would faithfully assist him in his undertakings; while foreigners would be less of a threat to his power as they would be dismayed by the loyalty of the Greeks to him. If he was eager for action he must cast a glance to the west and take note of the wars raging in Italy; let him wait and see and watch for the right time to make a bid for universal power. The present situation was not unfavourable for such a hope. He also

exhorted him to put off till quieter times his quarrels and wars with the Greeks, and direct all his efforts to that end: this would give him the possibility of making peace or war with them as he wished. If he waited for the clouds now gathering in the west to settle on Greece, 'then (he said) it was much to be feared that the truces and the wars, and in short the games we are at present indulging in with each other, will be so completely knocked out of our hands that we shall have to implore the gods to allow us the freedom of making war and peace with each other when we wish, and in short to have the power to settle our own disputes'.

(105) [. . .] This occasion and this conference were the first to involve the affairs of Greece, Italy and even of Africa.[3] For no longer did Philip nor the Greek leaders make war or peace with each other solely by reference to Greek affairs; they now all had their eyes on objectives in Italy. And the same soon happened to the islanders and the peoples of Asia; those who were displeased with Philip and some of those who had grievances against Attalus no longer inclined to Antiochus or Ptolemy or looked to the south or the east, but from this time cast their eyes to the west, some sending embassies to Carthage and others to Rome. Rome did the same with the Greeks, alarmed at Philip's audacity and fearing that he might join in the attack on them in their present situation.[4] [. . .]

(106) As soon as the Achaeans had put an end to the war and after the election of Timoxenus as general, they returned once more to their accustomed ways and habits, and together with the other cities of the Peloponnese they set out to restore their private fortunes, to cultivate the land and to renew the traditional sacrifices and festivals and all the local religious celebrations. For in most states these things had almost sunk into oblivion because of the continuous wars that had taken place. It has always somehow been the case that the Peloponnesians, who of all men are best suited to a peaceful and civilised way of life, have in former times at any rate had least enjoyment of it, being rather, as Euripides says (fr. 998 Nauck) 'excessive in labour and never resting with the spear'. It seems to me natural that this should happen to them: their desire for domination and love of liberty[5] involves them in continuous mutual wars, as they refuse to yield the first place to each other.

Polybius v.103.7–104; 105.4–8; 106.
1–5 (cf. *Staatsv.* III.520)

1. The Peace of Naupactus brought to an end the 'Social War' (see **58**).
2. The Second Punic War.
3. Polybius is here anticipating later developments.
4. See **61**.

5. On the conjunction of liberty and domination see J. A. O. Larsen, *CP* 57 (1962), 230–4.

60 Two letters of Philip V to Larisa in Thessaly followed by two decrees of the city (217 and 214)

The following inscription neatly illustrates (1) Thessaly's position in relation to Macedon, nominally independent but in practice controlled by the Macedonian kings (cf. Polybius IV.76.2; Livy XXXII.10.7–8), (2) the Macedonian kings' recurring preoccupation with manpower (see **73**), (3) Philip's awareness of the Romans and of Roman institutions.

Anancippus son of Thessalus, Aristonus son of Eunomus, Epigenes son of Jason, Eudicus son of Adamantus, Alexias son of Clearchus held the office of *tagos*;[1] Aleuas son of Demosthenes was gymnasiarch. King Philip sent the following letter to the *tagoi* and the city:

King Philip to the *tagoi* and the city of Larisa, greetings. Petraeus, Anancippus and Aristonus, when they came on their embassy, /   5
declared to me that because of the wars your city needs more inhabitants; until I think of others who are deserving of your citizenship, for the present I rule that you must pass a decree to grant citizenship to the Thessalians or the other Greeks who are resident in your city. For when this is done and all keep together because of the favours received, I am sure that many other benefits will result for me and the city, and the land will be more fully cultivated. Year 4, Hyperberetaeus 21.[2]

The city passed the following decree: /   10

On the 26th of Panamus a special assembly was held under the presidency of all the *tagoi*, since King Philip had sent a letter to the *tagoi* and the city, as Petraeus, Anancippus and Aristonus, when they came on their embassy, declared to him that because of the wars our city needs more inhabitants; until he thought of others who were deserving of our citizenship, for the present he ruled that we should pass a decree to grant citizenship to the Thessalians / or the other Greeks who are resident with   15
us. For when this was done and all kept together because of the favours received, he was sure that many other benefits would result for himself and our city, and that the land would be more fully cultivated. The city has voted to act in these matters as the king wrote in his letter, and to grant citizenship to the Thessalians and the other Greeks residing with us, themselves and their descendants, and to give them the same rights as the Larisaeans, choosing the tribe / they wish to belong to. The decree is   20
to be valid for all time and the treasurers are to hand it over to be inscribed on two stone stelae with the names of those who have been

given citizenship, and to place one in the sanctuary of Apollo *Kerdoios* (who brings gain) and the other in the acropolis; they shall provide whatever expense is incurred for this.

Later King Philip sent another letter to the *tagoi* and the city when Aristonus son of Eunomus, Eudicus son of Adamantus, Alexippus son of Hippolochus, / Epigenes son of Jason, Numenius son of Mnasaeus held the office of *tagos* and Timonides son of Timonides was gymnasiarch, as follows:

King Philip to the *tagoi* and the city of Larisa, greetings. I hear that those who were granted citizenship in accordance with the letter I sent to you and your decree, and whose names were inscribed (on the stele) have been erased. If this has happened, those who have advised you have ignored the interests of your city and my ruling. That it is much the best state of affairs for as many as possible to enjoy citizen rights, / the city to be strong and the land not to lie shamefully deserted, as at present, I believe none of you would deny, and one may observe others who grant citizenship in the same way. Among these are the Romans, who when they manumit their slaves admit them to the citizen body and grant them a share in the magistracies,[3] and in this way have not only enlarged their country but have sent out colonies to nearly 70 places.[4] And yet I even now exhort you to approach [the] matter with impartiality, / and to restore to their citizen rights those chosen by the citizens; if [any] have committed an unpardonable offence against the monarchy or the city or are not deserving for some other reason [to be included] on this stele, put off the decision on them till I am back from the [campaign][5] and can hear the cases. But warn in advance those who intend to lodge accusations against them, that they may not be seen to be acting in this way for [partisan] reasons. Year 7, Gorpiaeus 13.[6]

The city voted the following decree: /

On the 21st of Themistius, when Alexippus was presiding over a meeting of the assembly dealing with sacred matters, on the motion of Alexippus, the city decreed that all those who were granted citizenship and whose names were erased, the *tagoi* should [inscribe] them on a white board and display it themselves in the agora, and they should inscribe on two stone stelae the names of the others who were granted citizenship in accordance with the letter of the king, together with the (two) letters of the king, the earlier decree and the one passed today, and should place one in the sanctuary of Apollo *Kerdoios* / and the other in the acropolis in the sanctuary of Athena; the treasurers shall provide the expense incurred from the common revenues, and this decree is to be valid for all time.

The following were granted citizenship in accordance with the letters of the king and the decrees of the city: (there follows a list of names, incompletely preserved, which includes one from Samothrace, 142 from

Crannon in Thessaly and over 60 from Gyrtone, also in Thessaly).

*Syll.*³ 543; *IG* IX.2. 517; C. D. Buck,
The Greek Dialects (Chicago, 1955), 220–3

1. The chief magistrates of the city.
2. *Ca* September 217; on the date and context see C. Habicht in *Ancient Macedonia* I (1970), 273–9. For the wars mentioned by Philip V see Polybius v.99.1–5.
3. Inaccurate, if the reading is correct; only sons of freedmen were admitted to office.
4. An exaggeration; see E. T. Salmon, *Roman Colonization under the Republic* (London, 1969), 69.
5. In Illyria (Livy XXIV.40).
6. July–August 214.

61 Treaty between Hannibal and Philip V (215)

Shortly after the battle of Cannae Philip V approached Hannibal to secure an alliance; the text of the treaty as reproduced by Polybius is a Greek translation, made in Hannibal's chancellery, of the Punic original and was probably captured by the Romans from Philip's envoy Xenophanes. The aims of the signatories appear to be limited in scope (the version of the treaty given by Roman sources (Livy XXIII.33) is distorted and misleading). For Hannibal the treaty opened up a new war front against the Romans (the 'First Macedonian War' of 215–205), but he clearly did not envisage their total destruction; for Philip the treaty provided a useful ally and a recognition of his claims over parts of Illyria which had fallen under Rome's protectorate. But Rome's refusal to negotiate with Hannibal made the treaty increasingly irrelevant.

See further: E. J. Bickerman, *TAPA* 75 (1944), 87–102 (linguistic analysis) and *AJP* 73 (1952), 1–23 (historical evaluation); Walbank II (1967), 42–56, esp. 42–4; Errington (1971), 111–13.

This is a sworn treaty between Hannibal the general, Mago, Myrcan, Barmocar and all the members of the Carthaginian Senate who are with him and all the Carthaginians who are serving with him, and Xenophanes son of Cleomachus of Athens, the envoy sent to us by King Philip son of Demetrius on behalf of himself, the Macedonians and their allies; the oath[1] is taken before Zeus, Hera and Apollo; before the god of the Carthaginians, Heracles and Iolaus; before Ares, Triton, Poseidon; before the gods that accompany the army, the Sun, the Moon, and Earth; before the rivers, harbour and waters; before all the gods who possess Carthage; before all the gods who possess Macedon and the rest of Greece; before all the gods in the army who are witnesses to this oath.

Hannibal the general and all the members of the Carthaginian Senate who are with him, and all the Carthaginians who are serving with him, propose, subject to our mutual agreement, to make this sworn treaty of friendship and goodwill; we shall be friends, kinsmen and brothers, on the following conditions:

(1) King Philip and the Macedonians and the other Greeks who are their allies will protect the citizens (?)[2] of Carthage, and Hannibal the general and those serving with him, and the dependants of the Carthaginians who use the same laws, and the people of Utica and all the cities and peoples who are subject to the Carthaginians, and their soldiers and allies, and all the cities and peoples in Italy, Cisalpine Gaul and Liguria who are in alliance with us, or who may join our friendship and alliance in this country.

(2) On their side King Philip and the Macedonians and their allies among the other Greeks will be protected and defended by the Carthaginians in the army, and by the people of Utica, and by all the cities and peoples who are subject to the Carthaginians, and their allies and soldiers, and by all the peoples in Italy, Cisalpine Gaul and Liguria which may hereafter become our allies in Italy and those regions.

(3) We will not make plots or lay ambushes against each other, but with all zeal and goodwill and without deceit or hostile intention, we will be enemies of the Carthaginians' enemies, except for the kings, cities and harbours (?)[3] with which we have sworn agreements and friendships.

(4) And we too will be enemies of King Philip's enemies, except for the kings, cities and peoples with whom we have sworn agreements and friendships.

(5) You shall be our allies in the war we are fighting with the Romans until the gods give us and you victory; you shall give us such assistance as is necessary and as we mutually agree upon.

(6) And when the gods have given us victory in the war against the Romans and their allies, if the Romans decide to make a treaty of friendship, we (the Carthaginians) shall make it and include you in the same treaty of friendship, on the following conditions: the Romans are not to make war against you at any time; they are not to have power over Corcyra, Apollonia, Epidamnus, Pharus, Dimale, the Parthini, nor Atintania; they shall restore to Demetrius of Pharus all his friends who are now in the dominion of Rome.

(7) If the Romans make war on you or on us, we will give help to each other in the war, according to the need of either.

(8) Similarly if others do so, except for the kings, cities and peoples with whom we have sworn agreements and friendships.

(9) If we decide to withdraw or add anything to this sworn treaty, we will make such withdrawals or additions only by mutual agreement.

Polybius VII.9; Staatsv. III.528

1. Contrast the Punic oath form in this text with Greek oaths (see **33** n. 7).
2. Translation uncertain.
3. Probably a scribal error for 'peoples'.

62 Alliance between Rome and the Aetolian League (212 or 211)

The treaty between Rome and the Aetolian League, concluded during the 'First Macedonian War' as a move to embarrass Philip V and prevent him from joining Hannibal in Italy (see **61**), was Rome's first treaty with a Greek state of the mainland. The treaty is known chiefly from Livy's summary account (from Polybius) and from a fragmentary inscription found at Thyrrheum in Acarnania.

See further: Badian (1958), 56f., 293f. and *Latomus* 17 (1958), 197–208; Walbank II (1967), 162f., 179f., 599–601 and III (1979), 779 and 789; Errington (1971), 113–18; *Staatsv.* III.536.

(a) Livy

Such were the words and promises of the Roman commander, and they were confirmed by the authority of Scopas, who was at the time general of the Aetolians, and Dorimachus their leading citizen; they extolled the power and the majesty of the Roman people with less restraint and greater conviction. But the most powerful incentive was the hope of recovering Acarnania.[1] And so terms were drawn up to admit them to the friendship and alliance of the Roman people; and clauses were added (1) that should they so wish the Eleans, Spartans, Attalus, Pleuratus and Scerdilaedus would be included in the same treaty of friendship (Attalus was king of Asia[2] and the latter two kings of Thrace and Illyria respectively); (2) that the Aetolians should immediately wage war against Philip by land and the Romans should assist them with a fleet of not less than 25 quinqueremes; (3) that of the towns from Aetolia as far as Corcyra, the soil, roofs, walls and territory should belong to the Aetolians, and everything else should be the spoils of the Roman people,[3] who should help the Aetolians to secure possession of Acarnania; (4) that should the Aetolians make peace with Philip, they would specify in the treaty that the peace would only be valid if Philip refrained from attacking the Romans, their allies and those under their rule;[4] similarly, if the Roman people made a treaty with the king, they should take care to deny him the right to make war on the Aetolians and their allies.

These terms were agreed to, and were inscribed and deposited two years later by the Aetolians at Olympia and by the Romans on the Capitol, to invest the treaty with sanctity. The cause of the delay was that the Aetolian envoys were held back in Rome for a long time. [. . .]

Livy xxvi.24.7–15; *Staatsv.* III.536

(b) Inscription

. . . [towards] all these . . . let [the] magistrates of the Aetolians [do] as they wish to be done. And if the Romans capture by force any cities of
5 these / peoples let it be permitted to the Aetolian people to have these cities and (their) territories as far as the Roman people is concerned;[5] and [whatever] is captured by the Romans apart from the city and its
10 territory, / let the Romans have it. And if any of these cities is captured jointly by the Romans and Aetolians, [let] the Aetolians [be permitted] to have these cities and (their) territories as far as the Roman people is concerned.[6] And whatever they capture apart from the city, let it belong
15 jointly / to both parties. And if any of these [cities] join or come over to the side[7] of the Romans or the Aetolians, [let it be permitted] to the Aetolians to admit [to their] League (*politeuma*) these [men] and cities and
20 territories / [as far as the] Roman people [is concerned][8] . . . autonomous . . .

(the last 4 lines are too mutilated for continuous restoration and translation)

IG IX².1.241; *Staatsv.* III.536; Moretti II.87; cf. *SEG* XXV.626

1. On Aetolia and Acarnania see also **16**.
2. Or rather of Pergamum.
3. The clauses on booty are given in fuller detail in the inscriptional fragment of the treaty (next passage); on Aetolian privateering see **52**.
4. The Aetolians concluded a separate peace with Philip in 206 (Livy XXIX.12.1), which the Romans later declared a breach of the original alliance.
5. Or 'as far as lies in the power of the Roman people'.
6. See n. 5. Rome clearly did not envisage any territorial acquisitions in this area.
7. The difference in the meaning of the two verbs is not clear, but this clause appears in any case to contradict Flamininus' later interpretation of the treaty in 198 (Polybius XVIII.38.8–9) and the question of Polybius' (and Flamininus') sincerity is controversial.
8. See n. 5.

63 Nabis, tyrant/king of Sparta (207–192)

The Macedonian intervention in the Peloponnese (see **57**) resulted eventually in the defeat and flight of Cleomenes (222). His social reforms in Sparta were apparently left undisturbed by Antigonus Doson, but in any case there were many who had gained nothing from his reforms and social tensions persisted; this forms the background to the rise of Sparta's last and most violent 'tyrant' Nabis, who is presented in very hostile terms in the extant tradition.

See further: R. M. Errington, *Philopoemen* (Oxford, 1969), index s.v. Nabis; B. Shimron, *Late Sparta* (Buffalo, 1972), 53–78 (after Cleomenes), 79–100 (Nabis).

Nabis, tyrant[1] of Sparta, being now in the third year of his reign (205), did not venture on any important undertaking because of the recent defeat of Machanidas[2] by the Achaeans, but busied himself with laying the foundations of a long and oppressive tyranny. He destroyed utterly the last remaining members (of the royal houses?)[3] in Sparta, drove into exile those distinguished for their wealth or the fame of their ancestors, and distributed their property and wives to the most eminent of those who were left and to his mercenaries. The latter were composed of murderers, housebreakers, brigands and burglars. For generally speaking these were the kinds of men who sedulously flocked to him from every part of the world, men whose own country was closed to them owing to their impiety and crimes. He put himself forward as their champion and king[4] and used them as his attendants and bodyguards; it was clear therefore that his tyranny would be lasting and would enjoy a long reputation for lawlessness. Besides this he was not content to banish the citizens, but left no place secure for the exiles and no refuge safe. Some he caused to be pursued and assassinated on the road, while others he murdered on their return from exile. Finally in the cities where some of the exiles were staying, he would rent the houses next door to them by means of unsuspected agents; he then introduced Cretans[5] into them, to breach the walls and shoot arrows through the existing windows. In this way they killed the exiles, some standing up and others lying down in their own houses. No place was safe and there was not a moment of security for the unfortunate Spartans. In this way he destroyed the majority of them.[6]

Polybius XIII.6

1. Officially Nabis styled himself 'king' and he was in fact descended from the Eurypontid royal house, though he ruled without a colleague.
2. Nabis' predecessor on the Spartan throne, defeated and killed in 207 by the Achaeans (Polybius XI.11–18).
3. Words lost in the text.
4. Ironical.
5. Cretan mercenaries were a feature of the age (cf. **95** n. **4**) and Nabis had connexions with Crete (see Errington, *op. cit.*).
6. Exaggerated; Nabis' following, unlike that of Agis and Cleomenes (see **55, 56**), also included many enfranchised Helots.

64 The Peace of Phoenice between Rome and Philip V (summer 205)

See further: Badian (1958), 58–61; Walbank II (1967), 516f., 522; Errington (1971), 116–18 with n. 8, p. 281f.; *Staatsv.* III. 543.

Phoenice is a town in Epirus; the king (Philip V) conferred there first with Aeropus, Derdas and Philip, the magistrates of the Epirotes, and afterwards met P. Sempronius.[1] Amynander, king of the Athamanians and other magistrates of Epirus and Acarnania were present at the meeting. Philip the magistrate was the first to speak and requested simultaneously the king and the Roman commander to bring the war[2] to an end and to grant the Epirotes their pardon.

P. Sempronius laid down as conditions for peace that the Parthini, Dimallum, Bargullum and Eugenium should belong to the Romans, while Atintania should be ceded to Macedonia, provided Philip sent a deputation to the Senate and obtained this concession. When peace was agreed on these terms, the king included in the treaty Prusias, king of Bithynia, the Achaeans, Boeotians, Thessalians, Acarnanians and Epirotes; and the Romans included[3] Ilium, King Attalus, Pleuratus, Nabis tyrant of Sparta, the Eleans, Messenians and Athenians.

These terms[4] were written down and sealed, and a truce was made for two months, to give time to send envoys to Rome to ask the people to ratify the peace on these terms; all the tribes agreed to them, as now that the war was moving to Africa they wished to be free from all other wars for the time being. [. . .]

Livy XXIX.12.11–16; *Staatsv.* III.543

1. The Roman proconsul in Macedonia and Greece.
2. The 'First Macedonian War' (see **61, 62**); Philip's signing of this peace effectively cancelled his earlier alliance with Hannibal (see **61**).
3. The authenticity of the list of states and rulers allegedly included by Rome in the peace, and its significance for future Roman policy in the Hellenistic world, are controversial.
4. Livy fails to mention a non-aggression clause attested by Polybius XVI.34.7.

65 Philip V and the siege of Abydus (200)

The origins of, and responsibilities for, the outbreak of the 'Second Macedonian War' of 200–196 are very controversial and tie up with the wider question of Roman policy and the development of Roman 'imperialism'. This is not the place to attempt a summary of a very large debate; for modern views see e.g. F. W.

Walbank, *Philip V of Macedon* (Cambridge, 1940), 108–37; Badian (1958), 62–9; Errington (1971), 131–40; Will II (1967), 87–128; W. V. Harris, *War and Imperialism in Republican Rome* (Oxford, 1979), 205–8, 212–18.

Philip now[1] laid siege to Abydus by land and by sea, setting up a palisade in one part and a stockade in another. This action was not remarkable for the importance of the armaments used, nor for the ingenuity displayed in those works with which besiegers and besieged usually try to match each other's skill and craft, but more than any other it deserves to be remembered and recorded for the noble spirit and exceptional courage of the besieged. At first the inhabitants of Abydus, full of confidence in themselves, resisted vigorously Philip's armaments. Some of the engines he brought by sea they struck and dislodged with stones from their catapults, and others they destroyed by fire, so that the enemy had difficulty in pulling their ships out of danger. Against the siege works on land they resisted valiantly for a time, not despairing of prevailing over the enemy. But when the outer wall was undermined and collapsed, and when afterwards the Macedonians through their mines were approaching the wall built by the besieged in place of the fallen one, they then sent Iphiades and Pantagnostus as ambassadors and invited Philip to take possession of the city, on condition that he would allow the troops sent by the Rhodians and by Attalus[2] to depart under truce and would let all free persons find safety as they could, wherever they wished and with the clothes they were wearing. When Philip told them to surrender unconditionally or to fight bravely, they returned to the town. (31) The people of Abydus, on hearing the answer, met in an assembly and discussed the situation in a state of despair. They resolved, first to free the slaves, that they might have loyal auxiliaries on their side,[3] then to gather all the women in the sanctuary of Artemis and the children with their nurses in the gymnasium, then to bring together the silver and the gold in the agora, and similarly put all their valuable clothes on the Rhodian quadrireme and the Cyzicene trireme. After making these resolutions they acted unanimously on the decree, then met again in an assembly, and elected 50 of the older and more trusted men, who were still fit enough to execute the order. They bound them by oath in front of everyone else, that whenever they saw the inner wall being captured by the enemy, they should kill the children and women, set fire to the ships mentioned above and throw the silver and gold into the sea in accordance with the curses. After this they brought the priests forward and all swore either to defeat the enemy or to die fighting for their native city. On top of it all they slew victims and compelled the priests and priestesses to utter imprecations to meet the situation I have described. Having ratified these decisions they ceased countermining against the enemy and resolved that when the interior wall fell they would fight on the ruins of the wall and resist the enemy to death.[4]

Polybius XVI.30–31

1. Philip had been conducting a series of aggressive campaigns in the Aegean, Thrace, the Hellespont and Asia Minor since after the Peace of Phoenice (cf. **66, 68, 125, 133**). Rome, solicited by Rhodes and Attalus (next note) had already issued an (unsuccessful) ultimatum to Philip V earlier in 200, enjoining him not to attack any Greek state.
2. Rhodes and Attalus were brought together by their common fear of Philip's activities since 205 (see C. G. Starr, *CP* 33 (1938), 63–8); their appeal to Rome against Philip V and Antiochus III (see ch. 4) in autumn 201 helped to bring about the eventual Roman declaration of war. Cf. **152, 193, 198, 200**.
3. A practice frequently resorted to by Greek states in a military emergency (M. I. Finley, *Historia* 8 (1959), 157f.); see also **82**.
4. The spirit of the Greek *polis* was far from 'dead'. During the siege a Roman delegation issued another ultimatum to Philip V (autumn 200); its rejection by him was followed by the Roman declaration of war (the 'Second Macedonian War', 200–196).

66 The Athenians cancel honours previously voted to Philip V (199)

See further: J. Briscoe, *A Commentary on Livy Books* XXXI–XXXIII (Oxford, 1973), 150–2.

Then the Athenians, who had long kept in check their hatred of Philip,[1] now gave free rein to it as they looked forward to immediate assistance. There is never a shortage there of tongues ready to stir up the crowd; that kind of people is to be found in every free city, but particularly in Athens,[2] where oratory exercises the greatest influence, and it thrives on the support of the multitude. They immediately proposed a motion which the people ratified, to remove and destroy all the statues and portraits of Philip and the inscriptions on them, as well as those of all his ancestors, men and women, to cancel all the holidays, ceremonies and priesthoods instituted in honour of him and of his ancestors;[3] even the places where something had been placed or inscribed in his honour were to be put under a curse and it should be wrong in future to decide to place or dedicate anything there that religion allowed to place or dedicate in a holy spot; whenever the priests of the state offered prayers on behalf of the people of Athens, their allies, their armies and fleets, they should at the same time curse and execrate Philip, his children and his kingdom, his land and sea forces, and the entire race and name of the Macedonians. A clause was added to the decree, that if anyone hereafter proposed a motion dishonouring or disgracing Philip, the entire Athenian people would ratify it, while if anyone spoke or acted against Philip's disgrace and honoured him, he could be killed by anyone with impunity. A final clause was added that all the decrees once passed against the Peisistratids should be applied to Philip. Thus did the Athenians wage war against Philip with decrees and words, the only weapons they are strong in.⁴

Livy XXXI.44.2–9

1. Philip V had repeatedly attacked Athens in 200; cf. **198**.
2. Livy is drawing his account from Polybius who was very hostile to the Athenians of his day (F. W. Walbank, *Polybius* (Berkeley, 1972), 169 n. 81).
3. These honours were not divine in character; the Athenians had not established a divine cult of any of the Antigonids since Antigonus and Demetrius (see **34**).
4. Contrast this passage with the voting of religious honours to rulers (see **32**).

67 The strengths and weaknesses of the Macedonian phalanx (197)

Many considerations will easily prove that so long as the phalanx keeps its own formation and strength no one can resist it in a headlong clash or withstand its charge.¹ For since a fully armed man occupies in close battle formation a space of three feet; and since the length of the sarissae² is sixteen cubits (= *ca* 7.40 metres) according to the original design, though in practice it has usually been adjusted to fourteen (= *ca* 6.46 metres), from which one must further subtract four (= *ca* 1.85 metres) for the space between the hands and the counterweight behind the projecting part; it is clear that the sarissa must project ten cubits (= *ca* 4.62 metres) in front of the bodies of each soldier whenever he marches against the enemy holding the sarissa forward with both hands. And so the sarissae of the second, third, and fourth ranks project more, but the sarissae of the fifth rank still project two cubits (= *ca* 0.92 metres) in front of the men of the first rank, so long as the phalanx keeps its own formation as regards both depth and breadth [. . .] (30) And so it is easy to picture the likely appearance and strength of the whole phalanx when it moves to the attack with sarissae lowered and men drawn up sixteen deep. Of these, all those further back than the fifth rank cannot take part in the action with their sarissae; and so they do not level them man against man but hold them inclined above the shoulders of the men in front in order to protect the formation from above. For the sarissae are so closely packed together that they keep away any missiles which pass over the heads of the men of the front rank and might fall on those behind. By pressing with the weight of their bodies on those in front the men of the rear ranks make the charge (of the phalanx) very forcible and render it impossible for the men in the front rank to turn back. [. . .] (31) Why is it

127

then that the Romans win, and why are those who use the phalanx defeated? The reason is that in war the times and places for action are unlimited, while there is only one time and one kind of place which enables the phalanx to perform at its best. Now if the enemy was obliged to adapt to the times and places of the phalanx when about to fight a decisive engagement, the likelihood would be according to what has just been said that those who used the phalanx would always be victorious. But if it is possible to take evasive action and to do so early, what is left of the formidable character of the phalanx? It is generally agreed that the phalanx needs ground that is level and open, and which in addition is free from obstacles – I mean such things as ditches, ravines, depressions, ridges, and river beds. All these are enough to hinder and break up that formation. Everyone would agree that it is more or less impossible, or at least extremely rare, to find a piece of country of twenty stades (*ca* 3.5 km) and sometimes even more in which none of these obstacles is to be found. But supposing one could find such places, if the enemy refuse to come down to these but go round sacking the cities and the territory of one's allies, what is the use of such a formation? If it stays on the ground that suits it, it is unable to bring assistance to its friends and cannot even defend itself. The enemy will easily prevent the carriage of provisions when they exercise undisputed control over the open country. But if it leaves its proper ground and tries to take some action, it becomes an easy prey for the enemy. And again, even if the enemy does come down to level ground, but instead of engaging his entire army against the single charge of the phalanx at a single point of time, withholds a little of his forces from the conflict, it is easy to see what will happen from what the Romans do at present.

Polybius XVIII.29–31 (omitting 29.6–7; 30.5–11)

1. Polybius' comments are made in connexion with Philip's defeat by the Romans at Cynoscephalae (197).
2. See the discussion by M. M. Markle, *AJA* 81 (1977), 323–39.

68 The Roman settlement of Greece after the defeat of Philip V (196)

See further: F. W. Walbank, *Philip V of Macedon* (Cambridge, 1940), 172–85; Badian (1958), 69–75 and *Titus Quinctius Flamininus* (Cincinnati, 1970); Errington (1971), 151–5.

At about this time there arrived from Rome the ten commissioners who were to carry out the settlement of Greece,[1] with the Senate's decree on the peace with Philip. The main points of the decree were as follows: all the other Greeks in Asia and in Europe were to be free and enjoy their own laws,[2] Philip was to hand over to the Romans before the Isthmian festival the Greeks under his authority and the cities he had garrisoned, and should give their freedom to Euromus, Pedasa, Bargylia and Iasus, and also Abydus, Thasos, Myrina and Perinthus, and remove his garrisons from them.[3] Flamininus was to write to Prusias about the liberation of Cius in accordance with the Senate's decree. Philip should hand over to the Romans at the same time the prisoners and all the deserters, and likewise all decked ships except five and his 'sixteen'; he should pay an indemnity of 1,000 talents, half of this at once and half in instalments over a period of ten years. (45) When this decree was made public, all the other Greeks were filled with confidence and joy, and only the Aetolians, disappointed at not getting what they hoped,[4] sought to disparage the decree; it was nothing but words devoid of substance, they said. [. . .] Everyone could see from this that the Romans were taking over the 'fetters of Greece'[5] from Philip; the Greeks were changing masters and not recovering their freedom [. . .] (46) [. . .] When the time of the Isthmian festival came, the expectation of what was going to happen attracted men of the highest rank from almost the whole of the world. There was much varied talk all over the place of the festival: some said it was impossible that the Romans would withdraw from some of the places and cities, while others declared they would withdraw from the places that seemed most important while retaining others that appeared unimportant but could perform the same function. They had the ingenuity to provide a detailed list of these out of their own heads. Such was the general uncertainty that prevailed when the crowd had gathered at the stadium for the contest; the herald came forward, ordered the crowd to be silent through his trumpeter, and read out the following proclamation: 'The Senate of Rome and Titus Quintius the proconsul, after defeating King Philip and the Macedonians, leave the following peoples free, without garrison, without tribute, and in full enjoyment of their ancestral laws: the Corinthians, Phocians, Locrians, Euboeans, Achaeans of Phthiotis, Magnesians, Thessalians and Perrhaebians.'[6] As the herald began to speak a tremendous round of applause broke out; some did not hear the proclamation and others wanted to hear it again. The majority of people were incredulous and felt as though they were hearing the words in a dream, so unexpected was the event; they all shouted on another impulse for the herald and the trumpeter to come to the middle of the stadium and to repeat their message. In my opinion they wanted to see as well as to hear the speaker, so difficult did they find it to believe the proclamation. And when the herald came forward to the middle and silenced the clamour through his trumpeter, and then repeated the same proclamation in the same words as before, the applause was such that those who hear of it today would find it difficult to imagine. When finally the applause died down, no one paid any more attention to the athletes, but they were all talking to each other or to themselves, as men who had gone out of their senses. Indeed, after the competition they were so overjoyed that they nearly killed Flamininus in their display of gratitude. Some wanted to look him in the face and call him their Saviour (*Soter*);[7] others were eager to grasp his right hand; the majority threw garlands and fillets on him, and they very nearly tore the man apart. Though the expression of gratitude seemed extravagant, one could confidently say that it fell far short of the magnitude of the achievement. That the Romans and their general Flamininus should have pursued this policy, sustaining every expense and facing every risk for the freedom of the Greeks, was remarkable; that the power they had brought into action matched their policy was a great thing; but the greatest thing of all was that no accident had foiled their plan, but everything came to a successful issue at the right time, and in a single proclamation all the Greeks living in Asia and in Europe were made free, without garrison, without tribute and enjoying their own laws.

Polybius XVIII.44–45.1; 45.6; 46

1. On them cf. **154**.
2. On the 'freedom of the Greeks' cf. **29**, and for Rome's use of the slogan cf. **79**, **154**, **159**, **200**.
3. Cities conquered by Philip V in the years 202–200; cf. **65**.
4. The Romans regarded the treaty with Aetolia of 212/11 (see **62**) as obsolete; see further **69**, **70**, **72**.
5. The fortresses of Demetrias, Chalcis and Acrocorinth, through which the Macedonian king controlled mainland Greece (cf. Polybius XVIII.11.4).
6. These had all been controlled by Philip V and now became free as the other Greeks.
7. Numerous Greek states voted divine honours to Flamininus.

69 Aetolian negotiations with the Roman commander (191)

See further: Badian (1958), 84–7; Errington (1971), 171–5.

After the Roman capture of Heraclea,[1] Phaeneas the general of the Aetolians, seeing the danger that threatened Aetolia on all sides and realising what would happen to the other towns, decided to send an embassy to Manius Acilius[2] to ask for a truce and peace treaty. [. . .] When the truce was granted, Lucius (Valerius Flaccus)[3] came to Hypata and a lengthy discussion took place about the state of affairs. The

Aetolians sought to justify themselves by referring to their previous services towards the Romans,[4] but Valerius cut their enthusiasm short by saying that this kind of defence was unsuited to the present circumstances. The old friendly relations had been broken off by them; the Aetolians were responsible for the present state of hostility and those past services were of no help in the present state of affairs. He therefore advised them to stop justifying themselves, adopt a tone of supplication and beg the consul to pardon them for their errors. The Aetolians, after talking at length about the state of affairs decided to leave the whole matter to Acilius and entrusted themselves to the 'good faith' of the Romans (= *fides*), not realising what this meant but misled by the word 'faith' to expect they would be granted a fuller pardon. But with the Romans 'to entrust oneself to their good faith' is equivalent to 'surrendering unconditionally to the victor'. (10) Having made this decision the Aetolians sent off Phaeneas and others with Valerius to announce it at once to Acilius. They met the consul and started again to justify themselves as before, and finally declared that the Aetolians had decided to entrust themselves to the good faith of the Romans. Acilius interrupted them, saying 'Is that really so, men of Aetolia?' And when they answered in the affirmative, he said 'Well then, first of all none of you must cross over to Asia,[5] whether in a private capacity or by public decision, secondly you must surrender Dicaearchus and Menestratus of Epirus' (who happened at the time to have come to the assistance of the Aetolians at Naupactus), 'and also King Amynander and the Athamanians who deserted to your side with him.' Phaeneas interrupted him, saying 'What you are asking, consul, is unjust and ungreek'. To this Acilius answered, not so much because he was angry as because he wanted to make them realise their predicament and thoroughly frighten them: 'Do you still presume to put on Greek airs and talk about what is right and proper, after entrusting yourselves to my good faith? I could throw you all in chains and arrest you, if I wanted.' With these words he ordered a chain and iron collar to be brought and placed on the neck of each. Phaeneas and the others were thunderstruck and stood all speechless, as though paralysed in body and mind by this extraordinary turn of events. Valerius and a few others of the military tribunes there begged Acilius not to inflict any harsh treatment on the men present, as they were ambassadors. He agreed, and Phaeneas began to speak, saying he and the *Apokletoi*[6] were prepared to do as instructed, but they had to consult the general assembly (of the Aetolians) to obtain ratification of the orders. Acilius said he was right, and Phaeneas asked for a truce of ten days to be granted. This was also agreed and they departed with these terms; when they came to Hypata they told the *Apokletoi* what had happened and what had been said. The Aetolians on hearing this realised for the first time their error and the compulsion they were under. They therefore decided to sent messages to the cities and summon the Aetolians to discuss the Roman demands.[7] [. . .]

Polybius xx.9–10 (omitting 9.2–5; 10.15–17)

1. Heraclea in Trachis, near Thermopylae.
2. Manius Acilius Glabrio, consul in 191.
3. A legate of Glabrio.
4. See **62**, contrast their behaviour in **68**.
5. To assist Antiochus III whom they had incited to invade mainland Greece; cf. **159–161**.
6. A committee elected from the larger council of the Aetolians, which assisted the executive officials (especially the general) of the League; see Larsen (1968), 200–2.
7. The Aetolians refused to ratify the Roman terms; it was not till 189 that they were induced to submit (see **70**).

70 The Senate's peace terms for Aetolia (189)

See further: E. Badian (see **69**); Errington (1971), 184–6.

The Senate passed a decree which was confirmed by a vote of the people, and so the treaty was ratified; its detailed provisions were as follows: 'The people of Aetolia [shall preserve in good faith] the empire and majesty of the Roman people.[1] They shall not allow [enemy forces] to pass through their territory or cities against the Romans, or their allies or friends, and shall not provide them with supplies by public decision. [They shall have the same enemies as the Roman people], and if the Romans go to war against anyone, the people of Aetolia shall do so also.[2] The Aetolians shall surrender to the commander at Corcyra, within 100 days of the swearing of the oaths, all [deserters], runaway slaves and prisoners belonging to the Romans and their allies, apart from those who were captured in war, returned to their country and were captured again, and apart from those who were enemies of the Romans during the war between the Aetolians and the Romans. If any are not found during this period, when they are detected they shall be handed over without deceit; they shall not be allowed to return to Aetolia after the treaty is sworn. The Aetolians shall give to the consul in Greece 200 Euboean talents of silver not inferior to Attic currency; they may if they wish give gold in place of a third of the silver, at the rate of one mina of gold for ten of silver, within the first six years of the day when the treaty is ratified, in annual instalments of 50 talents; they shall deliver the money in Rome. The Aetolians shall provide to the consul 50 hostages, above the age of twelve but below forty, for a period of six years, as chosen by the Romans, but excluding any general or hipparch or public secretary or any who have previously been hostages in Rome; if any of the hostages dies they shall replace him. Cephallenia shall not be included in the treaty. Any territories, cities or men which were in the possession of the Aetolians, and were captured by the Romans or joined their friendship in the consulship of Lucius Quintius and Cnaeus Domitius (192) or subsequently, the Aetolians shall not seize them or anyone residing in them. The city and territory of Oeniadae shall belong to the Acarnanians.[3] The treaty was sworn on these terms and the peace concluded. [. . .]

Polybius XXI.32

1. The first known instance of a formula which later became almost standard in Roman treaties; it made explicit the moral obligations of Rome's clients to her.
2. Aetolia, the first Greek state on the mainland to make a formal alliance with Rome (see **62**), was thus also the first officially to lose her independence.
3. See **16**.

71 The Achaeans abolish Sparta's 'Lycurgan' constitution (188)

After the death of Nabis (see **63**), Philopoemen brought Sparta into the Achaean League (192), but the move provoked much internal tension in Sparta, which was not even quelled by the drastic action described in this passage. The continued reluctance of many Spartans to belong to the Achaean League (contrast **53** ch. 38) was aggravated by the social upheavals Sparta had experienced in previous decades (see **55, 56, 63**). The third-century attempts to revive Sparta's 'Lycurgan' constitution finally resulted in its destruction.

See further: R. M. Errington, *Philopoemen* (Oxford, 1969), chs. 7–11; B. Shimron, *Late Sparta* (Buffalo, 1972), 99–122.

Once the Spartans had been frightened in this way[1] they were ordered first to pull down their walls, then to expel from Laconia all the foreign auxiliaries who had been in the pay of the tyrants. All the slaves freed by the tyrants (there was a large number of them) were to leave before a certain day; the Achaeans would have the right to arrest, take away and sell those who remained. They were to abolish the laws and way of life of Lycurgus and were to adapt themselves to the laws and institutions of the Achaeans: in this way they would all belong to the same body and would agree more easily on all matters. No order was carried out more willingly by the Spartans than the destruction of the walls, and none with greater reluctance than the return of the exiles. A decree on their reinstatement was passed at Tegea in the federal council of the Achaeans, and when it was reported that the foreign auxiliaries who had been discharged and the enfranchised Spartans (this was the name they gave to those freed by the tyrants) had left the city and dispersed in the countryside, it was decided that before the (federal Achaean) army was disbanded the general should go with the light-armed troops to arrest men of that kind and sell them as booty; many were captured and sold. Permission was given by the Achaeans to restore with that money a portico at Megalopolis which the Spartans had destroyed. The Belbinatis, which the tyrants of Sparta had unlawfully occupied, was restored to the same city in accordance with an old decree of the Achaeans passed in the reign of Philip son of Amyntas. These measures broke the back of the Spartan state and made it for a long time subservient to the Achaeans;[2] but nothing did them so much harm as the abolition of the Lycurgan way of life after they had lived by it for 800 years.

Livy XXXVIII.34

1. The treacherous execution of 80 Spartans by Philopoemen at Compasion.
2. The whole account (from Polybius) underestimates the continued opposition in Sparta to the Achaeans.

72 Decree of the Amphictyonic Council in honour of a Thessalian (184–3)

An immediate result of the defeat of Antiochus III and the Aetolians by the Romans was the end of the long predominance exercised by Aetolia over the Amphictyonic League (see **48, 52, 58**). The Delphians sought successfully to ingratiate themselves with the Romans to recover their independence (see Sherk nos. 1, 37–39), but competition for influence within the Amphictyonic League remained fierce. The following decree of the Amphictyonic Council (unfortunately obscure in its allusions) attests indirectly the influence the Thessalians sought to exercise in the reorganisation of the League.

See further: Sherk nos. 1, 37–39.

In the archonship of Craton at Delphi (184/3), when Mnasidamus of Corinth was secretary of the Amphictyons, resolved [by the council] of the Amphictyons from the autonomous peoples and the democratic
5   cities:[1] since Nicostratus son of Anaxippus, / a Thessalian from Larisa, when sent as *hieromnemon*[2] by the Thessalian League to the Pythian festival in the archonship of Nicobulus at Delphi (186/5), displayed all his zeal together with the men sent by the people of Athens and the *hieromnemones*, so that the council of the Amphictyons should be
10   restored / to its original and traditional form, and presided over the

contest and the sacrifices with them, so that they would be performed in the best possible way; and when appointed by the council of the Amphictyons ambassador to Rome together with the Athenian Menedemus, / he approached the Senate, the consuls and the tribunes   15 and spoke about the object of his mission,[3] and achieved everything that was in the common interest of the Amphictyons and the other Greeks who choose freedom and democracy;[4] and when sent / as *hieromnemon* to   20 the session in late autumn in the archonship of Craton at Delphi (184/3), he offered a sacrifice together with the *hieromnemones*, returned with them to the sanctuary, and approached the assembly of the Delphians, and addressed them on the subject of his missions / to the Roman Senate, the   25 consuls and the tribunes, and invited the Delphians to preserve their goodwill towards all the Greeks and not to do anything contrary to the previous resolutions of the Greeks;[5] and / in all other circumstances   30 where the Amphictyons call upon him he has constantly shown himself zealous and devoted to the common good, and does not seek to evade any hardship or danger which his enemies[6] prepare for him. Therefore, so that all the Greeks may know / that the [Amphictyonic] Council   35 knows how to return adequate thanks to those who confer benefactions on them and on all the Greeks, with good fortune, be it resolved by the Amphictyonic Council to praise Nicostratus son of Anaxippus, a Thessalian from Larisa / and honour him with the god's crown and with   40 a bronze statue for his merits and for his constant devotion to the Amphictyonic Council [and the] other Greeks, and to place his statue in the sanctuary of Pythian Apollo. / The assembled *hieromnemones*   45 shall proclaim the crown and the statue at the next Pythian festival at the gymnastic contest; they shall also be proclaimed at the *Eleutheria*[7] at the gymnastic contest celebrated by the Thessalians.

Syll.[3] 613 A (but see G. Daux, *Delphes au IIe*
et au Ier siècle (Paris, 1936), 280–92)

1. This seems to be directed against the Aetolians (A. Giovannini in *Ancient Macedonia* I (1970), 147–54), but also by implication against Philip V (F. W. Walbank in *Ancient Macedonia* II (1977), 89–91, against Giovannini).
2. See **52** n. 2.
3. Unspecified.
4. See n. 1.
5. Another obscure allusion; possibly a conference of Greek states held in 186 to discuss the reorganisation of the Amphictyony.
6. Unspecified.
7. A festival at Larisa in Thessaly founded in 196 in honour of the Romans for their liberation of Greece (see **68**).

73 Philip's measures to rebuild Macedon (from 185)

See further: F. W. Walbank, *Philip V of Macedon* (Cambridge, 1940), 223f.; Rostovtzeff II (1941), 632–4 and III, 1470–2.

These measures[1] appeased the king's (Philip V) resentment against the Romans. For all that he never relaxed his efforts to build up his power in time of peace, for use in time of war whenever a favourable opportunity offered.[2] He increased the revenues of the kingdom, partly from (taxes on) agricultural produce and harbour dues but partly also from the mines, restarting old ones which had been left idle and opening up new ones in many places. To restore the country's previously flourishing population, which had been depleted in the disasters of the war,[3] besides seeking to increase the birthrate by compelling all to have children and to bring them up, he had even settled a large number of Thracians in Macedon.[4] The long respite from wars he had enjoyed enabled him to devote all his care to building up the resources of the kingdom.[5]

Livy XXXIX.24.1–4

1. Steps in the consolidation of Macedon's borders.
2. Livy's presentation of Philip's policy as warlike in intention is tendentious (cf. e.g. Errington (1971), 288 n. 30; see however E. S. Gruen, *GRBS* 15 (1974), 221–46).
3. See also **60**; it is in fact doubtful whether Macedon's population could have been described as 'flourishing' at any time during the third century. See also Livy XXXIII.3 (Philip's recruitment problems in 197).
4. See **77, 79** n. 4.
5. For the resources of Macedon see generally **79**.

74 Regulations on military discipline in the Macedonian army (reign of Philip V)

Livy's brief account of the reforms of Philip V makes no explicit mention of military reforms (see **73**). The following fragmentary inscription from Amphipolis, one of several texts dealing with military matters in the reign of Philip, preserves part of the code of discipline of the Macedonian army; it is not clear whether it belongs to the context of those reforms or dates from earlier in Philip's reign. The order of the fragments (two fragments of a text laid out on at least three columns) is uncertain; Moretti's text is followed here.

See further: F. W. Walbank, *Philip V of Macedon* (Cambridge, 1940), 289–94; Rostovtzeff III (1941), 1470 n. 37.

(A1) [. . . the watchmen] must not reply to the patrols, but must keep quiet and show that they are present and on their feet. *Concerning patrols.*
5 In each *strategia*[1] the tetrarchs must go the rounds in turn / without any

136

light and anyone who is sitting down or [sleeping] while on guard duty the tetrarchs shall fine one drachma for every offence and the secretaries (*grammateis*) shall obtain the payment [of the fine . . .]

(B1) . . . they shall punish according to the written rules those who are not bearing the arms appropriate to them: two obols for the *kottybos*,[2] the same amount for the *konos*,[3] three obols for the *sarissa*,[4] the same amount for the dagger, two obols for the greaves, a drachma for the shield. / In 5 the case of officers double the fine for the weapons mentioned, and two drachmas for the corslet and one drachma for the half-corslet. The secretaries and the chief attendants (*archyperetai*) shall receive the fines after reporting the offenders to the king.[5] / *Concerning discipline over war* 10 *booty.* [If] anyone brings booty to the camp, [the] generals[6] taking with them the speirarchs and tetrarchs [and] the other officers, and together with these the [attendants] in sufficient numbers shall go to meet them at a distance of three stades in front of the camp,[7] / [and they shall not 15 allow] those who captured the booty to keep it. And should any insubordination [of this kind] take place, the [officers?], speirarchs, tetrarchs and chief attendants shall pay a sum equivalent [to what each of them owes?] (the last 4 lines are very mutilated)

(A2) [. . . if they do not report] the offenders [to the king] they shall be fined three twelfths of a drachma (?)[8] which shall be given to the hypaspists[9] in case they were first to send in a written denunciation of the offenders. *Concerning the construction of the camp.* When they have completed the enclosure for the king and the rest of his quarters and an interval has been left, they shall straightaway build barracks for the hypaspists . . .

(B2) (The first 10 lines are very fragmentary) 10

[. . . the superintendent] of the court; and if [. . . they shall fine him] a twelfth of an obol[10] and the superintendent of [the court] shall do [the] same thing. *Concerning [foraging]. /* If anyone [forages] in [enemy] 15 territory, [a reward for his denunciation?] shall be promised and given [. . . And if anyone?] burns crops or [cuts] vines [or] is guilty [of any other offence, the generals shall promise?] a reward for his denunciation . . .

(A3) [. . .] [anyone who has been awarded?] a crown shall receive a double share [of the] booty, but nothing is to be given to the *cheiristes*,[11] [and] the 'friends'[12] of the king [shall adjudicate?]. *Concerning the watchwords.* They shall also take the [watchword . . . when?] they close the entrances to the [king's quarters . . .]

Moretti II.114

1. The different units of the Macedonian army are called (from larger to smaller) *strategia*, *speira* and *tetrarchia* (itself subdivided into four *lochoi*); the exact size of each is uncertain (*ca* 1,000, 250 and 60 respectively?).

2. The only known example of the word, perhaps analogous with the *kossymbos* which protected the belly.
3. A type of helmet.
4. See **67**.
5. Here and elsewhere in the inscription the military character of the Macedonian monarchy and court is evident.
6. Each general commands a *strategia* (see n. 1).
7. Concealment of booty would be much more difficult in the open field than in the camp (cf. Polybius x.17.1–5).
8. The precise sum indicated is unclear.
9. The hypaspists appear here as a military police while below they are shown as a royal bodyguard.
10. See n. 8.
11. Probably an official in charge of the division of the booty, who was expected to make a profit from his office.
12. See **25** and n. 3.

75 The mood in the Greek world on the eve of the Third Macedonian War (171)

In the consulship of P. Licinius and C. Cassius (171) it was not just the city of Rome and Italy, but all the kings and cities in Europe and Asia who anxiously turned their attention to the (impending) war between Macedon and Rome. Eumenes was moved by his old hatred and also by recent feelings of anger for having very nearly fallen like a sacrificial victim to the plot of the king (Perseus) at Delphi.[1] Prusias the king of Bithynia had decided not to resort to arms and to wait for the outcome; the Romans could not think it right for him to take up arms against the brother of his wife, and should Perseus win he would obtain his pardon through his sister.[2] Ariarathes the king of Cappadocia, besides promising personally to support the Romans, had identified himself with all the policies of Eumenes in war and peace ever since he had become his relative.[3] Antiochus,[4] it is true, was threatening the kingdom of Egypt, and despised the king's youth and the incapacity of his tutors; he believed that by provoking a dispute about Coele Syria he would gain a pretext for war and there would be no obstacle on his way as the Romans would be involved in the Macedonian war. Nonetheless, as regards the war, he had strenuously made every promise to the Senate through his own envoys and in person to their representatives. Ptolemy (VI Philometor) because of his age was still dependent on others; his tutors were preparing the war against Antiochus to stake their claim to Coele Syria, and at the same time were promising everything to the Romans for the Macedonian war. Masinissa[5] was helping the Romans by sending them grain and was getting ready to send to the war auxiliaries with elephants and his son Misagenes. He had laid his plans to meet any eventuality: should victory stay with the Romans his own position would remain the same as before; he would not make any further movement, since the Romans would not suffer him to use force against the Carthaginians. But if the power of Rome, which at the time was protecting the Carthaginians, was shattered, the whole of Africa would be his. Genthius the king of Illyria had given cause for suspicion to the Romans rather than taken a positive decision as to which side he would support, and gave the impression that he would join one side or the other on impulse rather than through careful consideration.[6] The Thracian Cotys, king of the Odrysians, had long taken the side of the Macedonians. (30) While these were the feelings of the kings about the war, among the free peoples and nations the common people sided, as usually happens, with the worse cause and favoured the king and the Macedonians;[7] the inclinations of the leading men could be seen to vary. Some backed the Romans with so little restraint that their excess of zeal destroyed their authority; of these a few were attracted by the justice of Roman rule, but a greater number believed they would be influential in their own cities if they had shown conspicuous devotion to the Romans. The second group was that of the king's flatterers; some were in debt and despaired for their future if the status quo persisted, and this drove them headlong to general revolution; others acted on their fickle temperament, as popular favour was moving more in the direction of Perseus. The third group consisted of the best and wisest citizens, who preferred to be under the Romans than under the king, if at least they were given the chance to decide which master they preferred; had they been given freedom to choose their fate they wanted neither side to become more powerful through the annihilation of the other, but rather that the forces on each side should remain intact and that peace should be preserved on a basis of equality. Their own states, placed between the two powers, would in this way be in the best position, as one side would always protect the weak against harm from the other. Such were their feelings as they observed in silence and from a position of safety the conflicts of the supporters of the two parties.

Livy XLII.29–30.7

1. Eumenes II of Pergamum had survived an attempt (?) on his life at Delphi in 172, allegedly instigated by Perseus (Livy XLII.15–16 and 18; see also **76**).
2. Prusias was married to Perseus' sister Apama.
3. Eumenes was married to Ariarathes' sister Stratonice; cf. **210**(c).
4. On Antiochus IV and Egypt see **164, 165**.
5. A Numidian ruler and client of Rome.
6. See also **76**.

7. The exact role of social divisions in the Greek world in determining attitudes towards Rome is controversial; cf. Rostovtzeff II (1941), 611–15; J. Briscoe in *Studies in Ancient Society* ed. M. I. Finley (London, 1974), 53–73; E. S. Gruen, *American Journal of Ancient History* I (1976), 29–60 (argues for a literary stereotype in Livy); D. Mendels, *Ancient Society* 9 (1978), 55–73. For one illustration of the divisions in Greek states towards Rome see **78**.

76 Letter (?) of the Romans to the Delphic Amphictyony, recounting grievances against Perseus (171–170?)

Though highly mutilated, and consequently very conjectural in restoration, the nature of the following inscription seems clear; it is a manifesto sent by the Romans (or by a Roman official) to the Delphic Amphictyony, listing the Roman charges against Perseus in the Third Macedonian War. The grievances listed are close to those known from the literary evidence (see especially Livy XLII.11–14, Eumenes' speech to the Roman Senate; Livy XLII.40, speech of Q. Marcius Philippus to Perseus; compare **75**). The Roman charges are largely flimsy; Perseus' real crime, in the Roman view, was probably that he sought to behave as an equal of Rome and not as her client.

See further: Errington (1971), 206–12; W. V. Harris, *War and Imperialism in Republican Rome* (Oxford, 1979), 227–33; F. W. Walbank in *Ancient Macedonia* II (1977), 81–94.

(the first 6 lines are too mutilated for continuous restoration)
[. . .] Perseus, contrary to what is proper [came with his army to Delphi during the sacred truce of the] Pythian festival;[1] [it was altogether] unjust [to allow him to enter or to participate in the offering to the oracle], the sacrifices, the competitions [or the common Amphictyonic Council of

10 the Greeks. For he] / called on the help of the [barbarians who live] across the [Danube, who on a former occasion massed together for] no [good purpose] but to enslave [all the Greeks, invaded Greece and] marched against the sanctuary [of Pythian Apollo at Delphi, with the intention of sacking] and destroying it, but they met [a fitting punishment at the hands of the gods, and most of them were killed].[2] And he (Perseus) broke the [sworn treaty which we made with his father and

15 which he himself renewed]. / And [he defeated and drove from their homes] the Thracians, [our friends and allies]. And [Abroupolis] whom we included in the [treaty with him as our friend and ally], he expelled from his kingdom.[3] Of the ambassadors [sent by the Greeks and the kings] to Rome to conclude an alliance, [he drowned] the [Thebans and sought to remove the others in various ways]. Indeed, he became so deranged [that he planned to poison the Roman Senate (!). And the

20 Dolopians] were deprived / of their freedom through [his attacks. In Aetolia he planned war and massacres] and [threw] the whole people into

a state of confusion [and strife. And in the whole of Greece] he constantly
acted [in the most detrimental way, planning] various other [crimes
including giving refuge to exiles from the cities. And] he corrupted the
leading statesmen, [courted at the same time the favour of the masses,
promised cancellation of debts and] caused revolutions,[4] [making] clear
[his policy towards the Greeks and Romans]. / As a result disasters   25
[beyond repair] have befallen the [Perrhaebi, Thessalians and Aetolians],
and the barbarians [have become an even greater source of terror to the
Greeks. He has long desired] war [against us],[5] his aim being to [render
us] helpless and enslave [all the Greek cities without anyone opposing
him; he bribed Genthius the Illyrian[6] and instigated him against us]. King
Eumenes [our friend and ally, he tried to assassinate[7] through the agency
of Euander], / at the time when [he went to Delphi] to fulfil [his vow, in   30
complete disregard of the safety guaranteed by the] god (Apollo) to all
who come [to visit him and attaching no importance to the sanctity and
inviolability of the city of Delphi which has been recognised] by all men,
[Greeks] and barbarians from the beginning [of time . . .]
(the rest of the inscription is too mutilated for continuous restoration)

Syll.[3] 643; Sherk no. 40 A

1. In 174.
2. See **48**.
3. Years earlier, in 179; Abroupolis had attacked Perseus, and in any case it is not
   clear that he was a friend and ally of Rome.
4. See **75** n. 7 for this Roman allegation.
5. For this Roman pretence see also **73**.
6. See **75**.
7. See **75**.

77 Perseus' forces in 171

The meeting of this council was held at Pella[1] in the old palace of the
kings of Macedon. 'Let us therefore wage war with the help of the gods',
the king (Perseus) said, 'since that is your opinion.' He despatched a
circular letter to his governors and assembled all his forces at Citium, a
town in Macedonia. He himself sacrificed a hundred victims in regal
style to Athena whom they call Alcidemus, and departed for Citium
with a group of wearers of the purple[2] and of attendants. All the troops
of the Macedonians and of the foreign auxiliaries had already gathered
there. He pitched camp in front of the city and drew up all his armed
forces in the plain; they added up to a total of 43,000 men, nearly half of
which consisted of soldiers of the phalanx, commanded by Hippias of
Beroea. From all the troops carrying a light shield (*caetrati*) 2,000 were

selected for their strength and the vigour of their youth: they themselves call this unit the *agema*, and it had as commanders Leonnatus and Thrasippus, from Euia.[3] The commander of the remaining troops with a light shield, who numbered nearly 3,000 men, was Antiphilus of Edessa. The Paeonians from Parorea and Parastrymonia, districts which neighbour on Thrace, and the Agrianes, to whom were also added Thracian settlers,[4] constituted a force of nearly 3,000 men. Didas the Paeonian, the assassin of the young Demetrius,[5] had armed and brought these together. There were also 2,000 Gauls under arms, under the command of Asclepiodotus. From Heraclea Sintice[6] 3,000 free Thracians had their own commander. An almost equal number of Cretans followed their own commanders, Susus of Phalasarna and Syllus of Cnossus.[7] The Lacedaemonian Leonides commanded 500 troops of mixed origins from Greece. He was said to be of royal blood and to have been exiled and condemned by a general meeting of the Achaean assembly when letters from him to Perseus were intercepted. Lycon the Achaean commanded the Aetolians and Boeotians whose numbers did not exceed 500. From these auxiliaries provided by so many peoples and nations a force of nearly 12,000 men was made up. As for cavalry, Perseus had collected from the whole of Macedon 3,000 men. Cotys, son of Seuthes, king of the Odrysian people, had come to the same place (Citium) with 1,000 picked cavalry and about the same number of infantry. And so the total numbers of the army added up to 39,000 infantry and 4,000 cavalry. It was generally agreed that, next to the army which Alexander took across to Asia,[8] no king of Macedon had ever had such a large number of troops.

Livy XLII.51

1. After the Roman decision to go to war. On the council of kings cf. **147** n. 4.
2. See **79** n. 8.
3. An emendation by P. Meloni.
4. See **73**.
5. The younger brother of Perseus, poisoned by Philip V in 180 for being a puppet of Roman policy (Errington (1971), 198–201).
6. See **79**.
7. See **95** n. 4.
8. See **3**.

78 Decree of the Senate concerning Thisbae in Boeotia (170)

In 172, during the build-up of the Third Macedonian War, a Roman delegation succeeded in breaking up the pro-Macedonian Boeotian League, though Haliartus, Coronea and Thisbae remained anti-Roman. Thisbae was induced in 171 to

surrender to a Roman army and was placed in the hands of a pro-Roman faction
(Livy XLII.63.12) which then deputised to Rome (in 170) to obtain a ruling from
the Senate on numerous matters relating to the city's surrender. The inscription
gives vivid evidence of the divisions in Greek cities (see **75** and n. 7) and of the
Roman need to protect their followers.

See further: Larsen (1968), 463–6; Errington (1971), 211 and 215–17.

Quintus Maenius son of Titus, praetor, consulted the Senate in the
Comitium on the 9th of October. Present at the writing (of the decree)
were Manius Acilius son of Manius, of the tribe Voltinia, / and Titus   5
Numisius son of Titus. Concerning the matters affecting them about
which the Thisbaeans spoke, requesting that they, who had remained in
our friendship, should be given an opportunity to explain the matters
that affect them; concerning this / matter it was resolved as follows: that   10
Quintus Maenius the praetor should appoint five senators who seem to
him suitable as regards the public interest and his own good faith.
Accepted. On the 14th of October; present at the writing (of the
decree) / were Publius Mucius son of Quintus, Marcus Claudius son of   15
Marcus, Manius Sergius son of Manius. Likewise concerning the matters
about which the same men spoke, viz. (their) territory, harbours,
revenues and mountains, it was resolved that what did belong to them
they should be allowed to have as far as we are concerned.[1] / Concerning   20
(their) magistracies, sanctuaries and shrines, that they themselves should
control them, about this matter it was resolved as follows: all those who
(came over) to our friendship before Gaius Lucretius led his army against
the city of Thisbae[2] should control them for the next ten years.
Accepted. / Concerning (their) territory, houses and belongings: it was   25
resolved that whoever owned any of these should be allowed to have
their own property. Likewise concerning the matters about which the
same men spoke, requesting that their men who had deserted (to the
Romans) and were exiles there should be allowed to fortify the citadel
and settle there, as they declared, it was resolved as follows: / that they   30
settle there and fortify the place. Accepted. It was resolved that they
should not fortify the city. Likewise concerning the matters about which
the same men spoke, that the gold which they had contributed for a
crown to be dedicated on the Capitol should be restored to them, as they
declared, so as to dedicate that crown on / [the] Capitol; it was resolved   35
to restore the gold on these terms.[3] Likewise concerning the matters
about which the same men spoke, that the men who were opposed to our
public interests and to theirs should be arrested; about this matter it was
resolved to do as seemed to the praetor Quintus Maenius to be consonant
with the public interest and his own good faith. / About their request   40
that all those who departed to other cities and had failed to present
themselves before our praetor should not be reinstated in their (former)

rank; concerning this matter it was resolved to send a letter to the consul Acilius Hostilius, that he should give his attention to this matter in
45 whatever way seemed to him consonant with the public interest and / his own good faith. Accepted. Likewise concerning the matters about which the same men spoke,[4] viz. the lawsuits of Xenopithis and Mnasis, that these women should be let out of Chalcis and (similarly) Damocrita daughter of Dionysius (should be let out) of Thebes; it was resolved to let these women out of these cities and not allow them to return to Thisbae.
50 Accepted. / Likewise concerning what they said about these women having brought vases full of money to the praetor; it was resolved to discuss this matter later in the presence of Gaius Lucretius. Likewise concerning the matters about which the same Thisbaeans spoke, the business partnership in grain and olive oil made by them with Gnaeus
55 Pandosinus;[5] about this matter / it was resolved to give them judges if they wish to have them. Likewise concerning the matters about which the same men spoke, requesting that the citizens of Thisbae going to Aetolia and Phocis should be given travel visas; about this matter it was resolved to give travel visas to the citizens of Thisbae and Coronea whenever they wish to go to Aetolia, Phocis, or any other cities.

Syll.[3] 646; Sherk no. 2; F. G. Maier,
Griechische Mauerbauinschriften I (Heidelberg, 1959),
no. 28 (in part)

1. I.e. Rome had initially confiscated these and was now returning them to the pro-Roman faction in Thisbae.
2. In 171 (Livy XLII.63.12).
3. I.e. the gold had been confiscated by the anti-Romans.
4. The next two requests are obscurely phrased and conjectural in interpretation.
5. An Italian businessman; the reference is probably to public lands leased to him on condition of paying part of the produce to the city of Thisbae.

79 The Roman settlement and partition of Macedon (167)

See further: J. A. O. Larsen in *An Economic Survey of Ancient Rome* ed. T. Frank, IV (Baltimore, 1938), 294–300; *id.* (1968), 295–300 and 475–82; Errington (1971), 221–6, 229–33; M. H. Crawford, *Economic History Review* 2nd series 30 (1977), 43–5.

A herald proclaimed silence and Paulus[1] read out in Latin what had been decided by the Senate and by himself in consultation with his council. Cn. Octavius the praetor, who was also present, translated the terms into Greek and repeated them. They were as follows: first of all the

Macedonians were to be free,² keep possession of their cities and lands, use their own laws, and appoint annual magistrates; they were to pay to the Roman people half of the tribute they had paid to the kings. Then Macedon was to be divided into four regions: the first part would comprise all the territory between the Strymon and the river Nessus; to this part were to be added across the Nessus to the east the villages, forts and towns which Perseus had controlled, except for Aenus, Maronea and Abdera, and across the Strymon to the west the whole of the land of the Bisaltae, with Heraclea which they call Sintice. The second region was to consist of the territory bounded in the east by the river Strymon, apart from Sintice, Heraclea and the Bisaltae, and in the west by the river Axius, with the addition of the Paeonians who dwell near the river Axius on the eastern side. The third part comprised the territory bounded by the Axius in the east and the river Peneus in the west; to the north Mt Bora forms a barrier; to this part was added the region of Paeonia which stretches from the west along the river Axius; Edessa and Beroea were also included in this part. The fourth region consisted of the territory beyond Mt Bora, bounded on one side by Illyria and on the other by Epirus. The capitals of the regions, where their assemblies would meet, were Amphipolis for the first, Thessalonica for the second, Pella for the third and Pelagonia for the fourth. He ordered that assemblies of each region should be appointed there, money brought in and magistrates appointed. He then ruled that there should be no right of intermarriage and no buying or selling of land or houses between inhabitants of one region and those of another. The gold and silver mines were to be closed down,³ but the working of the iron and copper mines was allowed. The tax on those working the mines was fixed at half of what they paid to the kings. He forbade the use of imported salt. When the Dardanians asked to be given back Paeonia, on the ground that it had been theirs and adjoined their boundaries, he announced that freedom was being granted to all who had been under the rule of Perseus. But after refusing them Paeonia he granted them the right to import salt; he ordered the third region to bring salt to Stobi in Paeonia, and fixed the price. He allowed the regions which had barbarians as their neighbours (and all had with the exception of the third) to maintain armed guards on their frontiers.

(30) This proclamation on the first day of the gathering met with a mixed response. The unexpected grant of freedom and the alleviation of the annual tax raised men's spirits; but the interruption of relations between one region and another seemed to them like breaking Macedon into pieces and leaving her like an animal torn into parts, each of which needed the other: so completely were the Macedonians themselves unaware of the size of Macedon, how easily it could be divided, how each part could exist on its own. The first region has the Bisaltae, men of

great courage (they live across the river Nessus and around the Strymon), and many peculiar kinds of crops, mines, and the strategic town of Amphipolis which forms a barrier on all the eastern routes of access into Macedon. The second part has the very populous cities of Thessalonica and Cassandrea and in addition Pallene, a land which is fertile and productive. The harbours of Torone, Mt Athos, Aenea and Acanthus also provide good outlets to the sea, some being suitably turned towards Thessaly and the island of Euboea, others towards the Hellespont. The third region has the famous cities of Edessa, Beroea and Pella, and the warlike race of the Vettii, and also a large population of Gauls and Illyrians, who are energetic farmers.[4] The fourth region is inhabited by the Eordaei, the Lyncestians and Pelagonians; next to these there is Atintania, Tymphaeis and Elimiotis. This whole region is cold, difficult to cultivate and harsh; the character of its inhabitants resembles that of the land. The neighbouring barbarians make them fiercer, giving them practice in war and intermingling their customs in peace. In this way the division of Macedon showed, by separating the advantages of its various parts, how great the country was as a whole. [. . .]

(32) After the interruptions caused by these investigations into foreign matters, the council of the Macedonians was again summoned; concerning the organisation of Macedonia it was announced that they must appoint senators (they call them *synhedri*) to form a council to govern the state.[5] Then they read out the names of the leading Macedonians who, it had been decided, were to be sent ahead to Italy together with their children above the age of fifteen.[6] This seemed at first a cruel act but was soon seen by the mass of Macedonians as having been done to protect their freedom. The names were those of the 'friends' of the king[7] and the wearers of the purple,[8] the commanders of the armies, the officers of the navy or of garrisons, men who had been accustomed to be humble in the king's service but to lord it arrogantly over others.[9] Some were immensely rich, others, though they did not possess comparable wealth, equalled them in their expenditure. All enjoyed a royal style of eating and dressing, but were devoid of affability and intolerant of the laws of freedom and equality. And so all who had held any post at court, even those who had served as ambassadors, were ordered to leave Macedon and to proceed to Italy; death was the penalty announced for anyone who disobeyed the order. Paulus gave laws to Macedon with so much care that he seemed to be granting them to loyal allies and not to defeated enemies – laws which not even use over a long period of time, the only real means of improving legislation, could prove by experience to be faulty.[10]

Livy XLV.29.3–30; 32.1–7

1. L. Aemilius Paulus, consul for the second time in 168, defeated Perseus at Pydna (22 June 168).
2. I.e. the Macedonian monarchy was abolished, the first of the Hellenistic monarchies to be overthrown by Rome, though Rome did not take over the country; the Macedonian people had no previous experience of republican self-government.
3. They were reopened in 158 and coinage was reintroduced.
4. An example of the Macedonian policy of settling barbarians in Macedon (see **73, 77**).
5. The detail of the institutions of the four Macedonian republics is controversial; see Larsen, *op. cit.*
6. After Pydna numerous Greek statesmen were victimised or deported to Italy, among them the historian Polybius; Epirus was devastated and 150,000 prisoners sold into slavery.
7. See **25** n. 3.
8. Hellenistic kings granted their 'friends' the right to wear purple as a mark of rank; see M. Reinhold, *History of purple as a status symbol in Antiquity* (Brussels, *Collection Latomus* 116, 1970), 29–36.
9. Contrast Cleomenes of Sparta (**56**(a)).
10. In fact after the settlement of 167 Macedon proved unstable and Rome eventually turned the country into a province in 146 after the revolt of the pretender Andriscus (cf. **193**).

80   The Roman treatment of Rhodes after Pydna (165)

Rhodes had initially been on the Roman side against Philip V (see **65**) then against Antiochus III, and increased her power as a result of the settlement of Apamea (see **161, 200**). After Pydna, the Roman attitude changed; it is not clear that past Rhodian actions were sufficient to justify Rome's new policy.

See further, on Rhodes' relations with Rome, Errington (1971), 192–4 and 249–52; E. S. Gruen, *CQ* n.s. 25 (1975), 58–71.

After this the Senate called in the Rhodians and listened to what they had to say. Astymedes came in and adopted a more moderate and better position than on his previous embassy. [. . .] He then went on to give a summary list of the losses the Rhodians had suffered: there was first the loss of Lycia and Caria, territories on which they had from the start spent a considerable amount of money, since they had had to fight three wars against them, and now they had been deprived of considerable revenues they used to draw from them.[1] 'But perhaps', he said, 'this was justifiable; you gave them to the Rhodian people as a favour because you were well disposed to us, and so when you cancelled the gift this seemed a justifiable thing to do, as you were now suspicious and at variance with us. But Caunus, at any rate, we purchased from the generals of Ptolemy and Stratonicea we received as a great favour from Antiochus and (or: son of) Seleucus;[2] from these two cities the Rhodian people drew an annual income of 120 talents. We have been deprived of all these revenues, although it was our wish to obey your instructions. It seems from this that you have imposed a heavier tribute on the Rhodians for their mistake than you have on the Macedonians who have always been your enemies. But the greater disaster to befall our city is the loss of the revenues from the harbour, since you made Delos a free port and deprived our people of the independence which guaranteed that the interests of the harbour and all the other interests of the city were properly defended. The truth of this is easy to see: in former times the harbour tax produced one million drachmas in revenue, but now [you have fixed it] at 150,000, so that your anger, men of Rome, has affected the chief revenues of the city all too severely. [. . .] And so, gentlemen, the Rhodian people, having lost its revenues, its independence and right of free speech, which previously it was prepared to make any sacrifice to defend, and having suffered enough blows, now asks and begs of you all to relax your anger, be reconciled and ratify the treaty (with us). May it thus become clear to all that you have laid aside your anger against the Rhodians and returned to your original attitude of friendship. For this is what the Rhodian people now needs, not an alliance of arms and soldiers.' These and similar words were used by Astymedes and he was thought to have spoken in a manner appropriate to the circumstances.[3] [. . .]

Polybius XXX.31 (omitting 3; 13–15; 19–20)

1. Lycia and Caria were granted by Rome to Rhodes in 188 after the defeat of Antiochus III; the grants were revoked after Pydna.
2. Caunus was acquired *ca* 191/90 from Ptolemy V; the date of the grant of Stratonicea, and the identity of the Seleucid kings mentioned, are conjectural.
3. The Senate granted the alliance (165/4), but it marked in effect the end of the long independence enjoyed by Rhodes in the Hellenistic age (see **39, 92–95**).

81 The depopulation of the Greek world in the second century

See further: J. A. O. Larsen in *Economic Survey of Ancient Rome*, ed. T. Frank IV (Baltimore, 1938), 418–22; Tarn and Griffith (1952), 100–4; Rostovtzeff II (1941), 623–32 and III, 1464–70.

In our time Greece was afflicted with a dearth of children and a general decline in population, which caused the cities to be deserted and the land to become unproductive, even though we were free from continuous wars and epidemics. Now if someone had suggested about this that we should send to consult the gods on what we needed to say or do to increase our numbers and make our cities more populous, would he not have seemed a foolish person when the cause is evident and the remedy lies with ourselves? For the evil quickly developed without anyone noticing when men turned to a life of empty pretensions, love of money and even idleness, and became unwilling to marry, or if they did to bring up the children they had, or as a general rule more than one or two so as to leave them wealthy and bring them up in a life of luxury.[1] For when there are one or two children, and war carries one away and illness the other, it is clear that the households must be left empty and, just as is the case with swarms of bees, similarly do the cities decline in numbers little by little and lose their strength. On this matter there is no need to ask the gods how we are to be delivered from such an evil; anybody will tell you that the surest remedy lies with the individuals themselves changing the objects of their ambition, or failing this, passing laws to enforce the rearing of children. There is no need here for prophets or prodigies.

Polybius XXXVI. 17. 5–10

1. Polybius' moralising view ignores social and economic causes such as the disturbed and uncertain conditions of the time; moreover his remarks apply primarily to upper class Greeks like himself and may not be equally true of the whole of the Greek world. Compare also his comments on Boeotia (see **84**).

82 The sack of Corinth by the Romans (146)

Because of the loss of most of Polybius' account (which was in any case biased against the Achaean leaders), the 'Achaean War' of 147/6 and the Roman settlement of Greece that followed are very imperfectly known. Pausanias, the chief extant source, is inaccurate in many details.

See further: J. A. O. Larsen in *Economic Survey of Ancient Rome*, ed. T. Frank, IV (1938), 303–11 and *id.* (1968), 489–504; Errington (1971), 236–41; on the Achaean War specifically see A. Fuks, *JHS* 90 (1970), 78–89 and E. S. Gruen, *JHS* 96 (1976), 46–69.

The Achaeans who had taken refuge in Corinth after the battle escaped from the city as soon as night fell, together with the majority of the Corinthians. Although the gates were opened, Mummius[1] first hesitated to enter Corinth, as he suspected some ambush lying within the walls; two days after the battle he stormed and burned Corinth. The Romans put to death the majority of the people found in the city, while Mummius sold the women and children into slavery; he also sold all the slaves who had received their freedom and fought on the side of the Achaeans[2] and had not been killed at once in the war. Mummius carried

149

off the most remarkable votive offerings and other works of art, and gave the less interesting ones to Philopoemen, the general sent by Attalus (II); even in my time there were spoils from Corinth at Pergamum. All the cities which had fought against the Romans had their walls razed and were deprived of their arms by Mummius even before the sending of the senatorial commission of advisers from Rome. When they arrived, Mummius overthrew the democracies and set up constitutions based on wealth;[3] tribute was imposed in Greece[4] and men of wealth were forbidden to acquire property abroad. All the federal councils, in Achaea, in Phocis, in Boeotia and everywhere else in Greece, were likewise dissolved.[5] A few years later the Romans were moved to pity for Greece, and restored to all their ancient federal councils and the right to acquire property abroad, and they cancelled the fines imposed by Mummius. He had ordered the Boeotians to pay 100 talents to the people of Heraclea and Euboea, and the Achaeans 200 to the Spartans. And so the Greeks obtained remission of these from the Romans, but a governor has continued to be sent (to Greece) up to my time.[6] The Romans call him governor not of Greece, but of Achaea, because when they subdued the Greeks the Achaeans were then the leading people in the Greek world.[7] This war came to an end in the archonship of Antitheus at Athens, in the 160th Olympiad, at which Diodorus of Sicyon was victorious. (17) It was then that Greece fell to the weakest point in its history, although parts of it had been ruined and devastated by the divinity from the beginning. [. . .]

Pausanias VII. 16. 7–17. 1

1. L. Mummius, consul in 146.
2. Cf. **65** n. 3.
3. This probably applies only to the states that had gone to war against Rome; see also **75** n. 7.
4. Misleading: Greece as a whole was not made tributary.
5. Again the measure probably applied only to the Leagues that had been on the anti-Roman side.
6. Greece was placed under the supervision of the Roman governor of Macedon, and not turned into a separate province as Pausanias implies; this only happened in 27 B.C. After 146 most of Greece was still theoretically 'free'.
7. Cf. **53** ch. 38.

4 The Greek cities: social and economic conditions

[*Note:* The texts in this chapter are grouped as follows: **83–98** texts arranged geographically; **99–116** aspects of economic life (public finances, coinage, market legislation, the corn supply); **117–131** aspects of society and religion; **132–137** relations between cities.]

83 A third-century description of central Greece

See further: Rostovtzeff I (1941), 210f. and III 1368f. (nn. 35 and 36); Walbank III (1979), 72.

(1.1) From here[1] to the city of Athens [is a distance of . . .] The road is pleasant, passes through countryside that is all cultivated, and offers pleasing scenery. The city itself is all dry and does not have a good water supply; the streets are narrow and winding, as they were built long ago.[2] Most of the houses are cheaply built, and only few reach a higher standard; a stranger would find it hard to believe at first sight that this was the famous city of Athens, though he might soon come to believe it. There you will see the most beautiful sights on earth: a large and impressive theatre, a magnificent temple of Athena, something out of this world and worth seeing, the so-called Parthenon, which lies above the theatre; it makes a great impression on sightseers. There is the Olympieum, which though only half-completed is impressively designed, though it would have been most magnificent if completed. There are three gymnasia: the Academy, the Lyceum and the Cynosarges; they are all planted with trees and laid out with lawns. They have festivals of all sorts, and philosophers from everywhere pull the wool over your eyes and provide recreation; there are many opportunities for leisure and spectacles without interruption. (2) The produce of the land is all priceless and delicious to taste, though in rather short supply. But the presence of foreigners, which they are all accustomed to and which fits in with their inclinations, causes them to forget about their stomach by diverting their attention to pleasant things. Because of the spectacles and entertainments in the city, the common people have no experience of

151

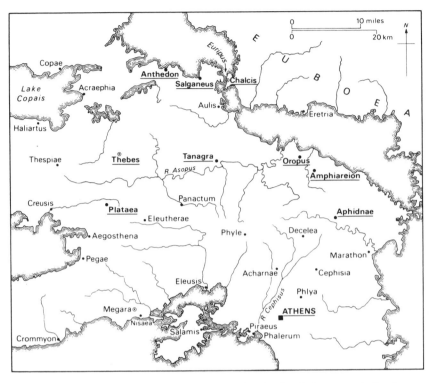

3 Central Greece (to illustrate **83**). Places mentioned in the description are underlined. Adapted from *CAH* VI, map 7

hunger, as they are made to forget about food, but for those who have money there is no city comparable in the pleasures it offers. The city also has many other delights; the cities which neighbour it are suburbs of Athens. [. . .] (6) From here to Oropus via Aphidnae and the sanctuary of Zeus Amphiaraus is about a day's journey for a traveller without luggage; the road is uphill. But the large number of inns, which have an abundance of all necessities, and the resting places, prevent travellers from feeling fatigue. (7) The city of Oropus belongs to Thebes. There are many retail traders here, and the greed of the customs collectors is not to be outdone; it is something which has long been congenial to them, and you could not improve on their wickedness. They collect customs on goods that are imported there. [. . .] (8) From there to Tanagra is a distance of 130 stades (*ca* 20 km.). The road passes through countryside that is planted with olive trees and is thickly wooded; it is completely free from the fear of robbers. The city lies on a rocky height; its soil is clayey and has a white appearance. The entrance halls of their houses and the encaustic paintings they display give the city a beautiful appearance. The city does not enjoy an abundance of agricultural produce, but it ranks first in Boeotia for its wine. (9) The inhabitants though wealthy are plain in their style of living; they are all farmers and not workmen. They know how to respect justice, good faith and hospitality. To their needy citizens and to wandering strangers they give from what they have and allow them to take freely;³ they are far removed from any unjust greed. It is the safest city in Boeotia for foreigners to stay in. You will find there a straight and strict dislike of evil because of the self-sufficiency and industriousness of the inhabitants. [. . .] (11) From there to Plataea is a distance of 200 stades (*ca* 35 km.). The road is somewhat deserted and stony, stretching towards Cithaeron, but not very dangerous. The comic poet Poseidippus describes the city: 'It has two temples, a stoa, and its name, and the bath and the fame of Serambus.⁴ Most of the time it is a desert, and only at the festival of the *Eleutheria*⁵ does it become a city.' The citizens have nothing to say except that they are colonists of the Athenians and that the battle between the Greeks and the Persians took place in their territory. They are Athenians among Boeotians. (12) From there to Thebes is a distance of 80 stades (*ca* 14 km.).⁶ The road is all flat and even. The city lies in the heart of Boeotia and has a circumference of 70 stades (*ca* 11½ km.).⁷ It lies on level ground, and is round in shape; the soil is dark in colour. Though an ancient city its streetplan is modern in design as, according to history books, it has already been destroyed three times⁸ because of the oppressiveness and arrogance of its inhabitants. (13) The Thebans are excellent horsebreeders; the land is all well watered, green and covered with hills, and has the largest number of gardens of any city in Greece. Two rivers flow through the land and water the whole of the plain below the city. From the Cadmea water also flows in underground channels which they say were built by Cadmus in ancient times. [. . .] (23) From there to Anthedon is a distance of 160 stades (*ca* 28 km.). It is a side road, though suitable for traffic; the journey goes through fields. The city is not large; it lies on the Euboean sea and has an agora all planted with trees and enclosed (?) by double colonnades. It has plenty of wine and fish, but is poor in corn because of the infertility of the soil. (24) The inhabitants are almost all fishermen who make their living from hooks, fishes, and also from purple shells and sponges; they have grown old on the shore, amid the seaweed and in their huts. They have red hair and are all slim; the tips of their fingernails are worn out, as they are devoted to working at sea. The majority are ferrymen and shipbuilders; they do not cultivate the land and in fact have none to cultivate, and they say they are descended from Glaucus the seaman, who is generally agreed to have been a fisherman. [. . .] (26) From Anthedon to Chalcis is a distance of 70 stades (*ca* 11½ km.). The road

153

follows the coastline as far as Salganeus; it is all flat and free from stones. On one side it leads down to the sea; on the other there is a not very high mountain, which is wooded and watered with streams. (27) The city of Chalcis has a circumference of 70 stades (*ca* 11½ km.),[9] more than the distance from Anthedon to it. It is all hilly and shaded, and has many springs, most of them salty; only one of them is somewhat brackish, though it is safe to use and cool, and flows from the spring called Arethusa, which is able to provide enough spring water to all the inhabitants of the city. (28) The city is well provided with public buildings, gymnasia, porticoes, temples, theatres, pictures, statues and an agora which is excellently situated for all trading purposes. (29) The stream which comes from Salganeus in Boeotia and the Euboean sea flows in the same direction and into the Europus; it passes along the harbour walls where there is the gate to the mart, which is next to the agora; the agora is spacious and enclosed by three colonnades. As the agora lies near the harbour and the unloading of the cargoes from the ships is quickly done, there is a large number of people who come by sea to the mart. The Euripus has two entrances and so it attracts the trader to the city. (30) Their land is all planted with olive trees; the sea is also productive. [. . .]

> Heraclides Creticus (?) 1, 1–2, 6–9, 11–13, 23–4, 26–30 (ed. F. Pfister, *Die Reisebilder des Herakleides* (Vienna, 1951)); see also K. Müller, *Fragmenta Historicorum Graecorum* II (Paris, 1848), 254–61; *id.*, *Geographici Graeci Minores* I (Paris, 1855), 97–106

1. The starting point in the description is not specified. The author of the work is unknown and is sometimes described as Ps. Dicaearchus and sometimes as Heraclides Creticus.
2. Contrast the description of Thebes in §12 below.
3. For support of the poor by the rich see **92**.
4. The identity of Serambus is obscure.
5. See **51**.
6. Overestimated, in fact *ca* 10 km.
7. Overestimated, in fact *ca* 7 km.
8. See **2**; the two other destructions belong probably to the mythical period.
9. Overestimated.

84 Chaos of public affairs in Boeotia (192)

See further: Rostovtzeff II (1941), 611f.; M. Feyel, *Polybe et l'histoire de Béotie* (1942), esp. 273–83; D. Hennig, *Chiron* 7 (1977), 119–48.

Public affairs in Boeotia had fallen to such a low state that for nearly twenty-five years justice had not been administered there, whether in private or in public cases.[1] The magistrates kept issuing orders for the despatch of garrisons or of national expeditions, and thus kept putting off the administration of justice; some of the generals would give allowances to the needy out of public funds.[2] The masses learnt in this way to listen to and invest with high office those who would enable them to escape punishment for their crimes and unpaid debts, and to expect occasional gratuities from the public funds as a favour from the magistrates.[3] No one contributed more to this [bad state of affairs] than Opheltas, who was always thinking up some new scheme apparently calculated to benefit the masses for the moment while sure to ruin everybody in future. To this was added another unfortunate craze. Men who died childless would not leave their property to their relatives, as had formerly been the custom in the country, but assigned it for feasts and drinking-parties to be shared in by their friends. Even many who had children apportioned the larger part of their property to their table mates, and as a result there were many Boeotians who had more feasts provided for them in the month than there were days in it.[4]

Polybius xx.6.1–6

1. On this problem see further **40** §6, **135, 209**.
2. Compare the Rhodian policy (see **92**).
3. On class divisions in Boeotia in the second century see **78** (Thisbae) and generally **75** and n. 7.
4. Compare **81**. Polybius' account of Boeotia is probably coloured by prejudice and its reliability is disputed.

85 The wealthy gentry of Elis in the third century

[. . .] During the devastation of the country[1] a large number of captives was made, but an even larger number made their escape to the neighbouring villages and strongholds. For the land of Elis happens to be thickly populated; it has an abundance of slaves and farm-stock, more so than the rest of the Peloponnese.[2] Some of the inhabitants are so fond of life in the country that, though they enjoy great wealth, they have not visited the law-court at all for two or three generations. This happens because those in government devote great care and attention to the country dwellers to make sure that justice is dispensed to them on the spot and they do not lack any of the necessities of life. It seems to me that this policy was thought up long ago and legislated for because of the extent of their territory, but especially because of the 'sacred' life they have led from the time when the Greeks granted them this concession owing to the Olympic Games; the land of Elis became holy and inviolate, and they have been sheltered from every danger and act of war.[3] (74) Later, because of the Arcadian claims over Lasion and the whole territory of Pisa,[4] they were compelled to defend their country and change their way of life; they no longer troubled themselves in the least about recovering from the Greeks their ancient and traditional immunity (*asylia*), but remained as they were. In my opinion they were wrong to neglect the future.

Polybius IV.73.5–74.2

1. In 219, during the 'Social War' (see **58, 59**).
2. Cf. Xenophon, *Hellenica* III.2.26.
3. The immunity Elis is supposed to have held is probably a fiction of fourth century Elean propaganda. On *asylia* cf. **151** and n. 5.
4. In 365–363.

86 Pirates and the slave trade

Though fictitious, this passage from the prologue of Menander's most recently discovered play shows how completely piracy and the slave trade were taken for granted as a reality of everyday life in the late fourth and early third centuries, and this remained true for the whole of Hellenistic history. For other examples, see **50, 52** with refs., **87–90, 92** with refs., **96, 98, 171**.

See further: H. A. Ormerod, *Piracy in the Ancient World* (Liverpool, 1924), esp. ch. 4; Rostovtzeff I (1941), 195–204 with III, 1360–6; II, 607–10 with III, 1458–60.

When they (the pirates) had seized the three of them, they did not think it worth their while to take away the old woman, but the child and the slave they took to Mylasa in Caria[1] and there offered them for sale in the market.[2] The slave was sitting there, holding his little mistress on one arm. [As they were being offered for sale] an officer came up, and asked their price. He was told it, he agreed, he [bought them]. A local slave, who was being sold a second time nearby, said to the slave: 'Cheer up, my friend, the Sicyonian officer has bought you, a very good and rich man.'

Menander, *The Sicyonian*, lines 3–15 (OCT)

1. Caria was a regular source of supply of slaves.
2. 'The pirate had a most useful place in the economy of the old world; he was the general slave merchant' (W. W. Tarn, *Antigonus Gonatas* (Oxford, 1913), 88).

87 Decree of Amorgos in honour of two men for help during an incursion of pirates (third century)

Resolved by the council and the people; Soterides son of Phidias of Cosyllus was president, Philoxenus son of Philothemis of Alsus moved: since, when pirates[1] / made an incursion into the countryside at night and captured a total of more than 30 girls, women and other persons both free and slave, and scuttled the ships in the harbour / and captured the ship of Dorieus, in which they sailed off with their captives and the rest of their booty; when all this had happened, Hegesippus and Antipappus, the sons of Hegesistratus, who were themselves prisoners, / persuaded Soclidas, the captain of the pirates, to release the free persons and some of the freedmen and slaves, and volunteered to act as hostages on their behalf, / and showed great concern that none of the citizen women or men should be carried off as booty and be sold, nor suffer torture or hardship, / and that no free person should perish;[2] thanks to these men the prisoners were saved (and returned) home without suffering harm; therefore be it resolved by the people, to crown Hegesippus and / Antipappus each with an olive wreath for their merits and the concern they showed for the citizens who were taken prisoners, and to proclaim this decree / at the Dionysia during the tragic contest; let the herald proclaim that the people crowns Hegesippus and Antipappus for their merits and the concern they showed for their / fellow prisoners. Let this decree be inscribed on a stele and placed in the sanctuary of Athena Polias, and let Hegesistratus[3] be responsible for the inscription.

Syll.[3] 521; *IG* xii.7.386

5
10
15
20
25
30
35
40

1. The identity of the pirates (e.g. Aetolians or Cretans) is not specified. On piracy see **86**.
2. Note the distinction drawn between the free prisoners and the slaves or ex-slaves. Cf. **107** l.6, **111** §1, **118** l.27, **216** ll.189–95.
3. The father of the men honoured; the inscription does not make clear how they secured their release.

88 Athens honours Eumaridas of Cydonia in Crete for rescuing victims of Aetolian pirates (217/16)

See further: Rostovtzeff I (1941), 199.

Gods. In the archonship of Heliodorus (229/8), in the eleventh prytany, of the tribe Cecropis, in the month Thargelion; Lysistratus son of Phylarchides of Oene moved: since Eumaridas both previously, / and at

5

the time when Bucris[1] overran the countryside and carried off to Crete a large number of the citizens and of the others from the city, performed many great services for the people and contributed money from his own
10 pocket for the twenty talents that had been agreed (as ransom) for / the prisoners; and (since) he lent money to the captives for their travel expenses; and (since) now, when the people (of Athens) has sent ambassadors so that good relations may be preserved with all the Cretans and so that this might be achieved if those who sail out are given the right to plunder (*laphyron*),[2] he pleaded his case so that everything should be
15 done in the best interest / of the people; and (since) he also took part in an embassy to Cnossus and her allies, and also gave letters to the ambassadors for his friends in Polyrrhenia, so that they would cooperate with them over the interests (of the people); and (since) he undertakes to show every care to ensure the preservation of good relations between the
20 people (of Athens) / and all the inhabitants of Crete; therefore, so that it may be manifest that the people is honouring those who display their favourable attitude in every circumstance, with good fortune, be it resolved by the people, to praise Eumaridas son of Pancles of Cydonia, and to crown him with a gold crown according to the law because of his
25 goodwill / and zeal towards the council and people of Athens, and to place a bronze statue of him on the acropolis. And it shall be possible for him in future to be honoured for the services he provides in a way that is fitting for the benefits conferred. The secretary of the people shall
30 inscribe this decree on a stone stele / and place it beside the statue. The treasurer of the military fund and the officials in charge of financial administration shall pay for the expense incurred in the dedication of the statue and of the stele.[3]

Syll.[3] 535; *IG* II[2].844.1

1. An Aetolian from Naupactus; on Aetolian piracy see **52**, on piracy in general see **86**.
2. I.e. the home state grants its nationals the right to seize lawfully any member of another state; see Rostovtzeff III (1941), 1458f. n. 7 and Walbank's note on Polybius IV.26.7. For Cretan piracy see also **89, 95**.
3. This inscription is the first of a group of three in honour of Eumaridas and his son Charmion attesting their friendly relations with Athens over several years.

89 Treaty between Miletus and Cretan cities against the purchase of citizens and slaves (after 260)

The agreements with the cities in Crete. (Decree) of the Cnossians. Resolved by the *kosmoi* and the city of Cnossus: concerning the matters

about which the Milesians sent the ambassadors Alcmeonides and
Evagoras, to reply to the ambassadors that / formerly when your   5
ambassadors came here we made the agreement, as the Milesians
requested,[1] and we placed it in the sanctuary of Apollo; and when the
sanctuary was burnt down you did well in sending the embassy so
that / the same agreement should be inscribed in your own city; [it   10
remained in force?] even though the agreement was not inscribed.[2] For
we think that you will receive from us all the concessions (detailed
below) and we shall preserve the friendship and goodwill which exists
from former times / towards each other as is just. And so that the other 15
Cretans should themselves make a treaty with you with greater willingness, we think it necessary to make a treaty as you have requested. A
Cnossian shall not knowingly purchase a Milesian who is a free man nor
a Milesian / a Cnossian. Anyone who purchases knowingly shall forfeit   20
the price paid and the person (bought) shall be free. If he purchases
unknowingly, he shall return the person and get back the price he paid. If
anyone buys a slave, he shall get back the price / he paid and return the 25
person. If he does not return it, he shall be brought at Cnossus before the
kosmoi and at Miletus before the presiding magistrates (*prytaneis*). The
magistrates in each state shall compel him to return the person to
whoever (rightfully) claims him, in accordance with the agreement. / If 30
any dispute arises about anything, a verdict shall be given at Cnossus by
the *kosmoi* and the council, and at Miletus by the overseers of the mart
within five days of the disputants coming before the magistrates. The
execution of the sentence against those convicted shall take place at
Cnossus in accordance with the law about *proxenoi* and at Miletus /   35
according to the law about the mart. Similar (decisions were taken by)
the Tylisians, Rhaucians, Chersonesians, Milatians, Eltynians, Herac-
leotes, Priansians, Apolloniates, Petraians, Itanians, Praisians, Istronians,
Olountians, Drerians, Latians, Eleuthernaians, Axians, Cydoniates,
Phalasarnians.[3]

Staatsv. III. 482 lines 1–39; *ICret*. I, p. 60f. no.6

1. The initiative comes from the Milesians, anxious to protect themselves against
   the activities of the Cretan pirates, on which see also **88, 95**; on piracy and the
   slave trade see **86**.
2. I.e. the Cnossians are reassuring the Milesians that the earlier treaty had
   remained in force even though the inscription recording it was lost in the fire.
3. There follow two further decrees on the same lines by Gortyn and Phaestus
   and their respective allies.

90 Itanos (Crete): oath of loyalty to the state (third century)

'Everywhere in Greece it is customary for the citizens to swear to preserve concord [cf. **51**] and everywhere they swear that oath' (Xenophon, *Memorabilia* IV.4.16). The context of the following oath from Itanos in Crete seems to be the enlargement of the citizen body by the ruling oligarchy, which sought to protect itself against revolutionary demands by the imposition of the oath on the new citizens. Cf. **91, 133, 182**, ll.64–78.

See further: R. F. Willetts, *Aristocratic Society in Ancient Crete* (London, 1955), 128f., 182, 184f., 226.

[God] is beneficent. [The following] oath[1] was sworn [by all] the Itanians, in the name of Zeus of Dicte, Hera, the [gods] at Dicte,
5 Athena / Polias, all the gods to whom sacrifices are offered in the sanctuary of Athena, Zeus Agoraeus and Pythian Apollo, over newly-
10 burnt offerings: I will not betray the city of Itanos / nor the territory or islands of the Itanians, and I will not introduce [enemies] (in the land) nor betray the ships [of] the Itanians, [and] I will [not] betray [any] of the
15 citizens / nor any of the belongings of the citizens. [And] I will not provoke an assembly or [conspiracy] for the harm of [the city] or of the
20 citizens, nor will I associate with anyone [else] who / [wishes] to do any of these things, [but] I will declare it to the magistrates. And I will not initiate a redistribution [of land] or of houses [or of] dwelling-sites nor a
25 [cancellation] of debts,[2] nor will I [bring] a corrupt suit / against [any] citizen for usurpation of citizen rights under [any] pretext. I will not plan any evil against [the city], and I will exercise my civic rights on a basis of
30 fairness and equality as regards all matters [sacred] / and human, [according to] the existing laws we use [concerning] sacred matters, the
35 laws we have now passed [and any] others we may pass in future / concerning either [sacred matters] or civil affairs, and I [will not desert] the city either in [war] or in [peace] as far as is [possible]. May those who
40 [honour] and respect the oath / be blessed with children, see their land produce crops and their flocks flourish, and may they and their children
45 enjoy [many other] blessings; but for those who break the oath / may their land be infertile, and may they be denied children and flourishing flocks, and may they perish miserably in their wickedness together with their [descendants].

Syll.[3] 526; *ICret.* III, pp. 89–91 no.8

1. For oaths see **33** n. 7.
2. For these revolutionary demands cf. **27**(a), **55–57, 75, 76**, cf. **84**. Contrast the emphasis on *homonoia* (**51**).

91 Oath of Dreros in Crete (*ca* 220?)

War between rival cities was an endemic feature of Cretan history, as shown for instance by the 'war of Lyttus' of 221/20 described by Polybius (IV.53.5–55) which may be the context of the following inscription (cf. also **124**). Whereas the oath of Itanos (see **90**) does not refer to any specific foreign threat, the oath of Dreros explicitly links loyalty to the state with the conflict of Dreros and Cnossus with another city, Lyttus.

See further: R. F. Willetts, *Aristocratic Society in Ancient Crete* (London, 1955), 119–21, 173, 182–5, 187; Walbank I (1957), 508–11.

God. Fortune. With good fortune. The *kosmoi* from the tribe Aithaleis /   5
were Cydilas, Cephalus, Pylus, Hippius, Bision; Philippus was
secretary; / the following oath was sworn by 180 ephebes (*agelai*) after   10
putting aside their boyhood garments (*panazostoi*);[1] I swear / by the   15
hearth in the prytaneum,[2] by Zeus Agoraeus, by Zeus Tallaeus, / by   20
Apollo Delphinius, by Athena Poliouchus, by Pythian Apollo, /   25
by Lato, by Artemis, by Ares, by Aphrodite, by Helios (the Sun),
by Britomartis, / by Phoenix, by Amphiona, by the Earth, by Heaven, by   30
the heroes, by the heroines, by the springs, by the rivers, / and by all the   35
gods and goddesses, that I will never be well disposed to the Lyttians in
any way or manner, / by night or by day. I will endeavour to do   40
whatever harm I am able to the city of Lyttus.[3] And I will not be bound
by any oath in lawsuits and [transactions]. / And I will be friendly to   45
Dreros and friendly to Cnossus, and I will not betray the city / of the   50
Drerians nor their forts nor those of the Cnossians; / and I will not   55
betray men of Deros or of Cnossus to the enemy, / and I will not initiate   60
factional strife (*stasis*), and I will oppose anyone who does, and I will not
form a conspiracy / in the city or outside it, and I will not join anyone   65
who does; / and if I hear that any are conspiring, I will report it to the   70
majority of the *kosmoi*; / and if I do not observe these undertakings, may   75
all the gods and goddesses by whom I swore be wroth against me, / and   80
may I die a most miserable death, myself and all my belongings, / and   85
may the earth not bear crops for me [nor] women [give birth] according
to [nature nor] flocks (give birth), / but if I [honour my oath] may [the]   90
gods by whom [I swore] be favourable [and grant many] blessings. And I
swear / by the same gods, that if the *kosmoi* do not bind by the same oath   95
which we have sworn the band of ephebes (*agela*) when they are putting
aside their boyhood garments,[4] / I will denounce them to the council   100
when / they lay down office, during the month of Comnocarius or of   105
Haliaeus; the council will fine each / of the *kosmoi* 500 staters within   110
three months of the day of the denunciation; / if they are insolvent, (the   115
council) will inscribe in the Delphinium the sum they have not

120 collected, / naming the individuals with their father's name and the sum
of money; any sum they have not collected they shall distribute to the
125 *hetaireiai*5 / in the city and to any Drerians who happen to be on guard
duty (away from the city). If the (members of) the council do not collect
130 the fine, they shall themselves / be [fined] twice the amount; the
135 collectors of the public funds will collect the fine and distribute it / to the
hetaireiai in the same way. [. . .]

> *Syll.*3 527, lines 1–136; *ICret.* II, pp. 84–8 no. 1; cf. *Staatsv.* III.584

1. See Willetts, *op. cit.*, 120f.
2. For the oath see R. F. Willetts, *Cretan Cults and Festivals* (London, 1962), index
s.v. oaths, Drerian. For other oaths see **33** n. 7.
3. Cf. Aristotle, *Politics* 1310 a 8: 'In some oligarchies nowadays they swear "I
will be hostile to the common people (*demos*) and plan whatever harm I can
against them".'
4. I.e. the oath is to be renewed annually by each new band of ephebes. On
ephebes cf. **117, 118**.
5. Clubs of adult citizens similar to the Spartan *syssitia*.

92 Strabo on Hellenistic Rhodes

See further: Rostovtzeff I (1941), 225–30; II, 676–91 and 771–8; P. M. Fraser and
G. E. Bean, *The Rhodian Peraea and Islands* (London, 1954); Préaux II (1978),
489–96.

The city of Rhodes lies on the eastern promontory (of the island); it
surpasses other cities so far in its harbours, streets, walls and other
constructions that I am unable to mention any other city that equals, let
alone surpasses this one. It is also remarkable for its good order (*eunomia*)
and for the care if devotes to the rest of its administration and especially
to naval matters; as a result it controlled the seas for a long time and
destroyed piracy,1 and became a friend to the Romans and to those of the
kings who were well disposed both to the Romans and to Greeks.2
Consequently it has preserved its independence and been adorned with
numerous votive offerings, the majority of which are in the (sanctuary
of) Dionysus and in the gymnasium, though there are others elsewhere.
[. . .] The Rhodians care for the common people (*demos*), although they
do not live under a democracy; they wish nonetheless to keep the mass of
the poor in good condition. And so the common people is provided with
food and the wealthy support those in need according to an old
tradition;3 they have liturgies4 for the provision of food, with the result
both that the poor receive sustenance and the city has no lack of available

manpower, particularly as regards the fleet. Some of the shipsheds were kept secret and access to them was forbidden to most people, and the penalty for spying or going inside was death. In Rhodes, too, as at Massilia and Cyzicus, they devote considerable attention to building works, the construction of war engines and the provisions of stores of weapons and other equipment, even more so than anywhere else.[5]

Strabo XIV.2.5 (652–3)

1. See **39, 94, 95**; on piracy in general see **86**.
2. See **93**.
3. For the support of the poor by the wealthy cf. **83** §9, **84, 113** 1.52; Tarn and Griffith (1952), 110; Hands (1968), 85. For the food supply of Greek cities see **112**.
4. See **40** n. 6.
5. It will be noted that Strabo derives the prosperity of Rhodes from her political and social stability and her consequent military power; he makes no mention of Rhodes' revenues from trade nor of her imperial income (see **39, 80, 200**).

93 The earthquake at Rhodes and the donations from foreign rulers and cities (227/6)

At about the same time the Rhodians, seizing the occasion presented by the earthquake which had taken place shortly before and in which the great Colossus and the larger part of the walls and dockyards had collapsed, used the incident in such a skilful and practical way that the disaster became a source of advantage to them rather than of damage. [. . .] Rhodian diplomacy enhanced the magnitude and importance of the disaster, while their envoys conducted themselves with dignity and seriousness in public audiences and at private meetings. In this way they made such an impression on the cities, and especially on the kings, that not only did they receive presents beyond measure but they even made the donors feel under obligation to them.[1] Hiero and Gelo[2] gave them 75 talents of silver [for the rebuilding of the walls? and] for the provision of oil in the gymnasia,[3] part at once and the rest very shortly after. They dedicated in addition silver cauldrons with their stands, and some water vessels, and added to all this (a sum of) ten talents for sacrifices and another ten for the enrichment of the citizens, with the intention that their present should add up to 100 talents. They granted furthermore exemption from customs to Rhodians sailing to their ports and presented Rhodes with 50 three-cubit catapults.[4] After making all these presents they still regarded themselves as under obligation and set up statues in the Exchange[5] at Rhodes showing the people of Rhodes being crowned by the people of Syracuse. (89) Ptolemy (III Euergetes) also promised them 300 talents of silver, a million artabas of wheat, timber for the construction of ten quinqueremes and ten triremes, consisting of 40,000 cubits of squared pine planking, 1,000 talents of bronze coinage, 3,000 talents of tow, 3,000 pieces of sail-cloth, 3,000 talents (of bronze?) for the repair of the Colossus, 100 architects with 350 workmen, and fourteen talents every year for their wages,[6] and in addition 12,000 artabas of wheat for competitions and sacrifices, and 20,000 for the supplying of ten triremes. Most of this he gave at once, as well as a third of the money promised.[7] In the same way Antigonus (Doson) promised to them 10,000 pieces of timber, varying from sixteen to eight cubits in length for use (in ships' hulls), 5,000 cross beams seven cubits long, 3,000 talents of iron, 1,000 talents of (solid) pitch and 1,000 (liquid) measures of tar, and in addition to all this 100 talents of silver.[8] His wife Chryseis also promised 100,000 (measures) of wheat and 3,000 talents of lead. Seleucus (II Callinicus) the father of Antiochus, besides granting exemption from custom dues to Rhodians sailing to his kingdom,[9] and besides giving ten quinqueremes fully equipped and 200,000 medimni of corn, gave them also 10,000 cubits of timber and 1,000 talents each of resin and hair.[10] (90) Similar gifts were made by Prusias (of Bithynia) and Mithridates (II of Pontus), and also by the dynasts ruling in Asia at the time, Lysanias, Olympichus[11] and Limnaeus. As for the cities which contributed, each according to its ability, it would be difficult to reckon their number. In fact, if one looks at the period at which the city of Rhodes began to be once more habitable, one would be very surprised at the great improvement achieved in a short time in regard to both private and public wealth. But when one considers the natural advantages of the site and the contributions from outside which have restored its former wealth, one is no longer surprised and in fact one feels that the result falls somewhat short of expectations.[12]

Polybius v.88–90.4

1. This was unusual: the acceptance of a gift was normally felt to create an obligation, cf. the rejection by the Achaeans of gifts from the kings (Polybius XXII.7–9) and cf. **56**(a).
2. Hiero II and his son Gelo, rulers of Syracuse.
3. Cf. **118**.
4. Catapults which could fire arrows three cubits long.
5. *Deigma*, a place for the display of goods and for trading.
6. Cf. **202** end.
7. For the close relations of Rhodes and Egypt see **39**.
8. For the resources of Macedon see **79**.
9. Cf. **161** §11.
10. For use in catapults.
11. Olympichus is attested epigraphically as a dynast in Caria (J. Crampa,

Labraunda III.1 (Lund, 1969)), but the other two are unknown. On dynasts in Asia Minor cf. **182** n. 6.

12. It goes without saying that although munificence was one of the qualities expected of, and practised by, Hellenistic kings (cf. **163**(b), **194, 217**) their generosities were not in fact indiscriminate and disinterested, but were addressed in the first instance to sanctuaries or states important enough to be worth courting, such as Hellenistic Rhodes.

94 The war of Rhodes against Byzantium to protect the freedom of the seas (220)

It was at this time that being hard pressed by the payment of the tribute,[1] the Byzantines started by sending embassies to the Greeks asking for their help and assistance in the present crisis; but when the majority paid no attention, they were compelled to introduce the levying of dues from ships sailing into the Black Sea. (47) The exaction by the Byzantines of a duty on goods brought from the Black Sea caused great loss and inconvenience to everyone.[2] There was general indignation and all the traders complained to the Rhodians, as they were thought to be the leaders (*prostatai*) of those who use the sea.[3] This was the origin of the war we shall now relate. The Rhodians were roused to action by their own losses as well as by those incurred by their neighbours, and they started by sending an embassy with their allies to the Byzantines, demanding the abolition of the duty. The Byzantines rejected their demands, convinced as they were of the justice of their cause from the arguments put forward at their meeting with the Rhodian ambassadors by Hecatodorus and Olympiodorus, who headed the government of Byzantium at the time. The Rhodians then departed after achieving nothing, and on their return voted to go to war against Byzantium for the reasons stated above.[4]

Polybius IV.46.5–47.6 (cf. *Staatsv* III.514 and 516)

1. Imposed on them by the Celts (cf. **48**) who settled in Thrace with their capital at Tylis near Byzantium.
2. On Byzantium and the Black Sea trade see **96**.
3. Rhodian intervention was therefore prompted in the first instance by the appeal of traders from states other than Rhodes.
4. The war ended when Byzantium agreed to abolish the duty they had introduced (Polybius IV. 52.5; *Staatsv*. III. 516).

95 Treaty between Rhodes and Hierapytna in Crete (*ca* 200?)

God. With good fortune.

(1) Resolved by the people, with good fortune: the priests and the sacrificers shall pray to the Sun and to Rhodos and to all the other gods

165

and goddesses and to the founding deities and to the heroes who possess the city and territory of the Rhodians, that what has been resolved
5 concerning the alliance may be of advantage to the Rhodians and / the Hierapytnians; when the prayer has been completed a sacrifice and a procession shall be offered, as resolved by the people.

(II) When the alliance has been ratified and the oaths have been sworn according to the written treaty, there shall be an alliance ⟨between the Hierapytnians⟩ and the people of Rhodes, and the Hierapytnians shall
10 assist / the people of Rhodes, and make available their city, harbours and naval bases, and shall be well disposed, friendly and allied for all time.[1]

(III) And if anyone attacks the city or territory of the Rhodians or subverts their laws, revenues or their established democracy,[2] the
15 Hierapytnians shall assist the Rhodians / with all possible strength. And if the people of Rhodes demands an auxiliary force from the Hierapytnians, the Hierapytnians shall provide that force within thirty days of the request of the Rhodians, consisting of 200 armed men, unless the
20 Rhodians need less; at least half of the men sent / shall be Hierapytnians.[3]

(IV) And if the Hierapytnians find themselves at war, they shall send as many men as they are able.

(V) To the men sent by the Hierapytnians the Rhodians shall provide transport for the journey from Crete to Rhodes. And if the Rhodians
25 demand an auxiliary force / within the first four years (after the signing of the treaty), from the day of the allies' arrival at Rhodes the Rhodians shall pay to every man a daily wage of nine Rhodian obols, and to every officer who commands at least 50 men a daily wage of two drachmas
30 each. /

(VI) And if the Rhodians demand an auxiliary force after the specified time, the other arrangements shall be the same, but from the day the allies sent by the Hierapytnians arrive at Rhodes, the Hierapytnians shall provide their wages to the allies sent by them for (the first) thirty days,
35 while the Rhodians shall give them for the rest of the time, / as specified.

(VII) And if a war arises between the Rhodians and a state in alliance with the Hierapytnians, if the Rhodians are victims of aggression, the Hierapytnians shall send an auxiliary force to the Rhodians, but if the Rhodians are the aggressors, it shall not be compulsory for the Hierapytnians to send
40 an auxiliary force to the Rhodians. /

(VIII) And if the Rhodians need (to recruit) a mercenary army in Crete,[4] the Hierapytnians shall provide safe conduct to the mercenary army in the city and also in their territory and the islands they control, to the best of their ability, and they shall do everthing to assist the Rhodians in recruiting a mercenary army. They shall not provide anyone else with a
45 mercenary army for use against the Rhodians / under any pretext, and

no Hierapytnian shall take part in a campaign against the Rhodians under any pretext, or he shall be liable to the same penalties as if he had taken part in a campaign against the city of Hierapytna, with the exception of those who have taken the field before (the conclusion of) this treaty.

(IX) The Hierapytnians shall give every assistance to the troops sent by the Rhodians, to the best of their ability, and shall take every care of them / as though they were their own citizens.   50

(X) And if pirates establish bases in Crete[5] and the Rhodians wage war at sea against the pirates or those who provide shelter or assistance to them, the Hierapytnians shall take part in the operations by land and by / sea with all possible strength at their own expense. The pirates who   55
are captured shall be handed over to the Rhodians together with their ships, while each of the allies shall take half of the rest (of the booty).

(XI) On these terms the Rhodians shall be well disposed, friendly and in alliance with the Hierapytnians for all / time, and the officers sent by the   60
Rhodians in command of the naval forces shall take care of the city of Hierapytna as though their own, doing everything that will assist the security and safety of the city of Hierapytna. And if any king or dynast[6] or anyone else / attacks the city of Hierapytna, (the Rhodians) shall come   65
to the assistance of the Hierapytnians in their city with all possible strength.

(XII) And if anyone deprives the Hierapytnians of their lawful revenues from the sea,[7] or subverts the established democracy of the Hierapytnians, and the Hierapytnians ask for an auxiliary force, / the Rhodians   70
shall send two triremes to the Hierapytnians; the Rhodians [shall provide the expenses for the triremes for a period of two months]; for the rest of the time [the Hierapytnians shall give for each] trireme 10,000 drachmas every month.

(XIII) And if [the Rhodians] find themselves at war [they shall send] whatever auxiliary force they are able.

(XIV) And if the Hierapytnians go to war [against anyone without] the agreement of the Rhodians, the Rhodians shall not be obliged to send an auxiliary force.

(XV) The Rhodians shall send an auxiliary force / within thirty days of   75
the Hierapytnians requesting it, with the exception of the war which has broken out between the Hierapytnians and the Cnossians and their allies; the Rhodians shall not be allies of the Hierapytnians in this war.

(XVI) No Rhodian shall take part in a campaign against the Hierapytnians under any pretext, or he shall be liable to the same penalties as if he had taken part in a campaign against the territory of Rhodes, with the exception of those who have taken the field before (the conclusion of) this treaty.

(XVII) And if / during a campaign which the Hierapytnians are waging   80 with the Rhodians to destroy a pirate base, any of those who provide shelter or assistance to the pirates wage war on the Hierapytnians because of this campaign, the Rhodians shall come to the help of the Hierapytnians with all possible strength, and anyone who acts in this way shall be an enemy of the Rhodians.

(xviii) And if the Hierapytnians recruit mercenaries from Asia for a war of their own, the Rhodians shall assist them in every possibly way to ensure the safe journey of the mercenary force to Hierapytna, but the Rhodians shall not assist in providing anyone with a mercenary force for

85 use against the Hierapytnians under any pretext. /

(xix) And it shall be permitted to amend the treaty, if both cities so decide and send embassies to each other; whatever is mutually agreed upon shall be valid.

(xx) And when the treaty is ratified the people shall elect at once five men; the men elected, together with the envoys who have come from Hierapytna, shall administer the customary oath on all the Rhodians of age, to abide by the alliance and the agreement concluded with the people

90 of Hierapytna, without deceit or evasion; if they abide by their oath / may all be well, but if they break it may the opposite happen.[8] The *prytaneis* shall forthwith administer the oath on the same terms to the envoys of the Hierapytnians in the assembly; the priest in charge of sacrifices shall provide the offerings, and the treasurers shall pay the sum specified by the law. So that the Hierapytnians may swear (the oath) to the people an envoy shall be elected; the person elected shall go to the Hierapytnians and administer the oath to them, on the same terms as specified for the Rhodians, and shall make clear the goodwill felt for the

95 Hierapytnians / by the people of Rhodes.

(xxi) And so that the resolutions concerning the alliance and the treaty might be inscribed on stelae and made manifest for all time, the people (of Rhodes) shall dedicate a stele at Rhodes in [the] sanctuary of Athena, and the sellers (*poletai*)[9] shall auction a contract, as instructed by the director of works, for making it out of 'Lartian' stone and for inscribing and dedicating in the sanctuary what was resolved by the cities concerning the alliance, at a cost of not more than 100 drachmas. The treasurers

100 shall provide the expense from the fund for expenses on decrees. / The Hierapytnians shall also inscribe (the alliance) and place it in their city in any sanctuary they wish at Hierapytna.[10]

(xxii) Diogenes son of Aristondas was elected as envoy to go to Hierapytna. Those who administered the oath in Rhodes were Hierombrotus son of Agesitimus, Aristolochus son of Peisistratus, adopted son of Archyllus, Timaratus son of Nicotimus, Nicomachus son of Aristarchus, Spartion son of Pheidianax.[11]

Syll.[3] 581; *ICret.* iii, pp. 31–6 no. 3A; *Staatsv.* iii.551

1. The treaty was probably concluded at the end of a war between Cretan cities (including Hierapytna) and Rhodes (Polybius XIII.4.1f. and 5.1). Rhodes is throughout the dominant partner in the treaty.
2. Rhodes was not a democracy in the fifth-century sense (cf. **53** n.1, **92**).
3. I.e. the rest may be mercenaries.
4. Crete was an important recruiting ground for mercenaries (cf. **63, 77, 224** ch. 65, **267**), mercenary service and piracy (next note) being two aspects of the same phenomenon; see e.g. R. F. Willetts, *Aristocratic Society in Ancient Crete* (London, 1955), 241–8.
5. On Cretan piracy see also **88, 89**; on Rhodes' policy against pirates see **92**.
6. Cf. **182** n. 6.
7. Such as custom or harbour dues as opposed to piracy.
8. See **33** n. 7.
9. See **48** n. 3.
10. The present text.
11. For a similar treaty between Rhodes and another Cretan city (Olus) see *Staatsv*. III.552; Y. Garlan, *BCH* 93 (1969), 160f.

96 Byzantium and the Black Sea trade

See further: Rostovtzeff I (1941), 585–602, esp. 589–91.

As far as the sea is concerned, the Byzantines occupy a position that is more secure and more advantageous than that of any other city in our part of the world, but as regards the land that position is in both respects most unfavourable. Their situation by sea at the entrance to the Black Sea enables them to prevent any trader from sailing into or out of the Black Sea against their will.[1] Since the Black Sea has an abundance of products which are of use to the rest of the world, the Byzantines have control over all of these. For those commodities which are indispensable to life, cattle and slaves,[2] are supplied to us by the countries around the Black Sea, as is generally agreed, in greater quantity, and of better quality than by any others; and as far as luxuries are concerned, they supply us with honey, wax and salt-fish in abundance. In return they receive from our part of the world the surplus olive oil and every kind of wine. With corn there is interchange; they give us some on occasion and sometimes import it from us.[3] Now the Greeks would have been deprived of all these resources or would have found trading in them quite unprofitable if the Byzantines had shown hostility and combined with the Celts, or still more with the Thracians, or had given up the place altogether. Because of the narrowness of the straits and the large number of barbarians living along its shores, the Black Sea would by common consent have become closed to navigation. The Byzantines probably draw themselves the greatest practical benefits from the peculiar situation of their town. Any surplus products they have are easily exported, while they can import easily and profitably anything they lack, without incurring any hardship or danger; but, as I have said, others derive many great advantages thanks to them. Hence as common benefactors of all, as it were, they deserve to gain not only gratitude but concerted support from the Greeks in the dangers they face from the barbarians.[4]

Polybius IV.38.1–10

1. See **94, 140**.
2. On the Black Sea slave trade see M. I. Finley, *Klio* 40 (1962), 51–9; M. H. Crawford, *JRS* 67 (1977), 122 n. 33.
3. The Black Sea regions were now less important for the corn trade than in the fifth and fourth centuries; see Rostovtzeff III (1941), 1462 n. 20. On the corn trade in general see **112**.
4. The Byzantines failed in fact to get any support from the Greeks when faced with increasing pressure from the Celts (see **94**). On the Thracians cf. **98, 153, 215**.

97 Olbia honours Protogenes for many services to the city (late third – early second century)

One of the most important features in the life of Greek cities in the Hellenistic age was the new and growing dependence on wealthy benefactors (*euergetai*), a phenomenon attested especially by numerous honorific decrees (for other examples see **43, 44, 98, 102, 110, 113, 119, 120, 215**). Probably most eloquent of all is the following decree from Olbia, a colony of Miletus on the Black Sea, where Protogenes, the citizen honoured, 'almost seems to carry the city on his shoulders' (Tarn and Griffith (1952), 108f.). The situation of Olbia, at the time under severe barbarian pressure, may have been extreme, though it was typical of many Greek cities with a barbarian hinterland (see **94, 96, 98, 215**). As usual the inscription reveals little of the basis of Protogenes' wealth, beyond the fact that he was obviously a great landed magnate, and though there are indications in the text of other wealthy men at Olbia, no one could compete with him. Olbia was in practice in his dependence, which makes all the more striking the outward observance on both sides of civic values and institutions: Protogenes, and others like him elsewhere, was simply honoured by his city for being a good citizen. On royal munificence cf. **93** and n.12.

See further: E. H. Minns, *Scythians and Greeks* (Cambridge, 1913), esp. 460–3 (cf. p. 641); Hands (1968); P. Veyne, *Le pain et le cirque* (Paris, 1976), ch. 2; Préaux II (1978), 520–4 (on the Greek cities of the Black Sea).

Side A

Resolved by the council and the people, on the twentieth (of the month); the magistrates and the Seven[1] moved: Heroson, father of Protogenes, has performed many great services for the city which involved the expenditure of money / and personal exertion, and Protogenes, having 5 taken over his father's goodwill towards the people has throughout his life constantly said and done what was best (for the city). First when King Saitaphernes[2] came / to Cancytus and asked for the gifts due for his 10 passage, and the public treasury was exhausted, he was called upon by the people and gave 400 gold pieces. When the magistrates pawned the sacred vessels / to repay the city's debt to Polycharmus for 100 gold 15 pieces and could not redeem them[3] and the foreign (creditor) was taking them to the moneyer,[4] he himself paid in addition the 100 gold pieces and redeemed (the vessels). When Democon / and his colleagues in office 20 bought wine cheaply for 300 gold pieces, but could not pay the price, he was called upon by the people and gave the 300 gold pieces. In the priesthood of Herodorus when there was a shortage of corn[5] and grain was being sold at five medimni for a gold piece, / and because of the 25 danger that was threatening the people thought it necessary to build a sufficient stock of grain, and invited those who had (grain) to do this, he was the first to come forward and promise[6] 2,000 medimni at ten medimni for a gold coin, and / whereas the others collected the price on 30 the spot he himself showed indulgence for a year and did not charge any interest. And in the same priesthood when the Saii[7] came along to collect the gifts, / and the people was unable to give them, and asked Pro- 35 togenes to help in this crisis, he came forward and promised 400 gold pieces. When he was elected one of the Nine[8] he made an advance of not less / than 1,500 gold pieces to be repaid from future revenues,[9] from 40 which many chieftains[10] were conciliated in good time and not a few presents were provided for the king (Saitaphernes) advantageously. / 45 When the equipment destined for the king's (palace) was auctioned in accordance with the decree (?), which required that those who bought it should receive 300 gold pieces from the city, Conon bought it, but since the magistrates were unable to give the money / as it was in the hands of 50 the tax collectors,[11] Conon (and his associates) cancelled the contract. Because of this the contract was sold three times, and Phormion bought it the third time; Protogenes then, seeing that / the city was risking great 55 danger, came forward himself to the assembly and gave the 300 gold pieces. Again in the priesthood of Plistarchus, when there was a severe shortage of corn and / grain was being sold at a medimnus and two 60 thirds for a gold coin, and it was clear that the price would rise further, and in fact the medimnus immediately reached the price of one gold coin and two thirds, and because of this the people was in deep distress and thought it / necessary to appoint a corn commission (*sitonia*), and that 65 the wealthy should render services for this purpose,[12] when the assembly met he was the first to promise 1,000 gold pieces for the purchase of

corn, which he brought and gave on the spot. Of these 300 were free
70   from interest / for a year, and 400 which he gave as gold he got back as
copper coins; and he was the first to promise 2,500 medimni of corn, 500
of which he gave at a rate of four medimni and a sixth for a gold coin,
75   and 2,000 at the rate of / two medimni and seven twelfths for a gold
coin. And whereas the others who had promised (grain) in this crisis
collected the price on the spot from the fund that had been set up, he
80   himself showed indulgence for a year and collected the price / without
charging any interest, and because of the eagerness of Protogenes a great
deal of money and a substantial amount of grain was provided for the
people. When King Saitaphernes came along to the other side of the
85   river[13] to receive favours,[14] and the magistrates / called an assembly and
reported on the presence of the king and on the fact that the (city's)
revenues were exhausted, Protogenes came forward and gave 900 gold
pieces, and when the ambassadors, Protogenes[15] and Aristocrates, took
90   the money and / met the king, and the king took the presents but flew
into a rage and broke up [his] quarters,[16] [. . . treated?] the magistrates
95   [unworthily? and so] / the people met together and [were] terrified [and
sent?] ambassadors to . . .

Side B

The largest part of the city along the river was not fortified, and (neither
100   was) the whole of the part along / the harbour and the part along the
former fish market as far as (the sanctuary or statue of) the hero Sosias.
Deserters were reporting that the Galatians (Celts) and the Sciri had
formed an alliance, that a large force had been collected and would be
105   coming during the winter, / and in addition that the Thisamatae,[17]
Scythians and Saudaratae were anxious to seize the fort,[18] as they
themselves were equally terrified of the cruelty of the Galatians. Because
110   of this many were in despair and prepared / to abandon the city. In
addition many other losses had been suffered in the countryside, in that
all the slaves[19] and the Half-Greeks[20] who live in the plain along the river
115   bank had been lost to us, no less than / 1,500 in number, who had fought
on our side in the city in the previous war, and also many of the
foreigners and not a few of the citizens had left. Because of this the
people met in an assembly in deep despair, as they saw before them
120   the / danger that lay ahead and the terrors in store, and called on all who
were able-bodied to help and not allow their native city, after it had been
preserved for many years, to be subjected by the enemy. When no one
125   would volunteer / for all or part of the demands of the people, he

promised he would himself build both the walls and would advance the whole cost of the construction, although not less than 1,500 gold pieces had been advanced by him.[21] / At once he brought to the assembly 500 gold pieces as deposits for the contractors, and auctioned the whole work through a herald,[22] and because the contractors made the payment from the available money he procured the city a substantial sum; and also when many / of the contractors were abandoning the work Protogenes completed the work himself for the city, and did not cause any loss to the people. After spending for both walls 1,500 gold pieces and having paid most of this sum, / he received back copper coins for 400 gold pieces. He restored the towers that were in bad condition, both towers near the great gates, the tower of Cathegetor, the tower near the carriage-way and the tower of Epidaurius; he also repaired / the granary, and repaired the gatehouse on the mart. Moreover, as the city was paying a freight-charge to the private individuals who transported the stones, since the public (transport) ships were in bad condition and did not have any tackle, he promised / to supply these too, and having spent on all this 200 gold pieces he produced an account forthwith. For this the people, after crowning him many times in the past, crowned him then as well for showing the account. Then, as the rest of the wall / near the tower of Posis up to the hill was incomplete, the people called on him to complete this and three other walls, Protogenes, not wishing to dis-oblige, undertook this / construction as well, for which he advanced 100 gold coins. When he was put in charge of the public finances and managed the city's most important revenues, he did not dispossess any of the tax collectors of what they had, and did not deprive anyone / of his means; and showing understanding for all the difficulties they were facing,[23] some he freed from their debts while to others he showed indulgence and remitted the interest (on the loans they had contracted) for as long as they wished. Having handled most of the city's affairs, he managed everything for three years in succession / in an upright and just way, submitting accounts at the specified time, receiving the income from the public revenues during his period in office as repayment (for his loans), although this had not in fact happened,[24] / and so freed the city from its debts and exempted it from the payment of interests. As affairs in the city were in a bad state because of the wars and the dearth of crops, and there were no resources available, and the people sought to meet this / by delaying the payment of debts month by month[25] and to provide usefully for creditors and debtors alike, although 6,000 gold pieces were owed to him and to his father, he was the first to leave it to the people to decide how they wanted [to deal] with him. When (the people) asked that [the debtors] should be freed from their debts, / he freed everyone from all debts and did not [charge] any (interest),

130

135

140

145

150

155

160

165

170

175

180

185

believing it more [glorious] for himself to enjoy [the] goodwill [of all]
than [his private advantage? . . .]

    (the last 5 lines are too mutilated for continuous restoration)

*Syll.*³ 495; F. G. Maier, *Griechische*

Mauerbauinschriften I (Heidelberg, 1959), no. 82 (Side B only)

1. Officials in charge of sacred matters.
2. A barbarian chieftain ruling on the eastern side of the river Hypanis (Bug),
   who extorted regular 'gifts' from Olbia.
3. For the indebtedness of Greek cities see also **100–103**.
4. To be melted down.
5. For the corn supply of Greek cities see **112**.
6. The publicly made offer of help is a regular preliminary to the help itself (cf.
   103, 110, 113, 119).
7. Probably the tribe ruled by Saitaphernes.
8. Probably a board of financial officials.
9. For this method of repaying public debts see also **40B, 100, 104**.
10. Probably petty rulers subjected to Saitaphernes.
11. They were in debt to the city, as the sequel of the decree shows (side B).
12. The assumption that the wealthy had a duty to spend for their community
    lies behind the phenomenon of the 'benefactors'; cf. **40B, 101, 103**.
13. The Hypanis (Bug).
14. Euphemistic.
15. It is not clear whether this is the same Protogenes.
16. I.e. made ready for hostile action, as the sequel shows.
17. This tribe and the Saudaratae were probably on the western bank of the Bug,
    between Olbia and the Celts and Sciri further inland. On the Celts cf. **48**.
18. The city of Olbia.
19. Probably a native servile people who worked the land for the Greeks (cf. D.
    M. Pippidi in *Problèmes de la terre en Grèce ancienne*, ed. M. I. Finley (Paris,
    1973), 63–82, esp. 75f.).
20. A people half-Greek and half-Scythian, cf. Herodotus IV.17.
21. The sum mentioned above (line 40).
22. On the auctioning of contracts for public works cf. **104**.
23. The tax collectors.
24. I.e. he falsified the city's accounts in its favour to show a nominal repayment
    of the money he had advanced (cf. n. 9).
25. Debts were repaid on a monthly basis.

98 Istria honours Agathocles for many services in defence of the city (ca 200–150)

Resolved by the council and the people; Dionysius son of Bianor was
epimenios;[1] Apollonius son of Cleombrotus moved: since Agathocles son
of Antiphilus, born of a father who was a benefactor, continues to be a

good and honourable man towards the city / and the citizens, showing   5
himself zealous in all the crises faced by the city, and constantly says and
does what is best for the people in all the magistracies, commissions and
appointments as *synedros*² which he holds; and when the [city] was in [a
state of confusion] and a [large] number of Thracian pirates³ were
attacking / the land and the [city, and the harvest] was imminent and the   10
citizens were in distress, he was [elected] commander of the archers and
took (with him) mercenaries, and [protected] the land and enabled the
citizens to gather in the crops without harm;⁴ and when the Thracians
[under Zoltes came with] / a larger force [to] Scythia and the Greek   15
cities [under the rule of King] Rhemaxus,⁵ he was elected ambassador
and [travelled across] enemy territory, passing through many tribes
without [avoiding any] danger, and persuaded the barbarians [not only
not to do any] harm / to our city but even to seek out [and return] all the   20
[flocks which] had been taken away [previously] by the pirates under the
command of [King] Zoltes, [and with] these he urged them (?) . . . the
city, to give five [talents? to make] a compact with the city / to protect   25
its livelihood;⁶ and after this, when they (the Thracians of Zoltes)
[invaded] the land, laid siege to Bizone⁷ and ravaged the land, and the
harvest was imminent, he was elected ambassador and travelled to the
(Thracian) army, and as the citizens had given him instructions to
redeem the land and the crops at [all] / cost, he persuaded Zoltes and the   30
Thracians at a cost of 600 gold pieces [not to invade] the land nor to
approach the city, which enabled [the] citizens to secure all the [crops]
from the land; again when elected ambassador to Thrace [and to] / their   35
commander [Zoltes] he renewed the agreement and [treaty that had
been] concluded [with] them; and noticing that a large force of [pirates]
was assembling, he [pointed it out] to Zoltes and revealed it to the
[citizens] on his [return], which caused their plot to [be] unsuccessful; /   40
and [when] the Thracians [broke] their oath and the [agreement, and]
made continuous raids, he was elected by the [people] general over the
land with full powers, and took volunteer troops from among [the]
citizens and the barbarians⁸ who had taken refuge [in the] city, and
defended and protected the land, / the flocks, [and the] crops until King   45
[Rhemaxus] could cross (the Danube); and when the king crossed back to
the [other side] (of the river), but did not leave a guard force [through
fear], and sent messengers [and asked] for the tribute while the land [was]
in a state of war, he (sc. Agathocles) was [elected] ambassador and
travelled / [on] a boat, and persuaded [King] Rhemaxus to provide 100   50
cavalrymen to serve [as an advance guard]; and when a heavier attack of
the Thracians fell on the advance guards and they retreated [across the
river] through fear, and the land was unprotected, he was [elected]
ambassador to [Phradmon] the [son] of the king, and / [persuaded] him   55

to provide an advance guard of 600 cavalrymen; [they overcame] the (enemy) armies, [defeated their commander] Zoltes and . . . of the Thracians . . .

Moretti II. 131; cf. *SEG* XXIV. 1095

1. President of the board of twelve *epimenioi*, a magistracy of Milesian origin (Istria was founded from Miletus), analogous to the Athenian *prytaneis*.
2. A magistracy, again of Milesian origin, probably concerned with the preparation and submission of decrees.
3. On piracy see **86**; for the whole situation compare **97**.
4. Compare **44, 50**.
5. This chieftain was probably based to the north of Istria across the Danube. As the sequel shows, the Greek cities had established a *modus vivendi* with him which they failed to secure with Zoltes and his Thracians, who appear in the inscription as newcomers in the picture.
6. Or: 'to provide for their (the Thracians') livelihood'.
7. A Greek city on the coast, some 120 km to the south of Istria.
8. Perhaps natives under Greek rule, cf. **97** n. 19.

99 Exemption from taxes for new citizens at Teos (*ca* 300)

The context of the following inscription is the incorporation of new citizens in the city of Teos, and the granting to them of exemption from various taxes and obligations for a period of a few years (for which cf. **40A** §9, **134**). The identity of the new citizens is unknown (there is probably no connexion with **40**). Though fragmentary and conjectural in restoration the inscription gives valuable evidence not just on the finances of Teos, but also on the society and economy of the Teans, or perhaps rather of the new citizens.

See further: Rostovtzeff I (1941), 181f.; III, 1355 n. 45 and 1374 n. 71; J. and L. Robert cited below.

[. . . in which] the other Teans share, [being exempted?] from taxes for a period of four [years]. They shall be exempted from the *choregia*, the . . ., the *boegia*, the *lampadarchia*,[1] and the tax (*epigraphe*) on all [the oxen] for ploughing they have and those which do not form part of a
5 team. / [And] their working oxen shall be exempted from (requisition for) all the public works which [the city carries out?]. And they shall be given exemption from taxes on pack animals and [slaves], whether they are hired labourers or wood carriers, and whatever they [do or] sell which is connected with the sale of timber, and from the tax on sheep [up to a number of . . .?]. Those who wish may raise pigs up to [the
10 specified] number / of sheep and they shall be exempt from tax. And they shall be exempt from [the other taxes] except the tax for the maintenance of doctors.[2] All the slaves who sell [charcoal?] or anything

else which is connected with the sale of timber shall [be] exempted³ from those taxes [as well]. And all those who make mantles or [woollen shawls?] or anything else from 'Milesian' wool whether rough or [fine / or any other material?], shall be exempt from the tax on these   15
whether they sell them on the spot [or export them]. Whatever they import for the making of the mantles . . . purple-dyeing, they shall be exempt [from the tax on these. And they shall be exempt from?] the tax on gardens and on beehives; and they shall be [exempt . . .] of all if they wish to export . . . / they shall be exempt for ten years, and [the   20
exemption is to run from] the month Leucatheon and the prytany of Aristippus.

> *SEG* 11.79; H. W. Pleket, *Epigraphica* 1 (Leyden, 1964)
> no. 22; J. and L. Robert, *Journal des Savants*
> (1976), 175–88

1. These are liturgies (see **40** n. 6) of a religious character: the *choregia* involved the training of a chorus for a dramatic festival, the *boegia* probably the provision of oxen for a procession followed by a sacrifice, the *lampadarchia* the expenses for the organisation of a torch race (cf. **118** ll. 71–83).
2. Cf. **124, 125**.
3. I.e. their owners are exempted.

100 Decree of Halicarnassus for the repayment of a public debt contracted for the building of a stoa (third century)

See further, on the finances of Greek cities: Jones (1940), 241–50; Tarn and Griffith (1952), 116–19; on public subscriptions: Rostovtzeff III (1941), 1463f.; Hands (1968), 39f.

(The beginning of the inscription is lost)
 . . . Callicles to the treasurers, and the treasurers shall give (the money) at once to the commissioners (*epimeletai*)¹ and the commissioners shall give it to the contractors in accordance with the plans. And so that those who have advanced money for the stoa which the people is dedicating to Apollo and to King Ptolemy² should be known to all, the / controllers   5
(*exetastai*) in whose period of office the stoa is completed shall inscribe on the side wall of the stoa the names and patronymics of all those who have advanced without interest sums of not less than 500 drachmas, prefacing the list with the words 'The following men gave to the people money without interest for the construction of the stoa'. They shall inscribe first the person who gave most. So that those who have advanced money should recover (their loans), / the revenues which have been earmarked   10
for (the construction of) the council house shall be assigned to them, once

the former creditors have been refunded.[3] There shall also be assigned to
them the revenues earmarked for the statues, viz. the two per cent tax[4]
and the tax for recording oaths,[5] once the former creditors to whom the
revenues had been assigned by decree have been refunded. There shall
also be assigned to them from the public revenues one talent every year
15 after / the creditors to whom six talents were assigned from the budget
of the city have received it with interest; the surplus is to go to the public
revenues. In addition shall be assigned to them the sum raised from the
stoa after the sale of the columns, the timber, the tiles and the bricks.[6] Let
those who farm out the construction works sell the columns up to the
20 court of justice / [at] the same meeting of the assembly, and let the buyer
pay the [money] within [thirty] days to the treasurers, and the [treasurers
. . .]

OGIS 46; H. W. Pleket, *Epigraphica* I (Leyden, 1964), no. 26.

1. The commissioners supervising the construction of the stoa.
2. Ptolemy II or III.
3. On this practice cf. **97** n.9; here the public revenues have already been assigned
   to other creditors who have a prior claim.
4. A tax on imports and exports, common to many Greek cities (cf. **80, 104,
   109**).
5. In sales between individuals the seller had to swear he was the legal owner of
   the goods he was selling; such oaths were publicly recorded.
6. Perhaps materials from an older building which was being demolished to
   make way for the new stoa.

101 Oropus opens a subscription for the construction (or repair) of a fortification (third century?)

See further: Hands (1968), 51, and see **100**.

Gods. Lysander moved: so that a source of money might be found for
the construction (or: repair) of the wall, and when the walls are
5 completed we might be of help / to ourselves and to the Boeotian
League, be it resolved by the people that the commissioners for the walls
and the polemarchs should raise a loan from any available source, at the
lowest possible rate of interest and should repay the money to the
10 lenders / in the year following the priesthood of Oropodorus, the capital
sum and the interest thereon. Those who have lent to the city for the
15 construction (or: repair) of a wall a talent or more at an (annual) rate / of
ten per cent are to be (called) *proxenoi* and benefactors (*euergetai*) of the
city of Oropus, themselves and their descendants, and shall be granted
the right to acquire land and a house, equality of taxation (*isoteleia*),
personal security (*asphaleia*), inviolability (*asylia*) in peace and war, by
20 land / and by sea and all the other rights enjoyed by citizens; their names

shall be inscribed with their father's name on a stone stele and placed in the sanctuary of Amphiaraus. As to those who lend to the city less than a talent, the people shall consider in their case / what honours each of them deserves to receive from the city. The polemarchs shall inscribe the decree on a stone stele and place it in the sanctuary of Amphiaraus; the treasurer shall provide the expense.

The following (were made) *proxenoi* and benefactors in accordance with the decree: Nicon son of Charmis.[1]

Syll.[3] 544; *IG* VII.4263; F. G. Maier,
Griechische Mauerbauinschriften 1 (Heidelberg, 1959), no. 26

1. There is only one name: any other subscribers there may have been contributed less than a talent.

102 Decree of Istria in honour of Hephaestion of Callatis for remission of a debt (*ca* 200–150)

Resolved by the council and the [people]; Dionysius [son of] Hieron was *epimenios*;[1] the magistrates [moved]: since Hephaestion [son of Matris] / from Callatis,[2] when the city owed him for [many] years for a [loan] made by his father 300 gold pieces [according to] a written agreement, and [considerable] interests had accumulated, / he proved himself a good and honourable man and showed [understanding] for the difficulties facing the city, and remitted [the] interest which amounted to 400 [gold pieces],[3] and [agreed] to recover the sum that was owed to him / according to the [written] agreement, which amounted to 300 gold pieces, without interest [over] a period of two [years]; for [these services] Hephaestion son of Matris from [Callatis] should be praised . . .

Moretti II.130

1. See **98** n. 1.
2. A Greek city some 70 km to the south of Istria (see **98**) on the Black Sea coast.
3. I.e. the interest is higher than the original loan; at a rate of 8⅓ simple interest the loan would have been sixteen years old.

103 Decree of Crannon (Thessaly) to eliminate debts by raising a subscription (*ca* 168–142?)

See further (on Thessaly): Rostovtzeff III (1941), 1467.

On the second day of the month Homoloios,[1] when Crateraeus son of Diodorus of Larisa was general of the Thessalians, and Pheidon son of

5   Cratippus, Antiphanes / son of Cratippus, Pheidon son of Eudoxus,
Pantauchus son of Agasicrates, and Anaxippus son of Marsyas were
tagoi, and Menander son of Philocles and Philocles son of Aristodamas
10 were treasurers; since the city / has numerous debts because of the wars
which have afflicted it[2] [and] the debts have now been dragging on for a
long time; Anaxippus son of Marsyas moved; the community (*koinon*) of
15 the city resolved / that it would be fitting and advantageous that all the
citizens should come to the help of the city, each according to his private
20 means, so as to free it if possible from all debts, and if not, from / the
majority; and that those who wish should declare to the city in the
assembly[3] the sum each wishes to contribute as a gift for the aforemen-
25 tioned debts; that the declaration should be made / while Crateraeus
holds the office of general, and that the city should praise those who
made such a declaration so that it should be manifest to all that the city
30 remembers its benefactors;[4] that the treasurers should take / care that
those who have declared (they would give money) should give the
money to the city as declared; that those who have declared (they would
give money) should be inscribed on a stone stele, each with his father's
35 name, as / they have made their declaration, the first to have done so
being inscribed first, and [then] the others who followed, according [to
the] sum offered [and] that the stele should be placed on [the acropolis in
40 the most] distinguished place;[5] / [. . . the] treasurers shall take care [that
a copy of the decree] should be inscribed [wherever it seems] suitable;
[the resulting expense shall be inscribed in the accounts of the city].

Moretti II.99

1. May–June.
2. Thessaly suffered from the war between Rome and Antiochus III in 191 and
   then from the war between Rome and Perseus in 171 and after.
3. See **97** n. 6.
4. The city has nothing to offer except gratitude.
5. The list of donors has not survived.

104 Extracts from the temple accounts of the Delian 'hieropoioi' (279)

The small Aegean island of Delos with its famous sanctuary of Apollo enjoyed
nominal independence for much of the Hellenistic period (from 314 to 167, after
which the Roman Senate restored it to Athenian control and made it a free port;
see **80**). The wealth of Apollo's sanctuary, which included land, houses, cash,
animals, offerings etc., as well as the temple buildings, was administered by an
annual board of two *hieropoioi* who published their accounts on stone every year.
This series of texts forms one of the most important sources of information on

the economic life of Delos and the Aegean in this period; many of the inscriptions are fragmentary or even lost altogether, but some are extensively preserved, including the accounts for the year 279. Although calculations of the total wealth of Apollo are approximate, it is clear that all told it was on a modest scale, and the island was in no position to be a great international moneylending centre, despite the fame of Apollo's sanctuary. For other texts on the economic life of Delos see **109, 114–115, 171**.

See further: J. A. O. Larsen in *Economic Survey of Ancient Rome*, ed. T. Frank, IV (Baltimore, 1938), 334–57; Rostovtzeff I (1941), 190f. and 230–6 with III, 1371–3; J. H. Kent, *Hesperia* 17 (1948), 243–338; R. Bogaert, *Banques et banquiers dans les cités grecques* (Leyden, 1968), esp. 131–65, 279–304.

Side A

[Gods. Account] of the *hieropoioi* who held office in the archonship of Hypsocles (279), Aristotheus son of Timothalus, Xenocles son of Philarchides. We received from the *hieropoioi* who held office in the archonship of Charmus (280), Hegias son of Phocaeus, Anaschetus son of Theoxenus, in the presence of the councillors, the secretary of the city Timesidemus son of Anticrates and the secretary of the *hieropoioi* Lysimachides son of Lysus: 18,648 drachmas and ¼ obol of silver coins; 10 drs. 1 ob. of gold (coins); 2 Ptolemaic gold 'cicadas',¹ a Phocaean gold coin; miscellaneous silver coins reckoned as 8 drs. of Alexander silver; /   5
from Aristocles son of Philon, 100 drs.; from Philaethus and Euclides who were *hieropoioi* in the archonship of Glauciades (281), 600 drs.

The following persons paid rent² for temple lands during our period of office: Apollodorus son of Xenomedes for the land of Porthmus, 1,320 drs.; Dorcon for the land at Pyrgi, 1,220 drs. ½ ob.; Aristeas son of Amphoterus for the land at Limnae, 397 drs. ½ ob.; Antigonus son of Anectus for the land at Rhamnus, 429 drs. [. . .]³

The following rents⁴ from temple property were paid in: from   16
Ephesus for the buildings in which Ephesus carries on a retail trade, 51 drs.; from Isus for the men's apartment in the house (called) Chareteia, 65 drs.; from Anapsychtides for the women's apartment, 95 drs.; from Soteles for the men's apartment which is one of those near the sea, 50 drs.; from the children of Diophantus for the men's apartment next to these, 17 drs.; from Autosthenes for the house which belonged to the children of Aristobulus, 39 drs. 4½ ob. [. . .]⁵

The following sums were also paid in: for the repayment of the money   25
which the city owes to the god,⁶ from the councillors in the archonship of Hypsocles (279): from the tax of one fiftieth (two per cent)⁷ together with the duty⁸ on it, 14,910 drs.; from the ten per cent tax on houses⁹ on behalf of Teisicles,¹⁰ 600 drs.; for the fishery-rights on behalf of Phillis,

530 drs.; for the ten per cent tax on wheat[11] on behalf of Gnosidicus, 120 drs.; the duty paid on these, 61½ drs.; and the subvention for the Dionysiac festival,[12] 2,056 drs. 4 ob.

The following persons paid interest[13] during our period in office: Gergyllus son of Pistoxenus, 100 drs.; Athenis son of Eurymanthes for the lands at Passirus, 60 drs.; Mnesalcus son of Telesarchides for the lands at Passirus which formerly belonged to Sosipolis, / 60 drs.; Andromenes son of Xenon, 20 drs. 5 ob.; Alexicratea on behalf of Arignotus, 20 drs. 5 ob. [. . .][14]

The following sums were also paid in: from Calodicus for the fish in the (sacred) lake,[15] 60 drs.; the surplus from the regular taxes, 272 drs.; from the collection boxes:[16] in the temple, 19 drs. 4 ob.; 1 Aeginetan (drachma), 2 Rhodian obols, 3 Epidaurian obols; from (the collection box) in the Asclepieion, 26 drs. 2¼ ob.; from (the collection box) in the Aphrodision, 4¼ ob. and 1 gold stater; for a dead goose,[17] 5½ drs.; for an Egyptian goose and the eggs of a goose, 1 dr. 2 ob.; for a partridge, 1 ob.; for the sale of timber from the gateway,[18] 8½ drs.; from the councillors in the archonship of Charmus (280) from the subvention for the Dionysiac festival,[19] 1,482½ drs.; from the councillors and the *hieropoioi* / in the archonship of Charmus (280), a further 200 drs., which Hypsocles son of Archestratus paid (in full) for the surety he provided for Amphistratus[20] son of Hypsocles; from the councillors in the archonship of Hypsocles (279), a further 175 drs. which Arignotus son of Antipater paid (in full) for the surety he provided for Diaetus son of Apollodorus for the construction around the theatre;[21] and from Anticrates son of Timesidemus in exchange for old silver,[22] 100 drs.; from Phaneas for the palm wood left over from the model, 6 drs.; from the pigeons' dung, 6 drs.; from the purple, 12 drs.; from the mulberries . . .

We auctioned the following contracts for works[23] in accordance with decrees of the people with the architect and the commissioners appointed by the people and in accordance with the written contracts: / Phaneas son of Caicus and Pisibulus of Paros contracted for making fifteen coffered compartments in the ceiling of the peristyle in front of the roof of the temple of Apollo, each compartment at a cost of 300 drs., on condition that they supply themselves everything that is needed for the work except the timber; we gave to them on the instructions of the commissioners and the architect the first payment of 2,250 drs., and when they had completed half of the work in accordance with the contract we gave them a second payment of 1,800 drs., and when they had completed the (whole) work and supplied it in good order in accordance with the contract we paid them on the instructions of the architect and the commissioners the (remaining) tenth, 450 drs. Salary to Nikon for dressing the top course of the / temple of Apollo, 5 drs.

(Salary) to Dinocrates for placing the fillet on the top course of the temple, 38 drs.[24] [. . .]

And we made the following payments on the instructions of the   76
architect and the commissioners for contracts for works issued before our period of office: to Croesus the contractor for the stones for the temple of Zeus Cynthius, for bringing and measuring the stones which were due up to the length of 1,004 feet, we made the second payment of 1,994 drs. ¼ ob. To Dinocrates for completing the roof of the temple of Asclepius we gave the (remaining) tenth, / 55 drs. On behalf of   80
Theophilus who contracted for making the tiles of the temple of Artemis, to Sosimenes and Timesidemus his sureties who completed the work in accordance with the contract, we paid the (remaining) tenth, 135 drs. Salary to the hired workers for cleaning the orchestra and the seats of the theatre and removing the pile of dust, as directed by the architect, 7 drs.

We also made the following payments: salary to the architect, 720 drs.; to the slave woman for her food, 120 drs.; to Dorus the servant, 156 drs.; to Leptines and Bacchius the stone workers for their food, 480 drs.; for their clothing, 34 drs.; salary to the secretary,[25] 80 drs.; to the herald, 60 drs.; to the temple warden of the Asclepieion, / 180 drs.; to the temple   85
warden of the god (Apollo), 60 drs.; to the overseer of the walls, 90 drs.; salary for the flute-girl who plays for the chorus of women, 120 drs. [. . .]

And we also spent the following sums in accordance with decrees of   114
the people: to Hermon for making watertight the roof of the banqueting hall in the island, / 12 drs.; to Hermon for plastering the roof of the stage   115
building, 12 drs.; to Dionysius for making watertight the roofs of the houses at the landing, 16 drs.; we also spent for the Thesmophoria in addition to what we received from the treasurer 75 drs.; for the sacrifice to Eilythuia, 25 drs.; in addition to the monthly revenue 'from the bowl'[26] we spent for the cleansing of the temple a further 14 drs. 1½ ob.; a cloak for Dorus the servant, 24 drs.; a stele from Philonides, 25 drs.; for the men who took the stele from the Asclepieion and brought it to the temple (of Apollo), 1½ dr.; for Dinomenes who inscribed the stele, at 300 letters a drachma, a total of 30,000 letters, salary 100 drs.; lead, 5 drs.; timber, 1 dr.; to the men who set up the stele, 2½ drs.; / for repairing the   120
collapsed part of the house in which Antigonus son of Timocrates lives, 10 drs.; a board of elm from Dinocrates for the fillet under the roof of the temple of Apollo, 15 drs.; salt, 2½ drs.; timber for the trenails, 4 ob.; half an amphora of pitch from Amphithales, 20 drs.

Total of the money we received and which was paid in during our period in office, 54,162 drs.; miscellaneous silver coins reckoned as 11 drs. of Alexander silver, 10 drs. 2 ob. of gold coins, 2 golden 'cicadas' and a Phocaean coin. Total of expenditure, 12,720 drs. The balance we handed over to the *hieropoioi* in the archonship of Menecrates (278), Demon son of Nicon, Pistes son of Xenon, in the / presence of the councillors and the secretaries, Antipater son of Demetrius (secretary) of the city and Clinodicus son of Clinodicus (secretary) of the *hieropoioi*, amounting to 41,442 drs. 2¾ ob. of silver, together with the 24,630 drs. which the people voted that the *hieropoioi* who are in office should always receive [during the transfer],[27] also the 'cicadas', 2 ob., the Phocaean coin, [11 drs.] of miscellaneous silver coins [and] 10 drs. 2 ob. [of gold].[28]

IG XI.2.161 A (extracts)

1. Coins with the type of a cicada, or possibly ornaments.
2. Annual rent on 10 year leases.
3. A further 16 entries follow, with sums ranging from 60 to 1,800 drs.
4. Annual rent on 5 year leases.
5. A further eleven entries follow, with sums ranging from 25 to 136 drs., total 882 drs. 2½ ob.
6. The city of Delos had 'borrowed' a large sum from Apollo and was repaying it out of its regular revenues (cf. **97** n. 9).
7. See **100** n. 4.
8. A duty paid by the tax farmer.
9. A tax paid by foreigners for renting accommodation (only Delians could own real estate in Delos).
10. Probably the tax farmer, as in the cases which follow.
11. From the small sum indicated this can only have affected a very small part of the grain sold in the island.
12. Probably money intended for dramatic festivals but not spent.
13. This rubric refers to arrears of interest due.
14. A further nineteen entries follow, with sums ranging from 2 drs. 2 ob. to 120 drs., total 638 drs.
15. I.e. fishing rights.
16. Collection boxes placed in the temples for individual offerings.
17. Animals kept by the temple; the *hieropoioi* made money for Apollo out of anything, however small.
18. Timber from the builder's model for the gateway, left unused and sold.
19. See n. 12.
20. A defaulting tenant; his surety paid for him. For loans and sureties cf. **206**.
21. A defaulting builder; see n. 23.
22. Probably débris of silver objects.
23. Building contracts are known from a number of Greek sanctuaries and follow a common pattern (cf. P. H. Davis, *BCH* 61 (1937), 109–20 for Delos; in general A. Burford, *The Greek Temple Builders at Epidauros* (Liverpool, 1969), ch. 4). At Delos contracts were issued by the 'architect' (in practice a Master of Works, cf. **216** l.152 at Pergamum) and the board of commissioners; half of the sum due to the contractor was paid before he

started work (and sometimes the state had to provide materials as well), the other half less one tenth was paid half way through, and the rest on completion of the work. The implication is that the contractors had little capital or resources of their own. They had to provide sureties (cf. n. 21 and see below): the state made sure to protect its interests.

24. Some works were carried out and paid for on a daily basis or by piece.

25. The secretary of the *hieropoioi*; the sum is too small to represent a full salary. The same applies to the herald, the temple warden of Apollo and the overseer of the wells. These posts probably had an honorific character which explains the lower payment.

26. An indemnity paid for sacrifices: the sacrifices involved the use of sacred vessels and the participation of the official clergy.

27. A reserve fund: the people decided that the sums in hand with the *hieropoioi* should not fall below a certain figure.

28. Side B of the inscription is a long inventory of sacred objects (cups, bowls, etc.) and materials owned by the god.

105 Decree of Gortyn on the use of bronze coins (mid–second half of third century)

The context of the following inscription is probably the issuing by Gortyn of a new bronze coinage to replace silver denominations below the drachma; the decree was needed to combat the suspicion against the new coins which, unlike silver, had no intrinsic metallic value. Cf. **215** ll.43–49.

See further: R. F. Willetts, *Aristocratic Society in Ancient Crete* (London, 1955), 131f., 187–91; A. E. Jackson, *NC* (1971), 37–51; J. R. Melville Jones, *NC* (1972), 39f.

[Gods. The following decision was taken by] the [city] after a vote with three [hundred] men being present:[1] one must use the bronze coinage which the city has issued; one must not accept the / silver obols. If   5 anyone accepts (the silver obols) or refuses to accept the (bronze) coinage or sells anything in exchange for grain,[2] he shall be fined five silver staters. Information (about such cases) is to be laid / before the *neotas* (the   10 body of young men),[3] and from the *neotas* the Seven chosen by lot shall give their verdict on oath in the agora.[4] Whichever party wins a majority of votes shall win, and the Seven shall exact the fine from the losing party, give one half [to the winning party] and the other half [to the city].

Syll.[3] 525; *ICret.* IV, pp.222–5 no. 162;
R. Bogaert, *Epigraphica* III (Leyden, 1976), no. 22

1. A quorum for decisions.
2. This implies that payments in kind are still being practised.
3. A formally organised body of young men above the age of nineteen

(ex-ephebes), such as existed in many Greek cities; see Willetts, *loc. cit.* Cf. **113, 118, 194, 201, 215**.

4. Or: 'the Seven in the agora chosen by lot shall give their verdict on oath'.

106 List of convictions for the counterfeiting of coins, from Dyme in Achaea (third–second century)

When Philocles was priest (*theokolos*), Damocritus registrar (*grammatistes*), Cleon president of the [council]; the city condemned [the follow-
5 ing men] to / [death] for stealing sacred property [and] striking [bronze] coins:[1] Thracion whose name may be [Antiochus], [Cratis] the
10 goldsmith, / [Cyllanius] whose name may be Pantaleon or something else, Moscholaus son of Moscholaus.

When Euphanes was president of the council: [Asclepiades] son of
15 Dromas. /

When Phileas was president of the council: . . .ias son of Olympichus.

Syll.[3] 530; H. W. Pleket, *Epigraphica* I
(Leyden, 1964), no.11

1. Probably bronze coins plated with silver (J. R. Melville Jones, *NC* (1972), 42f.). Death was the normal penalty for counterfeiting coins.

107 Amphictyonic decree concerning the Athenian tetradrachm (124–100)

Whereas Gortyn was merely concerned with the local enforcement of her own bronze coinage (see **105**), the following decree of the Delphic Amphictyony (cf. **48, 52, 72**) seeks to secure acceptance of the Athenian silver tetradrachm (but not other Athenian denominations) by all the Greeks. The measure may in fact be less ambitious than appears at first sight, for it seems that by this time the 'New Style' Athenian tetradrachms (see **111** n. 7) were in any case being widely used. Athens at this period was well in with the Delphic Amphictyony; whether the measure was prompted by any economic considerations and not simply by national pride is not obvious.

See further: Rostovtzeff III (1941), 1503 n. 9; G. Daux, *Delphes au IIe et Ier siècle* (Paris, 1936), 387–91.

When Polyon was archon at Delphi, on the thirteenth of the [month] of Daedaphorius,[1] it was resolved by the Amphictyons who came to Delphi, that all the Greeks should accept the Athenian tetradrachm for four drachmas of silver. If any of those who live in the cities, whether foreigner, citizen or slave, whether man / or woman, does not accept or 5 give in payment (the Athenian tetradrachm) as has been prescribed, the slave shall be scourged by the magistrates and the free man shall be fined 200 drachmas of silver.[2] The magistrates in the cities and the *agoranomoi*[3] shall [give] help in collecting from those who disobey the resolution the [specified] sum of money; half of the sum collected shall belong [to the person who brought] before the authorities the offending person / and 10 the other half shall belong to the city. If the magistrates [who hold office in] the cities or at the national festivals do not give help to those who bring [the offenders] before [them], they shall be tried before the Amphictyons [after an] investigation [has been made] in accordance with [the] laws of the Amphictyons. [Likewise] if the money [changers[4] who operate in the cities] and at the national festivals do not obey the resolution, it shall be permitted [to anyone who wishes to bring them before the] magistrates; / any (magistrate) who [refuses to give help to 15 persons who bring (offenders before them)] shall be prosecuted [in the same way as] is specified [against the other magistrates. Each of the *hieromnemones*[5] shall bring a sealed] copy of the resolution [to] his own city, and [the secretary] shall send [(copies of) the decree to all the Greeks, and inscribe it at] Delphi on the treasury of the Athenians[6] [in the sanctuary of the god, and similarly at Athens on the acropolis so that all] may know what [arrangements the Amphictyons] have made [in this matter].

Syll.[3] 729; H. W. Pleket, *Epigraphica* I (Leyden, 1964), no. 13

1. November.
2. Cf. **87** n. 2.
3. Officials concerned with the policing of markets; see **110**, **111**, **113**.
4. The multiplicity of coinages circulating in the Greek world (cf. **104**) required the presence of money changers in many Greek cities. Cf. **206** l. 32.
5. See **52** n. 2.
6. The present text.

108 Harbour regulations at Thasos (third century)

It is forbidden to haul up[1] a ship beyond the signposts, beyond the first one if the ship [has a tonnage of less than] 3,000 talents (*ca* 78 tons), beyond the second one if it has a tonnage of less than five [thousand talents] (*ca* 130 tons);[2] anyone who hauls up his ship in contravention of these rules shall pay a fine of five [staters] to the city; the *epistatai*[3] shall exact the fine. Should any dispute arise, / [the] *apologoi* [shall take them 5 to court] before a jury; they shall [communicate to the] *epistatai* the

sentence (and the amount of the fine), and the *epistatai* shall exact it. If they do not exact it, [they shall owe the fine themselves]. If the *apologoi* do not take (the culprits) to court, or do not communicate (the sentence and the amount of the fine) to the [*epistatai*], they shall be liable to prosecution by the incoming *apologoi* . . . [. . . the] *epistatai* (verb) those who haul up [a ship beyond the signposts] in contravention of the
10 decree; / [let anyone who] wishes [denounce? . . .]⁴

IG xii Supplement.348; H. W. Pleket,
Epigraphica i (Leyden, 1964), no. 9

1. The hauling up of ships within the harbour was still practised at Thasos.
2. On the size of ancient freighters cf. L. Casson in *Studi A. Calderini e R. Paribeni* i, ed. S. Pagani (Milan, 1956), 231–8 (p. 234 on this inscription) and *id., Ships and Seamanship in the Ancient World* (Princeton, 1971), 171 n. 23, 183f.
3. On the *epistatai* and *apologoi* at Thasos cf. F. Salviat, *BCH* 82 (1958), 204–6.
4. The measure seems designed as a policing operation (to prevent the harbour being cluttered up with smaller craft) with possible fiscal overtones (larger ships would mean higher import dues). There is of course no trace of protectionism; nothing is said in the text of the nationality of ships or the nature of their cargoes.

109 Law regulating the sale of wood and charcoal at Delos (*ca* 250–200)

[No one may sell] charcoal or logs¹ or [wood without using] the (official) measures for wood.² [No one] may sell these if he has bought them on Delos, nor even if he has bought any of these [on board] ship. He may sell (these goods) only after making the (statutory) declaration in his own
5 name. / He must not sell goods (i.e. wood or charcoal) which have been publicly auctioned after bidding successfully for them,³ nor sell wood, logs or charcoal belonging to someone else. No one is allowed to sell except the importers themselves and they must not sell at a higher or
10 lower price than / they stated in their declaration to the collectors of the two per cent tax (*pentekostologoi*).⁴ Before selling the importers must declare to the *agoranomoi*⁵ the price stated in their declaration to the
15 *pentekostologoi*. And if anyone sells (his goods) / in violation of the regulations, he shall be fined 50 drachmas, and any citizen who wishes may bring an accusation against him before the *agoranomoi*. The *agorano-*
20 *moi* shall introduce the cases before the / Thirty One during the month in which the accusation was made. The accuser must pay the (statutory) deposit to the court. If (the defendant) is found guilty, he shall pay back

the deposit to the accuser as well as two thirds of the prescribed fine, / and (shall pay) the remaining third to the public treasury. The agoranomoi shall collect the fines from the defendant within ten days of his condemnation, and they may not be called to account (for their action). If they are unable (to collect the fines), they shall declare so under oath and shall hand over the defendant and his possessions to the accuser, and they shall inscribe (these facts) on / the board where the other written statements are kept and shall hand it over to the council (to be deposited) in the record office.

Those who enjoy freedom from taxes (ateleia) (at Delos) and who import wood or logs or charcoal for sale according to the (official) measures for wood, shall declare to the agoranomoi / the prices they intend to charge before they begin selling, and they shall not be allowed to sell (their goods) at a higher or lower price than they stated in their declaration. Should anyone contravene the regulations, the agoranomoi shall not provide them with scales or with / measures for charcoal,[6] and they (the importers) shall pay to the city a fee of one drachma a day for the place where they store their wood, charcoal or logs until they remove them. The agoranomoi shall collect the fee from them, and they may not be called to account (for their action).[7]

Syll.[3] 975; IDélos 509; H. W. Pleket
Epigraphica I (Leyden, 1964), no. 10

1. Wood and charcoal were the normal fuels for heating and cooking.
2. On measures compare III, 231 n. 25.
3. On this clause see P. Gauthier, BCH 101 (1977), 203–8.
4. See 100 n. 4.
5. See 107 n. 3.
6. Compare III.
7. The intention of the law is clear: the Delians wish to enjoy stable prices for wood and charcoal and to protect themselves from speculation.

110 Decree of Paros in honour of a man for services especially as 'agoranomos' (second century)

Good fortune. Resolved by the council and people; Myrmidon son of Eumenes moved: since Cillus son of Demetrius is a good [man] and a benefactor of the city; and (since) previously / when he was agoranomos[1] he discharged his office [well] and justly and in accordance with the [laws], for which the people awarded him fitting honours; and (since) when he was elected to the same [office] in the archonship of Gorgus / he showed himself exceedingly industrious, and made every effort to ensure

that the people should enjoy prosperity and abundance and be supplied with bread and barley at the lowest prices and of the highest quality,[2] and
15 as regards the wage / labourers and their employers, he made sure that neither would be unfairly treated by compelling, in accordance with the laws, the labourers not to misbehave but to get down to work and the
20 employers to pay their wages to the / workers without having to be taken to court; and (since) he showed proper care for all the other duties of his office, avoiding no hardship, but behaving in conformity with the
25 laws and his whole mode of life and the / offices he held before he was *agoranomos*; therefore, so that the people may be seen to be rendering worthy honours to those who show surpassing zeal for the people, with
30 good fortune, be it resolved to praise Cillus son of Demetrius and / to honour him with a gold crown [and] a marble statue for his merits and for the zeal which he continuously displays for the people [and] to proclaim the crown at the tragic contest during the Great Dionysia,
35 proclaiming / [the] reasons why [the] people has crowned him; the magistrates in whose term of office the Great Dionysia are next celebrated shall take care of the proclamation of the crown. And Dexiochus came forward and said he was grateful to the people for the
40 honours / voted to his father, and that he would [give] himself the money for the statue and its dedication;[3] therefore, so that the statue should be made and placed as soon as possible in the office of the
45 *agoranomos* / wherever they wish, without disturbing [any] of the dedications, and the [decree] should be inscribed on a stone stele and [placed near] the statue, let Dexiochus see to this [as he] promises.

50 Dioscuri. / Resolved by the council and the people; Eumenes son of Eumenes moved: since Cillus son of Demetrius has in the past constantly been a good man towards the people and has benefited in every way the
55 city publicly and those who meet him privately, / and now when he was elected polemarch and happened to be serving as priest of the Dioscuri at the sacrifice of the Theoxenia, [wishing] to make more magnificent the festival in honour of the gods [and] to have everyone sharing in the
60 sacrificial offerings, he has come forward / [to] the people and promises[4] to give a public feast at the Theoxenia, be it resolved by the people to praise Cillus son of Demetrius for his piety to the gods and his goodwill to the people, [and] let him hold the public feast in the gymnasium.[5]

IG XII.5.129

1. See **107** n. 3.
2. On the food supply of Greek cities see **112**.
3. Cf. **215** n. 15.
4. See **97** n. 6.
5. On the wealthy benefactors of Greek cities see **97**.

111 Athenian decree concerning weights and measures (late second century)

See further: J. Day, *An Economic History of Athens under Roman Domination* (New York, 1942), 85f., 111–13.

(I) . . . [the measure? in the Skias[1]] or at Piraeus or [at Eleusis . . .] the owner of the measure shall be arrested . . . disputing about the measure . . . [the] magistrates [shall . . .?] the measure to the public bank . . . [the] / list of the goods to be auctioned; if he is a slave, he shall receive   5 [fifty strokes] of the lash,[2] and they (sc. the magistrates) shall destroy [the measure]; if the magistrates do not give assistance to individuals,[3] the Council of Six Hundred [shall compel them (to act)].[4]

(II) The magistrates whose legal responsibility it is shall make standard measures corresponding to the copies that have been made, for liquid measures, dry measures and weights, and shall [compel those who] sell goods in the agora or the workshops or the retail shops or the [wineshops] / to use these measures and weights, measuring all liquid   10 produce with the same [measure], and henceforward it shall not be allowed for any magistrate to make measures or weights [larger] or smaller than these; if any magistrate does this or fails to compel [the sellers] to sell with [these] he shall be fined 1,000 drachmas which will be consecrated to Demeter and Core, and any Athenian who wishes may make an inventory of his property to secure payment of the fine. [Similarly / they must make] equal and inspect the measures and weights   15 in future, and the Council of Six Hundred which is in session during the month of Hecatombaeon shall take care that no seller or buyer uses a measure [or] weight that is not true to standard, but only the correct ones.

(III)[5] Those who sell Persian nuts (walnuts), dried almonds, hazelnuts of Heraclea, pine-nuts, chestnuts, Egyptian beans, / dates and any other   20 dried fruits that are sold with these, and (also) lupines, olives and pine kernels, shall sell them with a measure of a capacity of three half *choinikes* of grain levelled off, selling them with this *choinix* heaped up, with a depth of five fingers and a width at the rim of one finger; similarly those who sell fresh almonds, [newly] picked [olives] and dried figs must sell them with a *choinix* heaped full, twice the size of the previously [mentioned one, / with a] rim three half fingers (wide), and they must   25 use measures (*choinikes*) made of wood; if [anyone] sells fresh almonds, newly picked olives or dried figs [in another way?] or with another type of measure [he must not sell less] than a medimnus of grain; if he [sells] in a smaller type of measure, the magistrate under whose [supervision he is] shall immediately sell [the] contents by auction, pay the price to the [public bank] and destroy the measure.

(IV)[6] The commercial mina shall weigh 138 [drachmas of wreath-bearing[7]
30 (silver)] / according to the weights at the mint and a make-[weight] of
twelve drachmas of wreath-bearing (silver), and everybody shall sell all
other goods with this mina except for those expressly specified to be sold
according to the silver (coin standard), and they shall place the beam of
the scales level at a weight of 150 drachmas of [wreath-] bearing (silver);
[the] commercial weight of five minas shall have a [make-] weight of one
commercial mina, so that when the beam of the scales is level it shall weigh
35 six commercial / minas; the commercial talent [shall have] a
make-weight of five commercial [minas], so that when the beam of the
scales is level it shall weigh one commercial [talent and] five commercial
minas; they must all correspond to the [measures] and [weights] in the mint.
(v) [So that] the measures and weights may remain for [future] time, [the
person] appointed to [provide] the measures and weights, Diodorus son
of Theophilus [of Halae], shall hand [then over] to the public slave
40 [appointed] in the Skias / and to the one at Piraeus along with the
[overseer?[8] and to the one at] Eleusis; they shall preserve [them] and shall
give copies of the [measures and weights] to the magistrates [and to] all
[others] who need them, and they shall not be allowed to [alter? them]
nor to remove [anything from the] buildings provided except the leaden
[and bronze] copies that have been made . . .
45 (VI) If they (sc. the public slaves) charge anybody money . . . / . . . the
prytaneis [who are in office] and the general in charge of [the] soldiers
shall [punish] the (public slave) [appointed] at the [Skias] with strokes of
the lash, [punishing] him according to [the] seriousness of the offence;
the overseer [of the harbour] who is appointed (shall punish) the (public
slave) at [Piraeus]; the hierophant [and the] men [who] are appointed
every [year] for the festival[9] (shall punish) the (public slave) at Eleusis.
(VII) [The public] slaves shall hand [over] to the public slaves [appointed
50 after] them / all the [measures and weights] together with an inventory;
if there is anything they do not hand [over], they shall [be made to
provide it] by those appointed to supervise them in accordance with the
decree, and [if they destroy any item, they] shall be made [to provide
other similar ones] in place of those destroyed; [they shall also deposit in]
the [Metroon][10] a written statement of the items they have received and
[handed over; if they do not] deposit [this statement they] shall not be
allowed to receive wages for any public service.
(VIII) Copies [are to be deposited in] the acropolis of the commercial
55 [talent] / the ten mina weight, the five mina weight, the double mina,
[the mina], the half mina, the quarter mina, the *chous* [and the *choinix*].
(IX) If anyone is caught committing an offence concerning the measures
and weights deposited [in the Skias], at Eleusis, at [Piraeus] and on the
acropolis, whether he is a magistrate or [a private citizen] or a public

slave, he will be punished in accordance with the law passed on [the punishment] of wrongdoers. [The council] of the Aeropagus shall be responsible and shall punish anyone who has committed an offence [in these matters] / in accordance with the laws passed about wrongdoers.   60 [The] man appointed to provide the [measures and] weights shall inscribe [this decree on stone] stelae and place them in the buildings in which the measures and weights are deposited.

From the same decree:[11]

[The] officials shall use the same measure with the [leaden] symbol, corresponding to that in the Skias, and must not charge more than three obols; the magistrates shall use the previously stamped measures, unless any of the sellers [or buyers] uses a stamped measure.[12]

H. W. Pleket, *Epigraphica* I (Leyden, 1964), no. 14; *IG* II². 1013 with *Hesperia* 7 (1938), p. 127 no. 27

1. I.e. the Tholus, a round building in the agora where the *prytaneis* took their meals (see *The Athenian Agora* XIV (Princeton, 1972), 41–6).
2. Cf. **87** n. 2.
3. Individuals who denounce culprits to them.
4. This first clause is concerned with the use of false measures.
5. On this clause see M. Crosby, *Hesperia* 18 (1949), 108–13.
6. The details and purpose of this clause are obscure and controversial; a mina of 150 drs. is introduced in addition to the existing mina of 138 drs. which is kept for certain transactions. See M. Lang and M. Crosby, *The Athenian Agora* X (Princeton, 1964), 2–4.
7. A reference to the so-called 'New Style' Athenian coinage (see **107**) introduced by Athens in 196/5 (? the date is disputed, cf. D. M. Lewis, *NC* (1962), 275–300 and M. Thompson, *ib.* 301–33); the reverse of the coin shows an olive wreath surrounding Athena's owl and a Panathenaic amphora.
8. See clause VI below.
9. The Eleusinian Mysteries.
10. The repository of state archives (see *The Athenian Agora* XIV (Princeton, 1972), 35–8).
11. On these last lines see M. Crosby, *Hesperia* 18 (1949), 111f.
12. The inscription does not make clear the purpose of the legislation on weights and measures. It is not obvious that anything more was involved than a simple market-policing operation. On measures cf. **109, 231** n. 25.

112 Ephesus honours Agathocles of Rhodes for selling corn cheap (*ca* 300)

One of the most important preoccupations of many Greek cities, large or small, was their food supply. The evidence illuminating this problem is abundant and varied (see **34** and n. 5, **40A** §§10 and 11, **43, 44, 50, 92, 96** and n. 3, **97, 110, 113–116, 156, 269** and n. 6).

See further: Rostovtzeff II (1941), 1248–52 and index svv. corn, grain; Tarn and Griffith (1952), 106–8; L. Casson, *TAPA* 85 (1954), 168–87; Hands (1968), ch. 7.

Resolved by the council and the people; Dion son of Diopithes moved: since Agathocles son of Hegemon of Rhodes,[1] when he was importing corn to the city amounting to 14,000 *hekteis*[2] and found that the grain in the agora was being sold at more than 6 drachmas (a medimnus), he was

5 persuaded by the *agoranomos*[3] and wished / to do a favour to the people, and sold all his grain more cheaply than it was being sold in the agora, be it resolved by the people, to grant citizenship to Agathocles of Rhodes on a basis of full equality, to himself and his descendants; the priests (*essenes*) shall allot him a tribe and *chiliastys*[4] and the temple administrators (*naopoioi*) shall inscribe these honours in the sanctuary of Artemis, where

10 the other grants of citizenship / are inscribed, so that all may know that the people knows how to return thanks to its benefactors. He was allotted the tribe Bembine and the *chiliastys* Aegoteus.

Syll.[3] 354

1. Honoured in a proxeny decree from Arcesine, *IG* XII.7.9 (*ca* 300).
2. 6 *hekteis* to 1 medimnus.
3. See **107** n. 3.
4. A subdivision of the tribe, cf. **116, 135** (Samos).

113 Decree of Samos in honour of Boulagoras for many services (*ca* 246–243)

Resolved by the council and the people, proposal of the *prytaneis*, concerning [the] motion put forward by Hippodamas son of Pantonactides, that Boulagoras son of Alexis, who has performed many services publicly for the city and privately for many of the citizens,[1] should be

5 honoured and crowned as resolved by the council and the / people; since Boulagoras, when previously estates in the territory of Anaia[2] which at the time was under the authority of King Antiochus[3] were being contested, and the citizens who had been deprived of their estates turned for help to the people and asked for an embassy to (be sent to) Antiochus to make them recover their property,[4] Boulagoras was appointed

10 ambassador and travelled / first to Ephesus, but when Antiochus broke camp he followed him as far as Sardis, and displayed every zeal and enthusiasm in opposing in his embassy the most illustrious of the 'friends'[5] of Antiochus, who happened to be in possession of the

contested estates, so that the people might get back the estates which had
been claimed at that time and restore them / to those who had been   15
deprived of them unjustly, and concerning these matters he brought back
letters from Antiochus to our city and to the commander under his
orders at Anaia and to the financial official (*dioiketes*),[6] thanks to which
those who had been deprived (of their estates) at the time recovered their
possessions and subsequently none of the subordinates of Antiochus ever
tried to lay claim to / what belonged to the citizens; and (since) when   20
chosen by the people on several occasions to be advocate (*proegoros*) in
public trials[7] he constantly showed himself eager and zealous and
procured many benefits and advantages to the city from the verdicts; and
(since) when elected by the people superintendent (*epistates*) of the
gymnasium in accordance with the law because of the failure of the
gymnasiarch,[8] he directed with fairness [and] / excellence the good   25
discipline (*eukosmia*) of the ephebes and the *neoi* (young men),[9] and
(since) during the present year a delegation of sacred envoys had to be
sent to Alexandria,[10] knowing that the people attaches the greatest
importance to the honours paid to King Ptolemy (III) and to his sister
Queen Berenice, since funds for their crowns[11] and the sacrifices which
the sacred envoys had to perform in Alexandria / were limited, and there   30
was no money to pay for the travel expenses of the leader of the sacred
embassy and the sacred envoys who were to bring the crowns (to
Alexandria) and perform the sacrifices, and no immediate source of
money was available, (Boulagoras) wishing that none of the honours
previously decreed to the king, the queen, their parents and ancestors
should be omitted, promised that he would advance from his own
pocket the money for that purpose / which amounted to little less than   35
6,000 drachmas; and when the people was suffering from a shortage of
corn[12] and the citizens because of the urgency of the need had appointed
three corn commissions (*sitonia*),[13] in all of these he was never short of
zeal and enthusiasm, but in the first corn commission he advanced all the
money for the deposit as voted by the people, and for / the second he   40
promised a sum equal to that provided by the most lavish contributors,
while for the third he not only contributed from his own pocket all the
money for the deposit, but also when the grain had been brought to the
city and the corn commissioner had lent money for it, he came forward
in the assembly and promised[14] that since there were no resources
available to refund the money, he himself would pay back the loan on
behalf of the city together with the interests / and all other expenses, and 45
he did this quickly and refunded the creditor without imposing any
written contract for these sums on the city and without requesting the
nomination of guarantors, but attaching the greatest importance to the
common good and the enjoyment of abundance by the people; and

(since) on all other occasions he continues to show himself eager and well
50   disposed, / giving the best [advice] to the people publicly and privately
to every citizen, reconciling those who have disputes and advancing
loans from his own private means to many of the needy;[15] therefore so
that we may be seen to be honouring good men and [encouraging] many
citizens to follow the same course of action, be it resolved by the people
55   to praise Boulagoras son of Alexis for his [excellence] / and for his
goodwill towards the citizens, and to crown him with a gold [crown] at
the Dionysia during the tragic contest; the agonothete[16] shall see to the
proclamation; the controllers (*exetastai*) shall inscribe this decree on a
stone stele and dedicate it in the sanctuary of Hera; the treasurer of the
sacred monies [shall provide] for the expense from the money available
60   to him from fines; / Hyblesius, Herodotus, Monimus, Demetrius were
[present].

SEG 1.366

1. On benefactors see **97**.
2. See **116** §§3–4. Compare the case of Samothrace, **269**.
3. Antiochus Hierax: see **144, 145, 197**.
4. Compare the mediation of Philippides in **43**.
5. See **25** n. 3.
6. Cf. **156** n. 5.
7. Trials which involved the interests of the city against individuals, e.g. over loans or state property.
8. I.e. the liturgy was proving too burdensome for its holder. On gymnasia cf. **118**.
9. See **105** n. 3.
10. To the *Ptolemaieia*, cf. **218**.
11. Crowns of gold, cf. **183** n. 1, **231** l. 59 and n. 15.
12. See **112**.
13. Their function was to purchase grain for the state; cf. **97, 114–116**.
14. See **97** n. 6.
15. See **92** n. 3.
16. See **43** n. 8.

114 Decree of Delos in honour of Aristobulus of Thessalonica, 'sitones' of Demetrius II of Macedon (239–229)

[Resolved by the] council and the people; . . . son of Teleson moved;
[since Aristobulus] son of Athenaeus [of Thessalonica], who is *proxenos*
5   and benefactor / [of the] sanctuary and of the Delians, when sent [by]
King Demetrius (II of Macedon) as corn commissioner (*sitones*),[1] stayed
(in Delos) for a long time behaving in a way that was [dignified] and
10   worthy of the sanctuary, [of the king] and of the people of Delos / [and]

196

has [displayed] every zeal and enthusiasm [over] the [interests of the sanctuary], of the king [and] of the people of [Delos] and [provides] benefits publicly to the city and privately to [those who] meet / him,   15 whatever [request any] Delian makes from him; so that all may know that the people knows how [to honour good men], be it resolved [by the council] and the people, to [praise] him and crown him with a laurel wreath / [and] that the sacred [herald] shall make the following proc-   20 lamation in [the] theatre at the festival of Apollo when the choruses of boys are competing: the people of Delos crowns Aristobulus son of Athenaeus of Thessalonica / with a laurel wreath for his excellence, his   25 [piety] towards the sanctuary and his goodwill [towards] King Demet-rius and the people of Delos. Antipater son of Callias put the motion to the vote.[2]

F. Dürrbach, *Choix d'inscriptions de Délos* (Paris, 1921)

no. 48

1. See **113** n. 13.
2. The exact importance of Delos as a centre of the corn trade in the Hellenistic world is controversial; it is emphasised e.g. by Rostovtzeff but doubted by Casson, both cited on **112**. See also **44** ll.53–55 with T. L. Shear, *Hesperia* Supplement 17 (1978), 30–2.

115 Decree of Histiaea found at Delos, in honour of a Rhodian in connexion with the corn supply (*ca* 230–220)

Side A

(In a crown) The people of Histiaea (crowns) Athenodorus son of Pisagoras. /   5
    The archons proposed that the council should submit to the people the following resolution: since Athenodorus son of Pisagoras of Rhodes continues to show his goodwill to the people and provides services privately to any citizen who is in need and publicly to the city, and (since) in every way he provided ready assistance to the corn commissioners (*sitonai*)[1] sent by the city / to Delos[2] and lent them money without   10 interest,[3] and enabled them to discharge their duties as quickly as possible, preferring the good of the city to his private gain; therefore, so that all may know that the people of Histiaea / knows how to honour its   15 benefactors and more people may compete to provide benefits to the city when they see worthy men being honoured; with good fortune, be it resolved by the people, to honour Athenodorus son of Pisagoras of Rhodes for his goodwill towards the city and to crown him with an

20   olive / wreath for his excellence and his goodwill towards the people of
Histiaea, to proclaim the crown at the procession of the *Antigoneia*,[4] and
that the agonothete[5] shall see to the proclamation; to grant him and his
descendants citizenship according to the law and precedence of access to
25   the council / and the people after sacred matters; to inscribe this decree
on a stone stele and dedicate it here (i.e. in Histiaea) in the sanctuary of
Dionysus and at Delos in the sanctuary of Apollo[6] after asking the
community (*koinon*) of the Delians for a place; the expense for the
30   inscription shall be provided by the / presiding treasurer.

Side B

Resolved by the council and the people; Parmenion son of Polybulus
moved; to grant to the Histiaeans the place in the sanctuary [which] they
are requesting, between the statues of Ophell[. . . and . . .]ikis for the
5   dedication of the stele on which are [inscribed] / the honours granted by
the Histiaeans to Athenodorus; Theophas son of Cleosthenes put to the
vote.

F. Dürrbach, *Choix d'inscriptions de Délos* (Paris, 1921),

no. 50; *Syll.*[3] 493

1. See **113** n. 13.
2. See **114** n. 2; the importance of Rhodes in the corn trade is emphasised by
Casson, *op. cit.*
3. Athenodorus need not have been a banker (R. Bogaert, *Banques et banquiers dans les cités grecques* (Leyden, 1968), 171f.).
4. A festival in honour of (probably) Antigonus Doson.
5. See **43** n. 8.
6. The present text.

116 A Samian corn law (after 188)

The following inscription gives the most detailed evidence available of the setting
up of a permanent fund by a Greek city, by public subscription, for the purchase
of corn which was to be distributed free to all Samian citizens (and not just the
needy). The measure will have been designed to palliate the shortages previously
experienced by Samos (cf. **113**). The funds were to be lent out at interest to
private borrowers and the interest from these loans (or, in case of default, the
interest from the sale of the security) was to finance the purchase of corn. The
fund was managed by commissioners (*meledonoi*; see §§1–3, 5, 8–9), elected
annually, who lent the money, collected the interest and made payments to two
men 'in charge of the corn supply' elected annually (see §5) to purchase corn from
the revenues of the goddess Hera from Anaia on the mainland (see §§3–4) and to
distribute it on a monthly basis to all citizens (see §7). In addition there was a corn

commissioner (*sitones* – see **113** n. 13) in charge of the purchase of corn from all other sources (see §§3–5). For the food supply of Greek cities see on **112**. On foundations cf. **119, 120, 156, 206**.

See further: Hands (1968), 95f.

(The beginning of the inscription is lost)[1]

(1) . . . of the wealthiest. They shall hold the election (of magistrates) during the month Cronion at the second meeting of the [assembly]. The presiding magistrates (*prytaneis*) shall summon the assembly [in the] theatre and order the members of the assembly to sit [according] / to   5
their *chiliastys*,[2] after placing signs and marking off [a spot] for each *chiliastys*; anyone who disobeys and does not sit in his own *chiliastys*, they shall fine one Samian stater. If he claims to have been unjustly fined he shall appeal, and judgement shall be given in the citizens' court / within   10
twenty days. The proposal and election[3] shall be carried out by members of the *chiliastys* themselves.

(2) At this assembly the *chiliastys* shall approve after examination the securities and the guarantors. The *prytaneis* shall inscribe the securities and the guarantors they (sc. the *chiliastys*) have approved / in the public   15
records. Similarly they shall enter in the public records (the names of) the commissioners (*meledonoi*) who have been appointed. When [the] election is about to take place, the herald of the city shall pray for the prosperity of those who have elected men they believe will / manage the   20
funds in the best way.

(3) (The commissioners) who are elected shall collect the interest from the borrowers and pay it to the men who have been appointed in charge of the corn supply. The latter shall purchase the corn that is collected from the tax of one twentieth / from Anaia,[4] and shall pay the goddess   25
(Hera) a price that is not less than that previously fixed by the people, (namely) five [drachmas] and two obols (a medimnus). The money that is left over, if the people decides not to buy any more corn, they shall keep themselves until the appointment of others in charge of the corn supply; they shall then pay the money to them. But if (the people) /   30
decides to buy more corn they shall immediately make the payment to the corn commissioner (*sitones*) who has been appointed.

(4) The latter shall purchase corn from the territory of Anaia in the way which seems to him most advantageous for the city, unless the people thinks it more advantageous to buy corn from another source. If not, / (the purchase) shall be made as the people decides. The *prytaneis* in   35
office during [the] month of Artemision shall put this matter on the agenda every year and introduce a motion.

(5) The people shall appoint every year, on the first day of the elections to magistracies, after the elective magistracies have been filled, / two men,   40

one from each tribe, to be in charge of the corn supply, each of them with property worth not less than three talents. They shall receive the interest from the commissioners (*meledonoi*) and shall pay the price of the corn together with any other expense incurred, and they shall measure
45   out / the corn. The people shall elect a corn commissioner (*sitones*) at the same assembly, with property worth not less than two talents.

(6) If (the people) so decides, the money from the interest shall be lent, if anyone wishes after providing adequate security and naming guarantors
50   to anticipate / and provide corn more advantageously. The men appointed in charge of the corn supply shall accept such security at their own risk.

(7) They shall distribute all the corn that has been bought to the citizens who are in residence according to their *chiliastys*, measuring out free to
55   each citizen every month / two medimni. They shall begin the distribution in the month of Pelusion and shall measure out (the corn) continuously for as many months as (the corn) suffices. They shall not measure out (corn) to anybody on behalf of anybody else except in case of illness. They shall carry out the distribution from the new moon until the tenth (of the month), and until the thirtieth to citizens who are abroad
60   if they come back. / They shall provide every month a register of the beneficiaries of the distribution and shall lodge it in the office of the public auditor with the names of the beneficiaries arranged according to their *chiliastys*.

(8) The members of each *chiliastys* shall be permitted to appoint the same man as commissioner (*meledonos*) successively for five years.
65   (9) If any of the / borrowers does not pay back the money, in whole or in part, the *chiliastys* shall sell the security; if there is a surplus it shall give it to the person who provided the security, but if there is a deficit it shall recover it from the guarantor. The *chiliastys* shall give the interest that is due to those who have been appointed in charge of the corn supply. If it
70   does not, / the members of the *chiliastys* shall not receive the corn that is due until they have paid the debt. If any of the commissioners (*meledonoi*) who have been appointed takes the money which he is supposed to lend but instead of lending it keeps it unjustly for himself, he shall owe (a fine of) 10,000 drachmas to the city. Similarly if he does not give the
75   interest / to the men appointed in charge of the corn supply, he shall pay the same fine, and the public auditors (*exetastai*) shall inscribe his property as being confiscated up to the amount of money he ought to have paid. In addition to the fine they shall inscribe him as deprived of his civic rights, and he shall remain so until he has paid. The members of the
80   *chiliastys* shall not receive / the corn that is due to them if they appoint a commissioner (*meledonos*) who has not paid the money. The members of the *chiliastys* may if they wish pay themselves the money which was not

given to the city by the commissioner (*meledonos*) or the borrower, either all of them or sharing it out between some of them; and when they have paid the money they shall receive distributions / of corn from the time when they pay.   85

(10) It shall not be permitted to anyone to use these funds nor the revenue from them for any other purpose than the distribution of free corn. If any *prytanis* puts forward a motion, or any orator proposes, or any president puts to the vote that these funds should be lent or diverted to any other purpose, they shall each be fined / 10,000 drachmas. Similarly if any   90 treasurer or commissioner (*meledonos*) or any of those appointed in charge of the corn supply, or any corn commissioner (*sitones*) gives or lends (these funds) for any other purpose than the distribution of free corn.⁵ [. . .]⁶

*Syll.*³ 976

1. The lost part of the inscription will have dealt with the setting up of the fund.
2. A subdivision of the tribe, cf. **112, 135**.
3. Of the *meledonoi*, cf. next §.
4. A district on the mainland, controlled by Samos (cf. **113**), where the goddess Hera had extensive estates.
5. Cf. the similar safeguards in **119, 120, 206**.
6. There follows a list of *ca* 120 contributors to the corn fund (cf. **125** n. 1); the sums given range from 50 to 1,000 drs., 100 being the most frequent figure.

117 The Athenian 'ephebeia' in the Hellenistic age (266/5)

In the years after the battle of Chaeronea in 338 the Athenian *ephebeia* was reorganised as a system of civic and military training, supported by the state and compulsory for all Athenian citizens between the ages of 18 and 20. After a gap in the epigraphic record from 303/2 to 267/6, the institution reemerges into light in a modified form: it has become annual (instead of lasting two years), voluntary, and in practice restricted to the children of wealthy citizens, as is implied by the considerable fall in numbers (from *ca* 600–700 ephebes annually in the late fourth century to *ca* 20–40 in the period after 267/6). In the second century the *ephebeia* acquired elements of literary and philosophical education, and its original character was further modified in the latter part of the second century when non-Athenians began to be admitted. For educational institutions elsewhere in the Greek world cf. **118–120**.

See further: C. Pélékidis, *Histoire de l'éphébie attique* (Paris, 1962); Hands (1968), 116–20, 169f.

[In] the archonship of Nicias [of the deme Otryne] (266/5), in the third prytany, of the tribe Acamantis, for which Isocrates of the deme Alopeke

was secretary; on the twenty-[sixth] of Boedromion, and the twenty-
sixth day of the prytany; [assembly]; of the presiding magistrates
(*proedroi*) Leocrates son of Leostratus [of the deme Oine] put the motion
5 to the vote / together with his colleagues in office; resolved by the
council and the [people, . .s]tratus son of Mynniscus of the deme
Pergase moved: since [the ephebes, who] have undergone their training
in the archonship of Menecles (267/6) when the city was [at war],¹ all
10 held their ground, [keeping] good order [and] obeying the laws / [and]
the *kosmetes*,² and [continued] throughout the year to perform the [guard
duties and all] the instructions given by [the] general for the guarding of
the Mouseion,³ as [ordered] by the people; therefore, since the others
who [held their ground] have also been honoured, so that [they] too may
15 be honoured [for] their deserts: / with good fortune, resolved by [the]
council, that the presiding magistrates [who] are in charge of the [next]
meeting of the assembly should bring forward the *kosmetes* after sacred
matters and raise this question, and communicate to the people [the
opinion of] the council, viz. that [the] council [resolves] to praise [the]
20 ephebes who have undergone their training / [in] the archonship of
Menecles, [and] to crown them [with a gold crown] in accordance with
the law for their [good] discipline and the zeal they constantly [show]
towards the people; they shall be granted a seat of honour in the
[competitions] celebrated by the city. Aminias son of Antiphanes of the
25 deme Cephisia, their [*kosmetes*], shall also be praised; / [so too] Hermodorus son of Heortius [of the deme Acharnae, the] physical trainer
(*paidotribes*),⁴ Philotheus son of Stratius of the deme Lamptra, [the
javelin] thrower, Mnesitheus son of Mnesitheus of the deme Copros,
[the artilleryman] and Sondrus [of Crete], the archer,⁵ [and] they shall be
30 crowned with an olive crown / [for their] good discipline [and] the
careful attention they constantly show towards the [ephebes]; the
secretary of the prytany shall inscribe this decree on a [stone] stele [and]
place it in the agora, and the officials in charge of financial [administra-
tion] shall provide the [expense] required for the stele. [. . .]⁶

*Syll.*³ 385; *IG* ɪɪ².665

1. The Chremonidean War (cf. **49, 50**).
2. The supervisor of ephebic education, similar in function to gymnasiarchs
   elsewhere.
3. Cf. **44** n. 3.
4. Cf. **118** n. 10.
5. These were all involved in training the ephebes in physical and military
   exercises.
6. There follows a list of names of the officials and the (33) ephebes honoured.

118   A gymnasiarchy law from Beroea (between 167 and 148)

On education in the Hellenistic world see further: Jones (1940), 220–5; Tarn and Griffith (1952), 95–8; H. I. Marrou, *A History of Education in Antiquity* (London, 1956), part II; Hands (1968), 116–30.

Side A

When Hippocrates son of Nicocrates was *strategos*, on the 19th of Apellaeus, at a meeting of the assembly, Zopyrus son of Amyntas, the gymnasiarch, Asclepiades son of Heras and Callipus / son of Hippostratus moved: since all the other magistracies are exercised in accordance with the law,[1] and in the cities[2] in which there are gymnasia and anointing is practised the laws on gymnasiarchs are deposited in the public archives, it is (therefore) appropriate that the same should be done among us and that the law which we handed over to the auditors (*exetastai*) should be inscribed on a stele and placed / in the gymnasium and also deposited in the public office; for when this is done, the young men (*neoteroi*) will feel a greater sense of shame and be more obedient to their leader,[3] and their revenues will not be wasted away as the gymnasiarchs who are appointed / will discharge their office in accordance with the law and will be liable to render accounts.[4]

    The city resolved that the law on the gymnasiarchy which Zopyrus son of Amyntas, the gymnasiarch, Asclepiades son of Heras and Callipus son of Hippostratus introduced, should be valid and be deposited in the public archives, and that the gymnasiarchs should use / it, and that the law should be inscribed on a stele and placed in the gymnasium. The law was ratified on the first of Peritius.

The Law on the Gymnasiarchy

The city shall appoint a gymnasiarch [at the same time] as the other magistrates, and he shall not be below (the age of) [30] nor above 60. The gymnasiarch who is appointed / . . . shall swear the following oath: [I swear by . . . Heracles] (and) Hermes[5] that I shall discharge the office of gymnasiarch in accordance with the law on the gymnasiarchy; as for all the things that are not [written] in the [law . . .] with the [greatest possible fairness . . .] without showing favour to a friend or / harming an enemy unjustly, nor will I appropriate any of the revenues which belong to the young men (*neoi*), nor will I knowingly allow anyone else (to do so) in any way or under any pretext; if I abide by my oath may I enjoy many blessings, but if I break it may the opposite happen.

    The gymnasiarch [who is appointed], when he enters / office, [shall summon] an assembly on the first of the month [of Peritius] in the [gymnasium to choose?] three men who once elected [shall swear the] following oath and . . . [. . .]

Side B

No one under the age of 30 may take off his clothes when the signal is lowered,[6] unless the leader gives his assent. When the signal is raised, no one else may do so unless the leader gives his assent, and no one may

5 anoint himself in another wrestling-school (*palaistra*) in the / same city. If he does, the gymnasiarch shall prevent him and fine him 50 drachmas.

All those who frequent the gymnasium shall obey whoever is appointed by the gymnasiarch to act as leader, as is specified for the gymnasiarch; whoever does not obey (the leader), the gymnasiarch shall

10 punish him with flogging, [and] he shall fine the / others.[7]

The ephebes[8] and those about the age of 22 shall practise javelin throwing and archery every day, when the boys have anointed themselves, and similarly if any other exercise appears to be necessary.

Concerning the boys: none of the youngsters (*neaniskoi*)[9] may enter

15 among the boys, nor talk to the boys, otherwise the gymnasiarch / shall fine and prevent anyone who does any of these things. The physical trainers[10] shall present themselves at the gymnasium twice every day at the time determined by the gymnasiarch, except in the case of illness or some other unavoidable impediment; if not, they shall report to the gymnasiarch. If any of the physical trainers appears to show disrespect

20 and not to present himself / before the boys at the appointed hour, he (sc. the gymnasiarch) shall fine him 5 drachmas every day. The gymnasiarch shall have the power to flog the boys and the physical trainers who show indiscipline, if they are not free, and to fine those who are free. He shall compel the physical trainers to make a review[11] of the

25 boys / three times a year every four months and shall appoint judges for them; he shall crown [the] winner with an olive branch.

Those who may not take part in the gymnasium: no one may (enter) the gymnasium and take off his clothes (if he is) [a slave], a freedman, or a [son] of these,[12] if he has not been to the wrestling-school (*palaistra*), if he is a paederast, or has practised a vulgar trade,[13] or is drunk, or mad.

30 If / the gymnasiarch knowingly allows any of these to anoint himself, [or] (does so) after someone has reported to him and pointed (this) out, he shall be fined 1,000 drachmas. To secure exaction of the fine, the informer shall hand over a report to the auditors (*exetastai*) of the city, and they shall lodge his name with the collector of public debts. [If] they do not lodge his name, or if the collector does not exact (the fine), they

35 shall also be fined the / sum, and one third shall be given to the successful prosecutor. If the gymnasiarch believes his name has been unjustly lodged, he may challenge the decision within [ten] days and be judged before the appropriate tribunal. The future gymnasiarchs shall also prevent those who appear to be contravening the law from anointing themselves. [If] not, they shall be liable to the same fines.

No one may insult the gymnasiarch / in the gymnasium, otherwise   40
(the gymnasiarch) shall fine him 50 drachmas. If anyone strikes the
gymnasiarch in the gymnasium, those present shall prevent him and not
allow him, and (the gymnasiarch) shall likewise fine [the] person who
struck (him) 100 drachmas, and in addition he shall be liable to
prosecution by the gymnasiarch in accordance with the public laws. Any
of those present who do not give help though able to do so shall be
fined / 50 drachmas.   45

Concerning the *Hermaia* (festival of Hermes): the gymnasiarch shall
hold the *Hermaia* in the month of Hyperberetaeus; he shall sacrifice to
Hermes and offer as prizes a weapon and three others for fitness (*euexia*),
good discipline (*eutaxia*) and hard training (*philoponia*) for those up to the
age of 30. The gymnasiarch shall draw up a list of seven men from those
on the spot, who are to judge (the contest of) good discipline;[14] he shall
draw lots for these and make the three who are selected swear / by   50
Hermes that they will judge fairly who seems to them to be in the best
physical condition, without favouritism or hostility of any sort. If the
judges chosen by lot do not do their duty and do not state on oath their
inability (to be judges), the gymnasiarch shall have power to fine the
recalcitrant the sum of 10 drachmas, and shall draw lots among the rest
to replace the defaulter. As for (the contests of) good discipline and hard
training, the gymnasiarch shall swear / by Hermes and judge for good   55
discipline who seems to him to be most well behaved of those up to the
age of 30, and for hard training who seems to him to have trained hardest
during the year of those up to the age of 30. The winners shall wear
crowns on that day and it shall be allowed to tie a headband on anyone
who wishes. At the *Hermaia* the gymnasiarch shall also hold a torch race
of the boys and of the youngsters. The money for the / weapons shall   60
come from the existing revenues. The *hieropoioi* (religious officials),
when celebrating the *Hermaia*, shall receive from each of those who
frequent the gymnasium not more than two drachmas and shall feast
them in the gymnasium, and they shall designate in place of themselves
others to serve as *hieropoioi* in future. The physical trainers shall also
celebrate the sacrifice to Hermes at the same time as the *hieropoioi*; / they   65
shall receive from each of the boys not more than one drachma, and they
shall divide up in shares the raw meat from the sacrifice. The *hieropoioi*
and the gymnasiarch shall not introduce any performers[15] during the
drinking. The winners shall dedicate the prizes they have received under
the following gymnasiarch within eight months. If not, the gymnasiarch
shall fine them 100 drachmas. The gymnasiarch shall have power to flog
and fine those who cheat and do not take part fairly / in the competi-   70
tions, and similarly if anyone hands the victory to another.

Selection of lampadarchs:[16] the gymnasiarch shall appoint from among those on the spot three lampadarchs in the month of Gorpiaeus, and those who have been chosen shall supply oil to the youngsters, each for ten days. He shall also appoint three lampadarchs of the boys; those who

75 are chosen shall supply oil / for the same number of days. If any of those chosen objects, or his father objects, or his brothers, or the guardians of orphans, alleging that he is not able to be lampadarch, he shall state on oath his inability within five days of being chosen. If the person appointed does not perform his duties or does not state on oath his inability, he shall be fined 50 drachmas and shall all the same provide oil and be lampadarch. Likewise if the person who has declared his inability on oath is shown to have done this without good reason, and is convicted

80 by the / gymnasiarch and the young men, he shall be fined 50 drachmas and shall nonetheless be compelled to provide the oil and be lampadarch. In place of a person who has declared on oath his inability with good cause, the gymnasiarch shall appoint someone else. He shall hold the torch race of the boys from among those who frequent (the gymnasium) who seem to him suitable, and similarly with the young men.

Concerning umpires: the gymnasiarch shall appoint umpires who

85 seem to him / suitable, for the torch race at the *Hermaia*, the long race and the other contests. If anyone complains against one of the umpires and says he has been unfairly treated by one of them, he shall call him to account in accordance with the public laws.

The gymnasiarch shall have control of the funds available for the young men and shall spend from them; when he leaves office he shall inscribe on a tablet the sum of the revenues together with any income

90 from fines or convictions / and what has been spent from these, and he shall display it in the gymnasium in the month of Dius of the following year; he shall hand it over within four months to the auditors (*exetastai*) of the city, and any who wish may examine his accounts with them. The balance of the revenue he shall hand over to the succeeding gymnasiarch within 30 days of departing from office. If he does not hand over his

95 accounts or the / balance as is prescribed, he shall pay a fine of 1,000 drachmas to the young men; the collector of public debts shall exact the fine from him when the *exetastai* have lodged his name; the gymnasiarch shall nonetheless hand over his accounts and the balance. The person who has purchased the revenue from the dirt[17] shall provide the service of keeper of the wrestling school (*palaistra*), carrying out the instructions of the gymnasiarch for everything that is appropriate in the gymnasium. If he does not obey or is in any way disorderly, he shall be flogged by the gymnasiarch.

100 Anyone who / steals anything from the gymnasium shall be liable to prosecution for sacrilege and shall be convicted before the appropriate tribunal. The gymnasiarch shall inscribe the motive for all the fines he

inflicted and shall proclaim them in the gymnasium, and shall display (the names of) [all those] fined on a whitewashed board; he shall report them to the collector of public debts who shall exact the fines and hand them over to the gymnasiarch in office. If anyone claims to have been fined unjustly, he may / lodge a complaint and be tried before the   105
appropriate magistrates; if the person fined wins his suit, the gymnasiarch shall pay to him one and a half times (the fine) and he shall be fined in addition one fifth and one tenth. Anyone who wishes may call the gymnasiarch to account within 24 months after his year of office, and suits about this shall be decided before the appropriate tribunals. / [. . .]   110

J. M. R. Cormack in *Ancient Macedonia* II (1977), 139–50;
for the text see *Bull.* 1978, 274

1. Laws regulating the duties of particular magistrates were common in Greek cities; cf. **119, 216**. For other texts on gymnasia and gymnasiarchs cf. **93, 113, 168, 215, 255, 266**; the following is the most informative single text extant.
2. The cities of Macedonia rather than Greek cities generally.
3. Cf. below side B, lines 6–10.
4. The sequel of the text implies the existence of disorders and irregularities in the gymnasium; these prompted the revision and publication of the law.
5. Patrons of gymnasia and education, cf. **119, 120, 215** l.78. On oaths cf. **33** n. 7.
6. The gymnasium remains closed until the signal is raised.
7. The distinction is between free and unfree persons, cf. side B ll.23f.
8. Three consecutive age groups are distinguished according to normal Greek practice, boys (*paides*), ephebes and young men (*neoi*); cf. **105** n. 3.
9. Here and below probably = the ephebes.
10. *Paidotribai*, cf. also **117, 119, 120**.
11. Cf. **120**.
12. On this restriction cf. **119, 120** (cf. also **87** n. 2).
13. Literally 'a trade of the agora'.
14. An engraver's error for 'fitness'.
15. Lecturers, singers, players, artists; cf. **215** ll.74f.
16. Cf. **99** n.1, **129** §IV.
17. *Gloios*: a mixture of oil and dirt scraped off the athletes' bodies, which had medical uses and was sold for revenue.

119 Foundation of a school at Miletus (200/199)

Ephebic institutions in the Hellenistic world were organised by the Greek cities, which appointed officials to supervise their education and constructed the necessary buildings (cf. **117, 118**). On the other hand schools for primary education are shown by the evidence to have been either privately run, or as in the case of this and the next text, to have owed their existence to the generosity of a wealthy benefactor, be he a member of the city concerned (cf. generally **97**), or a king (cf. **206**; Polybius XXXI.31).

See further: Hands (1968), 120–7, and see **118**.

(I) Resolved by the people, proposal of the *synedroi*: since Eudemus son of Thallion has chosen to benefit the people and to perpetuate for all time the memory of his own love of glory, and has promised[1] to give for the education of the free children[2] ten talents of silver / on behalf of himself and his brothers Menander and Dion, the Milesians have voted: to praise Eudemus for his zeal for the most worthy pursuits, and to commend him to the attention of the council and of the people.

(II) So that the management of these funds might be administered in the proper way,[3] Eudemus shall pay / the sum of money mentioned to the treasurers of the regular revenues at the time fixed in his promise, and the treasurers shall forthwith hand it over to the officials appointed to the management of the public bank,[4] and they shall enter it in the city's account under the heading 'the money given by Eudemus for the education / of the free children'; they shall inscribe the sum given and shall guard it carefully, and shall hand it over to the bankers appointed to succeed them, until the people decides about the revenue which is expected from it; if they fail to hand it over as prescribed, they shall owe to the people twice the amount. The assessors (*anataktai*) who administer / the revenues of the city shall put aside every year in their assessment 300 staters for the expected revenue from the money, and shall pay every month in their disbursements the sum due to each of the treasurers. If they fail to put it aside as prescribed, they shall each be fined 500 staters which shall be consecrated / to Hermes and the Muses.[5]

(III) Those who wish to be gymnastic trainers[6] or schoolteachers[7] shall register with the *paidonomoi*[8] appointed for the following year, and the registration shall take place every year from the full moon to the twentieth of the month of Artemisium, and they (sc. the *paidonomoi*) shall publish their names in the stoa of Antiochus;[9] on the 28th / of the same month, when the assembly meets, they shall place a tripod and a censer in the orchestra (i.e. in the theatre), and the priests of Hermes Enagonius[10] in the wrestling school (*palaistra*) of the boys, and of the Muses, and the sacred herald, and the *paidonomoi* who have been elected and are about to enter office, and Eudemus so long as he lives and after that / the eldest of Eudemus' descendants, shall burn frankincense to Hermes, the Muses and Apollo Musagetes.[11] The sacred herald shall pray before the assembly that all may be for the best for those who elect gymnastic trainers and school-teachers whom they believe will best look after the boys, and who declare their opinion without unjust partisanship; / if not, may the opposite happen. After this the *paidonomoi*   40 shall hand over to the secretary of the council the names of those who have registered, and he shall introduce them one by one; the priests and the sacred heralds shall administer an oath on each of those who comes forward. The oath sworn by the gymnastic trainers shall be as follows: 'I swear by Hermes that I have not solicited any / Milesian for his vote, nor   45 have instructed anyone else to canvass for me'; and he shall pray that those who honour their oath may prosper, but that the opposite may happen to those who break it. The schoolteachers shall swear a similar oath, except that they shall swear by Apollo and the Muses. The people shall elect and appoint from the candidates four gymnastic trainers / and   50 four schoolteachers.

(IV) The salary for each of the gymnastic trainers shall be fixed at 30 drs. a month, and for each of the schoolteachers at 40 drs. a month.[12] They shall perform such displays and other activities as are specified in the law concerning *paidonomoi*.[13] The gymnastic trainers who have been elected, / if they wish to go abroad and take athletes to one of the   55 'crowned' competitions,[14] may do so provided they obtain leave of absence from the *paidonomoi* and leave someone in charge of the boys in their place who is acceptable to the *paidonomoi*. And so that each of them may be paid his due regularly, the treasurers shall give the salary stipulated / to the gymnastic trainers and the schoolteachers on the first   60 of every month; if any (of the treasurers) does not give it, he shall be fined 500 staters which shall be consecrated to Hermes and the Muses, and the gymnastic trainers and schoolteachers may exact their salary from them in accordance with the law on *agoranomoi*.[15] The money set aside for this purpose in the / assessment may not be transferred to any   65 other purpose in any way; should anyone mention, propose or put to the vote (such a motion), or transfer (the money) or set aside less than is proposed, he shall be fined 500 staters which shall be consecrated to Hermes and the Muses.

(V) Once the salaries have been paid the *paidonomoi* shall take the balance of the money set aside for these purposes, and shall send / to   70 Apollo of Didyma as fine a bull as possible at the *Didymaea* every five years[16] and in the other years at the *Boegia*; they shall take part in the procession themselves together with the boys they have chosen, the supervisors of the boys who have been elected, Eudemus so long as he lives, and after this the eldest of Eudemus' descendants; / the *paidonomoi*   75 shall sacrifice the victims they have sent and shall share it out among all the boys and the others who are required to take part in the procession.[17]

(VI) The boys shall be released from their studies on the fifth of every month, and the *paidonomoi* shall inscribe this day too together with the

80 others as one of the school holidays, as / is prescribed in the law on *paidonomoi*.

(VII) So that the favourable disposition of the people and the love of glory displayed by Eudemus in this matter might be manifest to all, the *teichopoioi*[18] together with the director of works shall see to it that this decree is inscribed on [two stone] stelae, and one is placed in the wrestling school of the boys, in the [place] which seems to them 85 suitable, / and the other in the sanctuary of [Apollo] Delphinius[19] in the arcade dedicated by [Eudemus] son of Thallion; the people shall deliberate at the [appropriate] time on how Eudemus [is to be honoured worthily] for the zeal he has shown in this. The people resolved to inscribe [the decree] on a whitewashed board.[20]

Syll.[3] 577; H. W. Pleket, *Epigraphica* I (Leyden, 1964),

no. 34

1. Cf. **97** n. 6.
2. Cf. **118B**, ll.26–29, **120**.
3. For other foundations cf. **116, 120, 206**.
4. This public bank, attested by several inscriptions, seems to have had as its chief function the investment of funds from foundations such as that of Eudemus; cf. R. Bogaert, *Banques et banquiers dans les cités grecques* (Leyden, 1968), 256–62.
5. I.e. paid into the treasury of Hermes and the Muses, patrons of education (cf. also on Hermes **118** n. 5).
6. *Paidotribai*, cf. **118** n. 10.
7. Literally 'teachers of letters' (*grammatodidaskaloi*).
8. Supervisors of education; cf. **120, 213** (end).
9. Built by Antiochus I (A. Rehm, *Didyma* II (Berlin, 1958), 479; *OGIS* 213).
10. Who presides over contests.
11. Leader of the Muses.
12. The salaries mentioned here and in **120** are relatively low.
13. Cf. **118** n. 1.
14. The 'sacred' competitions in which the prize was a crown, as opposed to the far more numerous, but less prestigious, competitions in which money prizes were given (cf. Jones (1940), 231f.); cf. **42** l.72, **184**.
15. Cf. **118** n. 1; on *agoranomoi* cf. **107** n. 3.
16. Inclusively reckoned = every four years.
17. Participation by boys and ephebes in religious and other processions celebrated by the cities was common; cf. **206** ll.55–60, **213** (end), **215** l.36, **220** col.III.
18. Officials who looked after the city walls.
19. The present text.
20. For temporary display in addition to permanent exhibition on an inscription.

120 Foundation of a school at Teos (second century)

Fragment A

(I) [. . . and after the] selection [of the] gymnasiarch a *paidonomos*[1] is to be appointed not below [the age] of 40.

(II) And so that all the free children[2] might be educated just as Polythrus son of Onesimus in his foresight promised / to the people,   5
wishing to establish a most fair memorial of his own love of glory, he made a gift for this purpose of 34,000 drachmas.

(III) Every year at the elections, after the selection of the scribes, three schoolmasters[3] are to be appointed, who will teach the boys and the girls;[4] / the person appointed to the first class (literally 'task') shall be   10
given 600 drs. a year,[5] the person (appointed) to the second (class) 550 drs., and the person (appointed) to the third (class) 500 drs. Two physical trainers[6] are also to be appointed, and the annual salary of each is to be 500 drs. A lute player, one who plucks the strings or who uses a plectrum, is also to be appointed, / and the annual salary of the person   15
elected is to be 700 drs. He shall teach music and playing the lute by plucking the strings or using a plectrum to the children whom it is appropriate to select for the higher class and those who are a year younger than them, and (he shall teach) music to the ephebes. The *paidonomos* shall decide about the age of these children. / Should we add   20
an intercalary month (sc. to the calendar)[7] a supplement of the salary shall be paid for the month. The *paidonomos* and the gymnasiarch shall also hire a drill-sergeant and a teacher of archery and javelin throwing, subject to ratification by the people; they shall teach the ephebes and the children who have been registered to learn music. / The teacher of   25
archery and javelin throwing shall be given a salary of 250 drs., and the drill-sergeant 300 drs. The drill-sergeant shall teach for not less than two months. The *paidonomos* and the gymnasiarch shall see to it that the children and the ephebes practice their studies carefully, as each of them / is instructed to do according to the laws. If the schoolmasters   30
disagree with each other about the number of children, the *paidonomos* shall decide, and they shall obey his instructions. The reviews[8] which are to take place shall be held in the gymnasium by the schoolmasters and by the music teachers in the council chamber . . .

Fragment B

(IV) . . . if they do not pay the fine, they [may be compelled to do so].   35
Concerning the drill-sergeant and the teacher of archery and javelin throwing the procedure shall be as written above. If the treasurers in office or those in charge at any time / do not hand over the money as is   40

prescribed, or another magistrate or private citizen submits a motion, or acts, or proposes, or puts to the vote, or submits a law in contravention of this, or cancels this law in any way or under any pretext, (suggesting) that the money must be diverted or not spent for the purpose specified by the law, or allocated to [any] other ends than those laid down in this
45 law,[9] the action / shall be invalid and the subsequent treasurers shall earmark for this account in accordance with this law the equivalent sum of money [from the] revenues of the [city], and shall carry out all the other provisions in accordance with this law. [Anyone who] proposes or [does] anything in violation of this law or does not carry out any of the instructions (laid down) in this law shall be accursed, himself and his family, and shall be held guilty of sacrilege, and every step shall be
50 taken / against him which is prescribed in the laws concerning sacrilege. Anyone who does anything in contravention of this law concerning this money or does not carry out the instructions shall owe to the city (a fine of) 10,000 drs. Anyone who wishes may go to law against him whether in a private or a public suit, after the submission of the monthly accounts and at any time he wishes; no one may reject any of these suits on the
55 grounds that it does not meet the official time limit / or in any other way. The person convicted shall be fined double the amount, half of which shall belong to the city and be consecrated to Hermes, Heracles and the Muses,[10] and be earmarked to the above-mentioned account, and half to the successful prosecutor. The *euthynoi* (public examiners) shall carry out the collection of fines (arising) from these suits, as with the
60 other public suits. /

(v) The *timouchoi*[11] who are in office shall proclaim in addition to the curse, that anyone who diverts in any way or under any pretext the money given by Polythrus son of Onesimus for the education of the free children, or who allocates it to any other purpose than the one prescribed by the law, or does not carry out the instructions of the law, shall be
65 accursed, himself and his family. /

(vi) If the [treasurers] do not lend the money (at interest) as is prescribed or do not pay the (money due) to those in charge of the (children's) studies [in accordance with this] law, each of them shall owe to the [city] 2,000 [drs.], and [anyone who] wishes may take him to court . . . [the person convicted] shall be fined twice the amount, and [half . . .]

(the rest of the inscription is lost)

Syll.[3] 578

1. Cf. **119** n. 8.
2. Cf. **119** n. 2.
3. Cf. **119** n. 7.

4. The Milesian foundation (**119**) does not explicitly include girls as well as boys; the education of girls was relatively neglected.
5. Cf. **119** n. 12.
6. Cf. **118** n. 10.
7. Greek calendars were based on the lunisolar year and so required periodic adjustment by means of intercalary months (E. J. Bickerman, *Chronology of the Ancient World* (London, 2nd ed., 1980), 27–33). Cf. **196** §2.
8. Cf. **118** side B l.24.
9. Cf. the provisions in **116, 119, 206**.
10. Cf. **118** n. 5, **119** n. 5.
11. A title of public officials who at Teos pronounced public curses on behalf of the city (ML 30: fifth century).

121   Victory at the Nemean Games of a Sidonian prince (*ca* 200)

Inscriptions recording victories of athletes in the innumerable competitions celebrated throughout the Greek world (cf. e.g. **122**) are legion; the following text (from Sidon) is unusual in that it records the victory in a Greek competition of a Phoenician from Sidon, and thus illustrates indirectly the hellenisation of the Phoenician cities in the Hellenistic age (cf. also **218** n. 1, and on Palestine cf. **168, 276**).

(1) The city of the Sidonians (honours) Diotimus son of Dionysius,[1] judge,[2] who won the chariot race at the Nemean Games.

(2) Timocharis of Eleuthernae[3] made (the statue).

(3) When [in the vale] of Argos all the [competitors] drove from their seats [their swift horses] for the competition, [the people] of Phoronis[4] [bestowed on] you, Diotimus, a fine distinction, and you received the ever-memorable [crown]. For you were the first[5] of our citizens to bring back from Greece[6] the glory of a victory in the chariot race to the house of the noble sons of Agenor.[7] The sacred city of Cadmean Thebes[8] also exults when she sees her mother city made famous by victories. As for your father Dionysius, [his prayer] about the competition was fulfilled when Hellas raised this clear [cry]: 'Not only do you excel in your ships,[9] [Sidon], but also in your yoked [chariots which bring] victory'.

L. Moretti, *Iscrizione agonistiche greche* (Rome, 1953), no. 41; cf. E. Bikerman in *Mélanges R. Dussaud* I (Paris, 1939), 91–9

1. Both names are Greek.
2. 'Judge' = the Phoenician office of 'sufet'; Sidon retained her native institutions.
3. In Crete, a sculptor known from inscriptions to have been active in Rhodes and elsewhere in the late third century.

4. Argos.
5. A frequent theme in agonistic inscriptions.
6. The panhellenic competitions were open to Greeks only; admittance to them was therefore a mark of acceptance by the Greek world.
7. The first ruler of Sidon according to Greek mythology.
8. In Greek mythology Thebes was founded by Cadmus son of Agenor. Diotimus is anxious to integrate his native city into the framework of Greek legends (cf. E. J. Bickerman, *CP* 47 (1952), 65–81).
9. Sidon had long been a powerful maritime state (cf. **218** n. 1).

122 Victories of a tragic actor (Tegea, between 276 and 219)

The following is a series of dedications made by a tragic actor at his native city of Tegea, in commemoration of victories won at various competitions in the Greek world: one example among many of the mobility of the Greeks in the Hellenistic world, contrasting with the lack of mobility of the native populations of Asia and Egypt (cf. e.g. **190, 192**).

See further: Rostovtzeff II (1941), 1032–48, 1086–9.

(1) At [the] Great Dionysia [at] Athens, in the *Orestes* of Euripides.[1]

(2) At the *Soteria* [at] Delphi,[2] in the *Heracles* of Euripides and the *Antaeus* of Archestratus.

(3) At the *Ptolemaieia* at Alexandria,[3] in boxing in the men's category.

(4) At the *Heraea* (sc. at Argos), in the *Heracles* of Euripides and the *Archelaus* of Euripides.

(5) At the *Naia* at Dodona, in the *Archelaus* of Euripides and the *Achilles* of Chaeremon.

(6) And 88 prizes in the dramatic contests at the Dionysia in the cities[4] and in any other festivals celebrated by the cities.

Syll.[3] 1080; *IG* v.2.118

1. Extant, as also the *Heracles*; the other plays mentioned are lost.
2. Cf. **48**.
3. Cf. **218** and n. 4.
4. I.e. Greek cities.

123 Decree of the Dionysiac artists in honour of a benefactor (between 197 and 166)

A development of the period after Alexander was the foundation of associations of travelling actors and artists; the Athenian association was the earliest, followed by the Isthmian and Nemean, and in Asia Minor the association of Ionia and the Hellespont, together with other associations in the Hellenistic east. Like the numerous and proliferating private clubs and associations characteristic of the Hellenistic age and after (cf. **130**), the 'Dionysiac artists' modelled their organisation on the institutions of the democratic *polis*: they had magistrates and assemblies which passed resolutions, despatched or received envoys, and dealt with states and rulers as independent sovereign bodies. In Asia (or at least in Ptolemaic Egypt (cf. *OGIS* 51) and in the Pergamene kingdom), the associations were brought under royal control and used by the kings as instruments for the promotion of dynastic cults.

See further: C. B. Welles on *RC* 53, p.231–3; Rostovtzeff II (1941), 1048–50, 1085f. and index s.v. 'Dionysiac *technitai*', III, p. 1684; Hansen (1971), 460–4.

The association (*koinon*) of the Dionysiac artists (*technitai*) of [Ionia] and the Hellespont, and of those under the patronage of [Dionysus] Cathegemon[1] (crowns) Craton son of Zotichus,[2] their benefactor, for his merits and [the goodwill] which he constantly displays towards the association of the Dionysiac [artists]. /   5

[Resolved] by the association of the Dionysiac artists of Ionia and the [Hellespont and of those under the patronage of] Dionysus [Cathegemon]: since Craton son of Zotichus, the flautist, who was previously [priest of Dionysus and] agonothete,[3] performed his duties [as priest] with honour and glory, [and when judged] worthy of this honour by the assembly of the artists was appointed [a second time priest] of Dionysus and agonothete during the same year, and surpassed [all the] agonothetes [who preceded him] / in his spending, his generosity and his   10
[magnificence, and has conducted himself in a way that is fitting] and worthy of the association, and [has performed] everything that relates to honour and glory [for Dionysus], the Muses, Pythian Apollo and all the other gods [and similarly for the kings], the queens and the brothers of King Eumenes (II),[4] and the [association of the Dionysiac] artists, displaying his excellence, piety [and emulation on every occasion] / and   15
being always responsible for some benefaction both privately and publicly; so that the immortal glory conferred by the artists[5] [might be made manifest for all] time, whom (sc. the artists) the gods, the kings [and all the] Greeks honour, having granted to all [the] artists freedom from seizure (*asylia*) and security (*asphaleia*) [in war and] peace,[6] in conformity with the oracles of Apollo, in accordance with which [they compete in the contests of] Pythian Apollo, the Muses of Helicon, and [Dionysus, (being) at Delphi the] / *Pythia* and *Soteria*, at Thespiae the   20
Mouseia, at Thebes the [*Agriania*,[7] as they are reputed to be] the most pious of all the Greeks; with good fortune; resolution: so that [the company may be seen to be honouring] its benefactors in a way worthy of their benefactions, to crown [Craton son of Zotichus, the flautist,] their benefactor, every year for all time in the theatre, on the day when

the [assembly of the association is] celebrated, after the crowning of the cities,[8] with a crown in accordance with the law [for his merits and the
25 goodwill] / which he constantly displays towards the association of the Dionysiac artists; the agonothete who is in office on each occasion shall be responsible [for the proclamation of the crown]; three [statues of him are to be dedicated], one at Teos[9] in the theatre, so that the [agonothetes] every year, [during the] assembly [of the association] and when the city of Teos celebrates the *Dionysia* or any other [contest might crown the statue] of Craton with the crown specified by the law, with which the
30 [artists] traditionally [crown their] / benefactors; the second at Delos, so that it [may be] crowned there too [by the association of the Dionysiac] artists; the third wherever Craton dedicates it, so that [he might have] for all [time a memorial of his] piety [towards] the gods and of [his emulation] towards the kings and queens [and towards the brothers of] King Eumenes (II) and the association of the Dionysiac artists, [and also] of the gratitude of the company, seeing that [it honoured Craton] its
35 benefactor and repaid / thanks worthy of his benefactions; [the honours that have been granted shall be] inscribed on a stone stele and placed next to the statues [of] Craton; two [envoys are to be sent] to the people of Teos to ask for a place [in the theatre for setting up] the statue of Craton, and others to the people of Delos [who on arriving at Delos will] approach the people and the council and request [the Delians, who are
40 our friends and kinsmen] / to grant to the association of the artists the place for [setting up the statue of Craton].[10]

> G. Daux, *BCH* 59 (1935), 210–30 (F. Dürrbach,
> *Choix d'inscriptions de Délos* (Paris, 1921), 75)

1. Created by the Attalids for their cult of Dionysus Cathegemon (cf. **210, 213** ll.45f.), then amalgamated with the association of Ionia and the Hellespont which the Attalids brought under their control.
2. From Calchedon, known from several inscriptions to have been also priest of the cult of Eumenes II and founder of an association of *Attalistai* dedicated to the cult of Attalus I or II (*OGIS* 325, 326).
3. Organiser of the competitions celebrated by the association.
4. The references are to the Attalid family, the kings = Attalus I and Eumenes II, the queens = Apollonis and Stratonice (cf. **204**); on the brothers of Eumenes II cf. **193**.
5. The reference is now to all the Dionysiac artists in general, not just the associations of Asia Minor.
6. Attested for the Athenian association by a decree of Delphi, *Syll.*[3] 399.
7. In honour of Dionysus (L. Robert, *BCH* 59 (1935), 193–8).
8. Literally 'peoples'; this refers to honours voted by the association for Greek cities.
9. The headquarters of the association of Ionia and the Hellespont till the mid

second century (cf. **151**); the association was distinct from the city of Teos, as may be seen from the present text. See further Sherk no. 49.

10. This text originates from Delos.

124 Decree of Cnossus in honour of a doctor from Cos (221–219)

The *kosmoi* and the city of Cnossus to the council and people of Cos, greetings. Since, when the people of Gortyn sent an embassy to you concerning a doctor,[1] and you responded with zealous eagerness by sending to them Hermias the doctor, and when there was a revolution /   5 at Gortyn[2] and we came in accordance with our alliance to the battle [which took place at Gortyn] in the [city] and it happened that some of the citizens [and] of the others of our own number who had come to [the] battle were wounded and that many [fell] seriously ill from [their] /   10 wounds, Hermias being a good man showed then all his zeal on our behalf and saved them [from] great dangers, and otherwise he constantly gives assistance without stint to those who call upon [him], /   and on   15 another occasion when a battle took place near Phaestus [many] were wounded and similarly many were in danger because of their ailments, he displayed all his [zeal] in looking after them and [saved them] from great dangers, and [otherwise he shows / himself helpful to those who   20 call upon him . . .][3]

Syll.[3] 528; *ICret.* I, p.62 no. 7

1. Cos had a famous school of doctors, and Coan doctors were in great demand in the Greek world; requests for their services were addressed to the state of Cos (cf. S. M. Sherwin-White, *Ancient Cos* (Göttingen, 1978), 256–89; L. Robert, *Rev. Phil.* 52 (1978), 242–52; E. M. Craik, *The Dorian Aegean* (London, 1980), 107–31). Hermias worked in Gortyn as a public doctor (cf. **125**); his activity there is mentioned in a decree from Gortyn which refers to the same events (*ICret.* IV, p. 230–2 no. 168; see further Sherwin-White, *op. cit.*, 267f.). Both inscriptions emanate from Cos, which advertised in this way the services of its doctors.
2. For the context of these events cf. **91**.
3. The decree of Gortyn (n. 1 above) shows that Hermias asked for leave to return home after five years of absence.

125 Decree of Samos in honour of a public doctor (201–197)

Doctors in the Greek world were in great demand for their skills but in short supply. To palliate the deficiency many Greek cities kept doctors in public service; they were paid a retainer, but their services were not free (unless they waived their fees). The institution therefore fell significantly short of a state 'health service' and modern analogies are not applicable. For other examples in the Greek world cf. **99, 124, 264** §7.

See further: Rostovtzeff II (1941), 1088–94 and III, 1597–1600; L. Cohn-Haft, *The Public Physicians of Ancient Greece* (Northampton, Mass., 1956), cf. *Bull.* 1958, 85; Hands (1968), 131–9.

[Resolved by the council and the people, proposal of the presiding magistrates (*prytaneis*); concerning the] motion put [by . . . that Diodorus[1] son of Dioscurides] who has been a doctor in public service [among us for many years?], and has provided his services irreproachably
5 in accordance with his skill, / and during the restoration of the city[2] and the siege of the high points, when many were wounded, provided his services, should be praised and honoured, as resolved by the council and the people. The council also passed a motion to introduce these
10 matters / before the assembly held for the elections: since Diodorus son of Dioscurides, who took over among us the task of public doctor, has first for many years in the previous period through his own skill and care looked after and cured many of the citizens and of the others in the city
15 who had fallen seriously ill / and was responsible for their safety, as has frequently been vouched for by many among the people at the time when contracts are issued,[3] and when the earthquakes took place and
20 among us many suffered painful wounds of every sort / because of the unexpectedness of the disaster and were in need of urgent attention, he distributed his services equally to all and assisted them, and when the judges who had been invited[4] came to our city and some of them were
25 taken ill, and the people instructed him / to take care of them, in their case too he showed himself fair and blameless, and when the city was restored to the empire[5] of King Ptolemy (V), and many were wounded during the siege of the high points and during the daily encounters, he
30 considered no hardship / or expense to be of greater importance than the safety of all, and as for those who were [constantly] in need of [help], from his own means . . .

C. Habicht, *AM* 72 (1957), 233–41 at p. 233f.

1. A Samian, also attested as a contributor to the Samian corn fund (**116**): the medical profession could be lucrative.
2. Sc. to the Ptolemaic empire, cf. below.
3. The auctioning of contracts by the state was a public occasion.
4. Judges invited from another city to settle disputes, cf. **135**.
5. *Pragmata*, cf. **139** n. 3; taken over by Philip V and garrisoned by him in 201, Samos was restored to Ptolemaic rule (cf. **218** n. 3) some time between 201 and 197 (cf. Walbank II (1967), 505f.).

126 The miraculous cures at Epidaurus (late fourth century)

'In former times there stood many stelae within the precinct (sc. of Asclepius at Epidaurus) [. . .] The names of men and women who have been cured by Asclepius are written on them, and also what disease each of them suffered from, and how it was cured' (Pausanias II.27.3). The following are some of the texts seen by Pausanias at Epidaurus; similar miraculous cures are attested at other sanctuaries of Asclepius in the Greek world (e.g. at Cos). Contrast **124, 125**: in Greek medicine rational human skill and supernatural divine agency coexisted side by side.

See further: E. and L. Edelstein, *Asclepius* I and II (Baltimore, 1945), with full collection and translation of sources; W. K. C. Guthrie, *The Greeks and their Gods* (London, 1950), 242–53; L. Cohn-Haft, *The Public Physicians of Ancient Greece* (Northampton, Mass., 1956), 26–31.

God. Good fortune.
Cures of Apollo[1] and Asclepius.

(1) [Cleo] was pregnant for five years. After already five years of pregnancy she came as a suppliant to the [god] and went to sleep[2] in the innermost sanctuary. As soon as / she came out of it and was outside the   5
sanctuary,[3] she gave birth to a boy, who as soon as he was born washed himself from the fountain and walked about with his mother. After being granted this favour she wrote the following inscription on her dedication: 'It is not the greatness of the tablet that deserves admiration, but the divinity, as Cleo was pregnant with child in her womb for five years, until she went to sleep (sc. in the sanctuary), and the divinity restored her to health.'[4]

(2) A three-year / [pregnancy]. Isthmonice of Pellene came to the   10
sanctuary for offspring, and having gone to sleep saw a vision:[5] she thought she was asking the god that she should give birth to a [daughter], and Asclepius said she would be pregnant and he would fulfill any other request she made, but she said she did not demand anything else. She became pregnant and was with child in her womb for three years, until she approached / the god as a suppliant about the birth.   15
She went to sleep and saw a vision: she thought that the god was asking her whether she had not been granted everything she asked for and was pregnant. She did nothing about the birth, even though the god asked her whether she required anything else and said that he would do that as well; since she had now come to him as a suppliant about this / he said he   20
would also grant this to her. After this she came out of the innermost sanctuary hurriedly to be outside the temple, and gave birth to a daughter.

(3) A man with the fingers of his hand paralysed except for one came as a suppliant to the god, and when he saw the tablets in the sanctuary he

would not believe the cures and was rather contemptuous of the
25   inscriptions,[6] / but when he went to sleep he saw a vision: he thought
that as he was playing dice below the sanctuary and was about to throw
the dice, the god appeared, sprang on his hand and stretched out his
fingers, and when the god moved away, the man thought he bent his
hand and stretched out the fingers one by one, and when he had
30   straightened them all out, the god asked him / whether he still did not
believe the inscriptions on the tablets in the sanctuary, and the man said
he did. The god said: 'Since previously you would not believe them,
although they are not incredible, in future let [your name] be
'Incredulous'' '. When day came he went away cured.

(4) Ambrosia from Athens, [blind in one eye]. She came as a suppliant
35   to the god, and as she walked about / the sanctuary she ridiculed some of
the cures as [being] incredible and impossible, that persons who were
lame and blind should be restored to health [merely] by seeing a dream.
But when she went to sleep she saw a vision: she thought the god was
standing next to her [and saying] that he would restore her to health, but
she must [dedicate in] the sanctuary as a reward a silver pig, as a
40   memorial of her stupidity.[7] Having said / [this] he split open the diseased
eye and [poured in a medicine]. When day came she went away cured.
[. . .]

Syll.[3] 1168, lines 1–41; *IG* IV[2].1.121

1. Mentioned as father of Asclepius and possessor of the sanctuary, though the
   particular cures are not in fact credited to him.
2. The normal practice of 'incubation' in the sanctuary.
3. 'No death or birth may take place within the precinct' (Pausanias II.27.1).
4. The inscription was probably the source of the account.
5. Cf. Serapis, **131, 239, 261**.
6. A recurring theme: the god confounds his detractors.
7. Cf. n. 4.

127 The Delphic manumission records

The practice of manumitting slaves through a fictitious 'sale' to a god or goddess
is widely attested in the Greek world through numerous inscriptions; the
institution was even imported by the Greeks to the Near East (cf. *SEG* VII.15–26
recording manumissions at Susa through 'consecration' to the oriental goddess
Nanaia). The largest single group of texts originates from Delphi, and comprises
some 1,000 preserved texts recording over 1,200 manumissions; they span the
last two centuries B.C. and the first century A.D., with the majority of texts dating
from the second century B.C. The inscriptions provide much evidence, e.g. on
prices and origins of slaves, and on the institution of 'conditional release'

(*paramone*) whereby some slaves only gained their full freedom after the death of their owner. Manumission, whether in its full or its conditional form, offered an incentive to good behaviour for slaves, and for slave owners a means of replacing older slaves with new ones. 'Manumission reinforced slavery as an institution'; 'manumission and the slave market grew hand in hand' (Hopkins and Roscoe, *op. cit.* below, 148, 170).

See further: W. L. Westermann, *The Slave Systems of Greek and Roman Antiquity* (Philadelphia, 1955), 31–7; K. Hopkins (with P. J. Roscoe), *Conquerors and Slaves* (Cambridge, 1978), 133–71.

(a) Unconditional manumission

In the archonship of Tharres, in the month of Panagyrius, as reckoned by the people of Amphissa, and in the archonship of Damostratus at Delphi, in the month of Poitropius (144 B.C.), Telon and Cleto, with the approval of their son Straton, sold to Pythian Apollo a male slave[1] / whose name is Sosus, of Cappadocian origin, for the price of 3 minas of silver.[2] Accordingly Sosus entrusted the sale to the god, on condition of his being free and not to be claimed as a slave by anyone for all time. Guarantor in accordance with the law and the contract: Philoxenus son of Dorotheus of Amphissa. The previous / sale of Sosus to Apollo which took place in the archonship of Thrasycles at Delphi, and the provisions of the sale, namely that Sosus should remain with Telon and Cleto for as long as they live,[3] shall be null and void. Witnesses: the priests of Apollo, Praxias and Andronicus, and the archon Pyrrhias / son of Archelaus, and the Amphissians Charixenus son of Ecephylus, Polycritus, Aristodamus son of Callicles, Euthydamus son of Polycritus, Dorotheus son of Timesius, Demetrius son of Monimus. The contract is kept by the priest Praxias and Andronicus, and the Amphissians Polycritus and [Charixenus] / son of Ecephylus.

5
10
15
20

SGDI II. 2143

(b) Conditional manumission

When Panaetolus and Phytaeus were generals of the Aetolians, in the month of Homoloius, and in the archonship of Xeneas at Delphi and the month Bysius (167 B.C.), Critodamus son of Damocles, of Physce, sold to Pythian Apollo / a male slave whose name is Maiphatas, of Galatian origin, and a female (slave) whose name is Ammia, of Illyrian origin, for the price of seven minas of silver.[4] Maiphatas and Ammia shall remain with Critodamus for as long as Critodamus lives, doing for Critodamus what they are told to; / if they do not remain and do what they are told to, the sale shall be null and void. When Critodamus dies, Maiphatas and Ammia shall be free and the sale shall remain with the god / on condition that they are free and not to be claimed as slaves by anyone for their whole life, doing whatever they wish and going wherever they wish.

5
10
15

221

Guarantors in accordance with the law and the contract: Philon son of
20 Aristeas, Astoxenus son of Dionysius. Witnesses: the priests / Amyntas
and Tarantinus; private citizens: Dexicrates, Sotimus, Callimachus,
Euangelus, . . . chaeus, of Delphi, Lyciscus and Menedamus, of Physce.

SGDI II. 1854

1. Here and elsewhere literally 'body'.
2. = 300 drs. The prices paid by slaves for their freedom appear to correspond to
   the purchase price of slaves; it is not known how slaves were able to raise the
   money for their manumission, nor what proportion of the servile population
   did this.
3. Sosus had first been conditionally manumitted (cf. next text). Unconditional
   manumissions predominate in the second century but decrease in the first,
   with a corresponding increase in conditional manumissions, the terms of
   which become more stringent. Similarly the price paid by slaves for full
   freedom increases, while the price of conditional release remains more stable.
   This indicates that the supply of slaves at and near Delphi in this period was
   not keeping pace with demand. See Hopkins and Roscoe, *op. cit.*
4. = 700 drs. for the two slaves.

128 A calendar of sacrifices (Myconos, *ca* 200)

Gods. With good fortune. In the archonship of Cratinus, Polyzelus (and)
Philophron, when the cities united together,[1] the people of Myconos
resolved to offer the following sacrifices in addition to those previously
(existing) and the following changes were made concerning the pre-
5 viously existing sacrifices: /
On the fifth of (the month of) Poseidon, to Poseidon *Temenites*,[2] a
white ram of the finest quality, uncastrated; the ram is not brought into
the city;[3] the chine and the shoulder-blades are cut off; the shoulder-
blades are dedicated as offerings (to the god); the priest gets the tongue
and a shoulder.[4]   On the same day, to Poseidon *Phykios*, a white
10 uncastrated lamb; women may not participate (in the ceremony); and /
from the tax on fishing[5] the council shall purchase sheep for twenty
drachmas and provide them.[6]   On the same day, to Demeter Chloe,
two sows of the finest quality, one of them pregnant; the chine of the
pregnant one is cut off. The [council shall select] the sows; the magistrates shall give to the [sacrificer] the loin and a thigh-bone of the other
15 sow, two *choinikes* of barley-groats / and three *kotylai* of wine.
On the tenth of (the month of) Lenaion, for the crops, to the
accompaniment of a hymn, to Demeter, a pregnant sow who is bearing
her first litter, to Core (the Maiden), a full-grown boar, to Zeus

Bouleus,[7] a pig; the religious officials (*hieropoioi*) shall provide these from the sacred funds, and they shall provide wood and barley-groats. The magistrates and the priests shall make sure that the victims are of good quality; / if there is need to sacrifice anything to obtain good omens, the   20
hieropoioi shall provide it; any woman of Myconos who wishes may come to the festival and so too all the women living in Myconos who have been initiated into (the Mysteries of) Demeter.

On the eleventh (sc. of Lenaion) on the . . . to Semele, a sheep every year; a ninth part of it is burnt.[8]   On the twelfth (sc. of Lenaion), to Dionysus Leneus, a sheep every year; for the / crops, to Zeus Chthonios   25
and Ge Chthonia, black flayed sheep[9] every year; foreigners may not participate (in the ceremony); they shall have the feast on the spot.[10]

On the tenth of (the month of) Bacchion, at Deiras, to Dionysus Baccheus, a he-goat of the finest quality; the *hieropoioi* shall provide the cost and take part in the feast; they shall have the feast on the spot.

On the seventh of (the month of) Hekatombaion, / to Apollo Heka-   30
tombios, a bull and ten lambs; the chine of the bull is cut off; the priest is given the tongue of the bull and a shoulder; of the lambs sacrificed by the children a tongue (is given) to the priest and a tongue (is given) to each of the (two) children; of the lambs sacrificed by the bridegrooms a tongue (is given) to the priest and to each of the (two) bridegrooms.

On the / same day, to Acheloius, a fully grown sheep and ten lambs;   35
[three] of these, the fully grown and two others, [are slaughtered] at the altar, [and] the others in the river. The person working [the plot of land] at Sa . . . (which is consecrated to) Acheloius shall pay the rent [for it to Acheloius . . . and] shall consecrate this [in the treasury].

On the fifteenth, to Archegetes, a sheep every year . . . [. . .]

Syll.[3] 1024; F. Sokolowski, *Lois sacrées des
cités grecques* (Paris, 1969), no. 96

1. Myconos was originally divided between two separate cities; their union provided the occasion for the revision of the calendar of sacrifices (cf. **134**).
2. Who has a *temenos* (a sacred enclosure), but no temple.
3. To be led back in procession to the shrine outside the city.
4. It was regular practice for priests to receive a share of the sacrificial animals; cf. **129**.
5. Cf. **104** l.27.
6. Only the lamb is sacrificed to the god; the sheep are used for a collective feast following the sacrifice (cf. **130**).
7. Zeus as lord of the underworld.
8. The rest being eaten by the participants in the sacrifice.
9. Curiously the number of animals is not specified.
10. Cf. **215** n. 22.

129 Law of Priene on the priesthood of Dionysus (second century)

By the classical period it had become common for Greek cities to treat priesthoods as normal magistracies, to be filled by election or sortition, though certain cults (such as the Eleusinian Mysteries near Athens) remained the preserve of ancient families. Priesthoods conferred both status and material advantages on their holders. The practice of the sale of priesthoods seems to have been largely confined to Asia Minor and the neighbouring islands and never spread to the mainland of Greece. This in itself makes it difficult to explain it purely as a fiscal device to raise money. For priesthoods of the dynastic cults of rulers cf. **158, 175, 177, 210, 222** n.3; for native Egyptian priesthoods cf. **222, 227, 231, 246**.

See further: Jones (1940), 227–9; E. M. Craik, *The Dorian Aegean* (London, 1980), 193–208.

Rules for (the priesthood of) Dionysus Phleos. With good fortune. We are selling the priesthood of Dionysus Phleos on the following conditions:

(I) The purchaser (of the priesthood) shall be priest for life, and he shall
5   also be priest / of Dionysus Catagogius.[1] He shall be free of obligations on his person.[2] He shall also be granted free meals every day in the *prytaneum* (townhall) and in the Panionion.[3] He shall receive from the animals sacrificed by the city a leg, the tongue and the hide as shares from
10   the altar.[4] /

(II) He shall provide burnt-offerings, barley-corns, frankincense, and flat cakes, for an ox of a *tetarteus*, for a sheep of a half-*hekteus*, and for a sucking pig of two *choinikes*. He shall also have the right to a seat of
15   honour in the theatre and may wear any dress he wishes and / a golden ivy crown.

(III) He shall also perform the sacrifices in the theatre for Dionysus Melpomenus, and shall place frankincense (on the altar) and shall begin the libation, and shall offer the prayers on behalf of the city of Priene. He
20   may wear any dress he wishes / and a golden crown during the months of Lenaion and Anthesterion, and at the *Katagogia* he shall lead those who are escorting Dionysus back,[5] and may wear any dress he wishes and a golden crown.

25   (IV) If the priesthood fetches more than 6,000 drs.,[6] / its purchaser shall be exempt from the liturgies of lampadarch,[7] agonothete, *hippotrophos*,[8] the *architheoria*[9] and the gymnasiarchy.[10] If he purchases it for more than 12,000 drs., he shall be exempt from the trierarchy,[11] the
30   *oikonomia*,[12] the *neopoia*[13] / and the advance of money (to the state).[14]

(V) The purchaser shall pay to the *neopoios* immediately one tenth (of the price), and of the rest of the price (he shall pay) half during the month of Metageitnion in the same year, and half during the month of Anthesterion when Cleomenes is crown-bearer (*stephanephoros*). /

(vi) Athenopolis son of Cydimus bought (the priesthood) for 12,002   35
drs.,[15] and the tenth (is) 1,200 drs. 1 obol and 3 chalci.

Syll.[3] 1003; F. Sokolowski, *Lois sacrées de
l'Asie mineure* (Paris, 1955), no.37.

1. Cf. n.5 below.
2. This may include military service.
3. Cf. **40** n. 1.
4. Cf. **128** n. 4.
5. In procession to his temple, hence the name Dionysus Catagogius.
6. = 1 talent, a large sum.
7. Cf. **118B** ll.71–83; on liturgies cf. **40** n. 6.
8. This involved the obligation to keep horses.
9. The leadership of a sacred embassy; cf. **44, 113**.
10. Cf. **118**.
11. This must be an ancient rule, since the harbour of Priene had long been silted up.
12. Precise functions unknown, but clearly a burdensome obligation like the other liturgies involved.
13. The office of commissioner for the maintenance of temples.
14. Cf. **40B**.
15. An indication of the demand for the priesthood.

130 Decree of an Attic cult association (307/6)

The proliferation of private associations and clubs, religious and social in function, was characteristic of the whole of the Greek world after Alexander. The phenomenon is attested almost entirely by epigraphic evidence. The organisation of these associations, which were mostly very small (rarely more than 100 members), was modelled on that of the democratic *polis* (cf. also **123**).

See further: M. N. Tod, *Sidelights on Greek History* (Oxford, 1932), 71–96; Rostovtzeff III (1941), index p. 1668 s.v. Associations; W. S. Ferguson, 'The Attic Orgeones', *Harvard Theological Review* 37 (1944), 61–140, esp. 80f., 127–30; Tarn and Griffith (1952), 93–5.

[Gods]. The *orgeones*[1] leased the sanctuary of Egretes[2] to Diognetus son of Arcesilas of the deme Melite for ten years, at 200 drachmas every year, / to use the sanctuary and the houses which have been built there as   5
a sanctuary.[3] Diognetus shall whitewash the walls which require it; he shall build and construct / anything else whenever he wishes. When the   10
period of ten years elapses, he shall go away taking the timber, the tiles and the doorways,[4] but he shall not remove anything else. He shall also look after / the trees planted in the sanctuary, and should any be missing,   15
he shall replace them and hand over the same number. Diognetus shall

20 pay the rent to whoever is treasurer / of the *orgeones* every year, half of it,
100 drs., on the first of Boedromion, and the remaining 100 drs. on the
25 first of Elaphebolion. When the *orgeones* are sacrificing / to the hero (sc.
Egretes) in the month of Boedromion, Diognetus shall open the house,
where the shrine is, and give access to it, and provide a covered shelter,
30 an oven, couches, and tables for two sets of three / couches.[5] If
Diognetus does not pay the rent at the prescribed time or fails to carry
out the provisions of the lease, the lease shall be cancelled and he shall
35 forfeit / the timber, the tiles and the doorways, and the *orgeones* may
lease the sanctuary to anyone they wish. Should a property-tax be raised,
it shall fall on the *orgeones* in accordance with the assessment.[6] Diognetus
40 shall inscribe / this lease on the stele which is in the sanctuary.[7] The lease
comes into effect in the archonship following that of Coroebus (306/5).

Syll.[3] 1097; *IG* II².2499

1. Members of a religious association, 'sacrificing associates' (W. S. Ferguson).
2. A little-known Attic hero.
3. I.e. use the sanctuary in such a way as not to interfere with its religious function when required. The need of the *orgeones* to lease the sanctuary of Egretes is indicative of the lack of financial resources of such associations, which made them frequently dependent on the generosity of wealthy benefactors.
4. The sanctuary is leased without these, which the tenant supplies himself.
5. All these are required for the banquet of the *orgeones* (up to 30 in all), which follows the sacrifice (cf. **128**).
6. The obligation to pay property-tax when raised by the state sometimes fell on the tenant.
7. The text was inscribed on a previously used stele which was erased for the purpose.

131 The introduction of the cult of Serapis to Delos (*ca* 200)

See further: A. D. Nock, *Conversion* (Oxford, 1933), 48–56 and on Serapis cf. **239, 257, 261**.

Apollonius the priest had (this text) inscribed in accordance with an injunction from the god.[1] For Apollonius, my grandfather, who was an
5 Egyptian from the priestly class,[2] came from Egypt with his god, / and continued to celebrate the cult in accordance with ancestral tradition; he lived, it is thought, to the age of 97. My father Demetrius succeeded him and worshipped the gods in the same way; because of his piety he was
10 honoured by / the god[3] with a bronze statue which is dedicated in the temple of the god. He lived 61 years. When I inherited the sacred objects

and devoted myself carefully to his cult, the god told me in my sleep[4]
that a Serapeum of his own must / be dedicated to him and that he must   15
not be as before in a rented building; he said he would find a spot himself
where he should be set and that he would point it out. And that is what
happened. Now this spot was full of dirt,[5] and was advertised for
sale / on a little notice (displayed) in the passage to the agora. As the god   20
wanted this the purchase was completed and the sanctuary was rapidly
built in six months. And when some men[6] joined against us and the god,
and introduced a public suit against the sanctuary / and me,[7] involving a   25
penalty or a fine, the god promised to me in my sleep that we would be
victorious. Now that the trial is completed and we have won a victory
worthy of the god, we praise the gods and repay them adequate thanks.[8]

This is what Maiistas[9] writes about the sanctuary. [. . .]

Syll.[3] 663; *IG* XI.4. 1299; *SEG* XXIV.1158

1. Serapis.
2. Yet the whole family bears Greek names; the whole inscription is in Greek,
   and the cult imported by Apollonius to Delos is that of the hellenised Serapis
   rather than the original Osor-Hapi of Memphis (cf. **257**).
3. The god expressed his approval of the honour through an oracle.
4. Cf. **239, 261**.
5. A conventional theme, to contrast with the greatness of the god; in practice
   this quarter of Delos was not poor (cf. P. Bruneau, *BCH* Suppl. 1 (1973),
   111–36; *Bull.* 1974, 393).
6. Deliberately vague.
7. Hardly on religious grounds, but through jealousy of Apollonius.
8. A dedication by Apollonius and his followers is extant (*IG* XI.4.1290); this
   was not in fact the end of their tribulations (cf. *Syll.*[3] 664; Sherk no. 5).
9. An '*aretalogos*', i.e. a professional expounder of the 'virtues' (*aretai*) of the god;
   his poem which follows enlarges in Greek poetic style on the narrative of the
   inscription. The name Maiistas is unique; he need not have been an Egyptian.

132 Treaty between Hierapytna and Praisos in Crete (early third century)

See further: Tarn and Griffith (1952), 84f. (on *isopoliteia*); R. F. Willetts,
Aristocratic Society in Ancient Crete (London, 1955), 134f.

(Side A illegible)

Side B

. . . after settling his own private affairs[1] each in his / home state, (a   5
citizen of either state) who belongs to a tribe[2] may thus exercise political

10 rights (in the other state) with full participation / in all things divine and
15 human, provided he gives up his citizen rights / in his city of origin;[3] if a
   citizen of one state moves to the other state to exercise political rights
20 there, / a vote shall be taken at a plenary session of the assembly to
25 decide whether / he should [be granted] citizen [rights] or not; and if
30 three votes are cast in opposition / he shall not be a citizen;[4] the right of
35 pasturage (*epinoma*) shall be granted to the / Hierapytnian at Praisos,
40 except for the sacred enclosures / at Ardaniton and at Daron, and to the
45 Praisian at / Hierapytna; they shall not be harmed and shall be allowed to
50 return / each to their own land;[5] if the Hierapytnian wishes to set up a
55 farmstead / in the territory of Praisos, he must have a Praisian as
60 assessor; similarly / if the Praisian wishes to set up a farmstead at
65 Hierapytna / he must have a Hierapytnian as assessor;[6] dance choirs
70 and race contests / are to be common to both, to the Hierapytnians at
75 Praisos / and to the Praisians at Hierapytna.

(the rest of the inscription is mutilated)

Staatsv. III.554; *ICret*. III, pp. 78–81 no. 1.

1. Or: 'disposing of his property'.
2. Formal registration in a tribe was a precondition of citizenship, cf. e.g. **112**,
   135.
3. Or: 'provided he asks for permission from his city of origin', but in any case
   taking up actively the citizenship of another state normally implied forfeiting
   one's original citizenship.
4. I.e. this falls short of a full grant of *isopoliteia* (see **52**) whereby the right of
   taking up another state's citizenship once granted was not subject to scrutiny
   in individual cases.
5. A controversial clause, partly restored.
6. A citizen of one state who wishes to pasture in the other state for a longer
   period of time will be supervised by a citizen of the other state to prevent
   disputes arising; disputes over pasturing rights are a recurring feature of Greek
   history.

133 'Homopoliteia' of Cos and Calymnus (between 205 and 201/0?)

The *homopoliteia* of Cos and Calymnus illustrated by the following inscription is
similar to the commonly attested *sympoliteia* whereby two cities decided to fuse
together politically, but unlike the situation in **134** where two small states merge
on a basis of equality, Cos in this text is the larger and dominant partner. The
detailed clauses of the *homopoliteia* (the only occurrence of the word so far) are
unfortunately lost.

See further: Bagnall (1976), 103–5; S. M. Sherwin-White, *Ancient Cos* (Göttingen, 1978), 124–31.

Stasilas son of Lycophron moved: two commissioners shall be appointed from each tribe who shall administer the oath to the citizens in the agora in front of the town hall, and also a scribe for each tribe and a man to dictate (the terms of) the oath; one commissioner shall be appointed from each tribe to go to Calymnus / (and administer the oath) with a secretary 5 for them; they shall administer the oath where the general sent by the people instructs them; the sellers (*poletai*)[1] shall farm out now the provision for the citizens of two sets of sacrificial victims for the swearing of the oath here and in Calymnus; the sacrificial victims shall consist of a bull, a boar and a ram, all of them uncastrated; / the citizens 10 shall all swear from the young men upwards, beginning with the presidents and generals; of the others those who are present (shall swear) before the commissioners appointed here, the rest before the commissioners who are being sent to Calymnus; the commissioners shall administer the following oath:[2] I will abide by / the established 15 democracy,[3] the restoration[4] of the *homopoliteia*, the ancestral laws of Cos, the resolutions of the assembly and the provisions of the *homopoliteia*; I will also abide by the friendship and alliance with King Ptolemy[5] and the treaties / ratified by the people with the allies; I will 20 never set up under any pretext an oligarchy or a tyranny or any other constitution apart from democracy, and if anyone else establishes (such a régime) I will not obey, but I will prevent (him) as far as possible, and I will not take over under any pretext any of the forts or the acropolis, whether for my own / possession or in collaboration with someone else, 25 and I will not allow the territory of Cos to be diminished, but I will increase it to the best of my ability; I will be a just judge and a fair-minded citizen, taking part in elections and casting my vote without favouritism, according to what seems to me to be in the interest of the people;[6] all this is true by / Zeus, Hera and Poseidon; if I abide by my 30 oath may all be for the best, if I break it may the opposite happen. The [commissioners shall administer the oath] at once in the [assembly] over [burning] victims [in accordance with the] resolution of the [assembly . . .]

(the rest of the inscription is lost)

Staatsv. III.545

1. See **48** n. 3.
2. Cf. **33** n. 7; compare especially **90, 182** ll.64–78, both concerned with the same question of the loyalty of newly incorporated citizens.
3. Cf. **40A** §8, **48**.
4. The original *homopoliteia* probably took place by 205 and was then broken by the campaigns of Philip V in the Aegean (cf. **65, 125** end).
5. Probably Ptolemy V. On Cos and the Ptolemies cf. also **268**.
6. The oath gives a definition of the 'model citizen'.

134 'Sympoliteia' of Stiris and Medeon in Phocis (second century)

See further: Larsen (1968), 300–2.

Side A

God. Good fortune. When Zeuxis was general of the Phocians, in the
5 seventh month, convention / between the city of Stiris and [the] city of
Medeon.[1] The Stirians and Medeonians have formed a single city, with
10 their sanctuaries, their city, their territory, their harbours all /
unencumbered,[2] on the following conditions: the Medeonians are all to
be Stirians, equal and enjoying the same rights; they shall take part in the
15 same assembly and the same elections for magistracies as the / city of
Stiris, and those who reach the proper age shall judge all the cases which
come before the city; a *hierotamias* shall be appointed from among the
20 Medeonians / who shall offer the traditional sacrifices for the Medeonians which are (specified) in the law of the city, together with the
25 archons established at Stiris. The *hierotamias* shall receive / the money
which [the] archons (sc. in Medeon) used to receive, half a mina and the
share of the contributions to religious festivals which falls to the
30 *hierotamias*. The *hierotamias* shall judge together with / the archons the
suits which the archons judge, and he shall draw lots for the courts if it is
35 necessary to draw lots with the archons. It shall not be compulsory / for
those Medeonians to hold magistracies in Stiris who in Medeon have
been archons, judges of foreigners (*xenodikai*), collectors of debts (*prak-*
40 *teres*), *demiourgoi*, priests, high priests (*hierarchai*), and among / women
those who have held priesthoods, unless someone undertakes them
willingly.[3] Magistracies shall be filled from the Medeonians who have
not performed public functions and from the Stirians. The
45 administration / of the sanctuaries at Medeon shall be carried out as
required by the laws of the city. The [territory] of Medeon shall all be
50 Stirian and (the territory) of Stiris / shall [all] be Medeonian and jointly
owned. The Medeonians shall participate in all the sacrifices at Stiris and
55 the Stirians in all the sacrifices at Medeon. It shall not be permissible / for
the Medeonians to break away from the Stirians nor the Stirians from the
60 Medeonians. Whichever of the two sides does not abide by the written /
agreement shall pay to the side which does ten talents (*Side B*) and they
65 shall be liable to prosecution. / The convention shall be inscribed on a
stele and dedicated in the sanctuary of [Athena], and a sealed copy of the
70 convention shall be deposited with a private individual. / The convention (is) [with] Thrason of Lilaea. Witnesses: Thrason son of Damatrius
75 of Elatea, Eupalidas son of Thrason of Lilaea, Timocrates / son of
Epinicus of Tithorea.[4] The Stirians shall give to the phratry of the

Medeonians[5] within four years five minas of silver and / the place called   80
Damatrea.

Syll.[3] 647; F. Salviat and C. Vatin,
Inscriptions de Grèce centrale (Paris, 1971),
77–80

1. Two small neighbouring cities, both members of the Phocian League; proximity and kinship will have facilitated their political union (*sympoliteia*). The inscription does not specify the aims the two cities had in mind, but it is likely that for Medeon, which was in full decline, the move was intended to preserve her from total extinction. On 'synoecism' cf. **40**.
2. In extreme circumstances Greek cities sometimes had to offer their own public buildings as security for loans (cf. Appian, *Mithridateia* 63).
3. Compare **40A** §9.
4. These are all Phocian cities.
5. Presumably some cult association; the details are obscure.

135 Decree of Samos in honour of judges from Myndus (*ca* 280)

The recurring failure of many Greek cities to provide for the regular functioning of their own justice was characteristic of the Hellenistic age (cf. **40A** §6, **84, 209**). To palliate this deficiency there developed the institution of calling on other cities to provide a panel of judges to settle the lawsuits in suspense; Hellenistic rulers often acted as mediators in inviting such panels and may in fact been responsible for promoting the practice in the generation after Alexander, as a means of securing the internal stability of Greek cities (cf. **40A** §6, **125** ll.23–5, **268**). The institution is known from a large number of inscriptions honouring the judges after the completion of their mission.

   See further: J. A. O. Larsen, *CP* 38 (1943), 249–53; Tarn and Griffith (1952), 88–91; L. Robert in *Xenion. Festschrift für Pan. J. Zepos* I, ed. E. von Caemmerer (Athens, 1973), 765–82; Walbank III (1979), 335f.

Resolved by the council and the people, proposal of the *prytaneis* concerning the matters on which the council put forward a motion, that the judges who came from Miletus, Myndus and Halicarnassus[1] to settle the contracts (*symbolaia*) in suspense should be honoured; / since, when   5
the citizens were in disagreement with each other over the contracts in suspense, Philocles king of the Sidonians,[2] wishing the city to be in a state of concord (*homonoia*),[3] wrote a letter requesting the people of Myndus to send a panel of judges to settle the contracts in suspense, and the Myndians / showing every goodwill and eagerness to (see) the   10
citizens reconciled, appointed excellent men and sent them to the city, Theocles son of Theogenes and Herophantus son of Artemidorus, and (since) they settled the suits brought before them with fairness and

231

15 justice, / some by giving a verdict and others by conciliation, wishing the citizens who were in disagreement reconciled and living in a state of concord after being freed from mutual grievances, be it resolved by the
20 council and the people, to praise the people of Myndus / for sending the men, and to praise the men who came, Theocles son of Theogenes and Herophantus son of Artemidorus, for settling the suits fairly and advantageously, some by conciliation and others by giving a verdict, and to
25 crown them with a gold crown and to proclaim / the crown at the Dionysia during the tragedies, and to make them *proxenoi* and benefactors of the city, and to give them citizenship with full and equal rights, and to allot them to a tribe, a *chiliastys*, a *hekatostys* and a family (*genos*)⁴ as
30 the other Samians, and to grant / them a seat of honour at the contests celebrated by the city and to give them precedence of access before the council and the people after religious matters and matters concerning the kings,⁵ and the right of entry and exit from the port [in] war and peace
35 without reprisal or the need for a formal treaty; / the magistrates who are in office shall look after them should they need anything; and so that the people of Myndus may know what has been decreed, an ambassador shall be appointed to go to Myndus and give the decree to the council
40 [and] the people; the decree shall be inscribed on a stone stele / and dedicated in the sanctuary of Hera; the secretary of the council shall be responsible for the inscription; the treasurer shall pay for the expense of the stele and the inscription; a travel allowance will be provided to the
45 ambassador as fixed by the people. / Aeschylus son of Ampalidas was appointed ambassador.

SEG 1.363

1. The judges from Miletus and Halicarnassus were probably honoured in another inscription.
2. A Phoenician ruler, allied to the Ptolemies; cf. **218** n. 1.
3. See **51**.
4. Subdivisions of the tribe, *chiliastys* (cf. **116**) = a 'Thousand', *hekatostys* = a 'Hundred'.
5. Royal affairs are thus a formalised heading in the political agenda.

136 Megarian arbitration in a border dispute between Epidaurus and Corinth (242/1–235/4)

Unlike the different institution of foreign judges which developed in the Hellenistic age (see **135**), the practice of interstate arbitration had roots in earlier Greek history as far back as the Archaic age. Such arbitrations, known from literary evidence but especially from inscriptions, concerned particularly the settlement of boundary disputes, one of the most common sources of friction between Greek cities.

See further: M. N. Tod, *International Arbitration amongst the Greeks* (Oxford, 1913), p.14 no.xv and references p.191; *id.*, *Sidelights on Greek History* (Oxford, 1932), 39–68.

When Aegialeus was general of [the] Achaeans,[1] and Dionysius priest of Asclepius at Epidaurus,[2] the following verdict was given by the Megarians for the Epidaurians and Corinthians over the disputed land, the Sellanyon and the Spiraeon, when in accordance with the resolution of the Achaeans / they sent a panel of 151 judges; and when the judges came 5 on the spot and judged that the land belonged to the Epidaurians, and the Corinthians contested the delimitation, the Megarians sent again 31 men from the same panel of judges to fix the boundaries in accordance / with 10 the resolution of the Achaeans; they went on the spot[3] and fixed the following boundaries:[4] from the top of Cordyleion to the top of Halieion; from the Halieion to the top of Ceraunion; from the Ceraunion to the top of Corniatas; from the top of Corniatas to the road over the crest of / Corniatas; from the crest of Corniatas to the crest of Aneiae 15 above Scolleia; from the crest above Scolleia beneath Aneiae to the summit which overlooks the carriage-road which leads to Spiraeon; from the summit which overlooks the carriage-[road] to the summit on top of Mt Phagas; from / the summit on top of Mt Phagas to the summit 20 on top of Mt Aegipyra; from the summit on top of Mt Aegipyra to the summit of Mt Araea; from the summit of Mt Araea to the summit beneath Petra; from the summit beneath Petra to the summit which overlooks Schoenus; from the summit which overlooks Schoenus to the summit / which is over against Euorga; from the summit which over- 25 looks Euorga [to] the crest which overlooks Sycousia; from the crest which overlooks Sycousia to the summit which overlooks Pelleritis; from the summit which overlooks Pelleritis to the summit of Panion; from Panion to the crest which overlooks [Holcus]; from the crest / 30 which overlooks Holcus to the crest of Apollonion; from [the] crest which overlooks Apollonion to Apollonion. The judges who gave the verdict were the following: (151 names arranged according to the three Dorian tribes). Boundary commissioners chosen from among the same 85 judges: (31 names).

Syll.[3] 471; *IG* iv².1.71

1. Both Epidaurus and Corinth belonged to the Achaean League (see **53**) and so turned to the League first, which then referred them to Megara, also (at the time) a member of the League.
2. The inscription comes from Epidaurus.

3. Not every arbitration was decided by on-the-spot inspection (contrast *Syll.*[3] 683).

4. The disputed land is in the mountainous area on the Saronic Gulf.

137 Decree of Oropus in honour of an Achaean for help in the feud with Athens (*ca* 154–149)

While some inter-city disputes were settled peacefully by arbitration (see **136**), others led to violence. Such was the feud between Athens and the Boeotian border town of Oropus (see **83**), regularly claimed by Athens as her own and intermittently controlled by her. Though the events alluded to in the following inscription are related in Pausanias VII.11.4–8, obscurities remain. In 164 Athens sacked Oropus, whose inhabitants appealed to the Roman Senate for help; the Senate decided against Athens and instructed Sicyon (an Achaean city) to assess a fine, which was fixed at 500 talents. An Athenian embassy at Rome obtained a reduction of the fine (in 155), but trouble continued until the Achaean League intervened and secured the restoration of the Oropians.

See further: Larsen (1968), 486f.

Olympichus son of Hermodorus moved: since Hieron son of Telecles of Aegira[1] has constantly shown his goodwill towards the people of Oropus, speaking and acting in their interest on every occasion, and
5   when the greatest of calamities / and breaches of faith befell the Oropians and the magistrates and we (sc. Olympichus) had come to the meeting (*synodos*) (of the Achaean League) in Corinth, he organised a collection for us, and by his advice he induced the Achaeans to show
10   every concern for / our city and the sanctuary of Amphiaraus, since we also (i.e. like the Achaeans) continue to remain in the friendship and faith of the Romans; and (since) when the Achaeans resolved to call a meeting (*synkletos*) (of the Achaean League) at Argos about these matters, Hieron,
15   wishing to demonstrate on every occasion / his goodwill and excellence, welcomed into his own house all the Oropians who had come and sacrificed to Zeus the Saviour on our behalf, and [spoke] against the
20   Athenians and the other ambassadors who had come to oppose [us] / and induced the Achaeans not to allow a Greek city to be enslaved, (a city) which was in the friendship and faith of the Romans; and (since) through his concern and excellence we have recovered our native city and have
25   returned / with our children and wives; therefore, so that the Oropians may be seen to be mindful of the benefits which anyone has conferred on them, and that others may emulate the same conduct, in the knowledge that they will receive honours appropriate for their benefactions, with
30   good / fortune, be it resolved by the people of Oropus to honour Hieron son of Telecles of Aegira with a bronze statue for his merits and the

excellence which he continues to show to the people of Oropus, and to proclaim the erection of the statue at the great festival of Amphiaraus /   35 during the athletic contest.

*Syll.*³ 675; *IG* VII.411

1. An Achaean city; see **53** ch. 41.

5 The Seleucids and Asia

[*Note*: Texts **138–173** are arranged chronologically, **174–192** geographically.]

138 A Babylonian king list

The preservation of lists of kings was a centuries-old tradition in Babylonia, but the following text is the first known list of this kind for the Hellenistic period, and has provided important chronological evidence for the Seleucid kings.

See further: A. J. Sachs and D. J. Wiseman, *op. cit.* below; R. A. Parker and W. Dubberstein, *Babylonian Chronology 626* B.C.–A.D.*75* (Providence, 1956), 20–4 and Tables pp.36ff.; A. Aymard, *Etudes d'histoire ancienne* (Paris, 1967), 263–72.

Obverse

5 ... Alexander ... Philip, Alexander's brother, ... years there was no king in the land. Antigonus, the chief of the army ... / Alexander the son of Alex(ander[1] was reckoned as king until) year? 6 (= 306/5).[2] Year 7 (= 305/4), which is (his) first year, Seleucus (I) (ruled as) king. He reigned 25 years. Year 31, month VI (= late August–September 281), Se(leucus) the king was killed in the land (of the) Khāni.[3] Year 32 (= 280/79), An(tiochus) (I) the son of Se(leucus ruled as) king. He
10 reigned 20 years. / Year 51, (month) II, (day) 16 (= 1 or 2 June, 261): An(tiochus) the great king died. Year 52 (= 260/59), An(tiochus) (II) the son of An(tiochus ruled as) king. (In month) V of year 66 (= August 246), the following was heard in Babylon: 'An(tiochus) the great king [died ...]'. Year 67 (= 245/4), Se(leucus) (II) [the son of Antiochus (I)
15 ruled as king. / He reigned 20 years. He died month ..., day ..., year 86 (= 226/5)].

Reverse

[Year] 87 (= 225/4), Se(leucus) (III) [ruled as king. He reigned 3 years]. [Year] 90 (= 222/1), An(tiochus) (III) the king sat on the throne. He
5 reigned 35 [years. From year] 102 until year 119 (= 210/9 to 193/2), / An(tiochus) and An(tiochus), the sons of the king.[4] Year 125, month III,

236

the following was heard in Babylon: '(On) day 25 (= 3 or 4 July, 187), An(tiochus) the king was killed in the land of Elam.' The same year Se(leucus) (IV) his son sat on the throne. He ruled 12 years. Year 137, month VI, day 10 (= 2 or 3 September, 175), Se(leucus) the king died . . . / The same month An(tiochus) (IV) his son sat on the throne. He reigned 11 years. The same [year], month VIII (= 22 or 23 October, 175), An(tiochus) (IV) and An(tiochus) his son (ruled) as kings. [Year 1]42, month V (= between 30 July and 30 August, 170), at the command of An(tiochus) (IV) the king, An(tiochus) the (co-)regent, his son, was put to death.⁵ [Year 14]3 (= 169/8), An(tiochus ruled as) king (alone). [Year 148, month] IX (= between 19 November and 19 December, 164), it was heard that King An(tiochus) [died . . .] [. . .]⁶

A. J. Sachs and D. J. Wiseman, *Iraq* 16 (1954), 202–11

1. Respectively Alexander the Great, Philip Arrhidaeus, Antigonus the One-Eyed and Alexander IV; see ch. 2.
2. The dates are computed according to the Seleucid era (starting 1 Dios = October 312 in the Macedonian calendar and 1 Nisan = April 311 in the Babylonian). Alexander IV had in fact been killed in 310/9 (cf. **30**), but his reign was probably fictitiously extended.
3. See **46** (end).
4. An error: Antiochus III was brother and not son of Seleucus III. The co-regency of Antiochus III and his son (cf. **177, 184, 190**) follows a frequent pattern in Hellenistic kingdoms, cf. also **141–143, 189, 206, 209**.
5. The identity of this Antiochus is problematic; cf. Walbank III (1979), 284f.
6. The last five lines are seriously mutilated. For the Seleucids as kings of Babylon see also **141, 189**.

139 Decree of Ilium in honour of Antiochus I after his accession

When Nymphius son of Diotrephes was *epimenios*, and Dionysius son of Hippomedon was president (*epistates*), Demetrius son of Dies moved: since King Antiochus (I) son of King Seleucus (I), having in the beginning taken over the kingdom and pursued a glorious and honourable policy, has sought to bring back to peace and their former prosperity the cities of the Seleucis¹ / which were suffering from difficult times because of the rebels from his cause,² and after attacking those hostile to his interests,³ as was just, (has sought) to recover his ancestral rule;⁴ and therefore has embarked upon an honourable and just enterprise, and with not only the ready assistance of his 'friends' and his military forces⁵ in his fight for / his interests but also the goodwill and collaboration of the deity, has restored the cities to peace and the kingdom to its former state; and (since) now he has come to the provinces (*topoi*) this side of Mt Taurus with all zeal and enthusiasm and has at once restored peace to the cities and has advanced his interests and the kingdom to a more powerful and more brilliant position, / most of all through his own excellence but also through the goodwill of his 'friends' and his military forces; and therefore, so that the people might be seen to be well disposed to the king and to hold the same attitude, since previously at the time when he took over the kingdom it offered continuously prayers and sacrifices on his behalf to all the gods, with good fortune, be it resolved by the council and the / people, that the priestess, the temple-wardens and the *prytaneis* should pray to Athena of Ilium together with the ambassadors, that his presence (this side of Taurus) should be to the advantage of the king, his sister[6] and queen, his friends and his military forces, and that every other prosperity should attend the king and the queen, and that their interests and the kingdom should remain for them and prosper / as they themselves intend; and (be it resolved) that the other priests and priestesses should pray together with the priest of King Antiochus[7] to Apollo, the ancestor of his family,[8] to Nike, to Zeus and to all the other gods and goddesses. [After] the prayers the temple-wardens and the *prytaneis*, together with the priestess and the (royal) ambassadors shall perform the customary [ancestral] sacrifice,[9] while the generals together with the other priests (shall perform the sacrifice) to Apollo / and the other gods. When they are offering [the] sacrifice, the citizens and all the resident foreigners (*paroikoi*) shall wear crowns, and shall gather [in front of their homes] and offer sacrifices to the gods on behalf of the king and the people.[10] [And so that] the people [might be] seen [by all] to be helping in promoting what relates to honour and glory, (be it resolved) to praise him for the excellence and manliness he [constantly] displays, [and to set up] a golden equestrian statue [of him] / in the sanctuary of Athena in the [most] distinguished [place] on the step of white stone with the following inscription: 'The people of [Ilium (honours) King Antiochus] son of King Seleucus for his piety towards the sanctuary[11] (and) for being [the benefactor and] saviour of the people.' And (be it resolved) that the *agonothete*[12] and the [*synedroi*] should proclaim at the [Panathenaea during the] gymnastic contest [when the] city [of Ilium] / and the other cities crown with the [crown of valour Athena of] Ilium, making the proclamation . . . and (be it resolved) that [three] envoys should be appointed from among [all the men of Ilium, to] convey to him the greetings of [the people, and congratulate him on the good] health enjoyed by him, his [sister and queen, his children], / his friends and [military forces, and to convey (to him) the] honour [that has been voted to him], and to discourse on [the goodwill the people has constantly] shown [towards]

15

20

25

30

35

40

45

238

his father [Seleucus and the whole royal household] and to invite [him to . . .][13]

(the end of the inscription is lost)

OGIS 219; L. Robert, *American Studies in Papyrology* 1 (1966), 175–211; P. Frisch, *Die Inschriften von Ilion* (Bonn, 1975), no. 32.

1. See **174**.
2. A vague reference to serious disturbances at the accession of Antiochus I, possibly aggravated by Ptolemaic intervention.
3. Literally 'affairs' (*pragmata*), a word commonly used to describe the 'kingdom' or the 'state' of Hellenistic kings; cf. **125** l.26, **175**, **176**(b), **180**(b) (3), **182** l.5, **184**, **186**, **196** l.29, **203** l.32, **209** l.32, **230**.
4. Cf. **217** n. 8.
5. The conjunction of king, 'friends' (cf. **25** n. 3) and army is frequent; cf. **151** ll.23f.
6. An honorific title, cf. **156**, **158**.
7. This shows the existence of a cult of Antiochus I at Ilium (a cult of Seleucus I is attested by *OGIS* 212 (*Inschr. von Ilion*, no. 31), if correctly attributed); for other examples of cults of Seleucid rulers by Greek cities see **143**, **151**, **182**; for the cult of themselves set up by the Seleucids see on **158**.
8. See **186**.
9. To Athena of Ilium.
10. Cf. **271**.
11. On this theme see **163** n. 4.
12. Cf. **43** n. 8.
13. For Antiochus I and Ilium cf. too **180**; for the Seleucids and the Greek cities of Asia Minor see also **143**, **151**, **153–157**, **159**, **182–184**, **186**.

140 The coming of the Galatians to Asia Minor (278/7)

When the Galatians[1] arrived at Byzantium and ravaged the larger part of its territory, the Byzantines, weakened by the war, sent an embassy to their allies[2] asking for help. They all provided support within their means, and the people of Heraclea provided 4,000 gold pieces (the sum requested by the embassy). The Galatians who had made the attack on the Byzantines[3] repeatedly tried to cross into Asia but failed every time on the opposition of the Byzantines, but not long after Nicomedes[4] made a treaty with them with a view to bringing them across. The treaty was as follows: the barbarians were to be always well disposed to Nicomedes and his descendants, and would not make any alliance with anyone who sent embassies to them without the consent of Nicomedes, but would always be friends of his friends and enemies of those hostile to him; they would also if necessary be allies of the peoples of Byzantium, Tios,

Heraclea, Calchedon, Cieros and a few other tribal leaders. In conformity with this treaty Nicomedes brought over to Asia the mass of the Galatians. Their most conspicuous leaders were seventeen in number, and among these the most eminent and distinguished were Leonnorius and Luturius. At first it was believed that this crossing of the Galatians into Asia would bring about the ruin of the inhabitants, but the end result turned out to be to their advantage; for though the kings were anxious to destroy the democracy in the cites,[5] their action tended to strengthen it as they opposed the hostile Galatians.[6] Nicomedes, by arming the barbarians against the Bithynians at first, with the alliance of the people of Heraclea, established control over the country and massacred the inhabitants,[7] while the Galatians shared out the rest of the booty among themselves. The latter roamed over a vast area of country and then withdrew, and from the territory they had seized they cut off for themselves the country now called Galatia, dividing it into three parts and calling the inhabitants of each respectively the Trogmi, Tolostobogii and Tectosages. The Trogmi built the city of Ancyra, the Tolostobogii Tabia and the Tectosages Pisinus.[8]

Memnon of Heraclea, FGrH 434 F 11; Staatsv. III.469

1. I.e. the Celts, for whose coming cf. **48**.
2. A league of Greek cities (listed below) formed in 281 after the death of Lysimachus and in opposition to the Seleucids (Memnon, *op. cit.* F 6–7).
3. On Byzantium cf. **94, 96**.
4. Nicomedes, one of the two sons of Zipoetes the founder of the native monarchy of Bithynia, was in conflict with his brother Zipoetes.
5. Contrast **143, 182**.
6. The Galatians pillaged and blackmailed the Greek cities, but had nothing against Greek democracy as such.
7. Only in part.
8. There is no mention here of Antiochus I's war against the Galatians (cf. **142**). For the impact of the Galatians in Asia Minor cf. also **180, 183, 194** n. 5; for their use as mercenaries cf. also **149, 160**.

141 A Babylonian account of the reign of Antiochus I for the years 276–4

(10) . . . In that year[1] the king (Antiochus I) left his court, his wife and the crown prince in Sapardu[2] to keep a strong guard. He went to the province Ebirnari[3] and marched against the Egyptian army[4] (11) which was camped in Ebirnari. The Egyptian army fled before him. In Adar on the 24th the governor of Akkad despatched a great quantity of silver, cloth stuffs, furniture and gear (12) from Babylon and Seleucia, the royal city,[5] and 20 elephants which the governor of Bactria had sent to the king, to Ebirnari (13) to the king. Adar. In that month the general

assembled the royal army which was in Akkad from its head to its . . ., and in Nisan marched to Ebirnari to assist the king. (14) In that year they paid current prices in Babylon and the cities in copper coins of Greece.[6] In that year there was much scabies in the country. (15) In the 37th year (= 275/4), Antiochus (I) and Seleucus.[7] In the month of Adar on the 9th the governor of Akkad and the town magistrates of the king who went to Sapardu in the 36th year (= 276/5) to the king (16) returned to Seleucia, the royal city on the Tigris. They wrote (?) their rescripts to the Babylonians. In Teshri on the 12th (17) they brought the Babylonians out to Seleucia.[8] In that month the governor of Akkad acquired the seed-land, which they gave in the 32nd year (= 280/79) according to the king's wish for the food supply of the inhabitants of Babylon. (18) Borsippa and Kuthah, and the oxen, sheep and everything whatever which in the towns and cities according to the king's wish unto the Babylonians they gave, (19) for the king's household. In that year a quantity of bricks for rebuilding Esagila[9] were made above and below Babylon . . . with sun-dried brick in . . . (20) . . . There was a famine in Akkad. The people hired their children for silver. The people died of hunger. In that year there was much scabies in the country. (21) They paid current prices in Babylon and the cities in copper coins of Greece. In the 38th year (= 274/3), reigns of Antiochus (I) and Seleucus . . . (22) Observation of the firmament (?) from Teshri of the 38th year to the end of Adar of the 38th year, in the reign of Antiochus and Seleucus. [. . .]

S. Smith, *Babylonian Historical Texts* (Methuen, London, 1924), 150–9

1. The 36th of the Seleucid era in the Babylonian reckoning (see **138**), i.e. 276/5. For all dates see the tables in Parker-Dubberstein, *op. cit.*
2. Sardis in Lydia (cf. **181**, **185**).
3. Syria.
4. I.e. the forces of Ptolemy II Philadelphus; the reference is to the 'First Syrian War' between Ptolemies and Seleucids.
5. Seleucia on the Tigris, cf. **188**.
6. I.e. there was a scarcity of silver.
7. Seleucus, eldest son of Antiochus I was coregent (cf. **138** n. 4) till early 267, when he may have been executed for conspiracy (?), and was replaced as coregent by his younger brother Antiochus II, cf. **142**, **143**.
8. The purpose of the move is unclear; Pausanias 1.16.3 credits Seleucus with transferring colonists from Babylon to Seleucia on the Tigris.
9. The great temple at Babylon, cf. **189**.

142 Decree of two native villages in Asia Minor (January 267)

In the reigns of King Antiochus (I) and King Seleucus,[1] in the 45th year, in the month Peritius,[2] when Helenus was overseer (*epimeletes*) of the

district (*topos*),³ a meeting of the assembly was held and it was resolved
5 by the people of Neoteichos / and Kiddioukome:⁴ since Banabelos⁵ the
manager of the estates of Achaeus,⁶ and Lachares son of Papus, the
accountant (*eklogistes*)⁷ of the estates of Achaeus, have been their benefac-
10 tors on all occasions and both publicly and in private / have given
assistance to every individual during the war against the Galatians,⁸ and
as many of them had been taken prisoner by the Galatians, they reported
15 (the matter) to Achaeus and [ransomed them], / (it was resolved) to praise
them and to inscribe their benefaction on a stone stele, and to place it in
20 the sanctuary of Zeus at Babakome and that of Apollo at Kiddioukome, /
and to grant them and their descendants for all time a seat of honour
(*proedria*) at the public festivals, and to sacrifice to Achaeus the lord of the
25 district and saviour every year / an ox in the sanctuary of Zeus, and to
Lachares and Banabelos their benefactors two rams, <and?> in the
sanctuary of Apollo at Kiddioukome three sheep, so that others may
30 know that the people of Neoteichos / and Kiddioukome know how to
repay honours to those who have done them a favour.⁹

M. Wörrle, *Chiron* 5 (1975), 59–87; J. and L. Robert, *Bull.* 1976, 667

1. See **141** n. 7.
2. January 267: this inscription therefore places the victory of Antiochus I over
   the Galatians in *ca* 269–268.
3. The first attested example of this title in Seleucid administration.
4. Two native villages in Asia Minor; the Greek character of the inscription and
   the hellenisation of the two native communities are noteworthy.
5. A semitic name.
6. Grandfather of the Achaeus who revolted from Antiochus III (cf. **146, 193**);
   for other large estates in Asia Minor worked by native peasants (*laoi*), cf. **180,
   181, 185**.
7. Cf. **187**.
8. Cf. **140**.
9. This is the first text to show the native peasantry of Asia Minor speaking with
   its own voice; contrast **180, 181, 185**.

143 Decree of the League of Ionians for Antiochus I

. . . on the fourth day of the beginning (of the month) . . ., so that we
should [pass the day on which King Antiochus (I)] was born¹ in . . .
reverence [. . . To each person participating in the festival (?)] shall be
5 given / [a sum] equivalent to that given for [the procession and sacrifice ?
for Alexander].² And so that [King Antiochus and] Queen Stratonice³
[might know of the resolutions (?) of the League of] Ionians⁴ concerning
the honours, two [ambassadors shall be appointed . . .] from each

city, / . . . as ambassadors to King [Antiochus, and they] shall hand over   10
the present decree [to the king from the League] of the Ionian cities as
[. . . and shall do (?) whatever] good they can to the [League of cities].
The ambassadors [shall] also [invite] King / [Antiochus] to take [every]   15
care of the [Ionian] cities [so that in future] they might be free and under
[democracies,5 and might enjoy harmony (?)] in their political life
according to (their) ancestral [laws]. The ambassadors [shall] also
[represent] to him that [if he does this] he will be the cause [of many
blessings] to the cities / [and will at the same time follow the] policy of   20
his ancestors.6 [The ambassadors shall also] ask [King] Antiochus to
point to [the spot that] seems [to him . . .], in which [his] sacred
enclosure [will be established (?)] and the religious festival (*panegyris*)
[will be] celebrated.7 [And when] the ambassadors [have returned], the
city / [. . . the] sacrifice of the *Alexandreia* [will invite all the peoples]   25
who participate in the [sacrifice] to discuss [in accordance with the
resolution] of the council . . . and the furnishing . . ., the [contest (?), the
sacrifices] and the other arrangements / [to be made and the] time when   30
they are to be celebrated. [When the] decree [is ratified] the delegates
who are present from the cities shall offer a sacrifice to all the gods and
goddesses, and to the kings Antiochus <and Antiochus>8 and to Queen
Stratonice, and shall sacrifice perfect victims, and the delegates and all the
others in the city shall wear wreaths. / The priests and priestesses shall   35
open the sanctuaries and sacrifice with a prayer that the resolutions might
bring advantage to Kings Antiochus and Antiochus, to Queen Stratonice
and [to all] those who have a share in the honours.9 / This decree shall be   40
inscribed on a stele with the names and patronymics of the delegates who
have come from the cities, and shall be placed in the sacred enclosure
next to the altar of the kings. The peoples in each city shall also inscribe
this decree and the names and patronymics [of the] delegates, /   45
[and set it up in the place (?) which] seems to them most distinguished.
. . . Ephesians: Artemidorus son of Gorgo
. . . Lebedians: Cap . . ..
(the rest of the inscription is lost)
OGIS 222; H. Engelmann and R. Merkelbach, *Die Inschriften
von Erythrai und Klazomenai* II (Bonn, 1973), no. 504

1. On the celebration of the king's birthday cf. **222** n. 6.
2. This festival, celebrated by the League of Ionians (see n. 4), was probably
   established in Alexander's lifetime.
3. Stratonice, daughter of Demetrius Poliorcetes, wife of Seleucus I then of
   Antiochus I.
4. The ancient League of Ionians in Asia Minor, dissolved under the Persians,
   was seemingly revived by Alexander, cf. **40** n. 1.

5. Cf. **182**.
6. 'Ancestors' may only refer to Antiochus' father Seleucus I.
7. For divine honours paid to the Seleucids by Greek cities see **139** n. 7.
8. Antiochus II, son of Antiochus I, associated on the throne with him; cf. **141** n. 7.
9. This includes the followers of the king, cf. **139**.

144 Aradus in Phoenicia in the Seleucid empire

In former times the people of Aradus were ruled by their own kings, just like each of the other Phoenician cities. Subsequently, first the Persians, then the Macedonians and now the Romans changed their situation to the present state of affairs. The people of Aradus, then, together with the other Phoenicians were subjects of the Syrian kings (i.e. the Seleucids), who were friendly to them.[1] Then during the conflict between the two brothers Seleucus (II) Callinicus (the Victorious) and Antiochus called Hierax (The Hawk),[2] they joined the side of Callinicus and made a compact with him, which allowed them to receive refugees from his kingdom and not to surrender them against their will, though they were not to allow them to sail out (of their city) without the king's permission.[3] This was the source of great advantages to them; for the men who took refuge with them were no ordinary individuals but men in positions of great trust who feared for their lives. Being entertained by them they regarded their hosts as benefactors (*euergetai*) and saviours (*soteres*), and would remember the favour especially on returning to their own country. As a result the people of Aradus acquired much territory on the mainland,[4] most of which they still have today, and they prospered in other respects. In addition to their good luck they displayed foresight and were industrious in exploiting the sea; when they saw the neighbouring Cilicians acquiring pirate bases they never once collaborated with them in such an enterprise.[5]

Strabo XVI.2.14; cf. Staatsv. III.491

1. A powerful naval city, Aradus was essential to the Seleucids in their struggles against the Ptolemies for the control of Coele Syria (cf. **148**); the 'era' of Aradus dates from October 259 and probably reflects a grant of autonomy by Antiochus II. See also **178**, and cf. generally J. P. Rey-Coquais, *Arados et sa pérée* (Paris, 1975), esp. 149–61.
2. The 'fratricidal war' of *ca* 241–239 (?) which weakened the Seleucid empire (cf. **145, 197**), and left it divided until 226 between Antiochus Hierax in Asia Minor (cf. **113**) and Seleucus in the rest of the empire.
3. Whether this privilege is equivalent to a grant of *asylia* (see **151**) is disputed.
4. Aradus was located on an island some 2 km. from the coast.

5. Cf. **171**. Polybius v.68.7 mentions a treaty of alliance between Aradus and Antiochus III during the Fourth Syrian War in 218 (cf. **148, 149**).

145 The origins of the Parthian kingdom

See further: J. Wolski, *Berytus* 12 (1956–7), 35–52; Will 1 (1979), 301–8.

When the peoples beyond the Taurus revolted as the kings of Syria and Media, who also controlled those parts, were fighting with each other (?),[1] Bactria and all the territory near it was the first to be made independent by the men who enjoyed the confidence of the kings, namely Euthydemus[2] and his followers. Then Arsaces, a Scythian, at the head of some of the nomad tribes of the Dahae, who are called the Parni and live along the Oxus,[3] invaded Parthia and established control over it. Initially he was weak as he and his successors had to fight against men dispossessed of their territory, but later they became so powerful by seizing neighbouring lands through continuous successes in war that in the end they became masters of all the territory within (i.e. to the east of) the Euphrates. They also seized part of Bactria by reducing the Scythians, and even before this Eucratidas and his followers;[4] at present they rule so much territory and so many peoples that they have become as it were rivals of the Romans for the extent of their empire. The reason for this is their life-style and customs, which have many barbarian and Scythian elements, but which also have much that is conducive to leadership and success in war. (3) They say that the Parnian Dahae are migrants from the Dahae who live above Lake Maeotis,[5] whom they call Xandii or Parii; but it is not quite agreed that the Dahae are Scythians from above Lake Maeotis. At any rate some say that Arsaces derived his origin from them, while others say he was a Bactrian who was escaping from the growing power of Diodotus and his followers and so caused Parthia to revolt. [. . .][6]

Strabo XI.9.2–3

1. Text uncertain; the reference is presumably to the war of Seleucus II and Antiochus Hierax, cf. **144** and n. 2. The Parthian royal 'era' started in 247, but this could easily be later retrojection.
2. Presumably an error for 'Diodotus', the first Greek king of Bactria mentioned below, since Euthydemus ruled years later, cf. **150, 191**.
3. The Amu-Darya.
4. King of Bactria in the second century, cf. **191**.
5. Presumably the Aral Sea rather than the Sea of Azov (the more frequent use of the name 'Lake Maeotis').
6. Compare the version in Justin XLI.4.

146 The usurpation of Achaeus in Asia Minor

[. . .] Achaeus was a relation[1] of the Antiochus (III) who had taken over
the kingdom in Syria;[2] he had secured the position of power I have
mentioned more or less as follows. When Seleucus (II) the father of this
Antiochus (III) died, and Seleucus (III) the eldest of his sons succeeded to
the kingdom,[3] he (sc. Achaeus) accompanied him on his expedition over
the Taurus because of his kinship (this was about two years before the
events I am relating). For as soon as the younger Seleucus had succeeded
to the throne, on hearing that Attalus (I of Pergamum) had already
reduced all the country this side of Taurus under his power,[4] he was
eager to restore his position. He crossed the Taurus with a large army but
was treacherously killed by Apaturius the Gaul and Nicanor. Because of
his family connexion Achaeus at once avenged his murder and put to
death Nicanor and Apaturius, and took charge of the military forces and
of the whole administration with prudence and generosity. For though
he had the opportunity, and the support of the common soldiers was
pressing him to assume the diadem,[5] he chose not to do this but to
safeguard the royalty for Antiochus the younger of the sons, and by an
energetic march he regained all the country this side of Taurus. But as he
met with success beyond expectation, having shut Attalus up in Pergamum and secured control of everything else, he was carried away by
success and drifted off the proper course. He assumed the diadem, called
himself king, and was at the time the most powerful and feared of the
kings and dynasts[6] this side of Taurus.[7] [. . .]

Polybius IV.48

1. The exact relationship is unclear; cf. Walbank *ad loc*. On the elder Achaeus cf.
   142, 193. The context of this passage is the appeal to Achaeus by Byzantium in
   the war against Rhodes (see **94**).
2. See **147**.
3. In 225.
4. This had been achieved as a result of the 'fratricidal war' (**144** n. 2).
5. Cf. **36** n. 1.
6. Cf. **182** n. 6.
7. See also **147**. Achaeus' assumption of the royal title dates in fact from 220, and
   it was only after the 'Fourth Syrian War' that Antiochus III moved to
   overthrow Achaeus in Asia Minor (216–213).

147 The accession of Antiochus III and the revolt of Molon (223–220)

[. . .] Antiochus (III) was the younger son of Seleucus (II) called

Callinicus; when his father died and his brother Seleucus (III) succeeded to the throne because of his age, he at first went to live in the upper (i.e. eastern) provinces, but when Seleucus was treacherously killed while crossing the Taurus with his army, as I have mentioned before, he took over the kingdom and ruled himself, entrusting control of affairs this side of Taurus to Achaeus,[1] and placing the upper provinces of the kingdom in the hands of Molon and Alexander, Molon's brother, Molon being satrap of Media and his brother of Persis. (41) They viewed Antiochus with contempt because of his youth, and hoped that Achaeus would be an accomplice in their undertaking. They were particularly afraid of the cruelty and evil-doing of Hermeias, who at the time was the chief minister of the whole kingdom,[2] and so undertook to revolt and detach the upper satrapies. Hermeias was a Carian who was 'in charge of affairs', having been appointed to that position of trust by Seleucus (III) brother of Antiochus at the time when he made his expedition against Attalus (I of Pergamum). Invested with this authority he was jealous of all those who held an eminent position at court, and being cruel by temperament he would punish the mistakes of some by placing a sinister interpretation on them and would bring trumped up and false charges against others, showing himself a pitiless and harsh judge. But his chief ambition, to which he attached great importance, was to remove Epigenes, the man who had brought back the army which had gone with Seleucus, as he could see that he had eloquence and practical ability and enjoyed great popularity with the soldiers. With this aim in mind he kept vigilant, always ready to seize any opportunity or pretext against Epigenes.[3] When a meeting of the council[4] was held to discuss the revolt of Molon, and the king asked each member to give his opinion on how to deal with the rebels, Epigenes gave his view first, saying that it was essential to take control of the situation without delay, and in particular the king must proceed immediately to the provinces (*topoi*) and meet the crisis face to face. In this way (he said), Molon and his followers either would not even dare to stir up trouble, the king being present and showing himself to his peoples with an adequate army, or even if they had the audacity to pursue their attempt, they would rapidly be seized by the soldiers and handed over to the king. (42) While Epigenes was still speaking in this way, Hermeias in a fit of anger declared that he had long been scheming secretly to betray the kingdom, but now he had done a service in revealing his true intentions, by being anxious to expose the king's person, with few followers, to the rebels. For the time being he was content, as it were, to ignite suspicions and let them smoulder, and let go of Epigenes, having made an ill-timed show of bad temper rather than of real hatred. As for his own advice, he counselled against the expedition against Molon, being terrified of the danger because of his lack of military experience, but he urged a campaign against Ptolemy (IV), believing this would be a safe war because of Ptolemy's indolence.[5] On that occasion he overawed all the members of the council; he despatched against Molon Xenon and Theodotus 'Hemiolius'[6] with an army, and kept inciting Antiochus to take in hand the problem of Coele Syria,[7] with this one thought in mind, that if the young ruler was surrounded by war on all sides, he (Hermeias) would escape punishment for his former crimes and would avoid being deprived of his position of authority, because of the services he rendered and because of the trials and dangers that would continuously surround the king. In the end he forged[8] a letter supposedly sent by Achaeus and showed it to the king, to the effect that Ptolemy was encouraging him to make a bid for power and promising him naval and financial help in all his undertakings should he wish to assume the diadem[9] and display openly his claims to sovereignty, which he already enjoyed in practice while grudging himself the glory by refusing the crown that fate offered to him. The king was convinced by the letter and became prepared and anxious for the campaign against Coele Syria. (43) [. . .] In the meantime Molon had turned the troops from his satrapy into an army prepared for anything, by raising their hopes of profit and by the fears he inspired in their leaders as a result of showing them forged letters from the king that were threatening in tone. He had a ready ally in his brother Alexander and had secured his position in the neighbouring satrapies by winning the goodwill of their governors through bribery. He now marched out with a large army to meet the king's generals. Xenon and Theodotus were terrified at his approach and retreated to the cities. Molon secured control of the territory of Apolloniatis and was now provided with supplies in considerable quantities. Even before this the extent of his power made him formidable. (44) For all the royal herds of horses are entrusted to the Medes,[10] and they have incalculable quantities of corn and cattle. As to the strength and size of the country no one could easily give a fair idea. Media lies centrally in Asia but surpasses in size and altitude all the provinces in Asia when compared to them. And again it neighbours on the largest and most warlike peoples.[11] [. . .]

Polybius v.40–44 (with omissions)

1. On all this see **146**.
2. Literally 'in charge of affairs' (cf. **139** n. 3), an official post with powers equivalent to those of a viceroy, as Polybius' account shows.
3. Polybius' account is based on a source obviously hostile to Hermeias.
4. The king's council of 'friends' was a regular institution in all Hellenistic monarchies, cf. **25** n. 3, **77**, **164**, **167** ch. 149, **208**. Polybius' account gives a valuable insight into court politics.

5. Ptolemy III, though Polybius is thinking of Ptolemy IV.
6. Literally 'one and a half', probably a reference to his size.
7. This led to a short and unsuccessful campaign by Antiochus III in Syria in 221 (Polybius v.45–46); the war over Coele Syria was only resumed in earnest after the overthrow of Molon (see **148, 149**).
8. The letter could be genuine.
9. Cf. **36** n. 1.
10. For Median cavalry cf. **148, 160**.
11. Molon, who had in fact assumed the royal title, as shown by coins, was eventually defeated in 220 and committed suicide. Hermeias fell out of favour in the same year and was assassinated by Antiochus III (Polybius v.45–56).

148 The conflicting Seleucid and Ptolemaic claims to Coele Syria (winter 219/18)

See further: V. Tcherikover, *Hellenistic Civilization and the Jews* (Philadelphia, 1959), 52–5.

In fact at the time the ambassadors came back, Sosibius[1] and his followers were ready for every eventuality while Antiochus (III) was extremely anxious to secure as much diplomatic advantage over the envoys from Alexandria in his conferences with them as he had in force of arms. Hence when the ambassadors arrived at Seleucia[2] and began to discuss the detailed clauses of the treaty in accordance with the instructions of Sosibius, the king in self-justification minimised the recent disaster and the manifest injustice involved in the seizure of Coele Syria. In fact he did not even consider his action to be a breach of justice, as he was laying claim to places that belonged to him; the first conquest by Antigonus the One-Eyed and the rule exercised by Seleucus (I) over these places constituted, he said, the most solid and justifiable title to possession in virtue of which Coele Syria belonged to them and not to Ptolemy.[3] Ptolemy (I) had gone to war against Antigonus not for himself but to secure for Seleucus the rule over those places. He laid particular emphasis on the general agreement of all the kings, made at the time of their victory over Antigonus[4] when they met in conference and Cassander, Lysimachus and Seleucus all decided of one accord that the whole of Syria should belong to Seleucus. Ptolemy's envoys tried to establish the opposite point of view; they exaggerated the existing injury and emphasised its seriousness, and assimilated the betrayal of Theodotus[5] and the invasion of Antiochus to a breach of treaty; they put forward the rights of possession established under Ptolemy (I) son of Lagus, claiming that Ptolemy had collaborated in the campaign of Seleucus on the understanding that sovereignty over the whole of Asia would be attributed to Seleucus while Coele Syria and Phoenicia would fall to his own share. These and similar arguments were put forward frequently by both sides in their diplomatic exchanges and conferences, but nothing at all was achieved as the negotiation was conducted through common friends and there was no one in between to check and control the pretensions of the side which might appear to be in the wrong.[6] [. . .]

Polybius v.67; cf. Staatsv.III.447

1. The most influential figure at the Ptolemaic court (cf. **224** and n. 1). These negotiations were conducted during a four-month armistice in winter 219/18; Antiochus III had already occupied Coele Syria in 219.
2. Seleucia in Pieria (cf. **174, 176–177**), lost in the 'Third Syrian War' or 'Laodicean War' of 246–241 (cf. **220**) and just recaptured by Antiochus III from Ptolemy IV in 219 (Polybius v.58–9).
3. For this view of the rights of conquest and inheritance, cf. **30** n. 4, and cf. the wills of Attalus III (**211**) and Ptolemy VIII (**230**).
4. See **43** n. 5.
5. The Ptolemaic governor of Coele Syria, whose treachery enabled Antiochus III to invade Coele Syria (Polybius v.61–62).
6. For the sequel see **149**. For the Ptolemaic side cf. **224, 225**.

149 The army of Antiochus III at the battle of Raphia (217)

See further: Griffith (1935), 143f.; B. Bar-Kochva, *The Seleucid Army* (Cambridge, 1976), 128–41, and index s.v. Raphia.

At the beginning of spring (217), Antiochus (III) and Ptolemy (IV) having completed their preparations were intent on bringing the campaign to an end by a decisive battle. Ptolemy and his men departed from Alexandria with about 70,000 infantry, 5,000 horses and 73 elephants.[1] Antiochus perceiving their approach assembled his troops. These consisted of Dahae, Carmanians and Cilicians lightly armed numbering about 5,000; the Macedonian Byttacus had the charge and command of them. Under Theodotus the Aetolian, the man who had betrayed Coele Syria (to Antiochus),[2] were placed 10,000 men picked from the whole kingdom and armed in the Macedonian fashion, the majority of them Silver Shields.[3] The numbers of the phalanx amounted to 20,000 commanded by Nicarchus and Theodotus called 'Hemiolius'.[4] After them came 2,000 Agrianes and Persians, archers and slingers. With them were 1,000 Thracians, commanded by Menedemus of Alabanda. There were also Medians, Cissians, Cadusians and Carmanians adding up to about 5,000 men and placed under the orders of Aspasianus the Mede.[5]

The Arabs and some of their neighbours numbered about 10,000, under the command of Zabdibelus. The Thessalian Hippolochus commanded the mercenaries from Greece, and they numbered about 5,000; he also had 1,500 Cretans with Eurylochus and 1,000 Neocretans under the orders of Zelys of Gortyn. They were joined by 500 Lydian javelin-men and 1,000 Cardaces under Lysimachus the Galatian. The total number of cavalry amounted to about 6,000 men, 4,000 of whom were commanded by Antipater, the king's nephew, while Themison was in charge of the remainder. The army of Antiochus amounted to 62,000 infantry, 6,000 cavalry and 102 elephants.[6]

Polybius v.79

1. For the Ptolemaic side see **224**.
2. See **148** n. 5.
3. The élite royal guard; see Bar-Kochva, *op. cit.*, 59–66. Cf. **15** n. 9 for the time of Alexander.
4. See **147** n. 6.
5. On Media cf. **147** (end).
6. Antiochus' defeat at this battle postponed Seleucid hopes of reconquering Coele Syria for nearly two decades (cf. **154, 167**). On the Seleucid army cf. also **160**.

150 The Anabasis of Antiochus III (212–205)

The simultaneous rise of the Parthian and Bactrian kingdoms (cf. **145, 191**) effectively amputated the eastern provinces of the Seleucid empire. An attempt by Seleucus II to check Parthia failed, and it was not until 212 that Antiochus III embarked on his eastern expedition (the 'Anabasis'). Polybius' account of this grandiose campaign, reminiscent of Alexander's, is only preserved in fragments. In 212 Armenia was forced to recognise Seleucid overlordship and pay tribute (Polybius VIII.23), in 211–210 Media was invaded and the temple of Anaitis at Ecbatana plundered for its wealth (Polybius X.27; cf. **168**), in 209 a campaign against the Parthians led to a settlement but not the elimination of Parthian power (Polybius X.28–31), then in 208–6 Antiochus attacked and besieged unsuccessfully Euthydemus the Greek king in Bactria (Polybius X.49), and so was ready for an arrangement.

Euthydemus himself was a Magnesian[1] and he replied to (Teleas) the envoy that it was not right for Antiochus (III) to try to expel him from his kingdom. He had not himself revolted from the king, but had destroyed the descendants of others who had: that was how he had secured rule over Bactria.[2] He added further arguments to that effect and urged Teleas to show goodwill in mediating a settlement by inviting Antiochus not to refuse him the title and position of king. Should Antiochus refuse the request, there would be no security for either of them: large hordes of nomads were at hand who presented a threat to both of them, and the country would certainly be barbarised if they allowed them in.[3] With these words he sent Teleas back to Antiochus. The king had long been anxious to resolve the situation, and on hearing the report of Teleas he readily consented to a settlement for the above-mentioned reasons. After much toing and froing between the two sides by Teleas, Euthydemus finally sent his son Demetrius to ratify the agreement. The king received him and thought the young man worthy of royalty on account of his appearance, his dignified bearing and conversation; he first promised to give him one of his daughters (in marriage) and secondly he conceded the royal title to his father. On the other matters he concluded a written treaty and a sworn alliance,[4] and then broke camp after generously supplying his army with provisions and adding to his forces the elephants which Euthydemus had. He crossed the Caucasus[5] and descended into India, renewed his friendship with Sophagasenus king of the Indians and received more elephants,[6] raising their number to a total of 150, provisioned his army once more on the spot, and he himself broke camp with his troops while leaving behind Androsthenes of Cyzicus to bring back the treasure which the king (i.e. Sophagasenus) had agreed to give him. He traversed Arachosia, crossed the river Erymanthus,[7] passed through Drangene and reached Carmania, where he established his winter quarters as winter was now at hand (206/5). This was the extreme limit of the march of Antiochus into the interior, through which he subjected to his rule not only the satraps of the interior but the coastal cities and the dynasts on this side of Taurus,[8] and in a word he strengthened his kingdom by overawing all his subjects with his daring and energy. For it was this campaign which made him appear worthy of royalty, not only to the peoples of Asia but to those in Europe as well.[9]

Polybius XI.34

1. I.e. like Teleas; which Magnesia is uncertain.
2. Euthydemus had overthrown Diodotus II, son of Diodotus I the founder of the Greek kingdom in Bactria (cf. **145, 191**).
3. The major threat to Greeks and Iranians alike in Bactria.
4. The terms are unknown; in effect Antiochus III was recognising the independence of Bactria.
5. The Hindu-Kush.
6. Cf. Seleucus I before, **46** n. 8. Sophagasenus is otherwise unknown.
7. The Helmand.
8. Cf. **182** n. 6, and for Antiochus III in Asia Minor cf. **151, 153, 154**.
9. For this conception of royalty cf. **36, 37, 47**(a). It was probably after this campaign that Antiochus III assumed the title 'The Great'.

151 Antiochus III and Teos (204/3)

[Proposal of the] *timouchoi* [and generals: since King] Antiochus (III) . . .
favourable policy [and preserving . . . / . . .the] goodwill he shows and   5
which he inherited from his [ancestors], and . . . intends to . . .
manifold, and intends to be the common [benefactor] of the other Greek
[cities and] of our own city.[1] Previously, when staying in the region
beyond the Taurus, he was the cause of many benefits / to us; when he   10
came to our region[2] he settled affairs in an advantageous way, and when
he stayed in our city he saw that we were exhausted both in our public
and our private affairs because of the continuous wars and the great
burden of contributions we were bearing. Wishing / to display piety   15
towards the god[3] to whom he consecrated our city and territory, and
wanting to do a favour to the people and the association of Dionysiac
artists,[4] he came forward in person in the assembly and granted to our
city and territory (to be) holy (*hiera*), inviolate (*asylos*)[5] and free from
tribute (*aphorologetos*), and undertook to free us himself from the other
contributions we pay to King Attalus (I),[6] / so that by bringing about an   20
improvement in the city's fortunes he would receive the title not only of
benefactor of the people, but of its saviour. He stayed in the city with his
friends and the military forces which accompanied him,[7] and gave ample
evidence of the good faith he already shows / towards all men, and after   25
this has constantly been responsible for many favours to us, thereby
giving an example to all the Greeks of how he treats those who are his
benefactors and who are well disposed towards him; some of the
blessings which resulted in prosperity for our city he is now bringing
about, while others he will bring about in future. He wrote a letter to the
people in which he suggested the sending of an embassy [to / him] to   30
discuss the matters he said he was convinced would [benefit] the people
as well, and when the people sent as ambassadors Dionysius son of
Apollo . . ., Hermagoras son of Epimenes, Theodorus son of Zopyrus,
he declared to them [that] he had freed the city for all time as he had
promised of the tributes which we paid to King Attalus. Concerning these
matters he sent a letter in which he said he had instructed the /   35
ambassadors to report to us, and the ambassadors reported these matters
[to the people]. In the same way his sister[8] and queen Laodice[9] constantly
shares the same view as the king in [all circumstances] and . . . and in
good deeds towards the city she shows [herself] eager and zealous to
perform benefactions, and the people has received the greatest /   40
[blessings] from both of them. Therefore, so that we may be seen in
every [circumstance] to be returning adequate thanks to the king and to
the queen and to be surpassing ourselves in the honours paid to them in
proportion to the benefactions received, and so that all may see that the

45   [people] is fully disposed to repay gratitude, with good fortune, (be it resolved) to place side by side with / the statue of Dionysus marble statues¹⁰ of King Antiochus and of his sister and queen Laodice, as beautiful [and as] majestic as possible, so that since they have granted to (our) city and territory (to be) holy and inviolate and have exempted us from taxation and have granted these favours to the people and to the
50   association of Dionysiac artists, they might receive from / all [the] honours as far as [possible, and] might share in the temple¹¹ and the other honours enjoyed by Dionysus and be the joint [saviours] of our [city] and bestow blessings [on our] community. So that [these resolutions] might be put into effect two [commissioners] shall be appointed from all [the]
55   citizens to] supervise [the] making [and the] dedication of the [statues]. / The [money] for this shall be provided . . .¹²

P. Herrman, *Anadolu* 9 (1965), 29–159 at pp. 34–6

1. See **139** n. 13.
2. Before the discovery of this inscription (in 1963) Antiochus III's activity in Asia Minor in 204/3 was only attested in Caria (*RC* 38; cf. Polybius xv.35.13 and see also R. L. Pounder, *Hesperia* 47 (1978), 55–7) and the allegiance of Teos to the Seleucid cause was not attested before 190 (Livy xxxvii.27f.).
3. See **163** n. 4.
4. See **123** and n. 9.
5. The recognition of a city as 'holy and inviolate', a privilege much sought after in the Hellenistic world, meant that the city was in effect consecrated to a god and so made immune from arbitrary seizure or reprisals in peace time. It did not necessarily make it politically 'neutral': Teos is found in 190 actively supporting Antiochus III in his war against the Romans and being treated by them as a normal combatant city, though they had previously recognised her *asylia* (cf. **157** and Livy xxxvii.27f.). For other cases of *asylia* granted to cities or sanctuaries cf. **52, 85, 144** (?), **173, 178, 182, 184**. For Egypt cf. **231** l. 84 and n. 22.
6. Teos was previously under Attalid rule, cf. Polybius v.77.5 (in 218).
7. See **139** n. 5.
8. See **139** n. 6.
9. See **156, 158**.
10. These are cult statues (*agalmata*); on the cult of Seleucid rulers by Greek cities see **139** n. 7.
11. On this notion cf. **210**(c) and A. D. Nock, *HSCP* 41 (1930), 1–62.
12. There follows another decree regulating the religious honours to be paid to Antiochus III and Laodice.

152 The (alleged) secret pact between Antiochus III and Philip V (203/2)

The authenticity of the 'secret pact' whereby Philip V and Antiochus III are alleged to have agreed on a partition of the kingdom of the infant Ptolemy has been much debated. While Polybius believed in its historicity, he apparently knew nothing of its contents (cf. too III.2.8; the relevance of XVI.1.8f. is uncertain), nor does he seem to have regarded the pact as a cause of the Roman declaration of war against Philip V in 200 (cf. **65**).

See further: *Staatsv.* III.547 for a summary of modern views; R. M. Errington, *Athenaeum* 49 (1971), 336–54, for a sceptical view; W. V. Harris, *War and Imperialism in Republican Rome* (Oxford, 1979), 212f.; Walbank III (1979), 785.

Is it not astonishing that when Ptolemy (IV) was alive and had no need of their help, they (sc. Antiochus III and Philip V) were prepared to assist him, but when he died leaving a young son,[1] the preservation of whose kingdom fell on them according to the ties of nature, they urged each other on to partition the child's kingdom and to destroy the orphan without even putting forward the slightest pretext to justify their iniquity, as tyrants do, but acted in such a violent way like beasts of prey that they deserve to be said to live the life of fishes, among which it is said that though they are of the same species the destruction of the smaller is the food and livelihood of the larger? Who can look at this treaty as into a mirror and not see the impiety to the gods and the cruelty to men, as well as the unbounded ambition displayed by these two kings? [. . .][2]

Polybius XV.20; *Staatsv.* III.547

1. Ptolemy was 5 years old at his accession in 204.
2. Whatever the truth about the pact, Philip V proceeded to campaign in Thrace, the Aegean and Asia Minor in 202–201 (cf. **65**), while Antiochus III invaded Coele Syria in the 'Fifth Syrian War' (202–200), this time successfully, then moved into Asia Minor in 198–197 (see **153**).

153 Antiochus III in Asia Minor and at the Hellespont (197/6)

See further: J. Briscoe, *A Commentary on Livy Books* XXXI–XXXIII (Oxford, 1973), 320–2.

In the same year[1] King Antiochus, after wintering at Ephesus, sought to bring all the cities of Asia back to their former status within the empire.[2] He could see that the remainder would submit to his rule without difficulty, either because of their position in a plain or because they could place little reliance on their walls, weapons and soldiers, but Smyrna and Lampsacus were asserting their freedom and there was a danger that if they were granted what they sought, other cities might follow the example of Smyrna in Ionia and Aeolis, and of Lampsacus in the Hellespont.[3] And so he himself sent an army from Ephesus to besiege

Smyrna and ordered the troops stationed at Abydus to proceed to the siege of Lampsacus leaving only a small garrison behind. In fact he was not relying so much on the fear inspired by force, but through envoys he would send them conciliatory messages and reproach them for their rashness and obstinacy; he sought in this way to raise the hope that they would soon have what they were seeking, but only when it was sufficiently clear to themselves and to all others that it was from the king that they had obtained their freedom and that they had not seized it in favourable circumstances.[4] The reply to all this was that Antiochus should be neither surprised nor angry that they should not lightly accept seeing their hopes of freedom being put off. Antiochus himself sailed at the beginning of spring from Ephesus and made for the Hellespont, and ordered his land forces to cross from Abydus to the Chersonese. The land and sea forces made their junction near Madytus, a city on the Chersonese, which shut its gates to him and so he surrounded its walls with troops; the city surrendered when he started to move up his siege engines. The same fear induced the inhabitants of Sestus and the other cities in the Chersonese to surrender. From there he reached Lysimachea[5] simultaneously with all his sea and land forces. He found it deserted and almost completely lying in ruins (a few years before the Thracians had captured and sacked the city and set it on fire), and he became anxious to restore a distinguished city which enjoyed a favourable position.[6] And so he started work on every part of the project at once, the reconstruction of the roofs and walls, redeeming those of the people of Lysimachea who had fallen into slavery, searching out and bringing together those who had scattered in flight throughout the Hellespont and Chersonese, and enlisting new settlers whom he attracted by the hope of advantages and sought in every way to make as numerous as possible. At the same time, in order to dispel the fear of the Thracians, he set off in person with half of his land forces to ravage the neighbouring parts of Thrace, while the other half he left together with all his naval allies to work on the reconstruction of the city.[7]

Livy XXXIII. 38

1. 196, but the events mentioned belong in fact to 197/6.
2. On Antiochus III's hopes of reconstructing his ancestral kingdom cf. **148, 150, 154**.
3. On Lampsacus cf. **155**; on Smyrna cf. **182**.
4. Cf. **154**.
5. Cf. **45** n. 8.
6. On kings as founders or restorers of cities cf. **40**.
7. For an inscription recording a reciprocal oath of alliance between Antiochus III and Lysimachea, cf. P. Frisch, *Die Inschriften von Ilion* (Bonn, 1975), no. 45. On the Thracians cf. **96** n. 4.

154 The conference at Lysimachea between Antiochus III and the Roman envoys (196)

See further (on Rome and Antiochus III): E. Badian, *CP* 54 (1959), 81–99; Errington (1971), 156–67; W. V. Harris, *War and Imperialism in Republican Rome* (Oxford, 1979), 219–23.

[. . .] Just as Antiochus' designs in Thrace were going as he wished, Lucius Cornelius and his colleagues sailed into Selymbria; they were the ambassadors sent by the Senate to arrange a peace between Antiochus and Ptolemy (V).[1] (50) At the same time there arrived three of the ten commissioners,[2] Publius Lentulus from Bargylia and Lucius Terentius and Publius Villius from Thasos. Their presence was promptly reported to the king and they all met together a few days later at Lysimachea; and Hegesianax and Lysias, the envoys sent to Titus (Flamininus) also happened to arrive at this time. The private meetings of the king and the Romans were quite informal and friendly, but afterwards when they met in public council to discuss matters of state policy things took a very different turn. Lucius Cornelius demanded that Antiochus should give up all the cities in Asia under the rule of Ptolemy (V) which he had just captured, and he earnestly requested him to evacuate those under Philip (V). He also advised him to keep away from the autonomous cities.[3] Finally, he said he could not understand why he had crossed to Europe with such a large army and fleet: there was no other reasonable interpretation of his action than that he was seeking to attack the Romans. With these words the Romans fell silent. (51) The king on his side said he could not understand on what grounds they were arguing with him over the cities in Asia; the Romans had less right to do this than anyone else. He next asked them not to meddle at all in the affairs of Asia; he himself had not interfered in any way in Italian affairs. He said he had crossed into Europe with his army to recover possession of the Chersonese and the cities in Thrace: sovereignty over those parts belonged to him more than to any other. At first Lysimachus held power over this area, but when Seleucus waged war on him and was victorious,[4] the whole kingdom of Lysimachus fell to Seleucus as the spoils of war.[5] Subsequently, because of the distractions which hindered his predecessors, first Ptolemy (III) then Philip (V) had wrested this country from him and made it their own.[6] He had not acquired the country by taking advantage of Philip's difficulties but had recovered possession of it in virtue of his rights. The people of Lysimachea had been expelled by the Thracians unexpectedly and he was not doing any injustice to the Romans in bringing them back and resettling them;[7] he did this, he said, not with the intention of attacking the Romans but to provide a residence for (his son) Seleucus.[8] As for the autonomous cities of Asia they must obtain their freedom not from an injunction of Rome but through an act of favour on his part.[9] As for Ptolemy, he said he would be settling matters amicably with him; he intended not only to conclude friendship with him but to seal it with a marriage alliance.[10]

Polybius XVIII.49–51

1. Antiochus III had defeated Ptolemy V in the 'Fifth Syrian War'.
2. See **68**.
3. The Roman declaration of freedom for the Greeks included those in Asia (see **68**).
4. See **45, 46**.
5. Cf. **30** n. 4.
6. In *ca* 245–241 and 200 respectively.
7. See **153**.
8. The future Seleucus IV Philopator, installed as governor of the Seleucid possessions in Thrace; cf. **215** n. 3.
9. Cf. **153** and see generally **139** n. 13.
10. Peace was concluded between Antiochus III and Ptolemy V in 195, Ptolemy marrying Antiochus' daughter Cleopatra.

155 Decree of Lampsacus in honour of an ambassador to Massalia and Rome (196/5)

Lampsacus, one of the cities which resisted Antiochus III in 197 (cf. **153**), is shown by this inscription to have sought the help of Rome through the agency of Massalia, like Lampsacus a colony of Phocaea, and a city which had a long-standing treaty with Rome.

See further: Walbank II (1967), 614.

(The beginning of the inscription is lost)

. . . [in the decrees] inscribed above. [And when the people was seeking] with all [earnestness] and calling upon [men] to offer their services, and had voted [that / the] men who went on a mission on behalf of the city to the [Massaliotes] and the Romans should receive some honour from the [people] and that when they returned [the] council [should introduce a motion] on the honours to be granted to them, and when [some persons] had been put forward but refused, and some had actually been appointed / [and had declined] on oath because of the magnitude of the journey [and of the expenses involved], Hegesias was put forward and instead of declining on oath [he was appointed] and deemed worthy by the people; [he gave no thought to] the dangers involved in the journey abroad, but [attached less importance] to his own personal affairs than to

5

10

the [interests] of the city / [and accepted] the embassy; he travelled   15
abroad and [came to] Greece and together with his fellow-[ambassadors]
he met [Lucius][1] the Roman general in command of the naval [forces]
and discoursed at length to him to the effect that the people (of
Lampsacus), [who was related and] friendly to the Roman people,[2] had
[sent / them] to him, and that [with] his fellow-ambassadors he urged   20
and [beseeched] them since we are kinsmen of the [Romans, to take
thought] for our city so as to bring about [whatever seemed] advantageous to the people, for it was incumbent on [them always to]
champion the interests of the city because of [the] kinship [which
exists] / between them and us, which [they] too [recognised] and   25
because the Massaliotes are our brothers [and are friends] and allies of the
Roman people; [and when] they had received [from him] a suitable reply,
they were to transmit [them all to the city]. These raised the spirits of the
[people; / for in them] he (sc. Flamininus) declares that he recognises the   30
[close kinship] which exists between us and the [Romans, and he
promised] that if he should conclude friendship or an alliance with
anyone, he would include [in them] our city, and would protect [the
democracy], autonomy and peace (of the city) [and / that he would do   35
anything in his] power to favour us, and that if anyone [tried to harass us]
he would not allow this but would prevent it. And when (Hegesias)
[with his fellow-]envoys met the quaestor in charge of the fleet [. . . and
persuaded] him always to be responsible for some favour, [he also
received] a letter from him to [our] people / [which he saw] was in our   40
favour and deposited in [the public archives]. He then travelled
. . .[. . .and wishing to carry out fully] the mission for which he had the
decrees, he [sailed to Massalia], a long and dangerous journey, [presented
himself before / the Six] Hundred[3] and won them over to his side, and   45
secured [the appointment of ambassadors] to accompany [him from
Massalia to] Rome; and believing it would be useful, they [requested and
received from the] Six Hundred a suitable letter [on behalf of our people
to the people] of the Tolostoagian Galatians.[4] He then sailed [to / Rome   50
together with] his fellow-ambassadors and the envoys [sent] with [him
from Massalia] and negotiated with the Senate with [them, and listened
to the Massaliotes declaring] the goodwill and support they [constantly
show towards] them, and renewing the [friendship] which exists [with
them], and discoursing to them [about us, / to the effect that they (sc.   55
the Romans)] ought to be brothers of our people, [and that their policy]
should be in harmony with their kinship. He gave himself a report [on
the present state of affairs] and about the aims of the people [in sending
off the] embassy, and together with [his fellow-ambassadors] he urged
them [to show concern] for the [security] of their other close friends, /   60
[and] to take care of our city, [because of our kinship and] because of the

[friendliness] which exists between them and us [and because of the] introduction [provided] to us by the [Massaliotes, and asked] to be given [a letter] favourable to the people; and when [the ambassadors earnestly requested] that we should be included [in the / treaty] made between the Romans and the [king (Philip V),5 the Senate included] us in the treaty [with the king, as] they themselves state in their letter, and concerning [all other matters] the Senate [referred] them to Titus (Flamininus) the [Roman proconsul] and the ten commissioners [in charge of Greek affairs].6 / And having come to Corinth with [. . . and] Apollodorus he met the commander [and the ten commissioners, and spoke] to them on behalf of the people, and [urged them with all] zeal to take thought [for us and to help] in preserving [the autonomy] / and democracy of [our] city; on these matters he [received a friendly resolution] and letters to the kings [. . . and recognising that they were favourable] to him he sent them [. . . the people], as it had voted . . .7

(the end of the inscription is lost)

*Syll.*3 591; M. Holleaux, *Etudes* v (1957),
141–55; P. Frisch, *Die Inschriften von Lampsakos* (Bonn, 1978), no. 4

1. L. Quinctius Flamininus, brother of Titus, praetor in 199 and legate under his brother in Greece 198–194 B.C.
2. This fictitious connexion rests on Lampsacus' membership of the league of cities of the Troad and on Rome's alleged Trojan origin.
3. The aristocratic council of Massalia.
4. The precise object of this appeal to the Galatians is unclear; Massalia, a city with friendly relations with the Celts in the west, was a suitable mediator.
5. The peace treaty which concluded the 'Second Macedonian War'.
6. See **68, 154**.
7. The preserved part of the inscription makes no explicit reference to Antiochus III, who is only alluded to indirectly.

156 Letter of Laodice to Iasus in Caria (ca 195)

When Kydias son of Hierocles was crown-bearer (*stephanephoros*), letter. In the month of Elaphebolion. Queen Laodice to the council and people of Iasus, greetings. Having often heard my brother1 recall the / help he constantly provides to his friends and allies, and how when he recovered2 your city which had been afflicted by unexpected natural disasters,3 he restored to you your freedom and your laws, and for the rest he intends / to increase the citizen body4 and bring it to a better condition, and since it is my policy to act in accordance with his zeal and eagerness and because of this to confer a benefaction on those citizens who are

destitute, which would be of general advantage / to the entire people, I   15
have written to Strouthion, the financial official (*dioiketes*),5 to have
brought to the city every year for ten years 1,000 Attic medimni of corn
to be delivered to the people's representatives.6 You would do well
therefore to instruct the treasurers to receive / (the corn) and to utilise   20
the proceeds from the sale of a fixed amount of it, and (to instruct) the
presidents (*prostatai*) and any others you select to make sure that they
deposit the sum raised from this (to serve) as dowries for the daughters of
needy citizens,7 giving to each of the brides not more than 300
Antiochene drachmas. / If you continue to be (well) disposed towards   25
my brother and in general towards our house as is fitting, [and]
gratefully remember all our benefactions, I will try to help in securing in
every way the other benefits I intend to confer, acting in accordance
with / the wishes of my brother. For I know that [he] is very eager to   30
bring about the restoration [of the] city. Farewell.8

G. Pugliese-Carratelli, *Annuario* 45–6
(1967–8), 445–53; J. and L. Robert, *Bull.*
1971, 621; *SEG* XXVI.1226

1. Antiochus III; the title is honorific, cf. **139** n. 6.
2. It is not known when Iasus was previously in Seleucid possession; for Antiochus III in Asia Minor see **151, 153, 154.**
3. Probably a reference to an earthquake in 199/8.
4. Simply = 'improve their condition', not literally as in **190.**
5. Hardly the chief finance minister of the kingdom but a local official; cf. **113, 187.**
6. Cf. **112** on the corn supply of Greek cities.
7. An unusual benefaction, but suitable for a queen. On foundations cf. **116.**
8. There follows a (mutilated) decree of Iasus in honour of Laodice, on whom cf. also **151, 158.**

157 Letter of M. Valerius Messala to Teos (193)

(Letter) from the Romans. Marcus Valerius (Messala), son of Marcus, praetor, and the tribunes and the Senate, to the council and people of Teos, greetings. Menippus the envoy sent to us by King Antiochus (III)1 / and who was appointed by you to act as ambassador for your   5
city, handed over the decree (to us) and spoke himself with all zeal in conformity with it. We received the man in a friendly spirit, both because of his previous / reputation and because of his inherent excel-   10
lence, and we listened with goodwill to his requests. That we constantly attach the greatest importance to piety towards the gods may best be inferred from the favour which attends us / on the part of the divinity   15

because of this. Nonetheless we are convinced that there are many other signs which have demonstrated clearly to all the high honour we pay to the divinity. And so for these reasons, because of your goodwill towards us and because of the request of your ambassador, we decide that your city
20 and territory / are sacred, as at present, inviolate (*asylos*)[2] and free from taxation by the Roman people, and we shall endeavour to assist in increasing the honours paid to the god[3] and the privileges granted to you, provided you preserve in future your goodwill towards us.[4] Farewell.

Syll.[3] 601; Sherk no. 34

1. Antiochus III was still formally at peace with Rome.
2. Cf. **151**; this is one of several inscriptions recording acceptance of the *asylia* of Teos (cf. *Syll.*[3] 563–6).
3. Dionysus.
4. Cf. **151** n. 5.

158 Letter of a Seleucid governor to Laodicea in Media, with copy of an edict of Antiochus III (193)

The worship of living rulers by Greek cities is attested already in the time of Alexander and his successors (cf. **32, 139** n. 7). The setting up of dynastic cults by the rulers themselves was slower to develop. Antiochus I deified his father Seleucus after his death, and subsequent Seleucid rulers followed the practice, deifying their predecessors (cf. **177, 190**), but there is so far no proof of a cult of the ruler or his queen being established by that ruler in his lifetime before the reign of Antiochus III. For Ptolemaic practice see **217** and n. 12. It will be seen that, contrary to what is frequently asserted, these dynastic cults were not conceived by the rulers as a means of legitimising their power; rather, the rulers honoured themselves for their merits and achievements, and at the same time provided their followers with a means of displaying loyalty and achieving promotion through the tenure of priesthoods. Cf. P. A. Brunt, *JRS* LXIX (1979), 168–75.

Menedemus[1] to Apollodorus[2] and the magistrates and city of Laodicea, greetings. Appended below is [the] copy of the edict sent to us in writing
5 [by the king]. / Do you therefore conform to the instructions given and see to it that the edict is inscribed on a stone stele and dedicated in the
10 most distinguished sanctuary in the city. / Farewell. Year 119, on the 10th of the month of Panemus.[3]

King Antiochus (III) to Menedemus, greetings. Wishing to increase further the honours of our sister[4] and Queen Laodice, and believing this
15 to be most imperative for us, / not only because of the affection and care she shows in her life with us, but also because of her piety towards the deity,[5] we continue to perform affectionately everything that is fitting

and just [for her] to receive from us, / and in particular it is our decision   20
that just as chief-priests (*archiereis*) of ourselves are appointed throughout
the kingdom[6] so too chief-priestesses should be set up in the same
[provinces] who shall wear gold crowns with her portrait on them, and
who shall [also] be inscribed / on (business) contracts after the chief-   25
priests of our [ancestors] and ourselves.[7] Therefore since Laodice[8] has
been appointed in the provinces under [your] command,[9] [let] everything [be done] in conformity with what is written above and let the
copies of the letters be inscribed on stelae / and dedicated in the most   30
distinguished [places], so that [our good disposition] towards our sister
should be made manifest in these matters too now and for the future.
Year 119, [on the . . . of the month of Xandicus].[10]

L. Robert, *Hellenica* 7 (1949), 5–22

1. Governor of the satrapy.
2. The royal governor (*epistates*) at Laodicea, cf. **176, 209**.
3. June–July 193. Another copy of the same edict, also sent by Menedemus
   whose covering letter is dated on the 3rd of Panemus, has been found in the
   Zagros range on the road from Ecbatana to Seleucia on the Tigris (L. Robert,
   CRAI (1967), 281–96). The edict thus reached Media some two months later
   than the third known copy from Phrygia (*RC* 36–37, where the date should
   be corrected to 193).
4. Cf. **139** n. 6; on Laodice cf. **151, 156**. The daughter of King Mithridates II of
   Pontus, Antiochus III married her in 222 (Polybius v.43). Compare Apollonis in **204**.
5. On this theme cf. **163** n. 4.
6. I.e. Antiochus III had established a cult of himself before this, but the exact
   date is uncertain.
7. For the use of dynastic priesthoods for dating purposes cf. **190, 222** nn. 3, 14.
   On priesthoods generally cf. **129**.
8. Daughter of Antiochus III; in the text from Phrygia (n. 3 above) the
   chief-priestess is the daughter of a local dynast descended from Lysimachus
   (**202** n. 2).
9. I.e. every satrapy of the empire would have its chief-priestess.
10. March–April 193 (cf. n. 3 above).

159 Letter of L. Cornelius Scipio and his brother to Heraclea under Mt Latmus (190)

[Lucius Cornelius Scipio], consul of the Romans, [and Publius Scipio his
brother][1], to the council and [people] of Heraclea, [greetings]. Your
envoys Dias, Dies, Dionysius, . . . amandrus, Eudemus, Moschus,
Aristides, Menes, [excellent] men, [met] us / and handed over your   5
decree and spoke themselves in conformity [with the] detailed provisions

of the decree, and showed no lack [of zeal]. We [happen to] be favourably disposed to all the Greeks[2] and we shall endeavour, since you have placed yourselves in our [trust],[3] to show all possible care (for you), and always
10 [to be responsible] for some good. / We grant you your freedom, as we have to [the] other cities which have placed themselves under our care, and you will keep [under your control] the administration of [all] your own affairs in accordance with your laws, [and in] other matters we shall endeavour to be of help to you and to be always [responsible] for some
15 good. We accept the gifts and the [pledges] you are offering, / and we shall endeavour ourselves not to fall short in returning gratitude. We have also [sent] to you Lucius Orbius to look after your [city and] territory and to make sure that no one harasses you. Farewell.

Sherk no. 35 (Syll.[3] 618, misattributed)

1. P. Cornelius Scipio Africanus. War had broken out between Antiochus III and Rome in 192; Antiochus' invasion of Greece, incited by the Aetolians (cf. **69**), was repulsed (192–191) and the war shifted to Asia Minor (cf. **160, 161**).
2. For this propaganda pose cf. **68** n. 2.
3. I.e. *fides*, cf. **69**.

160 The army of Antiochus III at the battle of Magnesia (early 189)

See further: Griffith (1935), 144–6; B. Bar-Kochva, *The Seleucid Army* (Cambridge, 1976), 163–73 and see index s.v. Magnesia (battle of).

The king's battle line was more varied (sc. than the Roman), as it was made up of many peoples who differed in their weapons and their auxiliary forces.[1] There were 16,000 infantry armed in the Macedonian way, who are called the *phalangitae* (members of the phalanx). They held the centre of the battle line, and their front was divided into ten parts, each part being separated by a gap where two elephants were positioned. The battle line extended from the front to a depth of 32 men. These were the best troops in the king's army, and in general presented a frightening appearance, especially because of the elephants towering so high above the troops. The elephants themselves were huge, and their appearance was enhanced by their frontlets and crests, and by the towers placed on their backs, on which stood four soldiers in addition to the driver. To the right of the *phalangitae* the king placed 1,500 'Gallo-Greek' cavalry,[2] and next to these 3,000 mail-clad cavalry (they called them *cataphracti*). To these was added a squadron of about 1,000 cavalry, called the *agema*; they consisted of picked Median troops, and mixed cavalry of many races from the same region.[3] Next to these was placed a herd of 16 elephants in support. On this side was the royal guard, with its wing slightly forward; they were called Silver Shields from the kind of weapons they used.[4] Then came 1,200 Dahae, who were mounted archers, then 3,000 light-armed troops, consisting of Cretans and Trallians in almost equal numbers. Next to these came 2,500 Mysian archers. The extreme right wing was formed by a mixture of Cyrtaean slingers and Elymaean archers, to a total of 4,000. On the left wing, next to the *phalangitae* came 1,500 'Gallo-Greek' cavalry, and 2,000 Cappadocians armed in the same way; these had been sent to the king by Ariarathes. Then came a mixture of auxiliary forces of all kinds, 2,700 in all, and 3,000 mail-clad cavalry, and another 1,000 cavalry, the royal squadron, with lighter protection for themselves and their horses but otherwise equipped in the same way (sc. as the mail-clad cavalry); they were mostly Syrians, with an admixture of Phrygians and Lydians. In front of this body of cavalry were chariots armed with scythes and camels of the kind they call dromedaries. They had as mounts Arab archers, with slender swords four cubits long, which allowed them to reach the enemy from such a height. Then came another host, equal in numbers to the host on the right wing, consisting first of 'Tarentines',[5] then of 2,500 'Gallo-Greek' cavalry, then of 1,000 Neocretans and 1,500 Carians and Cilicians armed in the same way, and the same number of Trallians, and 3,000 men armed with a *caetra*[6]; these were Pisidians, Pamphylians and Lycians. Then were placed auxiliary forces of Cyrtaeans and Elymaeans in equal numbers to those on the right wing. (41) The king himself was on the right wing; Seleucus (his son) and Antipater (the son of his brother) he put in command of the left wing. The centre of the battle line was placed under three men, Minnion, Zeuxis and Philippus the master of the elephants. [. . .][7]

Livy XXXVII.40–41

1. Compare **149** and the pageant of Antiochus IV at Daphne (Polybius xxx.25–26).
2. I.e. Galatians, cf. **140**.
3. On Media cf. **147** (end).
4. See **149** n. 3.
5. See **28** n. 5.
6. A short Spanish shield.
7. Antiochus' defeat led to the Peace of Apamea (see **161**).

161 The Peace of Apamea between Antiochus III and the Romans (188)

See further: Badian (1958), 80–3; Errington (1971), 178–83; O. Mørkholm, *Antiochus IV of Syria* (Copenhagen, 1966), 22–32; Walbank III (1979), 156–62.

The detailed provisions of the treaty were as follows:

(1) There shall be peace for all time between Antiochus (III) and the Romans provided he carries out the terms of the treaty.

(2) King Antiochus and his subjects shall not allow any enemies to pass through their territory to attack the Romans and their allies and shall not supply them with anything; and similarly for the Romans and their allies with those attacking Antiochus and his subjects.

(3) Antiochus shall not make war against the islanders and the people of Europe.

(4) He shall evacuate the cities and territory . . .;[1] his soldiers shall not take anything out except the arms which they carry; should they happen to have removed anything, they shall restore it to these same cities.

(5) They shall not give shelter to refugees from King Eumenes,[2] be they soldiers or anyone else.

(6) If there be any from the cities captured by the Romans present in the army of Antiochus, they shall deliver them up at Apamea. If there be any <from the kingdom of Antiochus> present with the Romans and their allies, they will be allowed to stay if they wish or to leave.

(7) Antiochus and his subjects shall surrender the slaves belonging to the Romans and their allies, whether war captives or deserters, and any captive taken from anywhere. Antiochus shall surrender, if it is in his power to do so, Hannibal son of Hamilcar, of Carthage,[3] Mnasilochus of Acarnania, <Thoas> of Aetolia, Eubulidas and Philon of Chalcis, and all the Aetolians who have held public office.[4]

(8) He shall surrender all the elephants at Apamea,[5] and shall have none henceforth. He shall surrender his ships of war, their tackle and fittings, and in future shall not have more than ten undecked vessels, [and of these] none shall be driven [by more] than 30 oars nor with one man to each oar for the purposes of a war started by himself.[6]

(9) He shall not sail to this side (i.e. west) of the river Calycadnus <and> the promontory <of Sarpedon>, except for the purpose of bringing tribute, ambassadors or hostages.

(10) Antiochus shall not be permitted to recruit mercenaries from the territory subject to Rome nor to receive refugees from it.

(11) Any houses belonging to the Rhodians or their allies in the territory subject to King Antiochus shall belong to the Rhodians as before the outbreak of war.[7] Any money owed to them shall likewise be recoverable; and any property left behind by them shall be sought for and restored. Merchandise destined for the Rhodians shall be free from duty, as before the war.[8]

(12) If Antiochus has given to others some of the cities which he is required to surrender, he shall remove from them his garrisons and his

troops. And if any wish hereafter to desert to him, he shall not receive them.

(13) Antiochus shall give to the Romans 10,000 talents of best Attic silver over a period of ten years in annual instalments of 1,000 talents; each talent shall weigh not less than 80 Roman pounds. And he shall give 540,000 *modii* of corn.

(14) <He shall give to King Eumenes> 350 <talents> over the next five years, in annual instalments of <70> talents, at the same time as he makes his payments to the Romans, and in place of corn, as assessed by King Antiochus, 127 talents and 1,208 drachmas, which Eumenes agreed to accept as a satisfactory payment to himself.[9]

(15) Antiochus shall provide <twenty> hostages, over eighteen years of age but under 45, and shall change them every three years.[10]

(16) Any deficit in the money paid shall be made good the following year.

(17) If any of the cities or peoples who have been instructed not to make war on Antiochus take the initiative in hostilities, Antiochus shall be allowed to go to war. But he shall not exercise sovereignty over these peoples and cities and shall not receive them into his alliance.

(18) Any complaints arising between the two parties shall be referred to arbitration.

(19) If both parties wish by common agreement to add or subtract anything from the treaty, it shall be lawful to do so.[11]

Polybius XXI.43

1. The key words are missing; Livy's version (XXXVIII.38.4–5) reads here 'beyond the Taurus as far as the river Tanais and along that valley of the Taurus as far as the heights where it faces towards Lycaonia'. The exact details are controversial (cf. A. H. McDonald, *JRS* 57 (1967), 1–8), but in effect the Seleucids were excluded from any further role in western Asia Minor.
2. Eumenes II of Pergamum, Rome's ally in the war against Antiochus; his kingdom was substantially enlarged after the defeat of Antiochus (see **193, 200** with n. 11).
3. Hannibal had taken refuge with Antiochus III in 195; he then fled to the court of Prusias I of Bithynia, and committed suicide in 183 rather than be handed over to the Romans.
4. The Aetolians had incited Antiochus III to invade the Greek mainland in 192.
5. Cf. **169, 174**.
6. On the text of this clause cf. A. H. McDonald and F. W. Walbank, *JRS* 59 (1969), 30–9.
7. The Rhodians, like Eumenes II, had fought on the Roman side; cf. **65, 80, 92, 198, 200**.
8. See **93** ch. 89.

9. These heavy war indemnities, combined with the loss of territory (and hence of revenue), seriously affected Seleucid finances, cf. **168**. Antiochus III was in fact killed in 187 while plundering a native sanctuary in Elymais.

10. Cf. **162, 168, 169**.

11. The treaty did not in any way regulate Seleucid relations with the Ptolemies; on this cf. **164, 165, 168**.

162 The accession of Antiochus IV Epiphanes (175)

Antiochus, the younger brother of Seleucus IV who succeeded his father Antiochus III in 187, was detained as a hostage at Rome after the treaty of Apamea (cf. **161**) until eventually replaced by Demetrius, eldest son of Seleucus IV. In 175 Seleucus IV was assassinated by his minister Heliodorus, and the opportunity was taken by Antiochus, with Attalid backing, to occupy the Seleucid throne. This was the origin of the split in the Seleucid dynasty which accelerated its disintegration (cf. **169–173**). The following decree, found at Pergamum, probably originates from Athens, where Antiochus IV had resided before his accession, though it has also been attributed to Seleucid Antioch.

See further: O. Mørkholm, *Antiochus IV of Syria* (Copenhagen, 1966), 38–50.

(The first lines are too mutilated for continuous restoration)

10 . . . when Seleucus (IV) died [and since the calamity] invited this, as they[1] saw that the occasion was providing [an opportunity] for them to lay in store a favour as benefactors, they considered everything else to be of no relevance and placed themselves at his disposal, and accompanying

15 him / as far as the frontiers of his own kingdom, providing him with money, furnishing him with troops, crowning him with the diadem[2] and all other suitable apparel, offering sacrifices and exchanging pledges of

20 faith / with each other with all goodwill and affection, they helped in restoring King Antiochus (IV) to his ancestral kingdom in a memorable way. Therefore, so that the people may be seen to be foremost in repaying gratitude and may be seen to be honouring those who confer

25 benefits on itself and its friends / without being invited to do so, and to be raising fine deeds to everlasting memory now as previously, with good fortune, be it resolved by the council, that the presidents (*proedroi*) who are chosen by lot should lay the matter for discussion at the next meeting of the assembly, and should communicate the opinion of the

30 council / to the people, viz. that the council resolves to praise King Eumenes (II) son of King Attalus (I) and Queen Apollonis and to crown him with a gold crown for merit in accordance with the law, for his

35 excellence, goodwill and the devotion which he has shown / towards all men by his eagerness on behalf of King Antiochus and by the help he provided in reinstating him in his ancestral [kingdom]; and in the same way to crown Attalus[3] for assisting his brother Eumenes in everything

with diligence and in disregard of risk; and to praise his brothers / 40
Philetaerus and Athenaeus, and to crown each of them with a gold
crown for the goodwill and zeal which they displayed during the return
of King Antiochus; and to praise his parents, King Attalus and Queen / 45
Apollonis, and to crown them with a gold crown for merit for the
excellence and good qualities which they bequeathed to their sons by
looking after their education in an excellent and wise way;[4] and to
proclaim these crowns in the contests which [we celebrate], / and 50
likewise in those celebrated by King Eumenes with his brothers and the
people of Pergamum, and also in those celebrated by King Antiochus at
Daphne,[5] as is their custom. And so that the memory of this might
remain manifest for all time, (be it resolved) to inscribe this decree on
stone stelae / and to place one in the agora next to the statues of King 55
Antiochus, another one in the sanctuary of Athena Nicephorus and
another in the sanctuary of Apollo at Daphne,[6] and to entrust to the
generals the sending of the decree to the king, his mother and his
brothers, / this task to be carried out by them carefully and as soon as 60
possible.[7]

OGIS 248; M. Holleaux, *Etudes* II (1938), 127–47

1. The Attalids, cf. below. Attalid help in the accession of Antiochus IV was
   otherwise only briefly known from Appian, *Syrian Wars* 45.
2. Cf. **36** n. 1.
3. The future Attalus II.
4. See esp. **193, 204**.
5. See **174, 175, 177**.
6. Cf. n. 5.
7. On Athens and Antiochus IV see further L. Robert, *Ephemeris Archaiologike*
   (1969), 1–6.

163 Portrait of Antiochus IV Epiphanes

For his contemporaries, as for modern scholars, Antiochus IV has seemed a
bizarre and controversial ruler (for the Jewish view of him, cf. **168**). The
following characterisation is valuable not just as the portrait of an eccentric
personality, resentful of the constraints of royalty, but also for showing by
implication the type of behaviour normally expected from kings. For other royal
portraits see **199** and n. 2.

See further: O. Mørkholm, *Antiochus IV of Syria* (Copenhagen, 1966), esp.
55–63, 130, 181–3.

(a) Polybius

Antiochus Epiphanes, nicknamed from his actions Epimanes,[1] would
sometimes steal from the royal palace leaving his attendants behind, and

appear wandering about any part of the town with two or three companions. He was especially to be found among the silversmiths and goldsmiths, discussing like an expert questions of art with the workers in relief and the other craftsmen. He would also be found joining groups of common people and would drink in the company of foreign visitors of the humblest kind. Whenever he found any young men feasting together, he would come and join the party unannounced with fife and band, and most people would be so taken aback that they would get up and run away. Often he would take off his royal dress, put on a *tebenna* and go about the agora canvassing for office, shaking hands with some and embracing others and urging them to vote for him, sometimes as aedile (*agoranomos*) and sometimes as tribune (*demarchos*).[2] And when he got the office and sat on the ivory chair in accordance with the Roman custom, he would listen to the suits which took place in the agora and would give his verdict with great seriousness and attention. This was a source of embarrassment to respectable people, some of whom thought him easy-going, but others mad. In regard to giving presents, too, his behaviour was similar; to some he would give dice made of antelope bone, to others dates, to others gold. People he happened to meet and whom he had never seen before he would present with unexpected gifts. [. . .]

Polybius XXVI.I

(b) Livy

[. . .] However, there were two important and honourable activities in which he showed a truly royal spirit, namely gifts to cities[3] and worship of gods.[4] To the people of Megalopolis in Arcadia he promised he would build them a wall around their city, and paid the biggest part of the expense. At Tegea he began the construction of a magnificent marble theatre. At Cyzicus he deposited golden vases to cover one table in the Prytaneum – the town-hall where those who are granted this honour are fed at public expense. To the Rhodians he gave no particular present that was outstanding, but he lavished on them all manner of things as their needs required. As to his generosity towards the gods, the temple of Olympian Zeus at Athens can bear witness, the only temple in the world undertaken on a scale commensurate with the greatness of the god. But he also embellished Delos with magnificent altars and numerous statues, while at Antioch he promised to build among many other buildings in various places a magnificent temple of Jupiter Capitolinus, which would not merely have a ceiling panelled with gold but would even have its walls all covered with gold leaf; but he did not complete these as his reign was very brief.[5] He also surpassed all previous kings in the magnificence of the shows of every kind he offered.[6] Most of them conformed to his usual style and were staged by a large number of Greek artists, but he also put on a gladiatorial show in the Roman style. At first this caused more alarm than pleasure to men who were not used to such a spectacle, but later by multiplying the shows, and sometimes allowing the fighters to go only as far as wounds while sometimes even having fights without quarter, he familiarised men with this spectacle and made it popular, and filled most young men with an enthusiasm for arms. [. . .]

Livy XLI.20

1. *Epiphanes*: 'conspicuous, distinguished', of deities 'god manifest'; *epimanes*: 'mad'.
2. Roman magistracies; Antiochus IV had been a hostage in Rome (cf. **162, 168**). For Roman influence on him, cf. Mørkholm, *op. cit.*, 39f.
3. Cf. **93** and n. 12.
4. For this theme, cf. **18, 139, 151, 158, 167, 175, 178, 182, 184, 189, 204, 206, 210, 217** n. 9.
5. 175–164/3.
6. Cf. the pageant at Daphne in 166, Polybius xxx.25–26.

164   The Roman ultimatum to Antiochus IV in Egypt (summer 168)

After Antiochus III's conquest of Coele Syria and the settlement with Ptolemy V in 195 (cf. **154, 167**), peace reigned between the two monarchies until the reign of Antiochus IV, when the conflict flared up again in circumstances which are unclear (cf. **75**), though the initiative seems to have belonged to the Ptolemaic side (the 'Sixth Syrian War', 170–168). Antiochus invaded Egypt a first time in 169, posing as a champion of the young Ptolemy VI Philometor (nephew of Antiochus) against his brother Ptolemy VIII (on whom cf. **228–230**), but in his second invasion in 168 he seems to have intended the annexation of Egypt pure and simple, issuing coins and an edict in Egypt as king (*P. Tebt.* III, 698; *C. Ord. Ptol.*, 32) and perhaps being crowned Pharaoh at Memphis (*FGrH* 260 F 49a). At this juncture he was faced by the Roman delegates; Rome had just defeated Perseus at Pydna.

See further: O. Mørkholm, *Antiochus IV of Syria* (Copenhagen, 1966), 64–101; Errington (1971), 252–6.

When Antiochus (IV) had advanced against Ptolemy (VI) in order to take control of Pelusium, he was met by the Roman commander (C.) Popilius (Laenas). The king greeted him by voice from a distance and offered to him his right hand, but Popilius presented to him the tablet he had in his hand which contained the Senate's decree, and asked Antiochus to read it first. In my opinion, he did not want to display any mark of friendship before finding out the intentions of the recipient, whether he was a friend or an enemy. When the king had read it, he said he wanted to consult with his friends on these new developments,[1] but Popilius in reply did something which seemed insolent and arrogant to the highest degree. With a vine stick which he had in his hand he drew a circle around Antiochus and told him to give his reply to the message before he stepped out of that circle. The king was astounded at this arrogance and after hesitating for a moment said he would do everything the Romans asked from him. Thereupon Popilius and his colleagues shook him by the hand and all welcomed him graciously. The decree of the Senate required him to put an end at once to the war with Ptolemy. And so within a stated number of days Antiochus withdrew his army to Syria, deeply distressed at what had happened but yielding to present circumstances. Popilius and his colleagues settled matters in Alexandria and urged the kings to preserve harmony. [. . .] In this way the Romans saved the kingdom of Ptolemy while on the brink of ruin. Fortune so arranged matters with Perseus and the Macedonians, that after being reduced to the last extremity Alexandria and the whole of Egypt were given a fresh lease of life by the fact that Perseus' fate was the first to be decided. For if this had not happened or had not been certain, I do not believe that Antiochus would have obeyed the injunction.[2]

Polybius XXIX.27

1. Cf. **147** n. 4.
2. For an Egyptian view of these events cf. **165**, for a Jewish view cf. **168**.

165 The retreat of Antiochus IV seen through Egyptian eyes

The following text comes from a private archive in Egyptian demotic which belonged to an Egyptian priest contemporary with Antiochus IV, Hor of Sebennytos. The text is one of several drafts from this archive which refer to Antiochus' expulsion from Egypt in 168 (cf. **164**), an event which Hor claims to have foreseen in a dream. It was probably intended for inclusion in a petition to the Ptolemaic king to establish Hor's trustworthiness (the precise circumstances are unknown).

See further: J. D. Ray, *The Archive of Hor* (London, 1976), esp. 7–32, 125–9.

Recto

From Hor the scribe, a man of the town of Isis, lady of the cavern, the great goddess, in the nome (of) Sebennytos. The dream which told to me
5 of the safety of Alexandria / (and) the journeyings[1] of Antiochus (IV), namely that he would go [[that he would go]] by sail[2] from Egypt by year 2, Paoni, final day.[3] I reported the said matter (to) Irenaeus (?), who

was *strategos*, (in) year 2, Paoni, day 11.[4] Cleon (or Creon?), the agent of
Antiochus, had not yet / left Memphis.[5] (But) the said matters were   10
revealed immediately. He did not speak of them further, (but) he sent in
the hour (?) a letter. I gave it <(to) the Pharaohs>[6] in the Great Serapeum
which is in Alexandria,[7] in year 2, Epeiph, final day.[8] For every matter
which refers to this was compensation for you (at) the time in question
(for) that which concerns me, namely, the greatness towards that which
concerns the gods (in) your heart. / I brought it before you, for I came   15
to Alexandria with Diodotus the *strategos*, namely . . .
(the rest is erased)

Verso[9]

From Ḥor the man (of) the town of Isis, lady of the cavern,
the great goddess, (in) the nome (of) Seb(ennytos). (*Erasures*)
Irenaeus sent within the hour (?). Account of a letter: I gave it to the
Pharaohs / (in) the Great Serapeum which is in Alexandria, in year 2,   5
Epeiph, final day, (namely), the blessings which I reported in year 2,
Paoni, day 11 (when) Cleon, the agent of Antiochus, had not yet left
Memphis. I read out the salvation of Alexandria and every man who was
within it, / which happened through the good disposition (of) the   10
Pharaohs. None could controvert that which referred to the journeyings
of Antiochus and his army, namely, that he would leave Egypt <by sail>
by year 2, Paoni, final day. For there was a great matter measured within
the words written (in) the letter, (at) the time of paying heed to the
utterance in question. There came about the counsel of Isis, the great
goddess, / and Thoth, the three times great, in every matter which   15
concerned these things . . . (*more erasures*)[10]

J. D. Ray, The Archive of Ḥor (Egypt
Exploration Society, London, 1976), 14–20

1. I.e. the expulsion.
2. This detail is not mentioned in Polybius, cf. **164**.
3. 30 July 168.
4. 11 July 168. On the Ptolemaic *strategoi* cf. **231** n. 26.
5. Probably a governor installed by Antiochus IV at Memphis.
6. Ptolemy VI and VIII.
7. Cf. **232** §10.
8. 29 August 168.
9. A different draft of the same events.
10. Ḥor makes no explicit reference to the Roman intervention, though in
    another draft (Ray, *op. cit.*, 26) he refers to the sending of an embassy from
    Egypt to Rome known from literary evidence (Polybius xxx.16).

166 A Greek view of the Jews in early Hellenistic times

While the Greeks had long been acquainted with the other ancient civilisations of the Near East, it was only in the Hellenistic age that they became aware of the Jews. To Hecataeus of Abdera, an adviser of Ptolemy in his campaign in Palestine *ca* 320–318, we owe what is probably the earliest reference in Greek literature to the Jews (*ca* 315?; for the date cf. O. Murray against M. Stern, *JEA* 59 (1973), 159–68).

See further: M. Stern, *Greek and Latin Authors on Jews and Judaism* I (Jerusalem, 1974), 20–35; A. Momigliano, *Alien Wisdom* (Cambridge, 1975), 74–96, esp. 83f.

Now that we are about to relate the war against the Jews,[1] we think it appropriate to begin by summarising the main facts concerning the establishment of this people from the beginning and the customs which prevail among them. When in former times a pestilence broke out in Egypt, the common people ascribed the cause of their evils to divine intervention. For with many foreigners from all over the world living in their midst and using different customs concerning religion and sacrifices, their own ancestral cult of the gods had fallen into abeyance. And so the natives of the land assumed that unless they removed the foreigners they would never solve their troubles. The aliens were therefore immediately driven out of the country, and the most distinguished and energetic joined together and were cast ashore, as some say, in Greece and other places; they had outstanding leaders, most conspicuous of whom were Danaus and Cadmus. But the mass of the people were expelled into the land now called Judaea, which is not far from Egypt, and which at that time lay completely deserted. The colony was led by a man called Moses, who was outstanding both in wisdom and bravery. On taking possession of the country he founded many cities including the one which is most conspicuous, which is called Jerusalem. He also founded the Temple which they hold in greatest honour, introduced the honours and ritual paid to (their) god, established laws and organised the form of their state. He also divided the mass of the people into twelve tribes as he believed this to be the most perfect number, corresponding to the number of months which make up the year. But he did not fashion any images of the gods at all as he did not believe that God existed in human shape, but thought that only Heaven which surrounds the earth is divine and lord of the universe. The forms of sacrifice he established differ from those of other peoples, and so does their way of living. Because of their own expulsion from Egypt he introduced a way of life that was unsociable and hostile to foreigners. He picked out the men of greatest accomplishment who would be most able to lead the entire nation and appointed them priests, and prescribed how they should occupy themselves with the Temple and the honours and sacrifices (paid) to God. He also appointed them to be judges in the most important cases, and entrusted to them the guardianship of the laws and customs (of the nation). That is why the Jews have never had a king, but the leadership of the mass of the people is always vested in the priest who appears to excel in wisdom and virtue. They call him the High-Priest, and believe him to be the mediator of God's commands to them. According to (Hecataeus), it is he who in their assemblies and their other meetings proclaims what is ordained, and the Jews are so obedient in such matters that they immediately fall to the ground and do obeisance to the High-Priest who expounds (these commands) to them. The statement is even added at the end of their (code of) laws that 'Moses heard from God these words which he declares to the Jews'. The lawgiver also devoted much attention to the arts of war, and he compelled the young to practice bravery and endurance, and in general to put up with every kind of hardship. He also made military expeditions against the neighbouring peoples, and acquired much land which he distributed in lots, making the lots equal for private individuals but larger for the priests, so that they might have more considerable revenues and so might devote themselves continuously and without interruption to the worship of God. Private individuals were not allowed to sell their lots, to prevent some from greedily buying them up, and so causing hardship to poorer people and bringing about a decline in the population.[2] He compelled those who lived on the land to rear children,[3] and as the offspring was brought up at little expense the Jewish people was always very populous. He also made their customs with regard to marriage and the burial of the dead, which differ considerably from those of the rest of mankind. But when later they fell under foreign domination as a result of mixing with outsiders, under the rule of the Persians and of the Macedonians who overthrew them, many of the ancestral customs of the Jews were disturbed. Such is the account given by Hecataeus of Abdera concerning the Jews.

Diodorus XL.3 from Hecataeus of Abdera, FGrH 264 F 6

1. Pompey's capture of Jerusalem in 63.
2. The account is influenced by Greek experiences, notably the case of Sparta (cf. **55**).
3. Whereas Greeks practised the exposure of children.

167 Antiochus III and the Jews

As a result of the 'Fifth Syrian War', Judaea passed to the Seleucids after over a century of Ptolemaic rule (cf. **262, 275, 276**). Josephus has preserved three documents of Antiochus III relating to the Jews, which are probably authentic.

See further: E. Bickerman, *Revue des études juives* 100 (1935), 4–35 and *Syria* 25 (1946–8), 67–85; R. Marcus, *Josephus* VII (Loeb edition, 1943), 743–66; V. Tcherikover, *Hellenistic Civilization and the Jews* (Philadelphia, 1959), 79–89, 287f.

(138) King Antiochus (III) to Ptolemy,[1] greetings. Since the Jews, when we entered their country, at once displayed their enthusiasm for us, and when we arrived at their city received us magnificently and came to meet us with their senate, and have provided abundant supplies to our soldiers and elephants, and assisted us in expelling the Egyptian[2] garrison in the citadel, (139) we thought it right on our part to repay them for these services and to restore their city which had been destroyed by the accidents of war, and to repeople it by bringing back to it those who have been scattered abroad. (140) In the first place we have decided because of their piety to provide them with an allowance for sacrifices consisting of sacrificial animals, wine, olive oil and frankincense, to the value of 20,000 silver pieces, and sacred artabas of finest flour in accordance with their native law, and 1,460 medimni of wheat, and 375 medimni of salt. (141) I wish these grants to be made to them in accordance with my instructions, and the work on the Temple to be completed together with the stoas and anything else which needs to be built. The timber required for the woodwork shall be brought from Judaea itself, from the other nations and from Lebanon, and no one shall charge any duty on it. Similarly for the other materials needed for repairing the Temple in a more splendid way. (142) All the people of the nation shall govern themselves in accordance with their ancestral laws, and the senate, the priests, the scribes of the Temple and the Temple-singers shall be exempted from the poll-tax, the crown-tax and the salt-tax.[3] (143) To hasten the repeopling of the city, I grant to the present inhabitants and to those who come back before the month of Hyperberetaeus (*ca* October) freedom from taxes for three years. (144) We also remit for the future one third of their taxes to make good the injuries they have sustained. As for all those who were carried away from their city and are now slaves, I grant their freedom to them and to their children, and order the restoration of their property to them.

(145) Such was the content of the letter. And out of respect for the Temple he issued a proclamation throughout the whole kingdom[4] in the following terms: 'No foreigner shall be allowed to enter the precinct of the Temple which is forbidden to the Jews, except for those who are accustomed to doing so after purifying themselves in accordance with ancestral custom. (146) Nor shall anyone bring into the city the flesh of horses, mules, wild or tame asses, leopards, foxes, and hares, and generally of any of the animals forbidden to the Jews. Nor is it allowed to

bring in their skins, nor even to rear any of these animals in the city. Only the sacrificial animals used by their ancestors, necessary for a propitious sacrifice to God, shall they be allowed to use. Whoever transgresses any of these rules shall pay to the priests a fine of 3,000 drachmas of silver.'

(147) He also gave witness to our piety and good faith when during his stay in the upper satrapies[5] he heard of the revolt of Phrygia and Lydia, and wrote to Zeuxis, his general and one of his closest 'friends',[6] with instructions to send some of our people from Babylon to Phrygia. He writes as follows: (148) 'King Antiochus to Zeuxis, his father,[7] greetings. If you are in good health, it is well; I too am in good health. (149) On hearing that the people in Lydia and Phrygia are in revolt, I thought this required great attention on my part, and after discussing with my friends what ought to be done,[8] I resolved to move 2,000 Jewish families with their chattels from Mesopotamia and Babylonia to the strongholds and the most strategic places. (150) For I am convinced that they will be loyal guardians of our interests because of their piety to God, and I know that my ancestors have given witness to their loyalty and eagerness for what they are asked to do. I wish therefore to transfer them, although this is a laborious task, with the promise that they shall use their own laws. (151) When you have brought them to the places I have mentioned, you will give them each a place to build a house and a plot of land to cultivate and plant vines, and you will grant them exemption from taxes on agricultural produce for ten years. (152) Until such time as they obtain produce from the soil, corn shall be measured out to them to feed their servants.[9] To those who perform services (?)[10] shall be provided everything they need, so that by receiving this favour from us they might show themselves more devoted to our interests. (153) Show concern for their people as much as possible, so that it may not be troubled by anyone.' Concerning the friendliness of Antiochus the Great towards the Jews let the proofs we have given suffice.[11]

Josephus, *Jewish Antiquities* XII.138–53

1. The governor appointed by Antiochus III over Coele Syria after the conquest of the country; for epigraphic evidence concerning him cf. *Bull.* 1970, 627 and T. Fischer, *ZPE* 33 (1979), 131–8.
2. I.e. Ptolemaic.
3. Poll-tax: this is the only evidence for the Seleucid empire (cf. **202** l.10, Attalids); crown-tax: see **183** n. 1; salt-tax: also attested in Seleucid Babylonia (Rostovtzeff I (1941), 469–71).
4. Hardly likely: this applied only to Jerusalem.
5. Antiochus' great eastern expedition (see **150**).
6. Cf. **25** n. 3; on Zeuxis see Walbank II (1967), 503, 649.
7. A courtesy title.

8. Cf. **147** n. 4.
9. This passage gives the most explicit information available on the establishment of a military colony in the Seleucid empire; see G. M. Cohen, *The Seleucid Colonies* (Wiesbaden, 1978), 5–9. Cf. also **202** n. 2.
10. Meaning uncertain.
11. Toleration of native customs and religions was the norm in the Seleucid empire; cf. **141, 178, 189**.

168 Antiochus IV and the Jews

For over a century Judaea had existed peacefully as a state incorporated first in the Ptolemaic, then the Seleucid, empires (cf. **166, 167, 275, 276**). The conflict between Jews and Seleucids in the reign of Antiochus IV arose in the first instance, it appears, from divisions within the leading Jewish circles along cultural and political lines, one group being receptive to Greek cultural influences and turning for support to the Seleucid rulers. The story of the conflict, which led eventually to the emancipation from Seleucid rule of the Jewish nation and the assertion of its separate identity despite the assimilation of Hellenistic influences, is known almost solely from Jewish sources (though cf. Diodorus XXXIV.1), notably I *Maccabees* which covers the years 175–135 and dates probably from between 135 and 104 B.C., and (by a different author) II *Maccabees* which goes from the end of the reign of Seleucus IV to 160 and dates from between 124 and 63 B.C. but is abridged from an earlier (lost) work by one Jason of Cyrene.

See further: V. Tcherikover, *Hellenistic Civilization and the Jews* (Philadelphia, 1959), 152–203, 381–402, 404–9; O. Mørkholm, *Antiochus IV of Syria* (Copenhagen, 1966), 135–65; E. Schürer, *The History of the Jewish People in the Age of Jesus Christ*, rev. by G. Vermes and F. Millar I (Edinburgh, 1972), 137–63; M. Hengel, *Judaism and Hellenism* I (London, 1974), 277–309, and against him F. Millar, *Journal of Jewish Studies* 29.1 (1978), 1–21; A. Momigliano, *Alien Wisdom* (Cambridge, 1975), 97–122; E. Bickerman, *The God of the Maccabees* (Leyden, 1979, translated from the German edition, 1937).

From them[1] came forth a sinful shoot, Antiochus Epiphanes, son of King Antiochus (III), who after being a hostage in Rome[2] became king in year 137 of the kingdom of the Greeks.[3] In those days there came forth from Israel a lawless generation who persuaded many others by saying, 'Come, let us make a treaty with the peoples around us, since many evils have fallen upon us from the time we separated from them.' This proposal seemed good in their eyes, and some of the people eagerly went to the king, who granted them permission to practise the customs of the heathen. And they built a gymnasium[4] in Jerusalem in accordance with the customs of the nations. They became uncircumcised, gave up the holy covenant to join the yoke of the gentiles, and sold themselves to cause evil.[5] And when Antiochus felt his kingdom was firmly established, he decided to become ruler of the land of Egypt so as to reign over both kingdoms.[6] He invaded Egypt with a massive army of chariots and elephants and a large fleet. He waged war on Ptolemy king of Egypt, and Ptolemy turned away before him and fled, and many men were wounded and fled. They seized the Egyptian strongholds and captured the spoils of the land of Egypt. After defeating Egypt Antiochus returned in the year 143 (= 169); he marched against Israel and entered Jerusalem with a massive army. In his arrogance he penetrated the sanctuary, and seized the golden altar and the lamp for the light with all its fittings, and the table for the offering of the loaves, the libation vases, the cups, the golden censers, the veil, the crowns, the golden ornaments on the façade of the Temple which he stripped off completely. He seized the silver and gold and the precious vessels and took away the hidden treasures he found. He went away to his country taking everything,[7] shedding much blood and uttering words of extreme arrogance. [. . .]

The king then[8] issued a proclamation to the whole of his kingdom that they should all form one people and that they should each give up their own customs.[9] All the nations acquiesced in the royal edict. Many Israelites accepted his worship and sacrificed to idols and profaned the Sabbath. The king also sent letters by messenger to Jerusalem and the cities of Juda that they should follow customs alien to their land, banish holocausts, sacrifices and libations from the sanctuary and profane the sabbaths and festivals, defile the sanctuary and the holy men, build altars and sacred enclosures and idol's temples, sacrifice pigs and unclean animals, leave their sons uncircumcised, defile themselves with every kind of impurity and abomination, so as to forget the Law and change all their ordinances. Anyone who did not conform to the king's edict would be punished with death. In accordance with all these instructions he sent letters to the whole of his kingdom; he set up inspectors over the whole people and ordered the cities of Juda to sacrifice in each and every city. Many of the people joined with them, whoever abandoned the Law, and they caused great evil in the land, and drove Israel into all its secret hiding places. On the 15th day of Chislev in the year 145 (= December 167), he (sc. Antiochus) built the 'abomination of desolation'[10] on the altar, and in the cities of Juda around they built altars, and offered incense at the doors of houses and in the streets. Any books of the Law that were found were torn up and burnt.[11]

I *Maccabees* 1.10–25 and 45–56

1. The successors of Alexander the Great.
2. Cf. **162**.
3. I.e. the Seleucid era (cf. **138**) = 176/5.
4. Characteristic of Greek social life; cf. **118**.

5. For a much fuller account of the internal divisions among the Jews and the activities of the Jewish 'hellenizers' who prompted Seleucid intervention, see II *Maccabees* 3–4.

6. This refers to Antiochus' first invasion of Egypt (see **164**).

7. This is as much a sign of Antiochus' financial difficulties (cf. **161** n. 9) as of his wickedness.

8. In 167, after the second invasion of Egypt (see **164, 165**).

9. Both the scope and the intention of Antiochus' proclamation are enormously controversial, being interpreted by some as an attempt to impose Greek cultural and religious uniformity over his whole kingdom (which would represent a drastic departure from the usual Seleucid policy), by others as a measure of purely local character designed to break the Jewish rebellion against him. See the works cited above.

10. Under this phrase may lurk a reference to an altar of the Syrian god Baal-Shamen, worshipped by the troops left as garrison in the Citadel by Antiochus in 168; if correct, Antiochus' aim will not have been the enforcement of Greek cults on Jerusalem. Cf. e.g. M. Hengel, *op. cit.*, 294–7.

11. The Jewish resistance led by Mattathias and his sons (the Maccabees) caused Antiochus to rescind his proclamation (March 164); in December 164 Judas Maccabaeus purified and restored the Temple, but the struggle continued till the eventual liberation of Judaea from Seleucid rule (cf. **172**).

169 Demetrius I and the policy of the Senate towards the Seleucids (164)

See further: Badian (1957), 107f.; Errington (1971), 255f.; for a divergent view cf. E. S. Gruen, *Chiron* 6 (1976), 73–95 (Roman policy apathetic, not hostile).

Demetrius (I) son of Seleucus (IV) who had been long detained at Rome as a hostage[1] had for a long time felt that his detention was unjust. He had been given by his father Seleucus as a sign of his good faith, but after Antiochus (IV) had succeeded to the throne, he felt there was no reason why he should act as hostage for Antiochus' children.[2] Nevertheless up till this time he kept quiet, especially since he was powerless (he was still a child). But now having reached the prime of manhood he approached the Senate and made a speech in which he urgently requested them to restore him to his kingdom: it belonged to him, he said, rather than to the children of Antiochus. He spoke at great length on this theme and particularly appealed to the fact that Rome was his country and had nursed his youth, that the sons of senators were all his brothers, that the senators were his fathers because he had come to Rome as a small child, and that he was now 23 years old. All the senators on hearing this were inclined in their hearts to take his side, but the Senate as a body resolved to detain Demetrius and to help in securing the throne for the boy left (by

Antiochus). In my opinion the Senate acted thus out of distrust of Demetrius' age and a belief that the youth and weakness of the boy who had succeeded to the throne³ would be of greater advantage to their interests. This became clear from what followed. For they at once appointed as ambassadors Cnaeus Octavius, Spurius Lucretius and Lucius Aurelius and sent them to settle matters in the kingdom as decided by the Senate, since no one would oppose their instructions, as the king was still a boy and the leading men were glad that power had not been entrusted to Demetrius, which is what they had most expected to happen. Cnaeus Octavius and his colleagues set out with instructions to burn the decked ships, then to hamstring the elephants and in general to weaken the forces of the kingdom.⁴ [. . .]

Polybius XXXI.2

1. Cf. **161** §15, **162**.
2. Cf. **162**.
3. Antiochus V, still a minor.
4. Cf. **161** §8. Demetrius eventually escaped from Rome in 162 and secured the Seleucid throne. Compare the policy of the Senate towards Ptolemy VI and VIII, **229**.

170 Dynastic struggles in the Seleucid kingdom under Demetrius II (145)

See further: G. Downey, *A History of Antioch in Syria* (Princeton, 1961), 119–24.

Demetrius (II), now that the kingdom of Egypt was weakened and he alone was left,¹ assumed that he was free of all danger. And so he refused to seek the favour of the populace,² as was customary, and showed himself increasingly oppressive in the injunctions he issued. His behaviour became that of a cruel tyrant and he indulged in extravagantly lawless conduct of every kind. The cause of his behaviour was not just his own personality but the man who was in charge of the kingdom, an impious and unscrupulous man who incited him to every kind of wrongdoing, by flattering the young man and encouraging him to all the basest deeds.³ In the first place Demetrius was not content to punish his opponents in the war with moderate penalties but heaped unusual punishments on them. Then when the people of Antioch behaved towards him in their usual way, he gathered a large mercenary force against them, took away their weapons and of those who refused to hand them over some he killed in open combat and others he shot down in their homes with their children and wives. The disarming of the citizens caused a great disturbance, and so he set fire to the largest part of the city. He punished many of those who had been charged and confiscated their property for the royal exchequer. Such was the fear and hatred he inspired that many of the Antiochenes fled from their country and wandered about the whole of Syria, waiting for the right time to attack the king. Demetrius, openly hostile to them, carried out without interruption, massacres, exiles and confiscations of property, and surpassed by far the cruelty and bloodiness of his father. For his father had emulated not the moderation of a king but the lawlessness of a tyrant[4] and had involved his subjects in disasters beyond remedy. And so the kings from this house were hated for their lawlessness while those from the other house were loved for their moderation. Hence at this time there were continuous conflicts and wars in Syria, as the princes of each house constantly lay in wait for each other. The populace actually readily accepted the changes of rulers since the kings who returned (to power) always sought to ingratiate themselves (with the people).[5]

Diodorus XXXIII.4

1. Demetrius II, son of Demetrius I (cf. **169**), had rid himself of the pretender Alexander Balas (150–145 B.C.), and Ptolemy VI his 'protector' had been killed in battle against Balas.
2. Cf. **163**.
3. Lasthenes, a Cretan mercenary captain.
4. A stock contrast.
5. For examples of this outside Antioch, cf. **172, 173**.

171 The revolt of Diodotus Tryphon and the spread of piracy

The first place in Cilicia, then, is the fort of Coracesium, situated on top of a sheer cliff. Diodotus called Tryphon[1] used it as a base at the time when he detached Syria from the (Seleucid) kings and waged war on them, with a mixture of success and failure. Antiochus (VII) son of Demetrius (I) shut him up in a certain place and forced him to commit suicide. It was Tryphon, together with the worthlessness of the kings who succeeded each other in ruling Syria and also Cilicia, which caused the Cilicians to begin to organise pirate fleets.[2] For his own revolt provoked others to revolt at the same time, and the conflict between brothers resulted in making the country a prey to invaders. The export trade in slaves was a great incitement to wrongdoing, as it was very lucrative; prisoners were an easy catch, and the island of Delos provided a large and wealthy market not far away, which was capable of receiving and exporting 10,000 slaves a day. Hence the proverb: 'Merchant, sail in, unload, everything is sold'. The reason was that after the destruction of Carthage and Corinth the Romans became wealthy and used many slaves; the pirates seeing the easy gains to be made, blossomed forth in large numbers, acting simultaneously as pirates and as slave traders. They were assisted in this by the kings of Cyprus and of Egypt (i.e. the Ptolemies) who were hostile to the Syrians (i.e. the Seleucids); the Rhodians were not friendly to them either and so provided no help. At the same time the pirates, pretending to be slave dealers, carried on their misdeeds without interruption. Nor did the Romans concern themselves as yet very much with affairs beyond the Taurus, but they sent Scipio Aemilianus,[3] and others after him, to inspect the peoples and cities, and decided that it was the inadequacy of the rulers which had caused the problem to arise, though they were too ashamed to put an end to the line of succession descended from Seleucus Nicator which they themselves had recognised. This made the Parthians masters of the country; they took control of the land beyond the Euphrates,[4] and finally so did the Armenians, who acquired the land outside the Taurus as far even as Phoenicia, and overthrew the kings and the whole royal family as far as possible,[5] though they conceded the sea to the Cilicians. Then when the pirates had grown powerful the Romans were compelled to destroy them by war with an army,[6] though they had not hindered their growth. It is difficult to accuse them of negligence: they had other more pressing business on hand nearer to them and were unable to keep an eye on more distant matters. [. . .]

Strabo XIV.5.2

1. An ex-officer of the usurper Alexander Balas (**170** n. 1), but unlike him Diodotus did not pose as a ruler in the Seleucid line but as a self-made king (142/1–137). Cf. also **172**.
2. On piracy cf. **86** and refs.; Ormerod, *Piracy in the Ancient World* (Liverpool, 1924), ch. 6.
3. In 140–139; see A. E. Astin, *Scipio Aemilianus* (Oxford, 1967), 127, 138f., 177.
4. Cf. **145**; the Parthian occupation of Babylonia is dated to July 141.
5. In 83.
6. A reference to Pompey's campaign in 67; for new inscriptional evidence on Rome's policy in the East in the late second century see M. Hassall, M. Crawford, J. Reynolds, *JRS* 64 (1974), 195–220. Strabo's account is probably derived from Poseidonius, cf. H. Strasburger, *JRS* 55 (1965), 40–53.

172 Antiochus VII Sidetes and the independence of the Jews (139)

After the disastrous action of Antiochus IV (see **168**), the increasing weakness and divisions within the Seleucid kingdom enabled the Jews to extort more and more concessions from rival Seleucid rulers; these are detailed in I *Maccabees*, the following being the last to be mentioned in that work.

See further: E. Schürer (cf. **168**), 197–209.

Antiochus (VII) son of King Demetrius (I Soter) sent a letter from the islands of the sea[1] to Simon, priest and ethnarch of the Jews, and to the whole nation. Its contents were as follows:

'King Antiochus to Simon, the High-Priest and ethnarch, and to the Jewish nation, greetings. Since some pernicious men have seized the kingdom of our fathers and I wish to lay claim to the kingdom, so as to restore it to its former position, and I have raised a mercenary army and equipped warships, and I wish to land in the country to take vengeance on those who have devastated our land and laid waste many cities in my kingdom, I therefore now confirm to you all the remissions of tribute conceded to you by the kings before me, as well as all the other donations they have granted to you. I grant you the right to strike coins with your own types to be legal tender in your country.[2] Jerusalem and the Temple are to be free. You will keep all the weapons you have made and the strongholds you have built and which you control. Let everything which you owe to the royal treasury now and in future be remitted to you for the present and for all time. When we have restored our kingdom we will confer on you, your people and the Temple such great honours that your glory will be manifest all the world over.'[3]

I *Maccabees* 15.1–9

1. Rhodes. The letter dates from 139 when Antiochus VII was still engaged in his struggle with Diodotus Tryphon (cf. **171**).
2. The striking of coins was an attribute of sovereignty.
3. In fact once in power Antiochus VII turned against the Jews, eventually capturing Jerusalem in 131, but his death in the Parthian expedition of 130–129 deprived the Seleucids of their last ruler of stature and finally ended their control over Judaea.

173 Letter of Antiochus VIII concerning the freedom of Seleucia in Pieria (summer 109)

King Antiochus (VIII) to King Ptolemy (IX) also called Alexander, his brother, greetings. If you are well, it would be as we [wish]; we ourselves are in good health and remember you [affectionately]. The people of Seleucia in Pieria,[1] the city holy and inviolate,[2] / have [from the beginning] been devoted to our father, and have preserved their goodwill towards him steadfastly throughout, and [maintained] their affection towards us and displayed it [through many] fine deeds, especially

in the [most critical] circumstances which have [overtaken us].³ In /   10
[other respects] we have advanced them generously and worthily and
have brought them [to more conspicuous] honour. And now being
anxious to deem [them] worthy of the [first and greatest benefaction, we
have decided that for] all time they [shall be] free [and we have included
them in the treaties] we have made with each [other, / in the belief that in   15
this] way our [piety and generosity] towards our native city would be
more clearly demonstrated. [So that you too may be] acquainted [with
these concessions, it seemed to us] fitting [to write to you. Farewell].
Year 203, Gorpiaeus 29.⁴

    RC 71; *OGIS* 257; T. B. Mitford, *BSA* 56 (1961), 3f. no. 3

1. See **174, 176, 177**.
2. See **151**; Seleucia received the title 'holy' *ca* 145 and was 'holy and inviolate' by
   138.
3. Civil war between the two half-brothers Antiochus VIII and IX.
4. Summer 109, from which time Seleucia dated a new 'era'.

174 The heart of the Seleucid kingdom

See further: G. Downey, *A History of Antioch in Syria* (1961), esp. 54–86; H.
Seyrig in *The Role of the Phoenicians in the Interaction of Mediterranean Civilizations*,
ed. W. A. Ward (Beirut, 1968), 53–63 (more fully in French in *Syria* 47 (1970),
290–311); A. H. M. Jones, *The Cities of the Eastern Roman Provinces* (Oxford, 2nd
ed., 1971), 241–6.

(4) The Seleucis is the best of the parts (of Syria) I have mentioned; it is
called Tetrapolis and is so in fact because of its most prominent cities.
There are actually more cities there, but four are the largest, Antioch near
Daphne, Seleucia in Pieria, Apamea and Laodicea; they were said to be
sister cities because of the concord between them, and were founded by
Seleucus (I) Nicator.¹ The largest was called after his father, the strongest
after himself and of the others Apamea was called after his wife Apama²
and Laodicea after his mother. Appropriately for the Tetrapolis the
Seleucis was divided into four satrapies, as Poseidonius says (*FGrH* 87 F
65; Edelstein-Kidd F 251), as many as Coele Syria, while Mesopotamia
forms one satrapy. Antioch is itself a tetrapolis as it consists of four parts;
it is fortified both by a common wall and by a wall for each of the
foundations. The first was brought together by Seleucus (I) Nicator
when he moved the settlers from Antigonea, which Antigonus the son of
Philip had built nearby shortly before,³ the second was founded by the
mass of the settlers, the third by Seleucus (II) Callinicus and the fourth by
Antiochus (IV) Epiphanes.

4 North Syria (to illustrate **174**)
adapted from A. H. M. Jones, *Cities of the Eastern Roman Provinces* (Oxford, 2nd edn., 1971)

(5) Antioch, then, is the metropolis of Syria, and that is where the rulers of the country established their royal capital; in power and size it does not fall far short of Seleucia on the Tigris[4] and Alexandria in[5] Egypt. Nicator also brought together there the descendants of Triptolemus, whom I have just mentioned;[6] that is why the Antiochenes honour him like a hero and celebrate a festival on Mt Casius near Seleucia. [. . .] (6) Forty stades (= *ca* 7 km) away towards the sea lies Daphne, a small settlement, and a large shaded grove watered with springs, in the middle of which there is an inviolate enclosure and temple of Apollo and Artemis.[7] It is a custom of the Antiochenes and their neighbours to hold a religious festival there. The grove has a perimeter of 80 stades (*ca* 14 km). (7) Near the city flows the river Orontes, which has its source in Coele Syria, then goes underground and reappears at the surface; it flows through the territory of the Apameans towards Antioch, comes near the city and continues towards the sea near Seleucia. [. . .] (8) Near the sea there is Seleucia and Pieria, a mountain which adjoins the Amanus, and Rhosus which is situated between Issus and Seleucia; Seleucia was formerly called Water Rivers (*Hydatos Potamoi*). The city is a powerful stronghold which cannot be stormed.[8] [. . .] (9) Then there is Laodicea, a city most beautifully built on the sea and with a good harbour; its territory besides being fertile for other crops produces much wine. It supplies most of their wine to the Alexandrians,[9] and the mountain which lies above the city is completely planted with vines almost up to the summits. While the summits are a great distance away from Laodicea, as they slope up gently and gradually away from it, they dominate Apamea rising up to a sheer height above it. [. . .] (10) Apamea also has an acropolis[10] that is well walled for the most part; for it is a well-fortified hill in a hollow plain, which is made into a peninsula by the Orontes and a large lake that lies around it and empties itself (?)[11] into broad marshes and extremely large meadows suitable for pasturing cattle and horses. The city, then, enjoys this secure position (in fact it used to be called Chersonesus (= peninsula) because of this occurrence) and it has a large and fertile territory through which the Orontes flows; there are many townships in it. That is where Seleucus Nicator and the later kings kept the 500 elephants and the larger part of their army. It used to be called Pella by the first Macedonian settlers because most of the Macedonian troops lived there, and because Pella, the native city of Philip and Alexander, had become as it were the metropolis of the Macedonians. The war office and the royal studs were kept there, and they consisted of more than 30,000 mares and 300 stallions; and here too were the horsebreakers, drill-sergeants and all the military instructors who served for pay.

Strabo XVI.2.4–7, 8–10

287

1. See too **46** ch. 57.
2. A Persian princess married by Seleucus in 324 (cf. **14**).
3. Antigonus the One-Eyed, in 307/6 (Diodorus xx.47.5–6).
4. Cf. **46** ch. 58, **188**.
5. Literally 'near'; see **232**.
6. XVI.1.25.
7. Cf. on Daphne **162** (end), **175, 177**.
8. Cf. on Seleucia in Pieria **173, 176, 177, 220**; for a fuller description see Polybius v.58–9. Seleucia was initially intended to be the capital of the empire, but Antiochus I then moved the capital to Antioch.
9. Hardly before late Ptolemaic times; cf. Fraser I (1972), 167–9.
10. An emendation.
11. Text uncertain.

175 Letter of Antiochus III concerning the appointment of a chief-priest at Daphne (189)

(The beginning of the inscription is lost)

. . . he had been held in honour [and trust] by our brother[1] [and] has zealously given many great proofs of his devotion to us and our 5 interests,[2] and has spared neither his life nor his property / to promote our interests and has carried out all the tasks entrusted to him as was fitting, and for the rest has conducted himself in a manner worthy of his previous services to our interests; we (therefore) wished to keep him 10 with us as our collaborator, / but since he frequently pleaded his physical infirmity which resulted from the continuous strains he was under, and requested us to allow him to enjoy rest so that he could spend the 15 remainder of his life in uninterrupted / good health, we yielded to his entreaties, as we wished to show the esteem we have for him. Therefore it shall be our concern that in future he may receive all that pertains to 20 honour and / glory, (and) since the chief-priesthood[3] of Apollo, Artemis Daittae and the other sanctuaries whose sacred enclosures are at Daphne,[4] 25 requires a man who is our 'friend'[5] and who will be capable / of holding the post worthily of the zeal which our ancestors and ourselves have shown for the place and of our piety towards the gods,[6] we have appointed him chief-priest of these sanctuaries in the conviction that their 30 administration / would be fully and properly carried out by him. Give instructions (therefore) to enter him in public documents[7] as chief-priest 35 of these sanctuaries and to honour the man worthily of our / decision, and should he request that assistance be given in the performance of any of the duties concerned, to recommend those who are connected with the 40 sanctuaries and the others who are under his orders, with instructions / to comply with any written or spoken order he gives; and (give instructions) that a copy of this letter be inscribed on stelae and dedicated in the most distinguished places. Year 124, Dios 14.[8]

RC 44; *IGLS* III.2.992

1. Seleucus III, predecessor of Antiochus III.
2. See **139** n. 3.
3. To be distinguished from the chief-priesthoods of the dynastic cults (cf. **158**).
4. See **174** n. 7.
5. Cf. **25** n. 3.
6. Cf. **163** n. 4.
7. I.e. use his name for dating purposes, cf. **158** n. 7.
8. October 12, 189. With this text compare **210**.

176   Decree of Seleucia in Pieria and part of a letter of Seleucus IV (186)

(*a*) Proposal of Theophilus the governor (*epistates*)[1] and of the magistrates: since an injunction (*prostagma*) was handed to us from the king (= Seleucus IV) concerning Aristolochus, one of his 'honoured friends'[2] in residence with him, of which a copy is appended below, / and that it is   5
fitting, since the man is well disposed to our city, that he has resolved to come and settle here, and that on many occasions which affected the interests of the city he has spontaneously offered his help publicly to (all) the citizens and privately to individuals, / and (since) the ambassadors   10
sent to the king, Conon, Zethus, Androcles and Artemidorus, have reported on their return the zeal he has displayed before the king concerning the object of their mission, (it is fitting that) the city should display / its gracious welcome of the zeal and benefactions of such men,   15
so that others, realising what returns those who seek to do good obtain from the city, might be anxious to help the citizens and might be desirous / of acquiring citizenship in our city; be it resolved by the   20
people, to praise Aristolochus for his good disposition and to grant him citizenship in our city; the governor and the magistrates shall determine a place in the magistrates' office for the statue granted to him in the (king's) injunction; / the secretary shall register him as son of Aristolochus, in   25
the deme of Olympius and the tribe Laodicea. Year 126, on the 30th of the month Daisius.[3]
(*b*) King Seleucus to Theophilus and to the magistrates of Seleucia / in   30
Pieria[4] and to the city, greetings; Aristolochus, one of our 'honoured friends', has performed services with all goodwill to our father, our brother and ourselves,[5] and in the most critical circumstances has given assiduous proofs / of his zeal for our interests;[6] in all other respects we   35

289

show our care for him in a way worthy of the [goodwill] he displays, and we have honoured [him] with a bronze statue . . . which we wish to have set up in [your city . . .]

RC 45; *IGLS* III.2.1183

1. Cf. **158** n. 2. The inscription illustrates both royal control of the city and respect for civic forms by the king. Compare the relations of the Attalids with Pergamum, **195**.
2. A formal rank within the larger order of royal 'friends'; cf. **25** n. 3.
3. June 186.
4. Cf. **174** n. 8.
5. I.e. a loyal servant of Antiochus III as the man honoured in **175**.
6. Cf. **139** n. 3. Aristolochus could be expected to exert his influence at Seleucia on behalf of the king; cf. too **180**.

177 List of annual priesthoods at Seleucia in Pieria under Seleucus IV

Column A

. . . priests of the year one hundred and . . .;[1] (priest) of Zeus Olympius
5 and Zeus Coryphaeus,[2] / Niceratus son of Niceratus; (priest) of Apollo of Daphne,[3] Callicles son of [Diogenes]; (priest) of Apollo, Zenobius son
10 of Zenon; / (priest) of Seleucus (I) Zeus Nicator[4] and Antiochus (I)
15 Apollo Soter and Antiochus (II) Theos and Seleucus (II) / Callinicus and Seleucus (III) Soter and Antiochus[5] and Antiochus (III) the Great,
20 Diogenes son of Artemon; / (priest) of [King] Seleucus (IV),[6] Eucrates son of Anaxion; [sceptre-]bearer . . . son of Demetrius.

Column B

. . . priests of the year one hundred and . . . .: (priest) of Zeus Olympius,
5 the Saviour Gods / and Zeus [Coryphaeus], Andron son of
10 [Philophron]; (priest) of Apollo, Theophilus son of Ant . . .; / (priest) of Seleucus (I) Zeus Nicator and [Antiochus] (I) Apollo Soter and Anti-
15 ochus (II) Theos and Seleucus (II) [Callinicus and Seleucus (III)] Soter / and Antiochus and Antiochus (III) the Great, Aristias son of [Homerus]
20 grandson of Aristarchus; (priest) of King Seleucus (IV), / Numenius son
25 of [Numenius]; sceptre-bearer, Thoas son of Pythocles; / thunder-bearers, Hieron son of [Sozon, Iatron son of Iatragoras].

IGLS III.2.1184 (*OGIS* 245)

1. Here and in Column B the exact date is lost but lies within the reign of Seleucus IV.
2. I.e. 'Zeus of the mountain peak', the peak overhanging Seleucia (cf. **174**).

3. See **174, 175**.

4. These are dynastic cults of deceased kings set up by their successors, cf. **158**; for the assimilation of kings and gods cf. **182** ll. 12, 83.

5. Cf. **138** n. 4.

6. The cult of the living king (cf. **158**), identified by the royal title.

178 Letter of a Seleucid king about grants to Zeus of Baetocaece (date uncertain)

While acceptance of native cults was clearly the normal policy of the Seleucids (cf. **141, 167, 189**) their policy towards the landed wealth of many native sanctuaries is variously interpreted. It has been widely assumed that the earlier Seleucids appropriated much of this wealth (thus e.g. Welles *ad loc.*, Tarn and Griffith (1952), 134–41), but there is in fact no evidence for this view (T. R. S. Broughton in *Studies A. C. Johnson*, ed. P. R. Coleman-Norton (Princeton, 1951), 236–50; T. Zawadzki, *Eos* 46 (1952–3), 83–96). The present text, part of a dossier inscribed in Roman imperial times, has often been dated to the late Seleucid period and interpreted as a reversal of earlier Seleucid policy (thus e.g. Welles), but it may well belong to the reigns of Antiochus I or II (H. Seyrig, *Syria* 28 (1951), 200–2). The likelihood is that the Seleucids (and Attalids) increased rather than decreased the wealth of native sanctuaries.

Letter of King Antiochus. King Antiochus to Euphemus,[1] greetings. I have issued the memorandum which is appended below. Let action be taken as instructed on the matters which you are to carry out.

    A report having been brought to me about the power of the god Zeus of Baetocaece,[2] / I have decided to concede to him for all time the source   5 of the god's power, (namely) the village of Baetocaece,[3] formerly held by Demetrius, son of Demetrius and grandson of Mnaseas,[4] (who lived) at Tourgona (?) in the satrapy of Apamea, together with everything that appertains and belongs to it, according to the existing surveys,[5] and including the revenues of the present year, so that the revenue from this village / might be spent for the celebration of the monthly sacrifices and   10 the other things that increase the prestige of the sanctuary by the priest designated by the god, as is the custom. Fairs exempt from taxation are also to be held every month on the fifteenth and the thirtieth; the sanctuary is to be inviolate[6] and the village exempt from billeting,[7] as no objection has been lodged against this. Anyone who opposed any of the above-mentioned instructions / shall be held guilty of impiety. A copy   15 (of the instructions) is to be inscribed on a stone stele and placed in this same sanctuary. It will therefore be necessary to write to the usual officials so that action is taken in accordance with these instructions.

IGLS VII.4028 B and C; *RC* 70

1. An official, precise status unknown.
2. A native sanctuary in north Syria, in the territory of the Phoenician city of Aradus (cf. **144**); the report mentioned by Antiochus may in fact have emanated from Aradus.
3. For native villages cf. **142, 180, 181, 182** l. 45, **185, 187**; cf. also **212** n. 3.
4. Otherwise unknown, but probably a royal favourite who had been granted a large estate, cf. **142, 180, 181, 185**. There is no indication that the village of Baetocaece had previously belonged to the god.
5. Cf. **180, 185**.
6. See **151**.
7. An important privilege; cf. **249**.

179 Law on inheritance from Dura-Europus

Europus, a foundation of Seleucus I on the upper course of the Euphrates (cf. **46** ch. 57), has been excavated and though most of the evidence recovered dates from later times it is possible to reconstruct a picture of the city under the Seleucids. The following parchment dates from Roman times but probably reproduces a law of the original colony.

See further: Rostovtzeff I (1941), 482–9; C. Bradford Welles, *loc. cit.*; G. M. Cohen, *The Seleucid Colonies* (Wiesbaden, 1978), 19f., 66f., 69f.

Concerning [inheritance? . . .] law of the [registry office].
The inheritances of the deceased are to be handed down to the nearest
5   of kin. / The nearest of kin are as follows:
    (1) If the deceased has not left any [children] or if he has not adopted a son in accordance with the laws, his father or his mother if she has not married another man.
    (2) If neither (is alive), the paternal brothers of the father.
10   (3) If there are none / of these, the paternal brothers (of the deceased).
    (4) If there are none of these, but the father of his father (is alive), or the mother of his father, or the cousin on his father's side, the inheritance shall belong to them.
15   (5) If / there are none of these, the property shall fall to the crown.[1]
    The same rules shall also apply for the (other) rights and obligations of the next of kin.

C. Bradford Welles, *The Excavations at Dura-Europos,*
Final Report v. I: *The Parchments and Papyri*
(New Haven, 1959), 76–9 no. 12

1. I.e. the king retained a right of *escheat*. (Cf. **252** for Ptolemaic Egypt.)

180 Letters concerning gifts of land by Antiochus I to Aristodicides of Assos (*ca* 275?)

(a) Letter of Meleager to Ilium

Meleager[1] to the council and people of Ilium,[2] greetings. Aristodicides of Assos[3] has handed to us letters from King Antiochus (I), copies of which we append below. He also came to us in person and / said that although   5
many others were approaching him and offering him crowns[4] – and we ourselves have information on this point as embassies have come to us from certain cities – he wished that the land given to him by King Antiochus / should because of the sanctuary and because of his goodwill   10
towards you be attached to your city.[5] What he wishes to be granted to him by the city, he will explain to you himself. You would do well therefore to vote him all the privileges, to inscribe the terms of the grant he will make to you / and exhibit them on a stele to be placed in the   15
sanctuary, so that you may securely preserve for all time the grant that has been made to you. Farewell.

(b) Copies of three letters of Antiochus I

(1) King Antiochus to Meleager, greetings. We have given to Aristodicides of Assos / 2,000 *plethra*[6] of arable land, to be attached to the city of   20
Ilium or of Scepsis. Do therefore give instructions to assign to Aristodicides from the land which borders on Gergis or Scepsis,[7] wherever you decide, the 2,000 *plethra* of land, and attach it to the city of Ilium or of / Scepsis. Farewell.   25

(2) King Antiochus to Meleager, greetings. Aristodicides of Assos came to see us requesting that we give him in the Hellespontine satrapy Petra, formerly held by Meleager,[8] and in the territory of Petra / 1,500 *plethra*   30
of arable land and a further 2,000 *plethra* of arable land from the territory bordering on the portion already given to him. And we have given to him Petra, unless it has previously been given to someone else,[9] and the land / next to Petra, and a further 2,000 *plethra* of arable land because he   35
as our 'friend' has performed for us all the services he could with all goodwill and zeal.[10] Do you therefore investigate whether this Petra has not been previously given to someone else, and designate / it with its   40
neighbouring territory to Aristodicides, and from the royal land which neighbours on the land previously given to Aristodicides give instructions to measure out and assign to him 2,000 *plethra*, and to allow him to attach it / to any city he wishes in the country (*chora*) and the alliance   45
(*symmachia*).[11] Should the royal peasants (*basilikoi laoi*)[12] from the region of Petra wish to live at Petra for their own security, we have given instructions to Aristodicides to allow them to reside there.[13] Farewell. /   50
(3) King Antiochus to Meleager, greetings. Aristodicides came to see us

and said that he had not yet received the place called Petra and the land attached to it, concerning which we previously sent letters giving it to him, as it had been assigned to Athenaeus the commander of the naval
55 base, and he has requested / that in place of the territory of Petra be designated to him the same number of *plethra*, and that a further 2,000 *plethra* be granted to him, to be attached to any city he wishes in our
60 alliance, as we have previously written. Seeing therefore that he / is well disposed and zealous for our interests[14] we wish to treat the man with great consideration and have acquiesced in these matters too. He says that the land granted to him in the territory of Petra amounts to 1,500
65 *plethra*. Do therefore give instructions to measure out / and designate to Aristodicides the 2,500 *plethra*[15] of arable land and in place of the territory of Petra a further 1,500 *plethra* of arable land from the royal land which
70 neighbours on the land originally given / to him by us. And (give instructions) to allow Aristodicides to attach the land to any city he wishes in our alliance, as we have written in the previous letter. Farewell.

RC 13, 10–12; *OGIS* 221; P. Frisch, *Die Inschriften von Ilion* (Bonn, 1975), no. 33

1. The Seleucid governor of the Hellespontine satrapy; cf. **201** n. 3.
2. On Ilium and the Seleucids cf. **139**.
3. A Greek city in the Troad; on the places mentioned in this inscription see J. M. Cook, *The Troad* (Oxford, 1973).
4. Not literally, but refers to honours and presents of all kinds.
5. Royal land granted to a favourite and 'attached' to the territory of a city became the irrevocable property of the beneficiary, while the city to which the land was attached could derive fiscal advantages from this land besides the gain in prestige; cf. also **185**. Whether this improved in any way the status of the native peasants (thus e.g. Tarn and Griffith (1952), 134–8) is very doubtful (cf. P. Briant, *Klio* 60 (1978), 57–92, in a wider context, also K. M. T. Atkinson, *Antichthon* 2 (1968), 32–57). On Ptolemaic 'gift' land cf. **235** n. 15.
6. 1 *plethron* = 10,000 sq ft = *ca* 950 m² (depending on the size of foot).
7. Royal land, cf. below. On Scepsis cf. **31, 32**.
8. Not the governor.
9. The inefficiency and rudimentary character of the royal administration are astonishing, though this may be due to the effects of the Galatian invasion (cf. **140, 142**); contrast the more complex and efficient administration in **185** (also **187**).
10. On royal favourites cf. **113, 175, 176**, and generally **25** n. 3.
11. It is not clear whether these words are used in a technical sense and show that cities in the Seleucid empire fell into two distinct legal categories; in the next letter Antiochus I only refers to the 'alliance'.
12. On these cf. too **142, 181, 185**. For Ptolemaic Egypt cf. **231** n. 38.
13. Another probable indication of the Galatian threat (n. 9).

14. Cf. **139** n. 3.

15. More than Aristodicides asked, if this is not an engraver's error. The total size of his estate amounts to 8,000 *plethra*.

181   Loan (?) of money by the temple of Artemis at Sardis on the security of an estate (*ca* 200)

The following inscription is valuable for giving a detailed description of a large estate in Asia Minor comprising several native villages and the revenues from them (cf. also **142, 180, 185**), but the detailed interpretation of the text has many uncertainties: (1) the date and circumstances of the grant of the estate to Mnesimachus (if Antigonus in l. 2 is Antigonus the One-Eyed, one must suppose that the text was inscribed or re-inscribed at a much later date, *ca* 200), (2) the nature and purpose of the large loan by the temple of Artemis at Sardis to Mnesimachus which he is unable to repay, (3) the exact nature of the contract in col. II whereby the estate is made over to the temple.

See further (for a divergent view): K. M. T. Atkinson, *Historia* 21 (1972), 45–74.

Column I

. . . Chaereas having enquired . . . and later Antigonus awarded the estate (*oikos*) to me. But now since the temple-wardens are asking back from me the gold lent on [deposit] which belongs to Artemis, and I have no means of paying it back to them, these then are [the particulars of the] estate. The villages with the following names: Tobalmoura, a village in the plain of Sardis on the hill of Ilos; [to] this [village] also belong / other   5
villages, one called the village of Tandos, and Kombdilipia; the annual revenue (*phoros*) of the villages to the 'chiliarchy'[1] of Pytheas . . . is 50 gold pieces. And there is also a lot (*kleros*) at Kinaroa near Tobalmoura, with an annual [revenue] of three gold pieces. And there is another village Periasasostra in the Water of Morstas, with an annual revenue to the 'chiliarchy' of . . . arius of 57 gold pieces. And there is also a lot ⟨at⟩ the Water of Morstas at Nagrioa, with a revenue to the 'chiliarchy' of Sagarius son of Koreis of three gold pieces and four gold obols. And there is / another village at Attoudda called the village of Ilos, with an   10
annual revenue of three gold pieces and three gold obols.

Now from all the villages, from the lots, from the dwelling-plots which belong to them, from the peasants (*laoi*) with all their households and belongings, from the wine-vessels, from the dues paid in silver and in labour,[2] and from the other revenues from the villages and even more besides, when the division was made,[3] Pytheus and Adrastus received as a separate estate a farmstead at Tobalmoura, outside of which are the houses of the / peasants and the slaves and two gardens (requiring)   15 fifteen *artabas* of seed, and at Periasasostra dwelling-plots (requiring) three *artabas* of seed, and slaves living in this place, at Tobalmoura Ephesus son of Adrastus, Kadoas son of Adrastus, Heraclides son of Beletrus, Tuius son of Maneas Caecus; those dwelling at Periasasostra, Kadoas son of Armanandes, Adrastus son of Maneas.[4]

Column II

[. . . it shall] no longer [be permitted] to me or [to my descendants nor
. . .] nor to anyone else to redeem [anything]. And if anyone lays a claim
to any of the villages or lots or any of the other things listed here in
writing, I and my descendants shall guarantee possession and turn out
the rival claimant. If we do not guarantee possession or transgress this
5   written contract / in respect of the villages, the lots, the lands and all the
slaves, they shall fall to the treasury of Artemis, and the temple wardens
shall conduct legal proceedings and secure judgement on these matters
against the claimants as they wish, and I, Mnesimachus, and my
descendants shall pay to the treasury of Artemis 2,650 gold pieces,[5] and
for the produce and the fruit, if they (sc. the temple wardens) do not
receive the fruits that year for the treasury of Artemis, we shall also pay
10 whatever price in gold they are worth, / and for the buildings and the
plants belonging to Artemis or anything else they may do, we shall pay
whatever price in gold they are worth; and so long as we have not paid,
(the loan) will remain for us as a 'deposit' (*parakatatheke*) until we have
paid in full. And if the king on account of Mnesimachus takes away from
Artemis the villages or the lots or any of the other securities offered, I,
Mnesimachus, and my descendants shall immediately pay to the treasury
of Artemis the original amount in gold of the 'deposit', (namely) 1,325
15 gold pieces, / and we shall pay at once whatever is the value of the
buildings and of the plants of Artemis, and for the produce and the fruit,
if they do not receive the fruits that year for the treasury of Artemis we
shall also pay whatever price in gold they are worth; and so long as we
have not paid (the loan) will remain for me and for my descendants as a
'deposit' until we have paid in full to the treasury of Artemis. The
recovery (of the loan) so long as (repayment) has not been made by us, is
to be enforceable.

Sardis VII. 1 (Princeton, 1932), 1–7 no. 1;
R. Bogaert, *Epigraphica* III (Leyden, 1976), no. 36

1. A territorial division (a military settlement?); exact nature uncertain.
2. I.e. the *laoi* owe *corvées* to their masters. For compulsory labour in Ptolemaic Egypt see **251**.
3. Circumstances unknown.
4. Note the mixture of Greek and non-Greek names.
5. Double the original loan, cf. below.

182 Smyrna under Seleucus II

See further: C. J. Cadoux, *Ancient Smyrna* (Oxford, 1938), 113–27; G. M. Cohen, *The Seleucid Colonies* (Wiesbaden, 1978), 60–3, 77f.

(*a*) Lines 1–33, decree of Smyrna on the treaty with the inhabitants of Magnesia near Mt Sipylus. (*b*) Lines 34–88, treaty between the inhabitants of Smyrna and those of Magnesia. (*c*) Lines 89–108, decree of Smyrna concerning the soldiers at Old Magnesia and others not included in the treaty.

(*a*) Resolved by the people, proposal of the generals: since previously at the time when King Seleucus (II) crossed into Seleucis,[1] and many great dangers were threatening our city and territory,[2] the people preserved its goodwill and friendship towards him, and was not daunted at the enemies' invasion and gave no thought to the destruction of its property, but considered everything secondary to the maintenance / of its policy of   5 friendship and to defending the king's interests[3] to the best of its ability as it initially promised; and so King Seleucus, who shows piety towards the gods[4] and affection towards his parents, being generous and knowing how to repay gratitude towards his benefactors, honoured our city because of the goodwill and zeal displayed by the people towards his interests and because of the establishment in our city of the cult of his father Antiochus Theos (the god) and his father's mother Stratonice Thea (the goddess), in which are offered to them / great honours publicly by the people and in   10 private by each of the citizens,[5] and he guaranteed to the people its autonomy and democracy, and wrote to the kings, the dynasts, the cities and the peoples (*ethne*)[6] requesting that the sanctuary of Aphrodite Stratonicis[7] be recognised as inviolate and our city as holy and inviolate.[8] And now that the king has crossed over (sc. the Taurus) into Seleucis, the generals, being anxious that the king's interests should be safeguarded, sent a delegation to the settlers (*katoikoi*) at Magnesia[9] and to the cavalry and soldiers in the camp (*hypaithroi*), and despatched from among themselves / one man, Dionysius, to urge them to preserve for all time   15 their friendship and alliance with King Seleucus, and they promised that if they (sc. those at Magnesia) defended (the king's) interests and had the same enemies and friends (as the king), they would receive from the people and from King Seleucus every privilege and advantage, and gratitude worthy of their friendship would be repaid to them.[10] The men at Magnesia, being thus invited and being themselves anxious to maintain their friendship and alliance with the king and to defend his interests, eagerly accepted the requests of the generals and promised / to show the   20 same favourable attitude as our people towards all the interests of King Seleucus, and they have sent to us as ambassadors Potamon and Hierocles from the settlers and Apollonicetes from the soldiers in camp, to

negotiate with us and to bring the agreement for the friendship they wish
to be concluded. And when the ambassadors were brought before the
people they conversed on all matters in conformity with the terms of the
agreement. With good fortune, be it resolved to conclude the (treaty of)
friendship with the men at Magnesia in furtherance of all the interests of
25   King Seleucus, and to appoint three ambassadors to be sent to them, /
who will bring them the agreement as resolved by the people and will
discourse about its terms and will urge them to accept and observe the
terms of the agreement, and if the men at Magnesia do observe it, the
ambassadors who are to be appointed will administer to them the oath
written in the agreement. When the men at Magnesia have accepted this
and have jointly sealed the agreement and sworn, and when the
ambassadors have returned, let all the other provisions written in the
agreement be carried out, and let this decree be inscribed in accordance
30   with the law; let it be inscribed [on] / the same stele as the agreement will
be; and let the monthly presidents (*epimenioi*) of the council invite the
ambassadors who [have come] from Magnesia to a meal at the town-hall;
let Callinus the treasurer give to the ambassadors who are appointed
journey money from the city's revenues in accordance with the [law] for
the number of days laid down by the people. The number of days was
fixed at five, and the ambassadors appointed were Phanodemus son of
[Micion], Dionysius son of Dionytas, Parmeniscus son of Pytheas.

(*b*) When Hegesias was priest, Pythodorus *stephanephoros* (crown-
bearer), in the month of Lenaion, with good fortune: friendship was
35   concluded on the following terms by the people of Smyrna / and the
settlers at Magnesia, the cavalry and the infantry in the city, and [the
men] in the camp and the other inhabitants,[11] and the people of Smyrna
granted citizenship to the settlers at Magnesia, the cavalry and the
infantry in the city, and the men in the camp and the [other] inhabitants
of the city, on condition that the men at Magnesia preserve the alliance
with King Seleucus and goodwill towards his interests with all zeal for all
time, and that what they have received from King Seleucus they shall
preserve to the best of their ability and shall restore to King Seleucus.
They shall enjoy citizen rights together with the people of Smyrna in
40   accordance with the laws of the city, / without causing any civil
disturbance,[12] with the same enemies and friends as the people of
Smyrna. The men at Magnesia shall swear to the people of Smyrna and
the people of Smyrna to the men at Magnesia the oath appended to the
agreement. And when the oaths have been completed the grievances
which arose between them during the war[13] shall all be lifted and neither
side shall be allowed to accuse the other about what took place during the
war, whether through action at law or in any other way. If the clause is
violated, any accusation which is brought will be invalid. The settlers at

Magnesia, the cavalry and the infantry in the city, and the men in the camp shall be granted citizen rights at Smyrna on a basis of full equality with the other citizens. Similarly citizen rights [shall be granted] / to the   45
other inhabitants of Magnesia who are free and Greek.[14] The present secretaries of the divisions shall bring to the people the muster-rolls of the cavalry and infantry in the city at Magnesia and of the men in the camp, and the men appointed by the settlers at Magnesia (shall bring) the register of the [other] inhabitants. When the secretaries submit the muster-rolls and the men appointed the register of the other inhabitants, the auditors (*exetastai*) shall administer an oath at the Metroon with newly-burnt offerings [on the secretaries], to the effect that they have submitted to the best of their ability the register of the cavalry and [infantry] settlers who are with them, [those in the city and those who are in the] / camp, and on the men who are submitting the register of the   50
[other inhabitants, to the effect that they have submitted to the best of their ability the register of the] inhabitants of Magnesia who are free and Greek. [The] auditors shall hand over to the keeper of the records of the council and people the [registers which have been submitted], and he shall deposit them in the public record-office. [The auditors] shall allot all the names which have been submitted among the tribes and will inscribe them on the citizen-lists, and those who have been inscribed [on the] citizen-lists shall share in all the privileges enjoyed by the other citizens. Those who are enrolled as citizens at Magnesia shall use the laws of the people of Smyrna in their [contracts] with and accusations against people of Smyrna. / They shall accept in Magnesia the [legal] coinage of the   55
city. The men at Magnesia shall welcome the governor (*archon*) appointed by the people to take charge of the keys and to command the garrison of the city, and to preserve the city for King Seleucus. The people at Smyrna shall give as quarters for those who pack up and leave Magnesia houses with as many beds as the people decides,[15] from the time when the agreement is jointly sealed for a period of six months. The treasurer of the sacred revenues shall hire the houses together with the generals and shall provide the expense from the revenues of the city. The settlers at Magnesia, the cavalry and the infantry in the city, and the soldiers in the camp and / the others who are entered in the citizen body   60
shall swear the following oath:[16]

I swear by Zeus, the Earth, the Sun, Ares, Athena Areia, the Tauropolus, the Sipylene Mother, Apollo at Panda, all the other gods and goddesses, and the Fortune of King Seleucus:[17] I will abide by the treaty concluded with the people of Smyrna for all time, and I will maintain the alliance and the goodwill towards King Seleucus and the city of Smyrna, and what I have received from King Seleucus I will preserve to the best of my ability and return to King Seleucus, and I will not transgress any of

the terms of the agreement and I will not distort its written provisions in any way or by any means. I will behave as a citizen in a spirit
65 of / concord (*homonoia*),[18] without causing any civil disturbance, in accordance with the laws of the people of Smyrna and the decrees of the people, and I will help to preserve the autonomy and the democracy (of Smyrna) and all the other privileges granted to the people of Smyrna by King Seleucus, with the zeal at all time and I will not do harm to any of them nor suffer anyone else to do so to the best of my ability. If I notice anyone conspiring against the city or the lands of the city, or subverting the democracy and its equality (*isonomia*), I will inform the people of Smyrna, and I will help vigorously and with all zeal, and I will not abandon (the people of Smyrna) as far as I can. If I abide by my oath may I prosper, but if I break it may I be destroyed, myself and my [descendants].

The people of Smyrna shall swear to the men from Magnesia the
70 following oath: /

I swear by Zeus, the Earth, the Sun, Ares, Athena Areia, the Tauropolus, the Sipylene Mother, Aphrodite Stratonicis and all the other gods and goddesses: I will abide by the treaty concluded with the settlers at Magnesia, the cavalry and infantry in the city, the men in the camp and the others included in the [citizen] body for all time, without transgressing any of the terms of the agreement or distorting its written provisions, in any way or by any [means]. And I will be well disposed to King Seleucus and the settlers from Magnesia, those in the city and those in the camp, and the other [inhabitants of] Magnesia who are free and
75 Greek, and I will make them all / citizens, and their descendants as well, on a basis of full equality with the other [citizens], and I will allot them into tribes and enter them into any tribe they have drawn, and I will not do harm to any of them myself nor suffer anyone else to do so to the best of my ability. If I notice anyone conspiring against them or their descendants or their property, I will inform them as soon as possible and I will give help zealously. I will give them a share in the magistracies and the other public affairs of the city in which the other participate. If I abide by my oath may I prosper, but if I break it may I be destroyed, myself and my descendants.

The people of Smyrna and the men from Magnesia shall appoint men to the number they each think sufficient, to administer the oath to the mass
80 of citizens / in Smyrna and in Magnesia. They shall [administer the oath after giving public notice] on the previous day that those in the city should stay at home as the oath is about to be taken as laid down in the agreement. The men from Magnesia who have been appointed shall administer [the prescribed oath] to the people of Smyrna, and the men from Smyrna similarly to the men at Magnesia. Callinus [the treasurer

shall provide] the sacrificial victims for the taking of the oath at Smyrna from whatever funds the people votes, and likewise at Magnesia the treasurers to whom the people assigns the task. The people of Smyrna shall inscribe the agreement on stelae [of white stone and] consecrate them in the sanctuary of Aphrodite Stratonicis and at Magnesia on the Maeander in the sanctuary of Artemis [Leucophryene],[19] and the settlers in Magnesia (shall consecrate them) in the agora next to the altar of / Dionysus and the statues of the kings, and at Panda in [the sanctuary   85 of] Apollo and at Gryneon in the sanctuary of Apollo. The keeper of the records of the council and of the people shall inscribe copies of the agreement (and deposit them) [in the public record-office]. The agreements shall be jointly sealed, the one that is given to the people of Smyrna by whoever is appointed by the state (*koinon*) of Magnesia with their own signet and the existing state signet, and the one that is to be given to Magnesia by the generals and the auditors with the signet of the city and with their own. Let these arrangements be carried out by both peoples with good fortune.

(*c*) Resolved by the people, proposal of the generals: since the people continues to show concern for all the interests of King Seleucus and formerly helped to increase his kingdom / and preserved his interests as   90 far as possible, and had to suffer the loss and destruction of many of its possessions, and incurred many dangers in order to preserve its friendship with King Seleucus, and now being anxious to help in preserving and maintaining his interests as far as possible, has concluded a friendship with the settlers at Magnesia, and with the cavalry and infantry in the camp and the other inhabitants of Magnesia, so that they should preserve the alliance and the goodwill towards King Seleucus; and believing it necessary for the city to take over also the fort (called) Old Magnesia and to provide for its garrisoning, so that when it has been taken over by the city all the interests of King Seleucus in the vicinity might be more securely preserved, / they sent an embassy to the   95 inhabitants of the fort and invited them to opt for friendship with King Seleucus and to hand over the keys to the governor sent by the people, and to admit a garrison which would help them to preserve the fort for King Seleucus, promising that if they did this they would receive from the city every privilege and advantage, and the inhabitants of the fort, opting for friendship with King Seleucus with all zeal accepted the requests of the people and handed over the keys to the governor sent by the people and admitted the garrison sent by the city into the fort; with good fortune, be it resolved that they should be citizens / and that they   100 should enjoy the same rights as the other citizens, and that their two lots (*kleroi*), the one granted to them by Antiochus (I) Theos Soter (the god and saviour) and the one about which Alexander[20] wrote, should be exempt from the tithe and if the territory occupied by the former settlers at Magnesia is added to our city, the three lots shall remain as a free concession and they shall continue to enjoy their present exemption from taxation. Those of them who do not have a lot shall (each) be given a cavalryman's lot as a free concession from those lying near the fort. Timon and the infantrymen under Timon's command who were detached from the phalanx to guard the fort shall be granted citizen rights and the same exemption from taxation enjoyed by the others, and they shall remain in the fort. Omanes and the / Persians under Omanes and the men sent from Smyrna to guard the fort, Menecles and those under his command, shall be granted citizenship and the other privileges which have been voted to the others from Magnesia, and the people will see to it that they are given from the royal treasury their rations and pay and everything else which is normally given to them from the royal treasury.[21]

The decree is to be inscribed on the stelae to be consecrated in the sanctuaries by the people (of Smyrna) and [by the] men from Magnesia. It shall also be inscribed in the public records.

OGIS 229; *Staatsv.* III.492

1. Cf. **174**.
2. A reference to the 'Third Syrian War' or 'Laodicean War' of 246–241 (cf. **220–222, 274**) during which Smyrna remained loyal to Seleucus II while Magnesia near Mt Sipylus and the troops stationed there were clearly on the Ptolemaic side.
3. Cf. **139** n. 3.
4. On this theme cf. **163** n. 4.
5. On the cult of Seleucid rulers by Greek cities cf. **139** n. 7.
6. A shorthand description of the types of state known to the Hellenistic world. Kings = Antigonids, Seleucids, Attalids, Ptolemies; dynasts = petty rulers, as those frequently attested in Asia Minor (cf. **33, 93** n. 11, **146, 150, 197** n. 7, **202** n. 2, **223**); cities = Greek and other self-governing city-states; peoples = nations not organised on a city basis, as e.g. the Jews (cf. **166, 167**).
7. Cf. **177**.
8. On *asylia* cf. **151**; a decree of Delphi recognises Smyrna as 'holy and inviolate' (*OGIS* 228).
9. The exact identity of these 'settlers' (*katoikoi*) is much disputed; they are regarded by many as military settlers who have been granted land allotments in return for military service (cf. **167**), *katoikoi* and *katoikia* being used in a technical sense (cf. e.g. B. Bar-Kochva, *The Seleucid Army* (Cambridge, 1976), 22f.). For Ptolemaic military settlers cf. **252**.
10. Here as below Smyrna is implicitly claiming to speak for the king; under a profession of loyalty to Seleucus II the city is in effect extending its influence in the region.

11. I.e. the civilian population at Magnesia.
12. On the problems posed by the incorporation of new citizens cf. **133**.
13. Cf. n. 2 above.
14. Note the exclusions: all slaves and all the non-Greek natives.
15. Compare Teos and Lebedus in **40**.
16. See **33** n. 7.
17. Note the inclusion of the king's 'Fortune' in the oath.
18. Cf. **51**.
19. Cf. **184, 190**.
20. A Seleucid official.
21. Cf. n. 10 above.

183 Letter of Antiochus I or II to Erythrae

King Antiochus (I or II) to the council and people of Erythrae, greetings.
Tharsynon, Pythes and Bottas, your envoys, handed over the decree to
us in which you voted the honours, and brought the crown with which
you crowned / us, and likewise the gold offered as a present,[1] and they   5
themselves spoke about the goodwill which you have constantly felt
towards our house, and in general about the gratitude felt by the people
towards all benefactors, and also about the eminent position enjoyed by
the city under the former / kings, and they requested with every   10
earnestness and zeal that we should be well disposed to you and that at
the same time we should help in increasing the city's privileges in all that
relates to honour and glory. We have graciously accepted the honours
and the crown, and likewise the present (of gold), and we praise you for
your gratitude in all matters; / for you seem in general to pursue this line   15
of conduct. And therefore from the beginning we have constantly
maintained our goodwill towards you, as we can see the sincerity and
honesty of your conduct, and now we are even more attracted to you, as
we recognise your nobility from many other proofs, and not least from
the decree / which was handed over to us and from the words spoken by   20
your ambassadors. And since Tharsynon, Pythes and Bottas declared
that under Alexander and Antigonus (the One-Eyed) your city was
autonomous and free from tribute,[2] and our ancestors[3] were constantly
zealous on its behalf, and since we see that their decision / was just and   25
we ourselves wish not to fall short in (our) benefactions, we shall help to
preserve your autonomy and we grant you exemption from tribute,
including all the other taxes and [the] contributions [to] the Gallic fund.[4]
You will also have the [. . . and any] other privilege which we shall think
of or / [you will request from us]. We also invite you, remembering   30
[that you have always?] most earnestly tried . . . goodwill as is just and
[. . . in conformity?] with your previous actions . . . that you will

35 remember worthily [those from whom] you have received benefactions. / [Your] envoys [will report to you at greater length on these matters and] on the other subject of our discussion, and [we praise] them for all the other [things they did and] because of the zeal they showed [for the people's interests]. Farewell.⁵

RC 15; *OGIS* 223; H. Engelmann and R. Merkelbach
Die Inschriften von Erythrai und Klazomenai 1
(Bonn, 1972), no. 32

1. 'Presents' of gold to rulers on special occasions (e.g. accession, victories) were customary in the East and in the Hellenistic period often took the form of crowns; cf. **113, 167** §142, **231** n. 15.
2. Tribute was the norm unless the city was specially exempted; cf. **151**, also **167**.
3. Perhaps simply = 'father', if the letter is from Antiochus I; the letter is strikingly silent on Lysimachus, who had controlled the city in the early third century.
4. Probably a special tax to meet in some way Galatian pressure (cf. **140**).
5. For fragments of a decree of Erythrae following the king's letter cf. H. Engelmann and R. Merkelbach, *op. cit.*, no. 30.

184 Letter of Antiochus III to Magnesia on the Maeander recognising the festival of Artemis Leucophryene

After an apparition of Apollo and Artemis in their city, the Magnesians secured an oracle from Delphi in 221/20 on the strength of which they sought to raise the status of their festival in honour of Artemis Leucophryene and have it recognised in the wider Greek world. A first attempt failed, but a second attempt some fourteen years later was strikingly successful, as attested by a large dossier of inscriptions from the temple of Artemis at Magnesia which record the decrees or letters of acceptance by cities or kings (cf. *Syll.*³ 554, 557–62 and see **190**), but whereas the cities were for the most part willing to recognise in addition Magnesia as being 'holy and inviolate' (cf. **151**), the kings with the exception of Ptolemy IV make no mention of this.

King Antiochus (III) to the council and people of Magnesia, greetings. Demophon, Philiscus and Pheres, the sacred ambassadors (*theoroi*) sent to
5 us by you / to announce the contest and the other celebrations voted by the people in honour of Artemis Leucophryene, the patron goddess of
10 your city, met me at Antioch / in Persis,¹ handed me the decree and spoke themselves with enthusiasm in accordance with the terms of the
15 decree, urging me to recognise as 'crowned' and 'isopythian'² / the contest which you are celebrating in honour of the goddess every five

years.[3] Since therefore we have had from the beginning the friendliest disposition [towards] your people because of the goodwill it has shown to us / and our interests[4] in all circumstances, and wish to make clear our policy, we recognise the honours you have voted to the goddess, and intend to increase these in whatever respects you invite us or / we ourselves think of.[5] We have also written to those in charge of affairs[6] so that the cities may recognise (the celebrations) in the same way. Farewell.[7]

20

25

RC 31; OGIS 231

1. Cf. **190**; this represents a journey of well over 2,000 km.
2. I.e. equal in status to the Pythian games at Delphi; on the 'crowned' competitions cf. **119** n. 14.
3. Reckoned inclusively = every 4 years.
4. Cf. **139** n. 3.
5. Cf. **163** n. 4.
6. I.e. governors and officials.
7. There is a similar letter from Antiochus' son and coregent, RC 32.

185 A sale of land by Antiochus II to his divorced queen Laodice (254/3)

The following dossier comprises three documents: (1) a covering letter by Metrophanes, governor of the Hellespontine satrapy (cf. **180, 201** n. 3) to Nicomachus, a subordinate finance official (*oikonomos*), (2) a letter of Antiochus II to Metrophanes, (3) a report of a *hyparch* (full name lost), an official in charge of a subdivision of the satrapy. The lost portion of the text at the beginning comprised a letter from Nicomachus to the *hyparch*, attested by the last document. (For a different view of the contents of the stele cf. P. N. Lockhart, *AJP* 82 (1961), 188–92 but see *SEG* XIX.676). With this text, which gives important information on Seleucid administration and land tenure in Asia Minor, compare **142, 178, 180, 181**.

A [. . . the copy of the edict written] by him . . . and to the others . . . [to place] the stelae . . . / [and] in accordance with the letter sent by [the king] issue a contract[1] and give instructions to inscribe the sale and the survey[2] on two stone stelae, and to place [one] of these at Ephesus in the sanctuary of Artemis, and the other / at Didyma in the sanctuary of Apollo,[3] and to provide the money needed for this from the royal treasury. Take care that the erection of the stelae is carried out as quickly as possible, and write to us when it has been done. We have also written to Timoxenus the keeper of the records to enter / the sale and the survey in the royal archives at Sardis,[4] as instructed by the king.

5

10

15

B In the month of Daesius.⁵ King Antiochus (II) to Metrophanes, greetings. We have sold to Laodice⁶ Pannucome, the manor-house, and the land which is attached to the village – it is bounded by the territory
20 of Zelia and Cyzicus / and the ancient road, which was above Pannucome, [but] has been ploughed up [by] the peasants nearby so that they might appropriate the place (the road which now exists for [Pannucome] was constructed later) – together with any hamlets which are found in
25 this region, the peasants (*laoi*) who live there with all their household / and belongings,⁷ and with the revenues of the 59th year,⁸ at a price of 30 talents of silver,⁹ and also any of the peasants from this village who have moved to other places,¹⁰ on condition that she pays no taxes to the royal
30 treasury and that she will have the right / to attach the land to any city she wishes.¹¹ And similarly any who buy (the land) or receive it from her will own it lawfully and will attach it to any city they wish, unless Laodice has previously attached it to a city, in which case they will
35 exercise their property rights where the land has been attached / by Laodice. We have given orders to pay the price into the treasury at . . . in three instalments, the first in the month of Audnaeus¹² in the 60th year, the second in the month of Xandicus,¹³ and the third within the next
40 three months. / Give instructions to transfer to Arrhidaeus, the manager¹⁴ of the property of Laodice, the village, the manor-house, the land which is attached to it, the peasants, with their household and all their belongings, and to inscribe the sale in the royal archives at Sardis
45 and on five stone stelae, the first of these / to be placed at Ilium in the sanctuary of Athena,¹⁵ the second in the sanctuary at Samothrace, the third at Ephesus in the sanctuary of Artemis, the fourth at Didyma in the sanctuary of Apollo¹⁶ and the fifth at Sardis in the sanctuary of Artemis.¹⁷
50 And (give instructions) to survey the land at once / and mark it off with boundary stones, and to [inscribe] the survey in the stelae . . .

C . . . in the month of Dius, year . . . [Pannucome, the manor-house,
55 the land and the peasants living there. Transferred] / to Arrhidaeus, the manager of the property of Laodice, [by . . . c]rates the *hyparch*, the village, the manor-house and the [land] attached to it, in accordance with the instructions of Nicomachus the *oikonomos*, [to which] were appended the written instructions from Metrophanes and from the king to him,
60 according to which it was necessary to carry out the survey. From / the east, from the land of Zelia which adjoins that of Cyzicus, the ancient royal road which leads to Pannucome, above the village and the manor-house, as pointed out by Menecrates the son of Bacchius of Pythocome and Daos son of Azaretus and Medeius son of Metrodorus
65 both of Pannucome,¹⁸ / but which has been ploughed up by those living near the place; from this to the altar of Zeus which is above the

manor-house and which is, like the tomb, on the right of the road; from the tomb the royal road itself which leads through the Eupannese up to the river Aesepus. [The territory] was marked off with pillars according to the boundaries which have been pointed out.

Didyma II (Berlin 1958), 492 A–C, *RC* 19, 18, 20;
OGIS 225 (B and C only)

1. For the engraving of the stelae.
2. The following two texts.
3. The present inscription.
4. Cf. **181**.
5. *Ca* May.
6. Laodice, first wife of Antiochus II, divorced by him in 253; Antiochus then married the Ptolemaic princess Berenice. This led later (in 246–241) to the 'Laodicean War' or 'Third Syrian War' between Seleucids and Ptolemies (cf. **182** n. 2). Note the absence of royal titles for Laodice.
7. Compare **181**.
8. In the Seleucid era = 253.
9. A nominal sum, i.e. the sale was fictitious and intended to provide Laodice with financial security after her divorce.
10. Though the native peasants are not literally tied to the soil, they cannot escape their fiscal obligations by moving from the village in which they are registered.
11. See **180** n. 5.
12. December 253 – January 252.
13. March 252.
14. Cf. **142**.
15. Cf. **139, 180**.
16. Cf. **186**.
17. Cf. **181**. Note the extensive publicity given to the transaction.
18. Note the mixture of Greek and non-Greek names; cf. **142**.

186 Letter of Seleucus II to Miletus

King Seleucus (II) to the council and people of Miletus, greetings. Whereas our ancestors and our father conferred many great benefits on your city[1] because of the oracles rendered from the sanctuary (you have) / of Apollo Didymeus, and because of their kinship with the god   5
himself,[2] and also because of the gratitude shown by your people; and whereas we can see ourselves, from the policies you have constantly pursued towards our interests,[3] which our father's 'friends' have pointed out to us,[4] and from the speech / made by Glaucippus and Diomander,   10

307

your envoys who have brought the sacred crown from the shrine with which your people has crowned us, that you remain sincere and firm in your friendships and (that you) remember the benefactions you have

15 received, we welcomed the policy of your people, and / since we are anxious and attach the greatest importance to raising [your city] to a more distinguished position [and to increasing?] the privileges [you now have? . . .]

(the rest of the letter is lost)

Didyma II (Berlin, 1958), 493; *RC* 22; *OGIS* 227

1. Cf. Rostovtzeff I (1941), 174. Miletus was in the Ptolemaic orbit, at least intermittently, in the 270s and 260s (cf. **270**), then returned to the Seleucid fold in 259/8 when Antiochus II helped to free the city from the Ptolemaic officer Timarchus (Appian, *Syrian Wars* 65; cf. *OGIS* 226).
2. Cf. **34** n. 6, **139, 174** §6, **175, 177**. Seleucid coins show the head of Apollo on the reverse.
3. Cf. **139** n. 3.
4. Note the influence of the 'friends' (cf. **25** n. 3) of Antiochus II on the young ruler. The context of this inscription may be the display of loyalty by Miletus to Seleucus II during the 'Laodicean War' (cf. **185** n. 6).

187 Decree of Apollonia of Salbace in honour of a Seleucid official (date uncertain)

[. . . and in former] times [he has constantly shown himself] well [disposed publicly to the people][1] and privately to each [of the citizens; and when he was appointed cavalry] commander in charge of the [soldiers (stationed)] among [us], he [secured] perfect discipline,[2] [and

5 when ambassadors] / were sent concerning the [interests of the] people to Ctesicles the . . . and to Menander the financial official (*dioiketes*),[3] he devoted [himself zealously] when the ambassadors [departed and] after

10 travelling [with] them he was anxious that [all] / our demands should be granted. And furthermore when [Demetrius] the accountant (*eklogistes*)[4] summoned the ambassadors about the report made to him by [Demetrius] the official in charge of the sanctuaries[5] and [discussed] with them

15 the question of the 'sacred' villages, the Saleioi / of the mountains and the Saleioi of the plains[6] . . . he urged Demetrius not to modify in his administration any of the [previously] existing possessions of the people . . . but to allow them to remain as at [present], and not only did he

20 deliver to the [ambassadors] sent after this / [concerning] the villages just mentioned a [letter] for Demetrius [consonant with] the resolutions (of the people), but he even met [him] and spoke with enthusiasm, as the

25 [ambassadors] who heard him witnessed. And [in general] / he never

ceases to be responsible for some good to the citizens. Be it resolved by the council and people of Apollonia: the praise Philo . . . for his merits and for the goodwill he [constantly] displays towards the people; to grant him [and] / his descendants citizen rights and exemption from all taxes 30 [over which the] city has control;[7] and to invite him every year to [a seat of honour (*proedria*)] and to crown him with a gold crown during the gymnastic competition celebrated in honour of King [Seleucus].

L. and J. Robert, *La Carie* II (Paris, 1954), 285–302, no. 166

1. The decree emanates from Apollonia in Caria, founded (or at least established as a Greek city) by Seleucus I or Antiochus I.
2. Cf. **249**.
3. Cf. **113, 156** n. 5.
4. Cf. **142**.
5. The only known example of this post so far.
6. The point at issue concerned probably the question of revenues from native 'sacred' villages, i.e. villages built around a native sanctuary (cf. **178**).
7. This implies that some of the taxes of the city were controlled by the king; for other examples cf. Rostovtzeff III (1941), 1475 n. 54.

188 Seleucia on the Tigris

[. . .] Here too (sc. in Babylon) is the tomb of Belus, which is now completely in ruins; it is said that Xerxes destroyed it. It was a square-based pyramid of baked brick, a stade (*ca* 175 m) high and each of its sides also measured a stade. Alexander intended to restore it, but it was a great and time-consuming task (merely to clear away the heap of dust would have taken 10,000 men two months), and so the undertaking was not brought to completion; for the king soon fell ill and died, and none of his successors showed any interest. Even what was left of the city was neglected and ruined, partly by the Persians, partly by time, partly by the disdain shown by the Macedonians[1] for these matters, particularly after the foundation by Seleucus (I) Nicator of Seleucia on the Tigris, near Babylon, some 300 stades away (*ca* 52½ km).[2] For he and all the kings after him lavished their attention on this city and transferred their royal capital there.[3] Hence it has now grown larger than Babylon while Babylon is largely deserted, so that one would not hesitate to apply to it the words of a comic poet about Megalopolis in Arcadia: 'Megalopolis (= the great city) is a great desert'.[4] [. . .]

Strabo XVI. 1. 5

1. The Seleucids, frequently referred to by Strabo and other sources as the 'Macedonians' (cf. C. F. Edson, *CP* 53 (1958), 153–70).

2. Cf. **46** ch. 58; exact date uncertain, cf. R. A. Hadley, *Historia* 27 (1978), 228–30.
3. Capital for the eastern part of the empire only; cf. **141**.
4. Contrast **189**; Seleucid policy was clearly ambivalent, cf. also **46** ch. 58. For a view of Seleucia on the Tigris under the Roman empire, cf. Tacitus *Annals* VI.42: 'a powerful city, surrounded by walls, which had not been corrupted by barbarian ways but preserved the spirit of Seleucus its founder. Three hundred citizens chosen for their wealth or wisdom make up its senate, while the people has its share of power.'

189 Antiochus I as king of Babylon

See further: Rostovtzeff I (1941), 435–7; III, 1427f.

I am Antiochus, the great king, the legitimate king, the king of the world, king of Babylon,[1] king of all countries, the caretaker of the temples Esagila and Ezida,[2] the first (born) son of King Seleucus, the Macedonian,[3] king of Babylon.

When I conceived the idea of (re)constructing Esagila and Ezida, I formed with my august hands (when I was still) in the country Hatti[4] the (first) brick for Esagila and Ezida with the finest oil and brought (it with me) for the laying of the foundation of Esagila and Ezida. And in the month of Addaru, the 20th day, the 43rd year,[5] I did lay the foundation of Ezida, the (only) true temple of Nebo which is in Borsippa.

O Nebo, lofty son, (most) wise among the gods, splendid (and) worthy of all praise, first-born son of Marduk, child of Arua, the queen who fashioned all creation, do look friendly (upon me) and may – upon your lofty command which is never revoked – the overthrow of the country of my enemy, the fulfilment of (all) my wishes against my foes, constant predominance, a kingdom (ruled) in justice (to all), an orderly government, years of happiness, enough progeny be your permanent gift to the (joint) kingship of Antiochus and his son,[6] King Seleucus!

When you, Prince Nebo, born in Esagila, first-born of Marduk, child of Arua the queen, enter – under jubilant rejoicings – Ezida, the (only) true temple, the temple (befitting) your position as Anu (i.e. highermost of the gods), the seat which gladdens your heart, may – upon your trusty command which cannot be made void – my days (on earth) be long, my years many, my throne firm, my rule lasting, under your lofty sceptre which determines the borderline between the heaven and the nether world. May (only words of) favour be on your sacred lips with regard to me, and may I personally conquer (all) the countries from sunrise to sunset,[7] gather their tribute and bring it (home) for the perfection of Esagila and Ezida.

O Nebo, foremost son, when you enter Ezida, the (only) true temple, may there be on your lips (words of) favour for Antiochus, the king of all countries, for Seleucus, the king his son (and) for Stratonice, his consort, the queen!

J. B. Pritchard, ed., *Ancient Near Eastern Texts relating to the Old Testament* (Princeton University Press, 3rd ed., 1969), 317

1. The Seleucids, like Alexander before, posed as successors of the ancient Babylonian kings (cf. also **138, 141**). Contrast the style and terminology of this cuneiform inscription with the many Greek texts in this chapter.
2. Cf. **141**; on the Seleucids and native cults cf. **167, 178**.
3. Cf. **188** n. 1.
4. Syria.
5. = March 268.
6. Cf. **138** n. 4.
7. Compare the tone of **221**.

190 Decree of Antioch in Persis on its links with Magnesia on the Maeander (reign of Antiochus III)

(Decree) from the people of Antioch in [Persis]. When Heraclitus son of Zoes was priest of Seleucus (I) Nicator and Antiochus (I) Soter and Antiochus (II) Theos and Seleucus (II) Callinicus and King[1] Seleucus (III) and King Antiochus (III) / and his son King Antiochus,[2] in the first half-year, resolutions of a sovereign meeting of the assembly which were handed in by Asclepiades son of Hecataeus and grandson of Demetrius, the secretary of the council and the assembly, on the third of the waning month of Pantheus. / Resolved by the assembly on the motion of the *prytaneis*. The people of Magnesia on the Maeander are kinsmen and friends of our people and have performed many distinguished services for the Greeks [which] relate [to glory]. Formerly, when Antiochus (I) Soter / was eager to increase our city, as it was called after him, and sent (an embassy) to them about (the sending of) a colony, they passed an honourable and glorious decree, offered a sacrifice and sent a sufficient number of men of great personal excellence, as they were anxious / to help in increasing the people of Antioch.[3] As they were preserving their goodwill towards all the Greeks and wished to make manifest that they are admitting all deserving men to a share in all libations, sacrifices and other religious honours, when an oracle was rendered to them, / they proclaimed it throughout the whole of Greece and celebrated in honour of the patron goddess of their city sacrifices, a religious festival, a truce, and a 'crowned' competition to be held every five years[4] which would

5

10

15

20

25

311

consist of musical, gymnastic and equestrian events, (thereby) repaying
30   just thanks to their benefactress. / They have sent as ambassadors to our
people Demophon son of Lycideus, Philiscus son of Philius and Pheres
son of Pheres, who approached the council and the assembly, handed
over the decree from the people of Magnesia, and after 'renewing' their
35   kinship and friendship (with us) / spoke at length about the apparition of
the goddess and the services provided by the people of Magnesia to many
of the Greek cities, and invited (us) to recognise the 'crowned' competition which they celebrate in honour of Artemis Leucophryene, in
40   accordance with the oracle of the god.5 / The people in its reverence for
the gods we share with the Magnesians, and its wish to augment [its]
goodwill towards its kinsmen, and since [many] other cities have
previously voted [the same decisions] . . . believes it a matter of great
45   importance not [to let] pass [any suitable] opportunity / for displaying
privately [to each individual and] publicly to all the zeal [which] it
continuously displays [for the] interests of the people of Magnesia. With
good fortune, [be it resolved] by the council and the people, to [praise]
50   the people of Magnesia for their piety towards the gods and / for their
friendship and goodwill towards King Antiochus (III) and the people of
Antioch, and because if they make good use of their own advantages and
of the prosperity of the city, they will preserve their ancestral constitution, and (be it resolved) that the priests should pray to all the gods and
goddesses that their [constitution] should forever abide with the people
55   of Magnesia / for their good fortune, and (be it resolved to) recognise
the sacrifice, the religious festival, the [truce, the 'crowned' competition
as 'isopythian'] and the [musical, gymnastic and equestrian competition
which the people of Magnesia] celebrate [in honour of Artemis
60   Leucophryene] / because of the ancestral . . . [. . .]6 [and to send sacred
65   ambassadors] / to Magnesia [who will sacrifice to Artemis]
Leucophryene for the safety [of the king and of both the] cities, and [also]
to give them [journey money from the public treasury] to the amount
[voted] by the people [to be adequate and fitting for the] city [and to
70   appoint the sacred ambassadors in the . . . of the] month of Heraclius /
[when the other political offices] are appointed, and that those [who have
been appointed should be sent] from the [common] hearth [of the people;
and that presents should be given] by the treasurers [from the public
treasury to the] sacred ambassadors who have come [from Magnesia to
75   us, just as they are given] / to [embassies] from [rulers and
cities]. Let the sacred [ambassadors] join in the sacrifice [. . . in honour of
Artemis Leucophryene . . .]. The [citizens] who are victorious [in the
contest of the] Leucophryena shall have the [same honours and privileges
80   from] / the city as exist [for the victors at the Pythian festival according
to the] laws . . . [. . .]7 . . . so that friendship [might remain between]

the [cities for all] time. [A *theorodokos*][8] shall be appointed [by the people]
to receive the [sacred ambassadors who have come from] / the people of   85
Magnesia . . . [. . .][9]

Similar decrees were passed by the people of Seleucia on the Tigris, the
people of Apamea on the Selea, / the people of Seleucia on the Red Sea,   90
the people of Seleucia on the Eulaeus, / the people of Seleucia [on] the   95
. . . the people of [Antioch] on . . . the people of [Alexandria . . .][10]

OGIS 233

1. An incorrect use of the royal title for a dead king, cf. **177** and n. 6.
2. Cf. **138** n. 4.
3. One of the few indications of the origins of the settlers in the Seleucid
   foundations in the east. Note the (implicit) compulsion exercised by the
   king, cf. **40**.
4. Cf. **184** n. 3.
5. On all this cf. **184**. It will be noted that the decree says nothing about the
   recognition of Magnesia as 'holy and inviolate': this was a question of foreign
   policy which only the king could pronounce on (A. Giovannini, in *Ancient
   Macedonia* II (1977), 465–72, esp. 471).
6. Several fragmentary lines.
7. Several fragmentary lines.
8. A person appointed to receive officially the sacred ambassadors (*theoroi*).
9. Several fragmentary lines.
10. These are all Greek cities founded in the eastern part of the empire. On
    Seleucia on the Tigris cf. **188**.

191 The Greek kingdom in Bactria

The history of the Greek kingdom in Bactria, which began in the mid third
century and continued into the first century B.C., has rightly been claimed as
being of equal importance to that of the other Hellenistic kingdoms, yet it still
remains substantially a lost chapter of Hellenistic history. References in the
surviving literary sources are scanty (cf. also **145, 150**), archaeological and
epigraphic evidence is as yet limited compared to the western part of the
Hellenistic world (though cf. **192**), and the most important source of information
remains the coins issued by the Bactrian kings, which are among the finest of all
Greek coins.

See further, for discussion of the frequently obscure details: W. W. Tarn, *The
Greeks in Bactria and India* (Cambridge, 2nd ed., 1951) (very speculative); A. K.
Narain, *The Indo-Greeks* (Oxford, 1957).

Parts of Bactria adjoin Areia to the north, but most of it stretches beyond
it to the east; it is a large country and produces everything except olive
oil. The Greeks who made Bactria independent[1] became so powerful

because of the wealth of the country that they established control over Ariane and India, according to Apollodorus of Artemita (*FGrH* 779 F 7a),[2] and they subdued more peoples than Alexander did, especially Menander[3] (if it is true that he crossed the Hypanis (the Beas) towards the east and advanced as far as the Imaos), the conquests being due partly to himself and partly to Demetrius son of Euthydemus[4] king of the Bactrians. They not only controlled Patalene but also along the rest of the coast the kingdom of Saraostus and Sigerdis as it is called. In sum, says Apollodorus, Bactria is the ornament of the whole of Ariane; what is more, they extended their rule as far as the Seres and Phryni. (2) As to their cities, they possessed Bactria which they also call Zariaspa, through which flows a river of the same name which empties into the Oxus (the Amu-Darya), and Adrapsa and many others; one of these was Eucratidea, called after its ruler. The Greeks who established control of Bactria divided it into satrapies, two of which, those of Aspiones and Tapuria were taken away from Eucratides[5] by the Parthians. They also controlled Sogdiana which lies above Bactria to the east, between the river Oxus, which is the boundary between Bactria and Sogdiana, and the Jaxartes (the Syr-Darya). The latter separates the Sogdians from the nomads.

Strabo XI.11.1–2

1. From the Seleucids.
2. First century B.C., author of a *Parthian History* used and cited several times by Strabo.
3. Ruled *ca* 155–130? (Narain, *op. cit.*, 75–7, 99f.).
4. See **150**.
5. Eucratides I, ruled *ca* 171–155? (Narain, *op. cit.*, 53, 70, 73).

192 Delphic maxims from Ai-Khanoum in Bactria

The interest of this inscription lies not just in its contents (a set of maxims of conventional Delphic wisdom), but in the identity of its author, plausibly identified with the philosopher Clearchus of Soloi, a pupil of Aristotle, and in its place of origin. It is one of the Greek inscriptions found in the excavations of the Greek city at Ai-Khanoum in Bactria on the river Oxus (Amu-Darya), which have begun to reveal the vitality of Hellenism deep in central Asia, and its contacts with the Aegean world several thousand km away (cf. too **191**). The Greek name of the city, founded probably by Alexander or Seleucus I, is still unknown.

See further: P. Bernard, *Proceedings of the British Academy* 53 (1967), 71–95; excavation reports in *CRAI* since 1966; L. Robert, *op. cit.* below.

These wise sayings of men of former times, the words of famous men, are consecrated at holy Pytho;[1] from there Clearchus copied them carefully, to set them up, shining afar, in the precinct of Cineas.

When a child show yourself well behaved; when a young man, self-controlled; in middle age, just; as an old man, a good counsellor; at the end of your life, free from sorrow.[2]

L. Robert, *CRAI* (1968), 416–57

1. Delphi.
2. The original text was much longer.

6 The Attalids of Pergamum

193 An outline of Attalid history

Pergamum exercises a kind of preponderance over these places;[1] it is a famous city and prospered a long time together with the Attalid kings.[2] I must begin my next section here, and show briefly how the kings originated and the end to which they came. Pergamum was the treasury of Lysimachus the son of Agathocles, one of Alexander's successors; the top of the mountain is densely settled with people, while the mountain is conical in shape and ends in a sharp peak. Philetaerus, a man of Tieum, who was a eunuch from childhood,[3] had been entrusted with the custody of this fort and of the money, which amounted to 9,000 talents. [. . .] He was brought up well and proved worthy of this trust. For a while he remained well disposed to Lysimachus, but then quarrelled with Arsinoe his wife, who was slandering him, and so caused the place to revolt and pursued a policy of opportunism, as he saw that circumstances favoured a change. Lysimachus had become embroiled in a domestic crisis and was forced to assassinate his son Agathocles, then Seleucus (I) Nicator intervened and overthrew him but was then overthrown in his turn when Ptolemy Ceraunus treacherously killed him.[4] While such crises were taking place the eunuch remained in charge of the fort, and pursued a policy of making promises to and courting whoever was powerful and at hand. He remained in control of the fort and of the money for twenty years.[5] (2) He had two brothers, the eldest being Eumenes and the youngest Attalus.[6] To Eumenes was born a son called Eumenes like his father, and he took over Pergamum. He was already ruler (*dynastes*) of the places around and so he even defeated in battle near Sardis Antiochus (I) the son of Seleucus (I).[7] He died after ruling for 22 years. Attalus, the son of Attalus and Antiochis, the daughter of Achaeus,[8] then took over power, and was the first (Attalid ruler) to be proclaimed king after defeating the Galatians in a great battle.[9] He became a friend of the Romans and fought on their side against Philip (V) together with the Rhodian fleet.[10] He died an old man after a reign of 43 years,[11] and left behind four sons by Apollonis, a woman from Cyzicus,[12] Eumenes, Attalus, Philetaerus and Athenaeus. The (two) younger sons remained private citizens, while Eumenes the eldest of the others became king. He fought on the side of the Romans against Antiochus (III) the Great and against Perseus, and received from the Romans all the territory within the Taurus which had been under the rule of Antiochus.[13] Previously the territory around Pergamum did not include many places as far as the sea along the gulfs of Elaea and Adramyttium. This ruler embellished the city, planted the Nicephorium with a grove, and it was he who beautified the city with dedications and libraries and increased the settlement of Pergamum to its present size.[14] He reigned for 49 years[15] and left his rule to his son Attalus (III), whose mother was Stratonice, daughter of Ariarathes, king of Cappadocia.[16] He appointed his brother Attalus (II) as guardian of his son, who was very young, and of his empire (*arche*). After a reign of 21 years, Attalus died an old man after achieving many successes; for he helped Alexander (Balas) son of Antiochus (IV) to defeat Demetrius (I) son of Seleucus (IV),[17] and fought on the side of the Romans against the Pseudo-Philip,[18] and marched into Thrace and subdued Diegylis king of the Caeni,[19] and he killed Prusias (II of Bithynia) having incited his son Nicomedes against him,[20] and left the empire to Attalus his ward. The latter reigned five years and was called Philometor; when he died of illness he left the Romans his heirs. They turned the country into a province, giving it the same name as the continent of Asia.[21] [. . .]

Strabo XIII.4.1–2

1. Western Asia Minor as far as the Taurus.
2. On Pergamum under the Attalids see **195**.
3. The fact has been doubted.
4. On these events cf. **45, 46** (end).
5. On Philetaerus' policy cf. **194**.
6. In fact Attalus father of Attalus I must have been nephew and not brother of Philetaerus; cf. Hansen (1971), 26 n. 2.
7. In 262.
8. The elder Achaeus, cf. **142**.
9. Cf. **199** and on the Attalids and the Galatians cf. **194** n. 5.
10. Cf. **198, 200**.
11. 44 years, according to Polybius (cf. **199**).
12. Cf. **204**.
13. Cf. **200**.
14. On the building activity of Eumenes II at Pergamum cf. Hansen (1971), 245–84.
15. A manuscript error for 39 years.
16. On Stratonice cf. **204, 210**(c).
17. In 151/50; cf. **169**.
18. The pretender Andriscus who passed himself off as a son of Perseus and

raised a revolt in Macedon against Rome (149–148), after which Rome turned Macedon into a province.

19. In 145; Diegylis had given support to Andriscus and to Prusias II.
20. In 149.
21. See **211–214**.

194 Gifts of Philetaerus to Cyzicus (280/279 to 276/5)

Public munificence was characteristic of all Hellenistic monarchies (cf. **93** and n. 12) as well as of wealthy private individuals (cf. **97**), and this was true of the Attalids from the start, all the more so as compared with the other monarchies they were an upstart dynasty of doubtful social and political origins (cf. **193**). On Attalid munificence cf. also **198, 203, 206, 207** and generally L. Robert, *Etudes Anatoliennes* (1937), 84–6.

See further: K. M. T. Atkinson, *Antichthon* 2 (1968), 44–9 (speculative), and on Philetaerus' policy McShane (1964), 30–42; Hansen (1971), 14–21.

The following gifts were presented by Philetaerus son of Attalus to the people:[1]

When Gorgippides son of Apollonius was cavalry commander (280/
5   79), for (the celebration of) contests, 20 Alexander talents of silver / and 50 horses for the defence of the territory.

When Bouphantides (was cavalry commander) (279/8), when the land
10   had been ravaged by war,[2] exemption from taxation of the flocks / and of the other things which they sent away (to safety)[3] and of the cattle which they bought and took out of his territory.

When Phoenix (was cavalry commander) (278/7), a force to defend the
15   territory and the expenses incurred for this. /

When Poseidon (was cavalry commander) (277/6), for (the provision of) olive oil and a banquet for the young men (*neoi*),[4] 26 Alexander talents of silver.

When Diomedon (was cavalry commander) (276/5), during the war
20   against the Galatians,[5] / . . . medimni of wheat [. . . and . . .] medimni of [barley . . .]

(the rest of the inscription is fragmentary)

OGIS 748; cf. M. Holleaux, *Etudes* II (Paris, 1938), 1–8

1. Of Cyzicus on the Propontis, a city with close Attalid connexions, cf. **204** n. 1; the city founded a festival in honour of Philetaerus, the *Philetaereia*. Generosities of Philetaerus are also attested at Delos and on the mainland of Greece (Hansen, *op. cit.*, 19).
2. Possibly a war between Antiochus I and Nicomedes of Bithynia (cf. **140**).
3. I.e. to the territory of Philetaerus, who did not tax them; cf. **33**.
4. Cf. **105** n. 3.

5. On the Galatians cf. **140** and for the Attalid struggles against them cf. **193, 197, 199, 205, 208**.

195 Letter of Eumenes I to Pergamum and decree of Pergamum in honour of the generals

See further: Hansen (1971), 23f., 187–203.

(a) Letter of Eumenes

[Eumenes son[1] of Philetaerus to the people[2] of Pergamum, greetings; Palamander, Scymnus, Metrodorus, Theotimus,] Philiscus [the generals (*strategoi*) appointed[3] during the priesthood of . . .] appear [to have discharged] their official duties [well in all circumstances]; for they have justly performed their / [duties and everything else, and] have [not only]   5
administered [all the] revenues of the city and the sacred revenues [in] their period of office in a way that was advantageous to the people and the gods, but have also sought out (debts) passed over by the previous boards of generals, and by not sparing anybody who had kept anything back / they have restored these to the city. They have also cared for the   10
restoration of the sacred dedications, and so by restoring to order the departments mentioned have made it easy for the generals who succeed them to administer the public affairs by following their example. Therefore as we consider it just / not to pass over magistrates who act in   15
this way, so that those appointed after them might try to govern the people properly, we have decided ourselves to crown them at the Panathenaea and we thought we ought to write to you about them, so that you might consider the matter in the meantime and honour them as / you think they deserve. Farewell.   20

RC 23; *OGIS* 267 I

(b) Decree of Pergamum

Resolved by the people; Archestratus son of Hermippus moved:[4] since the generals appointed by Eumenes – Palamander, Scymnus, Metrodorus, Theotimus, Philiscus – have discharged their official duties well, in accordance with Eumenes' instructions, be it resolved by the people / to   25
praise Eumenes, because in all circumstances he shows care for the interests of the people and honours and crowns those citizens who give assistance towards this end, as he wishes to make the officials (*archontes*) who are appointed more zealous to devote care to sacred and civilian affairs. And so that the people / may clearly display to Eumenes their   30
zeal for such men, be it resolved by the people to crown them at the *Panathenaea* with a gold crown for their excellence and their devotion

towards Eumenes and the people. The treasurers who are in office shall
35 give to them every year at the *Eumeneia*[5] a sheep, which they / shall take
and sacrifice to Eumenes the benefactor, so that the people might be seen
by all to be showing its gratitude. The letter from Eumenes and the
decree shall be inscribed on a stone stele and placed in the agora, and the
treasurers (in office) in the priesthood of Arkeon shall provide the money
for the stele and the inscription.

OGIS 267 II

1. Adopted son, cf. **193**.
2. Addressed to the people only, not to the magistrates and council as well.
3. On the generals of Pergamum cf. also **211, 216**; they were appointed directly
   by the Attalids, not elected by the people, had wide supervisory powers over
   government and administration and the exclusive right of introducing
   measures to the assembly, except when the Attalid ruler gave a direct personal
   recommendation, as in this case. On Pergamum and the Attalids cf. too **193,
   197, 210**(c). Compare Seleucid relations with Seleucia, **176**.
4. A private citizen acting on Eumenes' advice.
5. An annual festival in honour of Eumenes.

196 Agreement between Eumenes I and his mercenaries, with reciprocal oaths (263–241)

The following inscription records a settlement between Eumenes I and his
mercenary troops at Philetaerea and Attalea after a mutiny (precise circumstances
unknown); the inscription gives valuable evidence of the conditions of service of
mercenaries (cf. **33**), though the interpretation of several clauses is controversial.

See further: Griffith (1935), 172f., 282–8, 312f. and generally 171–82 on Attalid
armies; Launey II (1950), 738–46; Hansen (1971), 22f., 231f.

The demands which Eumenes (I) son[1] of Philetaerus granted [to the]
soldiers [at] Philetaerea and those at Attalea:

(1) (Eumenes *or* the soldiers) will pay as the price of corn 4 drachmas a
medimnus, (and) as the price of wine 4 drachmas a *metretes*.[2]

5 (2) Concerning the / campaigning year: it will last a period of ten
months, and (Eumenes) will not introduce an intercalary month.[3]

(3) Concerning those who have fulfilled the regular number (of
months or years?) and have become idle (or: unfit for service?): they shall
receive pay for the period of time previously worked.[4]

(4) Concerning the money for the orphans (or: the rights of orphans):[5]
the next of kin shall receive (it *or* them) or anyone to whom (the soldier)
leaves (it *or* them by will).

10 (5) Concerning the taxes: / the freedom from taxation (granted) in the

320

44th year[6] shall apply; if any soldier becomes idle or seeks discharge, he shall be released and may take his belongings out of the country tax-free.

(6) Concerning the pay which (Eumenes) agreed to pay for the period of four months:[7] [the] pay agreed shall be given and shall not be reckoned as part of the (normal) pay.

(7) Concerning the soldiers decorated with crowns:[8] / they shall   15
receive their grain ration for the same period that they are awarded the crown.

The oath and the agreement are to be inscribed on four stone stelae, one of these shall be dedicated at Pergamum in the sanctuary of Athena,[9] another at Gryneum, another at Delos, and another at Mytilene in the sanctuary of Asclepius.

Oath sworn by Paramonus and the / officers and the soldiers under   20
their command at Philetaerea under Mt Ida, and Polylaus and the officers under his command and the soldiers at Attalea, and Attinas <the> hipparch and the cavalry under his command and Homoloichus and the Trallians[10] under his command:

I swear[11] by Zeus, the Earth, the Sun, Poseidon, Demeter, Ares, Athena Areia, the Tauropolus, / and all the gods and goddesses. I am   25
fully reconciled with Eumenes son of Philetaerus and I shall be well disposed to him and [to his] descendants and I shall not conspire against Eumenes son of Philetaerus nor shall I bear arms [against him, nor] shall I desert Eumenes, but I shall fight [for] him and his interests[12] and sacrifice my life for him.[13] / And I shall perform all other services with goodwill   30
and without hesitation, with all enthusiasm as far as I am able. If I discover anyone conspiring against Eumenes son of Philetaerus [or] acting [in any] way against him or his interests, I will [not] endure this, but I shall denounce at / [once] or as soon as I am able the person who   35
does any of these things to [Eumenes] the son of Philetaerus or to anyone I think [will reveal] the matter to him most quickly. I shall guard anything I receive from him, whether a city or a [fort or] ships or money or anything else which is handed to me, and I shall restore it correctly [and] justly to Eumenes son of Philetaerus or to anyone he orders, so long as [he] carries out / the terms of the agreement. I shall not accept   40
from the enemy any letters and shall not receive any ambassadors nor shall I send any to them.[14] If anyone brings (letters) to me, I shall take the letters sealed up, and deliver their bearers to Eumenes son of Philetaerus as quickly as possible, or shall take and deliver them to anyone I think will reveal the matter to him most quickly. / I shall not   45
distort this oath in any way or by any means. I release Eumenes son of Attalus[15] and those who have sworn with him from the oath once the terms of the agreement have been carried out. If I abide by the oath and maintain my goodwill towards Eumenes son of Philetaerus may I and

50 my descendants prosper, / but if I break the oath and violate any of the terms of the agreement, [may] I and my family perish.

Oath of Eumenes: I swear [by Zeus, the Earth,] the Sun, Poseidon, Apollo, Demeter, Ares, Athena Areia, the [Tauropolus] and all the other gods and goddesses. I shall be well disposed to Paramonus, the officers,

55 and the other mercenaries in the *strategia*[16] / of Philetaerea under Mt Ida who are under the orders of Paramonus, and to Arces and the guards under his command and to Philonides, and to the unpaid troops[17] who have sworn with them, to all these and to those who belong to them, and to Polylaus, the officers and all the other soldiers under his command [in]

60 Attalea, the infantry, cavalry and the Trallians, for as long as / they serve [with] us, and I shall not conspire (against them) nor shall [anyone] (conspire) through me. And I shall not betray them nor [any] of their possessions to any enemy, [nor (shall I betray) those who command?] them nor those appointed by their assembly (*koinon*) in [any] way [or by any means], nor shall I take up [arms] against them nor . . .

(the rest of the inscription is lost)

OGIS 266; *Staatsv.* III.481

1. Cf. **195** n. 1.
2. Either Eumenes is substituting money payments for rations, or the price soldiers pay for rations is being fixed. The prices mentioned for corn and wine are substantially lower than those attested elsewhere at this period.
3. Cf. **120** n. 7.
4. It is not clear whether this refers to a period of *months* or *years* of service; the clause may therefore concern either pensions for veterans or simply regular annual pay paid in arrears.
5. It is not clear whether this refers to a fund for orphans or to the guardianship of orphans. By protecting the orphans of soldiers Eumenes may have had in mind the future recruitment of troops.
6. 269/8, if this refers to the Seleucid era (the Attalids had not yet officially broken with the Seleucids); circumstances unknown.
7. Probably the period of the mutiny.
8. Literally 'crowns of white poplar'; the reference is probably to bonuses for distinguished service.
9. The present text.
10. Thracian mercenaries; cf. **269** l. 13.
11. See **33** n. 7.
12. See **139** n. 3.
13. Literally: 'and I shall fight as far as life and death'.
14. A possible indication of Seleucid involvement in the rebellion.
15. A cousin of Eumenes, not mentioned in the extant literary tradition (cf. **193**), and somehow compromised with the mutineers.
16. A military unit.

17. Probably a body of irregular troops not party to the oath of the regular troops which precedes.

197 Dedications by Attalus I to Athena at Pergamum for victories in battle (*ca* 238–227?)

See further: E. J. Bickerman, *Berytus* 8 (1943–4), 76–8; Magie II (1950), 737–9; Hansen (1971), 34–8, 242f., 302; McShane (1964), 59–61.

King[1] Attalus (dedicates) to Athena[2] (these) thank-offerings for battles waged in war:[3]

[From the] battle [in] Phrygia on the [Hellespont against] Antiochus (sc. Hierax).[4]

[From the] battle [near the] Aphrodision[5] against the Tolistoagian [and Tectosagian] Galatians[6] and Antiochus (Hierax).

From the battle near the springs of the river Caicus against the Tolistoagian Galatians.

From the battle near [. . . against] Lysias[7] and the [generals of Seleucus (III)].

[From the] battle [near Coloe against Antiochus (Hierax)].

[From the battle on the Harpasus in] Caria [against Antiochus (Hierax)].[8]

OGIS 273–279

1. Attalus was the first Attalid to assume the royal title, cf. **193, 199**.
2. Not called '*Nicephorus*'; the institution of the *Nicephoria* of Pergamum dates from the late 220s. On them and on their reorganisation in 182/1 cf. **204** n. 2, **209** n. 8, **210**(c) and C. P. Jones, *Chiron* 4 (1974), 184–9.
3. The exact sequence and chronology of these battles is conjectural; the monument itself dates from the years 226–223.
4. On Antiochus Hierax cf. **113, 144, 145**, cf. **199** n. 7; Hierax relied initially on the alliance of the Galatians. Note that Attalus refuses the royal title to his Seleucid rivals.
5. Just outside the city wall of Pergamum.
6. On the Galatians see **140, 194** n. 5.
7. Probably an independent dynast in Asia Minor, cf. **182** n. 6.
8. On the subsequent struggles between Attalus I and the Seleucids see **146, 147, 151**.

198 The visit of Attalus I to Athens (200)

The people of Athens sent ambassadors to King Attalus[1] to thank him for what had happened and at the same time to urge him to come to Athens to examine with them the present situation. A few days later the king, on hearing that Roman ambassadors had sailed into Piraeus,[2] and believing it to be imperative to have a meeting with them, put to sea in haste. The people of Athens, being informed of his presence, passed generous resolutions about the reception and general entertainment of the king.[3] Attalus then sailed into Piraeus; the first day he spent in negotiations with the ambassadors from Rome, and he was extremely pleased to see them recalling their former partnership in arms and being ready for the war against Philip.[4] Next morning he went up to the city in great pomp, accompanied by the Romans and the Athenian magistrates; for they were met not only by the magistrates together with the knights, but by all the citizens with their children and wives. And when they came together there was such a display of friendliness on the part of the crowd towards the Romans and still more towards Attalus that it could not have been exceeded. When he entered by the Dipylon Gate they placed the priestesses and priests on each side (of the street). They then opened all the temples, placed victims at all the altars and asked him to offer sacrifice. Finally they voted him honours greater than they had readily bestowed on any of their previous benefactors; for in addition to other distinctions they called a tribe after Attalus[5] and enrolled him among the eponymous tribal heroes. (26) They next summoned a meeting of the assembly and invited the king to speak, but when he declined and said it would be in bad taste to come before them and recount his benefactions to those who had received them, they ceased to demand his presence but asked him to state in writing what he thought to be the best course of action in the present circumstances. Attalus agreed and wrote a letter which the presiding magistrates presented to the assembly. The main points of his letter were as follows: he recalled his former benefactions to the people, enumerated his actions against Philip (V) during the present crisis, and finally urged them to take part in the war against Philip and solemnly declared that if they did not choose now to join resolutely the Rhodians, the Romans and himself in a policy of hostility, but threw away the opportunity and then wished to share in the peace which others had brought about, they would be failing to achieve the interests of their country. After this letter had been read out the people was ready to vote for war, both on account of Attalus' words and because of their goodwill towards him. And when the Rhodians came before them and spoke at great length on the same theme, the Athenians resolved to go to war against Philip.[6] [. . .]

Polybius XVI.25–26

1. In Aegina at the time (cf. **209** n. 1 for the Attalids and Aegina); Attalus and the Rhodians had assisted Athens against the attacks of Philip V (cf. **65** n. 2).

2. The purpose of this embassy is variously described in the sources; see J. P. V. D. Balsdon, *JRS* 44 (1954), 39–41.
3. Compare the reception of Demetrius over a century earlier, **34**.
4. In fact the formal decision for war had probably not yet been passed by the *comitia* in Rome.
5. Cf. **34** (end); the Athenians had recently abolished the tribes Antigonis and Demetrias created in 307.
6. For Athens' reaction to Philip V see **66**.

199 Portrait of Attalus I on his death (197)

Concerning King Attalus (I), who died at this time,[1] it is right that I should say something appropriate, as has been my practice with others.[2] Originally he had no other external advantages for royalty except wealth,[3] which when used with intelligence and boldness is indeed of great assistance in any undertaking, but without these qualities is usually the cause of disaster for most people and in fact of total ruin. [. . .] That is why one ought to admire this man's greatness of spirit, because he never sought to use his advantages for anything except the acquisition of royalty, and no greater or fairer goal can be mentioned than that. Moreover he took the first step in achieving this design not just by conferring benefactions and favours on his friends,[4] but also by achievements in war.[5] For it was by defeating the Galatians in battle,[6] the most violent and warlike people in Asia at the time, that he secured his position and first assumed the royal title.[7] And though he achieved this honour, and lived 72 years, 44 of these as king,[8] he lived a life of the utmost decency and respectability with his wife and children,[9] and preserved good faith with all his allies and friends, and died in the midst of a most glorious campaign, while fighting for the freedom of the Greeks.[10] Most of all, although he left four grown-up sons,[11] he had so secured his rule that the kingdom was handed down to his grandchildren without any disturbance.[12]

Polybius XVIII.41

1. Attalus I was taken ill at Thebes in spring 197 and died after being brought back to Pergamum.
2. For other royal portraits cf. **56**(a), **163, 204, 207, 223**; see also Eumenes II's eulogy of his predecessor, **200**.
3. Polybius does not mention here the work of Attalus' predecessors Philetaerus and Eumenes I (cf. **193**).
4. Cf. **25** n. 3, **207**.
5. Cf. **36**.
6. See **194** and n. 5.

7. Cf. **193**; it has however been suggested that it was Attalus' defeat of Antiochus Hierax (cf. **197**) rather than of the Galatians which provided the justification for his assumption of royalty (E. J. Bickerman, *Berytus* 8 (1943–4), 76–8).

8. Born 269 or 268, succeeded Eumenes I in 241.

9. On the family loyalty of the Attalids, which was in pointed contrast to dynastic conflicts of the Seleucids (see esp. **144, 145, 169–173, 220**) and Ptolemies (see **228–231**), see **204**.

10. On this theme cf. **29**, and for the Attalids as self-proclaimed champions of the Greeks cf. especially **194, 197, 203, 207**.

11. See **162, 193, 204**.

12. This refers to Attalus III, the last Attalid king, cf. **211–214**.

200 Eumenes II and the Rhodians at Rome (189)

At the beginning of summer following the Roman victory over Antiochus (III)[1] there arrived (in Rome) King Eumenes (II), the envoys from Antiochus and from the Rhodians, as well as those from the other states. For immediately after the battle nearly all the states in Asia began sending ambassadors to Rome, because at that time all hopes for the future for everybody lay with the Senate. The Senate gave a gracious welcome to all who arrived, but the most splendid reception both in the escort sent out to greet him and in the gifts provided for his stay was granted to Eumenes, and after him to the Rhodians. When the time for the audience came, they invited the king first and asked him to declare freely what he wanted to obtain from the Senate.[2] [. . .] (19) He said therefore that he would not say anything further about his own concerns, but would keep <to his view> and leave the decision entirely to them; but there was one point which worried him about the Rhodians, and it was this which prompted him to speak about the present situation. They had come to defend the interests of their country with no less eagerness than he himself wished to promote his own kingdom in the present circumstances; but their words gave an impression quite different from their real purpose, and this was easy to discover. 'When they enter they will say that they have come not to request anything from you nor with the wish of harming me in any way, but are ambassadors for the freedom of the Greeks who live in Asia. They will say that this is not so much a favour to them as a duty which is incumbent on you and which follows from what has already been achieved.[3] Such will be the impression their words seek to convey, but their true intentions will be shown to be the exact opposite. For if the cities are set free, as they urge, their power will be increased many times over, while my own will in a way be destroyed. For the name of freedom and autonomy would completely draw away from my rule not only those who are to be freed now but even those previously subject to me, when it will be clear that you are pursuing this policy, and it will bring them all over to the side of the Rhodians.' [. . .] (20) 'As for me', he continued, 'though on every other matter I would, if necessary, be prepared to yield without argument to my neighbours, as far as your friendship and my goodwill towards you are concerned I will never, so far as I can, yield to anyone alive. I imagine that my father[4] if he were alive, would have said the same. For he was the first of nearly all the peoples of Asia and Greece to become your friend and ally,[5] and he preserved that friendship most nobly till his last day, not only in intention but in actual deeds. He took part in every one of your wars in Greece and provided the highest number of infantry and naval forces of all your other allies, contributed the largest amount of supplies and faced the greatest dangers, and finally ended his life while actively involved in the war against Philip (V), as he was urging the Boeotians to join your friendship and alliance. When I took over the kingdom, I maintained my father's policy – it was not possible to take it any further – but I surpassed him in what I did. Circumstances brought me to a more burning test than happened in his case. Antiochus (III) was anxious to offer me his daughter in marriage and to bind together (our kingdom) through ties of blood;[6] he offered to hand over at once the cities which had previously been detached from me;[7] he then promised to do everything if I took part in the war against you. Yet far from accepting any of these offers I fought on your side against Antiochus with the largest number of infantry and naval forces of all your other allies, I contributed the largest share of supplies to meet your needs in the most critical circumstances, and I exposed myself without hesitation to all dangers together with your commanders. Finally I submitted to being cut off and besieged in Pergamum itself, and risked my life and my kingdom because of my goodwill towards your people. (21) [. . .] What then am I asking for, and what do I claim to obtain from you? I will tell you frankly, since you have invited me to speak my mind to you. Should you decide yourselves to continue holding certain parts of Asia this side of Mt Taurus, which were previously subject to Antiochus, this is what I would most wish to see happening; for I believe the best guarantee of safety for my kingdom would be for me to have you as neighbours and especially to share in your power. But should you decide not to do this but to evacuate Asia completely, there is no one to whom you could yield more justly the prizes won in the war than to me. It may be objected that it is more honourable to free those who are enslaved. Yes, if only they had not dared to fight with Antiochus against you, and since they submitted to do this it is much more honourable to show proper gratitude to your true friends than to do a benefaction to those who have been your enemies.'

(22) After making this effective speech, Eumenes withdrew; the Senate was favourably impressed by the king and what he had said and was anxious to favour him in every possible way. [. . .] After them[8] the Rhodians entered, and after a few brief words (of introduction) about their particular services to the Romans, they quickly went on to speak about their own country. It was a very unfortunate accident, they said, that in their embassy the nature of the problem should place them in opposition to a king with whom they had the friendliest relations in public and in private. It was the belief of their country that the most honourable course of action and the one most appropriate for the Romans was that the Greeks in Asia should be liberated and obtain their autonomy, mankind's most prized possession; but this was least in the interest of Eumenes and his brothers. For it was the nature of monarchy to hate equality and to seek to reduce all, or at least the majority, to the status of obedient subjects.[9] Yet though this was the case, they were confident, they said, of achieving their objective, not because they had more influence with the Romans than Eumenes, but because their suggestions were clearly more just and obviously of greater advantage to all. If it was not possible for the Romans to repay Eumenes except by handing over to him the autonomous cities, they might well be at a loss in the present circumstances: they would either have to slight a true friend or to neglect their own honour and duty and so to obscure and nullify the purpose of their own actions. But if it were possible to cater adequately for both alternatives, who could be in any further doubt about the matter? In fact, as at a lavish banquet, there was enough and to spare for everybody.[10] [. . .] (23) It was open to the Romans, therefore, to strengthen their friends substantially without forfeiting the glory of their own policy. Their purpose in war was different from that of other men; all other people went to war with the intention of conquering and seizing cities, supplies, and ships, but the gods had freed the Romans from the desire for these, by placing the whole world under their power. [. . .] Therefore, the most splendid of all their achievements was the liberation of Greece; if they now brought that work to completion, their fame would reach its height, but if they neglected to do so, even their previous achievements would be clearly diminished.[11] [. . .]

Polybius XXI. 18–23 (with omissions)

1. At the battle of Magnesia, cf. **160**.
2. The authenticity of the arguments attributed by Polybius to Eumenes and to the Rhodians is doubted by some (cf. McShane (1964), 149f.).
3. On the issue of the 'freedom of the Greeks' cf. esp. **29**, and for Roman use of the theme cf. **68** n. 2.
4. Attalus I, on whose policy cf. too **193, 198, 199**.

5. It is not certain whether there was any formal treaty of alliance.
6. *Ca* 193–191.
7. See **151, 153, 154**.
8. A delegation from Smyrna.
9. With this view of Attalid relations with the Greek cities contrast esp. **199, 203, 207**.
10. On the 'empire' of Rhodes see **80**.
11. For the Peace of Apamea which followed see **161, 201** n. 3, **202** n. 2. **215** n. 3.

201 Decree of Apollonia on the Rhyndacus (?) in honour of an Attalid governor (post 188?)

See further: Hansen (1971), 108f.; Walbank III (1979), 527f.

Resolved by the council and the people;[1] Menemachus son of Archelaus moved: since Corragus son of Aristomachus, the Macedonian,[2] when he was appointed general (*strategos*) of the regions (*topoi*) about the Hellespont,[3] continuously applied all his / enthusiasm and goodwill to the improvement of the people's condition and made himself serviceable both publicly and in private to all the citizens who had dealings with him, and when he took over[4] the city he requested from the king[5] the restoration of our laws, / the ancestral constitution, the sacred precincts,[6] the funds for cult expenses and the administration of the city,[7] the oil for the young men (*neoi*)[8] and everything else which originally belonged to the people,[9] and as the citizens were destitute because of the war,[10] he supplied at his own expense / cattle and other victims for the public sacrifices and after mentioning the matter to the king he secured the provision of corn for sowing and for food, and he enthusiastically assisted (the king) in preserving the private property of each of the citizens / and in providing those who had none with some from the royal treasury, and as exemption from all taxes had been granted by the king for three years,[11] he secured a further exemption for two years, wishing to restore the citizens to a state of prosperity and increase, / acting in conformity with the king's policy; so that the people may be seen to be rendering adequate thanks to its benefactors, be it resolved by the people, [to praise] Corragus the general and [to crown him] with a gold [crown . . .][12]

   M. Holleaux, *Etudes* II (Paris, 1938), 73–125 (*SEG* 11.663)

1. City unknown, perhaps Apollonia on the Rhyndacus.
2. Note the emphasis on Macedonian descent; Corragus may be identical with the Attalid officer mentioned in Livy XXXVIII.13.3 (in 189) and XLII.67.3 (in 171).

3. The technical administrative designation for Hellespontine Phrygia, added from the Seleucid to the Attalid kingdom by the Peace of Apamea (see **161, 200**), previously under the Seleucids designated as a satrapy (cf. **180**(b)).
4. Probably simply as governor, not through capture in war.
5. Probably Eumenes II or Attalus II.
6. Confiscated by the king.
7. Apparently the king had been providing subsidies to the city.
8. Cf. **105** n. 3, **118**.
9. Although the inscription does not say so, these requests will probably have been granted.
10. Probably the war against Antiochus III (cf. **200**), though possibly one of the wars between the Attalids and their neighbours in Asia Minor (Bithynia, the Galatians).
11. A normal period for tax exemptions, cf. **40A** §9, **167** §143, **202**.
12. For other texts on Attalid governors and administration see **202, 205, 209**.

202 Letter of Eumenes II to an official concerning remission of taxes (181)

See further: Rostovtzeff II (1941), 645–8 and III, 1477 n. 61; Hansen (1971), 184f.; Walbank III (1979), 173f.

King Eumenes (II) to Artemidorus.[1] I have read the comments you appended to the petition submitted by the settlers in the village of the
5 Cardaces.[2] Since after investigating you find / that their private affairs are in a weak condition, as their trees are not yielding much fruit and their land is of poor quality, give instructions that they may keep the piece of land they bought from Ptolemy[3] and the price they did not pay because most of them have no resources left, and (give instructions) not
10 to exact the money: / and since they must pay for each adult person a poll-tax (*syntaxis*)[4] of four Rhodian drachmas and an obol, but the weak condition of their private affairs makes this a burden to them, (give instructions) to exempt them from the arrears (of this tax) for the sixteenth year (= 182/1), and of one Rhodian drachma and one obol[5]
15 from the seventeenth year (= 181/80); and for all those / whom they (i.e. the Cardaces) introduce[6] from the outside,[7] (give instructions) that they be granted exemption from all taxes for three years,[8] and for those who have previously left the area (*topos*) but now wish to return, exemption for two years; and (give instructions) that they may repair the fort they previously had, so as to have a stronghold, so long as they
20 [provide] themselves the rest of the expenditure, / while I myself will

330

pay for a skilled craftsman (*technites*).⁹ (Year) 17, the 4th day from the end
of (the month of) Dius.

M. Segre, *Clara Rhodos* IX (Rhodes, 1938), 190–207;
F. G. Maier, *Griechische Mauerbauinschriften*
I (Heidelberg, 1959), no. 76

1. The Attalid governor of the region of Telmessus in Lycia.
2. Barbarian mercenaries (cf. **149** at Raphia), probably settled in the region of
   Telmessus by Antiochus III after his conquest of the area from the dynast (cf.
   182 n. 6) Ptolemy son of Lysimachus (cf. **158** n. 8 and esp. **271**; F. W.
   Walbank, *loc. cit.* above and II (1967), 481). Compare the settlement of Jews in
   Lydia (**167**). After the Peace of Apamea (**161, 200** n. 11), Telmessus was
   attributed by the Romans to Eumenes II.
3. Perhaps the grandson of Ptolemy son of Lysimachus (previous note).
4. Cf. **167** n. 3; possibly imposed by Eumenes in 182/1.
5. Translation uncertain; it is not clear whether the poll-tax is being reduced *by* 1
   dr. 1 ob. or *to* 1 dr. 1 ob.
6. As settlers; cf. Antiochus III and the repeopling of Jerusalem, **167**.
7. From outside the kingdom of Eumenes.
8. Cf. **201** n. 11.
9. For the provision of workmen by kings cf. **93**.

203 Letter of Eumenes II to the Ionian League (winter 167/6)

Although Eumenes II had consistently followed his father Attalus' pro-Roman
policy (cf. **75, 76, 200**), the growth of Attalid power resulting from the Peace of
Apamea (cf. **161**) lead to increasing Roman suspicion of Eumenes and attempts to
undermine his kingdom in Asia Minor (cf. too **208**). But, as Polybius noted
(XXXI.6.6, in 163), Rome's hostility towards Eumenes increased his popularity in
the Greek world, as shown for instance by the following decree of the Ionian
League passed shortly after the Senate had insulted Eumenes by refusing him
admission to Italy.

See further: Badian (1958), 98–100, 102–5, 294f.; McShane (1964), 177–86;
Walbank III (1979), 415f.

King [Eumenes (II) to the League of Ionians,¹ greetings]; of the ambassadors sent by you Menecles did not come before me,² but Irenias and
Archelaus met me at Delos and handed over / a fine and generous   5
decree, in which you began by stating that I had chosen from the start the
finest deeds and showed myself the common benefactor of the Greeks,³
that I had faced many great battles against the / barbarians,⁴ displaying   10
all zeal and care to make sure that the inhabitants of the Greek cities
should always live in peace and enjoy the best state of affairs, receiving
[glory] in exchange [for] the [attendant] danger and [hardship, / and]   15

choosing to [stand firm in] what [concerned the] League, in conformity
with the policy of my father, (and that) I had demonstrated on many
occasions my attitude in these matters, both in public and in private,
being well disposed to each of the cities and helping each of them to
20   achieve many of the things that relate to distinction / and glory, which
through my actions [demonstrated?] my love of glory and the gratitude
of the League. And you passed a resolution, in order that you might
25   always be seen to be repaying worthy honours to your benefactors, / to
crown me with a gold crown for valour, and to set up a golden statue in
any place in Ionia I wished, and to proclaim these honours both in the
competitions you celebrate and in those celebrated in each of the
30   cities, / [and to convey to me the greetings] of the League, [and to rejoice
in the fact] that both I [and] my advisers[5] are in good [health and that] my
interests[6] [are] in a satisfactory state, and to urge [me when seeing] the
gratitude of the people to show [proper] care for ways of [increasing the
35   prosperity] of the League of [Ionians] / and ensuring that it constantly
enjoys the [best condition]; in this way and in future I [would obtain
everything] that relates to honour and glory. [And in conformity with
all] the detailed provisions (of the decree) your [ambassadors] spoke
[with] great enthusiasm, [relating] the [great] eagerness [and] purity of
40   the goodwill felt by the whole / people towards me. I [accept graciously]
the honours (voted) and having never failed so far as lies [in my] power
to secure some [glory and honour] both [to all in common] and to every
45   individual in each city, / I shall try now not to depart from this purpose.
May events turn out as I wish, for in this way my actions themselves will
50   demonstrate my policy more convincingly to you. / And so that in
future by celebrating a day in my name at the festival of the Panionia you
might make the whole festival more distinguished, I shall assign to you
55   sufficient sources of revenue / which will enable you to [celebrate] my
memory in a fitting way. As to the gold statue [I shall make it] myself,
since I wish [the] favour [not to cost anything] to the [League.[7] I wish] it
60   to be consecrated [in the] sacred [enclosure] which has been voted / to
me by the Milesians. For since you were celebrating the festival in that
city when you voted the honour to me, and Miletus is the only Ionian
65   city to date to have dedicated a sacred enclosure to me, / and regards
itself as related to me on account of the people of Cyzicus,[8] and has
performed many famous and memorable actions on behalf of the
Ionians, I thought it most suitable that the dedication (of the statue)
should be made there. As to a detailed statement of my goodwill towards
70   all of you together / and towards each city, your ambassadors have
heard me and will report to you. Farewell.[9]

RC 52; *OGIS* 763; M. Holleaux, *Etudes* II
(Paris, 1938), 153–78

1. See **143** n. 4.
2. The reason for this is unknown.
3. On this Attalid posture cf. **199** n. 10; on 'benefactors' cf. generally **93** and n. 12, **97**.
4. The Galatians, cf. **194** n. 5. They had started a new war against the Attalids in 168, received indirect encouragement from Rome in 167, and though defeated in 166 were granted their autonomy by the Senate. Cf. further **208**.
5. Literally 'relatives'.
6. Cf. **139** n. 3.
7. For Attalid financing of honours to themselves cf. **206**.
8. See **204** n. 1.
9. For honours paid by Greek cities to the Attalids see **209** n. 7.

204 Decree of Hierapolis in honour of Apollonis, wife of Attalus I (*ca* 167–159)

See further: Hansen (1971), 44f., 100, 455f.; Walbank III (1979), 211f.

Decision of the generals Apollonius son of Matron, Apollonius son of Hermogenes, Apollonides son of Phalangites: since Queen Apollonis[1] Eusebes (the pious), wife of King Attalus (I) the god and mother of King Eumenes (II) Soter (the saviour),[2] has departed to the gods,[3] after displaying in a glorious / and fitting way among men her own virtue,   5 because of her piety towards the gods[4] and her reverence towards her parents, [just as] her life with her husband was distinguished and she consorted with her children in (a spirit of) complete harmony, and being blessed with beautiful children born in wedlock she left behind great sources of praise of her glory / having earned conspicuous gratitude   10 from her children; and so having displayed in her life everything that relates [to honour] and glory, she has lived a distinguished and fitting life, having reared children with the help of fortune and having consorted nobly with King Eumenes Soter and Attalus Philadelphus and Philetaerus / and Athenaeus, and left no small proof of her piety   15 towards the gods by a [most] magnificent deed, and left a most beautiful and praiseworthy [sign] of her own excellence in her harmonious relations with her children, and [always behaved] with goodwill in all circumstances towards Queen Stratonice[5] [wife] of King Eumenes [Soter], / believing that the woman who shared her son (also) [shared] in   20 her own [affection]; and so submitting to . . . she achieved immortal honour . . . to all the Greeks [and especially to King] Eumenes Soter and her [other children . . .]

OGIS 308

333

1. A woman from Cyzicus, a city with close Attalid connexions, cf. **193, 194, 203, 210**; on her cf. also **123, 162**, and on the Attalids as a 'model family' cf. **193, 199, 207, 210**. Compare Antiochus III and Laodice, **158**.

2. Eumenes II assumed this title not later than December 184 for a victory over Prusias of Bithynia and the Galatians in the war of 186–183. This provided the occasion for the reorganisation of the *Nicephoria* (**197** n. 2).

3. A regular formula to describe the death of rulers, cf. **211, 215** l. 16; the exact date of Apollonis' death is uncertain.

4. Cf. **163** n. 4.

5. Cf. **193, 210**(c).

205 Letter of Attalus (future II) to Amlada in Pisidia (ca 160)

See further: Hansen (1971), 203, 206f.

Attalus[1] to the city and elders of Amlada,[2] greetings. Your envoys Oprasates son of Cila . . . nus, Nalagloas son of Cilarius, and Menneas[3] came before [us] and spoke about the object of the mission you entrusted
5   to them, and requested / that your hostages should be released and that we relieve you of the debt of 9,000 drachmas you incurred in the war against the Galatians[4] [for the purpose of] repairs[5] and of the 2 talents which you pay annually, since you are hard pressed in many ways and are [at present] in a weak condition. Therefore as I saw that you had
10   repented of your / former errors and that you were carrying out my instructions zealously, [I showed] care for you [and] as a favour to Oprasates and to the [city, I gave] instructions to exempt you from 3,000 drachmas of the tribute (*phoros*) and the [payment] (*telesma*), and of the
15   other 9,000 drachmas [which] / you owed to us [in addition]. And I have freed your hostages . . .
(the rest of the inscription is lost)

RC 54; *OGIS* 751

1. The future King Attalus II, brother and collaborator of Eumenes II.
2. A Pisidian city, only partially hellenised, as shown by the non-Greek names and the absence of the normal institutions of the council and the people.
3. The only Greek name, possibly a second name of Nalagloas.
4. Amlada had revolted against the Attalids in the Galatian war of 168–166, cf. **203** n. 4.
5. Allusion unclear.

206 A foundation by Attalus II at Delphi (160/159)

See further: Hansen (1971), 292–5, 395, 459f.

Resolved by the city of Delphi in a plenary assembly and with the legal number of votes: since King Attalus (II)[1] son of King Attalus (I), when we sent as envoys to him previously Praxias son of Eudocus and Callias son of Emmenidas concerning the education of the children, and a second time Praxias son of Eudocus / (and) Bacchius son of Agron,[2] and he is our friend by ancestral tradition and well disposed to our city, and shows a pious and holy disposition towards the gods,[3] he listened favourably to our requests and sent to the city 18,000 Alexander drachmas of silver for the education of the children[4] and 3,000 drachmas for the honours and sacrifices,[5] so that his donation might remain / in perpetuity and the salaries of the teachers might be regularly paid and the expense for the honours and the sacrifices might be provided from the interest on the loan of the money;[6] with good fortune, be it resolved by the city, that the money should be consecrated to the god and that it should not be allowed to any magistrate or any private individual to use (this money) for any other purpose and in any way, / whether by a decree or by a resolution;[7] if anyone whether a magistrate or a private individual does any of these things, he shall be prosecuted by the *mastroi*[8] for stealing sacred money, and the *mastroi* shall register him for recovery of eight times the sum of money involved in the decree or otherwise transferred, and the decree or resolution shall be null and void; any surplus left over from the interest after the salaries have been paid / to the teachers as is laid down shall be brought to the *probouloi*[9] and the people and the resolution passed shall be final. The three commissioners appointed by the people shall lend the money at a rate of interest of 1 in 15 (= 6.66%) in the month of Amalius (= January) in the archonship of Amphistratus; those who wish to borrow money shall register their names with the commissioners who are appointed / and provide a field as security;[10] loans shall be of a minimum of 5 minas; the borrowers shall provide sureties approved by the commissioners; the same persons shall be sureties and guarantors of the securities provided; when (the commissioners) have lent (the money) and inscribed the (names of the) borrowers and the securities provided on two whitewashed boards, they shall read them out in the assembly; the securities offered shall be / substantial and free from servitude;[11] (the commissioners) shall deposit one of the boards in the temple and the other in the public archives; the expenses and the travel money may be paid for from the profits of exchange[12] and those who have handled (the exchange) shall render an account to the city. In future the appointment of the commissioners and the administration (of the fund) are to be as follows: the interest from the 18,000 drachmas shall be spent on [the] / teachers, while from the (interest from the) 3,000 drachmas the honours and sacrifices shall be carried out by the commissioners for [the] *Attaleia* as follows: the magistrates in office shall draw up in the month of Poitropius (= December) at the

statutory meeting of the assembly every year a list of three commissioners from the names put forward and chosen by a vote of the people; the
commissioners who are appointed shall swear an oath like the other
40 magistrates and shall collect / the interest on the money in the month of
Endyspoitropius (= April) before the fifteenth, and they shall deposit the
sum for the teachers in the temple in the month of Heracleius (= May),
and the following year they shall pay the teachers every month and
render an account to the city; if they do not act as is prescribed . . . (gap
of 4 lines) . . . [they shall perform] the [sacrifice, the honours and the
45 public banquet on the thirteenth of] the [month of Heracleius / and] shall
render an account [to the *mastroi* during the same] month; if they fail to
do this, the *mastroi* shall [bring an action] against them for stealing [sacred
money] in accordance with the [law of the *mastroi*]; the commissioners
shall sacrifice three full grown oxen which the citizens shall provide for
50 Apollo, Leto / and Artemis together with the other victims [as is]
prescribed,[13] (sacrificing) in the name of King Attalus and calling the
sacrifice *Attaleia*; they shall use the meat at the public banquet and 40
measures of wine, and they shall have the victim ready on the twelfth of
55 the month of Heracleius (= May), and on the / thirteenth[14] the priests of
Apollo and of the other gods, the *prytaneis*, the magistrates (*archontes*) and
the children wearing crowns shall take part in the procession, and the
procession shall go from the threshing floor[15] to the temple; and when the
priests of Apollo have taken part in the procession, they shall make a prayer
60 and proclaim the name of the sacrifice as being the *Attaleia* / as is
customary; so that these resolutions might be conspicuous, the decree
shall be inscribed on the statue (base) of King Attalus; the borrowers
shall pay back to the city all the money in the fifth year; if they do not pay it
65 back as is prescribed, their securities shall belong to the city / and the
commissioners who lend the money shall have authority to sell them; if the
sale of the securities does not realise the sum of money which was pledged to
the city, the borrower himself and his sureties shall be liable to action by
70 the commissioners in office for recovery of the deficit, / in any
way they wish, just as they do with other public and sacred matters; if the
borrowers do not pay the interests to the commissioners before the
fifteenth of the month of Endyspoitropius (= April), they shall be liable
75 to action by the commissioners for recovery / of the interest on each loan
plus one half; the commissioners shall hand over to the city the money
raised in the month of Boathous (= September) as the law lays down for
other surplus income; the commissioners who are appointed shall lend
80 the money again / at a rate of interest of 1 in 15; if the commissioners do
not hand over the money at the prescribed time, they shall be deprived of
their civic rights and shall be registered by the succeeding commissioners
for recovery of this sum plus one half; loans take effect from the month

336

of Amalius (= January) / in the archonship of Amphistratus; Praxias son 85
of Eudocus, Bacchius son of Agron,[16] Xenon son of Boulon were
appointed commissioners for five years.

> *Syll.*[3] 672; G. Daux, *Delphes au IIe et au Ier*
> *siècle* (Paris, 1936), 686–92, cf. 497–511 and
> 682–98; F. Sokolowski, *Lois sacrées des cités*
> *grecques* (Paris, 1969), no. 80 (in part).

1. Associated on the throne by his brother Eumenes II by 161/60.
2. These embassies also visited Eumenes II and obtained gifts from him (*Syll.*[3]
   671 and G. Daux, *op. cit.*); the insistence and cynicism of the Delphians are
   noteworthy. On Attalid generosities to the Greeks cf. **194**.
3. Cf. **163** n. 4.
4. On educational foundations in Greek cities cf. **119, 120**.
5. On Attalid financing of honours to themselves cf. **203**.
6. On foundations and their administration cf. **116, 119, 120, 156**.
7. A decree of the people or a resolution of the council.
8. Delphic magistrates who supervised finances.
9. The council at Delphi.
10. On loans and securities cf. **104**, ll. 40ff.
11. I.e. they may not be claimed by someone else.
12. Delphi used a different (Aeginetan) coin standard from that of the Attalids;
    on money-changers cf. **107** n. 4.
13. This refers to a previous decree on the *Eumeneia* and *Attaleia*.
14. The day after the celebration of the *Eumeneia*.
15. The open space below the terrace of Apollo's temple; on processions cf. **119**
    n. 17.
16. Two of the envoys originally sent to Attalus II, cf. above.

207 An estimate of Eumenes II on his death (159)

King Eumenes (II) was completely exhausted in bodily strength, but the
brilliance of his mind remained unimpaired. He was a man who in most
respects was second to none of the kings of his time, and who in the most
serious and honourable matters was greater and more distinguished than
them.[1] First, he received a kingdom from his father which was reduced
to a very few insignificant towns and raised his power to rival that of the
greatest dynasties of his time; in this he did not for the most part have the
helping hand of fortune, nor did he rely on any sudden new turn of
events, but he owed it to his intelligence, industry and political skill.[2]
Then he was very anxious to win a good reputation, and conferred
benefactions on more Greek cities than the other kings of his time, and
enriched privately very many men.[3] In the third place, although he had
three brothers who were grown up and active he kept them all obedient

to himself, acting as his guards and preserving the prestige of the kingdom. And that is something which is rarely seen to happen.[4]

Polybius XXXII.8

1. Cf. the portrait of Attalus I, **199**.
2. Polybius does not make explicit here that the increase in the size and power of Eumenes' kingdom was due to the Roman settlement after the defeat of Antiochus III (see **161, 200**).
3. On the generosities of Eumenes II cf. **201–203, 206**.
4. On this theme cf. **204** and n. 1.

208 Letter of Attalus II to Attis, priest of Cybele (156)

The following text is the last and most explicit from a series of letters addressed by Eumenes II and Attalus II to Attis, a Galatian priest of the native cult of Cybele at Pessinus in Phrygia, and dating from 163 to *ca* 156. The letters are unusual in being genuine private letters not meant for publication, unlike most of the preserved royal letters of the Hellenistic period which were official in character; as a result they are frequently allusive in content and sometimes very frank. (The reasons for the publication of this dossier about a century later are unknown.) The background to this letter is the continued attempt by the Attalids to check the Galatians (cf. **203** n. 4) in collaboration with the priest Attis, a supporter of the Attalids.

See further: McShane (1964), 186f.; Errington (1971), 246f.; A. N. Sherwin-White, *JRS* 67 (1977), 64.

[King Attalus (II) to Attis the priest, greetings; if you were well, it would be] as I wish; I too was in good health. When we came to Pergamum I called together not only Athenaeus,[1] Sosander,[2] and Menogenes[3] but also
5 many others / of my advisers,[4] laid before them what we had discussed at Apamea[5] and told them what we had decided. A very elaborate discussion ensued,[6] and to begin with everybody inclined to the same view as we did, but Chlorus was extremely insistent in emphasising the
10 Roman factor and advising that in no way should anything / be done without consulting them. At first few shared his point of view, but after this as we kept examining the matter day after day, his advice made a greater impression on us, and to go ahead without consulting them seemed to involve considerable danger. If successful, the result would be
15 jealousy, displeasure and hostile suspicion, as / they had felt towards my brother,[7] and if we failed, certain destruction. For (it seemed that) they would not stir a finger but would look on with satisfaction, as we had undertaken such a great project without (consulting) them. But now should we suffer any reverse – may heaven forbid – we would get help as

we had acted in everything with their assent and would fight back / with   20
the goodwill of the gods. I have therefore decided to send to Rome on
every occasion messengers to report continuously [doubtful] cases, while
[we] ourselves make [careful] preparations [to defend] ourselves [in case
of need . . .]

RC 61; *OGIS* 315 VI

1. Younger brother of Attalus II, cf. **162, 193, 204**.
2. See **210**.
3. A high-ranking courtier, cf. *OGIS* 290–296.
4. Literally 'relatives', a court-title.
5. Apamea on the Maeander; the decision mentioned was to take military action
   against the Galatians.
6. Cf. the meeting of Antiochus III's council, **147** with n. 4.
7. Cf. **203**.

209 Decree of Aegina in honour of a governor under Attalus II

See further: Hansen (1971), 167, 204, 463; R. E. Allen, *BSA* 66 (1971), 1–12.

With good fortune, resolved by the council and the people:[1] the people
has obeyed all those who have been sent to (govern) the city and has
complied as far as was possible with the wishes of each of them, and
Cleon one of the 'bodyguards' (*somatophylakes*)[2] of King Attalus (II)
Philadelphus came to the island / and stayed for sixteen years, and in that   5
period he demonstrated his orderliness in his conduct of public affairs
and in his personal life and dealt with everybody in a fair and [just way]
with complete integrity, / and did not lay hands on any private property   10
or show any willingness to act improperly or abuse his authority, but
sought to settle most disputes, and as for those who would not be
reconciled he referred them to the fine and just laws dispensed to us by
the kings, according to the injunctions (*prostagmata*) issued (by them) for
[a period of time] / and to the laws,[3] so as to secure fair jurisdiction for   15
the weakest [against] the strongest [and] for the humblest against the
richest;[4] and of the lawsuits which were brought in during those years,
the majority he brought to a settlement [while those which] were
referred [to him] he settled / so that [those] who had lawsuits were   20
[thoroughly] satisfied; and he [conducted himself] otherwise in a way
that was orderly and worthy of the king and of the city, wishing as far as
possible not to cause harm to anyone, but to do good as is just both
publicly and privately to [each] citizen, in conformity with / the policy   25
which our kings constantly maintain towards the [city], making himself

easy of access to those in the city, to those who came from the king and
to the foreigners in [residence] here; for these reasons the people has
frequently sent envoys to the kings and requested them to confer the

30 greatest of favours / on the [people] by allowing him to remain in charge
of the city. For these reasons and because he has behaved [honourably]
and justly towards the king's interests,⁵ [as in all] other matters, [with]
excellence and justice, be it resolved by [the] council and the people, to

35 praise Cleon / son of Stratagus, [of Pergamum, the governor (*epistates*)]⁶
of the city, and to honour him with a gold [crown and] a bronze statue
for his excellence [and] the goodwill he [constantly] displays [towards]
King Eumenes (II) and King [Attalus] (II) Philadelphus and Queen
Stratonice and Attalus [son of King] Eumenes and the people of

40 Aegina, / and [to proclaim the crown] at the [theatrical contest] of the
Attaleia, the *Eumeneia*⁷ and the *Nicephoria*⁸ and at the tragic performances
at the *Dionysia*, [and] to entrust this responsibility to the generals [who
are in] office; he shall be a citizen (of Aegina) [and so too] his
[descendants], and he shall be enrolled in any tribe and deme he [wishes];

45 he shall enjoy the right of free meals (*sitesis*) / at the town hall for life.
The secretary of the people shall inscribe (this decree) [on a] stele to be set
up in the Attaleum, and the treasurer shall provide the expense for the
engraving and the dedication (of the stele); the generals shall be responsible for the dedication (of the stele), so that when these arrangements are

50 executed it will be seen that the people will honour worthily / to the best
of its ability those who deserve well of the king and conduct themselves
well and justly towards the people. The generals shall convey [this]
decree to the king, so that the resolutions may be implemented with his
assent.

55   The council / (and) the people (honour) Cleon, son of Stratagus, of
Pergamum.⁹

OGIS 329; *IG* iv.1

1. Of Aegina; the island was purchased by Attalus I from the Aetolians for 30
   talents in *ca* 210 and became a naval base (Polybius xxii.8.10; cf. McShane
   (1964), 107; R. E. Allen, *op. cit.*).
2. A court-title in the Hellenistic monarchies, in Cleon's case obviously devoid
   of practical functions. Cf. **254** n. 1 for Ptolemaic Egypt.
3. Laws had permanent validity.
4. On this problem cf. **84** and n.1; Cleon's judicial functions obviously were (or
   became) regular and not merely incidental to his office.
5. Cf. **139** n. 3.
6. Cf. **158** n. 2.
7. For the honours paid by Greek cities to Attalid rulers cf. **194** n. 1, **198, 203,
   204, 206, 215** ll. 26–30.

8. A festival instituted on the model of the *Nicephoria* of Pergamum (cf. **197** n. 2).

9. Compare **201**. The implication of such decrees is that governors could be expected to be oppressive.

210 Letters of Attalus II and III concerning the priesthoods of a friend (142–135)

See further: Hansen (1971), 440f., 451f., 469.

(a) Letter of Attalus II to Athenaeus

[. . .][1] / King Attalus (II) to Athenaeus his cousin, greetings. Sosander,[2]   5
our 'comrade'[3] and your son-in-law, was appointed by my brother the
king[4] priest of Dionysius Cathegemon, and performed the rites in very
many triennial[5] festivals with piety and worthily of the god, and with
affection towards by brother and towards us / and towards all others. It   10
had happened that in previous (triennial) festivals he suffered from a disease
of the tendons, and though he was able to perform the sacrifices with us
he could not perform the processions and some of the other religious
rites, and so we decided that his son Athenaeus should take over as priest
so that he might perform all the rites that Sosander was unable to
perform. / Since therefore the appropriate rites were celebrated on that   15
occasion in a pious way [as was fitting], and Sosander has now died, and
it is necessary for a priest to be appointed, I and Attalus my brother's
son[6] have decided that Athenaeus his son should preserve this priesthood
as well, since it so happened / that he was [initiated] into the priesthood   20
while his father was still alive, and since we believe that Dionysus
himself has so wished, and that the man is worthy both of this charge for
the god and of our whole house. So that you too may know that we have
conferred [this] honour as well on Athenaeus, I have decided to write to
you. / Year 18, Audnaeus 19.[7] Athenagoras (brought the letter) from   25
Pergamum.[8]

(b) Letter of Attalus III to Cyzicus

King Attalus (III) to the council and people of Cyzicus,[9] greetings. I am
sure that you are aware that Athenaeus son of Sosander, the former priest
of Dionysus Cathegemon and the 'comrade' of my father, is our
kinsman, since Sosander married the daughter of Athenaeus / son of   30
Midias – Athenaeus the cousin of my father – and begat him. As he was
worthy of our house, Attalus my uncle gave him first – with my
approval and when Sosander was still alive – the hereditary priesthood of
Zeus Sabazius[10] which we hold in the highest honour, and later – after

35 the death of Sosander, / because of his personal excellence and his piety
towards the deity and his goodwill and faith towards us – we thought
him worthy of the priesthood of Dionysus Cathegemon as well, as we
believed, I and Attalus my uncle, that he deserved this honour too, and
would conduct such great mysteries in a fitting manner, as is made clear
40 in (the records for) the / eighteenth year of his reign.[11] Knowing
therefore that on his mother's side he is one of your citizens I have decided
to write to you enclosing the other instructions and the benefactions
made in writing by us concerning him, so that you may know how
affectionately we feel towards him.[12] Year 4, Dius 7.[13] Menes (brought
45 the letter) from Pergamum. /

(c) Letter of Attalus III to Pergamum

King Attalus (III) to the council and people of Pergamum,[14] greetings;
since Queen Stratonice my mother,[15] the most pious of all women and
one who showed the greatest affection towards my father and towards
myself, displayed piety to all the gods[16] and in particular to Zeus
50 Sabazius, whom she introduced as an ancestral god[17] / to our native city,
and whom, as he stood by and assisted us in many actions and through
many dangers, we decided because of his manifestations[18] to include in
the sanctuary together with Athena Nicephorus.[19] We believed this place
to be worthy and fitting for him, and we gave instructions in accordance
55 with this concerning the sacrifices, processions and mysteries / which
are to be celebrated in his honour before the city at the appropriate time
and place. We have also appointed for him a hereditary priest, my friend
Athenaeus, who is outstanding in piety and excellence and in his constant
good faith towards us.[20] Therefore, so that the honours to the god and
the benefactions made to Athenaeus might remain undisturbed and
unchanged for all time, we decided that the instructions (*prostagmata*) we
60 have issued in writing / should be included in your sacred laws.[21] Year 4,
Dius 4.[22] Lytus (brought the letter) from Pergamum.

RC 65–67; OGIS 331 II–IV

1. The preserved part of the inscription contains the very end of a decree of
   Pergamum passed in accordance with the request of Attalus III (cf. (c) below).
2. Cf. also **208**.
3. Literally 'brought up with' (*syntrophos*), an honorific title; cf. Hansen. *op. cit.*,
   201f.
4. Eumenes II.
5. Inclusively reckoned = biennial. On Dionysus Cathegemon cf. **123** n. 1.
6. The future Attalus III, officially regarded as Eumenes' son, though his descent
   is disputed (cf. Walbank III (1979), 417f.).
7. 25 December 142.

8. From the royal archives.

9. See **204** n. 1.

10. See next letter.

11. This shows the existence of an official royal 'diary'.

12. Attalus III makes no explicit request from Cyzicus, but the city would be expected to honour Athenaeus in consequence.

13. 8 October 135.

14. For the Attalids and Pergamum see **195**.

15. Cf. **193, 204**. Compare the case of Laodice, **158**.

16. Cf. **163** n. 4.

17. From Cappadocia.

18. On divine epiphanies cf. too **184, 190**.

19. I.e. make him 'share the temple' (*synnaos*; cf. **151** n. 11) of Athena Nicephorus, on whom cf. **197** and n. 2.

20. Compare **175**. On priesthoods cf. **129**.

21. To be given the permanence of city laws; Pergamum duly passed a decree, cf. n. 1 above.

22. 5 October 135.

211 Decree of Pergamum after the death of Attalus III (133)

Much the most noteworthy feature of the short reign of Attalus III (139/8 to 134/3) was the will by which he left the Roman people heir to his kingdom, yet Attalus' motives for this decision are far from clear (the ancient sources provide no explanation, cf. **193** end). Suggested possibilities include (a) the wish to deny the succession to Aristonicus (cf. **212** – Attalus was himself childless), (b) the wish to preempt serious social disturbances (such as actually broke out) if a strong power did not take over, (c) the wish to ensure himself against assassination by rivals, assuming the terms of the will were public knowledge beforehand (cf. the analogy of the will of Ptolemy VIII in 155, see **230**). It should not be assumed that the will necessarily represented Attalus' ultimate intentions; it merely came into force through his premature death (contrast the long reigns of other Attalid rulers, **193**). Modern literature on the end of the Attalid kingdom and the revolt of Aristonicus which followed is very bulky, by contrast with the scantiness of the ancient sources.

See further (on **211–214**): Magie I (1950), 30–3, 147–58 and notes; Hansen (1971), 147–63; J. Vogt, *Ancient Slavery and the Ideal of Man* (Oxford, 1974), 93–102 and index s.v. Aristonicus; C. P. Jones, *Chiron* 4 (1974), 190–3; V. Vavřínek, *Eirene* 13 (1975), 109–29; A. N. Sherwin-White, *JRS* 67 (1977), 66–70.

In the priesthood of Menestratus son of Apollodorus, on the nineteenth of the month Eumeneius,[1] resolved by the people, motion of the generals:[2] [since] King Attalus (III) Philometor and Euergetes, having [departed] from among men,[3] / left our [native city] free, having   5 attached to it also the [civic] land (*chora*) which he designated,[4] and (since) it is necessary for the will to be ratified by the Romans, and it is [essential] for the safety of all that the [undermentioned] classes (of men)

10 should share in citizen rights because of the [complete] goodwill / which they have showed towards the people;[5] with good [fortune, be it resolved] by the people, to grant citizen rights to the [undermentioned classes]: to those who are registered in the lists of the resident [foreigners], to the soldiers who are settled in [the city] and the country-

15 side (*chora*),[6] and similarly to the Macedonians and [Mysians] / and to the settlers (*katoikoi*) who are registered in the citadel and in [the] old [city], and to the Masdyeni and . . . and to the policemen (*paraphylakitai*) and to the other mercenary soldiers (*epikouroi*) who are settled or own property in [the city] or the countryside, and similarly to their wives and

20 children. / The descendants of freedmen shall be transferred to the class of resident foreigners, and so too the royal slaves, both the adults and the young men, and similarly the women[7] except for those who were bought in the reigns of King Philadelphus (Attalus II) and King

25 Philometor (Attalus III) and those who were taken over / from property which became royal,[8] and similarly the public slaves. All the settlers, both men and women, who have left at the time of the <death> of the king or leave the city or the countryside, shall be deprived of their rights

30 and their property confiscated by the / city.[9] On the fourth day of the end of the month, resolved by the people, motion of the generals: since in the decree [which was passed] concerning the grant of citizen rights [to those registered in] the lists of the resident foreigners [and / to the other

35 classes] mentioned in the [decree, and concerning the transfer to (the category of)] resident foreigners of the [descendants of freedmen and the royal slaves and] the public slaves . . .

(the rest of the inscription is lost)

OGIS 338

1. Named after Eumenes I or II.
2. See **195**.
3. See **204** n. 3.
4. I.e. Attalus III granted freedom to Pergamum and its civic territory; it is not certain whether other Greek cities in the Attalid kingdom were similarly treated (cf. Plutarch, *Tiberius Gracchus* 14.2).
5. Although Aristonicus is not mentioned (cf. **212**), Pergamum's move is an obvious bid for support in the struggle that broke out on Attalus' death; it is not known whether the unrest had started even before the death of Attalus.
6. It is not clear whether this refers to the territory of Pergamum or to the whole of the Attalid kingdom; on these various categories of soldiers, see Griffith (1935), 177–82; Launey II (1950), 664–9.
7. Who belong to these categories.

8. Property confiscated by the crown.
9. A hint that Aristonicus may have had supporters in the city of Pergamum and not just in the countryside (**212**).

212 The revolt of Aristonicus

After Smyrna there is the small fort of Leucae, which Aristonicus caused to revolt after the death of Attalus (III) Philometor.[1] Aristonicus was reputed to be a member of the royal family and intended to seize the kingdom for himself.[2] He was expelled from there after being defeated in a sea battle near the territory of Cyme by the Ephesians, but went into the interior and quickly collected a large band of destitute men and of slaves whom he had incited with a promise of freedom, and he called his followers the *Heliopolitai* (citizens of the sun-state).[3] He first stole into Thyatira by surprise, then secured control of Apollonis, then sought to gain other fortresses, but he did not hold out for long and the cities promptly sent a large force (against him).[4] Nicomedes of Bithynia came to the rescue and so did the kings of Cappadocia.[5] Then five Roman ambassadors arrived,[6] followed by an army and the consul Publius Crassus,[7] then by Marcus Perperna who put an end to the war by capturing Aristonicus alive and sending him to Rome.[8] Aristonicus ended his life in prison while Perperna died of illness, and Crassus was killed in battle when some people attacked him near Leucae. Manius Aquillius (then) came as consul with ten envoys[9] and organised the province in the form of government which survives to this day.

Strabo XIV.1.38

1. Strabo makes no mention here of the will of Attalus III (see **193** (end), **211**).
2. A bastard of Eumenes II (?) Aristonicus assumed the title of Eumenes (III) and issued coins under that name for four years (E. S. G. Robinson, *NC* 14 (1954), 1–8); his aims were initially dynastic before he turned to social revolution.
3. A tantalising indication, and the starting point of much modern speculation; cf. e.g. Rostovtzeff II (1941), 808 and III, 1523f. (n.81); J. Vogt, *op. cit.* on **211**, 69–71; V. Vavřínek, *Eirene* 13 (1975), 121–9. Whatever the exact nature and sincerity of his appeal to the dispossessed and the rural classes of Asia Minor (on whom cf. **178** n. 3), Aristonicus' following was (or became) a varied one, cf. **211** n. 9; the coins he issued (n. 2 above) originate from the upper Caicus valley, an area of intensive Graeco-Macedonian military settlement from which he must have drawn support (L. Robert, *Villes d'Asie Mineure* (Paris, 2nd ed., 1962), 261–71).
4. Of the Greek cities only Phocaea is known to have joined his side; cf. **211, 213, 215**.

5. Also the rulers of Pontus and Paphlagonia; after the war they all received from Rome territorial grants from the former Attalid kingdom.
6. In 132; note the slowness of the Roman response (A. N. Sherwin-White, *JRS* 67 (1977), 68).
7. In 131.
8. In 130.
9. In 129.

213 Decree of Pergamum or Elaea after the revolt of Aristonicus

5   [. . . resolved by the council] and the [people / . . .] son of Nicanor, . . .
son of Dionysius, . . . son of [Archias . . .] son of Menander, Polystratus
10   son of Menon, / the generals moved: [since] our people, [preserving]
from the beginning its [goodwill] and friendship towards the Romans,
[has] provided [many great proofs] of its policy in the most [critical
15   circumstances], / and similarly in [the war against] Aristonicus[1] applied
[all] zeal and [faced] great [dangers] both on land and [at] sea, [wherefore]
20   the people of Rome, observing the [policy] / of our [people] and
[welcoming] its goodwill, has [admitted] our people to [friendship] and
alliance, and (since) a bronze tablet has been dedicated at [Rome] in the
25   temple [of] Jupiter Capitolinus / on which have been recorded the decree
passed by the [Senate] concerning the alliance and also the [treaty], and it
is fitting that [they] should also be inscribed [among] us on two bronze
30   tablets, to be [placed] in the sanctuary / of Demeter and [in the] council
chamber [next] to the statue of [Democracy]; be it resolved by [the]
council and the [people], that the auditors of public accounts (*exetastai*)
should issue a [contract] through the appropriate officials for the making
35   of [the] tablets and for their / [engraving, and] similarly for two marble
stelae into which [the] tablets shall be fitted once completed. A copy of
[this] decree shall be inscribed [verbatim on the] stelae, and [when] the
40   dedication / [of the stelae] has been completed, [the] crown-bearer
(*stephanephoros*), [the] priests and the [priestesses] and the magistrates
shall [open] the temples [of the gods] and make an offering of frankincense with (the following) [prayer on behalf] of the citizens: 'For the
45   good fortune [and safety] of / our people [and the] Romans and the
[association of artists] of Dionysus [Cathegemon],[2] may the friendship
and [alliance] with the Romans remain for us for [all] time.' A sacrifice
50   [as magnificent] as possible shall be offered to / Demeter and to Core,
[the] patron goddesses of [our] city, and [likewise] to [Rome][3] and to all
the other [gods] and goddesses. The day (of the sacrifice) [shall be] a
[holy day] and [the] children shall be released from their [lessons] and the
55   slaves / from their work. After the sacrifice a parade shall be held by

346

[the] children and the young men (*neoi*),[4] to be supervised by the *paidonomos*[5] [and] the gymnasiarch. [The] resulting expense [for] the making [of the] tablets and for everything else / shall be provided by the   60 treasurers Eucles and [Dionysius from] the [revenues] they administer.

Syll.[3] 694; F. Sokolowski, *Lois sacrées de l'Asie Mineure* (Paris, 1955), no. 15 (lines 31–61 only)

1. See **211, 212, 215**.
2. See **123** and n. 1.
3. I.e. the deified goddess Rome, a cult which spread in the Greek world in the second century B.C., first attested at Smyrna in 195 (Tacitus, *Annals* IV. 56); see R. J. Mellor, *Thea Rome: the Worship of the Goddess Roma in the Greek World* (Göttingen, 1975).
4. Cf. **105** n. 3, **119** n. 17.
5. See **119, 120**.

214 Decree of the Senate concerning Pergamum (133–129)

See further: T. Drew-Bear, *Historia* 21 (1972), 75–9, 86; A. N. Sherwin-White, *JRS* 67 (1977), 68.

[Decree of] the Senate.[1]
Caius Popillius, son of Caius, [praetor][2] consulted with [the Senate] on the . . . / . . . of . . .;[3] concerning the speech [he made about the] affairs   5 [of Pergamum?], and the instructions [to be given to the praetors] who are setting off to Asia,[4] that [all the] regulations, gifts, exemptions and penalties laid down [in Asia] by the [kings up to] the death of Attalus (III), [should be] / valid, concerning this matter the Senate [resolved] as   10 follows; [concerning the matters] about which Caius Popillius, son of Caius, praetor [spoke], (the Senate) [made the following resolution] about this matter: [that] all the regulations, penalties,[exemptions (and) gifts] made by King Attalus and the [other kings],[5] / in so far as they   15 were made up to one [day before] the death of Attalus (III), that these [should be valid] and that [the praetors] going to Asia [should not disturb the will] but allow (the provisions) to remain [all] valid [as the Senate] decided. [. . .]

Sherk no. 11; *OGIS* 435

1. This copy of the Senate's decree was set up at Pergamum in Greek: the Senate's ratification of the will of Attalus III involved confirmation of Pergamum's autonomy (see **211**).
2. Otherwise unknown.

3. A date in the latter part of the year, but the exact year is uncertain and much discussed; cf. Sherk, Sherwin-White, *opp. citt.*
4. I.e. future governors of the province.
5. Text uncertain, perhaps: '[that] all the [gifts], regulations . . . made by King Attalus and the other (rulers)' (Drew-Bear, *op. cit.*, 86).

215 Decree of Sestus in honour of Menas (after the end of the Attalids)

[In the priesthood] of Glaucias son of Cillaeus, in the month of [Hyperberetaeus . . . resolved] by the council and the people; Menander son of Apollas moved: [since Menas son of Menes] has [from] his earliest manhood believed it the finest course of action to make himself useful [to his native city],[1] and has not spared any cost or expense, and has not
5 avoided any hardship / or danger, nor has taken into account the losses to his private fortune which those serving as envoys suffer,[2] but considered all these things of secondary importance and attached the highest priority to loyalty and devotion to his native city, and wished always to achieve some useful advantage for the people through his own enthusiasm and to secure for himself and his descendants everlasting
10 fame through the gratitude of the people; / and he [served] on many embassies [to] the kings, in which together with his fellow envoys he achieved everything to the advantage of the people, and held loyally the positions of trust assigned to him; and when he was negotiating with Strato the general (*strategos*) of the Chersonese and of the Thracian districts (*topoi*)[3] and received the most favourable reception from him
15 because of his integrity in matters of trust, / he induced him to do a service to the city[4] and he himself showed enthusiasm in his dealings with all the citizens; and after the kings had departed to the gods,[5] and when the city was in a dangerous situation through fear of the neighbouring Thracians[6] and because of the other difficult circumstances arising out of the sudden emergency,[7] Menas constantly said and did
20 what was best and most honourable, exerting himself unhesitatingly / for all the city's interests, and he readily undertook the embassies to the generals sent to Asia by the Romans and to the envoys who were despatched,[8] and in these embassies the people did not fare badly in any matter, but was successful in everything because of the hardships endured by the envoys, and when he was despatched to other peoples in critical circumstances together with his fellow envoys, he secured
25 favourable results for his native city, / and in wartime conditions he has constantly shown himself a good man towards the people, and when he was appointed priest of King Attalus[9] he behaved in a way worthy of the

348

people, sustaining nobly every expense that fell on him, showing consideration not only for the citizens [and] the other inhabitants of the city, but also for the foreigners in residence, / conferring on his native 30 city the good reputation (he enjoyed) with the foreigners; and when he was appointed gymnasiarch, he showed concern for the good discipline of the ephebes and the young men (*neoi*),[10] and took charge of the general good order of the gymnasium honourably and in a spirit of emulation;[11] and he built the bathing-room and the building [next to it], and he dedicated a statue of white stone, and he built in addition the unfinished parts which were required; / and at the birthday feast of the king[12] when 35 sacrificing every month on behalf of the people he instituted parades (or: races) for the ephebes and the young men,[13] and celebrated javelin and archery contests, and provided oil for anointing, and through (the example of) his own emulation he encouraged the young men to exercise and train hard, for which the people welcomed his zeal and eagerness / 40 and allowed him to commemorate his deeds in inscriptions,[14] and deemed him worthy of being praised in decrees, and the ephebes and young men crowned him and the ephebarch, and though he accepted the honour he freed them from the expense involved, and made the dedication of the weapons at his own expense;[15] and when the people decided to use its own bronze coinage,[16] so that the city's coin type should be used as a current type / and the people should receive the 45 profit resulting from this source of revenue,[17] and appointed men who would safeguard this position of trust piously[18] and justly, Menas was appointed and together with his colleague in office showed suitable care, as a result of which the people thanks to the justice and emulation of these men has the use of its own coinage, and in the other magistracies / 50 and liturgies to which the people had appointed him, he has shown himself impartial and just, wishing to act in accordance with his achievements and not to fall short in any way of his goodwill towards the people, and to preserve with dignity and justice the positions of trust assigned to him; and when he was invited a second time to act as gymnasiarch he submitted to this in difficult circumstances, as [we] had been worn out / for many years because of the incursions of the Thracians 55 and the wars which were engulfing the city,[19] in the course of which everything in the fields was carried off, and most of the land was not sown, and the dearth of crops which recurred continuously reduced the people publicly and every individual citizen privately to penury, and Menas was one of the many to be afflicted; but he put aside all this, as [he could see] / that the people was grateful and knew how to honour good 60 men, and he surpassed himself in the expenses he incurred and in his zeal; for when he entered office on the new moon he celebrated sacrifices for Hermes and Heracles, the gods consecrated in the gymnasium,[20] on

behalf of the safety of the people and of the young men, and he organised
65   races and contests of javelin and archery, and on the last day / he offered
a sacrifice and invited to the sacrificial rites not only those who have
access to the gymnasium[21] but all the others as well, giving a share in the
sacrificial rites even to the foreigners; and every month when celebrating
the appropriate sacrifices on behalf of the young men, he treated the gods
who preside over the gymnasium with generosity and magnificence, by
instituting javelin and archery contests and organising races, giving to
70   the young men a share in the / victims sacrificed by him, and encouraging through his zeal the young men to exercise and train hard, which
would cause the minds of the younger men by competing for bravery to
receive a suitable training in moral excellence; and he gave a share in the
offerings connected with the gymnasium to those undergoing gymnastic
training for use at home,[22] extending his beneficence even to the
foreigners who have admission to the gymnasium; and he dealt in a
75   friendly way with all those who gave lectures,[23] / wishing in this too to
secure for his native city glory through men of education; and he looked
after the education of the ephebes and the young men, and showed care
for the general good order of the gymnasium, and he provided scrapers[24]
and supplied oil for anointing, and celebrated a contest in honour of
Hermes and Heracles in the month of Hyperberetaeus, offering as prizes
for the competitions for the young men and ephebes weapons with an
80   inscription and bound / in shield-cases, on which he inscribed the names
of the victors and (which he) immediately dedicated in the gymnasium;
and he offered second prizes; and he offered prizes for the boys and prizes
for armed combat for the ephebes and the men,[25] and similarly for
archery and javelin-throwing; and he offered weapons as prizes for the
long race, for good discipline, hard-training and fitness (*euexia*); and after
celebrating a sacrifice to the gods mentioned and after promoting their
85   fitness (*euandria*) in accordance with the law, he invited to the / sacrificial
rites all the members of the gymnasium[26] and the foreigners who share in
the common rights (*koina*), entertaining them in a magnificent way and
worthily of the gods and of the people. Therefore, so that the people may
be seen to be honouring excellent men and to be welcoming those who
from their earliest manhood have shown zeal concerning matters of
public interest, and not to be falling short in returning gratitude, and so
90   that others seeing the honours which are paid by the people / to excellent
men, should emulate the finest deeds and be encouraged towards
excellence, and public interests might be furthered when all are striving
to achieve glory and are always securing some benefit to their native city;
with good fortune, be it resolved by the council and the people, to praise
Menas son of Menes for all the services mentioned and for the goodwill
which he constantly displays towards the people, and to allow him to

350

dedicate the weapons with his name inscribed and / (mention of the fact)   95
that he was crowned by the ephebes and the young men; and to have him
crowned by the people every year at the gymnastic contest during the
religious festival with a gold crown, with the following proclamation
being made by the herald: 'The people crowns Menas son of Menes, who
held the office of gymnasiarch / twice honourably and zealously, and   100
showed himself a good man towards the people.' He and his descendants
are to be invited to a seat of honour (*proedria*) at all the competitions
celebrated by the people; the agonothete who is in charge every year shall
organise the proclamation of the crown; and since he wishes in these
matters too to do a favour to the people on account of the present tight
circumstances of the public finances and (is willing to) assume the
expense for the statue from his private means,[27] he shall take care
that / the statue set up is as beautiful as possible, and shall inscribe the   105
present decree on a stele of white stone and place it in the gymnasium.

OGIS 339

1. On 'benefactors' cf. generally **97**.
2. Cf. **155**.
3. Organised as a satrapy by Antiochus III (see **153, 154**), then handed over to the Attalids by the Peace of Apamea (see **161, 200**) and placed under a 'general' (*strategos*), cf. **201**.
4. Perhaps the sending of a force to defend Sestus.
5. Cf. **204** n. 3.
6. Cf. **96** and n. 4.
7. The war of Aristonicus, cf. **211–213**.
8. Cf. **212**.
9. Attalus II or III; cf. **209** n. 7.
10. Cf. **105** n. 3.
11. On gymnasia and gymnasiarchs, cf. **118**. See H. I. Marrou, *A History of Education in Antiquity* (London, 1956), 280–4 on this inscription.
12. Cf. **222** n. 6.
13. Cf. **119** n. 17.
14. The people allowed him to put his name and mention of the office he held on dedications to the gods.
15. It was not uncommon for the honorand to finance his own honours, cf. below; see **110** and for the kings themselves **203, 206**.
16. As opposed to an imported coinage; note the emphasis on civic pride in the issue of coinage. On this passage cf. J. R. Melville-Jones, *NC* (1972), 39–43 (at p. 43); L. Robert, *Rev. Num.* (1973), 43–53.
17. By issuing token bronze coins and not silver (cf. **105**).
18. The duties of mint-masters involved the choice of types which were religious in character (e.g. heads of deities).
19. See nn. 6 and 7.
20. See **118** with n. 5.

21. Here and below, literally 'those who share in the (athlete's) oil'.
22. Normally the meat from the sacrificial victims was consumed on the spot and not to be removed elsewhere; cf. **128** l. 26.
23. Public lectures from itinerant speakers; cf. **118** ll. 66f.
24. For cleaning oneself.
25. Boys, ephebes, men: age-groups in athletic competitions. Cf. **234**.
26. Literally 'the anointed'.
27. See n. 15.

216 The municipal administration of Pergamum under the Attalids

See further: Hansen (1971), 191–8.

. . . one of the *astynomoi*, dedicated the royal law at his private expense.[1]

Column I

5

10

15

20

25

30

35

. . .[2] [they (sc. the *astynomoi*) shall make an inspection and give a verdict as appears to them] just. [And if] they do not obey even so, / [the] generals (*strategoi*)[3] shall inflict on them [the] legal punishment and assign to the collector of fines (*praktor*) the task of collecting the fine; the *astynomoi* shall issue a contract for the restoration of the place to its original condition within / ten days, and shall exact from the offenders one and a half times the cost, and shall pay the sum due to the contractors and the rest to the treasurers. And if the *astynomoi* do not act / as the law lays down, the generals shall issue the contract, and the *astynomoi* shall be charged the [[remainder of the]][4] cost and shall be fined in addition / 100 drachmas. The guardians of the law (*nomophylakes*) shall exact (this sum) from them immediately. The same procedure shall apply in the case of other offenders. Concerning the roads in the territory (of the city) the / main roads shall be not less than twenty cubits (*ca* 30 ft) wide and the others not less than eight (*ca* 12 ft), except if some people use footpaths in their neighbourhoods to communicate with each other. [Those] who own property along the [roads] shall keep them / clean and passable [and also] the neighbourhood up to a distance of . . . stadia, [contributing] to the costs and to the [repairs. And] if they do not [obey, the . . .] shall take securities / [from them . . .]

Column II

50

[. . . the *amphodarchai*[5] shall] compel [those who have] thrown out [. . .[6] / to clean up the] place, as [the law lays down. If they fail to do this], they (sc. the *amphodarchai*) shall report (them) [to the *astynomoi*].

352

The *astynomoi* [shall issue a contract together with the] *amphodarches* and
shall exact [the resulting expense / from the offenders immediately] and   55
[shall] fine (them) [ten drachmas?]. If any of the [*amphodarchai* fails to
carry out any] of his written instructions [he shall be fined by] the
astynomoi twenty drachmas for [each offence]. The / sums [collected]   60
from the fines [shall be given] from month to month [to the treasurers]
and they shall be available should [the need arise?] for the purpose of
cleaning [the streets], but they [shall] not be transferred [to] any other
purpose. / The *astynomoi* shall have charge of collecting [the] fines and of   65
[everything] else. [If] they fail to carry out any of the written instructions, they shall be fined by the generals and the overseer of the city[7] 50
drachmas for each / offence and this fine shall also be assigned to the   70
purposes mentioned above. *Concerning digging up (the streets).* If anyone
digs up soil or stones on the streets or makes clay or bricks or lays out
open / drains, the *amphodarchai* shall prevent them. If they do not   75
comply, the *amphodarchai* shall report them to the *astynomoi*. They shall
fine the offender five drachmas for each offence and / shall compel (him)   80
to restore everything to its original state and to build underground
drains. If private citizens still refuse to obey, they shall issue a contract
(for repairs) within ten days and shall exact from the offenders one and a
half times the resulting expense. / Similarly they shall compel already   85
existing drains to be built underground. If the *astynomoi* fail to do any of
this they shall themselves be liable to the same / fines. *Concerning*   90
payments. If anyone fails to pay his share of the cost of the contract for
(removing) the refuse from the streets which are cleaned at public
expense, or (fails to pay) the fines, the *amphodarchai* shall seize securities
from them / and lay them as a pledge before the *astynomoi* on the same   95
day or the day after, and if no one has not sworn within five days to
claim back the goods seized as securities, they shall sell them either in the
phratry[8] or in the agora when it is full / in the presence of the *astynomoi*, 100
and they shall pay the proceeds . . .

Column III

They shall make an inspection[9] and if they (sc. the walls) seem to them to
be in need of repair, the owners shall repair them. / If any of them refuse   105
to do this, the *astynomoi* shall issue a contract together with any of the
injured parties who is willing. They shall exact immediately three fifths
of the resulting expense from / the offender and two fifths from the   110
other person, and shall pay (the money) to the contractors. As regards
party-walls which are in need of repair or have collapsed, if the
neighbours use the whole walls / to the same extent, they shall contri-   115
bute equally to the building costs. But if one neighbour has a building
along the party wall while the other has an open space, the former shall

120 contribute two thirds to the building costs / and the latter one third. They shall pay in the same proportions if one has a two-storey building along the wall and the other a single-storey building. If anyone destroys

125 party walls, / summons shall be lodged before the *astynomoi*, and if they are shown to be guilty and lose their case, they shall pay the cost for the damage done. It shall not be permissible to put up additional buildings

130 against party walls / nor to dig through them nor to do any other damage to them without the consent of the owners. As for neighbouring walls which cause offence to the residents, if the owners wish to lay out open passages (*peristaseis*) on the side of the neighbours' free-standing

135 (walls), / provided they cause no offence to the neighbours, they [shall] not be prevented from doing so provided they make them not more than a cubit wide and cover them immediately with stone blocks, after the

140 outer wall of the / open passage has been securely built, if there are no rocks where the blocks are to be placed. When covering it (the builders) shall not make the foundation higher than the rest of the open ground except for what is needed to allow the water to drain away. The builders

145 shall be owners / of the open passages, though the neighbours shall be owners of the spaces above them once they are covered up, provided they do not use it for any purpose detrimental to others' walls. They (sc.

150 the builders) shall lay out the entrances to the open passages / from their own houses. But if that is not possible according to the verdict of the architect[10] together with the *astynomoi*, the neighbours shall provide access to those who enter for the purpose of cleaning, and similarly when

155 there is a collapse / and (open passages) need to be repaired. Concerning those who enter with spiteful intent the *astynomoi* shall decide and if they convict him they shall fine him five drachmas. No one shall dig a trench

160 against someone else's wall / or a party wall, nor place wine-jars, nor plant anything nor do anything which would damage the wall. If anyone does and the owner brings a charge (against him), the *astynomoi* shall

165 examine the case and give a verdict / according to what seems just to them. Concerning the walls of other peoples' houses which threaten to collapse, when the neighbours give notice of the damage . . .

Column IV

170 / They shall [compel] (them) to clean the water-pipes. *Concerning the fountains.* Concerning the fountains in the city and in the suburbs it shall

175 be incumbent on the *astynomoi* to make sure they are clean / and that the pipes which bring and remove the water flow freely. If any need to be repaired, they shall notify the generals and the superintendent of the sacred revenues, so that contracts (for repair work) are issued by these

180 (officials). / No one shall be allowed to water animals at the public fountains nor to wash clothes or implements or anything else. Should

anyone do any of these things, if he is a free man[11] / his animals, clothes   185
and implements shall be confiscated and he shall be fined 50 drachmas,
but if he is a slave and if he has done any of these things with the consent
of his master, the same goods shall be confiscated and / he himself shall   190
receive 50 strokes of the whip in the pillory, while if he has acted without
his master's consent, everything he has[12] shall be confiscated and he shall
receive 100 strokes of the whip in the pillory and he shall be held in the
stocks for ten days and on his release / he shall receive not less than 50   195
strokes of the whip before being released. Anyone else who wishes may
arrest those guilty of offences concerning the fountains, and anyone who
brings an offender or who lays the goods seized before the *astynomoi* /   200
shall receive half of the proceeds from these goods, while the rest shall be
assigned to the repair of the sanctuary of the Nymphs. *Concerning the
cisterns.* The *astynomoi* who are in office shall draw up a list of the cisterns
then existing in the houses / and shall hand over the list in the month of   205
Pantheios to the generals and they shall make sure that the owners make
(the cisterns) watertight and that none of the existing cisterns get choked.
They shall fine those who commit any of these offences / 100 drachmas   210
for each cistern [and] compel them to clean them up. If any of the cisterns
happen to be already choked, they shall notify this to the owners so that
they clean them up / within eight months. If they (sc. the owners) fail to   215
do this, they (sc. the *astynomoi*) shall fine them the same sum and shall
compel them to clean up (the cisterns). They shall hand over the proceeds
from the fines from month to month to the treasurers, and this money
shall be available for the cleaning / and construction of cisterns, but shall   220
not be transferred to any other purpose. As to those who own cisterns
and cause damage to their neighbours by not [making] them water-tight,
the *astynomoi* shall [compel] them to comply by [fining] them, and
if / any lawsuits arise as a result, the *astynomoi* shall exact reparation and   225
pay it to the injured parties. Should any of the *astynomoi* fail to deposit at
the town-hall the list of cisterns for which he is responsible, or fail to act
in accordance with / the provisions of the law, the guardians of the law   230
shall fine him 100 drachmas and assign these to the same revenues.
Concerning the public toilets. The *astynomoi* shall take care of the public
toilets / and of the sewers which run from them, and [any sewers   235
which] are [not] covered and . . .

(the rest of the inscription is lost)

G. Klaffenbach, *Die Astynomeninschrift von
Pergamon* (Berlin, 1954), reproduced in *SEG* XIII. 521;
OGIS 483

1. The inscription was set up in late Hellenistic or Roman imperial times (cf.
Bull. 1956, 243), but the law itself dates from the Attalid period (on such laws

cf. **118** and n. 1). Although *astynomoi* are attested in several Greek cities, including classical Athens (Aristotle, *Constitution of Athens* 50.2), the Pergamum inscription is much the most informative source on their functions.

2. The inscription is laid out on 4 columns; a large part of the first two is lost. The preserved part of column 1 concerns roads.

3. On the *strategoi* of Pergamum cf. **195** and n. 3.

4. These words may be intrusive (Klaffenbach).

5. Officials entrusted with the care of streets (*amphodon* = street).

6. Refuse, probably.

7. A royal appointment, a post probably created in the second century (he is absent in **195**), and comparable to the Attalid governor in Aegina (see **209**) and in other cities of the Attalid kingdom.

8. A kinship group; sale in the phratry would make it easier for the goods to be redeemed by the family of the offender.

9. This section concerns walls.

10. A public official with the duties of a master of works; cf. at Delos **104** n. 23.

11. For other cases of grading of statuses cf. **87** n. 2.

12. When he was at the fountain.

7 The Ptolemies and Egypt

[*Note:* The texts in this chapter are grouped as follows: **217–231** texts arranged chronologically; **232–262** Egypt under the Ptolemies (mainly chronologically); **263–279** Ptolemaic activity outside Egypt.]

217 A poem in praise of Ptolemy II Philadelphus

The Syracusan poet Theocritus was active at the Alexandrian court under the reign of Ptolemy II. The following is an example of official poetry composed under royal patronage for the glorification of Hellenistic rulers.

See further: Fraser I (1972), 666f. and II, 933f. (n. 388); F. T. Griffiths, *Theocritus at Court* (Leyden, 1979), esp. 71–82.

[. . .] Zeus son of Cronus cares for august kings,[1] but preeminent is the one whom Zeus has loved from the moment of his birth. Prosperity attends him in abundance, and vast is the territory he rules, and vast the sea.

Countless countries, and countless nations, helped by the rain of Zeus, cause their crops to grow, but none is as productive as the lowlands of Egypt when the Nile in flood waters and breaks up the soil,[2] nor does any have as many towns of men skilled in work. Three hundred cities are built there, then three thousand in addition to thirty thousand, and twice three and three times nine besides;[3] over all these mighty Ptolemy rules as king. In addition he cuts off for himself a part of Phoenicia, Arabia, Syria, Libya and of the dark-skinned Ethiopians. He gives orders to all the Pamphylians, to the Cilician spearmen, to the Lycians and to the warlike Carians, and to the islands of the Cyclades, since his are the finest ships that sail the seas.[4] All the sea and land and the roaring rivers are ruled by Ptolemy, and about him gather a host of horsemen and a host of shielded warriors, equipped with glittering bronze.[5]

In wealth he could outweigh all the kings, so great are the riches that come daily from everywhere to his opulent home;[6] his people go about their occupations in security.[7] No enemy by land has crossed the teeming Nile to raise the battle cry in villages that do not belong to him, nor has he leaped in arms on to the shore from a swift ship with hostile intent to seize the herds of Egypt. So great is the man who reigns over the broad plains, fair-haired Ptolemy, a skilled spearman, who as a good king cares deeply for the preservation of his fatherly inheritance,[8] and adds to it himself. And yet in his wealthy house the gold does not lie useless in piles like the wealth of the ever-toiling ants. Much of it is received by the glorious homes of the gods,[9] where he always offers first fruits together with other offerings, and many are the gifts he has made to mighty kings, many to cities, and many to his trusted companions.[10] Nor has any man come to the sacred competitions of Dionysus,[11] skilled in raising a harmonious song, to whom he has not presented a gift worthy of his art. And so the spokesmen of the Muses (i.e. poets) celebrate Ptolemy in return for his benefactions. For a man blessed with wealth what more beautiful goal could there be than to win a good reputation among men? [. . .] Alone of men of former times and of those whose footsteps are still warm in the dust they trod, he has founded temples fragrant (with incense) to his dear mother and to his father;[12] in these temples he has set up beautiful statues (of them) in gold and ivory, as helpers[13] to all men living on earth. And as the months come round he burns on the reddened altars many fat thighs of oxen, he and his noble wife, the best of women, who holds in her embrace her husband in their palace, cherishing with all her heart her brother[14] and husband. [. . .]

Theocritus XVII, 73–130

1. On this theme cf. also **234** n. 3.
2. References to the Nile flood are of course numerous, cf. **219, 222** ll. 13–15, **227** ll. 24f., **232** §7, **242, 251, 256** ll. 169–73, **259** n. 4.
3. I.e. 33,333 (villages rather than 'cities'). Cf. Diodorus 1.31 (from Hecataeus of Abdera, cf. **166**): 'In ancient times (Egypt) had more than 18,000 large villages and cities, as one may see from entries in their sacred records, while under Ptolemy son of Lagus they numbered more than 30,000 [. . .] It is said that in former times the total population was about seven million and has remained no less in our time.' On the population of Egypt cf. Rostovtzeff II (1941), 1137–40.
4. On the 'empire' of the Ptolemies outside Egypt cf. generally **218, 221, 223, 265**, and for particular areas cf. **21** §§ 10–12, 17, **266–279**. Theocritus' list is not strictly complete or accurate. On the Ptolemaic navy cf. **219**.
5. On the military character of the Ptolemies cf. also **219–221, 223**.
6. On the wealth of the Ptolemies cf. also **219, 232**; generally Rostovtzeff I (1941), 407–11.
7. Cf. **219** (last §), **223**.
8. On this notion cf. also **139** (beginning), **153** n. 2, **172, 223**.
9. On this theme cf. **163** n. 4, **218** ll. 22f., and for the Ptolemies' relations with native Egyptian cults cf. **222, 227, 231, 235**.

10. On royal munificence cf. **93** and n. 12, and on the king's 'friends' cf. **25** n. 3, **224** n. 2.

11. I.e. dramatic festivals. The Ptolemies claimed descent from Dionysus, cf. **219, 221**, and generally Fraser I (1972), 201–7. For the Ptolemies as patrons of the arts cf. also **232** §8.

12. Antiochus I did deify his father Seleucus, cf. **158**, but Ptolemy II went further and deified his sister-wife Arsinoe and himself. For the dynastic cults of the Ptolemies cf. **218, 219, 221, 222** and n. 3, **227, 231** l. 78, **235**, and see generally Fraser I (1972), 213–46.

13. Ptolemy I and Berenice were deified as *Theoi Soteres*, i.e. 'Saviour Gods'.

14. Literal: the Ptolemies adopted the Egyptian custom of brother–sister marriages, cf. Fraser I (1972), 117f.

218 Decree of the League of Islanders on the acceptance of the 'Ptolemaieia' (ca 280)

The 'League of Islanders', which included the smaller islands of the central Aegean (cf. **21** and n. 1, **268**) was founded by Antigonus the One-Eyed in 315/14 and subsequently controlled by his son Demetrius Poliorcetes before it passed into Ptolemaic hands by *ca* 286 where it remained for some 30 years. The League is not mentioned in extant literary sources and the evidence for it is purely epigraphic. Like other Leagues founded under royal patronage (cf. **42**) it was used as an instrument of royal control.

See further: I. L. Merker, *Historia* 19 (1970), 141–60; Fraser I (1972), 224, 231f.; Bagnall (1976), 136–58; T. L. Shear, *Hesperia* Supplement 17 (1978), 30–44.

[Resolved] by the delegates (*synedroi*) of the Islanders; concerning the matters about which [Philocles] king of the Sidonians[1] and Bacchon the [nesiarch[2] wrote] to the cities, that they should send delegates to Samos[3] to / discuss the (question of the) sacrifice, the sacred envoys (*theoroi*) and   5
the contest which King Ptolemy (II) is instituting in honour of his father in Alexandria,[4] to be equal in rank with the Olympic Games [and (concerning which)] Philocles and Bacchon have [now conversed] with the [delegates] who have arrived from the cities, be it / resolved by the   10
common body (*koinon*) of the delegates, since King Ptolemy (I) Soter (the Saviour) has been responsible for many great blessings to the Islanders and the other Greeks, having liberated the cities,[5] restored their laws, / reestablished to all their ancestral constitution and remitted[6]   15
their taxes, and (since) now King Ptolemy (II), having inherited the kingdom from his father, continues to show the same goodwill and concern for the Islanders and / the other Greeks, and is offering a sacrifice in honour   20
of his father and instituting a gymnastic, musical and equestrian contest to be equal in rank with the Olympic Games, preserving his [piety] towards

the gods[7] and maintaining his goodwill towards his [ancestors], and
25 (since) for this purpose he is inviting / [the] Islanders and the other
Greeks to [vote] that the contest should be equal in rank with the
Olympic Games, and (since) it is fitting that all the Islanders, who were
the [first] to have honoured Ptolemy Soter with godlike honours[8] [both
because] of his [public benefactions] and because of his [services] to
30 individuals, / should collaborate [in other matters with King] Ptolemy
(II) at his invitation and should now [vote with all] zeal in accordance
35 with [his wish . . . to grant] worthy honours / [. . . of] their goodwill,
[to accept] the sacrifice and [to send] the sacred envoys at the [appropriate
season for] all time to come, as instructed by the king; [and] that the
contest should be equal in rank with the Olympic Games, and that the
40 victors / [from the Islanders] should enjoy the same honours which are
[written down in] the laws among each of the Islanders for the victors at
the Olympic Games; and to crown King Ptolemy son of King Ptolemy
45 Soter with a [golden] crown for merit / [worth] a thousand staters, for
his excellence and his goodwill towards the Islanders, and that the
delegates should inscribe this decree on a stone stele and [set it up at]
Delos next to the altar of [Ptolemy] Soter. [In] the same way let the cities
50 participating in the council (*synedrion*) pass this / resolution, inscribe it
on stone stelae and consecrate it in the sanctuaries in which the other
honours are inscribed in each city. The delegates shall appoint three
55 sacred envoys to go / to Alexandria, sacrifice to Ptolemy Soter on behalf
of the League (*koinon*) of Islanders and hand over [the] crown to the king.
The money for the crown, for the journey and expenses of the sacred
60 envoys shall be contributed by the cities, each / [according to] its share,
and they shall give it to the person [designated by Bacchon]. Glaucon of
[Cythnus, . . . of] Naxos, Cleocritus of Andros were appointed sacred
envoys.

Syll.[3] 390

1. A Hellenised ruler of Sidon, allied to the Ptolemies and admiral of their fleet;
   cf. **135** and I. L. Merker, *op. cit.*, 143–50; Bagnall (1976), index s.v. Philokles;
   M. Wörrle, *Chiron* 8 (1978), 225–30.
2. On Bacchon cf. **268** and I. L. Merker, *op. cit.*, 150–2; Bagnall (1976), index
   s.v. Bacchon. The 'nesiarch' was (probably) a royal appointee who acted as
   the king's delegate towards the islanders; it is not clear that he was subordinate
   to Philocles the admiral.
3. The council of the League usually met on Delos; it is not clear whether Samos,
   a naval base of the Ptolemies, formally belonged to the League (Bagnall
   (1976), 80 and n. 2). Cf. **113, 125**.
4. I.e. the quinquennial *Ptolemaieia*, cf. **44, 113, 122, 217** nn. 12 and 13, **219, 234**
   n. 5. The attempt to raise the status of the *Ptolemaieia* to equal that of the

Olympic Games and to involve the Greek world in its celebration was far more ambitious than anything practised by the other Hellenistic monarchies.
5. A reference to Ptolemy I's campaigns in Greece and the Aegean in 310–308 when he posed as 'champion of the Greeks' (cf. **29** and n. 9).
6. The Greek word could mean either 'lighten' or 'remove', cf. I. L. Merker, *op. cit.*, 151 n. 46.
7. Cf. **217** n. 9.
8. Presumably therefore earlier than Rhodes (cf. **39**(b)); cf. too **267** and see generally **32**.

219 The great procession at Alexandria in 271/70

The following passage, reproduced by Athenaeus from a work by Callixinus of Rhodes entitled *On Alexandria* (*FGrH* 627; cf. Fraser I (1972), 513 and II, 738f. n. 152), describes a procession held in Alexandria which may have been part of a celebration of the *Ptolemaieia* of 271/70 (cf. **218**).

See further: Fraser (1972), index s.v. Ptolemy Philadelphus, 'Pompe' (vol. III, p. 65).

After speaking of very many other things and enumerating herds of animals, he (sc. Callixinus of Rhodes) adds: 'One hundred and thirty Ethiopian sheep, three hundred Arabian, twenty Euboean; twenty-six Indian oxen, all white, eight Ethiopian, one large white she-bear, fourteen leopards, sixteen panthers, four lynxes, three young panthers, one giraffe, one Ethiopian rhinoceros.[1] Next, on a four-wheeled carriage Dionysus[2] at the altar of Rhea, having taken refuge when pursued by Hera, with a golden crown, and Priapus standing next to him wearing a golden ivy-crown. (Then) statues of Alexander[3] and Ptolemy, wearing ivy-crowns made of gold. The statue of Virtue standing next to Ptolemy had an olive-crown made of gold. Priapus stood next to them with a golden ivy-crown. The city of Corinth,[4] standing next to Ptolemy, was crowned with a golden diadem. Beside all these were placed a stand for drinking vessels full of golden cups and a golden mixing bowl with a capacity of five measures. This four-wheeled carriage was followed by women wearing expensive clothes and ornaments; they were given the names of cities, some from Ionia and the rest the Greek cities which were established in Asia and the islands and had been under Persian rule; they all wore golden crowns. On other four-wheeled carts were carried a (Bacchic) thyrsus of gold, 90 cubits long (= 135 ft) and a silver lance 60 cubits long (= 90 ft), and on another one a golden phallus 120 cubits long (= 180 ft), painted over and bound with golden fillets, with a gold star at its extremity, the circumference of which was six cubits (= 9 ft).

Though the things that have been mentioned in these processions were many and varied, we have selected only those which contained gold and silver. For there were many objects displayed worth mentioning, a multitude of wild animals and horses, and 24 huge lions. And there were other four-wheeled carts carrying not only statues of kings but many of gods as well. [. . .] (202 f) After these marched the cavalry and infantry, all of them equipped in wonderful fashion.⁵ The infantry numbered about 57,600, and the cavalry 23,200. All of these took part in the procession wearing each their appropriate uniform and the panoply suitable to each.' But apart from the panoplies these troops were all wearing, there were very many others stored away. Merely to set down the number of them is not easy; but Callixinus gave a list. 'In the contest men were honoured with gold crowns and even with statues. Ptolemy (I) was the first, then Berenice, and they were honoured with three statues in golden chariots and with sacred precincts at Dodona. The total expense in <Rhodian> currency amounted to 2,239 talents and 50 minas, and all this money was counted to the officials in charge before the end of the spectacle thanks to the enthusiasm of those who awarded the crowns. Ptolemy (II) Philadelphus their son (was honoured with) two golden statues in chariots of gold, mounted on columns one of six cubits (= 9 ft), five of five cubits (= 7½ ft) and six of four cubits (= 6 ft).'

What monarchy [. . .] has ever been so rich in gold?⁶ Certainly not any that seized the wealth of the Persians and of Babylon, or worked mines, or owned the Pactolus (in Lydia) which carries down gold dust. It is only the Nile, a river truly called 'streaming with gold', which with its unlimited provision of food carries down pure gold which is harvested without danger,⁷ so that all men have sufficient supplies, (gold) that in the manner of Triptolemus is sent forth to every land. [. . .] Philadelphus surpassed many kings in wealth, and applied himself enthusiastically to all kinds of equipment, so that he surpassed all in the number of ships as well. The largest ships he had were two 'thirties', one 'twenty', four 'thirteens', two 'twelves', fourteen 'elevens', thirty 'nines', thirty-seven 'sevens', five 'sixes', and seventeen 'fives'.⁸ He had twice as many ships ranging from 'fours' to war galleys (?). The ships sent to the islands and to the other cities he ruled⁹ and to Libya numbered more than 4,000. Need I even mention the number of volumes, the building of libraries and the gathering at the Museum,¹⁰ when these things are in everyone's memory?

Athenaeus, *Deipnosophistae* v 201 b–f,
202 f–203 e (= Callixinus of
Rhodes *FGrH* 627 F 2)

1. For Ptolemy II's interest in animals cf. **278, 279**.
2. Cf. **217** n. 11.

3. On the Ptolemies' exploitation of the fame of Alexander cf. **222** n. 1.
4. I.e. a personification.
5. Cf. **217** and n. 5.
6. Cf. **217** and n. 6. On the Ptolemies' gold mines cf. **263**.
7. Cf. **217**, nn. 2 and 7.
8. The exact types of ships involved are uncertain. They probably had several rowers per oar (up to 8?), and in some cases superimposed banks of oars (up to 3), and the very largest ships (the 'thirty' and the 'twenty') may have been double-hulled. Ptolemy II's fleet represented the culmination of the naval 'arms race' which flourished in the early Hellenistic period. See L. Casson, *Ships and Seamanship in the Ancient World* (Princeton, 1971), 97–123, 137–40.
9. Cf. **217** n. 4.
10. Cf. **232** §8, **262**.

220 The opening stages of the Laodicean (or Third Syrian) War (246/5)

By the treaty which ended the 'Second Syrian War' Antiochus II repudiated his wife Laodice by whom he had two children (cf. **185** and n. 6) and married Berenice, daughter of Ptolemy II Philadelphus and sister of Ptolemy III Euergetes, by whom he had a son. At the death of Antiochus II war over the succession broke out between the sons of the two wives (the precise circumstances and responsibilities are unclear); Berenice appealed to her brother Ptolemy III and this provided the starting point of the 'Third Syrian War' (246–241). The following is an account, preserved on papyrus, of the opening stages of the war when Ptolemy III invaded Syria, ostensibly written by the king himself (or at least in his name), as appears from internal evidence. On the war cf. also **182**(a), **221**, **222**, **271**, **274**.

Column II[1]

[. . .] . . . and having sailed along the coast to Soloi in [Cilicia] they seized the [money] which was deposited [there] and brought it / to   5
Seleucia.[2] This amounted to 1,500 (talents) [of silver which] Aribazus the [general] in Cilicia intended to send to Ephesus to Laodice, but the men of Soloi and ⟨the⟩ [soldiers] on the spot had agreed among themselves, and Pythagoras and Aristocles and their men had [vigorously] come to the rescue / and . . . and they had all shown themselves gallant men,   10
and so these funds were seized and the city and its citadel came into our hands . . . Aribazus escaped and sought to cross the Taurus, / but some   15
of the local people cut off his [head] and brought it to Antioch.[3] [As for us], after getting the [ships ready], at the beginning of the first watch we embarked on as many ships as the harbour at Seleucia was likely to admit and we sailed along the coast / to the fort called Posideum, and we   20
dropped anchor at about the [eighth] hour of the day. From there we

25 sailed at dawn and reached Seleucia. The priests, the [magistrates, the] other citizens, the officers and the soldiers were all wearing crowns / and came to meet us at the harbour.[4]

Column III

... goodwill [towards us] and . . . into the city . . . [the] offerings
5 [which were ready . . . on the altars] they had / [set up] . . . and the honours in the mart . . . During that day . . . but on the next day . . .
10 as far as is possible (?) . . . in which (sc. ships?) we received / . . . [all] those [who had sailed] with us [and the local] satraps and [generals and the other] officers who were not [on duty . . . in] the city and the
15 [citadel] . . . allowing / . . . for they were astonishing . . . [After] this [we came] to Antioch and [there] we [found] such preparations and . . .
20 that [we] were amazed. For outside the gate [there came to meet] us / the . . . satraps and the other officers [and soldiers], the priests, the boards of magistrates and [all the] young men [from] the gymnasium and the rest of the [crowd] . . . wearing [crowns], and they brought out all the sacred objects to the road in front of [the gate]. Some of them greeted us
25 with their right hand, / while others . . . with applause and shouting.

Column IV

(12 lines missing) . . . next to each house . . . they (or: we?) never
15 ceased to / . . . since for us there were many who . . . Nothing pleased us so much as the enthusiasm [they showed]. Then since . . . the offerings which were ready . . . and of private individuals, we poured
20 libations, and now / that the sun was setting we immediately went in to see (our) sister,[6] and after this we turned to practical business. We gave audience to the officers and soldiers and the other authorities in the
25 land, and held council on [matters of state]. / Furthermore, for a few days . . .

(the rest of the papyrus is lost)

FGrH 160; cf. M. Holleaux, *Etudes* III
(Paris, 1942), 281–310

1. Column I concerns the attack and capture of (probably) a Cilician city; the text is very mutilated.
2. Cf. **174** n. 8.
3. Cf. **174** §§4 and 5.
4. For such royal receptions cf. **34, 198**.
5. Cf. **119** n. 17.
6. I.e. Berenice, yet according to Justin 27.1.7 she had been murdered by Laodice before the arrival of Ptolemy III; it may be that the official Ptolemaic account of the war deliberately suppressed the fact to preserve the propaganda justification for Ptolemy's invasion (cf. also Polyaenus VIII.50).

221 An epigraphic account of Ptolemy III's 'Third Syrian War'

This inscription, copied by the traveller Cosmas Indicopleustes at Adulis on the Red Sea in the sixth century A.D., but now lost, gives an account of the 'conquests' of Ptolemy III during the 'Third Syrian War' (cf. **220**). Though written in Greek the inscription is more reminiscent of the grandiloquent victory reports and records of the achievements of eastern kings than of any Greek texts (cf. also **189**).

King Ptolemy (III) the Great, son of King Ptolemy (II) and Queen Arsinoe, the Brother-Sister Gods (*theoi adelphoi*), children of King Ptolemy (I) and Queen Berenice the Saviour Gods (*theoi soteres*), descended on his father's side from Heracles son of Zeus and on his mother's side / from Dionysus[1] son of Zeus, having taken over from his   5
father the kingdom of Egypt, Libya,[2] Syria, Phoenicia, Cyprus, Lycia, Caria and the Cyclades islands,[3] marched out into Asia with a force of infantry and cavalry, a fleet / and elephants from the Troglodytes and   10
Ethiopia, which his father and he himself were the first to hunt from these places, and (which) they brought to Egypt and equipped for use in war.[4] Having secured control of all the territory within (i.e. to the west of) the Euphrates and of Cilicia, Pamphylia, Ionia, the Hellespont, /   15
Thrace, and of all the forces in those places and of the Indian elephants,[5] and having reduced to his obedience all the rulers in the provinces (*topoi*), he crossed the river Euphrates, and having subdued Mesopotamia, Babylonia, Susiana, Persis, Media and all the remaining territory as far as / Bactria,[6] and having sought out all the sacred objects that were   20
removed from Egypt by the Persians and having brought them back to Egypt[7] together with the rest of the treasure from the provinces (*topoi*), he sent his forces across the dug out rivers (i.e. canals)[8] . . .

(the rest of the inscription is lost)

OGIS 54

1. See **217** n. 11.
2. I.e. Cyrenaica (cf. **264**).
3. See **217** n. 4.
4. Cf. **278, 279**.
5. I.e. the Seleucid elephants (cf. **150** n. 6).
6. The reality of these grandiose (and ephemeral) conquests is usually doubted (though cf. Dittenberger's commentary); Ptolemy III may not have advanced further into the Seleucid empire than Babylon (Appian, *Syrian Wars* 65).
7. Cf. **222**, l. 11.
8. Reference unclear, but perhaps to the canals in Egypt, to which Ptolemy III was recalled by internal disturbances (Justin 17.1.9). Ptolemy's return enabled Seleucus II to regain the initiative.

222 Decree of the Egyptian priests in honour of Ptolemy III and Berenice (4 March 238)

In the reign of Ptolemy (III) son of Ptolemy (II) and Arsinoe, the Brother-Sister Gods (*theoi adelphoi*), in the ninth year, when Apollonides son of Moschion was priest of Alexander[1] and of the Brother-Sister Gods and of the Benefactor Gods (*theoi euergetai*), when Menecratea was basket-bearer (*canephoros*)[2] of Arsinoe Philadelphus, on the 7th of the month Apellaeus and the 17th of the Egyptian month Tybi (= 4 March 238);[3] decree; the high-priests, the prophets, those who enter the holy of holies for the robing of the gods, the *pterophoroi*,[4] the sacred scribes
5 and / the other priests who have assembled from the temples throughout the land[5] for the 5th of Dios (= November), when the birthday of the king is celebrated,[6] and for the 25th of the same month, when he received the monarchy from his father, and who held a session on that day in the temple of the Benefactor Gods at Canopus, declared: since King Ptolemy son of Ptolemy and Arsinoe, the Brother-Sister Gods, and Queen Berenice his sister and wife, the Benefactor Gods, constantly confer many great benefactions on the temples throughout the land and increase more and more the honours of the gods,[7] and show constant care for Apis and Mnevis[8] and all the other famous sacred
10 animals in the country / at great expense and outlay, and (since) the king on a campaign abroad[9] brought back to Egypt the sacred statues that had been taken out of the country by the Persians and restored them to the temples from which they had initially been taken,[10] and (since) he has maintained the country at peace by fighting in its defence against many nations and their rulers, and (since) they have provided good government (*eunomia*) to all those in the country and to the other subjects of their kingdom, and (since) when on one occasion the rise of the river (i.e. the Nile)[11] was insufficient and all the inhabitants of the country were terrified at what had happened and remembered the disaster that
15 occurred / under some of the previous kings, under whom it happened that all the people living in the land suffered from a drought, they showed their care for the residents in the temples and the other inhabitants of the country, and showed much foresight and sacrificed a large part of their revenues for the salvation of the population, and by importing corn[12] into the country from Syria, Phoenicia and Cyprus and many other places at great expense, they saved the inhabitants of Egypt, bequeathing to men of today and to posterity an immortal benefaction and the greatest memorial of their own excellence. In return for this the
20 gods have granted them a stable rule / and will bestow all other blessings in future. With good fortune, be it resolved by the priests in the country to increase the honours which already exist[13] in the temples for King

Ptolemy and Queen Berenice, the Benefactor Gods, and to their parents the Brother-Sister Gods, and to their grandparents the Saviour Gods, and (be it resolved) that the priests in all the temples throughout the land should also be called priests of the Benefactor Gods and should be inscribed in all public documents,[14] and that the priesthood of the Benefactor Gods should also be engraved on the rings they wear; and (be it resolved) that in addition to the four 'tribes' of the body of priests living in each temple which exist at present another one should be designated, to be called the fifth / tribe of the Benefactor Gods, since,   25 with good fortune, it happened that the birth of King Ptolemy son of the Brother-Sister Gods took place on the 5th of Dios, which has been the beginning of many blessings for all mankind; shall be enrolled in this tribe those who have held the priesthood since the first year and those who will have been assigned to it up to the month of Mesore in the 9th year, and their descendants for all time; those who have previously been priests up to the first year shall remain in the same tribes in which they were before, and similarly from now on their descendants shall be assigned to the same tribes as their fathers. In place of the twenty priest councillors who are chosen / every year from the existing four tribes,   30 five being appointed from each tribe, there shall be twenty-five priest councillors with the addition of five from the fifth tribe of the Benefactor Gods. The members of the fifth tribe of the Benefactor Gods shall participate in the purification and all the other rites in the temples, and they shall have a head of the tribe as exists for the other four tribes. And since festivals of the Benefactor Gods are celebrated every month in the temples in accordance with the previous decree, on the 5th, the 9th and the 25th, and that festivals and public religious assemblies are celebrated every year for the other greatest gods, / a public religious assembly shall   35 be celebrated every year in the temples and throughout the whole country in honour of King Ptolemy and Queen Berenice, the Benefactor Gods, on the day when the star of Isis rises, which the holy books consider to be the new year, and which takes place at present in the ninth year on the first day of the month Payni (= 19 July), when the Little and the Great Boubastia are celebrated, the crops are gathered and the river (sc. the Nile) rises.[15] And should it happen that the rise of the star moves to another day within four years, the religious assembly shall not be moved but shall be celebrated in the same way on the first day of Payni, when it originally took place in the 9th year; the celebration shall last for five days / and shall include a wearing of wreaths (*stephanephoria*),   40 sacrifices, libations and the other appropriate rites. [. . .][16]

The *epistates* in charge in each temple[17] and the high-priest and the scribes of the temple shall inscribe this decree on a stone or bronze stele in sacred letters (i.e. hieroglyphs), Egyptian letters (i.e. demotic), and

75 Greek letters,[18] and shall consecrate it / in the temples of the first, second and third rank, so that it may be seen that the priests in the country honour the Benefactor Gods and their children, as is just.

OGIS 56 (omitting lines 40–73)

1. Alexander was buried at Alexandria where he received a divine cult (note the absence of the predicate '*theos*', otherwise used of deified Hellenistic rulers: Alexander was thought of as a full god). Cf. **232** §8, also **219** (beginning).
2. A sacred basket was carried in the procession in honour of Arsinoë Philadelphus; cf. Fraser I (1972), 225, 229f.
3. For similar prescripts cf. **227, 244, 248**, and for the dynastic cults of the Ptolemies cf. **217** n. 12. The priests and priestesses of these dynastic cults were appointed by the kings themselves from among their Greek and Macedonian entourage (no native Egyptians are attested); cf. Fraser I (1972), 222f. On priesthoods generally see **129**.
4. Priests wearing a hawk's wing on their heads.
5. The Egyptian priesthood was the only organised and articulate native body in Ptolemaic Egypt; cf. **227, 231**.
6. On the celebration of the king's birthday cf. **143, 215** l. 35, **227, 234** n. 3, **267**.
7. Cf. **217** n. 9.
8. The sacred bulls at Memphis and Heliopolis respectively, frequently singled out from among other Egyptian sacred animals; cf. **227** l. 31, **231** l. 77, also **261** on Serapis.
9. A reference to the 'Third Syrian War', cf. **220, 221**.
10. Cf. **221** ll. 20–22.
11. Cf. **217** n. 2.
12. Egypt was otherwise a regular grain exporter to the Greek world.
13. I.e. divine honours were already being paid by the Egyptian priests to the Ptolemies.
14. For the practice cf. **158** (n. 7), **227** l. 51 and above n. 3.
15. Cf. **217** n. 2.
16. Lines 40–46: reform of the calendar; lines 46–73: institution of a cult in honour of a deceased daughter of Ptolemy III. For a full translation of the inscription see Sir E. A. Wallis Budge, *The Rosetta Stone* (1929), 254–65.
17. Cf. **231** n. 17.
18. Cf. **227** l. 53f.

223 Ptolemy IV Philopator and the policy of his predecessors (221)

After his father's death, Ptolemy (IV) who was called Philopator put to death his brother Magas and his followers and took over power in Egypt. He felt freed from internal threats thanks to his efforts and to the action just mentioned, and felt that fortune had released him from foreign perils, as Antigonus (Doson) and Seleucus (III) had died, and Antiochus (III) and Philip (V), who had succeeded them on the throne, were very young and had barely reached manhood. Consequently he felt secure in his present position and conducted his reign with too much ostentation; he made himself invisible and difficult of access[1] to his courtiers and to the other officials who governed Egypt, and showed himself indifferent and frivolous towards those in charge of foreign affairs, though his predecessors had devoted not less but more care to them than to their rule in Egypt itself.[2] For they threatened the kings of Syria (i.e. the Seleucids) by land and by sea, as they were masters of Coele Syria and Cyprus; their sphere of control included the dynasts[3] in Asia and also the islands, as they were masters of the most important cities, strongholds and harbours along the whole coast from Pamphylia to the Hellespont and the region of Lysimachea.[4] They kept a watch on affairs in Thrace and Macedonia through their control of Aenus and Maronea and of even more distant cities.[5] In this way, having extended their reach so far and having shielded themselves at a great distance with these possessions, they never worried about their rule in Egypt.[6] That was why they rightly devoted much attention to foreign affairs. [. . .]

Polybius v. 34

1. Contrast Cleomenes III, **56**(a).
2. On the Ptolemies' foreign possessions cf. **217** n. 4. On Polybius' unfavourable presentation of Ptolemy IV cf. also **225**; the contrast with his predecessors may be overdrawn. Contrast Polybius' favourable royal portraits, **199, 207**.
3. Cf. **182** n. 6.
4. Cf. **153**.
5. Cf. **269**.
6. On the security of Egypt cf. **217** n. 7. However, Ptolemy I faced the threat of an invasion of Egypt twice, by Perdiccas in 321/20 and by Antigonus the One-Eyed in 305; cf. too **221** n. 8. Whether the foreign policy of the Ptolemies in the third century was 'offensive' or 'defensive' in intention has been much discussed (cf. Will I (1979), 153–208; Walbank III (1979), 772). Whatever the truth, and whether the antithesis is correct or not (cf. P. Vidal-Naquet, *RPh* 41 (1967), 271f.), Ptolemaic propaganda emphasised the military character of their dynasty's achievements, cf. **217** n. 5.

224 Preparations for the 'Fourth Syrian War' by the ministers of Ptolemy IV (219/18)

See further: Griffith (1935), 118–25.

Agathocles and Sosibius, at that time the chief ministers in the kingdom,[1] then held council together and took what steps they could from the means at their disposal to meet the present crisis. They decided to proceed with the preparations for the war and in the meantime to slow down Antiochus' (III) advance by sending embassies and pretending to confirm him in his previous opinion of Ptolemy (IV), namely that he would not fight, but would negotiate and use his 'friends'[2] to try to persuade him to evacuate Coele Syria. When these decisions were taken, Agathocles and Sosibius were assigned to this mission and carefully sent off the embassies to Antiochus. At the same time they sent envoys to Rhodes, Byzantium and Cyzicus, and also to Aetolia, and invited them to send delegates to discuss a settlement. The arrival of these embassies, by going backwards and forwards between the two kings, gave them ample opportunity to secure a breathing-space and the time needed to prepare for the war. They established themselves at Memphis and kept on negotiating with them, but also received the envoys from Antiochus and displayed every sign of courtesy in their meetings. Meanwhile they summoned and concentrated at Alexandria the mercenaries in their pay from the cities abroad.[3] They also despatched recruiting officers[4] and gathered pay for the soldiers present and to come. They were no less active with the remaining preparations, taking turns to go on continuous flying visits to Alexandria, to make sure nothing was missing in the preparations for the projected undertaking. The manufacture of weapons and the choice of men and their distribution they entrusted to Echecrates of Thessaly and Phoxides of Melite, and also to Eurylochus of Magnesia and Socrates of Boeotia; Cnopias of Allaria (in Crete) was also with them. They were very fortunate to secure these men, as they had served with Demetrius (II) and Antigonus (Doson) and had acquired some experience of real war and in general of operations in the open field. They took in hand the troops and trained them as best they could in military operations. [. . .] (65) Each of these men held a command appropriate to his personal experience. Eurylochus of Magnesia commanded about 3,000 of what is called the Royal Guard (*agema*). Socrates of Boeotia had 2,000 peltasts under his command. Phoxidas the Achaean and Ptolemy son of Thraseas, and with them Andromachus of Aspendus, were associated in the task of training the phalanx and the Greek mercenaries to the same use, while Andromachus and Ptolemy commanded the phalanx and Phoxidas the mercenaries; the phalanx numbered about 25,000 men[5] and the mercenaries 8,000. The palace cavalry, who numbered about 700, were trained by Polycrates, and similarly those from Libya and the native cavalry; they numbered about 3,000 and Polycrates commanded them all. Echecrates of Thessaly who had given excellent training to the cavalry from Greece and the entire body of mercenary cavalry, who numbered about 2,000, performed the greatest services in the battle itself. Cnopias of Allaria was second to none in the dedication he showed to those under his orders: he had all the Cretans, who numbered about 3,000, including 1,000 Neocretans over whom he had set Philon of Cnossus.[6] They also armed 3,000 Libyans in the Macedonian way, commanded by Ammonius of Barce. The Egyptian contingent constituted a phalanx of about 20,000, under the orders of Sosibius.[7] A force of Thracians and Galatians had also been collected, some of them from the military settlers (*katoikoi*) and their descendants, numbering about 4,000,[8] while the others were recently recruited; they numbered about 2,000 and were commanded by the Thracian Dionysius. Such was, in its numbers and in its different elements, the army that was being got ready by Ptolemy.[9]

Polybius v.63 and 65

1. On Sosibius cf. **148, 226**, on Agathocles cf. **226**, on the 'Fourth Syrian War' cf. also **148, 149**.
2. Cf. **25** n. 3 and for the king's 'friends' in the Ptolemaic kingdom cf. **217, 228, 232** n. 2, **239, 257, 259, 260**(c), **270, 276**; see generally Fraser I (1972), 101–5 and L. Mooren, *The Aulic Titulature in Ptolemaic Egypt* (Brussels, 1975), with prosopography.
3. I.e. in the Ptolemies' foreign possessions (**217** n. 4).
4. Cf. **226** and Griffith (1935), 254–63.
5. Polybius' figure has been questioned (Griffith, *op. cit.*, 122f.; Walbank *ad loc.*); see however Walbank III (1979), 773.
6. On Cretan mercenaries cf. **95** n. 4; on the Ptolemies and Crete cf. **267**.
7. For the effects of this cf. **225**.
8. On the Ptolemaic system of military settlements in Egypt cf. **252**.
9. For mercenaries in Ptolemaic service cf. also **274**.

225 The internal consequences of the battle of Raphia

See further: W. Peremans in *Préaux* (1975), 393–402.

(*a*) Immediately after this[1] Ptolemy (IV) became involved in the war against the Egyptians. For this king, by arming the Egyptians for the war against Antiochus (III), took a decision which though acceptable for the present involved a miscalculation for the future. For they were elated by the success at Raphia and could no longer endure to take orders, but looked out for a figure to lead them as they believed they were now able to fend for themselves. And that is what they achieved not long after.

Polybius v.107.1–3

(*b*) After the conclusion of the war over Coele Syria, King Ptolemy (IV) Philopator, of whom I am now speaking, gave up all honourable

371

pursuits and turned to a life of abandonment such as I have just described.[2] But late in life[3] he was compelled by circumstances to become involved in the war I have mentioned, a war which apart from the savagery and lawlessness each side displayed to the other, involved no regular battle, sea-fight, or siege, nor anything else worth mentioning.[4]

Polybius XIV.12.3–4

1. The 'Fourth Syrian War' (cf. **224**).
2. Cf. **223**.
3. The war started in 207/6; upper Egypt escaped from Ptolemaic control till 186.
4. I.e. a guerilla-type war. For disturbances in Egypt and tension between the natives and the immigrants cf. **221** n. 8, **227, 228, 231, 245**(?), **256** (n. 19), **257**. See generally C. Préaux *CE* 11 (1936), 522–52 and Préaux 1 (1978), 389–98.

226 The accession of Ptolemy V (204)

Two or three days later, having constructed a platform in the largest court of the palace, they[1] called together the bodyguard and the household troops, and also the officers of the infantry and cavalry. When these had come together, Agathocles and Sosibius ascended the platform and began by acknowledging the death of the king and queen[2] and proclaiming the customary period of mourning for the people. Then they placed a diadem[3] on the boy and proclaimed him king, and read out a forged will,[4] in which it was written that the king left Agathocles and Sosibius guardians of the child. They exhorted the officers to show goodwill towards the child and preserve his throne. They then brought in two silver urns, one of which was supposed to contain the king's bones and the other those of Arsinoe; in fact one of them did have the king's bones, but the other was full of spices. Having done this they immediately completed the funeral ceremony, and now the whole truth about Arsinoe's fate was made clear to the world. For now that her death was revealed men asked how it had come about. [. . .] No one cared about the king, but only about Arsinoe; some recalled her orphanhood, others the insults and maltreatment she had suffered from her earliest years, and on top of all this, her miserable end. The people fell into such a state of despair and grief that the city was filled with groans, tears and unending lamentations. Yet prudent observers could see that this was not so much a sign of their goodwill towards Arsinoe as rather of their hatred for Agathocles. The latter, after depositing the urns in the royal vaults, gave instructions to put off mourning, and at first gave two months' pay to the soldiers in the conviction that the hatred felt by the common soldiers would be blunted by their desire for gain. He then administered to them the oath they were accustomed to swear at the proclamation of the kings. He sent away Philammon, who had been in charge of the murder of Arsinoe, by appointing him 'Libyarch'[5] of the province of Cyrene, and entrusted the child (sc. the young Ptolemy V) to Oenanthe and Agathoclea.[6] After this he despatched Pelops son of Pelops to Asia to King Antiochus (III), to urge him to preserve their alliance and not to transgress the treaty with the child's father,[7] and Ptolemy son of Sosibius to Philip (V) to arrange matters concerning the marriage-alliance[8] and to ask for help should Antiochus attempt a serious breach of his compact with them. He also chose Ptolemy son of Agesarchus as ambassador to Rome,[9] not with a view of his hastening to carry out his mission, but because he thought that once he reached Greece and met the friends and relatives he had there, he would stay on the spot; for it was his (i.e. Agathocles') aim to remove all men of distinction. He also sent Scopas the Aetolian to recruit mercenaries in Greece,[10] giving him a large sum in gold for advance payments.[11] He did this with two objectives in mind: one was to use the mercenaries so recruited for the war with Antiochus,[12] another was to send away the existing mercenary troops to the forts in the country (sc. in Egypt) and the military settlements (*katoikiai*),[13] while he used the fresh recruits to fill up and renew the household troops, the palace guards and similarly the guards in the rest of the city (sc. Alexandria). It was his belief that the men recruited and paid by him would not sympathise with the previous soldiers as they knew nothing of them, but would place in him all their hopes of safety and success, and so would readily assist him and execute his instructions.[14]

Polybius xv.25.3–18

1. Probably Agathocles and Sosibius, on whom cf. **224** n. 1.
2. Ptolemy IV had died prematurely aged 35 (on the chronology cf. Walbank II (1967), 435–7). Arsinoe had been murdered by Agathocles' sister Agathoclea.
3. Cf. **36** n. 1.
4. On royal wills cf. **211, 230**.
5. It is not clear whether this is a technical term referring to an established post; cf. Bagnall (1976), 33f., 239.
6. Respectively mother and sister of Agathocles.
7. The treaty concluded after the battle of Raphia.
8. Perhaps a proposal for a marriage between Ptolemy V and a daughter of Philip V.
9. Probably to warn Rome of the danger presented by Antiochus III to Egypt.
10. Cf. **224** n. 4.
11. On this practice cf. Griffith (1935), esp. 292f.

12. The anticipated 'Fifth Syrian War' (cf. **167**).
13. Cf. **252**.
14. In fact Agathocles, his mother and sister were all to be lynched by the Alexandrian crowd, the first instance of its active interference in Ptolemaic politics (Polybius xv.26–33); this was to become a regular feature of the decline of the Ptolemies (cf. **228**). See Fraser I (1972), 81f., 118f.

227 Decree of the Egyptian priests in honour of King Ptolemy V (27 March 196)

The following text is a translation of the Greek version of the famous trilingual 'Rosetta stone' discovered in 1799, which made possible the decipherment of hieroglyphs. It consists of a decree of the Egyptian priesthood in honour of the young Ptolemy V Epiphanes, similar in character to the earlier decree from Canopus (see **222**), though comparison with that text reveals the increasing 'egyptianisation' of the Ptolemaic dynasty from the time of Ptolemy IV, and the need of the Ptolemies to conciliate the powerful native priesthood.
　　See further: Rostovtzeff II (1941), 713–15; Walbank II (1967), 435–7, 624f.

In the reign of the young one,[1] who has received royalty from his father, the lord of crowns, whose glory is great, who established Egypt and is pious towards the gods,[2] the conqueror of his enemies,[3] who restored the life of men, the lord of the Thirty-Year festivals,[4] like Hephaestus (i.e. Ptah) the Great, a king like the Sun (= Rā), the great king of the upper and lower regions,[5] son of the Father-Loving Gods (*theoi philopatores*), approved by Hephaestus, to whom the Sun granted victory, the living image of Zeus (= Amun) son of the Sun, Ptolemy the everliving, beloved of Ptah, in the 9th year, when Aetus son of Aetus was priest of Alexander, the Saviour Gods, the Brother-Sister Gods, the Benefactor Gods, the Father-Loving Gods and / the God Manifest and Beneficent (*theos epiphanes eucharistos*), when Pyrrha daughter of Philinus was *athlophoros*[6] of Berenice Euergetis, when Areia daughter of Diogenes was basket-bearer (*canephoros*) of Arsinoe Philadelphus, when Irene daughter of Ptolemy was priestess of Arsinoe Philopator, on the 4th of the month Xandicus and the 18th of the Egyptian month Mecheir (27 March 196);[7] decree; the chief priests, the prophets, those who enter the holy of holies for the robing of the gods, the *pterophoroi*, the sacred scribes and all the other priests who assembled before the king from the temples throughout the land to Memphis for the festival of the reception of royalty to the everliving Ptolemy, beloved of Ptah, God Manifest and Beneficent, which he received from his father, having come together in the temple at Memphis on this day, declared:[8] since King Ptolemy the everliving, beloved of Ptah, God Manifest and Beneficent, born of King Ptolemy

5

and Queen Arsinoe, Father-Loving Gods, has conferred many benefits on the temples and / those who dwell in them and on all the subjects in 10 his kingdom, being a god born of a god and goddess – just as Horus son of Isis and Osiris, who avenged his father Osiris – and being benevolently disposed towards the gods, has dedicated to the temples revenues in money and corn, and has sustained many expenses to bring Egypt to a state of prosperity and to establish the temples, and has given away freely from his own means, and of the revenues and dues he receives from Egypt some he has completely remitted and others he has reduced,[9] so that the people[10] and all others might enjoy prosperity during his reign, and he has remitted the debts to the crown which were owed by the people in Egypt and those in the rest of his kingdom, which were considerable, and he has freed those who were in the prisons and who were under accusation for a long time from the charges against them; and he has ordered that the revenues of the temples and the grants which are made to them annually in corn / and money, and also the proper quota 15 (*apomoira*) which is assigned to the gods[11] from vineyards and gardens and the other possessions of the gods, should remain as they were in his father's time; and with regard to the priests he has ordered that they should pay no more as their fee for consecration[12] than they were required to pay under his father and up to the first year (sc. of Ptolemy V's reign); and he has released the members of the priestly class from the annual obligation to sail down the river (i.e. the Nile) to Alexandria;[13] and he has ordered that men[14] shall no longer be pressganged for the navy, and has remitted two-thirds of the tax on byssus cloth paid by the temples to the royal treasury,[15] and has restored to order whatever things were neglected in former times, taking care that the customary celebrations should be offered to the gods as is fitting; and he has also dispensed justice to everybody, just like Hermes (i.e. Thoth) the Great and Great; and he has ordered further that those soldiers (*machimoi*)[16] who come back, and the others who were rebellious / during the period of 20 disturbances,[17] should return and keep possession of their own property; and he has made sure that the cavalry and infantry forces and ships should be sent out against those attacking Egypt by sea and by land,[18] and has sustained great expenses in money and corn so that the temples and all the people in the land might be in safety; and having gone to Lycopolis in the Busirite nome, which had been occupied and fortified for a siege with an abundant stock of weapons and other supplies[19] – for the disaffection was now of long standing among the impious men who had gathered there and who had done much harm to the temples and the inhabitants of Egypt – and having encamped against it he surrounded it with mounds and trenches and massive fortifications; and when the Nile rose to a great height in the 8th year (198/7) and was about to flood the

25 plains as usual,[20] / he held it in check by damming in many places the mouths of the canals, for which he spent no small sum of money, and having stationed cavalry and infantry to guard them, in a short while he took the city by storm and destroyed all the impious men in it, just as Hermes (= Thoth) and Horus, the son of Isis and Osiris, subdued formerly those who had rebelled in the same places. When he came to Memphis to avenge his father and his own royalty, he punished in a fitting way all the leaders of those who rebelled in his father's time, who had [disturbed] the country and done harm to the temples, at the time when he came there for the performance of the appropriate ceremonies for his reception of royalty;[21] and he has remitted the debts of the temples to the royal treasury up to the 8th year (198/7), which was no small amount of corn and money, [and] similarly the dues on the byssus cloth

30 which had not been delivered to the royal treasury / and of those delivered (he has remitted) the cost of checking them, up to the same period; and he has freed the temples from the (tax of one) artaba for each arura of sacred land, and also the (tax of one) jar of wine for each arura of vineyards; and he has bestowed many gifts on Apis and Mnevis and the other sacred animals in Egypt,[22] much more than the kings before him, showing consideration for what belonged [to] them in every respect, and for their burials he gave what was needed lavishly and splendidly, and what was paid to their special shrines, with sacrifices and religious assemblies and the other [customary observances], and he has maintained the privileges of the temples and of Egypt in accordance with the laws, and has adorned the temple of Apis with lavish work, spending on it no small sum of gold [and silver] and precious stones, and he has founded temples and shrines and altars, and has restored those in need of repair, in

35 the spirit of a beneficent god in matters relating [to] / religion; and having discovered what temples were held in the highest honour, he has restored them during his own reign, as is fitting; in return for these things the gods have granted him health, victory, power and [all] other blessings, and his royalty shall remain with him and his children for all time.

With good fortune. The priests of all the temples throughout the land have resolved to increase greatly the [honours] existing [in the temples] for King Ptolemy the everliving, beloved of Ptah, God Manifest and Beneficent, and also those for his parents the Father-Loving Gods, and those for his grandparents the Benefactor Gods [and those] for the Brother-Sister Gods and those for the Saviour Gods. A statue of King Ptolemy the everliving, God Manifest and Beneficent, shall be set up in each temple in the [most] distinguished [place], to be called (statue) of Ptolemy the avenger of Egypt, and beside it shall stand the chief god of each temple presenting to him the weapon of victory, which shall be

constructed [in the Egyptian] / fashion, and the priests shall worship the   40
statues three times a day and shall put upon them the sacred dress, and
perform the customary rites as for the other gods at [festivals and]
religious assemblies. A statue and a [golden] shrine shall be established
for King Ptolemy, God Manifest and Beneficent, born from King
Ptolemy and Queen Arsinoe, the Father-Loving Gods, [in each] temple
and they shall be placed in the innermost sanctuaries together with the
other shrines, and in the great religious assemblies, in which the shrines
are carried in procession, the [shrine] of the God Manifest and [Beneficent
shall also] be carried. And so that the shrine may be clearly marked now
and in future, it shall be surmounted by the ten golden crowns of the
king, with an asp fixed on them [as with all] the crowns with asps in the
other shrines. In the centre of them shall be the crown called *Pschent*,
which he (sc. the king) put on when he entered the [temple] at Memphis
[to] celebrate [there] / the ceremonies for the reception of royalty. And   45
there shall be placed on the square around the crowns, beside the
above-mentioned crown, [golden] symbols [which shall proclaim that]
they are those of the king who made illustrious the upper and the lower
country.[23] And since the 30th of Mesore (*ca* 7 October), on which the
king's birthday is celebrated,[24] and also [the 17th of Phaophi] (*ca* 28
November) on which he received the royalty from his father, have been
recognised as name-days in the temples, for they were the sources of
many blessings, these days shall be celebrated as festivals [and religious
assemblies in the] temples [throughout] Egypt every month, and in them
sacrifices, libations and the other customary celebrations shall be performed, as in other religious assemblies . . . in the temples. And a
festival and religious assembly shall be celebrated every [year] for the
everliving, beloved of Ptah, King Ptolemy, God Manifest and Beneficent
[in the temples throughout the] / country from the first day of Thoth for   50
five days, during which they shall wear wreaths as they perform the
sacrifices, libations and other appropriate rites. And [all the priests] shall
also be called priests of the God Manifest and Beneficent in addition to
the other names of the gods whom they serve, and his priesthood shall be
entered in all documents[25] and [engraved on the rings they wear]. And
private individuals may also celebrate the festival and set up the shrine
mentioned above and keep it in their houses, celebrating [the customary
rites in the monthly and] annual [festivals], in order that it may be well
known that the people in Egypt magnify and honour the God Manifest
and Beneficent, as is customary [for them. This decree shall be inscribed
on stelae] of hard stone, in sacred, native and Greek letters,[26] and
placed in every [temple] of the first, second [and third rank, next to the
statue].

SB 8299; *OGIS* 90 (cf. *SEG* xviii.634)

1. Ptolemy V was 13 at the time.
2. Cf. **217** n. 9.
3. Cf. **221**.
4. Identification uncertain.
5. This refers to the sun, not to Ptolemy V.
6. Literally 'prize-bearer', but the precise functions are unknown; cf. Fraser I (1972), 219, 225.
7. On such prescripts cf. **222** n. 3.
8. Cf. the similar gathering of priests at Canopus (**222**).
9. On these remissions and 'benefactions' characteristic of the decline of the Ptolemies, cf. **231**.
10. *Laos:* the native Egyptians.
11. Cf. **235**; the 'gods' here probably refer to the deified Ptolemaic rulers.
12. Cf. **231** ll. 80–2.
13. The precise purpose of the journey is not clear (possibly celebration of the king's birthday, cf. **222** n. 6); it may have involved expensive 'presents' to the rulers.
14. Probably men working on temple land; on pressganging for the Ptolemaic navy cf. **250** n. 1.
15. Weaving was a royal monopoly, but the temples were allowed to produce a certain amount of cloth for their own uses, as with oil, though subject to a tax (cf. **256** ll. 86–117 and n. 8).
16. A word used of the native Egyptian soldiers, on whom cf. also **231** ll. 44–48; it is not clear whether it refers here specifically to those recruited by Ptolemy for the 'Fourth Syrian War' (cf. **224, 225**).
17. The disturbances in Egypt which spread after the battle of Raphia (see **225**).
18. There is no mention here of the loss of Syria as a result of the 'Fifth Syrian War'.
19. On these events cf. Walbank III (1979), 204 on Polybius XXII.17.
20. Cf. **217** n. 2.
21. Apparently the first time a Ptolemaic ruler was crowned Pharaoh at Memphis according to Egyptian rites.
22. Cf. **222** n. 8.
23. The Pharaohs were kings of 'Upper (i.e. southern) and Lower (i.e. northern) Egypt.'
24. Cf. **222** n. 6.
25. Cf. **222** n. 14.
26. Cf. **222** l. 74.

228 The revolt of Dionysius Petosarapis (early 160s) and disturbances in Upper Egypt

See further: Fraser I (1972), 119f.; Walbank III (1979), 468.

(*a*) Dionysius called Petosarapis,[1] one of the 'friends'[2] of Ptolemy, sought to seize power for himself and so caused great danger to the kingdom.

For as he was the most influential man at court and surpassed all the Egyptians on the field of battle, he despised both of the kings because of their youth and lack of experience.[3] Pretending that he had been incited by the elder brother to murder his kinsman, he spread a story among the masses to the effect that the younger Ptolemy was the target of a plot by his brother. When the crowd[4] rushed to gather at the stadium and tempers were raised to such a pitch that they were making ready to kill the elder brother and hand over the kingdom to the younger, news of the disturbance was brought to the palace. The king sent for his brother and defended himself with tears in his eyes, begging him not to place any trust in a man who was seeking to appropriate the kingdom and who had nothing but contempt for their youth. If he still had any doubts and was apprehensive, he urged him to take over both the diadem[5] and the realm. The youth quickly cleared his brother of any suspicion, and the two of them put on royal dress and came out before the crowd, making a public demonstration of harmony. Dionysius, foiled in his attempt, took himself out of the way, and at first by sending messages to those soldiers who were ready to revolt he sought to persuade them to share his hopes, but then withdrew to Eleusis[6] and welcomed all those who were turning to revolution, and when a group of seditious soldiers had been collected, numbering about 4,000 . . . The king marched against them and was victorious, killing some and pursuing others, and forced Dionysius to swim naked across the river and to withdraw among the Egyptians, where he incited the masses to revolt.[7] Being an energetic man and finding himself enthusiastically welcomed by the Egyptians, he soon found many willing followers.

Diodorus XXXI.15 a

(*b*) Yet another disturbance took place in the Thebaid, as a revolutionary fervour fell on the masses.[8] King Ptolemy advanced against them with a large army and easily restored control over the other parts of the Thebaid. But the town called Panopolis[9] is situated on an ancient mound and because it is difficult of access it is thought to be a strong position; so the most active of the rebels gathered there. Ptolemy <seeing?> the desperation of the Egyptians and the strength of the place, laid siege to it and after enduring every kind of hardship he captured the city, punished the culprits and returned to Alexandria.

Diodorus XXXI.17 b

1. Otherwise unknown (cf. *PP* 14.600), and a rare example of a high-ranking Egyptian or Graeco-Egyptian at the Ptolemaic court.
2. Cf. **224** n. 2.
3. The two brothers Ptolemy VI and Ptolemy VIII, now in their twenties, had

379

been temporarily reconciled by Roman intervention (cf. **164**). For their
subsequent relations cf. **229, 230**.
4. On the growing political role of the Alexandrian populace cf. **226** and n. 14.
5. Cf. **36** n. 1.
6. A suburb of Alexandria.
7. On disturbances in Egypt cf. generally **225** and n. 4.
8. This need not be directly connected with the previous passage.
9. Cf. **231** l. 154 and n. 32.

229 Rivalry between Ptolemy VI and Ptolemy VIII and partition of the kingdom (163/2)

See further: Badian (1958), 108–10.

After the (two) Ptolemies had partitioned the kingdom,[1] the younger
Ptolemy (VIII) arrived in Rome wishing to cancel the partition he had
made with his brother; he said that it was not of his own free will but
under the force of circumstances that he had carried out what he had been
told to. He urged the Senate to assign Cyprus to him; for if this were
done he would (still) have a share far inferior to his brother's.
Canuleius and Quintus testified in favour of Menyllus, the envoy from the elder
Ptolemy (VI), by saying that the younger Ptolemy owed Cyrene and his
life to them (sc. the senators), so great was the anger and resentment felt
by the common people against him; and that when control of Cyrene
was granted to him against his hope and expectation, he was only too
glad to accept it, and slaughtered victims and exchanged mutual oaths
about this with his brother. Ptolemy (VIII) contradicted all this. The
Senate, seeing that the partition had been completely [ineffective?], but
wishing at the same time to make a division of the kingdom that would
be politically effective, since they[2] were responsible for it, granted the
demands of the younger Ptolemy for their own self-interest. Decisions of
this kind are now very frequent with the Romans; they rely on the
mistakes of others to increase and secure their own empire in a
statesmanlike way, by doing favours and appearing to confer benefactions on the offenders. That is why, seeing the greatness of the Egyptian
kingdom and fearing that should it ever find a leader he might become
excessively arrogant,[3] they appointed as ambassadors Titus Torquatus
and Cnaeus Merula to establish Ptolemy in Cyprus and carry out at once
the king's design and their own. They despatched them immediately
with instructions to reconcile the brothers and to secure Cyprus for the
younger without recourse to arms.[4]

Polybius XXXI. 10

1. On their earlier relations cf. **164, 228**. Strife broke out again between them and was temporarily settled in 163 by the partition here described; it is not clear whether Rome played any direct role in this partition.
2. The phrase is ambiguous, cf. Walbank *ad loc.*
3. Compare Roman dealings with the Seleucids, **169**.
4. In fact Ptolemy VI refused to give up Cyprus; whether Ptolemy VIII then tried to secure it by force is not clear. For the subsequent relations of the two brothers cf. **230**.

230 The will of Ptolemy VIII (March 155)

The prolonged conflict between the two Ptolemies (cf. **164, 228, 229**) culminated in an (alleged) assassination attempt in 155 by Ptolemy VI on his elder brother. This probably provides the context for the will of Ptolemy VIII, by which he bequeathed his 'kingdom' to the Romans in case he died childless, the first such example of a will by a Hellenistic ruler in favour of Rome (cf. **148** n. 3, **211**). Ptolemy's intention was probably to insure himself against future assassination attempts. The will remained in fact invalid; Ptolemy VI died in 145 and Ptolemy was able to restore the unity of the kingdom (for the sequel cf. **231**).

See further: Walbank III (1979), 477, 553f.

In the fifteenth year, in the month of Loios (March 155). With good fortune. This is the will[1] of King Ptolemy (VIII) the younger, son of King Ptolemy (V) and Queen Cleopatra (I), Gods / Manifest (*theoi epiphaneis*), a copy of which has been sent to Rome. May I with the favour of the gods exact suitable vengeance from those who hatched against me this impious plot and decided / to deprive me not only of my kingdom but even of my life.[2] Should any mortal fate befall me before I can leave behind heirs to the throne, I bequeathe the kingdom that belongs to me[3] to the Romans, / for whom I have from the beginning preserved our friendship and alliance with sincerity.[4] To them also I entrust the task of protecting my interests,[5] praying to them in the name of all the gods and with their own consent, that if any (enemies) / attack either the cities or the country (*chora*), they should give help with all their power in accordance with the friendship and alliance we concluded with each other and (in accordance with) justice. I make witnesses of these arrangements Capitoline Jupiter, / the Great Gods, the Sun and Apollo Archegetes, with whom the text of these arrangements is consecrated. With good fortune.

SEG IX.7

1. Or rather an abridged version published epigraphically for propaganda purposes.
2. A reference to the assassination attempt mentioned by Polybius XXXIII.11.2.

3. The scope of this is ambiguous; Ptolemy VIII only controlled Cyrene at the time. On Cyrene and the Ptolemies cf. **264**.
4. For Ptolemy VIII's relations with Rome cf. **164, 229**.
5. Cf. **139** n. 3.

231 The 'amnesty decree' of Ptolemy VIII, Cleopatra II and Cleopatra III (118)

The end of Ptolemy VIII's prolonged conflict with his brother (cf. **230**) was but one stage in his turbulent reign. Much of the latter part of it was taken up with a grim dynastic struggle between himself, his sister-wife Cleopatra II and his niece-wife Cleopatra III (cf. Fraser I (1972), 121–3). The struggle was only officially terminated in 124 with a formal reconciliation between the royal trio, after which they issued in 118 a long series of 'benefactions' or 'indulgences' (*philanthropa*) substantially preserved (though perhaps in an abridged form) in a papyrus from the archives of the village-scribe Menches (cf. **260**). This long text is but one in a series of such royal edicts which goes back to the reign of Ptolemy IV and sought to arrest the spread of disturbances and abuses in the country (cf. also **227**). The royal proclamations provide abundant evidence for the disturbed conditions in Egypt in the second century, further aggravated by the long civil war which had divided the country: brigandage and insecurity, accumulated arrears of taxes, usurpations of royal land, and especially corruption and oppression by the government's own officials. In response the royal authority proclaims a general amnesty, remission of taxes and arrears, condemnation of official abuses, privileges to those whose labour contributes to the royal treasury, and concessions to the growing power of the native clergy (cf. **227**). It goes without saying that the proclamations of 118 were no more effective than those which preceded them. On 'maladministration' in the Ptolemaic kingdom, and the official attitude to the problem, cf. also **245, 246, 256** ll. 224–33, **258–260, 272, 273, 276**. The evidence is unusually abundant and explicit compared to the other monarchies (cf. e.g. **13, 187, 209**).

See further: Préaux (1939), index p. 633; Rostovtzeff II (1941), 713–36, 870–914 (esp. 878ff. for a commentary on the text).

[King] Ptolemy (VIII), and Queen Cleopatra his sister, [and Queen] Cleopatra his wife, grant an amnesty to all their subjects [in] the [kingdom], for involuntary and voluntary offences, [accusations, condemnations] and suits of all kinds up to the 9th of [Pharmouthi in the] 52nd
5   year / except for [those] guilty of wilful [homicide] and sacrilege.

They have also decreed that those who have fled [because they were charged] with brigandage and other offences shall return to [their homes], resume their former occupations [and recover those] of their belongings [which were seized] for [these reasons] but which [have] not
10   yet been sold. /

And [they remit to all] the arrears [for the] period [up to the] 50th year, in respect of taxes in kind and [money taxes] except for hereditary lessees who have provided a security.[1]

Likewise for those who are in arrears in respect of the (half-artaba tax?) and . . . / and the (two-artaba tax),[2] the tax for guards (*phylakitikon*),[3]   15 the *naubion*,[4] [similar] taxes of this kind and the tax on embankments (*chomatikon*)[5] up to the [same period].

[. . .] And [they have decreed that] . . . / (sc. customs officials) shall   25 not seize goods unless they discover at the harbours in Alexandria, on the wharf, goods on which tax has not been paid or prohibited merchandise;[6] [these] they shall bring to the *dioiketes*.[7]

Similarly for those who [travel] on foot from the city (sc. Alexandria) inland along the land route which leads . . ., and those (who travel) from one tongue of land / [to] another, no toll is to be [requested] or   30 exacted in any way [except for] the legal duties . . .

[Similarly concerning] those who import goods through the market for foreigners . . . [except if . . .] the seizure takes place [at] the gate . . . /   35

And they have decreed that all the cleruchs[8] and all the holders of sacred land[9] or other 'relinquished' land (*en aphesei*),[10] both those who have encroached on royal land[11] and the others who hold more land than they are entitled to, shall evacuate / all the excess land they hold, declare   40 themselves and pay a year's rent; they shall then be released from arrears up to the 51st year, and shall retain legal possession . . . (sc. of what they have).

[The élite native corps], the native soldiers with holdings of 10 aruras or 7 aruras, [and their] / officers and the other members [of the native   45 corps, and the] native marines and those of . . . [shall have possession] of the holdings (*kleroi*) they have occupied up to the [52nd year] and shall [not be liable to accusation] or confiscation.[12]

And [they remit] to all the arrears of the work-tax (*leitourgikon*).[13] /   50

And they have decreed that [the sacred land] and [the] other sacred [revenues] which belong to the temples shall remain their [legal] possession, and that they shall [also receive] the quota (*apomoira*) which they used to receive from vineyards, orchards and other land.[14]

Similarly the sums allocated to them or what they have received from the royal treasury as subsidies to the temples and the other sums granted to them / up to [the] 51st year shall be paid regularly as [with] the other   55 revenues, and no one shall be allowed to take anything from them.

[No one] shall forcibly seize anything which is consecrated to the gods, nor shall apply compulsion to those in charge of the sacred revenues, nor shall appropriate villages or lands or other sacred revenues, nor shall exact the tax on associations, the 'crowns'[15] or the artaba-tax /   60 on what is consecrated to the gods,[16] nor shall exercise illegal patronage over the sacred land under any pretext, but its management shall be left to the priests.

And they have remitted to the overseers (*epistatai*) of the temples[17] and to the chief priests and priests [the] arrears both for the tax for overseers 65 and the valuations [of the] linen cloths up to the 50th year.[18] /

Similarly (they have remitted to) those who hold in the temples priestly positions, or posts as prophet or scribe, [or any other] functions, the arrears up to the 50th year in respect of the emoluments demanded on certain occasions.

Similarly (they have remitted to) those who have made excessive 70 profits (sc. from office) the fines up to the same period. /

Similarly for those in the lesser temples, shrines of Isis and feeding-places of ibises and hawk-shrines and Anubis-shrines [and] others of the same kind, . . . up to the same period.

[. . .] And they have decreed that the expenses for the burial of Apis and Mnevis[19] shall be met from the royal treasury, [as] with those (sc. members of the royal family) deified after their death.[20] Similarly with 80 the sums for the other sacred animals. /

The posts of prophet, the priestly offices, and the posts of scribe which have been purchased for the temples from the sacred revenues, and for which their holders have paid the price, shall remain the legal possession of the temples, but the priests [may] not make these over to others.[21]

And they have decreed that nobody shall be [removed] or forcibly taken away from places which enjoy the right of asylum[22] under any 85 pretext. /

And since it is reported that those holding the posts of *sitologoi*[23] and of *antigrapheis*[24] [make use of] larger measures than the standard bronze measures deposited in every nome[25] . . . in measuring what is due to the royal treasury, [and] that consequently the peasants are asked (an incorrect amount of) [*choinikes*], they have decreed that the *strategoi*,[26] those in charge of the revenues[27] and the royal scribes (*basilikogrammateis*)[28] shall test the measures as exactly as possible in the presence of those concerned in (sc. paying) the revenues, the peasants, 90 the priests, / the cleruchs and the other holders of 'relinquished' land . . . and they shall not hold more than two . . . allowed for errors . . ., and those who break these rules shall be punished [with death].

And they have decreed that the peasants who cultivate vineyards [or] orchards throughout the country, if they plant them in land that has been 95 flooded or is dry / between the 53rd and 57th year, shall be exempt from taxation for a period of five years from the time of planting, and that [from the] sixth year for a further three years they shall be taxed in the fourth year a reduced amount, and that from the ninth year they shall pay

the same taxes as the other owners of taxable (or: productive) land.²⁹
Cultivators in the territory of Alexandria shall be granted a [further]
three years' extension in addition to the privileges (granted) to those in
the countryside.

And they have decreed that those who have bought from the crown
houses or vineyards or orchards / or other . . . or boats or anything else   100
in any way, shall remain their legal owners, and their houses shall be
exempt from billeting.³⁰

[Similarly] the leases in kind concluded [with the peasants] shall
remain [valid . . .]

[. . .]³¹ And they have decreed that the owners of houses which have
been destroyed or burnt shall be allowed to rebuild them according to the
prescribed / measurements.   150

And (they have decreed) to allow those . . . [from the] villages in the
same way . . . to rebuild the private houses and the temples up to a
height of 10 (cubits) except for the inhabitants of Panopolis.³² /   155

No one shall collect any contributions from the peasants, the
workers in government monopolies (*hypoteleis*), those involved with the
revenues, bee-keepers and the others, for the benefit of *strategoi*, the
chiefs (*epistatai*) of the policemen (*phylakitai*), the chief policemen
(*archiphylakitai*),³³ the *oikonomoi*,³⁴ their agents / or the other officials, in   160
any way.

Neither the *strategoi* nor those in official positions nor their subordinates nor any other persons / shall appropriate royal land of good quality   165
from the cultivators or cultivate it of their own choice.

Exemption from billeting is granted to the Greeks serving in the army,
[the] priests, the cultivators / of royal land, the . . ., the wool-weavers,   170
[all] the other weavers, the swineherds, the gooseherds, the . . ., the
makers of sesame oil and castor oil, the [bee-keepers], the beer-brewers,
provided they pay their dues to the royal treasury, each of them / for one   175
house in which he lives; as for the other houses liable to billeting not
more than half shall be occupied.³⁵

And they have decreed that the *strategoi* and the other officials shall not
pressurise / any of the inhabitants of the countryside for personal   180
services, nor requisition any of their animals for their own private
purposes, nor impose on them the feeding of calves or sacrificial animals,
nor compel them to provide geese, fowl, wine / or grain for payment or   185
for the renewal of their office³⁶ nor force them to work without
payment, under any pretext.

And they remit to the policemen in the country the penalties entered
against them for negligence in the royal inspections and for / the loss of   190
crops, and the sums given to them for arrears and for other reasons and
which have disappeared up to the 50th year.

And (they have decided to) free from the consequent (penalties) those who have not delivered to the royal treasury against payment the

195 oil-yielding produce[37] from cleruchic, sacred / and other land up to the same period, and those who have failed to provide transport for the assembly (?). Likewise those who have failed to supply reeds and light

200 material for the embankments. /

Likewise (they free) the royal peasants[38] and the . . . and the [holders] of 'relinquished' land who have not planted the [required . . .][39] up to the 51st year from the consequent penalties, provided the planting is

205 done starting from the 52nd year. /

Likewise (sc. they offer amnesty to) those who have cut down trees on their own property in violation of the published ordinances.[40]

And they have decreed concerning suits brought by Egyptians against Greeks, viz. by Greeks against Egyptians, or by Egyptians against

210 Greeks,[41] with regard to all categories of people / except those cultivating royal land, the workers in government monopolies and the others who are involved with the revenues, that the Egyptians who have made contracts in Greek with Greeks shall give and receive satisfaction before

215 the *chrematistai*, while the Greeks / who have concluded contracts in Egyptian (sc. with Egyptians) shall give satisfaction before the *laokritai*[42] in accordance with the laws of the country (i.e. Egyptian laws). The suits of Egyptians against Egyptians shall not be taken by the *chrematistai* to their own courts,[43] but they shall allow them to be decided before the

220 *laokritai* in accordance with / the laws of the country.

And they have decreed that the collectors of private debts must not under any pretext arrest the royal peasants, the workers in the govern-

225 ment monopolies nor the others whom the previous ordinances forbid / to be brought up for accusation (? or: to be enslaved?)[44] but that the exactions of their debts shall be made on their goods in so far as they are

230 not excluded by this ordinance. /

And they have decreed concerning the royal peasants that (the collectors of debts) shall not sell at least one house in which their agricultural implements are stored (?), nor their cattle, nor their other

235 implements for / cultivation, whether [as arrears to the royal treasury?] or to the temples, nor for any other debt, under any pretext. In the same way (they must not sell) the workshops of the weavers in linen, byssus

240 and wool,[45] / nor of other similar workers, under any pretext; others may not acquire them nor use the implements for weaving linen and making byssus, except the workers in the royal monopolies [and]

245 the / byssus-makers, and they shall use them in the temple themselves for the provision of royal dues and the dressing of the other gods.

Those in official positions and others may not impose on the linen-

386

weavers, / the byssus-makers and the makers of clothes work without   250
payment or at reduced wages.

And they have decreed that no one may requisition boats under any
pretext for his own personal use. /   255

Neither the *strategoi* nor all the other officials in charge of royal, city or
sacred matters shall arrest anyone for some private debt or offence or in
pursuit of a private emnity, nor shall they keep him [imprisoned] in
their / houses or in other places under any pretext. If they have a   260
grievance against someone, they shall bring it before the tribunals
appointed in each (case *or* nome), and they shall receive and give
satisfaction in accordance with the ordinances and regulations.

C.Ord.Ptol. 53; *P.Tebt.* 5; cf. *Sel.Pap.*

II.210

1. Other leases being for fixed and limited periods; cf. Préaux (1939), 496.
2. Various taxes on land.
3. A tax for guarding the public granaries (Préaux (1939), 131f.).
4. Cf. **251**.
5. Cf. Préaux (1939), 182, 398f. On the maintenance of embankments cf. also **242**.
6. On taxation of foreign imports at Alexandria cf. **236** col. 52, **237**.
7. Cf. **235** n. 8.
8. On the Ptolemaic cleruchs (military settlers) cf. **252**.
9. Land belonging to native temples, cf. **227** l. 30, **235** col. 36; cf. Rostovtzeff I (1941), 280–4 and III, 1383f.; Préaux (1939), 480–91; Préaux I (1978), 378f.
10. This category of land is controversial in interpretation; cf. Crawford (1971), 93–5; J. C. Shelton, *CE* 46 (1971), 113–19; *P. Tebt.* IV (1976), p. 3.
11. Land owned by the king, cf. also **253, 256, 259**. See Rostovtzeff I (1941), 277–80 and III, 1382; Préaux (1939), 491–514; Préaux I (1978), 370–2.
12. I.e. the holdings become in effect private property and do not revert to the crown; contrast **252**.
13. Probably a payment from cleruchs in place of personal service (Préaux (1939), 398).
14. Cf. **227** l. 15, **235**.
15. On the 'crowns' see also **183** n. 1, **275**(a); cf. Préaux (1939), 394f.
16. This concession was ignored in practice; cf. Crawford (1971), 99 n. 10.
17. Officials appointed by the kings to supervise the administration of temples; cf. **222** l. 73 and Rostovtzeff I (1941), 282.
18. Cf. **227** n. 15.
19. Cf. **222** n. 8.
20. Cf. **217** n. 12.
21. Priestly appointments had important revenues and perquisites attached to them; they were purchased from the crown (cf. **227** l. 16) and treated in practice by their holders as their private possession. Cf. Préaux (1939), 489f.
22. See Rostovtzeff II (1941), 899–903 on the spread of grants of *asylia* by the kings to native Egyptian temples in the second century; cf. **151** n. 5.

23. Keepers of the royal granaries, cf. **256** l. 126.
24. Checking clerks, controllers, cf. **235, 236**.
25. Cf. **235** col. 25, **236** col. 40, **248, 260**(c). See also on measures **109, 111**.
26. The governor of the nome, the largest administrative unit in Ptolemaic Egypt; his functions, initially military as the title indicates, became civilian in character from the reign of Ptolemy III. Cf. **165, 255, 257, 259**.
27. A title which appears in the second century, frequently combined with the post of *strategos*.
28. Scribes of the nome (cf. **235** cols. 33 and esp. 36, **248, 253**), as opposed to the scribes of the subdivisions of the nome, the toparchy (*topogrammateis*, cf. **260**(b)) and the village (*komogrammateis*, cf. **244** (end), **256** l. 46, **260**).
29. On the anxiety of the authorities to get the land cultivated cf. **259, 260**(b).
30. Cf. also below ll. 168–77 and **249**.
31. Lines 103–33 largely lost, lines 134–46 repeat lines 147–67.
32. Cf. **228**(b), but this need not explain the exception here.
33. The former were chiefs of police for the whole nome, the latter for a single village; on the latter cf. **235** col. 37, **246, 250, 253**.
34. See **256** and n. 1.
35. Cf. **249**.
36. See **260** and nn. 1, 2.
37. See **236**.
38. The 'royal peasants' were the cultivators of crown land; cf. **253, 259**. For the Seleucid empire cf. **180** n. 12.
39. A possible reference to the 'sowing schedule', cf. **253**.
40. Cf. **256** l. 191–211.
41. Often corrected to 'Egyptians', but see J. Modrzejewski (next note).
42. *Chrematistai:* tribunals of Greek judges active in the countryside of Egypt (cf. **255**); *laokritai:* tribunals of Egyptian judges applying native Egyptian law. On this passage see J. Modrzejewski in Préaux (1975), 699–708. The legislation in favour of the native tribunals was in practice ineffective.
43. Even if written in Greek.
44. Cf. **275**(b).
45. Cf. **256** ll. 87–117 and n. 8.

232 A description of Alexandria

See further: Rostovtzeff I (1941), 415–20; Fraser I (1972), 7–37.

Since Alexandria and its vicinity form the largest and most important part of this work, I must begin with them.[1] The coast from Pelusium as one sails towards the west as far as the Canobic mouth is about 1,300 stades long (*ca* 227.5 km); this is what I have called the base of the Delta. From there to the island of Pharos is a further 150 stades (*ca* 26.25 km). Pharos is an oblong island, very close to the mainland, and forms with it a harbour with two entrances. The shore has the shape of a bay, as it has

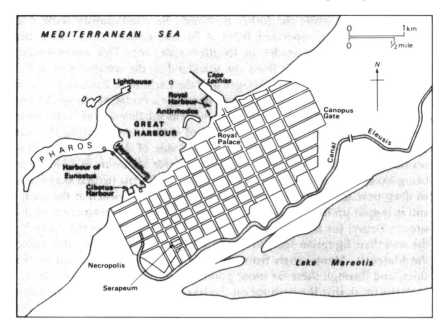

5 Hellenistic Alexandria (to illustrate **232**)
from A. Aymard and J. Auboyer, *L'Orient et la Grèce antique* (Paris, 6th ed., 1967), p. 442

two promontories jutting out into the sea; between these lies the island
which closes the bay, for it stretches lengthwise along the shore. Of the
extremities of Pharos the eastern one lies closer to the mainland and to
the promontory which faces it (this promontory is called Lochias), and
this makes the entrance of the harbour narrow; in addition to the
narrowness of the channel there are also rocks, some under water and
others above, which at all times roughen the waves that strike them from
the open sea. The extremity of the islet (sc. Pharos) is also a rock, washed
all round by the sea, with on top of it a tower magnificently built of
white stone, several storeys high, which bears the same name as the
island. This was dedicated by Sostratus of Cnidus, a 'friend'[2] of the
kings, for the safety of sailors, as the inscription declares. For since the
coast was harbourless and low on both sides, and also had rocks and
shallows, those who were sailing there from the open sea needed a high
and brilliant sign to enable them to make straight for the entrance of the
harbour. The western entrance does not offer easy access, though it does
not demand so much caution. It too forms another harbour, that of
Eunostus (i.e. 'of happy return') as it is called; it lies in front of the closed
harbour which was dug out artificially.[3] The harbour which has its
entrance on the side of the tower of Pharos which I have mentioned is the

389

Great Harbour, while the (other harbours) lie continuously with it in their recess, being separated from it by the embankment called the Heptastadium (i.e. 7 stades in length = 1,225 m). This embankment forms a bridge stretching from the mainland to the western part of the island, and leaves only two passages into the harbour of Eunostus, which are bridged over. This work formed not only a bridge to the island but also an aqueduct, at least when the island was inhabited. But in our time the deified Caesar (Julius Caesar) reduced it to a desert during the war against the Alexandrians,4 as it was on the side of the kings. But a few seamen do live near the tower. As for the Great Harbour, in addition to being excellently closed by the embankment and by its natural shape, it is so deep near the shore that the largest ship can be moored at the stairs, and it is split up into several harbours. [. . .] (7) The advantages of the site are many; for first the place is washed by two seas, in the north by the so-called Egyptian sea and in the south by Lake Mareia, also called the Mareotis. Many canals from the Nile fill it, from above and on the sides, and through these far more goods are imported than from the sea, with the result that the harbour on the lake was much wealthier than that on the sea; and here the exports from Alexandria are greater than the imports. [. . .] In addition to the wealth of the goods carried in both directions, to the harbour on the sea and to that on the lake, the purity of the air is also worthy of note. This is also a result of (the site) being washed by two seas, and of the favourable timing of the Nile's rise.5 For in the other cities that are situated on lakes the air is heavy and stifling during the heat of summer. [. . .] But at Alexandria at the beginning of summer the swelling Nile fills up the lake as well and prevents any stagnant water from fouling the rising air. It is also then that the Etesian winds blow from the north and from this vast open sea, so that the Alexandrians enjoy a most pleasant time in summer. (8) The shape of the area of the city is like a cloak (*chlamys*);6 the long sides of it are those that are washed by the two seas, and have a diameter of about 30 stades (*ca* 5.25 km) while the isthmuses form the short sides, each of them 7 or 8 stades wide (*ca* 1,225 to 1,400 m) and cut off on one side by the sea and on the other by the lake. The whole city is criss-crossed with streets suitable for the traffic of horses and carriages, and by two that are very wide, being more than 1 plethrum (*ca* 30 m) in breadth; these intersect each other at right angles. The city has magnificent public precincts and the royal palaces, which cover a fourth or even a third of the entire city area. For just as each of the kings would from a love of splendour add some ornament to the public monuments, so he would provide himself at his own expense with a residence in addition to those already standing, so that now, to quote Homer (*Odyssey* XVII.266) 'there is building after building'. All however are connected with each other and with the

390

harbour, even those that lie outside it. The Museum also forms part of the royal palaces; it has a covered walk, an arcade with recesses and seats (*exedra*) and a large house, in which is the dining-hall of the learned members of the Museum.[7] This association of men shares common property and has a priest of the Muses, who used to be appointed by the kings but is now appointed by Caesar (i.e. the emperor). The so-called *Sema* (tomb) is also part of the royal palaces; this was an enclosure in which were the tombs of the kings and of Alexander. For Ptolemy son of Lagus got in ahead of Perdiccas and took the body from him when he was bringing it down from Babylon.[8] [. . .] He gave it burial in Alexandria,[9] where it now lies, though not in the same sarcophagus. The present one is made of glass, while Ptolemy placed it in one made of gold. [. . .]

(9) In the Great Harbour at the entrance on the right there is the island and the tower Pharos, and on the other side are the rocks and the promontory Lochias with the royal palace. As one sails into the harbour there are on the left the inner royal palaces, which are joined to those on Lochias and have groves and many colourful lodges. Below these lies the artificially dug harbour which is not visible and is the private property of the kings, and Antirrhodos, a small island in front of the dug harbour which has both a royal palace and a small harbour. They gave it this name as being a rival of Rhodes. Above it lies the theatre, then the Posideum, a kind of headland jutting out from the so-called Emporium, with a sanctuary of Poseidon. [. . .] Then come the Caesareum, the Emporium and the storehouses; after them the shipyards as far as the Heptastadium. So much for the Great Harbour.

(10) Next after the Heptastadium comes the harbour of Eunostus, and above this the artificial harbour which is also called Cibotus (the 'Chest'); it too has shipyards. Further beyond this there is a canal fit for ships which stretches as far as Lake Mareotis. Beyond the canal only a little of the city is left. Then there is the suburb Necropolis in which are many gardens and tombs and installations suitable for the embalming of corpses. Within the canal there is the Serapeum[10] and other ancient precincts which have been virtually abandoned because of the construction of the new buildings at Nicopolis; for example there is an amphitheatre and a stadium and the quinquennial[11] competitions are celebrated there, while the old buildings have fallen into neglect. In a word, the city is full of dedications and sanctuaries; the most beautiful building is the Gymnasium which has porticoes over a stade (*ca* 175 m) in length. In the middle (of the city) are the law-courts and the groves. There is also the Paneium, an artificially made height, conical in shape and resembling a hill, and ascended by a spiral stair. From the top one has a panoramic view of the whole city lying below. The broad street which

runs lengthwise stretches from Necropolis along the Gymnasium as far as the Canopus gate; there there is the so-called Hippodrome and the other . . . that lie parallel as far as the Canobic canal. After passing through the Hippodrome one reaches Necropolis; it has a settlement on the sea no smaller than a city. [. . .][12]

Strabo XVII.1.6–10 (with omissions)

1. On the foundation of Alexandria cf. **7**.
2. Cf. **224** n. 2; on Sostratus cf. also **44**; Fraser *op. cit.*, 19f.; T. L. Shear, *Hesperia* Supplement 17 (1978), 22–5.
3. The 'Cibotus' mentioned below, §10.
4. In 48–47 B.C.
5. Cf. **217** n. 2.
6. Cf. **7** n. 3.
7. On the Museum cf. Fraser, *op. cit.*, 312–19; on the Library, not mentioned by Strabo, cf. **262**.
8. Cf. Diodorus XVIII.28; Pausanias 1.6.3; 1.7.1.
9. According to the Parian Marble (**21** §11) and Pausanias (previous note), Alexander's body was first buried at Memphis before being brought to Alexandria, where he was provided with a divine cult, linked to the Ptolemies' own dynastic cult; cf. **222** nn. 1 and 3.
10. Cf. **165, 261**.
11. Inclusively reckoned = every 4 years.
12. Strabo's description does not deal with the population and constitution of Alexandria, on which cf. Fraser, *op. cit.*, chs. 2–3. On the economic life of Alexandria cf. also **174** §9, **231** ll. 25–35, **237, 238, 248**.

233 Decree of Ptolemais in honour of its magistrates (reign of Ptolemy II or Ptolemy III)

While Alexander's conquest of Asia brought about the spread of Greek-type cities in Asia, especially under the Seleucids (cf. **40, 46** ch. 57 and n. 12), Ptolemaic Egypt followed a different line. Apart from the old treaty port of Naucratis in the Nile Delta (cf. **234** n. 7) only two new Greek cities were founded there in the Hellenistic age, Alexandria (cf. **7, 232**) and Ptolemais in Upper Egypt, founded by Ptolemy I probably as a counterweight to the ancient Egyptian city of Thebes (for a decree referring to its foundation and augmentation with fresh Greek colonists, cf. P. M. Fraser, *Berytus* 13 (1960), 123–33). The civic life of Ptolemais is illustrated by a number of inscriptions.

See further: Fraser III (1972), index s.v. Ptolemais Hermiou (p. 64).

Resolved by the council and the people; Hermas son of Dorcon of (the ward) Megistos[1] moved: since the presiding magistrates (*prytaneis*) who were colleagues of Dionysius son of Musaeus in the eighth year,[2]

Dionysius son of Musaeus of (the ward) Hyllus, Hippias son of Dion of
(the ward) Megistos, / Cratius son of Procritus of (the ward) Philotera,[3]   5
Cissus son of Nearchus of (the ward) Andania, Heliodorus son of
Nicomachus of (the ward) Danae, Neoptolemus son of Theodorus of
(the ward) Caranus, have governed the city well and worthily, (and)
when they saw some citizens not behaving properly and causing a
considerable uproar / at sessions of [the] council [and] meetings of the   10
assembly, particularly during [elections] when they had gone [as far as
resorting to violence and] impiety, they took note of this [depravity,
inflicting (on them) the] penalties prescribed by the laws, which caused
the [city to return to better order]; they [then] voted that the council [and
the] law-courts [should be recruited] from pre-selected men; the younger
men were incensed at this / but the other [citizens who were selected   15
thought that?] the city would be better [governed] and concerning the
matters they thought would benefit the city . . .
(the last line is seriously mutilated and the rest of the inscription lost)

OGIS 48

1. The names of the wards are derived from gods, heroes, and the royal family
   (n. 3).
2. 278/7 or 240/39.
3. A sister of Ptolemy II; cf. **274** n. 2.

234 List of victors in a competition

To King Ptolemy (II), son of the Saviours (*Soteres*),[1] Heraclides son of
Leptines from Alexandria, who organised the competition (as agonothete) and was the first to offer bronze vessels as prizes, in the
eighteenth year, on the twelfth of Dystros,[2] on the birthday festival (sc.
of the king), when Amadocus instituted the *Basileia*,[3] (dedicated) the list
of victors. / [*see overleaf*]

Trumpeters:
Theodorus son of Straton, Thracian
  Heralds:
Hephaestion son of Demeas, from Tarentum
  In the torch race, first lap:
10 Ptolemy son of Amadocus, Thracian
  In the torch race, (last lap):
Dionysius son of Stephanus, from Halicarnassus
  In the long race (*dolichon*), boys:[4]
Aenesis son of Patamusus, Thracian
15   Men:
Ptolemy son of Bubalus, Macedonian
  In the sprint (*stadion*), boys:
Ptolemy son of Amadocus, Thracian
  Ptolemaikoi:[5]
20 Cineas son of Alcetas, Thessalian[6]
  Beardless:
Cineas son of Alcetas, Thessalian
  Men:
. . . son of Parmenion, Macedonian
25   In the double stade race [children]:

. . .

Boxing, boys:
Chrysermos son of Amadocus, Thracian
  Ptolemaikoi:
Demetrius son of Artemon, from Naucratis[7]
  Beardless:
Stratippus son of Menoetius, Macedonian
  Men:
Bastakilas son of Amadocus, Thracian
  Boxing and wrestling (*pankration*), *Ptolemaikoi*:
Amadocus son of Satocus, Thracian
  Beardless:
Stratippus son of Menoetius, Macedonian
  Men:
Ptolemy son of Hadymus, Macedonian
  In the armed race:
Mnesimachus, son of Aminocles, Boeotian
  Dressage:
Ptolemy son of Amadocus, Thracian
  In the *stadion* race, foals:
Lycomedes son of Ctesicles, from Samos[8]
  Adult horses:

. . .

L. Koenen, *Eine agonistische Inschrift aus Ägypten und frühptolemäische Königsfeste* (1977), cf. *Bull.* 1977, 566

1. Ptolemy I and Berenice.
2. 8 March 267.
3. A festival of Zeus celebrated in Alexandria and founded to commemorate the birthday of Ptolemy II (Fraser 1 (1972), 194f., 232); cf. **217** for Zeus as protector of kings and **222** n. 6 for the celebration of royal birthdays. The festival mentioned in this inscription was organised by Amadocus (probably the father of several of the victors listed below) in the Egyptian countryside on the model of the Alexandrian festival; the participants were Ptolemaic cleruchs (cf. **252**) who demonstrated in this way their loyalty and gratitude to the dynasty.
4. Boys, beardless, men: age groups in competitions. Cf. **215**.
5. Competitors admitted under the rules in force for the *Ptolemaieia* (cf. **218**).
6. Probably identical with a priest of Alexander in 263/2 (cf. *PP* 17.215).
7. A citizen from Naucratis, one of the three Greek cities in Egypt (cf. **233**); the other victors identify themselves by their country or city of origin outside Egypt.
8. Probably honoured in a decree from Ptolemais for his devotion to Ptolemy II or III and to the city (*OGIS* 47, cf. *PP* 17.219).

235 The 'apomoira' for Arsinoe Philadelphus

The so-called 'Revenue Laws' of Ptolemy II Philadelphus come from one of the longest of Ptolemaic papyri, which deals with the farming of a number of royal revenues. The papyrus is not fully preserved and there is a gap of several lines at the top of each column. The best preserved parts concern (1) a royal decision to divert the quota (*apomoira*) of produce from vineyards and orchards, which used to be paid to the native Egyptian temples, to the cult of Ptolemy II's deceased and deified sister-wife Arsinoe (the following passage), and (2) regulations for the oil monopoly (see **236**). For later references to the *apomoira* cf. **227** l. 15, **231** ll. 50–3.

See further: B. P. Grenfell and J. P. Mahaffy, *Revenue Laws of Ptolemy Philadelphus* (Oxford, 1896); Préaux (1939), 165–81.

[In the reign] of Ptolemy (II) son of Ptolemy [and his son] Ptolemy, year 27 (259/8) . . . (gap of *ca* 7 lines) . . . [the] sixth of the wine [produced . . .], and from the [cleruchs] who are performing military service[1] and who have planted their [own] holdings (*kleroi*) (sc. with vines), and from the land [in the] Thebaid which requires special irrigation and from . . . [the] tenth. (col. 24)

For the orchards, in accordance with the [annual] valuation, the sixth in silver . . .[2]

[*Concerning*] *the gathering and collection* (sc. of the grapes). [The] cultivators shall gather the grapes when the season [comes], and when (col. 25) they begin to do so they shall report to the manager of the farm or (col. 25) [to the] tax-farmer,[3] and if he wishes to inspect [the vineyards] they shall show them to him . . . (gap of *ca* 7 lines) . . . When the cultivators wish to make the wine, they shall summon the manager of the farm in the presence of the *oikonomos*[4] and of the [*antigrapheus*][5] or of their agents, and when he has come, the cultivator shall make wine and measure it with the measures available at each place once they have been tested and sealed [by the] *oikonomos* and the *antigrapheus*, [and] he shall pay the *apomoira* in accordance with the result of the measuring.

If the cultivators do not comply with [any of] these regulations in accordance with the law, they shall pay double the *apomoira* to the tax-farmers.

(col. 26) [Those who own] implements for making wine shall register [with the manager] of the farm when . . . (gap of *ca* 7 lines) . . . [and when] they are about [to make wine, they shall exhibit] the seal placed on them to show it is intact. [Anyone who fails] to register, or to produce his [implements in accordance] with the law, or to bring them for [sealing] when the farmer wishes to seal them, or to [exhibit the] seal placed on them, shall pay forthwith to the tax-farmers the amount of the loss they estimate they have made. If the cultivators gather the grapes ahead of time and make wine . . . the wine in the vats or in . . . and when [they hear?] the first notice of the auction[6] announced in the town or village in which they [live], the cultivators shall register on the same day [or on the] day after, and they shall point out the wine [and the] vineyard from [which] they gathered the grapes ahead of time.

Agreements

(col. 27) [The] tax-farmer, when . . . (gap of *ca* 7 lines) . . . he [shall seal the copy of the] agreement and [give it] to the cultivator. In the agreement (the tax-farmer) shall declare under the [royal] oath that he has entered [in the] agreement the whole produce and the wine made ahead of time [and] reported to him by the cultivator, and has not taken away or let out of his hands any of it. The *oikonomos* or his representative shall keep the other agreement, once it has been sealed by the cultivator. The cultivator shall [declare] under the royal oath that he has exhibited all the produce and declared all the wine made ahead of time, and that he has honestly entered the resulting *apomoira*. And there shall also be [copies] (of the agreements), (col. 28) which shall not be sealed.

(col. 28) . . . (gap of *ca* 7 lines) . . .

[But if] a dispute arises (sc. between the cultivator and the tax-farmer) about the greater or [smaller] amount of the produce, the *oikonomos* and the *antigrapheus* shall decide, and the agreements shall be sealed in accordance with their decision.

If the tax-farmer fails to make an agreement with one of the cultivators, when the cultivator wishes to do so, he shall not exact payment of the tax.

But the *oikonomos* or the *antigrapheus* shall make an agreement with the cultivator, and having brought the resulting *apomoira* to the royal treasury they shall enter it, but shall not put down its value to the credit of the tax-farmers.

Against confusion of produce. If (the tax-farmers) mingle taxable produce with produce which is tax free . . . (col.29) as though belonging to this category . . . (gap of *ca* 7 lines) . . . (col. 29)

The owners [of orchards shall register] with [the] tax-farmer [and the] local [representative] of the *oikonomos* and the [*antigrapheus*], stating their name, the village in which they live, and [their assessment of the value] of the revenue from their [orchard, and if] the tax-farmer agrees, they shall [draw up] with him a double agreement which shall be sealed as is prescribed [in] the law, and the *oikonomos* shall exact the sixth on this basis.

But [if] the tax-farmer objects to the assessment he may seize the crop, and shall pay (sc. the cultivator) by instalments from what he sells from day to day. When the cultivator has received the equivalent of his assessment, the surplus shall belong to the tax-farmer, and the cultivator shall pay the sixth to the [*oikonomos*]. Should the sale of the crop fail to reach the value of [the] assessment, the *oikonomos* shall exact (the difference) [from] the tax-farmer and . . .

. . . (gap of *ca* 9 lines . . . [. . .] . . . [Should] they (sc. the farmers) fail to be present themselves at the [right time] or fail to send their qualified representatives in accordance with the law, or hold back the cultivators [in any other way] even though the latter [are giving] notice, summoning them and carrying out their [obligations], the cultivators may [in accordance] with the provisions (of the law) act in the presence of the agent of the *oikonomos* and of the *antigrapheus* without incurring any penalty. When [the] tax-farmer comes, they shall show him [the produce and] shall furnish [at once] all particulars of everything they have done. The [agent] of the *oikonomos* and of the *antigrapheus* shall give (sc. the tax-farmer) a written statement of the produce and of the *apomoira*, cultivator by cultivator. (col. 30)

Transport of the apomoira. The cultivators (sc. shall transport) the resulting *apomoira* of the . . . (gap of *ca* 7 lines) . . .

. . . he shall [pay] to [the tax-] farmers [the] cost of [transport] which is owed to them. [. . .][7] (col. 31)

Stamping of receipts. The *oikonomos* shall set up stores in each village, and shall give himself a stamped receipt to the [cultivator?] for what [he has] received . . . (corrector's hand: [the *oikonomos*] shall transport (the wine) from [the vats? . . .]).

(col. 32) . . . (gap of *ca* 7 lines) . . . (The cultivator) shall provide [pottery for the] store and wax; the pottery shall be of watertight jars, sealed with [pitch] and sufficient for the wine [collected for the] tax-farmers.

The *oikonomos* and the *antigrapheus*, [. . . days before] the cultivators gather the grapes, shall pay to the cultivators the price of the [pottery] which each must provide for the *apomoira* on his own produce, at a rate fixed by the *dioiketes*,[8] who shall pay them the price through the royal [bank][9] in the nome. [The cultivator] on receiving the price, shall supply [pottery] of the best quality. If [the] price is not given to him, he shall supply the pottery, and shall recover the price for it from [the *apomoira*] which he has to pay, [at a price of . . . drachmas] for a [*metretes*] of wine

(col. 33) of eight *choes* . . .

. . . (gap of *ca* 7 lines) . . .

All the [surplus wine] shall be examined [by the *oikonomos*, and] with the assistance of the tax-farmer, the *antigrapheus* and [his] agent, he shall sell it with them, giving [time] for the [purchasers] to settle their accounts. He shall exact [payment and shall enter it] in the account of the tax-farmers to their credit.

The royal scribes[10] shall notify [to the] tax-farmers within 10 days of the [opening of the public auction][11] the number of vineyards or of orchards [in] each nome, the [number] of aruras they contain, [and] the number of vineyards or of orchards, belonging to persons on [the tax-list], which paid taxes to the temples before the [22nd] year.

If they fail to give this notice or are shown to have done it incorrectly, they shall be tried and condemned, and shall pay to the tax-farmers 6,000 drachmas for each offence of which they have been convicted and twice the amount of the loss.

All the owners of vineyards [or] orchards who are on the [tax-list] and

(col. 34) [paid] to the temples the sixth [up to] the 21st year, [shall pay the] sixth (col. 34) [to (Arsinoe) Philadelphus? . . .]

. . . (gap of *ca* 5 lines) . . .

[The tax-farmers shall appoint sureties for a sum one twentieth above (the price for the tax)] within 30 days of their purchasing (the tax). [Payments ?] of the money shall be [made every] month from the month of Dius to . . .

The value of the wine received from them [for the royal] treasury shall be credited (to them) in the instalments (due from them).

Balancing of accounts. When all the produce relating to the tax has been [sold], the *oikonomos* shall take with him the tax-[farmer], his associates and the *antigrapheus* and shall balance the accounts with the (chief) tax-[farmer and his] associates, and if there is a profit, he [shall pay] to the chief tax-farmer and his associates through the royal bank the amount of the profit due to each of them according to his share in the company.

But if there is a deficit, he shall exact from the chief tax-farmer, his associates and their sureties the amount each of them owes.[12] These payments shall be due within the [first] three months of [the] following year. [If he fails to . . .]

    (col. 35 omitted)

    . . . (gap of *ca* 6 lines) . . . [make sure that these] prescriptions are [observed]. Farewell. Year 23, Daisius 5 (= 13 June 263).

    The royal scribes in the [nomes throughout the] country shall draw up a list, each for the nome of which [he is] scribe, of the number of aruras of vineyards [and] orchards, and of the produce from these cultivator by cultivator, from year 22. They shall set apart the sacred [land][13] and its produce so that [the] rest . . . (sc. may be determined) from which the sixth must be paid to (Arsinoe) [Philadelphus], and they shall hand over to the agents [of Satyrus][14] a written statement of these. Similarly the [cleruchs] who have vineyards or orchards in the holdings they received from the king and all the other owners of vineyards or orchards, or holders of them *en doreai*,[15] or who cultivate them in any other way, must each for his part register the amount of land (they have) and its produce, and pay the sixth of the produce to Arsinoe Philadelphus for sacrifices [and] libations.

    . . . (gap of *ca* 7 lines)

    [King] Ptolemy [to all the] *strategoi*, [hipparchs], officers, nomarchs, [toparchs],[16] *oikonomoi*, *antigrapheis*, royal [scribes], Libyarchs[17] and chiefs of police,[18] greetings. We have sent to you copies of the [ordinance which] requires payment of the sixth to (Arsinoe) Philadelphus. [Take care therefore] that these instructions are carried out. Farewell. Year 23, Dius 2. (= November–December 263)

    [All those who] have vineyards or orchards, [whatever] their tenure, shall all give to the agents of Satyrus [and to] the accountants (*eklogistai*) appointed as agents of Dionysodorus, [nome by] nome, a written statement, drawn up by themselves, or their managers, or [those cultivating] their property, from year 18 to [year 21], (indicating) the amount of produce and to which temple they used to give the sixth, and the annual amount. Similarly the priests (shall make a statement) from which property they used to receive (the sixth), and the annual amount of wine or money. Similarly the royal scribes and the . . . shall give . . . written statements of these . . .

P. Revenue Laws cols. 24–37 (ed. J. Bingen, *SB Beiheft* I, 1952); for cols. 36–37 see also *C.Ord.Ptol.* 17–18

(col. 35)

(col. 36)

(col. 37)

---

1. See **252**; the cleruchs are more favourably treated, paying a quota of 1/10th instead of 1/6th.

2. Vineyards are taxed in kind, orchards in money.
3. It will be seen that the tax-farmers do not in fact collect the taxes themselves; their role is to underwrite the king's revenues and protect him against loss (cf. col. 34). See Rostovtzeff I (1941), 328–30 and for tax-farmers in the Ptolemaic kingdom see also **236, 256, 258, 265** and (outside Egypt) **271, 275, 276**.
4. See **256** and n. 1.
5. Cf. **231** n. 24.
6. The auction of the tax-farming contracts.
7. Omitted is a list of different rates for different nomes.
8. The chief minister in the Ptolemaic kingdom after the king himself; cf. **231** l. 27, **236** cols. 38, 41, 46, 51, **237–247** (Apollonius), **253, 254, 256, 258, 260, 265, 266** (Thera), **273** (Cyprus), **275** (Syria). On the Seleucid *dioiketai* cf. **187** n. 3.
9. Banking rights were farmed out by the Ptolemies to individual contractors (most known bankers in Ptolemaic Egypt are Greeks). The banks, branches of which were to be found even in the villages in the countryside, served as agencies for payments to and by the crown, and also received private deposits and engaged in moneylending at high rates of interest (24% was the legal maximum, over twice the rates found elsewhere in the Greek world). Cf. col. 34 below, **236** col. 48, **238, 247** l. 86, **256** ll. 117–34, and see Préaux (1939), 280–97; Rostovtzeff I (1941), 404–6 and II, 1282–8.
10. Cf. **231** n. 28.
11. See n. 6.
12. This makes clear the function of the tax-farmers from the king's point of view.
13. Cf. **231** n. 9.
14. The *dioiketes* (n. 8 above).
15. 'Gift' land granted by the king to favourites, on a revocable basis; cf. **236** col. 43f., **240, 241** and (outside Egypt) **271** n. 2. For Seleucid practice cf. **180**. See generally M. Rostovtzeff III (1941), index s.v. *Doreai* (p. 1685).
16. Chiefs of the nomes and chiefs of the toparchies respectively; cf. **236** cols. 41–42, **256** ll. 131–3.
17. Identification uncertain; possibly officials in charge of law and order in the nome on the edge of the Libyan desert.
18. Cf. **231** n. 33.

236 The oil monopoly of Ptolemy II Philadelphus

Royal monopolies were a feature of the economy of Ptolemaic Egypt; the best known of these, and one of the most important, was the oil monopoly, described at length in the 'Revenue Laws' of Ptolemy II (cf. **235**). The monopoly extended to all kinds of oil-bearing plants (though not to olive oil) and affected every kind of land in Egypt, with only nominal concessions to the native Egyptian temples' own production of oil. The royal administration prescribed in detail what surface of land was to be sown with what oil-bearing plants, at least as far as royal land was concerned (cf. **253, 256** ll. 49–62). Every stage in the process, from planting to production and retailing was supervised by royal officials and tax-farmers, and the royal administration fixed all the prices to be paid or charged. The intention of these elaborate regulations was clearly purely fiscal: to ensure the king's revenues, not to improve production. Cf. also **256** ll. 87–117 and n. 8.

See further: Préaux (1939), 65–93; Rostovtzeff I (1941), 302–5.

Year 27, Loios 10 (= 1 September 259). We will correct (*altered to:* we have corrected) this in the office of Apollonius the *dioiketes*.[1] (col. 38)

. . . (gap of *ca* 5 lines) . . . (sc. the cultivators shall be paid as follows:) for an artaba [of sesame] containing [30] *choinikes*, [prepared] for grinding, [8] drachmas, for an artaba of croton containing 30 [*choinikes*], prepared for grinding, 4 dr., for an artaba of cnecus, prepared [for] grinding, 1 dr. 2 obols, for an artaba of colocynth, 4 ob., and for linseed, 3 ob. (col. 39)

If the cultivator does not wish to [provide] produce ready for grinding, he shall measure it out from the threshing-floor after cleaning it with a sieve, and he shall measure out in addition, for the further preparation for grinding, 7 artabas of sesame for every [100], the same amount of croton and 8 artabas (for every 100) of [cnecus].

They shall receive from the cultivators for the tax of 2 dr. payable on sesame and for the tax of 1 dr. payable on croton, sesame and croton at the price fixed [in] the tariff, and they shall not exact payment in silver.

The cultivators shall not be allowed to sell sesame or croton to anyone else (sc. than to the tax-farmers).[2]

. . . (gap of *ca* 5 lines) . . . [of the *antigrapheus*][3] from [the komarch[4] and they shall] give [to the] komarch a sealed receipt for what [they received] from each [cultivator]. If they fail to give the receipt the komarch shall not let (the produce) out of the village. If he does, he shall pay a fine of 1,000 dr. to the royal treasury and five times the amount of the loss incurred because of this by the tax-farmers. (col. 40)

They shall sell the oil in the countryside at a rate of 48 dr. in copper for a *metretes* of sesame oil or of cnecus oil containing [12] *choes*, and at a rate of 30 dr. for a *metretes* of castor oil, [colocynth] oil and lamp oil (*corrected to:* They shall sell the oil in the countryside both sesame and cnecus oil, and castor oil, colocynth oil and lamp oil at the rate of 48 dr. in copper for a *metretes* containing 12 *choes*, and 2 ob. for a *kotyle*).[5]

In Alexandria [and] the whole of Libya (they shall sell it) at a rate of 48 dr. for a *metretes* of sesame oil and 48 dr. for a *metretes* of castor oil (*corrected to:* a rate of 48 dr. for a *metretes* of sesame oil and castor oil, and 2 ob. for a *kotyle*), and they shall provide [an adequate supply] for those who wish to buy oil, selling it [throughout] the country in all the cities

[and] villages . . . with [measures]⁶ which [have been] tested by [the *oikonomos*⁷ and the] *antigrapheus*.

(col. 41) . . . (gap of *ca* 5 lines) . . . [. . .] They shall show the land sown to the tax-farmer together with the *oikonomos* and the *antigrapheus*, and if after measuring it they find that the (right) number of aruras has not been sown, the nomarch, the toparch,⁸ the *oikonomos* and the *antigrapheus* shall, each of them who is responsible, pay 2 talents to the royal treasury, and to the tax-farmers 2 dr. for every artaba of sesame which they ought to have received, and 1 dr. for every artaba of croton, together with the profit (they would have made) on the (sesame) oil and the castor oil. The *dioiketes* shall exact payment from them. [. . .]

Before the season comes for sowing the sesame and the croton, the *oikonomos* shall give to the nomarch in charge of the nome or to the toparch, if he wishes, for the sowing of [each arura] of sesame 4 dr., and for each arura of croton 2 dr. And he shall receive from the threshing-floor in return for . . .

(col. 42) . . . (gap of *ca* 5 lines) . . . [. . .] When the [season] comes for collecting the sesame, the croton and the cnecus, the cultivators shall give notice to the nomarch and the toparch, and where there are no nomarchs or toparchs, to the *oikonomos;* and they shall summon the tax-farmer. The tax-farmer shall go with them to the fields and assess (sc. the crops).

The [native peasants (*laoi*)] and the other cultivators shall assess their [own] crops each by kind before they gather them, and they shall draw up an agreement on the estimate with the tax-farmer, in duplicate and sealed. The native peasants shall state in writing on oath the area of land they have each sown, and with what kind of crops, [and] the amount of each peasant's estimate, and they shall seal the agreement, and the representative of the nomarch or [of the] toparch shall also seal it.

(col. 43) . . . (gap of *ca* 5 lines) . . . [. . .] The nomarch or the person in charge of the nome shall give out the seed for the fields, cultivator by cultivator, 60 days before the crop is gathered. If he fails to do this or does not show the cultivators who have sown the prescribed number (of aruras), he shall pay to the tax-farmer the prescribed fine, and shall exact payment himself from the disobedient cultivators.

[All] those throughout the country who enjoy exemption from taxes, or who hold villages and land [*en doreai*⁹ or] as a source of revenue, shall measure out all the sesame and croton they produce, and the other kinds of produce included in the oil (monopoly), leaving aside a sufficient amount for seed, and shall receive the value of it in copper at a rate of 6 dr. for an artaba of sesame, 3 dr. 2 ob. for an artaba of cnecus.¹⁰ If they do not measure out all [the] sesame . . .

(col. 44) . . . (gap of *ca* 5 lines) . . . to be a factory, and shall designate their choice by putting a stamp on it.

402

No oil-factory shall be set up in villages which are held *en doreai*.

They shall deliver to each factory a sufficient quantity of sesame, croton and cnecus.

They shall not give permission to the oil-workers appointed in each nome to move to another nome. [Should] any of them move, they may be arrested by the tax-farmer, the *oikonomos* and the *antigrapheus*.

No one shall harbour oil-workmen. If anyone harbours them knowingly, or fails to bring them back when told to do so, he shall be fined 3,000 dr. for every oil-worker and the worker shall be liable to arrest.

. . . (gap of *ca* 5 lines) . . . and from [the] surplus of the oil that is sold (*corrected to:* produced) he (sc. the *oikonomos*) shall divide up to the oil-workers 3 dr. for a *metretes* containing 12 *choes* (*corrected to:* 2 dr. 3 ob.); of this sum the oil-workers and those who pound the crop shall receive 2 dr. (*corrected to:* 1 dr. 4 ob.) and the tax-farmers 1 dr. (*corrected to:* 5 ob.).   (col. 45)

But if the *oikonomos* or his representative does not give to the oil-workers their wages, or their share in the profits of the sale, he shall pay to the royal treasury a fine of 3,000 dr., their wages to the workmen, and (to the tax-farmers) double of whatever loss they suffer because of them.

If the *oikonomos* and the *antigrapheus* fail to set up the oil-factories as prescribed or do not deliver a sufficient quantity of crops and the tax-farmers suffer because of this, they shall pay the resulting deficit [and] (shall pay) to the tax-farmers twice the amount [of their loss].

[The] *oikonomos* and [the] *antigrapheus* [shall supply the tools] in each [factory].

. . . (gap of *ca* 5 lines) . . . when he (sc. the *oikonomos*) comes (to the factory) to pay the wages (?) he shall not cause any hindrance to the detriment of the tax-contract.   (col. 46)

If he fails to provide (the tools) or harms the interests of the tax-contract, he shall be judged by the *dioiketes* and if condemned shall be fined 2 talents of silver and twice the amount of the damage caused.

The tax-farmers and the clerk appointed by the *oikonomos* and the *antigrapheus* [shall have] authority over all the oil-workers in [the] toparchy, [the] factories and the tools, [and] they shall place [seals] on the tools [when] they are not being used.[11]

They shall compel the oil-workers to work [every] day and shall stay beside them. They shall make into oil every day not less than 1$\frac{1}{2}$ artaba (*corrected to:* 1 artaba) of sesame for every mortar, or 4 artabas of croton, or 1 artaba of cnecus. They shall pay as wages [. . . dr. for] 4 [artabas] of sesame, 4 dr. for . . . artabas of [croton] and 8 [dr. for . . . artabas] of cnecus.

(col. 47) . . . (gap of *ca* 5 lines) . . . Neither the *oikonomos* nor the tax-farmer shall under any pretext make [an arrangement] with [the] oil-workers [concerning the] flow of the oil,[12] nor shall they leave the tools in the factories unsealed when they are not in use. If they make an arrangement with some of the oil-workers or leave the tools unsealed, each guilty person shall pay to the royal treasury a fine of 1 talent of silver plus the amount of any loss made by the tax-farmers.

The clerk appointed by the *oikonomos* and the *antigrapheus* shall draw up a list of the names of the dealers in each city and of the retailers, and shall arrange with them together with the tax-farmers [how much] oil and castor oil they must take and sell every day, and in Alexandria they shall make an arrangement with the traders and draw up a contract [with] each of them, [on a monthly basis] with those in the [countryside, and with those in Alexandria . . .]

(col. 48) . . . (gap of *ca* 5 lines) . . . [. . .] The amount of oil and cici (castor oil) which the dealers and retailers have agreed to dispose of in every village shall be supplied in full of each kind by the *oikonomos* and the *antigrapheus* before the beginning of the month to every village, and they shall measure it out every five days to the dealers and the retailers and collect the price on the same day, if possible, and if not within five days, and they shall pay it into the royal bank,[13] and the expenses for the transport shall be paid for from the tax-contract.

The oil which it has been arranged that each (sc. of the dealers and retailers) shall take, shall be offered for auction ten days before the beginning of the month and they shall write out and publish the highest bid every day for ten days in the capital of the nome and in the village, and they shall make a contract with the successful bidder.

(col. 49) [. . .] . . . (gap of *ca* 4 lines) . . . [Nor shall they . . .] under any pretext . . . mortars . . . nor presses nor any other implements used in the [manufacture] (sc. of the oil). If not, they shall pay to the royal treasury 5 talents and to the tax-farmers five times the amount of the loss. Those who already have any of these shall register within 30 days with the tax-farmer and the representative of the *oikonomos* and the *antigrapheus* and shall exhibit the mortars and presses.

The tax-farmers and the representative of the *oikonomos* and the *antigrapheus* shall transfer these to the royal oil-factories.

If anyone is found manufacturing oil from sesame, croton or cnecus in any way, or purchasing the oil and cici (castor oil) (*corrected to:* sesame oil, cnecus oil, or castor oil) from anywhere except from the tax-farmers, the king shall judge his case, and he shall pay to the tax-farmers 3,000 dr. and shall be deprived of the oil and the produce. The payment shall be exacted by the *oikonomos* and the *antigrapheus*; if he is unable to pay, he shall surrender himself to . . .

404

[. . .] . . . (gap of *ca* 3 lines) . . . under any [pretext] nor to bring it   (col.
(sc. oil) to [Alexandria] apart from the royal store (?). Any persons who   50)
import more than they require for their personal needs for three days
shall be deprived both of the goods and of the means of transport, and
shall pay in addition a fine of 100 dr. for every *metretes*, and for more or
less in proportion.

The cooks shall use up the lard every day in the presence of the
tax-farmer. They shall not sell it on its own to anyone under any pretext,
nor melt it down, nor store it away.[14] If they do, they shall each (*corrected
to:* both the seller [and the] buyer) pay to the farmer of the oil-tax for
every day (*corrected to:* for every piece bought) 50 dr.

The oil-workers in the temples throughout the country shall register
with the tax-farmer and with the representative of the *oikonomos* and of
the *antigrapheus* the number of oil factories in each temple, and the
number of mortars [and presses] in each factory, (col. 51) and [shall   (col.
exhibit the factories and provide the] mortars and [presses to] be sealed.   51)
[. . .] . . . (gap of *ca* 3 lines) . . . If [they fail to] register [or do not]
exhibit or provide (sc. the mortars and presses) to be sealed, those in
charge of the temples shall pay, each of them who is guilty, 3 talents to
the royal treasury and to the tax-farmers five times the amount of the loss
they estimate they have incurred. When they wish to manufacture
sesame oil in the temples, they shall summon the tax-farmer and the
representative of the *oikonomos* and of the *antigrapheus* and manufacture
the oil in their presence. They shall make in two months the amount of
oil they registered they would use in a year, and shall obtain the castor oil
they use from the tax-farmers at the established price.

The *oikonomos* and the *antigrapheus* shall send to the king an account of
both the cici (castor oil) and the (sesame) oil used for each temple, and
shall also give (one) to the *dioiketes*. No one may sell to anybody oil
manufactured for the temples; if they do, [they shall be] deprived (col.   (col.
52) [of the oil] and shall also be fined [100 dr. for a *metretes* and for] more   52)
or [less in proportion].[15]

[. . .] . . . (gap of *ca* 2 lines) . . . [it shall not be allowed] to bring (sc.
imported oil) into the country for sale, whether from Alexandria,
Pelusium or anywhere else. Any persons who do so shall be deprived of
the oil and shall be fined in addition 100 dr. a *metretes*, and for more or
less in proportion.

As for persons who bring foreign oil for their private needs, those who
bring it from Alexandria shall register in Alexandria, pay a duty of 12 dr.
a *metretes*, and for <more or> less in proportion, and shall obtain a
voucher before they import it.[16]

Those who bring it from Pelusium shall pay the duty at Pelusium and
obtain a voucher.

The collectors at Alexandria and Pelusium shall credit the duty to the nome into which the oil is imported.

Any persons who bring (sc. foreign oil) for their private needs and do not pay the duty or obtain a voucher shall be deprived of the oil and shall in addition be fined 100 dr. a *metretes*. [. . .]

(col. 53) [. . .] But if when they give up the contract they leave behind more (oil), they shall receive from the *oikonomos* as price for sesame oil 31 dr. 4½ ob. a *metretes* (*corrected to:* 28 dr. 3 ob.), for castor oil 21 dr. 2 ob. a *metretes* (*corrected to:* 20 dr.), for cnecus oil 18 dr. 4 ob. a *metretes* (*corrected to:* 17 dr. 1 ob.), for sesame 8 dr. an artaba, for croton 4 dr. an artaba, for cnecus 1 dr. 3 ob. (*corrected to:* 1 dr. 2 ob.).[17] [. . .]

(col. 54) [. . .] The tax-farmers shall also appoint clerks at Alexandria and Pelusium for [the] oil imported [from] Syria to [Pelusium] and Alexandria, and they shall seal the stores and supervise the issue of the oil.

The clerk of the oil-contract appointed by the *oikonomos* shall hold a balancing of accounts every month [with] the tax-farmer in the presence of the *antigrapheus*. He shall enter in his books the amount of the different kinds of produce he has received and the amounts (of oil) (col. 55) he has

(col. 55) produced and [sold] (*corrector's addition:* [at the price] specified [in the] tariff) [. . . except] the (oil) which is [set] apart, and the price of the [produce received] which is [prescribed] in [the] tariff . . . together with the [jars] and the other [expenses], at a rate of 1 dr. an artaba of sesame, . . . for [croton], 2 ob. for cnecus, [. . . for colocynth, . . . for linseed, . . . dr. for . . . artabas made into sesame oil], 1 [dr.] 1 ob. for 5 [artabas made into castor oil, . . . dr.] for 9 artabas made into cnecus oil, 1 dr. for 7 artabas made into lamp oil, 1 dr. 1 ob. for 12 artabas made into colocynth oil, and the share of the surplus which it is instructed to divide between the oil-worker and the tax-farmer, and all the expenses for the transport of the produce.

The pay for the tax-farmers shall be given to them from their share of the surplus.

Added by corrector: In Alexandria the wages for (the manufacture of) sesame oil and the brokerage and the pay (sc. of the tax-farmers) shall be given in accordance with the proclamation made at the time of the sale.

Search. If the tax-farmers or their subordinates wish to make a search, alleging that [some people] have contraband oil or (illegal) oil-factories,[18] they shall conduct a search in the presence of the [representative] of the *oikonomos* or of the *antigrapheus*. If [the] representative of the *oikonomos* or of the *antigrapheus* does not comply when summoned or does not stay until the search is conducted, he shall pay to the tax contractors twice the amount (of the oil) they estimate (to be concealed) and the tax-farmers

(col. 56) may (col. 56) conduct [a search within . . .] days [. . .]

If he (sc. the tax-farmer) fails to find [what] he said he was seeking, he may be required by the person whose property is being searched to take an oath in a temple that he has not made the search for any other than its declared purpose and the interests of the oil-contract.

If he fails to take the oath on the same day or the day after, he shall pay the person who demands the oath twice the value he estimated (the contraband oil) at before he made the search.

The tax-farmers shall appoint sureties for a sum greater by one twentieth (than that which they have undertaken to pay), and they shall pay the taxes they collect[19] every day to the bank, and the monthly instalment before the middle of the following month.

The oil-workers shall receive their wages from the (oil) that is manufactured, not from the (oil) that is stored.

P. Revenue Laws, cols. 38–56; *W. Chrest.*229;
*Sel. Pap.*II.203

1. Cf. **235** n. 8.
2. Cf. **235** n. 3.
3. Cf. **231** n. 24.
4. The village chiefs; cf. **256** n. 3.
5. These prices are more than double those current in the Greek world outside Egypt; cf. cols. 50 and 52 below for the restrictions and customs barriers on imported oil.
6. Cf. **231** n. 25.
7. Cf. **256** and n. 1.
8. Cf. **235** n. 16.
9. Cf. **235** n. 15.
10. Though exempted from the tax mentioned in col. 39 they are paid at a lower rate for their produce.
11. Cf. **256** ll. 136–59.
12. The point of this prohibition is not clear.
13. Cf. **235** n. 9.
14. To prevent lard being used as a substitute for oil.
15. On the Ptolemies and the native temples cf. also **222, 227, 231, 235**.
16. The earliest known example of a protective customs barrier (as opposed to a purely fiscal device); for taxes on imports to Egypt cf. **237**.
17. Compare the prices in col. 40.
18. These and other abuses are in fact known to have taken place; cf. **256** ll. 136–54, and *W. Chrest.* 300–303.
19. Allusion unclear.

237 Valuation of goods imported to Egypt by Apollonius (May–June 259)

The following papyrus, from the large archive of Zenon, the personal agent of Apollonius, *dioiketes* of Ptolemy II Philadelphus (cf. also **238–46**, esp. **240** n. 2),

consists of an account of goods imported into Egypt for the benefit of Apollonius
and others on two ships, captained by Patron and Heraclides respectively,
together with the details of the taxes paid on them. The goods are listed
according to the rates of tax levied, respectively 50%, 33⅓%, 25% and 20%.
These rates are far higher than those practised elsewhere in the Greek world (cf.
100 n. 4), though in line with the high rate of taxation internally in Egypt. The
small sums on the left-hand side refer to an inland toll (*diapylion*) paid between
Pelusium and Alexandria. Cf. also **231** ll. 25–35, **236** col. 52.

See further: Préaux (1939), 371–9; Fraser I (1972), 148–50.

Column I

Valuation [at Pelusium] of the goods [imported] . . . for [Apollonius]
and the others on the boats captained by Patron and Heraclides.

    Year 27, Artemisius.

5   Belonging to Apollonius, [on the boat captained by] Patron:

2 dr. 3 ob.   5 [jars of] grape syrup at 12 dr., 60 dr.

3 dr. 4 ob.   11 half [jars] at 4 dr., 44 dr.

    And [on the boat captained by Heraclides]:

10   3 ob.   1 [jar] of filtered wine, 12 dr.

1 dr.   [2 jars of] ordinary wine at 3 dr., 6 dr.

[1 dr. 2 ob.]   [4 half jars of grape syrup at] 4 dr., 16 dr.

[1 ob.; 1 dr. 3 ob.]   [1 half jar of white oil], 30 dr.[1]

[¼ ob.; 1 ob.]   [1 jar], 4 dr.

    The 50% tax on these goods, (total value) [172 dr.]

15   The 50% tax on this sum, [86 dr.]

    On the boat captained by Patron:

[33 dr.]   [70] Chian jars of wine [at 18 dr.], 1,260 [dr.]

1 dr.   [4] Chian half jars [at 9 dr., 36 dr.]

[1 dr. 3 ob.]   [3] Thasian jars [at 20 dr., 60 dr.]

20   [And] on the boat captained by [Heraclides]:

3 dr.   [9 jars] of dried figs [at 8 dr.], 72 dr.

30 dr. 3 ob.   [61] Chian jars of wine at 18 dr., 1,098 dr.

3 ob.   [2] Chian half jars [at 9 dr., 18 dr.]

2 dr.   [4] Thasian jars at 20 dr., 80 dr.

25   The 33⅓ tax on these goods, (total value) 2,624 dr.

    The 33⅓ tax on this sum, 874 dr. [4 ob.]

84 dr.

Column II

On the boat captained by Patron:

2 dr. 2 ob.   7 half jars of honey from Theangela at
                    12 dr., 84 dr.

2 ob.   1 of Rhodian honey, 12 dr.

2 ob.	1 jar of Attic honey, 20 dr.	30
2 ob.	1 half jar of Lycian honey, [12 dr.]	
1 dr.	smaller (jars) . . .	
1 dr. 2 ob.	[4 half jars] of Coracesian honey, [48 dr.]	
5 ob.	. . . of Chalybonian honey . . .	
	Small jars [containing 3 *kotylai*?]	35
	of Chian cheese . . .	
	of other cheese . . .	
1 dr.	of dried fish . . .	
	of fish pickled in the season . . .	
5 dr.	5 jars of [belly of tunny fish] / at 20 dr.,	40
	[100 dr.]	
3 dr.	. . . of salted fish at 16 dr., . . .	
2 dr.	. . . of mullet at dr., . . .	
	2 earthenware jars of wild-boar meat at 2 dr.,	
	[4 dr.]	
	2 jars of Samian earth at 10 dr., 20 dr.	45

And on the boat captained by Heraclides:

2 ob.	1 half jar of honey, 12 dr.	
¾ ob.	1 Chian jar containing 10 *choinikes* of Pontic	
	nuts, 6 dr. 1½ ob.	
	1 basket of hard nuts containing 1¼ artaba	
	1 half full basket [containing ¾ artaba]	50
	(total) 2 artabas at 12 dr. an artaba, 24 dr.	
	[4 large baskets] of pomegranate seeds (total)	
	2 artabas at 2 dr. an artaba, 4 dr.	

Column III

	1 jar of wild-boar meat, 5 dr.	
	1 pot (of the same), 2 dr. 3 ob.	
	2 jars of venison at 3 dr., 6 dr.	
	2 small pots of goat-meat, 4 dr.	55
	1 basket of hard sponges, 8 dr.	
	(1) of soft (sponges), 12 dr.	
	1 jar of Chian [cheese], 5 dr.	
	The 25% tax [on these goods, (total value)	
	859 dr. 4½ ob.]	
	The [25% tax on this sum, 214 dr. 5½ ob.,	
	1 chalcus]	60

On the boat captained by Patron:

1½ chalcus	[22½ minas] of pure wool in [a chest], at 2 dr.	
	[3 ob.] a mina, [56 dr.], 1½ ob.	

The 20% tax on these goods, [(total value)
56 dr. 1½ ob.]

65 The 20% tax on this sum, [11 dr. 1½ ob.]

Total value of the goods [which pay the 50% tax,
172 dr.]

The 50% tax on this sum, 86 dr.

(Total value) of the goods which pay [the 33⅓
tax], 2,624 dr.

The 33⅓ tax on this sum, 874 dr. 4 ob.

70 (Total value) of the goods which pay the 25%
tax, 859 dr. 4½ ob.

The 25% tax on this sum, 214 dr. 5½ ob.
1 chalcus

(Total value) of the goods which pay the 20%
tax, 56 dr. 1½ ob.

The 20% tax on this sum, 11 dr. 1½ ob.

(Total tax paid) 1,186 dr. 5 ob. 1 chalcus

The *trierarchema*,[2] 1½ ob.

75 The *diapylion*, 112 dr. 3 ob. ¼ 1 chalcus

The 1% tax,[3] 37 dr. ¼ ob.

(Total of these) 149 dr. 5 ob. [1 chalcus]

Grand total, 1,336 dr. 4 ob. ¼

Less the rebate of ¼,[4] 9 dr. 1¼ ob.

Leaves 1,327 dr. 2 ob. ¾ [. . .]

Verso: Year 27, Artemisius. The valuation we have received from Bubalus of the goods imported / for Apollonius from Syria[5] to Pelusium.

P. Cairo Zen. 59.012, lines 1–79

1. Cf. **236** col. 52.
2. A tax for the upkeep of the navy.
3. Perhaps a local harbour tax.
4. On the 1% tax.
5. I.e. goods from the Aegean or beyond will have been re-exported from Syria.

238 Letter to Apollonius concerning the gold coinage of Ptolemy II (ca 24 October 258)

See further: Préaux (1939), 267–80; Rostovtzeff I (1941), 402 and III, 1417 n. 201; Bagnall (1976), 176; Will I (1979), 175–9.

Demetrius[1] to Apollonius, greetings. It is well if you are in good health and everything else is as you wish. As for me, I am devoting myself to

what you wrote me to do: / I have received 57,000 (drachmas?) of gold 5
which I minted and returned. We would have received many times as
much, but as I have written to you before, the foreigners / who come 10
here by sea, the merchants, the forwarding agents,[2] and others, bring
their own fine local coins and the *trichrysa*,[3] to get them back as new
coins, in accordance with the ordinance which instructs / us to take and 15
mint them,[4] but as Philaretus (?)[5] does not allow me to accept them, we
have no one to refer to on this matter, and are compelled / not to accept 20
them. The men are furious since we refuse (the coins) at the banks[6] and at
the . . . and they cannot send (their agents) into the country / to 25
purchase merchandise, but they say their gold lies idle and that they are
suffering a great loss, since they brought it from abroad and cannot easily
dispose of it to others even at a lower price. As for the people in the city
(sc. Alexandria) they are all reluctant to use the worn / gold coins.[7] 30
For none of them knows to whom he can refer and after adding a little[8]
get back fine gold or silver in exchange. In the present circumstances, / I 35
see that the king's revenues are suffering no small loss.[9] I have therefore
written to inform you, and if you think fit, write to the king about it and
tell me / to whom I can refer on these matters. For I believe it is 40
advantageous that as much gold as possible should be imported from
abroad and that the royal coinage should always be fine and / new, at no 45
expense to the king.[10] It is not proper for me to say in writing how some
people are treating me, but as soon as you are back you will hear . . .
Write / to me on these matters that I may follow your instructions. 50
Farewell. Year 28, Gorpiaeus 15.

P. Cairo Zen. 59.021; *Sel. Pap.*II.409

1. Probably the master of the mint in Alexandria.
2. *ekdocheis*, precise meaning uncertain, cf. Fraser II (1972), 319f. n. 428.
3. Gold pentadrachms of Ptolemy I, now superseded by a new issue of gold coins.
4. Ptolemy I had already fixed a different (lighter) weight standard for Ptolemaic coins as compared with those of the other Hellenistic monarchies which followed the example of Alexander in adopting the Attic standard. Ptolemy II then instituted a monopoly of Ptolemaic coins in Egypt (as already practised by some Greek cities before); traders bringing foreign coins to Egypt therefore had to get them reminted at a rate fixed by the authorities.
5. Reading uncertain.
6. Cf. **235** n. 9.
7. Cf. n. 3.
8. I.e. paying a supplement.
9. A regular preoccupation with the royal administration, cf. **236, 256** ll. 233f., **259**.
10. Cf. also **219, 263**; the Ptolemies were even more dependent on foreign supplies for their silver.

239 Petition to Apollonius concerning the building of a sanctuary to Serapis (ca 12 February 257)

See further: Fraser I (1972), 116f., 257–9, 273, and see **261**.

To Apollonius, greetings from Zoilus of Aspendus, [one of . . .] and who was also introduced to you by the 'friends'[1] of the king. As I was worshipping the god Serapis[2] (and praying for) your good health and the prosperity of King Ptolemy (II), it happened that Serapis [enjoined] to
5   me several times / in my dreams to sail to visit you and [tell you about] this injunction: a . . . must be built to him together with a precinct (*temenos*) in the Greek quarter near the harbour,[3] and [a priest] must be appointed, [and] sacrifices performed at the altar on your behalf. As I [beseeched him . . .] to release me from [this task] here, he caused me to
10   fall seriously ill / so that [I] was in danger for my life. I prayed [to him (saying) that if] he restored [me] to health I would undertake the obligation and carry out his instructions. As soon as I had recovered, there arrived somebody from Cnidus who set about to build a Serapeum on this spot and who brought stones along. Later the god told him not to
15   build (the sanctuary), and he / went away. When I came to Alexandria and hesitated to approach you about these matters but (only discussed) the business you had agreed about, I had another relapse for four months. That is why I was unable to come and see you immediately. It is therefore right, Apollonius, for you to follow the god's commands so
20   that Serapis may be merciful to you and may greatly increase your / standing with the king and your prestige, and make you enjoy good bodily health. Do not therefore fear that the expense will prove to be great, for it will cost you very little; I shall jointly supervise all these works. Farewell.
    Verso: From Zoilus about Serapis. To Apollonius. Year 28, Audnaeus 9. At the harbour of Berenice.

P. Cairo Zen. 59.034

1. Cf. **224** n. 2.
2. See **257** and esp. **261**.
3. Exact place unknown.

240 Petition from Egyptian peasants to Apollonius (October–November 257)

See further: M. Rostovtzeff, *A Large Estate in Egypt in the 3rd C. B.C.* (Madison, 1923), 73f.; on the Zenon archive cf. C. C. Edgar in *P. Mich. Zen.* (1931), 1–50.

To Apollonius the *dioiketes* greetings from the farmers from [the] Heliopolite nome, from the village of Philadelphus[1] in the Arsinoite nome, from your 10,000 aruras.[2] After you gave us 1,000 [aruras] from the 10,000, and we had worked and sown these, Damis[3] took away from us 200 (?) aruras, and when [we] objected, he arrested three of our elders[4] until he compelled them to sign an act of renunciation.[5] And though [we were] willing to vacate the 1,000 aruras and asked / him to allow us time to work and sow them, even then he would not agree, but allowed the land to remain unsown. And there is another scribe, an Egyptian, [one of the] wicked men,[6] who does not allow the city to be settled but chases away those who are there. And there are many mistakes in the 10,000 aruras as there is nobody who knows anything about agriculture.[7] We therefore urge you, if you think fit, to call some of us in and listen to what we want to tell you. For twenty days have elapsed since our arrival. [We] wish . . . we are unable to . . ., but have spent everything we had / when we arrived. Farewell.

P. Lond. 1954

1. I.e. Philadelphia.
2. The large estate (*ca* 2,500 ha.) granted by Ptolemy II to Apollonius the *dioiketes*, well known through the archives of Zenon, agent of Apollonius and manager of the estate; cf. also **241, 244** and see **235** n. 15 on *ge en doreai*. The estate returned to the crown early in the reign of Ptolemy III. The archive of Zenon sheds remarkable light on the dynamism and entrepreneurial spirit of the new governing class of Egypt in the early Ptolemaic period; whether this spirit was characteristic of the whole of Ptolemaic Egypt, let alone throughout its history, is another matter. The standard account of Rostovtzeff *op. cit.* above, cf. also 1 (1941), esp. 420–2, may be too optimistic in this respect. Cf. e.g. J. Bingen in *Problèmes de la terre en Grèce ancienne*, ed. M. I. Finley (Paris, 1973), 215–22; D. J. Crawford, *ib.* 223–51.
3. Later attested as nomarch (*PP* 881 and 10.071; cf. **244**), but he does not appear to have an official position here.
4. Cf. **251** ll. 23f.
5. Of the contract between the peasants and Apollonius for the cultivation of the estate.
6. Possibly Anosis, village scribe of Philadelphia, cf. **244** (end).
7. An indication of the resentment felt by the Egyptian peasants against the attempts of the Greek immigrants to upset their traditional methods of agriculture; cf. **253, 256** ll. 49–59.

241 The estate of Apollonius the 'dioiketes' at Philadelphia (26 December 257)

Artemidorus[1] to Panacestor,[2] greetings. As I was coming from Boubastis to [Memphis], Apollonius ordered me to visit you if possible, and if

not to send one of my men to convey you his instructions. For he had heard that the 10,000 aruras³ were not being sown all over. He therefore instructed me to tell you to have the wood cleared away and the land
5   irrigated, / [and if possible] to sow the whole of the land, but if not that as much as . . . should be sown with sesame and that no part of the land should be left uncultivated. Since [then] I [am] unable to come in person through pressure of work,⁴ I have sent you a letter so that you may know and [act] accordingly. For he gave instructions to hire and put to work numerous . . . men to do the hoeing and sowing (?) and others to assist
10   them. Do this, then, while it is still time / to sow. I have also told Zenon and Artemidorus at [Memphis], as Apollonius instructed me, to supply you with as much copper as you need for the purpose. Take delivery of it, for it will be given to you. And they said . . . (sc. that they had given) . . . 10,000 drachmas to Maron.⁵ Farewell. Year 29, Apellaeus 2. [. . .]

P. Cairo Zen. 59.816

1. A doctor in the service of Apollonius (*PP* 10.160 and 16.582).
2. Zenon's predecessor at Philadelphia (*PP* 100).
3. See **240** n. 2.
4. Or: through illness.
5. A manager of the estate (*PP* 10.289).

242 A tender to Apollonius the 'dioiketes' for repairing embankments at Memphis (257)

See further: M. Rostovtzeff, *A Large Estate* (see **240**), 53f., 62.

[. . .] To Apollonius the *dioiketes*, greetings from Harmais.¹ At the city
10   of Memphis the [various] / embankments (measure) 100 *schoinia*.² Of these, those of the Syro-Persian (district) (measure) 12 *schoinia*, those of Paasu 7, those above [the] quay of Hephaestus and those below 4, those in the city together with the king's palace 23, those of the Carian (quarter) . . ., those of the Hellenion 3, beyond Memphis those to the west of the royal garden 20, and those to the [east . . .], and those to the north 5 (*schoinia*) 30 (cubits). For heaping up these embankments a sum of 1 (talent) 5,500 (drachmas) was given in [the 28th (year)] when the rise (sc. of the river) was 10 cubits, 3 palms, 1⅙ fingerbreadths, and in the 27th (year) a sum of 1 (talent) 1,300 (drachmas) was given when
15   [the] / river rose 10 (cubits) 6 (palms), 2⅔ fingerbreadths.³ I now undertake to heap up for you these same embankments, starting from the

base of the embankments to a rise of 12 cubits, to the satisfaction of the *oikonomos*[4] and the director of works,[5] for a payment of 1 (talent) from the royal treasury. According to established practice we shall be provided with spades, which we will return. Farewell.[6]

PSI 488, lines 9–19; *Sel.Pap.*II.346

1. An Egyptian.
2. 1 *schoinion* = *ca* 45 m.
3. Note the precision of the measurements, officially recorded by the 'Nilometer' at Memphis (Diodorus 1.36.11f.; Strabo XVII.1.48); on the Nile flood cf. **217** n. 2.
4. See **256** and n. 1.
5. The director of works (*architechton*) in the nome.
6. On embankments cf. too **231** n. 5; **256** ll. 197–211.

243 Record of lamp oil assigned to the retinue of Apollonius (January 256)

The following text is part of a record of daily disbursements of lamp oil made to the large retinue of Apollonius the *dioiketes* during his travels of inspection in Egypt. It is one of (probably) many such lists of materials assigned from the stores of Apollonius to his retainers. For the life-style of a *dioiketes* cf. also **254**.

Year 28, Apellaeus.
Daybook of the castor oil[1] spent for daily disbursement.

1st	For the accounting office of Athenagoras	1 cotula	5
	And for that of Demetrius	1 cotula	
	For that of Dionysodorus	½ cotula	
	For the scribe's office of Iatrocles	1 cotula	
	For that of Artemidorus	½ cotula	10
	To Philon for the bakery	½ cotula	
	To Bannaeus for the storeroom for the silverware	¼ cotula	
	For the steward's house	¼ cotula	
	To Philistus and Menodorus	¼ cotula	15
	To Pyron, for the steward's record books	⅛ cotula	
	To Herophantus	⅛ cotula	
	To Heraclides the groom, / for the horses	¼ cotula	20
	To Solon, for the horses of Amyntas	¼ cotula	
	To Eubulus	¼ cotula	
	Total for the day	6¼ cotulas	
2nd	To the same	6¼ cotulas	25

3rd	To the same	6¼ cotulas
4th	To the same	6¼ cotulas
5th	To the same	6¼ cotulas
6th	To the same	6¼ cotulas

30 To Philon the baker, for the man preparing
food for the festival[2]   1 cotula
Total   7¼ cotulas

| 7th | To the same | 7¼ cotulas |

35 And that added for Philon   1 cotula
Total   8¼ cotulas

| 8th | To the same | 8¼ cotulas |
| 9th | For the Isis festivals | |

Subtracting that given for the accounting
40 offices of Athenagoras, Demetrius / and
Dionysodorus, and the ½ cotula for the
scribe's office of Iatrocles, to the rest
3¼ cotulas
45 And to Helenus for a hand lamp, / 8 cotulas
Total   11¼ cotulas

10th To the same, subtracting from that given
to Helenus for a hand lamp, 3 cotulas,
remainder   8¼ cotulas
50 And that reassigned for the scribe's office
of Iatrocles   ½ cotula
Total   8¾ cotulas

P. Cornell 1, lines 1–52

1. Cf. **236** on the oil monopoly.
2. The Isis festivals mentioned below, a four-day Egyptian festival celebrated by Apollonius and his retinue.

244 A lease of land from the estate of Apollonius (August 256)

In the reign of Ptolemy (II) son of Ptolemy (I) Soter, in the 30th year, when Alexander son of Leonidas was priest of Alexander and of the Brother-Sister Gods, and Prepusa daughter of Demetrius was basket-bearer (*canephoros*) of Arsinoe Philadelphus, in the month of Panemus, and the 10th of the Egyptian month Epeiph.[1] Hegesarchus son of Theopompus and Theopompus son of Hegesarchus and Nicodemus son of Hegesarchus, all three Macedonians 'of the *epigone*',[2] have contracted
5 to work / for one year, from Zenon son of Agreophon, of Caunus, [in the service of] Apollonius the *dioiketes*, from the 10,000 aruras given by

416

the king to Apollonius the *dioiketes* at Philadelphia in the Arsinoite nome,[3] 100 aruras of seed-land in the 3rd basin[4] which stretches from north to south, at a rent of 7⅛ artabas of wheat for every arura, free from risk and not subject to any deduction. There shall be given as seed for the land bearing wheat ½ artaba to the arura, / and for the land bearing barley   10 an amount in proportion, and for expenses 1 artaba of barley for each arura, and for weeding ½ an artaba of barley and for wood cutting, should brushwood be found, whatever amount is judged sufficient to be given for each arura. Hegesarchus, Theopompus and Nicodemus shall measure out the corn for rent at the granary in Philadelphia, in accordance with the ordinance on corn collection[5] in the month of Daesius in the 31st year, and they shall similarly repay whatever corn they receive for seed, / for weeding, for expenses and whatever money they may borrow   15 for the brushwood, or corn instead of money, at the rate of 1 artaba of wheat for 1 dr. 2 ob. of copper, and a proportionate amount for barley. Hegesarchus, Theopompus and Nicodemus shall sow two thirds of the land they have contracted to work with wheat and one third with barley.[6] If they fail to carry out the terms of the agreement, Zenon may let the land to others. Any loss they cause to the / income of Apollonius,   20 or whatever they may owe by way of rent and loans, they shall pay forthwith one and a half times the amount to Zenon, and Zenon or his representative may enforce exaction on them, their sureties and all their belongings, both on one and on all, as in the case of (debts) to the crown.[7] Sureties for payment in full of the obligations in the contract: the contracting parties for each other, and Ammonius son of Theon, of Cyrene, one of the assistants (?).[8] / This contract shall be valid wherever   25 produced. Witnesses: Damis son of Cleon,[9] Sostratus son of Cleon, both of them from Helena, Theopompus son of Aristion, from Thessaly, doctor, Diodorus son of Zopyrus, from Magnesia, in the service of Apollonius the *dioiketes*, Agathinus son of Pyrrhus, from Cyrene, one of the assistants, Anosis son of Totorchois, from Sais, village-scribe of Philadelphia.[10] Keeper of the contract: Damis.

P. Col. 54, lines 1–29

1. Cf. **222** n. 3.
2. A status designation frequently found in the papyri, but its precise meaning is quite uncertain (= simply 'private individual', 'civilian' ?); cf. J. F. Oates, *YCS* 18 (1963), 5–129 and Fraser I (1972), 49f. and II, 134 n. 110.
3. Cf. **240** with n. 2.
4. An area enclosed by dykes.
5. Cf. **256** ll. 131–3; the full scope of this is unknown.
6. It is not certain that there is any official policy behind this.
7. Cf. **275**(b).

8. Exact meaning uncertain.
9. Cf. **240** n. 3.
10. Cf. **240** n. 6.

245 Letter of complaint to Zenon from a non-Greek (*ca* 256–255)

. . . to Zenon, greetings. You do well if you are keeping in good health.
I too am in good health. You know that you left me in Syria with
Crotus[1] and that I carried out all the instructions in connexion with the
5 camels and that I was blameless towards you. And when you ordered /
to pay me my salary (Crotus) gave me nothing of what you had
ordered. And when I requested many times that Crotus should give me
the salary you had ordered but he gave me nothing at all and told me to
go away, I held out for a long time waiting for you,[2] but when I ran out
10 of necessities / and was unable to obtain these from any source, I was
compelled to run away to Syria to avoid dying of hunger. I have
therefore written to you to inform you that Crotus is responsible. And
when you sent me again to Philadelphia to Jason, and I did everything I
15 was told to, / for nine months now he gives me nothing of what you
ordered, neither oil nor grain, except every two months when he also
pays the (allowance for) clothing. And I am in distress summer and
winter. And he tells me to accept ordinary wine for salary.[3] But they
have treated me with contempt because I am a barbarian.[4] I therefore
request you, if you please, to order them to let me have what is owed to
20 me / and in future to pay me regularly, so that I do not die of hunger
because I do not know how to speak Greek (*hellenizein*).[5] You would
therefore do well to treat me with respect. I pray to all the gods and to
the spirit (*daimon*) of the king that you may be in good health and come
quickly to me so that you may find out for yourself that I am
25 blameless. / Farewell.
(*Verso*) To Zenon.

P. Col. 66

1. An agent of Apollonius in Syria and Palestine (*PP* 16.418); the writer of the
   letter was connected with Apollonius' camel trade in Syria and Palestine.
2. Zenon returned from Syria to Egypt in spring 258 and did not come back.
3. A calculated slight.
4. The writer's exact nationality (Egyptian, Arab, etc.) is not clear.
5. Or perhaps: 'act like a Greek'. The letter is written in Greek, but could have
   been the work of an interpreter. On tensions between Greeks and natives cf.
   225 n. 4.

246 Letter to Zenon from two 'hierodouloi' of Boubastis

To Zenon, the *hierodouloi*[1] of Boubastis, who are feeders of cats,[2]
greetings. The king[3] rightly granted exemption from compulsory
labour[4] to men of this profession throughout the country / and   5
Apollonius[5] did the same. We are men from Sophthis. But Leontiscus[6]
forcibly sent us to work at the harvest, and in order to avoid troubling
you, we carried out the work / imposed on us. But now Leontiscus has   10
sent us a second time to go and make bricks. There are two of us. He is
protecting the brick-makers at Sophthis, Amerois and Besas, who ought
to be doing the work now, / as it suits his own ends.[7] Please therefore 15
conform yourself to the order issued by the king and Apollonius the
dioiketes.[8] For apart from you we have no one else present here to appeal
to.[9] / Farewell.   20

P. Cairo Zen. 59.451

1. I.e. members of the personnel of the native temples.
2. See **251** l. 25.
3. Ptolemy II Philadelphus.
4. On compulsory labour see **251**.
5. The *dioiketes* (cf. **235** n. 8).
6. *PP* 4583; the *archiphylakites* of the nome, cf. **231** n. 33.
7. On maladministration by officials cf. **231** and refs.
8. On the problem of the frequent ineffectiveness of official edicts cf. esp. **231**,
   249, 258, 259, 272.
9. The men may have been forced to work on Apollonius' estate (**240** n. 2).

247 Register of an official postal station (*ca* 255)

The following text is part of the daybook of an official postal station (exact
location unknown), recording the despatches handed in by couriers to the station
masters and forwarded by the latter to other couriers. The rolls or letters from
the north of the country emanate from the king and Apollonius the *dioiketes* to
various officials, those from the south from officials to (mainly) the king and
Apollonius. It will be seen that Apollonius' correspondence is almost as extensive
as that of the king himself (cf. also **256** ll. 244f., **265**).

　　　. . . 6 rolls, of which 3 were for the king together with a [letter],
　　　. . . for Theogenes the money-carrier, . . . for Apollonius the
　　　[*dioiketes* . . .]
16th　　. . . [delivered] / to Alexander 6 rolls; of these 1 roll was for   55

[King] Ptolemy (II), 1 roll for Apollonius the [*dioiketes*] and 2 letters were received in addition to the roll, 1 roll for Antiochus the Cretan, 1 roll for Menodorus, 1 roll wrapped in another (?)

60   for Chel . . .,¹ / and Alexander delivered them to Nicodemus.

17th   Morning hour, Phoenix the younger, son of Heraclitus, a Macedonian holding 100 aruras,² delivered to Aminon 1 roll and the price for Phanias,³ and Aminon delivered it to Theochrestus.

65   18th   At the first hour, Theochrestus delivered to Dinias 3 rolls from the upper (i.e. southern) country; of these 2 rolls were for King Ptolemy, 1 roll for Apollonius the *dioiketes*, and Dinias delivered these to Hippolysus.

70   18th   At the sixth hour, Phoenix the elder, son of Heraclitus, a Macedonian holding 100 aruras in the Heracleopolite nome, one of the first soldiers in the company of E . . ., delivered 1 roll for Phanias, and Aminon delivered it to Timocrates.

75   19th   At the eleventh hour, Nicodemus delivered to Alexander from the lower (i.e. northern) country . . . rolls; of these 1 roll was from King Ptolemy to Antiochus in the Heracleopolite nome, 1 roll for Demetrius the officer in charge of the supply of

80   elephants / in the Thebaid,⁴ 1 roll for Hippoteles the agent of Antiochus [left in charge?] at Apollonopolis the Great, 1 roll from

85   King Ptolemy to Theogenes the money-carrier, / [1 roll] for Heracleodorus in the Thebaid, [1] roll for Zoilus, banker⁵ in the Hermopolite nome, [1 roll] for Dionysius, *oikonomos*⁶ in the Arsinoite nome, . . . (3 lines missing) . . .

90   20th   At the . . . hour, Lycocles delivered [to Aminon] 3 rolls; of these 1 roll was for [King Ptolemy from . . .] the elephant country below Th . . ., 1 roll for Apollonius the *dioiketes*, 1 roll for

95   Hermippus member of [the] / company of workmen (?), and Aminon [delivered] them to Hippolysus.

21st   At the sixth hour, . . . delivered to Phanias from the lower country two letters . . . And Horus delivered to Dionysius . . .

100   22nd   At the first hour, A . . . delivered to [Dinias] 16 rolls; of these . . . rolls were for King Ptolemy from the elephant country below Th . . ., 4 rolls for Apollonius the *dioiketes* . . ., 4 rolls for

105   Antiochus the Cretan, and Dinias [delivered] them / to Nicodemus.

22nd   At the twelfth hour, Leon delivered [to Aminon] from the upper country [. . . rolls] for King Ptolemy, and Aminon delivered them to [Hippolysus].

23rd   At the morning hour, Timocrates [delivered . . .] rolls from the

110   upper country / [. . . to Alexander]; of these [. . . rolls] were for King Ptolemy, 1 roll [for Apollonius] the *dioiketes*, 1 roll for

. . . the money-carrier, [1 roll for . . .] and Alexander [delivered them to . . .]

P.Hib. 110, lines 51–114; *W.Chrest.*
435; *Sel.Pap.*II.397

1. The identity and status of these three men is unknown.
2. A cleruch like his brother (l. 71), cf. **252**, but it is not clear why they have the right to use the official post.
3. Allusion unclear.
4. On him cf. Fraser I (1972), 178 with II, 305f. n. 365. On the elephant hunts of the Ptolemies cf. **278, 279**.
5. Cf. **235** n. 9.
6. Cf. **256** and n. 1.

248 Receipt from a boat captain for transporting barley to Alexandria (251)

See further: Préaux (1939), 143–7; Fraser I (1972), 147.

[. . .] In the reign of Ptolemy (II) son of Ptolemy (I) Soter, in the 34th (year), when Neoptolemus son of Phrixius was priest of Alexander and of the [Brother]-Sister Gods, and Arsinoe daughter of Nicolaus was basket-bearer of Arsinoe Philadelphus, / on the 24th of the month of Mesore (= 13 October 251).[1] Dionysius the boat captain acknowledges that he has loaded [on to] the boat of Xenodocus and Alexander, on [which the pilot] is Ekteuris son of Pasis, of Memphis, through / Nechthembes the agent of the royal scribes,[2] for conveyance to the royal granary at Alexandria, with a sample,[3] four thousand eight [hundred] artabas [of barley, pure, unadulterated and sifted] grain, with the measure [and smoothing-rod][4] / which he [himself] brought from [Alexandria], with [just] measurement,[5] and [I make] no [complaint].[6]

*P. Hib.*98 (*W. Chrest.*441; *Sel. Pap.*II.365)

1. Cf. **222** n. 3.
2. Cf. **231** n. 28.
3. Designed to show that the cargo had not been tampered with in transit.
4. For levelling grain in a measure.
5. Cf. **231** n. 25.
6. On the supplying of Alexandria with grain cf. **256** ll. 70–87.

249 Letter of Ptolemy II Philadelphus on the billeting of troops (mid third century)

The practice of billeting government officials and especially troops on the local population, widely used in the ancient world (cf. **50, 178, 187**), was particularly needed in Ptolemaic Egypt because of the limited space available for permanent habitation because of the annual Nile flood. The burden was not restricted to the native population, though it fell most heavily on them. Though conceived as a personal and revocable privilege granted by the king, it came to be regarded by the beneficiaries as a hereditary right, and was open to obvious abuse, despite repeated royal legislation. Cf. **231** ll. 99–101, 168–177, **272** (in Cilicia), and on the Ptolemaic cleruchs cf. **252**.

See further: Préaux (1939), 387–92, 477–80; Rostovtzeff III (1941), index s.v. Billeting; *C. Ord. Ptol.* 1, 5–10, 84.

King Ptolemy (II) to Antiochus,[1] greetings. Concerning the billeting of soldiers we hear that there has been increased violence as they (sc. the soldiers) are not receiving lodgings from the *oikonomoi*[2] but break into
5   the houses themselves, / expel the inhabitants and settle there by force. Give instructions therefore that in future this is not repeated, but that preferably they provide themselves with accommodation.[3] If nevertheless the *oikonomoi* must give them quarters, let them give only what is
10   strictly necessary; and when the soldiers leave these quarters, / they must vacate them after putting them back in good order, and must not leave them until they return, as [we hear] is happening at present: they let out the houses or place seals on them when they leave. Be particularly
15   [careful] about Arsinoe near / Apollonopolis, so that [should] soldiers come none is billeted there,[4] but that they stay rather in Apollonopolis. Should there be any need for them to stop in Arsinoe, let them build
20   themselves huts, as their predecessors have done. / Farewell.

*C. Ord. Ptol.*24; *Sel. Pap.*II.207

1. Precise position uncertain.
2. Or: 'as they do not occupy lodgings assigned to them by the *oikonomoi*.' On the *oikonomoi*, cf. **256** and n. 1.
3. I.e. construct barracks.
4. Arsinoe, named after Ptolemy's sister-wife, is privileged for that very reason.

250 Ordinances of Ptolemy II concerning internal security in Egypt

The evidence for internal insecurity in Egypt from the end of the third century is abundant and explicit (cf. **225**). The following measures edicted by Ptolemy II

show the problem to have been endemic in Ptolemaic Egypt even in the period of
its greatest prosperity.

See further: *P. Hib.* II (1955), pp. 97–103.

. . . and if he (i.e. the policeman) does not bring (sc. the culprit to the
police station) he shall be liable to the [same] fine as the brigand.
Similarly with [the] sailors who are branded and the . . . of the fleet,[1]
the policemen . . . shall bring all those who are caught to [the]
commanders [of the] / guard posts.[2] If they do not bring them and have   90
been convicted (of this) [themselves], they shall be sent to the ships.[3]
[Those] who harbour[4] the sailors shall be liable to prosecution by the
crown.[5] Brigands, other criminals and royal sailors are to be arrested
wherever they are and no one shall protect [them] from arrest;[6] /   95
whoever prevents or . . . shall himself be liable to the same fines as the
[brigand] or the deserter from his [ship]. Similarly with those who
receive [stolen property] from brigands or (any other) criminal or
[harbour] them, [they shall be liable to] the same fines [as] / prescribed   100
. . . no one shall free them or he [shall be liable to . . .] they shall
conduct a search . . . (3 fragmentary lines). . . . / [no] one shall go at   105
night . . . (4 lines mostly lost). . . . a verdict on [them] shall be given
by [the judges][7] / to whom the duty [has been assigned] of judging   110
brigands; [those] who sail [on] the river are to moor before . . . at the
[appointed] places; at night . . . (sc. they are not to sail); [those] who are
overtaken [by] bad weather . . . (sc. and forced) / to [moor] on the bank   115
are to go to [the . . .] relevant authorities and report to the [policemen
the] reason [and] the place where they have moored. The chief of police[8]
shall provide them with an adequate [guard] to protect them where they
are moored [from any] / violence. Any envoys sent by the [king] on an   120
urgent boat trip who [wish to sail] at night shall receive an escort from
them (sc. the police) and . . .

P. Hib. 198, lines 85–122

1. Sailors for the Ptolemaic fleet were recruited from free natives and also from
   various pressed men; cf. **227** l. 17, **251** l. 30, **256** l. 219.
2. Guard posts placed throughout the country.
3. I.e. they shall take the place of the sailors.
4. Cf. **236** col. 44.
5. Or: 'shall be liable to the penalties for theft from the crown.'
6. I.e. they may not enjoy the right of asylum, cf. **231** n. 22 and cf. **256** ll.
   215–22.
7. Identity unknown.
8. Cf. **231** n. 33.

251 Compulsory labour on canals and dykes (242/1?)

Compulsory labour was traditional in ancient Egypt and continued under the Ptolemies (see also **181** n. 2 on Asia Minor). The following text is a report from an official to the *oikonomos* of the Theban toparchy concerning compulsory labour on canals and dams. The official reckons (in col. I, omitted here) 1,080 persons in the toparchy each owing 30 *naubia* a year (a cubic measure = a little over 1 m³, but also used as a unit of reckoning labour), i.e. 32,400 *naubia*, to which a further 60 are added (the reason for this is not clear). There follows a list of persons exempted from (or unable to provide) *naubia*, which are subtracted from the total, then a list of *naubia* actually performed.

See further: Préaux (1939), 395–400; N. Lewis, *Inventory of Compulsory Services in Ptolemaic and Roman Egypt, American Studies in Papyrology* III (New York, 1968).

Column II

	The elders[1] who guard the dams and embankments	53
	The elders, the infirm, and the young[2]	61
25	The inhabitants of Somphis who bury the cats[3]	21
	Those assigned to the receiving measures of the state granaries[4]	5
	Those who have discharged their obligations in the Pathyrite nome	15
30	Those assigned to the fleet[5]	2
	Among the Greeks[6]	1
	Runaways	37
	Also the keepers of mummies	21
35	Dead	7
	Subtract	282
	Whose *naubia* (total)	8,460
	This leaves as *naubia*	24,000

40 Labour has been performed on the following up to Payni 30th: / On the canals:

Column III

	On the canal of Philon, as it is called, whose outlet lies in the Pathyrite nome	*naubia*	4,120
	On Paneiomis		2,240
45	On that of Amasis		670
	On Pabebynis		1,555
	On that of Philon in the city		335
	On that of Dorion		60
	On the canals (total)		8,980

On the dams:		50
On that at Godoba	1,150	
On that at Godobera	70	
On that at the frontier	280	
On that leading to Coptus	90	
On the potter's dam	300	55
On the dams (total)	1,890	

On the embankments:		
On that to the east of Somphis	540	
On that to the west of the same	660	
On that to the east of the marshes	180	60

Column IV

On that on the land of Pachnumis son of Portis	150	
On that on the land of Callibius	100	
On the embankments (total)	1,630	65

Total	*naubia*	12,500	

And for the quarters of the *strategos*[7] are

expended	*naubia*	1,200	
For the same (total)	*naubia*	13,700	
This still leaves		10,300	70

From these the labour performed by the cultivators
on the locks of the canals and on the embankments,

which we shall add up to Mesore 30th[8]	4,150	75
This leaves	6,150[9]	

UPZ II.157, cols. II–IV

1. Cf. **240**.
2. All unable to work.
3. Cf. **246**.
4. Measures prescribed for use by officials in charge of revenue; cf. **231** n. 25.
5. Cf. **250** n. 1.
6. Perhaps soldiers serving in the Greek ranks; it is not clear whether this shows
   that Greeks in general were altogether exempted from corvées.
7. Perhaps guard duties.
8. I.e. 2 more months (*ca* August–October). The translation is uncertain.
9. How these are to be used is not explained.

252 Official correspondence concerning cleruchs (December 239–January 238)

While the Ptolemies shared with the other Hellenistic kings in the east the same need to attract and fix in their lands a permanent military force, the technique they adopted was different. Military settlers (cleruchs) in Ptolemaic Egypt were not established as communities, as in the Seleucid empire (cf. **182** n. 9), but were granted as individuals the use of plots of land, varying in size according to rank (up to 100 aruras). These were frequently leased by the cleruchs to others. Initially the holdings were conceived as precarious and revocable, e.g. in case of death as the following text shows, but in practice they gradually became the hereditary possession of their owners, a development eventually sanctioned by the kings themselves, cf. **231** ll. 36–48. For evidence on cleruchs and cleruchic land cf. also **224, 226, 234, 235**, cols. 24, 36, **247** l. 61, 70, **255, 275**(b) and on billeting cf. **249**.

See further: Préaux (1939), 463–77; Rostovtzeff I (1941), 284–7; Crawford (1971), 53–85.

Artemidorus. I have written below a copy of the letter to Nicanor [for
5 your] information. [Year 9], Phaophi [29]. /
To Nicanor. The cavalrymen listed below have died; therefore take back [their] holdings (*kleroi*) for the crown. At Boubastis, of the corps of Epimenes, Sitalces [son of. . .], captain . . .; at Theogonis, of the corps of Lacon, . . . machus son of Sca . . ., captain; at Tebetnu, of the corps
10 of Sosipolis, / Ammonius son of A . . . Year 9, Phaophi 29.
Choiak 4. Artemidorus to Asclepiades, greetings. The cavalrymen listed below have died; therefore take back their holdings for the crown.
15 At Heraclea / in the division of Themistes, of the corps of Damon, Leagrus son of Dionysophanes, captain, of the same corps, Philonides son of Artemidorus, officer; at Hiera Nesus in the division of Polemon, of the corps of Lichas, Ebryzemis son of Ziochorus, officer. Year 9, Athur 28. [. . .]

P. Hib. 81

253 Preliminary reports for the sowing schedule (September 232)

The 'sowing schedule' (*diagraphe sporou*), an important institution in the economy of Ptolemaic Egypt, illustrates at once the extent of administrative control over agriculture in Egypt and the limited effectiveness in practice of that control (at least as far as 'royal land' was concerned (cf. **231** n. 11); it is not clear whether it applied to other categories of land as well). Every year at the time when the Nile flood was receding (i.e. when the surface of irrigated land could be precisely determined), a schedule was drawn up locally by government officials (toparchs, royal scribes, chiefs of police), but not by the cultivators themselves, laying down what surfaces were to be sown with what crops. Several papyri attest the importance attached to the schedule by the administration, including the *dioiketes* himself (cf. **236, 256** ll. 49–62), but they also show clearly the reluctance of the Egyptian peasantry to be restricted to the prescribed crops and the difficulties of enforcing the schedule in practice (cf. **231** ll. 200–3).

See further: P. Vidal-Naquet, *Le bordereau d'ensemencement dans l'Egypte ptolémaique* (Brussels, 1967); Crawford (1971), 25f.

Recto

Apollonius[1] to Leon,[2] greetings. Appended is a copy of the (letter) from Athenodorus the *dioiketes*. Complete therefore the sowing schedule with the usual officials and in conformity with his [instructions], and have it ready so that [we] ourselves may give it before the appointed time / to   5
Leucippus the chief of police;[3] (do this) in the knowledge [that should] a delay occur you will be sent before the *dioiketes*. Farewell. (Year) 15, [Mesore . . .]

Athenodorus to Apollonius, greetings. Complete the sowing schedule of the land [in the district?] for the 16th (year) with the help of the [royal] / scribe[4] and other suitable persons, and send [it] preferably   10
sooner, but at the latest [by the . . .] of Mesore,[5] drawn up by individual and by village and in [summary], to Leucippus the chief of police. For we have written to him [that] you would send him [these] documents at that date, to be forwarded / to us in the city (i.e. Alexandria) together with   15
people [to] bring them back. (Year) 15, Epeiph . . . (August–September 232).

Verso

To Leon.
(Year) 15, Mesore 9, Apollonius. Copy of the (letter) from Athenodorus the (*dioiketes*) concerning the sowing schedule for the 16th (year).

P. Yale 36

1. Precise official position unknown (an *oikonomos?*).
2. Brother of Apollonius and toparch (cf. **231** n. 28) of Philadelphia; on him see further R. S. Bagnall, *GRBS* 15 (1974), 215–20.
3. Cf. **231** n. 33.
4. Cf. **231** n. 28.
5. Mid-October at the latest.

254 Preparations for the visit of a 'dioiketes' (January 225)

Requisition of supplies, transport and lodging (cf. **249**) for government officials was an ancient custom in Egypt, and in Ptolemaic times affected all classes of the population. Goods requisitioned were sometimes paid for, sometimes not (as here); the practice was open to obvious abuse (cf. **231** ll. 178–87).

See further: Préaux (1939), 392–4; Rostovtzeff I (1941), 315f. and index s.v. 'requisitions'.

Amenneus to Asclepiades, greetings. In accordance with your letter we have got ready for the visit of Chrysippus [the *archisomatophylax*][1] and *dioiketes*[2] 10 whiteheaded birds, 5 domestic geese, 50 fowls; of wild birds 5 (we have) 50 geese, 200 fowls, 100 pigeons; we have also borrowed / 5 riding donkeys and their . . ., and we have got ready the 40 pack-asses; we are now making the road. Farewell. [Year] 22, Choiak 4.

Verso.

To Asclepiades. Year 22, Choiak 7. Amenneus about the gifts prepared.

W. Chrest. 411; *Sel. Pap.* II.414

1. Literally 'commander of the (king's) bodyguard'; this became in the second century a court title. Cf. **262**, Fraser I (1972), 103, and L. Mooren *op. cit.* on **224** n. 2.
2. Cf. **235** n. 8.

255 A petition to Ptolemy IV concerning a gymnasium (27 February 221)

As the centres of physical and intellectual education of the Greeks (cf. **118**), gymnasia became in the Hellenistic east the distinguishing mark of Greek social life, established by the Greek immigrants deep in Asia and in Egypt. In Ptolemaic Egypt they appear to have been privately founded and maintained, though with royal blessing; as well as being centres of Greek culture they were closely connected with military life and the cult of the kings (cf. also **266**, at Thera), hence devotion to the life of the gymnasium was a means of expressing loyalty to the dynasty (cf. also **234**). The following text is a type of petition (*enteuxis*) of which numerous examples are known (see *P. Ent.*), nominally addressed to the king as the supreme dispenser of justice, but in practice handled by the office of the *strategos* (cf. **231** n. 26).

See further: Rostovtzeff I (1941), 324f. and II, 1058–61; Launey II (1950) ch. 14 (pp.836–869 on the Ptolemies).

To King Ptolemy (IV) greetings from Aristomachus, a Macedonian of the corps Eteoneus, a cleruch with an 80 arura holding.[1] I am wronged by [Dallus]. Apollodorus, who was registered as a Nagidian from the corps of Chrysermus, a commander of 500 men and a cleruch, [built] a gymnasium [at Samaria], where he had his holding, and consecrated it

with the following inscription: To King Ptolemy, Apollodorus (dedicated) the gymnasium. When Apollodorus died and left property
situated partly at Alexandria / and partly in the village mentioned above,   5
Polyclitus inherited this property, and I represent Polyclitus at law as
manager of the property [left] at Samaria, in accordance with a decision
of the *chrematistai*[2] who judged current suits in the district Alpha,[3]
Leonidas, Hegesianax, . . . ophius, with the assistance of Hegesippus
the *eisagogeus*,[4] in year 20, the 21st. Already previously, before this
decision . . . as I was managing [the buildings?] and they [were
decaying?] after the death of Apollodorus, I pulled down the apartment
built above the [gymnasium] / as it was collapsing, with the agreement   10
of Aphthonetus the former *strategos*, in year 16 through a petition. I built
buttresses against the buildings, and instead of the . . . and others which
were worn out I added props . . . next to the porch on [which is the]
inscription, I rebuilt it after it collapsed so that . . . with a prop. In the
same way, after the decision I am repairing everything which is
[decaying / . . . and I represent?] Polyclitus after the decision men-   15
tioned above. Now Dallus and the woman who is said to be his wife
. . . in the gymnasium itself, which is no concern of theirs . . . and as I
[was telling?] them to get out . . . (gap of 2 lines) . . . [I therefore] urge
[you, Sire, to instruct / Diophanes the *strategos* to write] to Agathocles   20
the chief police officer to summon Dallus before him . . . (sc. and
compel him) to get out and to pay a fine . . . when this is done thanks to
you, Sire . . . Farewell.

[To Agathocles: reconcile them if possible; if] not send them so that
justice is done to them in accordance with the laws. Year 1, Gorpiaeus
30, Tybi 13.

Verso

Year 1, Gorpiaeus 30, Tybi 13. Aristomachus against Dallus, concerning
buildings.

P. Ent. 8

1. Cf. **252**.
2. Cf. **231** n. 42.
3. One of the five quarters of Alexandria; cf. Fraser I (1972), 34f.
4. The magistrate who introduced the case before the 3 *chrematistai*.

256 The duties of an 'oikonomos' (late third century)

See further: M. Rostovtzeff on *P. Tebt.* 703.

[. . .] (Column 1 almost completely lost)[1]

(Sc. You must inspect) . . . and the water-ducts which run through [the]
30 fields, / whether the intakes into them have the prescribed depth and
whether there is sufficient space in them; the peasants are used to
35 [leading] water from these to the land each of them sows. Similarly /
with the canals mentioned from which the intakes go into the above-
mentioned water-ducts, (you must inspect) whether they are solidly
made and whether the entries from the river are kept as clean as possible
40 <and> whether in general / they are in good condition.

During your tour of inspection try as you [go] about to encourage
everybody and make them feel happier; you should do this not only by
45 words, but also should any of them / have a complaint against the
village-scribes² or the village chiefs (*komarchai*)³ about anything to do
with agriculture, you should investigate the matter and as far as possible
put an end to such incidents.

50 When the sowing has been completed, / it would not be a bad thing if
you made a careful tour of inspection; for in this way you will get a
precise idea of the sprouting (of the crops), and you will easily see what
has not been properly sown or left altogether unsown,⁴ and you will
55 [know from] this those who are guilty of negligence, / and it will be
known to you [whether anyone] has used the seeds for other purposes.⁵

You must consider it one of your most imperative duties to make sure
60 that the nome is sown with the crops specified in the sowing schedule. /

And if there are any who are in difficulties because of their rents or are
even [completely] worn out, you must not [let the matter pass] without
making an enquiry.

You must draw up a list of both the royal and the private cattle used in
65 cultivation / and show all possible care that the [calves] of the royal
herds, as soon as they are old enough to eat hay, are placed in the [calf]
70 byres.⁶ /

You must take care that the corn in the nomes – apart from the corn
which is used on the spot [for] seed and that which cannot be transported
75 by water – is conveyed . . .; in this way / [it will be easy to load it onto]
the first [ships] to arrive, and you must [never] show any laxity in
80 dealing with this matter. . . . (3 fragmentary lines) . . . / You must
also take care that the prescribed cargoes of corn, of which we are
sending you a list, are brought down to Alexandria at the right
85 time, / [not] only in the right numbers but also tested and suitable for
use.⁷

Visit also the weaving-houses in which the linen is woven and devote
90 the utmost care / to ensure that [as many] of the looms are in use as
possible, and that the weavers provide the embroidered stuffs prescribed
for the nome.⁸ And if any of them are in arrears with the items
95 ordered / they must be charged the prices specified in the ordinance for

430

each kind. Show particular care that the linen is of good quality [and] has (the number of) threads prescribed in the ordinance. Visit / also [the   100 washing] houses in which [the] raw [flax] is washed and the . . . [and] make a list, and report so that castor oil and natron might be supplied for washing.

. . . (several fragmentary lines) . . . . and should there be any surplus / from the amount booked in the first month, it shall be booked   110 in the next month as part of the monthly quota. All the looms which are not being used should all be taken to the / capital of the nome, deposited   115 in the store-houses and sealed up.

Audit the accounts of revenues, if possible village by village (and this does not seem impossible / if you devote yourself earnestly to the   120 matter), but if not, by toparchies. Allow in the audit only what is paid to the bank[9] in the case of money taxes / and (only) what has been   125 measured to the *sitologoi*[10] in the case of corn dues and of oil-bearing produce. Should there be any deficit in these, compel / the toparchs and   130 the tax-farmers[11] to pay to the banks the prices specified in [the] ordinance in the case of the corn debts,[12] and in the case of the oil-bearing produce according to the liquid product for each kind.

You must / devote care to all the matters written in the [memoran-   135 dum], and especially to what concerns the oil-factories.[13] For if you give sufficient attention to them, you will increase considerably the sale in the nome / and the thefts will be stopped. Such a result would be achieved if   140 on every occasion you inspected the workshops in [the] locality and the storehouses for both dry and liquid produce, [and] sealed them up. /   145 And (make sure) that the amounts measured out to the oil-workers are not greater than what is going to be used in the oil-presses which exist in the factories. You must take care that as far as possible / all [the presses]   150 are used, and if not, as many as possible, and keep an eye as closely as possible on [the] remainder; for . . . stuffing them with straw . . . to place a seal on them, / and the superfluous implements of the presses   155 which are not being used must be brought to [the same] spot and sealed up [in] the storehouses. And if . . . / know that apart from the   160 payments . . . you will fall into considerable disrepute, which it will [not] be easy for you to [dispel]. . . . (2 obscure lines) . . . /   165

And since the revenue from the pasture tax (*ennomion*) is also one of the most important, it would be particularly increased if you [carry] out the registration (sc. of cattle)[14] in the best possible way. The most suitable season for doing this is the month of Mesore (*ca* August); for at this time / since the [whole] land is covered by water,[15] the cattle-breeders   170 send their herds to the highest spots, since they are unable to scatter them in [other] places.

Take care also that goods offered for sale / are not sold at a higher   175

price than those prescribed.[16] All those which do not have fixed prices, and for which the dealers may fix any price they wish, you must also
180 inspect carefully, and after fixing a reasonable / profit for the goods that are being sold, you must compel the . . . to dispose of them.

Take care to inspect the calf-byres, and devote special care to ensure
185 that / corn is supplied in them until (the time for) green food, and that the amount prescribed is used for the calves every day and . . . is
190 provided correctly, from the locality itself and, should / they need additional supplies from outside, from other villages as well.

You must also take care that the planting of the local trees is done at
195 the right season, in case of the mature ones, / willows and mulberry trees, but around the month of Choiak (*ca* December) for acacias and tamarisks.[17] Of these the rest must be planted on the royal embankments, while [the young plants] must be placed [in] beds [so that] they
200 may be treated with all possible / care at [the time] of watering, and when necessary [and] the time for planting comes, then . . . place (them) [on?] the royal embankments.[18] The contractors must look after
205 them / and make sure that the plants are not damaged by sheep or by anybody else. In your other tours of inspection check whether there are
210 [any] cut trees on the embankments or in the fields, / and make a list of them.

Make a list also of the royal houses and the gardens attached to them,
215 and what each needs by way of attention, and report to us. /

Take care also that the question of the native soldiers (*machimoi*) is settled in accordance with the memorandum which we drew up concerning the men who abandoned their work and . . . sailors,[19] in order that
220 . . . / . . . those who fall into your hands may be held until they are sent to Alexandria.

Take especial care that no act of extortion or any other misdeed is
225 committed. / For everyone who lives in the country must clearly know and believe that all such acts have come to an end and that they have been
230 delivered from the previous bad state of affairs, / and that [nobody] is allowed to do what he wishes, [but] everything is arranged for the best.[20] And (so) you will make the countryside safe and . . . (sc. will increase) the revenues in no small way[21] . . .
235 Now it is not easy to include everything / and to convey it to you through memoranda, [because of the] complexity of the circumstances arising from the present situation. And so that as far as possible nothing
240 [is neglected] and concerning / the instructions set down in the [memorandum] . . . and concerning unforeseen circumstances that arise report
245 (to me) in the same way so that . . . (2 fragmentary lines). For since / it is necessary to transact [everything] through letters[22] . . . (2 fragmentary lines) . . . you must arrange for them to write . . . about each of

the / instructions sent, especially . . ., and if not, stating the reason, so   250
that . . . and that none of the [instructions given here] is [neglected]. If
[you] do this / you will carry out your duty and your whole security will   255
be assured.

Enough about these matters; I thought it well to set down in writing in
the memorandum what I said to you when sending you to the nome. / I   260
thought it was your most important duty to [behave?] with special care,
integrity, and in the best possible way . . . (several obscure lines) . . .
and after this, to behave in an orderly and upright way in your district, to
avoid bad company, to steer away from [all] disreputable collusion, / to   275
believe that if you show yourself to be above reproach in these matters
you will be held worthy of higher offices,²³ to keep the memoranda in
your hands, and to report on everything as has been ordered. /

P. Tebt. 703 (cf. *Sel. Pap.*II.204)

1. This text, one of the most instructive of all Ptolemaic papyri, is a
   memorandum from (probably) a *dioiketes* (**235** n. 8) to a subordinate
   oikonomos appointed by him, and conveying instructions of a general kind as
   to his duties (Pharaonic precedents are known for instructions of this type to
   officials). On the role of the *oikonomos* see also **231** l. 159, **235, 236, 242, 247,
   249, 251**, and outside Egypt **266, 275**.
2. Cf. **260**.
3. Cf. **236** n. 4, **275**(a).
4. A reference to the 'sowing schedule' (*diagraphe sporou*), cf. **253**.
5. Cf. **236** col. 41–43.
6. Cf. also ll. 183–91 below.
7. Cf. **248**.
8. The control of the linen industry described in ll. 87–117 is reminiscent of the
   organisation of the oil monopoly (cf. **236**). See also **227** ll. 17f., **231** ll. 63f.,
   239, 249f.
9. Cf. **235** n. 9.
10. Cf. **231** n. 23.
11. Cf. **235** n. 3.
12. Cf. **244** n. 5.
13. On this section cf. generally **236**.
14. Cf. **275**(a).
15. Through the Nile flood (cf. **217** n. 2).
16. As with oil (**236** col. 40).
17. Trees were in short supply in Egypt, hence the administration's interest in
    them (cf. **231** ll. 205f.; *P. Cairo Zen.* 59. 157).
18. On the maintenance of embankments cf. **231** n. 5, **242, 251**.
19. Cf. **250** and n. 1, and for flight from work by natives cf. **231** ll. 6–9, **251** l. 33.
    What precise disturbances are referred to here and in the next lines is not
    clear; cf. **221** n. 8, **225** for possible contexts.

20. A recurring profession by the royal administration, cf. **231, 258**.
21. Cf. **238** n. 9.
22. On the paperwork of the Ptolemaic administration cf. **247**.
23. The *dioiketes* controlled administrative appointments, cf. **260**(b).

257 The 'recluses' of the Great Serapeum at Memphis (161/60)

One of the most intriguing series of second century papyri is a group of texts (just over 100) relating to a group of persons, mostly Greeks and Macedonians though Egyptians are also found, who describe themselves as 'recluses' (*katochoi*) who are 'held in detention' in the great temple of Serapis at Memphis (on Serapis cf. **131, 239, 261**). During their period of 'detention', which may be anything from a brief period to many years, they may not leave the precinct of the sanctuary though they continue to communicate with the outside world. They are not priests themselves, though they take part in temple and cultic activities and receive remuneration accordingly. How and why this 'detention' begins and ends is not made clear, and the problem has eluded a definitive solution. A plausible analogy is that of the religious novitiate of worshippers of Isis described (some three centuries later) in Apuleius, *Metamorphoses* XI. On this view the *katochoi* at Memphis are novices of the god Serapis, whose 'detention' is ordered by the god appearing to them in a dream (cf. **126, 131, 239, 261**), and comes to an end in the same way when they are ready for initiation. As well as illustrating the life of the great sanctuary the texts give incidental evidence on tensions between Greeks and Egyptians at this period (cf. **228** and generally **225**).

See further: *UPZ* I (1927); Rostovtzeff II (1941), 734–6; Fraser I (1972), 250, 253f. and II, 403 n. 505.

To Dionysius, *strategos*[1] and one of the 'friends' (sc. of the king),[2] from Ptolemy son of Glaucias, a Macedonian, one of those 'held in detention' for twelve years in the great Serapeum in Memphis.[3] As I have suffered
5 grave injustice / and my life has been frequently endangered by the temple cleaners whose names are listed below, I am taking refuge with you in the belief that in this way I would best secure justice. For on Phaophi 8th in the 21st year (= 9 November 161) they came to the
10 Astarteum, which is in the sanctuary,[4] and in which / I have been living 'in detention' for the number of years mentioned above; some of them had stones in their hand and others sticks, and they tried to force their way in, in order to seize the opportunity to plunder the temple and to put
15 me to death because I am a Greek, like men laying a plot / against my life. But when I anticipated them and shut the door of the temple, and shouted to them to withdraw in peace, they did not go away even so. When Diphilus, one of the worshippers held 'in detention' by Serapis
20 besides me, / expressed indignation at their conduct in such a temple,

434

they pushed him back, handled him very roughly and beat him up, so that their lawless brutality was clear for all to see. When these same men treated me in the same way on Phaophi of the 19th year (= November 163), I immediately addressed a petition to you,⁵ / but as I had no one to   25
look after the matter further, they were let off scot-free and became even more arrogant. I therefore ask you, if you please, to order them to be brought before you, so that / they may receive the punishment they   30
deserve for all these misdeeds. Farewell.

Mys, clothes-dealer; Psosnaus, yoke-bearer; Imouthes, baker; Harembasnis, corn-dealer; Harchebis, doctor for internal diseases; Po . . ., carpet-weaver; Stotoetis, porter; and others with them, whose names / I   35
do not know.⁶

UPZ I.8

1. Cf. **231** n. 26.
2. Cf. **224** n. 2.
3. *PP* 7334; Ptolemy's detention lasted *ca* 20 years.
4. A precinct of the goddess Astarte, of Phoenician origin, within the temple complex, where the 'recluses' lived.
5. Cf. **255, 259**.
6. The names are all Egyptian, though Mys could be a Carian.

258 Maladministration by officials (25 October 156)

Dioscorides¹ to Dorion,² greetings. Appended is a copy of the letter to Dorion.³ In the knowledge that the same instructions are directed to you, make sure that nothing is done in violation of them and no evil action is kept hidden from us. Farewell. Year 26, Xandicus 1, Thoth 25. /   5
To Dorion. The king and the queen⁴ attach great importance to justice being done to all their subjects in the kingdom.⁵ Now many people are coming down the river (sc. the Nile) to the city (sc. Alexandria) and are lodging complaints against you, your subordinates and especially the tax-farmers⁶ for abuses of power / and fraudulent exactions, and some   10
even allege blackmail. We wish you not to lose sight of the fact that all this is incompatible with our rule of conduct and no less with your safety, should anyone be convicted of having done harm to one of the people concerned. Therefore take care yourself that no action of this kind is repeated / and that no one suffers any harm from anybody, and   15
particularly from tax-farmers who try to use blackmail, and send instructions to the same effect to all concerned without fail.⁷

UPZ I. 113

1. The *dioiketes* (cf. **235** n. 8).
2. A *hypodioiketes*, subordinate to the *dioiketes*.
3. Probably financial manager (*epimeletes*) of the Memphite nome.
4. Ptolemy VIII and Cleopatra II (cf. **231**).
5. Cf. **256** n. 20.
6. Cf. **235** n. 3.
7. On maladministration in the Ptolemaic kingdom, especially in the second century, cf. **231, 246** n. 8.

259 Petition to the 'strategos' from the royal peasants of Oxyrhyncha (*ca* 138)

To Phanias, [one of the] 'first friends',[1] *strategos* and manager of the revenues,[2] from the royal peasants[3] at Oxyrhyncha.[4] We have done our
5 best / to follow your exhortations, and we have sown the royal lands[5] which we cultivate. We have borrowed much money to prevent any
10 delay (in our payments); we have brought our crops / to the royal threshing-floor and have delivered them to the royal store. But we are wary of the illegal exactions practised by some (officials) whose conduct
15 is not / of the best and who transgress the existing ordinances relating to the peasants and the letters to the police chiefs (*epistatai*) on the same
20 matters emanating from you.[6] / We (therefore) beseech you, if you think fit, to assist us and the royal (revenues)[7] and to give instructions to write
25 to Demetrius and Stephanus the police chiefs to comply / with the (ordinances) mentioned and not to allow anyone to make illegal exactions from us nor to force their way into the threshing-floors, but to send
30 such men / before you, without excuses of any kind, so that you may examine their case publicly. If this is done we shall be able to pay our
35 rents in full / thanks to your help, and [the] king [shall] suffer no loss. [Farewell.][8]

P. Tebt. 786

1. Cf. **224** n. 2.
2. Cf. **231** nn. 26, 27.
3. Cf. **231** n. 38.
4. The village of Oxyrhyncha was situated high up and so received less benefit from the Nile flood (cf. *P. Tebt.* 787). By the late second century the number of royal peasants there had dropped from 140 to 40 (*P. Tebt.* 803) owing to difficulties in cultivation and pressure from officials.
5. Cf. **231** n. 11.
6. Cf. **246** n. 8.
7. Cf. **238** n. 9.
8. The Egyptian peasants made use of a Greek scribe versed in the official style.

260 Menches, village scribe of Kerkeosiris

The archives of Menches, a partly hellenised Egyptian who was village scribe (*komogrammateus*, cf. **231** n. 28) of Kerkeosiris in the Fayum from before 119 to 111/10, provide important information on the life of an Egyptian village in late Ptolemaic times (cf. also **231**). Menches' duties included providing his superiors with regular reports on lands, crops and rents due in his village, supervising public works and irrigation, and a concern for law and order, though he himself had no powers of jurisdiction.

See further: *P. Tebt.* I (1902) and IV (1976); G. M. Harper, *Aegyptus* 14 (1934), 14–32; Crawford (1971) and *JHS* 99 (1979), 221f.; L. Criscuolo, *Aegyptus* 58 (1978), 13–101.

(a) Menches' application for the post (25 May 119)

From Menches the village scribe of Kerkeosiris.[1] On being appointed to the post of village scribe previously held by me / I will pay at the village   5
50 artabas of wheat [and] 50 artabas of pulse, consisting of 20 artabas of lentils, / 10 of bruised corn, 10 of pease, 6 of mixed seeds, 3 of mustard,   10
1 of parched pulse, total 50. Total 100 artabas. / Year 51, Pachon 6. And   15
Dorion[2] (will pay) 50 artabas of wheat and 10 of pulse, (consisting of) 3 of bruised corn, 3 of pease, 3 of mixed seeds, 1 of mustard, total 10. Total 60 artabas.

P. Tebt. 9

(b) Menches' appointment (20 August 119)

Asclepiades[3] to Marres, greetings. Menches has been appointed by the *dioiketes*[4] to the post of village scribe of Kerkeosiris on the understanding that he shall cultivate at his own expense 10 aruras of the land around the village which has been registered as uncultivated at a rent of 50 artabas, which he shall pay / in full every year from the 52nd year to the royal   5
treasury, or he shall make up the deficit from his private means.[5] Give him the papers of his office (*or:* 'the certificate of his appointment') and take care that he carries out what he has promised. Farewell. Year 51, Mesore 3. (*Verso*) To Marres the *topogrammateus*.

P. Tebt. 10; *Sel. Pap.* II.339

(c) Receipt from Menches to Dorion (119)

Menches son of Petesuchus, village scribe of Kerkeosiris in the division of Polemon, in the Arsinoite nome, to Dorion son of Irenaeus, one of the '(first) friends'.[6] I acknowledge that there has been measured out (to me) / from you in the 51st year 100 artabas [of wheat] by the official   5
standard[7] and justly [measured], (the wheat) being new, pure and [sifted], and also 20 (artabas) of lentils, [13] of bruised corn, [13 of pease], 10 of mixed seeds,[8] [4] of mustard, [1 of parched pulse], / total 61 of   10

437

pulse, 100 (of wheat). And from the 52nd year you will [measure out] (to me) every [year] 50 (artabas of wheat), pure and [sifted], by the official standard [and justly measured] as written above [without lawsuit] / or judgement or any [. . . or] twice [the above-mentioned] amount or [as price for each artaba] 2,000 drachmas (of copper) and [. . . to be consecrated] to the Benefactor [Gods. This receipt] shall be valid wherever [it is produced].

15

P. Tebt. 11

1. The addressee is unidentified, perhaps deliberately so if Menches' promise is correctly interpreted as a bribe to secure his reappointment (cf. next note). See however L. Criscuolo, *op. cit.*, 18–22.
2. As can be seen from (c) below, where he is identified, Dorion paid this amount to Menches and in addition the amounts promised by Menches himself. He may have been purchasing in this way the favour of Menches (cf. **231** ll. 184–6, where the practice is denounced, also **246**).
3. The royal scribe of the nome (cf. **231** n. 28).
4. Cf. **235** n. 8.
5. The administration is anxious to have the land fully cultivated (cf. **231** ll. 93–8, **259**) and Menches on his side is anxious to secure a post he obviously regarded as worthwhile.
6. Cf. **224** n. 2.
7. Cf. **231** n. 25.
8. There is an extra artaba of mixed seeds; the reason is unknown.

261 The (alleged) introduction of Serapis to Egypt by Ptolemy I

The rapid spread of the cult of Serapis through much of the Greek world after Alexander is a remarkable phenomenon of the Hellenistic age, but the question of the 'origins' of his cult is surrounded with legend, as may be seen from the following passage. Despite Tacitus' account, it is most probable that Serapis was derived from native Egyptian traditions: the sacred Apis bulls of Memphis (cf. **222** n. 8) were after their death identified with Osiris and worshipped as Osor–Hapi = Serapis in Greek. In what sense this god was 'created' by Ptolemy I is not clear, nor is it certain that any deliberate political intention lay behind his introduction to Alexandria, although this has often been postulated. See also **131, 239, 257**.

See further: Fraser I (1972), 246–76 and notes; III (Index), p. 70 s.v. Serapis.

The origin of the god (sc. Serapis) has not yet been related by Roman writers; the account of the Egyptian priests is as follows. King Ptolemy, the first of the Macedonians to establish firmly the power of Egypt, while he was providing Alexandria, which had recently been founded,[1] with walls, temples and cults, saw in a dream a young man of exceptional beauty and of more than human size, who instructed him to send his most trusted friends to the Pontus (the Black Sea) to bring back his image. This would bring prosperity to his kingdom, and the home which welcomed him would be great and famous. At the same time the young man seemed to him to rise up in the sky enveloped in a mighty conflagration. Ptolemy was struck by the portent and the miracle, and revealed the night's apparition to the Egyptian priests who are accustomed to understanding prodigies of this kind. And since they knew too little about the Pontus and the outside world, the king turned to Timotheus of Athens, a member of the family of the Eumolpids whom he had summoned as being a priest of the Eleusinian Mysteries, and asked him what was this cult and who was this deity. After searching for persons who had been to the Pontus, Timotheus learnt that there was a city there, Sinope, with nearby a temple of Jupiter Dis which had long been famous among the (local) inhabitants, and that next (to the image of the god) stood one of a woman generally called Proserpine (= Demeter). But Ptolemy, as kings do, was quick to take fright, but when he had recovered a sense of security, he turned more to pleasure than to religion, gradually neglected (the matter) and turned his attention elsewhere, until the same apparition, but now more frightening and urgent, predicted doom for him and his kingdom if his orders were not carried out.[2] Then Ptolemy ordered the sending of envoys with gifts to King Scydrothemis, who at that time ruled Sinope, and instructed the envoys as they were about to depart to consult Pythian Apollo (i.e. at Delphi). They journeyed safely by sea, and the answer of the oracle was clear: they must go and bring back the image of his father, but leave that of his sister. (84) When they reached Sinope they produced the gifts, the prayers and the instructions of their king to Scydrothemis, who hesitated, being at times fearful of the deity and at times terrified by the threats and the opposition of the people, and often he would be influenced by the gifts and the promises of the envoys. Three years elapsed in the meantime and Ptolemy did not relax his zeal or his prayers, and kept increasing the dignity of his envoys, the number of ships and the amount of gold (offered). Then Scydrothemis saw a threatening apparition which enjoined him not to delay any further the execution of the god's orders. As he still hesitated he was harassed by various calamities, by diseases and clear signs of divine anger which increased every day. He summoned an assembly and recounted the orders of the deity, the visions he and Ptolemy had had, and the disasters that were falling on them. The crowd rebuffed the king, and was jealous of Egypt; they feared for themselves and surrounded the temple. This is what gave rise to the widespread report that the god himself had boarded the ships moored to the shore, and remarkably, three days later after crossing such a large expanse of sea, they landed at Alexandria. A temple commensurate with the size of the city was built in the district called Rhacotis;[3] there had existed a small shrine dedicated from of old to Serapis and Isis. Such is the most widespread account of the origin and coming of the god. I am well aware that there are some who say that he was brought from Seleucia, a city in Syria, in the reign of the third Ptolemy, while others relate that the same Ptolemy was responsible for introducing him from his ancient home of Memphis,[4] a city formerly famous and a pillar of ancient Egypt. As for the god himself many liken him to Asclepius for his healing powers,[5] some to Osiris, the most ancient deity of that people, many to Jupiter (= Zeus) as lord of the universe, and the majority to Dis because of his own obvious attributes or through elaborate interpretations.

Tacitus, Histories IV.83–84

1. Cf. **232**.
2. Cf. **126, 131, 239**.
3. Cf. **232** n. 10.
4. Cf. **257**; this version is probably nearest the truth.
5. Cf. **126**.

262 The Ptolemies and the Jews

Greeks and Macedonians formed the most important immigrant element in Ptolemaic Egypt, but other foreign settlers were also represented. Jews had in fact been settled in the country before Alexander. Under the Ptolemies there was a Jewish quarter in Alexandria and papyri attest the presence of Jews in the Egyptian countryside as military settlers, farmers, tax-gatherers, policemen, etc. Palestine was under Ptolemaic control for over a century until taken over by the Seleucids (cf. **166–8, 172, 275, 276**). The 'Letter of Aristeas to Philocrates' is the work of an Alexandrian Jew writing in Greek under a pseudonym in (probably) the mid second century. It includes the famous (though probably fictitious) story of the translation by royal command of the Pentateuch into Greek (the Septuagint).

See further: V. Tcherikover and A. Fuks, *Corpus Papyrorum Judaicarum* I (Cambridge, Mass., 1957), 1–47; Fraser I (1972), 320–35 (on the Library at Alexandria), 697–703 (on 'Aristeas'), with notes.

(a) (9) When Demetrius of Phalerum[1] was placed in charge of the king's Library he was provided with large sums of money to collect, if possible, all the books in the world. He purchased some and transcribed others, and brought to completion the king's[2] design as far as he was able. (10) When he was asked in my presence, 'How many thousands of books are there?' he replied, 'Over 200,000, Sire, and I shall endeavour in a short while to bring up the number to 500,000 with the remainder. I have been told that the laws of the Jews deserve to be transcribed and included in your Library.'³ (11) 'What then prevents you from doing this,' the king said, 'everything you need is at your disposal.' Demetrius replied, 'A translation is needed; in their country the Jews use their own script, just as the Egyptians use their arrangements of letters, and they also have their own language. They are believed to use Syrian (= Aramaic), but this is not so, and their dialect is different.' When the king learnt of these details he said a letter would be sent to the High Priest of the Jews to bring the above-mentioned design to completion. [. . .]

(b) (35) King Ptolemy to Eleazar the High-Priest, greetings and good health. Since it happens that many Jews have been settled in our country, some of whom were transplanted from Jerusalem by the Persians during their period of rule, and others came as captives to Egypt in our father's train – (36) of these he enrolled many in the army at high rates of pay, and similarly when he judged their leading men⁴ to be reliable he founded fortresses which he gave them, in order to keep the Egyptian people in fear; and since we have taken over the kingdom, we deal with all men in a very humane way, but particularly so with your own countrymen – (37) we have given their freedom to over 100,000 prisoners of war,⁵ paying their owners the proper value in money and putting right any harm done through the impulses of the crowd. It was our intention to perform a pious deed and to dedicate a thank-offering to the greatest god, who has kept our kingdom in peace and in the greatest renown throughout the whole inhabited world. We have enrolled in the army those in the prime of age, and those capable of being in our service and who are deserving of trust at the court we have appointed to official positions. (38) Now as we wish to show favour to them, to all the Jews in the inhabited world and to those of future generations, we have decided to have your Law translated from the Hebrew language you use into Greek, so that they too may be available in our Library together with the other royal books. (39) It would therefore be a good action on your part and one worthy of our zeal if you selected elders of distinguished life, experienced in the Law and capable of translating, six from each tribe, so that agreement may be reached among the majority, since the enquiry concerns a matter of great importance. We believe that the completion of this task will bring us great fame. (40) Concerning this matter we have sent Andreas, one of the *archisomatophylakes*,⁶ and Aristeas, men we hold in esteem, to discuss the question with you, and to bring dedications to the Temple and 100 talents of silver for sacrifices and other expenses. You would do us a favour and do a friendly act if you wrote to us about anything you desire, and your wishes shall be fulfilled as quickly as possible. Farewell.

'Aristeas to Philocrates' (ed. M. Hadas, 1951)
I. 9–11; V. 35–40

1. Philosopher, man of letters and politician (cf. **20**), Demetrius went to the Ptolemaic court after his expulsion from Athens. He may have advised Ptolemy I on the establishment of the Library at Alexandria, though he did not hold the post of Librarian.
2. Ptolemy II, but this is impossible since Ptolemy II exiled Demetrius on his accession.
3. The intention is not implausible, but there is every reason to believe that the translation was carried out by Jews for the benefit of the many Jews who had adopted Greek as their language.
4. Or: 'the Jews already in the country'.
5. The figure is exaggerated, but the fact may be correct.
6. Cf. **254** n. 1; the form of the title is anachronistic for the reign of Ptolemy II, cf. L. Mooren, *op. cit.*, 27–31, 78f.

263 The gold mines in southern Egypt

See further: Préaux (1939), 253–61; Rostovtzeff I (1941), 381–3; Fraser I (1972), 173–6; J. F. Healy, *Mining and Metallurgy in the Greek and Roman World* (London, 1978), index s.v. Agatharchides.

At the extremity of Egypt and in the territory which adjoins both Arabia and Ethiopia there is a place which has many large gold mines, where gold is extracted in large quantities but with much hardship and expense. For the earth is naturally black and contains veins and seams of marble which are extremely white and surpass in brilliance everything which shines naturally, and the overseers of the mining activity produce the gold with the help of a multitude of workmen. For the kings of Egypt assemble there those condemned for criminal offences, prisoners of war and even those who have been convicted on unjust charges and placed under custody because of their hostile attitude, and not only these individuals but sometimes all their relatives as well, and they condemn them to the gold mines. In this way they punish those found guilty and procure considerable revenues from their toil.[1] Those who have been condemned – they form a great multitude and are all bound in chains – labour ceaselessly by day and through the whole night, without any respite, and they are carefully cut off from any chance of escape. They are watched over by guards of barbarian soldiers who speak different

languages, which makes it impossible for anyone to corrupt any of the
guards by conversation or some friendly contact.[2]

Diodorus III.12.1–3

1. The Nubian mines had been exploited by the rulers of Egypt before the
   Ptolemies; though the most important gold mines available to them, they
   were costly to exploit, and in any case the Ptolemies had to look to foreign
   trade to supplement their supply of gold (cf. **238**).
2. A detailed description of the mining activity follows; the passage is derived
   from the second-century writer Agatharchides' lost work *On the Red Sea*.

264 Ptolemy I and Cyrene (321)

Cyrenaica, the earliest possession to be acquired by Ptolemy I outside Egypt,
remained Ptolemaic until bequeathed to Rome by Ptolemy Apion in 96 B.C. The
context of the following inscription is most probably the first intervention by
Ptolemy I in 322–321 (Diodorus XVIII. 19–21; cf. also **21** §§10, 11), when Ptolemy
was appealed to by Cyrenaean oligarchs in a struggle against a Spartan
condottiere Thibron and the Cyrenaean democrats. The inscription outlines the
new constitution subsequently established for Cyrene, most probably by
Ptolemy himself acting as mediator in the conflict. The new constitution was
oligarchic in character, favouring wealth and age, though more broadly based
than the previous constitution. The city preserved its independence nominally,
but Ptolemy enjoyed a special personal position in it; Ptolemaic influence was
further secured by the imposition of a garrison under Ophellas, a fact not
mentioned in the inscription. By the second century, if not earlier, Cyrenaica was
regarded by the Ptolemies as fully integrated in their kingdom (cf. **229, 230**).

See further: J. A. O. Larsen, *CP* 24 (1929), 351–68; Fraser I (1972), 48f. and II,
132 n. 101; Bagnall (1976), 25–37, esp. 28f.

[Good fortune?]. Shall be citizens[1] [the men] born from [a Cyrenaean
father] and a Cyrenaean mother, and [those born from] the Libyan
women between Catabathmos and Authamalax,[2] and those born from
the [settlers (*epoikoi*)] from the cities beyond Thinis,[3] whom the Cyre-
naeans sent as colonists [and / those] Ptolemy designates,[4] and those   5
admitted by the body of citizens (*politeuma*),[5] in conformity with the
following laws.
(1) The body of citizens (*politeuma*) shall consist of the Ten Thousand.
The members shall be the exiles who fled to Egypt, [whom] Ptolemy
shall designate, and any whose permanent property[6] together with that
of his wife is estimated at twenty Alexander minas[7] and which the
assessors will have declared unencumbered; and any to whom are owed
twenty Alexander minas / together with his wife's permanent property   10

443

(?) if it has been estimated to be worth not less than the debt and the interest – and the debtors shall make a counter-declaration on oath, even if neighbours do not have the (required) census rating[8] – these also shall belong to the Ten Thousand provided they are not below the age of 30. The Elders (*gerontes*) shall choose as assessors from the Ten Thousand 60 men who are not below the age of 30, after swearing the oath prescribed

15 by the law. The men so chosen shall make an estimation as / is written in the laws. For the first year the list of citizens shall be made up from the previous census lists.

(2) The Council shall consist of 500 men appointed by lot and not below the age of 50; they shall serve as councillors for two years, and in the third year they shall eliminate by lot half of their number, then they shall let two years elapse.[9] If the number is insufficient, they shall select by lot

20 the others from those over 40 years of age. /

(3) There shall be 101 Elders (*gerontes*), appointed by Ptolemy. In case of an (Elder) who dies or resigns, the Ten Thousand shall appoint another man to make up the 101 from those not below the age of 50. It shall not be permitted to appoint the Elders to any office except that of general in war (time). The priests of Apollo shall be appointed from those who

25 have not held the priesthood / and are not below the age of 50.

(4) Ptolemy shall be general for life.[10] Besides him five generals shall be appointed from those who have not yet held the office of general and are not below the age of 50; if a war breaks out, (they shall be appointed) from the entire civic body. If another war breaks out outside Libya, the

30 Ten Thousand shall decide [whether / the] same men shall be generals or not; if they decide that they shall not be, (the generals) shall be appointed from the entire body of citizens.[11]

(5) There shall be nine Guardians of the Law (*nomophylakes*) (appointed) from those who have not held this office, ⟨not below the age of . . .?⟩ and five ephors (appointed) from those who have not held this office, not below the age of 50.[12]

(6) The Elders shall have the powers which the Elders had in peace

35 time,[13] [the] / Council those the Council (had), the Ten Thousand those the Thousand[14] (had). The Elders, the Council and the Fifteen Hundred chosen by lot from the Ten Thousand shall judge all capital cases. They shall use the previous laws in so far as they do not conflict with this ordinance (*diagramma*). The magistrates shall be subject to rendering accounts in accordance with the existing laws. Anyone arrested by the

40 generals and facing a criminal charge before the Elders and the Council / shall have the right to be tried according to the laws or by Ptolemy, whichever he chooses, for a period of three years. In future he shall be tried according to the laws. No exile may be condemned without the consent of Ptolemy.

(7) Any member of the body of citizens[15] who is in public employment as doctor,[16] gymnastic trainer, teacher of archery, horse-riding or armed combat, or herald at the town hall (*prytaneum*), shall be excluded / from the magistracies reserved to the Ten Thousand.[17] Anyone belonging to these categories [who is chosen by lot shall resign from office]. [. . .] (the rest of the text is too mutilated for continuous restoration and translation)[18]

45

SEG IX. 1; on the text cf. P. M. Fraser,
Berytus 12 (1958), 120–7

1. Passive citizens, as opposed to the 'Ten Thousand' defined below.
2. The boundaries of Cyrenaica.
3. Location unknown.
4. Ptolemy does not yet have the royal title (cf. **36**).
5. I.e. the 'Ten Thousand'.
6. 'Permanent property, such as land or flocks of which the fruits alone are consumed' (*LSJ*⁹, p. 2044).
7. I.e. ½ talent, not a very high figure.
8. Neighbours act as witnesses.
9. Compressed and ambiguous; it is not clear whether councillors serve normally for two or four years.
10. In practice Ptolemy did not hold office himself but designated a substitute.
11. The 'Ten Thousand'.
12. The functions of both offices, taken over from the previous constitution, are not further defined.
13. I.e. before the strife which prompted Ptolemy's intervention.
14. The previous body of active citizens.
15. The 'Ten Thousand'.
16. See **125**.
17. It is not clear whether this clause implies prejudice against the professions indicated or is intended to guarantee the independence of the magistrates.
18. The end of the inscription includes a list of the first set of magistrates to be appointed.

265 Taxes in Egypt's foreign possessions (late third century, 219/8 or 202/1?)

The following papyrus consists of a series of abstracts of letters from the office of the *dioiketes* (cf. **235** n. 8) to officials in the Ptolemies' foreign possessions (cf. **217** n. 4). It is unique of its kind, but obscure in detailed interpretation through its brevity and the gaps in the text. It shows at least the close and regular supervision exercised by the office of the *dioiketes* over the taxation of the Ptolemaic empire (cf. **247** in Egypt, **266**).

See further: R. S. Bagnall, *JEA* 61 (1975), 165–80; *id.* (1976), 108–10, 162, 166f., 224–9.

[. . .] To Aphrodisius:[1] concerning the money and grain and the other revenues which exist in the districts (*topoi*) in Lesbos and Thrace,[2] to
10 inform me whether he has received part of them, / and concerning Heraclitus and the (accounts?) to send so that it may be executed (?).

To Callimedes: (sc. to send) the (copy) (sc. of this letter) and to send
15 the (revenues?) from Ca . . . /

To Nicostratus: (we) have written that the sale of the contract for the money revenues in Lycia[3] for the 4th (year) has increased to 6 (talents) 1,312 (drachmas) and 4 obols,[4] (and that) we have given our assent for the future as well (?).

Another (letter): concerning the gate toll (*diapylion*),[5] about which (we)
20 have written that the sale fell short / by 2 (talents) 1,366 (drachmas), to [send] the account of the wine imported by the merchants from the 16th (year) every year [so that it may be set] against the deficit.

[. . .]
30 To . . .: concerning Zethus and . . . es / [who] undertook the contract for purple[6] in Lycia for five (years), (and) concerning whom it was written that they had raised the annual revenue of 1 (talent) 1,800 (drachmas) of silver and the (revenue) of the 4th year . . .

R. S. Bagnall, *JEA* 61 (1975), 168f. (*P. Tebt.*
8; *W. Chrest.* 2)

1. The precise title and functions of this and the other officials below are not known.
2. Cf. also **269**.
3. Cf. also **271**.
4. On the issuing of contracts for the collection of taxes cf. **276**.
5. Cf. **237** at Alexandria.
6. A tax on the production of purple or possibly a monopolised industry.

266 Letter of Ptolemy VI to an officer at Thera concerning the payment of troops (13 August 163)

See further: Bagnall (1976), 123–34.

King Ptolemy (VI) to Apollonius,[1] greetings. We have received the letter to which you had appended the copy of the memorandum handed over
5 by the soldiers stationed at Thera, / and in conformity with their request we have given instructions to Diogenes the *dioiketes*[2] to give to them the
10 lands seized by the *oikonomos*[3] for the royal treasury, / (namely) the Teisagoreion, the Carcineion, the lands called Callistratea and those which Timacrita had, the annual revenues from which he declared to be

111 Ptolemaic drachmas, so that they may spend these on the sacrifices /   15
and the oil.⁴ Farewell. Year 18, Audnaeus 15, Epeiph 15.⁵

C. Ord. Ptol. 33; *OGIS* 59; *IG* XII.3.327

1. The commander of the Ptolemaic garrison at Thera; Ptolemaic presence on
   the island is attested epigraphically from the time of the Chremonidean war
   (**49, 50**) and was probably continuous till 145.
2. Cf. **235** n. 8.
3. The chief financial official in the island, answerable to the *dioiketes* himself and
   not to the garrison commander; on the post of *oikonomos* in Egypt cf. **256** and
   n. 1.
4. For the gymnasium (where the inscription was found); on the connexion
   between gymnasia and military life cf. **255**.
5. Appended to the letter is a long list of names of officers and soldiers of the
   garrison who contributed to the restoration of the gymnasium.

267 Decree of Itanos in Crete in honour of Ptolemy III (*ca* 246)

See further: Bagnall (1976), 117–23.

With good fortune. Since King Ptolemy (III), having received the city of
Itanos and its citizens from his father King Ptolemy (II) and his
ancestors,¹ continues to benefit (the citizens) well and gloriously, / and   5
to preserve with goodwill their enjoyment of the same laws they had
when he took them over, resolved by the council and the assembly: the
park next to the gate shall be consecrated as a sacred enclosure² of King
Ptolemy and Queen Berenice / the sister³ and wife of King Ptolemy; the   10
city shall offer a sacrifice every year at their birthday festival⁴ in honour
of King Ptolemy and Queen Berenice, and shall celebrate a race. The
kosmeteres in office with Soterius shall inscribe this decree / on a stone   15
stele and dedicate it in the sanctuary of [Athena Polias]. The expense shall
be paid [from the] revenues of the city.

*Syll.*³ 463; *ICret.* III, pp. 83–5 no. 4

1. It is not clear how literally this is to be taken; Ptolemaic presence at Itanos is
   only first attested in 266 (*OGIS* 45) under Ptolemy II during the Chremonidean war (**49, 50**), when a garrison may have been established. There is much
   evidence for Ptolemaic relations with Crete, an important source of mercenaries (cf. **95** and n. 4), but it is only at Itanos at the eastern end of the island that
   regular Ptolemaic control is attested.
2. Itanos is unable or unwilling to pay for the construction of a temple. On
   divine honours for the Ptolemies cf. **218** and n. 8.
3. Cousin.
4. Cf. **222** n. 6.

268 Decree of Naxos in honour of the Ptolemaic 'nesiarch' and the island of Cos (ca 280)

See further: Bagnall (1976), index s.v. *dikastes*, esp. 232; S. M. Sherwin-White, *Ancient Cos* (Göttingen, 1978), 90–108 on Cos and Ptolemy II Philadelphus.

[Since Bacchon son of Nicetas, the 'nesiarch',[1] came to the city of Cos[2] in accordance with the instructions of King] Ptolemy (II) and [the League of Islanders, and asked for] judges and [arbitrators to] decide on the
5 contracts which were [disputed],[3] and the city of / [Cos] sent excellent men, [who came] to us and concerning the disputes arising [from the contracts] and the other [matters entrusted] to them by the city,
10 reconciled [advantageously the] majority of the disputants by [inviting] / them many times before them, while they gave a verdict for the others with all [justice], and as they had spent [much] time [on] the lawsuits and
15 the [judges] wished [to go back] to their homes, [our] people / [invited] them together with Bacchon [the nesiarch] to stay [in the city *or:* with us] and to [assist] the Naxians by carrying out [to the end] the [other matters entrusted to them], and they being desirous [of doing us a favour in these
20 matters] as well / showed [every zeal for our people in order to carry out everything] in a way worthy [of both our cities and of the mission entrusted to them . . .].[4]

M. Holleaux, *Etudes* III (Paris, 1942), 27–37
fragment A; *OGIS* 43

1. The restoration is virtually certain; on Bacchon and the League of Islanders cf. **218**.
2. On Cos and the Ptolemies cf. also **133**; Ptolemy II was born there, cf. **21** §19.
3. On this institution cf. **135**.
4. Fragment B (from the same decree?) records honours voted to the judges from Cos.

269 Decree of Samothrace in honour of a Ptolemaic governor (reign of Ptolemy III)

See further: Bagnall (1976), 159–68, but see P. Gauthier, *Historia* 28 (1979), 76–89.

Side A

. . . Hegesistratus [. . . moved; since Hippomedon] son of Agesilaus, the Lacedaemonian,[1] [appointed by] King Ptolemy (III) [general (*strategos*) of the] Hellespont and the Thracian provinces (*topoi*),[2] is
5 [piously] / disposed towards the gods and honours the [sanctuary] with

sacrifices and dedications, and when he came to the island he was eager to take part in the [Mysteries],[3] and (since) [he shows] every care for the security of the fort[4] by sending to guard it cavalry [and] / infantry, missiles and catapults [and] men to operate them, and (since) when requested to advance money for the salary [of the] Trallians[5] he [gave it], and (since) he wishes [always] to oblige our city in everything it requests and is [favourably] disposed towards the people, / and shows every concern both publicly for the city and in private to those individuals who approach him, acting in conformity with the king's policy, and (since) the [council] has passed a preliminary motion concerning praise for him to the effect that the citizenship and the other privileges granted by [the] citizens / should be inscribed on a stele [and] consecrated in the sanctuary of [Athena]; with good [fortune],

Side B

[be it voted by the people, to praise Hippomedon . . .] . . . (6 mutilated lines) . . . [and the] presidents (*proedroi*) and the [agonothete shall be responsible for the proclamation] when [the people celebrates . . . the contest . . .] . . . (3 mutilated lines) . . . in conformity with the [policy] of the king and of the / queen and to grant to our city the export of corn tax-free, from the Chersonese and from any other place which seems suitable to him (sc. Hippomedon);[6] and the ambassadors shall discuss with him the question of the fortress[7] and shall invite him to cooperate with our city, so that once it is completed citizens should be settled / who shall receive land allotments and cultivate the land, so that from the revenues (sc. from these settlements) sacrifices might be celebrated and first fruits might be consecrated to the gods on behalf of the king and the [queen . . .][8]

(the rest of the inscription is lost)

Syll.[3] 502; *IG* XII.8.156; P. M. Fraser,
Samothrace II.1 (1960), 39f.

1. Hippomedon's father was adviser to Agis of Sparta (Plutarch, *Agis* 6 and 16; cf. **55**); on Hippomedon cf. R. S. Bagnall, *JEA* 61 (1975), 179f.
2. Acquired under Ptolemy III, cf. **221, 223, 265**. The island of Samothrace was not in fact under direct Ptolemaic control, but had possessions on the mainland (cf. Samos, **113, 116**) which formed an enclave in Ptolemaic dominions.
3. The Mysteries of the 'Great Gods' of Samothrace (the Cabiri), widely respected in the Greek world though of non-Greek origin.
4. On the mainland.
5. Thracian mercenaries (cf. **196** l. 23) hired by Samothrace.
6. This is commonly taken since Rostovtzeff (I (1941), 335 and III, 1399 n. 131) to imply that the Ptolemies normally controlled the corn trade in their foreign

possessions (i.e. imposed Ptolemaic produce on them); but the passage merely shows that the *export* of corn from places controlled by the Ptolemaic governor was regulated, a practice commonly found elsewhere (cf. Antigonus in **40** §10). See Gauthier, *op. cit.* On the corn supply of Greek cities cf. **112**.

7. On the mainland.
8. For the offering of honours to the gods 'on behalf of' rulers, cf. **271, 279**; Fraser 1 (1972), 226f. with notes.

270 Letter of Ptolemy II to Miletus (*ca 262/1*)

See further: Bagnall (1976), 173–5.

King Ptolemy (II) to the council and people of Miletus, greetings.[1] I have previously showed all zeal on behalf of your city, both through a gift of land[2] and by showing concern in all other matters, as was fitting since I
5 saw that our father was favourably disposed to your city / and had been the cause of many benefits to you, as he had released you from harsh and burdensome taxes and from harbour duties which some of the kings had imposed.[3] And now, as you have preserved dutifully your city and your friendship and alliance with us[4] – for my son and Callicrates[5] and my
10 other 'friends' who are with you[6] have written about the display / you have made of your goodwill towards us – we acknowledge this and give you unstinted praise, and we shall try to repay the people with benefactions, and we urge you to preserve for the future the same favourable attitude to us, so that we may show even greater care for your city in the light of your good dispositions. We have given instructions
15 more fully to Hegestratus / to discuss these matters with you and to convey to you our greetings. Farewell.[7]

RC 14

1. Cf. **186** and n. 1 for Miletus and the Seleucids.
2. In 279/8; no details are known.
3. It is not clear to what date in Ptolemy's reign these benefactions belong. 'Some of the kings' refers, with studied vagueness, to Antigonus the One-Eyed.
4. Miletus at the time was under attack by the Seleucids and Ptolemaic control was waning; cf. **186** n. 1.
5. Callicrates of Samos, admiral of Ptolemy II; see H. Hauben, *Callicrates of Samos* (1970).
6. Cf. **25** n. 3, **224** n. 2; note the influence of the king's 'friends' who are present on the spot.
7. There follows a decree of Miletus in praise of Ptolemy II and his son, the citizens and ephebes all taking an oath of loyalty to him.

271 Decree of Telmessus in Lycia in honour of a Ptolemaic official (February 240)

Ptolemaic control of Lycia was for long attested only from the time of Ptolemy II (cf. **217, 221, 265**), but new inscriptional evidence has shown the presence of a Ptolemaic administration already in 288, and the dynasty's control may in fact date as far back as Ptolemy I's campaign in 309 (Diodorus xx.27.1). Lycia was finally taken away from the Ptolemies by Antiochus III in 197 (cf. **153**).

See further: Bagnall (1976), 105–10; M. Wörrle, *Chiron* 7 (1977), 43–66 and 8 (1978), 201–46, esp. 218–25.

With good fortune. In the reign of Ptolemy (III) son of Ptolemy (II) and Arsinoe, the Brother-Sister Gods, in the seventh year, in the month of Dystrus, in the second year of the priesthood of Theodotus / son of   5
Heraclides, at a plenary meeting of the assembly, resolved by the city of Telmessus: since Ptolemy son of Lysimachus,[1] when he took over the city[2] from King Ptolemy[3] son of Ptolemy (and found it) in a bad /   10
[condition] because of the wars,[4] and (since) in [other matters] he continues to show care publicly for the [citizens] and in private for each individual, and seeing that the citizens were [hard pressed] in every way he gave them exemption[5] from [taxes] on fruit trees and on pasturing; and whereas previously they were harshly taxed on the / corn dues, all   15
pulses, millet,[6] sesame and lupine, he made them pay a tithe in accordance with the law,[7] measuring out . . . [to the] farmer and the collector of the tithe, and he exempted (them) from all other taxes /   20
attached to the [tax] on corn; be it resolved by the people of Telmessus, to praise Ptolemy [the Epigone][8] for the goodwill he continuously shows towards the city of Telmessus, and to set up on his [behalf][9] / an altar to   25
Zeus the Saviour in the most conspicuous place in the agora, and to sacrifice every year on the 11th of the month Dystrus a three-year-old ox; all the citizens and the resident foreigners (*paroikoi*) shall assemble together for the sacrifice.[10] [And] if / the magistrate (*archon*) and the   30
citizens do not perform the sacrifice every year, they shall be guilty in the eyes of all the [gods], and the magistrate shall be fined 1,000 drachmas which shall be consecrated to Zeus the Saviour, [unless] he is [prevented] by war from [performing] the sacrifice. / The magistrate shall inscribe   35
this decree on a stone stele and place it in the sanctuary of Artemis in the most conspicuous place, and the resulting expense shall be charged to the city.

OGIS 55; *Tituli Asiae Minoris* II.1

1. Cf. **202** n. 2.
2. Probably as a 'gift' (*en doreai*) from the king (cf. **235** n. 15), yet a decree from Telmessus of 279 praises Ptolemy II for exempting the city from being made a *dorea* (M. Wörrle, *Chiron* 8 (1978), 201–46).

3. Most probably Ptolemy III Euergetes.
4. A reference to (probably) the 'Third Syrian War' (cf. **220–222**).
5. Ptolemy son of Lysimachus appears in the inscription to be acting on his own authority.
6. Two kinds of millet are referred to in the text.
7. The sense of the passage is disputed. The words 'in accordance with the law' might go with 'they were harshly taxed'; nor is it clear whether a new tithe is being substituted for an older and more complex system of taxes.
8. I.e. son of Lysimachus.
9. Cf. **269** n. 8.
10. Cf. **139**.

272 Letter of Ptolemy IV (?) to an official at Soloi in Cilicia

See further: Bagnall (1976), 114–16.

. . .[1] that you did not have any time and had not carried out an inspection, and that the city was oppressed in no small way in this
5 fashion. For (they said that) in addition the soldiers camping in disorder / were occupying not only the outer but the inner city as well, which even under King Alexander was never subjected to billeting,[2] and that they were especially pressurised by the supernumeraries,[3] for they are the men
10 who occupy the greater part of the houses. / Now I believe that I gave you instructions [on] these matters face to face;[4] even [if] this is not so, you [ought to have shown the greatest care . . .]

RC 30

1. The beginning of the letter (lost) probably detailed the complaints made by Soloi to the king. On maladministration in the Ptolemaic kingdom cf. **231**.
2. Cf. **249**.
3. Non-combatants who provided supporting services.
4. Cf. **246** n. 8.

273 A Ptolemaic governor in Cyprus (180–165)

The strategic location of Cyprus, and its mineral and agricultural wealth (cf. **222** ll. 16–18), led to Ptolemaic intervention in the island from the earliest days of the dynasty (cf. **21** §17). Lost to Demetrius and Antigonus in 306 (cf. **21** §21, **36, 46** ch. 54), Cyprus was regained by Ptolemy I in 294 (Plutarch, *Demetrius* 35), and remained thereafter in the possession of the dynasty (cf. **229**) till annexed by Rome in 58 B.C. (it was temporarily restored to Cleopatra VII by Caesar and Mark Antony). Epigraphic evidence for the Ptolemaic presence (governors and military forces) is abundant, though it reveals little of the administration of the island.

See further: Bagnall (1976), 38–79 and Appendices A and B.

Ptolemy, the general (*strategos*) in command of Cyprus,[1] was in no way like an Egyptian,[2] but was a prudent man who displayed practical ability. For having taken charge of the island when the king (Ptolemy VI) was still a child, he showed himself very careful in the collection of money, but would not give anything to anybody, though he was frequently asked to by the king's financial officials (*dioiketes*)[3] and was the subject of bitter abuse for refusing to give anything away. But when the king came of age,[4] he collected a large sum of money and sent it on (to Egypt), with the result that Ptolemy (VI) himself and the members of his court praised him for his previous financial stringency and refusal to give anything away.

Polybius XXVII.13

1. The supreme Ptolemaic official in the island; the post is attested as a regular one from Ptolemy IV and may well have existed before.
2. Not in a literal racial sense; Polybius' bias is apparent.
3. Either local representatives of the *dioiketes* in Alexandria (cf. **235** n. 8), or successive holders of the post of *dioiketes*.
4. In 169.

274 Mercenaries in Ptolemaic service in Syria (second half of the third century?)

From comparison with similar inscriptions the following list of names, found just north of Laodicea in Syria, is most probably from a dedication made jointly by a group of mercenaries. Internal evidence and the origins of the mercenaries indicate that they were probably in Ptolemaic service during the second half of the third century. Their presence may well be connected with the 'Third Syrian War', cf. **220–222**.

   . . . from Cyrene
   . . . from Etenna[1]
   . . . from Cyrene
   . . . from Boeotia
   . . . from the ward Philoterea[2]   5
   . . . from Aspendus
   . . . from Phocis
   . . . from Thrace
   . . . from Miletus

10 Diotimus from Salamis[3]
Nicanor from Boeotia
Menippus
Demagoras from Salamis
Onetor from Salamis
15 Philippus from Cyrene
Heraclitus from Pisidia
Micion from Heraclea
Theocretus from Cyrene
Agis from Lysimachea
20 Pyrrhichus from Macedon
Simonides from Thessaly
Agesimachus from Athens
Bithys from Thrace
Damasis from Salamis
25 Cleon from Thessaly
Apollonius from Etenna
Dion from Cyrene[4]

J. P. Rey-Coquais, *Syria* 55 (1978), 313–25

1. In Pisidia, cf. **279**; see G. E. Bean, *Klio* 52 (1970), 13–16.
2. Of either Alexandria or Ptolemais (cf. **233** n. 3); the name of the city being omitted within Egypt and the Ptolemies' foreign possessions.
3. In Cyprus.
4. Cf. also **224** on Ptolemaic mercenaries.

275 Two ordinances of Ptolemy II on the registration of livestock and of natives in Syria and Phoenicia (April 260)

On the Ptolemies and Syria see also **21** §12, **46** ch. 52, **148, 217, 221, 223, 224, 274, 276**.
See further: Rostovtzeff I (1941), 340–51; Bagnall (1976), 11–24.

(a) . . . (sc. the owners of flocks shall declare) to the [*oikonomos*[1] sent out] to each hyparchy,[2] within a period of 60 days from the date of publication of the [ordinance], the [livestock] which is subject to taxation
5 and that which is exempt . . . get a receipt.[3] If / anyone [does not act in accordance] with these instructions, their livestock [shall be confiscated and] they shall be [liable] to the [fines] fixed in the ordinance. [As regards] the livestock which has not been registered prior [to the] publication [of the ordinance, they shall be exempted] for the previous
10 years [of the] pasture-tax (*ennomion*), the [crown][4] / and the [other fines],

454

[but] from [the 25th (year) they shall] pay the taxes village [by village] . . . All those who . . . [make their] declaration [under] other names, the [king] shall decide [on their] case [and their] / belongings shall be 15 confiscated. [Similarly . . .] . . . [Those] who have bought the tax-contracts for the [villages],5 and the village chiefs (*komarchai*) shall also declare within [the] same period [the] livestock which [is in] their villages, whether subject to taxation / or exempt, the names of their 20 owners, their fathers' names, their place of origin and the names of those who tend the cattle, and similarly all (the livestock) they know has not been registered up to the month of Dystrus in the 25th year; the declaration is to be made under oath in the king's name. Henceforth (the tax-payers) shall make their declaration every year at the same time, and they shall pay the taxes as / is laid down in the king's letter, during the 25 appropriate months in accordance with the ordinance. Anyone who does not carry out any of the above-mentioned prescriptions shall be liable to the same fines as those who declare [their] livestock under the names of others. Anyone who wishes may give information (against culprits), in which case he shall receive, from the fines collected in accordance / with 30 the ordinance, the amount prescribed in this ordinance, and one third of the property confiscated for the crown.

C. Ord. Ptol. 21

(*b*) By order of the king. All those in Syria and [Phoenicia] who have purchased a free native or [have] seized [and] detained him or [acquired him] in another way6 . . . / (sc. shall declare him) to [the *oikonomos*] set 5 up [in each] hyparchy within twenty days of the date of publication of the ordinance. If anyone does not declare (him) or does not produce (him), the slave shall be confiscated from him and he shall further be fined 6,000 drachmas7 for each slave, to be paid into the royal exchequer / and the king shall give a verdict on his case. Any informer 10 shall be given . . . (drachmas) for each slave. All those who demonstrate that the slaves they have declared and produced were already slaves when they [purchased them], shall have these returned to them. As to the / slaves sold [in] the royal public auctions, should any of them claim 15 to be free, their [possession] shall be guaranteed to the purchasers. All the soldiers and other settlers8 in Syria and Phoenicia who live with native women / [whom] they have taken need not declare them. And in future 20 no one shall be allowed to purchase or to accept as security free natives under any pretext, except for those handed over by the manager of the revenues in Syria and Phoenicia for execution (of a debt), / against 25 whom execution may be carried out even on their person, as is laid down in the law on tax-farming.9 Otherwise (offenders) shall be liable to the same fines (sc. as those mentioned above), and similarly for the sellers

30 and those who give (sc. free natives) as securities. To the / informers
shall be given 300 drachmas for every person from the sums raised.

C. Ord. Ptol. 22

1. Cf. **256** n. 1.
2. The basic administrative unit in Syria–Phoenicia.
3. On the registration of livestock cf. **256** ll. 165–73.
4. Cf. **231** n. 15.
5. Cf. **235** n. 3.
6. Cf. **231** ll. 221–30 (in Egypt).
7. = 1 talent.
8. Soldiers on active duty and military settlers (cf. **252**).
9. I.e. only royal officials may 'enslave' natives in execution of crown debts.

276 A tax collector in Syria

See further: V. Tcherikover, *Hellenistic Civilization and the Jews* (Philadelphia,
1959), 127–34, and see **275**.

(168) Now Joseph,[1] after sending to his friends in Samaria and borrowing money, prepared what he needed for his journey, clothes, cups and
beasts of burden (this cost him about 20,000 drachmas), and he came to
Alexandria. (169) It so happened at that time that all the leading men and
magistrates from the cities of Syria and Phoenicia were coming there to
bid for the collection of taxes. The king would sell these rights every year
to the influential men in each city.[2] [. . .] (175) When the day came on
which the (right to collect the) taxes of the cities were to be sold, the men
with the greatest influence in their native lands put in their bids. When
the taxes for Coele Syria, Phoenicia and Judaea together with Samaria
added up to 8,000 talents,[3] (176) Joseph came forward and accused the
bidders of conspiring to offer the king a low price for the taxes, and
undertook to pay himself twice the sum and to send to the king the
property of those who had offended against his house; for (the king) sold
this right together with the taxes. (177) The king was pleased to hear this
and said he would confirm to him the sale of the (right to collect the)
taxes, as he would increase his revenues; (178) and when he asked
whether he had sureties to provide,[4] Joseph made a very clever reply:
'Yes,' he said, 'I will provide excellent persons whom you will not
distrust.' When the king asked him to say who they were, Joseph replied
'Yourself, King, and your wife, as sureties for each other's share.'
Ptolemy laughed and gave him the (right to collect the) taxes without
sureties. (179) This annoyed greatly those who had come from the cities

456

to Egypt, for they felt they had been upstaged. And so they returned in shame each to their own country.

(180) But Joseph received from the king 2,000 infantry (he had requested a military force to bring compulsion on any persons in the cities who looked down on him), and after borrowing 500 talents from the 'friends'⁵ of the king in Alexandria, he set out for Syria. (181) When he came to Ascalon and asked the people for the tribute, they refused to give him anything and insulted him as well; he then arrested some twenty of their leading men and put them to death, and sent their property, which added up to 1,000 talents, to the king, telling him also what had occurred. (182) Ptolemy was impressed by his determination and praised him for his actions, and allowed him to do anything he wished.⁶ The Syrians were terrified at the news, and with the execution of the men of Ascalon as a grievous example before them of (the risks of) disobedience, they opened their gates, admitted Joseph readily and paid the tribute. (183) When the people of Scythopolis tried to insult him and refuse him the tribute which they used to pay without argument, he executed their leaders as well and sent their property to the king. (184) Having thus collected a great deal of money and made considerable profits from farming the taxes, he used his means to perpetuate his existing power, thinking it wise to preserve the origin and basis of his present good fortune from the riches he had himself acquired. (185) And so he sent many gifts secretly to the king and to Cleopatra⁷ and to their 'friends' and to all influential figures at·court, purchasing their goodwill by these means. (186) He enjoyed this good fortune for 22 years. [. . .]

Josephus, *Jewish Antiquities* XII. 168f.,
175–86

1. From the influential Jewish family of the Tobiads, and nephew of the High Priest Onias who had fallen out with the Ptolemies. The story of Joseph illustrates the penetration of Hellenism in Judaea, Joseph himself being an example of a hellenised Jew, deliberately 'international' in outlook (cf. **168**, also **121**). The story is placed by Josephus under Ptolemy V (cf. n. 7) but must belong to the third century, before the Seleucid conquest of Syria (**167**).
2. On tax-farming in Egypt cf. **235** n. 3; unlike the system described in the 'Revenue Laws', the tax-farmers in Josephus' account both underwrite and collect the taxes in Syria.
3. The figure is impossibly high.
4. Cf. **235** col. 34, **236** col. 56.
5. Cf. **224** n. 2.
6. This can hardly be literally true; contrast the official denunciations of maladministration in **231, 256** ll. 224–33, **258, 272**.
7. Ptolemy V and Cleopatra, daughter of Antiochus III; see n. 1.

277 Ptolemy II and the Red Sea

Then there is an isthmus which reaches to the Red Sea near the city of Berenice;[1] the city has no harbour, but provides suitable landing-places thanks to the favourable configuration of the isthmus. It is said that Philadelphus was the first to open up this road, which is waterless, with an army and to provide stations, as though for merchants travelling on camels,[2] and that he did this because the Red Sea is difficult to navigate, especially for those who sail out from the innermost recess.[3] Experience showed how very useful this was, and nowadays[4] all the goods from India and Arabia, and those from Ethiopia which are carried along the Arabian Gulf, are brought to Coptus, which is the emporium for merchandise of this sort. [. . .]

Strabo XVII.1.45

1. Berenice Trogodytice on the west coast of the Red Sea, connected by a desert road to Coptus in southern Egypt, and the most important of Philadelphus' foundations aimed at developing Egypt's eastern trade (Fraser I (1972), 176–9; Préaux (1939), 353–66).
2. Possibly an intrusive gloss.
3. The Gulf of Suez; Ptolemy opened the canal from the Red Sea to the Nile.
4. The use of the direct sea route from Arabia to the Indus mouth, and the consequent growth of Indian trade, did not start till the late second century with the discovery of the monsoon (Fraser I (1972), 180–4).

278 The animal hunts of Ptolemy II

The second Ptolemy, who was keenly interested in the hunting of elephants and who offered great rewards to those who performed the exploit of capturing the most valiant beasts, spent a great deal of money on this pursuit and collected a large number of war elephants,[1] but also made known to the Greeks other animals they had never seen and which astonished them.[2] And so some of the hunters, seeing the generosity of the king's presents, gathered together in sufficiently large numbers and decided to risk their lives, and to capture one of the large snakes and bring it back to Alexandria to Ptolemy. It was a great and amazing undertaking, but fortune smiled on their designs and brought about a successful outcome to their venture [. . .] They brought the snake back to Alexandria and presented it to the king, an astonishing spectacle which those who hear about it cannot believe. By starving the snake of food they wore down the beast's strength and gradually tamed it so that it became astonishingly domesticated. Ptolemy gave the hunters the re-

458

wards they had deserved, and kept the snake which was now tamed and offered the greatest and most remarkable spectacle to the foreigners who came (by sea) to his kingdom.[3]

Diodorus III.36.3–5; 37.7–8

1. Cf. **279** with n. 6.
2. For Ptolemy II's interest in animals cf. also **219**, *P. Cairo Zen.* 59.075.
3. Egypt was famous for its tourist attractions; for the Ptolemaic period cf. e.g.
   P. Tebt. 33 (*Sel. Pap.* II. 416); *P. Lond.* 1973.

279 Dedication of the elephant hunters (reign of Ptolemy IV)

See further: Préaux (1939), 34–7; Fraser I (1972), 178f. and notes; H. H. Scullard, *The Elephant in the Greek and Roman World* (London, 1974), 123–37.

On behalf of[1] King Ptolemy (IV) and Queen Arsinoe and Ptolemy the son,[2] Parent-Loving Gods, descended from Ptolemy (III) and Berenice, Benefactor Gods, / to Ares Nicephorus[3] Euagrus,[4] Alexander son of 5 Syndaeus of Oroanda,[5] the deputy sent out together with Charimortus the general in charge of the hunting of elephants,[6] and / Apoasis son of 10 Miorbollus from Etenna,[7] the leader, and the soldiers under his command (sc. made this dedication).

OGIS 86

1. Cf. **269** n. 8. The find place of this inscription is unknown.
2. The future Ptolemy V Epiphanes.
3. Who brings victory.
4. Who brings success in the hunt.
5. In Pisidia.
6. Mentioned by Strabo XIV.4.15 and Polybius XVIII.55.2. On the elephant hunts of the Ptolemies cf. **219, 221, 247** n. 4, **278**.
7. Cf. **274** n. 1.

Table of rulers

Note: The years are regnal years, i.e. years during which the rulers had the royal title. The numbering of rulers within a dynasty is mostly a modern convention. The lists are simplified and show only the main facts.

The ANTIGONIDS of Macedon

Antigonus I Monophthalmus	306–301
Demetrius Poliorcetes	306–283
Antigonus II Gonatas	283–239
Demetrius II	239–229
Antigonus III Doson	229–221
Philip V	221–179
Perseus	179–168

Note: Antigonus I never ruled Macedon, Demetrius I only 294–288/7, and Antigonus II only from 276.

The SELEUCIDS (see **138** for fuller details)

Seleucus I Nicator	305–281
Antiochus I Soter	281–261
Antiochus II Theos	261–246
Seleucus II Callinicus	246–225
Seleucus III Soter	225–223
Antiochus III the Great	223–187
Seleucus IV Philopator	187–175
Antiochus IV Epiphanes	175–164
Antiochus V Eupator	163–162
Demetrius I Soter	162–150
Alexander Balas	150–145
Antiochus VI Epiphanes	145–142
Antiochus VII Sidetes	138–129
Demetrius II Nicator	129–125
Cleopatra Thea	126
Cleopatra Thea and Antiochus VIII Grypus	125–121
Seleucus V	125
Antiochus VIII Grypus	121–96

460

Antiochus IX Cyzicenus   115–95

Note: The last rulers in the dynasty are omitted.

The ATTALIDS of Pergamum (cf. **193**)

Philetaerus	283–263
Eumenes I	263–241
Attalus I Soter	241–197
Eumenes II Soter	197–160
Attalus II	160–139
Attalus III	139–133
(Eumenes III, i.e. Aristonicus	133–129)

Note: Neither of the first two Attalids assumed the royal title, cf. **193, 199**; on Eumenes III/Aristonicus cf. **212** n. 2.

The PTOLEMIES

Ptolemy I Soter	305–283
Ptolemy II Philadelphus	283–246
Ptolemy III Euergetes I	246–222
Ptolemy IV Philopator	222–204
Ptolemy V Epiphanes	204–180
Ptolemy VI Philometor	180–145
Ptolemy VII Neos Philopator	145–144
Ptolemy VIII Euergetes II Physcon	145–116

Note: The last rulers in the dynasty are omitted.

Chronological table

Note: The chronology of the Hellenistic period is riddled with uncertainties, particularly as regards much of the third century; many of the dates listed below are approximate and subject to revision. For discussion of problems of detail see Will I (1979) and II (1967, 2nd ed. forthcoming), and in general E. J. Bickerman, *Chronology of the Ancient World* (2nd ed., 1980), with numerous chronological tables.

356	Birth of Alexander
336	Assassination of Philip; accession of Alexander. Alexander *hegemon* of the 'Corinthian League' (**2**)
335	Alexander campaigns in Thrace and Illyria. Revolt and destruction of Thebes (**2**)
334	(Spring) Start of Alexander's invasion of Asia. Battle of the Granicus. Conquest of Asia Minor (**3–5**)
334/3	Alexander winters at Gordium
333	(November) Battle of Issus
332	Alexander rejects Darius' peace offers (**6**). Siege of Tyre. Alexander conquers Syria. Surrender of Egypt to Alexander
331	Foundation of Alexandria (**7**). Alexander visits the oracle of Ammon at Siwah (**8**)
	(1 October) Battle of Gaugamela (cf. **10**). Agis III of Sparta defeated at Megalopolis (cf. **10**)
330	Destruction of Persepolis (**9**). Darius murdered by Bessus. Execution of Philotas and Parmenion
329	Alexander in Bactria
328	Murder of Clitus. Execution of Callisthenes (or 327) (cf. **11**)
327	Alexander marries Roxane. Invasion of India
326	Battle of the Hydaspes, defeat of Porus. Mutiny of the troops at the Hyphasis (**12**)
325	Alexander crosses Gedrosia. Nearchus sails to the Persian Gulf. Unrest in Alexander's empire (**13**)
324	Alexander returns to Susa. Mass marriages (**14**). Decree on the restoration of Greek exiles (**16**). Mutiny at Opis (**15**). Death of Hephaestion at Ecbatana
323	(10 June) Death of Alexander at Babylon. Settlement at Babylon (**22**)
323–322	Revolt of Greeks in Bactria. Lamian War in Greece (**23, 26**)

322	Cyrene conquered by Ptolemy (**264**). Perdiccas conquers Cappadocia
321–320	Coalition against Perdiccas. Death of Perdiccas in Egypt
320	Settlement at Triparadisus (**24**)
319	Death of Antipater; regency of Polyperchon (**25**)
318–316	Coalition of Cassander and Antigonus against Polyperchon and Eumenes (cf. **28**)
317	Demetrius of Phalerum set up by Cassander as ruler in Athens (**23**, cf. **34**). Death of Philip Arrhidaeus
316	Agathocles seizes power in Syracuse (**27**)
316/315	Antigonus executes Eumenes (**46** ch. 53)
315	Cassander executes Olympias (cf. **29**). Seleucus expelled from Babylon by Antigonus (**46** ch. 53). Cassander rebuilds Thebes (cf. **29**)
315–311	Coalition against Antigonus
314	Antigonus proclaims the 'freedom of the Greeks' (**29**). Foundation of the League of Islanders (cf. **218**)
312–311	Seleucus recovers Babylon; beginning of the Seleucid era (**46** ch. 54, **138**)
311	Peace treaty between the Diadochi except Seleucus (**30–32**)
311–306	Agathocles at war with Carthage; invasion of Africa (cf. **27**)
310	End of the Argead dynasty (**30**). Ptolemy annexes Cyprus (cf. **273**)
308	Seleucus begins the reconquest of the east (cf. **46**, ch. 54–5)
307	Demetrius liberates Athens from the control of Cassander. Demetrius of Phalerum exiled (**34**, cf. **262**)
306	Demetrius defeats Ptolemy at Cyprus. The Successors assume the royal title (306–304) (**36, 46** ch. 54)
305–304	Demetrius' fruitless siege of Rhodes (**39**)
ca 303	Seleucus settles with Chandragupta in India (**46** ch. 55)
302	Demetrius refounds the 'League of Corinth' (**42**)
301	Defeat and death of Antigonus at Ipsus (**43, 46** ch. 55); partition of his kingdom (cf. **148**)
300–299	Foundation of Seleucia in Pieria and Antioch (**174**)
297	Death of Cassander in Macedon (cf. **45**)
294–288/7	Demetrius king in Macedon (cf. **45**)
288/7	Coalition against Demetrius; Demetrius expelled from Macedon (cf. **44, 45**)
287 or 286	Athens revolts from Demetrius (**44**)
285–281	Lysimachus king of Macedon (**45**)
284–281	Achaean League reconstituted (**53**)
283	Death of Demetrius. Death of Ptolemy I
281	Defeat and death of Lysimachus at Corupedium; assassination of Seleucus I; Ptolemy Ceraunus ruler in Macedon (**45, 46** ch. 62, **193**). Accession of Antiochus I (**139**)
280–275	Campaigns of Pyrrhus in Italy and Sicily (**47**)
280–279	Celtic invasion of Macedon and Greece (**48**)

206	Aetolian peace with Philip V
205	Peace of Phoenice between Rome and Philip V (**64**)
204	Accession of Ptolemy V Epiphanes (**226**)
204–203	Antiochus III in Asia Minor (**151**)
203/2	(Alleged) secret pact of Antiochus III and Philip V against Ptolemy V (**152**)
203–200	Campaigns of Philip V in northern Greece, at the Straits and in the Aegean (cf. **65**). Appeal of Rhodes and Attalus I to Rome (cf. **198, 200**)
202–200	Fifth Syrian War: Antiochus III gains Coele Syria from Ptolemy V (cf. **167**)
200–196	Second Macedonian War: Rome against Philip V
197	Philip V defeated at Cynoscephalae (cf. **67**). Antiochus III in Asia Minor (**153**, cf. **154, 155**)
196	Flamininus proclaims the 'freedom of the Greeks' (**68**). Antiochus III in Thrace (**153, 154**). Ptolemy V consecrated Pharaoh at Memphis (**227**)
195	Peace between Antiochus III and Ptolemy V (cf. **154**)
194	The Romans evacuate Greece
192–188	War of Rome against Antiochus III. Antiochus III invades Greece, invited by the Aetolians
192	Sparta forced into the Achaean League (cf. **71**)
191	Defeat of Antiochus III at Thermopylae; he evacuates Greece. Roman armistice with the Aetolians (**69**)
189	Defeat of Antiochus III at Magnesia (**160**). Aetolia submits to Rome (**70**), loses control of Delphic Amphictyony (cf. **72**)
188	Treaty of Apamea between Rome and Antiochus III; settlement of Asian affairs (**161**)
185 onwards	Philip V rebuilds Macedon (**73**, cf. **74**)
180	Philip V executes his son Demetrius (cf. **77**)
175	Accession of Antiochus IV Epiphanes (**162**)
172	Eumenes II denounces Perseus of Macedon at Rome
171–167	Third Macedonian War: Rome against Perseus (**75–78**)
170–168	Sixth Syrian War: Antiochus IV Epiphanes invades Egypt twice (**164, 165**)
168	Perseus defeated at Pydna. End of the Macedonian monarchy. Delos declared a free port by Rome (**80**). Pergamum and Rhodes weakened (**80, 203**). Antiochus IV expelled from Egypt by Rome (**164, 165**)
167	Epirus plundered by the Romans. Macedonia divided into four republics (**79**)
167	Rising of the Maccabees in Palestine (**168**)
164	The Temple at Jerusalem rededicated
163	Roman mission to Syria (**169**). Partition of the Ptolemaic kingdom between Ptolemy VI and Ptolemy VIII (**229**)
160	Defeat and death of Judas Maccabaeus
155	Will of Ptolemy VIII bequeathing Cyrenaica to Rome (**230**)

149–148	Fourth Macedonian War: rising of the pretender Andriscus (cf. **193**)
146	War between Rome and the Achaeans; sack of Corinth (**82**) Macedon made a Roman province
142	Independence of the Jews
142–137	Revolt of Diodotus Tryphon (**171**)
141	The Parthians annex Babylonia
133	Death of Attalus III; his kingdom bequeathed to Rome (**211**)
132	Revolt of Aristonicus of Pergamum (**212, 213**)
130	Defeat of Aristonicus by Rome. Defeat and death of Antiochus VII against the Parthians
129	Roman organisation of the province of Asia (cf. **214**)
118	'Amnesty decree' of Ptolemy VIII, Cleopatra II and Cleopatra III (**231**)

Bibliography

Note: This is only a select bibliography. For fuller references to modern literature up till 1940 see Rostovtzeff III (1941); for more recent work see Préaux I and II (1978); for political history specifically see Will I (1979) and II (1967). See also the bibliographical reports on Greek history (including Hellenistic) by E. Will in *Revue Historique* 238 (1967), 377–452; 246 (1971), 84–150; 251 (1974), 123–64; 257 (1977), 365–427; 262 (1979), 407–73.

For bibliography on the ancient sources see pp. 1–7.

General

A. Aymard, *Etudes d'histoire ancienne* (Paris, 1967)

E. Badian, *Foreign Clientelae* (Oxford, 1958)

C. B. Welles, *Royal Correspondence in the Hellenistic Period* (New Haven, 1934)

Cambridge Ancient History, vols. VI–VIII (Cambridge, 1927–1930) (a new edition is in preparation)

V. Ehrenberg, *The Greek State* (London, 2nd ed., 1969), Part II

R. M. Errington, *The Dawn of Empire* (London, 1971)

M. Holleaux, *Etudes d'épigraphie et d'histoire grecques*, 6 vols., ed. L. Robert (Paris, 1938–1968)

A. Momigliano, 'Introduzione all' Ellenismo' in *Quinto Contributo alla storia degli studi classici* (Rome, 1975), 267–91

C. Préaux, *Le monde hellénistique. La Grèce et l'Orient (323–146 av. J.C.)*, 2 vols. (Paris, 1978) (the best introduction and survey)

M. Rostovtzeff, *The Social and Economic History of the Hellenistic World*, 3 vols. (Oxford, 1941)

W. W. Tarn and G. T. Griffith, *Hellenistic Civilization* (London, 3rd ed., 1952)

F. W. Walbank, *The Hellenistic World* (London, 1981)

E. Will, *Histoire politique du monde Hellénistique*, 2 vols. (Nancy, 1966 and 1967, 2nd ed., 1979–1982) (the best account of political history)

Id., *Le monde grec et l'Orient*, vol. II (Paris, 1975), 335–645

Special aspects

H. Bengtson, *Die Strategie in der hellenistischen Zeit*, 3 vols. (Munich, 1937–52)

E. J. Bickerman, *Chronology of the Ancient World* (London, 2nd ed., 1980)

P. Brulé, *La piraterie crétoise hellénistique* (Paris, 1978)

Bibliography

S. K. Eddy, *The King is Dead. Studies in the Near Eastern Resistance to Hellenism* (Lincoln, Nebraska, 1961)

H. van Effenterre, *La Crète et le monde grec de Platon à Polybe* (Paris, 1948)

Y. Garlan, *War in the Ancient World. A social history* (London, 1975)

W. Gawantka, *Isopolitie* (Munich, 1975)

G. T. Griffith, *The Mercenaries of the Hellenistic World* (Cambridge, 1935)

C. Habicht, *Gottmenschentum und griechische Städte* (Munich, 2nd ed., 1970)

A. R. Hands, *Charities and Social Aid in Greece and Rome* (London, 1968)

A. H. M. Jones, *The Greek City from Alexander to Justinian* (Oxford, 1940)

Id. and others, *The Cities of the Eastern Roman Provinces* (Oxford, 2nd ed., 1971)

M. Launey, *Recherches sur les armées hellénistiques*, 2 vols. (Paris, 1949–50)

H. I. Marrou, *Histoire de l'éducation dans l'antiquité* (6th ed., 1965)

A. Momigliano, *Alien Wisdom. The Limits of Hellenization* (Cambridge, 1975)

C. Nicolet and others, *Rome et la conquête du monde méditerranéen*, vol. II (Paris, 1978)

M. P. Nilsson, *Geschichte der griechischen Religion*, vol. 2 (Munich, 3rd ed., 1974)

Id., *Die hellenistische Schule* (Munich, 1955)

H. A. Ormerod, *Piracy in the Ancient World* (Liverpool, 1924)

The Princeton Encyclopaedia of Classical Sites, ed. R. Stilwell and others (Princeton, 1976)

Alexander the Great

E. Badian, 'Alexander the Great, 1948–1967', *The Classical World* 65 (1971), 37–56 and 77–83

H. Berve, *Das Alexanderreich auf prosopographischer Grundlage*, 2 vols. (Munich, 1926)

Entretiens Hardt 22 (1976): *Alexandre le Grand, image et réalité*

R. Lane Fox, *Alexander the Great* (London, 1973)

P. Goukowsky, *Essai sur les origines du mythe d'Alexandre*, vol. I (Nancy, 1978)

Greece and Rome 12.2 (1965)

P. Green, *Alexander the Great* (London, 1970)

G. T. Griffith, ed., *Alexander the Great: the Main Problems* (Cambridge, 1966)

J. R. Hamilton, *Alexander the Great* (Oxford, 1973)

N. G. L. Hammond and G. T. Griffith, *A History of Macedonia*, vol. 2 (Oxford, 1979)

J. Seibert, *Alexander der Grosse (Erträge der Forschung* 14) (Darmstadt, 1972)

W. W. Tarn, *Alexander the Great*, 2 vols. (Cambridge, 1948)

U. Wilcken, *Alexander the Great*, ed. E. N. Borza (New York, 1967)

Macedon and the Greek mainland

Ancient Macedonia, 2 vols., ed. B. Laourdas and C. Makaronas (Thessalonica, 1970 and 1977)

J. Briscoe, 'The Antigonids and the Greek States, 276–196 B.C.' in *Imperialism in the Ancient World*, ed. P. D. A. Garnsey and C. R. Whittaker (Cambridge, 1978), 145–57 and 314–19

G. Daux, *Les Aitoliens à Delphes* (Paris, 1937)

W. S. Ferguson, *Hellenistic Athens* (London, 1911)

C. Habicht, *Untersuchungen zur politischen Geschichte Athens im 3. Jahrhundert v. Chr.* (Munich, 1979)

H. Heinen, *Untersuchungen zur hellenistischen Geschichte des 3. Jahrhunderts v. Chr., Historia Einzelschriften* 20 (Wiesbaden, 1972)

J. A. O. Larsen, *Greek Federal States* (Oxford, 1968)

W. W. Tarn, *Antigonus Gonatas* (Oxford, 1913)

R. Urban, *Wachstum und Krise des Achäischen Bundes, Historia Einzelschriften* 35 (Wiesbaden, 1979)

F. W. Walbank, *Aratos of Sicyon* (Cambridge, 1933)

Id., *Philip V of Macedon* (Cambridge, 1940)

The Seleucids

B. Bar-Kochva, *The Seleucid Army* (Cambridge, 1976)

E. J. Bikerman, *Institutions des Séleucides* (Paris, 1938)

G. M. Cohen, *The Seleucid Colonies, Historia Einzelschriften* 30 (Wiesbaden, 1978)

G. Downey, *A History of Antioch in Syria from Seleucus to the Arab Conquest* (Princeton, 1961)

H. Kreissig, *Wirtschaft und Gesellschaft im Seleukidenreich* (Berlin, 1978)

O. Mørkholm, *Antiochus IV of Syria* (Copenhagen, 1966)

W. Orth, *Königlicher Machtanspruch und städtische Freiheit* (Munich, 1977)

H. H. Schmitt, *Untersuchungen zur Geschichte Antiochos' des Grossen und seiner Zeit, Historia Einzelschriften* 6 (Wiesbaden, 1964)

The Attalids

E. V. Hansen, *The Attalids of Pergamum* (Ithaca, N.Y, 2nd ed., 1971)

J. Hopp, *Untersuchungen zur Geschichte der letzten Attaliden* (Munich, 1977)

R. B. McShane, *The Foreign Policy of the Attalids of Pergamum* (Urbana, Ill., 1964)

The Ptolemies

R. S. Bagnall, *The Administration of the Ptolemaic Territories outside Egypt* (Leyden, 1976)

D. J. Crawford, *Kerkeosiris: an Egyptian village in the Ptolemaic period* (Cambridge, 1971)

P. M. Fraser, *Ptolemaic Alexandria*, 3 vols. (Oxford, 1972)

W. Huss, *Untersuchungen zur Aussenpolitik Ptolemaios' IV* (Munich, 1976)

W. Peremans and E. van't Dack, *Prosopographia Ptolemaica*, 8 vols. to date (Louvain, 1950–75)

C. Préaux, *L'Economie royale des Lagides* (Brussels, 1939)

Ead., 'L'Economie lagide: 1933–1958', *Proceedings of the IXth International Congress of Papyrology* (Oslo, 1961), 200–32

Bibliography

Ead., *Les Grecs en Egypte d'après les archives de Zénon* (Brussels, 1947)

Das Ptolemäische Ägypten. Akten des internationalen Symposions . . . September 1976 in Berlin (Berlin, 1978) (*non vidi*)

J. Seibert, *Untersuchungen zur Geschichte Ptolemaios' I* (Munich, 1969)

Addenda (1984)

W. L. Adams and E. N. Borza, edd. *Philip II, Alexander the Great and the Macedonian Heritage* (Lanham, 1982)

R. E. Allen, *The Attalid Kingdom. A Constitutional History* (Oxford, 1983)

R. S. Bagnall and P. S. Derow, *Greek Historical Documents: The Hellenistic Period* (Chico, 1981)

A. B. Bosworth, *A Historical Commentary on Arrian's History of Alexander*, vol. 1 (Oxford, 1980)

P. Briant, 'Des Achéménides aux rois hellénistiques: continuités et ruptures', *Annali della Scuola Normale Superiore di Pisa*, Serie III, vol. IX.4 (1979), 1375–1415.

Id., 'Colonisation hellénistique et populations indigènes, II' *Klio* 64 (1982), 83–98

P. A. Brunt, *Arrian. History of Alexander and Indica*, vol. 2 (Loeb edition, Cambridge, Mass. and Lond, 1983)

K. Buraselis, *Das hellenistische Makedonien und die Ägäis* (Munich, 1982)

D. J. Crawford, J. Quaegebeur, W. Clarysse, *Studies in Ptolemaic Memphis* (Louvain, 1980)

E. S. Gruen, *The Hellenistic World and the Coming of Rome*, 2 vols. (Berkeley, 1984)

P. Goukowski, *Essai sur les origines du mythe d'Alexandre. 2: Alexandre et Dionysos* (Nancy, 1981)

N. G. L. Hammond, *Three Historians of Alexander the Great* (Cambridge, 1983)

A. J. Heisserer, *Alexander the Great and the Greeks. The Epigraphic Evidence* (Norman, 1980)

J. Hornblower, *Hieronymus of Cardia* (Oxford, 1981)

S. Hornblower, *The Greek World 479–323 B.C.* (London, 1983)

Cl. Orrieux, *Les Papyrus de Zénon* (Paris, 1983)

P. W. Pestman, ed. *A Guide to the Zenon Archive*, 2 vols. (Leiden, 1981)

G. E. M. de Ste Croix, *The Class Struggle in the Ancient Greek World* (London, 1981)

A. E. Samuel, *From Athens to Alexandria: Hellenism and Social Goals in Ptolemaic Egypt* (Louvain, 1983)

L. Schober, *Untersuchungen zur Geschichte Babyloniens und der Oberen Satrapien von 323–303 v. Chr.* (Frankfurt, 1981)

A. N. Sherwin-White, *Rome and the Greek East* (London, 1984)

P. Vidal-Naquet, 'Flavius Arrien entre deux mondes', in *Arrien. Histoire d'Alexandre*, tr. P. Savinel (Paris, 1984), 309–94

Addenda (1989)

A. B. Bosworth, *From Arrian to Alexander* (Oxford, 1988)

Id., Conquest and Empire: The Reign of Alexander the Great (Cambridge, 1988)

S. M. Burstein, *The Hellenistic Age from the Battle of Ipsos to the Death of Kleopatra VII*, Translated Documents of Greece and Rome 3 (Cambridge, 1985)

Cambridge Ancient History, vol. VII part 1: *The Hellenistic World*, 2nd ed. (Cambridge, 1984)

Cambridge Ancient History, Plates to Volume VII part 1 (Cambridge, 1984)

N. G. L. Hammond and F. W. Walbank, *A History of Macedonia*, vol. 3: 336–167 B.C. (Oxford, 1988)

A. Kuhrt and S. Sherwin-White, edd., *Hellenism in the East* (London–Berkeley, 1987)

Index of ancient sources

A Literary Sources

Aeschines III.132–4: **10**

Appian, *Syrian Wars* 52–55, 57–58, 62–63: **46**

'Aristeas to Philocrates' I.9–11 and v.35–40: **262**

Arrian, *Alexander* I. 17: **4**; II. 14: **6**; III.1.5–2.2: **7**(a); III. 3–4: **8**; IV. 10.5–12.5: **11**; v.28–29.1: **12**; VI.27.3–5: **13**; VII.4.4–5: **14**; VII.1.1–4: **17**; VII.8–9 and 11: **15**

Arrian, *FGrH* 156 F 1, §§1–8: **22** (a); F 9, §§ 34–38: **24**

Athenaeus, *Deipnosophistae* v 201 b–f, 202 f–203 e: **219**; VI 253 b–f: **35**

Demetrius of Phalerum, *FGrH* 228 F 39: **20**

Diodorus III.12.1–3: **263**; III.36.3–5 and 37.7–8: **278**; VI.1.2–10: **38**; XVII.14: **2** (b); XVII.17.3–4: **3** (b); XVII.70–72: **9**; XVIII.3.2–5: **22** (b); XVIII.4.1–6: **18**; XVIII.8.2–7: **16**; XVIII.48.4–50: **25**; XIX.9: **27** (a); XIX.27.2–29: **28**; XIX.61–62.2: **29**; XIX.105.1–4: **30**; XX.81 and 100.1–4: **39**; XX.102.2–4: **41**; XXXI.15 a and 17 b: **228**; XXXIII.4: **170**; XL.3: **166**

Hecataeus of Abdera, *FGrH* 264 F 6: **166**

Heraclides Creticus (?) I (extracts): **83**

Josephus, *Jewish Antiquities* XII.138–153: **167**; XII.168–9 and 175–186: **276**

Livy XXVI.24.7–15: **62** (a); XXIX.12.11–16: **64**; XXXI.44.2–9: **66**; XXXIII.38: **153**; XXXVII.40–41: **160**; XXXVIII.34: **71**; XXXIX.24.1–4: **73**; XLI.20: **163** (b); XLII.29–30.7: **75**; XLII.51: **77**; XLV.29.3–30 and 32.1–7: **79**

I Maccabees 1.10–25 and 41–56: **168**; 15.1–9: **172**

Memnon, *FGrH* 434 F 11: **140**

Menander, *The Sicyonian* ll. 3–15: **86**

Pausanias I.9.5–10: **45**; I.25.3–6: **23**; VII.16.7–17.1: **82**

Plutarch, *Agis* 5–6.1 and 7.5–8: **55**
Alexander 10.6–11: **2** (a); 15: **3** (a); 26.3–10: **7** (b); 68.3: cf. **13**
Cleomenes 10–11 and 13: **56**; 16: **57**

Demetrius 8–10: **34**; 18: **36**
Pyrrhus 8.1–7 and 14: **47**
De Alexandri Magni Fortuna aut Virtute I.328 C–329 D: **19**

Polybius II.37.7–44: **53**; IV.25–26.2: **58**; IV.38.1–10: **96**; IV.46.5–47.6: **94**; IV.48: **146**; IV.73.5–74.2: **85**; V.34: **223**; V.40–44 (in part): **147**; V.63 and 65: **224**; V.67: **148**; V.79: **149**; V.88–90.4: **93**; V.103.7–106.5 (in part): **59**; V.107.1–3: **225** A; VII.9: **61**; XI.34: **150**; XIII.6: **63**; XIV.12.3–4: **225** B; XV.20: **152**; XV.25.3–18: **226**; XV.35.1–6: **27** B; XVI.25–26: **198**; XVI.30–31: **65**; XVIII.29–31: **67**; XVIII.41: **199**; XVIII.44–46 (in part): **68**; XVIII.49–51: **154**; XX.6.1–6: **84**; XX.9–10 (in part): **69**; XXI.18–23: **200**; XXI.32: **70**; XXI.43: **161**; XXVI.1: **163** A; XXVII.13: **273**; XXIX.21.1–6: **20**; XXIX.27: **164**; XXX.31: **80**; XXXI.2: **169**; XXXI.10: **229**; XXXII.8: **207**; XXXVI.17.5–10: **81**

Ps. Dicaearchus: see Heraclides Creticus

Strabo XI.9.2–3: **145**; XI.11.1–2: **191**; XIII.4.1–2: **193**; XIV.1.38: **212**; XIV.2.5: **92**; XIV.5.2: **171**; XVI.1.5: **188**; XVI.2.4–10: **174**; XVI.2.14: **144**; XVII.1.6.–10: **232**; XVII.1.45: **277**

Suda s.v. *Basileia* (2): **37**

Tacitus, *Histories* IV.83–84: **261**

Theocritus XVII.ll. 73–130: **217**

B Inscriptions

AM 72 (1957), 233–41 (C. Habicht): **125**

Anadolu 9 (1965), 34–6 (P. Herrmann): **151**

Annuario 45–6 (1967–8), 445–53 (G. Pugliese-Carratelli): **156**

Archaiologikon Deltion 22 (1967), 38–52 (B. C. Petrakos): **50**

BCH 59 (1935), 210–30 (G. Daux): **123**

BCH 99 (1975), 51–75 (R. Etienne and M. Piérart): **51**

R. Bogaert, *Epigraphica* III (1976), no. 22: **105**; no. 36: **181**

Chiron 5 (1975), 59–87 (M. Wörrle): **142**

C Papyri

General index